Atiyeh

ATIYEH

Governor Vic Atiyeh and the Transformation of Oregon

James Moore

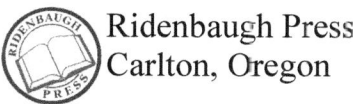
Ridenbaugh Press
Carlton, Oregon

ATIYEH: Governor Vic Atiyeh and the Transformation of Oregon
Copyright ©2025 by James Moore. All rights reserved. No part of this book may be reproduced or transmitted in any form, by any information storage or retrieval system, without written permission from the publisher, except in case of brief quotations used in critical articles or reviews.
Printed and bound in the United States of America.

10 9 8 7 6 5 4 3 2 1

Library of Congress Cataloging in Publication Data

Moore, James.

ATIYEH: Governor Vic Atiyeh and the Transformation of Oregon

Bibliography

1. Atiyeh, Victor. 2. Governors-United States-Biography. 3. Oregon. State-Biography.

I. Moore, James. II. Title.

ISBN 978-0-945648-57-4 (softbound)

Cover design by Randy Stapilus.

Cover picture: Vic Atiyeh delivering a speech during his inauguration as newly elected governor of Oregon. Victor Atiyeh Collection, Pacific University. (Portion of picture also opposite the title page.)

Ridenbaugh Press
P.O. Box 834, Carlton OR 97111
Phone (503) 852-0010
www.ridenbaugh.com

Table of Contents

Foreword *by Jeff Mapes*	1
1 Preparing	6
2 Legislating	34
3 Running and governing	93
4 Balancing resources	152
5 Managing crisis	222
6 Developing and taxing	288
7 Coping with Rajneeshees	350
8 Building relationships	419
9 Moving on	478
Acknowledgments	524
Index	526

Foreword

by Jeff Mapes

I first met Vic Atiyeh in early 1984 shortly after becoming a reporter for *The Oregonian*. I was on one of my first visits to the state Capitol when it came time for one of Atiyeh's weekly media availabilities. I followed five or six reporters up the stairs from the basement press room to the governor's ceremonial office on the second floor. The Legislature was out of session and our footsteps echoed through the empty halls.

I didn't know a lot about Oregon politics. I had just arrived after four years as a Washington correspondent for a chain of small newspapers. I was a small fish in Washington, but I had seen most of the nation's well-known politicians in action, from President Reagan to Teddy Kennedy. I expected to find the Oregon Capitol sleepy in comparison.

Atiyeh certainly fed into that impression as he presided over his get-together with reporters. He was friendly enough but low-key. Ronald Reagan he was not. It wasn't a big news day, so the reporters struggled to draw anything interesting out of him. I remember that the Rajneeshees – the religious cult causing so much consternation in eastern Oregon – came up. Atiyeh didn't have much new to say.

I can't say I was impressed. It didn't help that the veteran journalists in Salem were already turning their attention to shinier objects. Atiyeh was in the last two years of his second term and people were talking about the next governor's race. And once the

1985 legislative session started, the ambitious Democrats who ran the Legislature – as they did for every year of Atiyeh's governorship – were drawing the most headlines.

House Speaker Vera Katz and Senate President John Kitzhaber were particularly mediagenic. The "Kitz and Katz Show" made for great copy. You had an ER surgeon who dressed like a cowboy and a brash, brainy Jewish woman from New York. And they embodied the politics of the Big Idea, talking up sweeping reforms for taxes, health care and education. They were firmly in the mold of Oregon's most iconic governor, Tom McCall, who brought the state the Beach Bill, the Bottle Bill and Land Use. Those issues captured the public imagination and visibly transformed Oregon. Even his famous quip on national TV urging people to visit but not to stay only seemed to encourage more folks to move here.

Democrat Neil Goldschmidt and Republican Norma Paulus also had plenty to say about Atiyeh when they faced off in a high-stakes governor race in 1986. Both promised to shake up state government and get the state moving economically. Each portrayed Atiyeh as part of the staid status quo. It was true that Atiyeh was not an avatar of the Big Idea. His most famous quote may have been, "If it ain't broke, don't try to fix it."

Gradually, though, I came to understand that my off-the-cuff assessment of Atiyeh was wrong. The truth is that he had helped his beloved Oregon – my new state – with more skill than I've seen from most leaders. First, I had to understand true economic pain, something I had never really experienced growing up in the San Francisco Bay Area (perpetually booming in the 1960s and 1970s) and then working in Washington, D.C. (which with its permanent federal workforce was insulated from the worst of economic downturns).

In contrast, Oregon was devastated by the early 1980s recession. The slump was triggered by Federal Reserve Chairman Paul Volker's determination to end sky-high inflation. The Fed jacked up interest rates to the point that homebuilding crashed, forcing Oregon's dominant timber industry to shed tens of thousands of jobs. Oregon's unemployment rate reached 12% by the end of 1982. When I arrived a year later, I could still see plenty of boarded up storefronts and foreclosed homes. I felt like I had moved to Appalachia.

I realize how much Atiyeh had been required to make brutally hard decisions. In the depths of the recession, he joined the Democrats to increase Oregon's income tax, something that was especially painful for a Republican governor who had always prided himself on his fiscal conservatism. Atiyeh even managed to sell the tax hike in a way that avoided sparking a ballot referendum over the tax. In a state where almost anything of real controversy ends up on the ballot, that's no small feat. He angered his friends in the state's business community by raiding a workplace insurance fund to balance the state's operating budget. And he had to hear himself described as heartless for his cuts to safety net programs.

At the same time, Atiyeh worked hard to diversify Oregon's economy. As it became clear Oregon could no longer rely so heavily on timber, Atiyeh redoubled his efforts to sell the state to the electronics industry – or to anybody else he could conceivably entice. At one point he even tried to persuade General Motors to build a new auto plant in Coos Bay. That was a Hail Mary pass that came up far short.

As the years passed, however, Atiyeh's efforts at economic diversification began to bear fruit. As Oregon moved on to other governors, Atiyeh's work gained new appreciation. I remember interviewing Kitzhaber after he won the governorship in 1994 and being surprised when he told me he saw Atiyeh as a role model to follow. While they came from different sides of the political divide, Kitzhaber said he appreciated Atiyeh's steadiness and commitment to helping Oregon prosper. The two also shared a long period of service in the Legislature that taught them the nuances of Oregon's major issues.

I've thought more about Atiyeh and his legacy after reading Jim Moore's impeccably well-researched biography. What Moore shows is that Atiyeh provided a master class in how to govern from the center. This is a valuable skill that political, civic and even business leaders ignore all too often – and at their peril.

This applies to leaders of both the left and right. The most enduring accomplishments in American history are those that build bipartisan support, or at least grudging acceptance from the political party that was originally in opposition.

In Atiyeh's case, his instincts were that of a businessman who learned in his two decades in the Legislature that government had an important role to play – and just that what role was often depended on the situation. At times he could be a shape shifter. He was seen as a staunch conservative in the 1978 Republican gubernatorial primary when he defeated McCall in his comeback bid. By the time Atiyeh was running for re-election in the depths of the recession, he was willing to take on President Reagan for the economic policies that were hurting the state.

Atiyeh also showed his instincts for governing from the political center when he helped cement McCall's most important legacy: Oregon's statewide land use restrictions on urban sprawl. Atiyeh made changes aimed at providing more certainty to businesses and developers on where they could and could not build. At the same time, he opposed a 1982 ballot measure promoted by conservatives to gut the program.

In many ways, I compare Atiyeh to President Dwight D. Eisenhower, another Republican who knew how to work the political center. During his two terms, Eisenhower accepted Social Security – a centerpiece of FDR's New Deal. Eisenhower kept the U.S. active in international institutions and resisted isolationism. Like Atiyeh, Eisenhower more than once turned aside pressure from the right of his party, often so deftly that conservatives and liberals alike didn't realize what was happening. Both Ike and Vic weren't afraid to be boring to mask their behind-the-scenes maneuvering.

Atiyeh had a long final chapter in Oregon politics as an ex-governor and elder statesmen. He and Democrat Barbara Roberts, who also has had a lot of years as an ex-governor, were both regulars at ceremonial events and memorial services for prominent figures.

Atiyeh never did have a successor from his own party. For the rest of his life, he would be known as Oregon's last Republican governor. For years after he retired, Atiyeh was a regular at Republican conferences offering his own advice on how the party could succeed. Perhaps his skills weren't transferrable. It didn't help Republicans that for years after his governorship, they were more interested in purging the moderate-to-liberal Republicans who once dominated statewide offices than they were in learning how to govern from the center. And at a certain point, the state shifted so much to the left that it was hard to see what the Republican Party could do, even as it finally did nominate several moderates for governor.

Regardless, I still think that there's a bit of Vic Atiyeh's DNA in any governor or legislator who wants to figure out how to get things done. His story is well worth telling, even for students of government outside of Oregon.

Atiyeh always liked the aphorism that you can get a lot done if you don't worry about who takes credit for it. Still, he was human. I always enjoyed watching him – usually standing next to Roberts or one of the other ex-governors –after being introduced at the ceremonial opening of each legislative session. He'd wave, break out that almost shy smile of his and enjoy the applause of his former colleagues. He was a man of the institution who had the pleasure of knowing that he knew how to make it do some of its best work.

1 Preparing

Vic Atiyeh held office during an exciting time in Oregon politics. Entering elective office with the state's centennial, Atiyeh was part of a golden age for the state legislature, which at the time was truly coequal with the governor in terms of creating and implementing policy ideas.

The policies that made Oregon's government famous nationwide—the Beach Bill, the Bottle Bill, Oregon's statewide land use laws—all were big debates in the 1960s and 1970s. These became known as the Oregon Story. Atiyeh was on the frontline of some of these issues—whether in support or opposition—but he was always working to master the intricacies of these proposed laws so that he could cast votes he was comfortable with. With his election as Oregon's governor in 1978, he saw his job as ensuring that all these changes were solidified and incorporated firmly into Oregon's political system. He wanted them to be successful in the decades after the excitement of creating these new concepts.

Atiyeh's political aim was simple: leave Oregon better than it was when he started in politics and poised for the challenges ahead.

Atiyeh was largely successful in his goals, but he would be faced with problems not seen in Oregon since the 1930s. Oregon's worst recession since the Great Depression hit just as Atiyeh was seeking his second term. His responses to this recession would help establish Oregon as a player in the global economy in ways that were just not possible during the timber years.

This would be his legacy. Charismatic Tom McCall, Oregon's governor from 1967 to 1975, still lays claim to credit for the Oregon Story. In the ensuing decades, hundreds of thousands of people visited and moved to Oregon to experience that story. But when those people settled in Oregon, they were working in the economy Vic Atiyeh had helped come into being in the mid-1980s.

A Rug-Selling Family

Victor Atiyeh grew up and worked for much of his adult life in a retail family. The history of the Atiyeh Brothers Oriental Rug company in Portland and other cities showed young Victor what innovation, customer service, and loyalty to principles could accomplish. Sooner or later, many of those who engaged with him in politics came to understand that a big part of Victor's understanding of the political world, and especially public finance, grew from his knowledge of retailing.

Victor's father, George, came from Amar El-Husn, part of the Ottoman Empire in modern-day Syria. Tucked into a valley below the Crusader castle Krac du Chevalier, Amar had a long history as a Christian village. Located about 120 miles northwest of Damascus, and quite near the modern border with Lebanon, Amar epitomized change in the late Ottoman Empire—it was a village of emigrants, local villagers who left to find their futures in countries around the world.[1] George Atiyeh's older brother Aziz emigrated to the United States in 1897. Aziz was nineteen years old as he joined the Amar enclave in Pennsylvania, settling ten miles from Allentown in South Bethlehem, where he entered the linen business.[2] Aziz sent for his brother George to help out with

---

1   Anton Escher, "The Arab American Way: The Success Story of an American Family from a Syrian Village in Global Diaspora," *American Studies Journal* 52 (2008), DOAJ Database of Open Access Journals.

2   Edward Atiyeh, "Atiyeh Bros. Inc. 1900–2008," (Unpublished manuscript, 2008), 1, Scan of loose leaf binder, Atiyeh Collection, Pac. Univ. Archives.

the growing business, with George arriving in the United States on April 1, 1900. The business of A. Atiyeh and Brother was established with a bank account in Allentown.[3]

Around 1900, Aziz heard of business opportunities in the American West. The East Coast was filled with similar linen companies, so it was harder to make a living. Aziz began to make trips to Portland, Oregon, to explore the possibilities there and conduct business, leaving seventeen-year-old George to run the business in Pennsylvania. Within a few years Aziz made the transition from being a peddler to opening an actual store. The business first appeared in newspaper mentions in May 1903 as Atiyeh and Khoury at 411 Washington Street in Portland. George moved out to Portland in the late summer or early fall of 1903.[4] A partnership with David Khoury was over by September 1903 and A. Atiyeh and Bro., Importer of Oriental Rugs, settled into the new city.[5]

1905 was a big year for the new firm. First, A. Atiyeh and Brother took on the name that has lasted to this day, Atiyeh Brothers.[6] Second, the Lewis and Clark Exposition brought thousands of visitors to Portland, and thousands of potential customers to Atiyeh Brothers. The company also displayed rugs at the Exposition, winning gold medals. The next year the company was on the road, playing up its award-winning merchandise in other up and coming towns in the American West: "A part of Atiyeh Bros.' exhibit at the Lewis and Clark Exposition which obtained the GOLD MEDAL after a most critical inspection by leading connoisseurs."[7] The company also won more medals and

---

3 Aziz Atiyeh, "Aziz E. Atiyeh and Brother Bank Deposit Book," South Bethlehem National Bank, January 1901–August 1902, (1901–1902), Atiyeh Brothers archive, Tigard, OR.

4 *Oregonian*, "David Khoury," 14 September 1903.

5 Ed Atiyeh, "Atiyeh Bros. Inc. 1900–2008," 1–2; "Linda Atiyeh Emergency Passport Application," Consulate General, U.S. Department of State, (18 January 1921), Atiyeh Collection, Pac. Univ. Archives.

6 *Oregonian*, "Oriental Rug Sale," Advertisement, 28 March 1905; *Portland City Directory*, (Portland, OR: R. L. Polk, 1905).

7 *Tribune* (Salt Lake City), "Richest of Oriental Rugs," Advertisement, 1 May 1906. Capitalization in the original.

grand prizes at the Alaska-Yukon Exposition in Seattle in 1909, the 1915 Panama-Pacific Exposition in San Francisco, and the 1916 Panama-California Fair in San Diego. The company even represented the Ottoman Turkish government at the San Francisco exposition.[8]

In the 1920s the one company became two. George stayed in Portland to run the store; Aziz moved to New York to run a wholesale and importing business. Both brothers had ownership of both companies, but it was George who became firmly planted in the Portland business community.

George became a U.S. citizen in 1913. He had married in 1907, but his wife died by 1909.[9] At some point after World War I, he decided to marry again. He had met Linda Asly in Beirut. Linda was born in 1898 in Beirut, still a part of the Ottoman Empire. Her family was in the shipping business, so it is likely that George met Linda through Atiyeh Brothers' shipping of Oriental rugs through the port. In the early 1940s, Linda told a friend of hers that it was an arranged marriage.[10] Victor himself had a strong suspicion it was an arranged marriage as well, but, as he thought of it in 2013, when he had the chance to put it to his parents, "I didn't ask some questions I should have asked."[11]

Linda and George were married in Beirut at the end of December 1920. They embarked on a long honeymoon trip to Turkey, Egypt, Greece, and France, finally arriving at Ellis Island at the end of April 1921.[12] The laws at the time granted Linda American citizenship through marriage, so she entered the United

---

8 Ed Atiyeh, "Atiyeh Bros. Inc. 1900–2008," 2–3; "Atiyeh Brothers Awards," Atiyeh Brothers, 1905–1915. Atiyeh Brothers store, Tigard, OR.

9 *Daily Review* (Decatur, IL), "Telephoned Sister News of Marriage," 3 May 1907; Linda Atiyeh Anderson, *The Atiyeh Brothers, Richard, Victor, and Edward*, (Portland, OR: Apple iPhoto book, 2011), 3, Atiyeh Collection, Pac. Univ. Archives.

10 Donna Campbell, interviewed by Jim Moore, "Atiyeh interview," Raleigh Hills, OR, 26 June 2015. Summary notes, 6, Atiyeh project, Moore collection.

11 Victor Atiyeh, interviewed by Pat Amedeo, "Arlington Club Oral History," Oral history, recorded by Arlington Club, Portland, OR, 10 September 2013. Transcript, 14, 15, Atiyeh Collection, Pac. Univ. Archives.

12 Anderson, *Atiyeh Brothers*, 4–5

States as an immigrant, but also as a citizen. Linda was pregnant with twins as they headed to Portland to set up house.

Richard and Edward Atiyeh were born in October 1921, nine months and one week after their parents' marriage. The boys were baptized a year later by the Syrian Orthodox bishops of Brooklyn and Beirut (who married Linda and George in 1920), and Jerusalem at the family home in a rite that was described as "an interesting event" on the *Oregonian* and *Oregon Journal* society pages.[13] Sixteen months later, on February 20, 1923, the birth of Victor George Atiyeh was also announced on the *Oregonian* society page.[14] His baptism in October 1924, also at home, was presided over by the Syrian Archbishop of New York and North America, who actually lived in Mexico.[15]

As young Victor became aware of the world, he experienced the highs of the roaring 1920s and the lows of the Great Depression. His view of the world was forged in those childhood days as he watched his family's business negotiate a challenging business climate.

The Portland store and George Atiyeh faced a threat in 1924 when Victor was just one and the twins were two and a half. The first Saturday in May city officials raided the Atiyeh home during a party and confiscated "a large collection of fine wines and liquors."[16] A few days later the federal government stepped in, backing a truck up to the Portland central police station and taking the haul to the federal customs house. Federal prohibition agents were especially interested in the "specially devised container" that had transported the contraband alcohol from New York to Portland. Both the city and the federal government filed charges against George. Two months later George pleaded "guilty

---

13 *Oregon Journal*, "Baptism Is Picturesque: Greek Church Rites Used," 17 September 1922; *Oregonian*, "Society News,", 8 September 1922; Hazel Handy, "Mrs. Morrison Hostess to Auxiliary," *Portland Oregon Journal*, 7 September 1922; Anderson, *Atiyeh Brothers,* 8.
14 *Oregonian*, "Society News," 22 February 1923.
15 Anderson, *Atiyeh Brothers,* 45.
16 *Oregonian*, "Liquors Are Removed: Government Takes Charge of Intoxicants Seized in Raid," 6 May 1924.

to possession and transportation of liquor in violation of the prohibition act and to false marking of a package transported in interstate commerce" in Federal district court and was fined $500 (almost $6,800 in 2015).[17] The prosecutors were particularly interested in the "hermetically sealed case containing 28 quarts of genuine Scotch whisky" shipped from Brooklyn, New York, to the Atiyeh Brothers store in Portland. While Prohibition was often ignored by Portland's elite (one report noted 100 speakeasies in the city in the mid-1920s),[18] this federal conviction focusing on shipping, the lifeblood of the Atiyeh Brothers business, could have had serious consequences.

The Atiyeh boys knew about this incident from their parents. Ed Atiyeh recalled that the family "always got a good laugh" from the story. George "was disturbed because he felt the government agents did not destroy the liquor when they found it. Someone must have enjoyed it."[19]

During the Great Depression in the 1930s, Atiyeh Brothers experienced the same economic hardships as other businesses. In the fall of 1929 an Atiyeh Brothers representative, Fred Atiyeh (son of Aziz) was in Persia to buy rugs. George was able to get a message to Fred, telling him, "Don't spend the money!" He came back with the money and no rugs, and Atiyeh Brothers had enough cash to survive some of the early hard times of the growing Great Depression.[20] George was optimistic that the economy was changing for the better at the beginning of 1930, but by 1933 he joined with thousands of employers in President Roosevelt's plan to bring "back more employment with shorter

---

17 *Oregonian*, "Whisky Owner is Fined: Portland Merchant to Pay $500 on Federal Court Order," *Oregonian* 8 July 1924.

18 E. Kimbark MacColl, *The Growth of a City: Power and Politics in Portland, Oregon, 1915 to 1950.* (Portland, OR: Georgian Press, 1979), 276–277.

19 Edward Atiyeh, Email to Jim Moore, "Interesting Finding About Your Father," 3 August 2015.

20 Tom Atiyeh, interviewed by Jim Moore, "Atiyeh interview," Sherwood, OR, 28 July 2015. Summary, 13.

hours and higher wages by signing" an agreement with "the bureau of foreign and domestic commerce."[21]

George Atiyeh never laid off any of his employees, and he went into debt to keep the store going. He would sell rugs at whatever price it took to get some income for the business. The tensions among businesses competing for scarce consumer dollars were intense. At one point an Atiyeh Brothers salesman "waylaid one of the owners of another store and beat him up."[22] Victor never knew the details, and he did not find out how hard the Depression was on the business until he took over running it in the 1940s. The Great Depression was a difficult time, but the boys were shielded from it as much as possible.

By the mid-1930s Atiyeh Brothers was in good enough shape to move out of its location and into bigger accommodations in downtown Portland. The store had moved several times in its first decades, but it was always in the same three or four block area. The opening of this new location brought Portland's mayor, its chief of police, and much of the Chamber of Commerce to its grand opening.[23]

Childhood, then War

The Atiyeh home in northeast Portland on Holladay Street was near what was then called Sullivan's Gulch, the location of the Interstate 84 freeway and the Max light rail line today. In the gulch was a Hooverville, a place where people squatted in a

---

21 *Oregonian*,"3000 Oregon and Idaho Employers Heed President's Call: Largest Response of Any Single Day in Drive to Provide Higher Wages and New Employment; Totals for First Week Soar Up Past 8000 Mark as Returns Pour in From All Sections of Two States," 3 August 1933.

22 Victor Atiyeh, interviewed by Clark Hansen, "Tape 1," Oral history, recorded by Oregon Historical Society, Portland, OR, 24 November 1992. Transcript, 25, Atiyeh Collection, Pac. Univ. Archives.

23 *Oregonian*, "Atiyeh Opening Is Set for Today: Two-Day Open House Marks 35th Anniversary," 18 January 1935; *Oregonian*,"Retail Meet Speakers Praise George Atiyeh," 7 March 1935; *Oregonian*,"Atiyehs to Open New Rug Store," 13 January 1935; *Oregonian*, "Rugs to You, Mr. Atiyeh," Photograph with caption, 10 March 1935.

makeshift shanty town.[24] Victor remembered people "knocking on our door for a little food. They always said they would…want to do a little work…."[25] The boys did not really notice the impact of the Great Depression in their home lives, but they were very aware that there were widespread hard times.

The Atiyeh sons did not identify themselves as Arab, but rather as Americans. Their parents did not teach them Arabic; they did not live in the southeast Portland neighborhood where most other Arabs lived, and they grew up in the Episcopalian church, not the Syrian Orthodox church into which they were all baptized. They attended Portland public schools until they graduated from Washington High in 1941. At home the boys would play roller hockey on neighborhood streets, football in a local sandlot, occasional games of kick the can, interspersed with a lot of bicycle riding.[26]

As the boys grew older, they started doing outdoor chores around the house. There was household help for inside tasks like washing and ironing, but the boys became the main labor force for mowing the lawn and the like. Every third week each of the boys would take turns going down to Atiyeh Brothers to work.[27] They would work in the basement cleaning rugs and doing general tasks. Ed remembered learning "how to mix the Ivory Flakes and scrub by hand. It 'took at least a week for a rug to dry.'"[28] At the end of the day their father would pay that day's worker $5, if they earned it. "Richard always got his five dollars; I didn't always get my five dollars," recalled Victor.[29] Victor

---

24   Jewel Lansing, *Portland: People, Politics, and Power 1851–2001*, (Corvallis, OR: Oregon State University Press, 2003), 317–318; Carl Abbott, *Portland in Three Centuries: The Place and the People*, (Corvallis, OR: Oregon State University Press, 2011), 112–113.

25   Victor Atiyeh, "Tape 1," 24.

26   Victor Atiyeh, "Tape 1," 16.

27   Edward Atiyeh, Email to Jim Moore, "Vic's Biography," 8 December 2016, Atiyeh Collection, Pac. Univ. Archives.

28   Helen L. Mershon, "Governor-Elect's Roots Show Family 'Closeness': Those Atiyeh Boys," *Portland Oregon Journal*, 16 November 1978, Atiyeh Collection, Pac. Univ. Archives.

29   Victor Atiyeh, "Tape 1," 20–21.

remembered that he always wanted to be doing something else, knowing that he could work at the store if he wanted to. This yearning to find his own way lasted a lifetime, eventually leading him into politics.

Ed and Victor were active in Boy Scouts. Victor loved scouting, but the troop he and Ed joined was becoming disorganized. They switched to become Sea Scouts, boating out on the Columbia River on the Sea Scout ship *Columbia*, among other activities.[30]

Unknowingly, the Atiyeh boys grew up to appreciate demographic diversity. Their neighborhood and their schools were examples of the famous American melting pot. The 1930 and 1940 Census records show that their immediate neighbors were of widely scattered national and ethnic origins.[31] Victor remembered that

> in Holladay School and in Washington High School we were a whole mix of people. At Holladay School we had Japanese, most of which, of course, were interned during the war.... We went to school with them. A lot of Italians there, we were Syrian, a lot of blacks. It was just a good mix of people. ...We're just all going to school together, we're all friends from playing ball together or going to school together. There was just nothing unusual about it. That probably—that did have some effect on my later life, that is, in terms of thinking of people being very comfortable. Some people have to force themselves to not discriminate. To me, it was no forcing. I mean, these were just people I grew up with. I mean, we were all on the same level.[32]

---

30   Victor Atiyeh, interviewed by Clark Hansen, "Tape 3, side 1," Oral history, recorded by Oregon Historical Society, Portland, OR, 1 December 1992. Transcript, 58, Atiyeh Collection, Pac. Univ. Archives.

31   "Census," Bureau of the Census, Department of Commerce, Oregon, Multnomah County, District 376, (1930); "Census," Bureau of the Census, Department of Commerce, Oregon, Multnomah County, District 37-322, (1940).

32   Victor Atiyeh, interviewed by Clark Hansen, "Tape 2," Oral history, recorded by Oregon Historical Society, Portland, OR, 1 December 1992. Transcript, 34, Atiyeh Collection, Pac. Univ. Archives.

Ed Atiyeh remembered that his father George never showed any prejudice in his dealings with customers, business associates, or personal friends. The Atiyeh Brothers store was always open to all customers. From this background, it never occurred to Victor or his brothers to even talk about race when they dealt with people. Ed did not remember race or ethnicity being an issue when the boys were growing up, nor does he remember this being an issue after the boys ran Atiyeh Brothers from the 1940s to the 1980s.[33] Decades later people around Victor felt that he was frustrated at being treated differently because of his Syrian background, especially by the Portland business community.[34]

There was a time in the 1970s when being an Arab could have become a political issue. As the gasoline shortages caused by Arab oil producing countries were being talked about in an Oregon Senate committee meeting in February 1974, Vern Cook (D-Portland) "said, 'the Arabs are blackmailers.' Then he noticed Sen. Victor Atiyeh…break out in a grin. So did Cook. 'Present company excepted,' Cook said."[35] Atiyeh's political persona was built on his solid retail background and his years in the legislature. Did his Arab heritage become an issue because of the embargo? As it turned out, no.

One of the far-reaching events in the lives of young Victor and his brothers was a long trip to Syria in the summer of 1929, when Victor was six years old, and the twins were seven The Syria trip created treasured memories that lasted to the end of his life. Transportation in the region was made easier because George had purchased a Franklin Sedan automobile in Portland and had it shipped to Beirut. A driver was hired in Beirut to drive the family during its stay in the Levant. The family drove northeast from Linda's family home to George's home in Amar. This village of

---

33 Ed Atiyeh, "Atiyeh interview #2," 3–4.
34 Pat Amedeo, interviewed by Jim Moore, "Atiyeh interview," Santa Rosa, CA, 24 March 2015. Summary notes, 3.
35 *Oregon Statesman* (Salem), "Ccok Pulls Words from Frying Pan," 18 February 1974; AP, "Cook Amends Arab Remark," *Oregonian*, 19 February 1974.

emigrants erected a welcome sign (in English) atop an arch of palm fronds at the family house. The boys remembered "eating, riding on an Arabian horse (our family raised them), and sightseeing" at the nearby Krac de Chevalier castle.[36] The next time Victor would visit Amar would be as Oregon governor in 1984. He took pictures of the places he remembered from 55 years earlier, even noting that "the beds in which we slept were still there!"[37]

Victor excelled at school in the early grades. He skipped a grade in elementary school, so he was about in the same class year as his older brothers. At that time, Portland high schools graduated two classes a year, so there would be a January group of graduates, then a June group. Ed and Richard graduated in January 1941, Victor in June 1941. In high school Victor tried out basketball, track and field, golf, football, and baseball. He ended up being a credible football player. A big kid, Atiyeh went through sports until he found something that worked with his body (he broke an arm and a leg along the way), and that he really enjoyed.[38] A cyst from that broken leg would change Victor's life in college. Golf was the family pastime, and something that Rich and Ed loved as well. Ed even caddied for Victor when Victor was on the golf team at Washington High. Victor played golf up until his death. He never practiced. Rich and Ed would work at their games, but they were never as good as Victor. "It used to annoy us," Ed remembered.[39]

Football ended up being Atiyeh's sport in high school and college. He started out as a fullback on the freshman team. Then, playing behind an all-city back, Atiyeh moved to kicking kickoffs and extra points to get in the game on the varsity squad. With just a couple of games left in the season of Atiyeh's junior year, the

---

36 Anderson, *The Atiyeh Brothers*, 24.
37 Anderson, *The Atiyeh Brothers*, 25.
38 *Oregonian*, "Young Ball Player Breaks Right Ankle," 30 May 1937, 74; Mershon, "Governor-Elect's Roots."; W. Scott Jorgensen, *Conversations with Atiyeh*, (Carlton, OR: Ridenbaugh Press, 2014).
39 Ed Atiyeh, "Atiyeh interview #2," 5.

coach asked if Atiyeh would play as a lineman to replace an injured teammate. Victor jumped at the chance to be in the game all the time, instead of just trotting out for kicks, telling the coach, "I want to play football."[40] He got his letters in football both his junior and senior years. The big kid had found his athletic niche. His senior year in 1940 Atiyeh was named a Portland city all-star, even though his Washington high school team was 0-6-2 that year.[41] Victor won a football scholarship to the University of Oregon. At U of O Atiyeh never played varsity football.[42] In his first two years, his coaches were saving him for his last two years, so he played as a JV guard during his time on campus, along with some extra-point kicking in his first year. In the final game of the 1942 season, he almost came in at the end of the Civil War game against Oregon State, but the coach decided not to risk Atiyeh's future eligibility for varsity football.[43]

By high school, Victor had a close group of friends around him. His closest friends were Jim Campbell and Tom Galt. Jim's girlfriend, Donna Shulson, remembered hours of being together at school involved in the myriad activities of busy teenagers. Victor also had a steady girlfriend, Dolores Hewitt, another half-year younger than Victor, Jim, and Donna. These four decided to "locker together" in the 1940–41 school year. "What a mess," reminisced Donna, "But it was fun." Victor stayed in touch with his close high school friends as long as they lived, saying of all three in 1993, "to have that kind of friendship is very rare."

Victor first noticed Dolores Hewitt during his senior year in high school. He saw a pretty girl come out a door at school, and he said to himself, "Gee whiz, where did she come from?" She

---

40 Victor Atiyeh, "Tape 2," 31.
41 Don Taylor, "Teurman and Atiyeh Cup Winners," *Washington High School, Portland (OR) Washingtonian*, 20 May 1941, Atiyeh collection. Pacific University Archives, Forest Grove, OR; Wayne Thompson, "Wink from Pros Deepened Atiyeh's Love for Football," *Portland Oregonian*, 14 November 1978.
42 *State Journal* (Reno, NV), "22 Sophomores Will Report to Oregon's Coach," 6 September 1942; Harry Crawford, "Oregon Ready to Open Grid Drill Sept. 10," *Ogden (UT) Standard-Examiner*, 3 September 1942.
43 Thompson, "Wink from Pros."

had been at Washington for three years, but this was the first time Victor noticed her. He found out her name, but he also discovered that she had a boyfriend, so that was that. But soon, Victor found out that Dolores had broken up with her beau, so he began contemplating asking her out. As he remembered, there was a problem—"I was a very bashful kind of guy."[44] A friend reminded Victor of the upcoming Christmas dance and told him to invite Dolores. Victor did not know her phone number, so he started calling all the Hewitts in the phone book, asking for Dolores. After several wrong numbers, he found her, invited her to the dance, and they became high school sweethearts. Victor later learned that he had called the correct number early on, but that Dolores' father was just tired of all the phone calls for his daughter at dinner time. When his future son-in-law called, he had testily replied, "Nobody here by that name."

The brothers headed off to the University of Oregon together in the fall of 1941. It would be years before Richard and Ed graduated. Victor would never get his degree. Their father encouraged them to explore classes and major in whatever they wanted. There was no pressure at all for any of them to join Atiyeh Brothers after graduation. Victor's initial plan was to major in art or design to become a commercial artist. His father tersely ended that plan when he told Victor, "You're nuts."[45] So Victor became a pre-law student for no particular reason that he could remember.

The Atiyehs joined Phi Gamma Delta fraternity (the Fijis), along with Jim Campbell and Tom Galt. Victor played on the frosh football team, beating the Oregon State frosh squad, but missing an extra point kick in the effort. All that changed on a Sunday morning in December 1941. The Japanese attack on Pearl Harbor instantly upended the lives of most American men of that age.[46] Among the Fijis, there were some who immediately began

---

44   Victor Atiyeh, "Tape 2," 32.
45   Victor Atiyeh, "Tape 2," 41.
46   "Living Thoughts of World War II: Correspondence of Epsilon Omicron Fijis 1943–1945," (Unpublished manuscript, 1995), Collection of Letters, Phi Gama

to talk of joining the military. Others waited to see what would happen, but it was clear by the spring of 1942 that all able-bodied young men would be going into military service.

Over the course of the 1942–43 school year many of Victor's classmates joined the military. Victor tried to be one of them, but he ended up being rejected by the Army. His broken leg from playing baseball as a freshman in high school had created a cyst that caused him to fail the military physicals. He was very upset, but there was nothing he could do to change the medical findings.[47] After three physicals, he finally got a letter telling him he was discharged from the military. He tried to get drafted, but the same officials who had given him his Army physicals oversaw the draft board, so he was immediately rated 4-F, not available for the draft for medical reasons. They did not even process him. Victor then tried the Merchant Marines, but they rejected him as well.[48] Later, Victor successfully joined the Coast Guard temporary reserves, and spent twelve-hour shifts, one day a week, patrolling the docks in the Portland harbors.

Victor completed his sophomore year in June 1943. He never returned to college as a student.[49]

In 1944, as the war was raging and young men were in short supply on college campuses, as well as in the professional sports leagues, Atiyeh received interest from several professional football teams. The Chicago Cardinals, New York Giants, and Cleveland Rams all indicated they wanted him to play.[50] But when an actual contract arrived from the Green Bay Packers, Atiyeh

---

    Delta Epsilon Omicron Chapter, University of Oregon, Atiyeh Collection, Pac. Univ. Archives.

47   Ed Atiyeh, "Atiyeh interview #2," 3.

48   Victor Atiyeh, "Tape 2," 38.

49   Scott Morrell, Email to Jim Moore, "University of Oregon Registrar Historical Information Request," 9 June 2015.

50   Arch Wolf, Letter to Victor Atiyeh, "Chicago Cardinals' Interest," 3 June 1944, Atiyeh Collection, Pacific University Archives, Forest Grove, OR; Chas. F. Walsh, Letter to Victor Atiyeh, "Cleveland Rams' Interest," 31 May 1944, Atiyeh Collection, Pacific University Archives, Forest Grove, OR; John V. Mara, Letter to Victor Atiyeh, "New York Giants' Interest," 31 May 1944, Atiyeh Collection, Pac. Univ. Archives.

had some decisions to make.[51] By the third week in June Victor let all the teams know that he was flattered, but that he needed to concentrate on getting through the next three years of law studies.[52]

The last week in June 1944, Victor was planning to work at the Atiyeh Brothers store for the summer, continue his work with the Coast Guard Temporary Reserve, and prepare to enter law school after another year at U of O, having just turned down an offer to play professional football.

By the end of July 1944, just five weeks later, he was newly married, his father had died, and Victor had taken over management of Atiyeh Brothers, starting a career in the rug business that would last 35 years.

Becoming an Adult—Five Major Events in One Year

In the summer of 1944, with deployment into combat zones growing ever closer, Richard and Ed had a leave to return to Portland before shipping out. They suggested that Victor and Dolores get married during their visit, so a wedding was put together within a week. This was the first major event.

On July 5, 1944, Dolores Hewitt and Victor Atiyeh were married in the chapel at Portland's Trinity Episcopal Church. Dolores had a single attendant, her sister, while Richard was Victor's best man, and Ed, along with two other friends on leave from the military, served as ushers. Dolores in her bridal gown

---

51 Curley Lambeau, Telegram to Victor Atiyeh, "Green Bay Packers' Interest," 27 May 1944, Atiyeh Collection, Pacific University Archives, Forest Grove, OR; E. L. Lambeau, Letter and contract to Victor Atiyeh, "Green Bay Packers Offer," 6 June 1944, Atiyeh Collection, Pac. Univ. Archives.

52 Victor Atiyeh, Letter to E. L. Lambeau, "Response to Green Bay Packers Offer," 20 June 1944, Atiyeh Collection, Pacific University Archives, Forest Grove, OR; Victor Atiyeh, Letter to Chas. F. Walsh, "Response to Rams' Interest," 20 June 1944, Atiyeh Collection, Pacific University Archives, Forest Grove, OR; Victor Atiyeh, Letter to John V. Mara, "Response to Giants' Interest," 20 June 1944, Atiyeh Collection, Pacific University Archives, Forest Grove, OR; Victor Atiyeh, Letter to Arch Wolf, "Response to Cardinals' Interest," 20 June 1944, Atiyeh Collection, Pacific University Archives, Forest Grove, OR

was the featured photo on the first page of the *Oregonian* society section for Sunday July 16, 1944.[53] This was a wedding that, while quickly put together, showed the social status of the Atiyeh family in the community. The newlyweds moved into an apartment in the west hills of Portland, in the West Sylvan area.

Richard and Ed returned to their Army unit to prepare for European deployment. In the third week in July, their father, George, had a massive heart attack that left him in a coma. Richard and Ed quickly got emergency leave, traveled across the country for the second time in a month, and were able to see their father before his death on July 31, 1944. The second major event.

George Atiyeh's death was noted with an *Oregonian* news article and editorial.[54] His business acumen was extolled, as well as his role within the community. One trait that was singled out in the editorial "was his modesty, there were few who knew that their friend and acquaintance was by way of being a famous authority on a subject which demands far more than casual knowledge." The Oriental rug expert kept his nationally renowned talents, known to those in the trade, quiet among his Portland circle of friends. This penchant for modesty about abilities and expertise was something inherited by his youngest son, Victor.

Victor, the 21-year-old son who was not in the military due to his leg injury, took over the family business. Event number three. His natural ability to learn, as well as his growing knack for observing and understanding human nature, was put to the test very quickly. Victor had no training from his father on how to run the store. "We were taught a lot about the cleaning and repair end of the business. Management we had to learn for ourselves." Victor recalled,

---

53 *Oregonian*, "Miss Hewitt, Mr. Atiyeh Married Here Recently in Trinity Church Chapel," 16 July 1944; Ed Atiyeh, "Atiyeh interview #2," 4.

54 *Oregonian*, "Death Claims Rug Dealer," 2 August 1944; *Oregonian*, "Passing of Mr. Atiyeh," Editorial, 3 August 1944.

All of a sudden now I've got the management of the whole company. I had never talked to my dad about that. I know about the cleaning. So, I keep my eyes open. It was not pleasant. Salesmen would argue about whose customer it is because they got commission, and they'd come and say, "My customer," and he'd say, "My customer," and I'm supposed to decide whose customer it is. These weren't particularly pleasant times, but I just kind of keep my mouth shut and my eyes open, and it worked out.[55]

Atiyeh Brothers had several employees who had been with the company for decades, characterized as a group of "experienced, Middle Eastern salespeople" who were aggressive. Victor knew that if he managed them with a heavy hand, he would be in trouble. Using his "mouth shut, eyes open" strategy, Victor began to figure out how to manage these older men. He never confronted anybody, but he used strategies based on his sense of human nature to guide the salesmen to the right choices.

Victor had planned to go to law school. His brothers had both shown interest in someday running the family business, but Victor had not. When George Atiyeh had been alive, he and Victor had argued about how to pursue goals, either in the business or on a more personal level. Victor felt that his father did not "really believe" that Victor "was ever going to be in the rug business. Ed and Rich, yes, but I don't think he ever thought I was really going to be" working at Atiyeh Brothers.[56] Those close to Victor noticed that his heart was never really in the business in the same way as his brothers.[57]

By the fall of 1944, as World War II entered its fourth year for the United States, most of Victor's close male friends and his brothers were serving overseas. Richard and Ed, after months of training in Auburn, Alabama, at the Army Specialized Training Program (astp) for officers, were sent to Belgium with the 106th

---

55 Victor Atiyeh, "Tape 3, side 1," 64.
56 Victor Atiyeh, "Tape 3, side 1," 66.
57 Campbell, "Atiyeh Interview," 1.

Infantry Division, just a few months after the June 1944 D-Day landings. Relatively inexperienced soldiers, the 106th moved into place in Belgium on December 11, 1944, during a legendary cold spell. Richard and Ed remembered it being so cold in the foxholes that they cut holes in their mummy sleeping bags to wear like coats.[58] Within days, on December 16, the German counterattack known as the Battle of Bulge hit the 106th with full force. On December 19, 1944, two of the three regiments in the 106th surrendered to the Germans. Among those taken prisoner were Richard and Ed Atiyeh. The two brothers had been separated in the fierce fighting; their platoon was broken up in the confusion. They were taken prisoner, separately, the next day. The prisoners were kept in two large compounds. A fellow prisoner was moved from the compound that held Richard to the other, where Ed was being held. He passed the news to Ed that Richard was alive; Richard did not know what had happened to Ed until Richard's release in the spring of 1945.[59]

Back home, nothing was known about the Atiyeh brothers for almost three months. This was the fourth major event in Victor's life since July 1944.

Ed was liberated from a German camp on April 1, 1945, Easter Sunday, by an American armored division. After a few weeks in a hospital, he was on the plane back home. A month later, Richard was freed from his Polish open-pit coal mining camp and on the same track.[60] They finished out their war service recuperating, together, at an army facility in Santa Barbara, California. Ed did not share the details about his experiences with his family until the 50th anniversary of the Battle of the Bulge in 1994. For Richard it took longer: sixty-four years after their capture he finally revisited his wartime diary in 2008. But the brothers did talk among themselves. Victor knew quite a few details of Ed's

---

58 Dana Tims, "Atiyeh Twins of Raleigh Hills Share Memories of World War II Experiences," *Portland OregonLive*, 3 November 2011, http://www.oregonlive.com.
59 Victor Atiyeh, "Tape 2," 48.
60 Tims, "Atiyeh Twins Share Memories of WWII."

and Richard's harrowing experiences by the time he was interviewed for an oral history in 1992.

A fifth life-altering event took place at this same time. Victor and Dolores were expecting their first child by the autumn of 1944.[61] Along with all the other events, they were going to be a family of three in the spring of 1945. But the happy addition to the family did not happen. The baby was stillborn.[62] Victor and Dolores discovered they had Rh factor incompatibility. In the mid-1940s there was no effective treatment. When their child, Tom, was born in 1947, he was one of the first babies in the Portland area to get a life-saving transfusion and survive to be a healthy baby boy.[63]

With World War II raging to its end in Europe in May 1945 and in the Pacific in August 1945, many families experienced the stresses and tragedies that Victor and Dolores did, albeit in their own ways. Victor's good friend Tom Galt survived the war but was the only original member in his company by the end. Jim Campbell served in China out of an airbase. He survived, but his younger brother was killed during the American invasion of the Philippines in the spring of 1945—at almost the same time Victor and Dolores lost their child.[64] When Vic became governor, his close friend Jim Campbell consistently refused to travel with him to Japan; Jim never got over the death of his brother during the war. Twelve fellow fraternity brothers were killed—fighting as glider pilots, naval officers, and infantry soldiers, including four who had listened together in December 1941 as the news of Pearl Harbor came out of their house radio. In Victor's words, "That's the way the war went."[65]

Five major life events, personal glories, tragedies, and challenges all within ten months, and living within the context of

---

61   "Living Thoughts of World War II."
62   Ed Atiyeh, "Atiyeh interview #2," 1; Campbell, "Atiyeh interview," 3.
63   Helen Mills, Conversation to Jim Moore, "Atiyeh interview," 15 October 2013, Atiyeh project, Moore collection.
64   Campbell, "Atiyeh interview," 3; Victor Atiyeh, "Tape 2," 50.
65   Victor Atiyeh, "Tape 2," 50.

so many friends being caught up in the war. As Victor's nephew Bob said, "That had to have shaped who he was."[66] Nephew David marveled, "After that, maybe nothing was really as much of a challenge or insurmountable when you think of all the things he had to deal with at that point."[67]

Running the Store

Victor was officially appointed vice president and manager of Atiyeh Brothers, and elected to the board, on April 2, 1945. His uncle Aziz, in New York running the wholesale and importing business, continued as the president of the company.[68] As Victor's brothers left the military and ended their rehabilitation in Santa Barbara, Edward returned to work at Atiyeh Brothers as well. Richard re-entered the University of Oregon, earning his degree. When he was done, he came to work for the store while Ed went to Eugene to finish his degree. At the end of 1945, the transition to the new generation was completed at Atiyeh Brothers. Aziz resigned, Victor was elected president, Richard was elected vice president and got a spot on the board, and their mother, Linda, continued as the secretary-treasurer of the company. Atiyeh Brothers continued, but with a different set of brothers. Between 1946 and 1948, Aziz's remaining shares were purchased so that he was completely removed from the company in Portland. At the same time, Aziz purchased George's (passed on to his sons) partnership in the New York wholesale and importing business.

Linda Atiyeh died in March 1950, aged 51. Her husband had died at 61. Each of their three sons would live more than 90 years. With Linda's death, the Atiyeh boys purchased all the remaining shares of Atiyeh Brothers, splitting the stock among themselves

---

66 Bob Atiyeh, interviewed by Jim Moore, "Atiyeh interview," West Linn, OR, 4 February 2015. Summary notes, 5.
67 David Atiyeh, interviewed by Jim Moore, "Atiyeh interview," Tigard, OR, 30 July 2015. Summary, 6.
68 Ed Atiyeh, "Atiyeh Bros. Inc. 1900–2008," 10

equally.[69] From 1944 to 1950, the Atiyeh generations had completely shifted from the founders to the sons.

Through the 1950s Atiyeh Brothers brought a good living to Richard, Ed, and Victor. They settled into their roles, jointly making big decisions about the businesses but specializing in different areas of the companies' needs. Victor and Richard managed the retail store. Within the rug world, they had different focuses: Victor was the area-rug specialist while Richard worked on a relatively new floor covering concept, wall-to-wall carpets.

Since Victor had been working at the company as an adult longer than Richard and Ed, they accepted him as the president. But the three brothers made all major decisions together. Later, the three would shift board positions (e.g., becoming secretary-treasurer or vice president), but all three always had the top spots in the company.

Victor's management style continued to form during these early years. Aside from learning about management by keeping his mouth shut and his eyes open, he learned how to hire people. The trick in retail is that the workers must be able to work independently in order to understand customers and meet their needs. Victor learned to assess potential hires for their ability to make decisions on their own, within the larger goals of the store. Victor was very good at picking people. His management style was to give people a task, then leave them alone. Ed said Victor was "very astute about people."[70]

Victor's problem-solving capabilities also came to the fore as he and his brothers ran the company on their own. After the company branched out in 1949 and constructed a cleaning plant, Atiyeh Brothers was still washing customer rugs by hand with a mix of gelatin Ivory Soap. The brothers and a manager would make all the deliveries and pickups. Once a rug was picked up, the four of them would meet in the evening at the cleaning plant

---

69   Ed Atiyeh, "Atiyeh Bros. Inc. 1900–2008," 12.
70   Edward Atiyeh, interviewed by Jim Moore, "Atiyeh interview #1," Raleigh Hills, OR, 18 October 2014. Summary notes, 2.

to roll out all the rugs, measure them, and prepare them for cleaning. At some point, Victor said, "Why don't we measure them in the customers' homes?" This great idea was adopted, and the four stopped having to work several nights a week.[71]

Ed described Victor's personality as working very well with the company's needs. Victor never let anything bother him. Richard and Ed would take their frustrations home, but Victor never did. Victor would think ideas out before implementing them, and he had empathy for other people's feelings. The three brothers knew their strong points and their weak points. Whenever there were conflicts, they would talk them out and come to some final decision. And whatever happened, they were brothers and a family unit—they carpooled to the store every day from their neighboring homes.

Dolores and Victor's marriage produced a son, Tom in 1947. At about the same time they moved to a house in the Broadmoor neighborhood, just down the hill towards Beaverton from their West Sylvan apartment, buying one of the first ten houses built in the development.[72] Daughter Suzanne was born in 1952, bringing the family to four. They moved to a larger home fourteen years later, and aside from eight years living in Salem as governor, Victor and Dolores would live in the neighborhood until Victor's death 67 years later. A few years after Victor and Dolores moved to Broadmoor, Richard and his family bought the house next door. A couple of years later, Ed and his family moved in a few blocks away. Richard's family eventually moved within the neighborhood to a bigger house, but the three Atiyeh boys lived within a short walk of each other for decades.

The Road to Politics

The trio of Atiyehs always had a strong public service ethos. While Victor was the only one to enter politics, and only one

---

71 Ed Atiyeh, "Atiyeh interview #1," 2; Ed Atiyeh to Moore, 8 December 2016.
72 Victor Atiyeh, "Tape 3, side 1," 59–60; Tom Atiyeh, "Atiyeh interview," 14.

other Atiyeh gave elected office a try in 1984 (Richard's son, George), community and civic involvement was something that all three of the brothers took to heart.[73] Suzanne Atiyeh, Victor's daughter, told of her father and his brothers being taught "to bear responsibility as an honor."[74]

George Atiyeh had been a staunch Republican. Ed Atiyeh remembered that his father's business philosophy made him a Republican.[75] George did not agree with Franklin Delano Roosevelt's New Deal policies, saying that they were bringing socialism to the United States. George had a collection of anti-Democratic Party items in his office at Atiyeh Brothers—it was never shown to the public. Through the 1930s, George would have an election-night gathering at the family home. His Republican friends would come over to listen to the radio as election results came in from across the country. Ed remembered that after a couple of hours, they would get quiet, then they would go home with the Republican presidential candidate being defeated by FDR, yet again.

Victor did not think that his father being a Republican was the reason that he himself became a Republican. "I'm a Republican not because my dad was a Republican, which he was, [but because] I'm comfortable in the Republican party and the general attitude of Republicans.... My philosophy does not permit me to be a Democrat. So, it's not a matter of I inherited it, it's just something that I believe in."[76]

---

73 David Atiyeh, "Atiyeh interview," 8; *Statesman-Journal* (Salem) "Bennett, Opponent File," 16 December 1983; UPI, "Political Junkies Trek to Salem: Jam House Chambers to Watch Candidates Filing," *Coos Bay (OR) World*, 7 March 1984; Charles E. Beggs, "Demos Lose Two, Keep Two in State," *Salem (OR) Statesman-Journal*, 17 May 1984.

74 "State Memorial for the Honorable Vic Atiyeh," Memorial service, recorded by Oregon Legislative Media, Salem, OR, 3 September 2014. DVD, 1:28:45, Atiyeh project, Moore collection

75 Ed Atiyeh, "Atiyeh interview #1," 3.

76 Victor Atiyeh, interviewed by Clark Hansen, "Tape 60," Oral history, recorded by Oregon Historical Society, Portland, OR, 10 September 1993. Transcript, 63, Atiyeh Collection, Pac. Univ. Archives.

Some of Victor's earliest strong political memories come from the 1940 election. Roosevelt was running for his third presidential terms, and Victor was indignant. His indignation was not about FDR's policies, although it is not hard to imagine that George Atiyeh created an atmosphere that painted FDR in a negative light. Victor was mad about that unprecedented third term. He recalled thinking to himself that if FDR "thinks that he's the only one that can run this nation, then he doesn't understand our democracy."[77] Victor remembered that he was not interested in politics, and certainly was not planning a political career at the time—it "just *never* occurred to me"—but the seeming unfairness of Roosevelt wanting that monarch-like third term really struck him.[78]

During the U of O years, a group within the Fiji fraternity house would regularly gather to talk about politics. Ed Atiyeh remembered, "We all felt that our legislature was lacking in having senators and representatives with business experience. Victor said if we would support him, he would run for public office."[79] In a 1941 letter to his parents, Victor had kidded around about being their "politician-voiced son."[80] Victor's political bent showed through in the introductions to the various circular letters that went out to members of his fraternity during World War—he would provide a little bit of analysis and context based on his reading of the news back at home, something that his fraternity brothers at their various posts around the world might not be getting.

Beginning in 1949, Victor's name began to be known as part of a group of downtown business leaders.[81] There were celebrations

---

77 Victor Atiyeh, "Tape 2," 46.
78 Victor Atiyeh, "Tape 2," 46. Italics underlined in transcript.
79 Edward Atiyeh, Email to Jim Moore, "Interview Last Saturday," 22 October 2014, Atiyeh project, Moore collection.
80 Victor Atiyeh, to George Atiyeh and Linda Atiyeh, "Letter," 11 December 1941, Atiyeh Collection, Pac. Univ. Archives.
81 *Oregonian*, "Merchants to Place Stress on Oregon-Made Products," 23 October 1949; *Oregonian*, "Groups Post U.F. Quotas, United Fund Gift Goal," 28 October 1955; *Oregonian*, "Volunteers Listed in U.F. Campaign, Chairman, Aides Named for Groups," 5 July 1956; *Oregonian*, "TV-Radio Highlights: 10:00," 11 September

of Oregon-made products in 1949 and 1950—Victor was on the committee to make these events happen. In the mid-1950s, Victor was one of the leaders working to raise money for the United Fund charity. Victor was also a prominent local gun collector, cofounding the Oregon Arms Collectors in 1955.

By the second half of 1957, there was a change in the way Victor appeared in news accounts. He was taking on more of a civic leadership role and moving toward a political life. In the fall of 1957, he appeared with the Multnomah County sheriff and another guest on a local television talk show.

Atiyeh's natural bent toward politics was countered by his loyalty to the business and to the work it took to be successful. But there were limits to that loyalty as well. It may have been that Victor was unhappy working at the store from the beginning. "He couldn't do things the way he wanted to," remembered Jim Campbell's wife, Donna.[82] There was some inevitable tension in the three-headed managerial relationship because the brothers knew each other so well. Victor never did anything about this tension, and he loved his brothers dearly, but it was there.[83]

Jim Campbell talked to his friend Victor more bluntly about adding something more substantial to Victor's life. In about 1957 he told Victor, "You have to get out of the store. You are very unhappy."[84] Victor and Jim had a series of conversations in which Jim encouraged Victor to explore other options—developing one of his hobbies into more fulfilling work, jumping into politics—something that would get Victor out of the store more often.

There was also the civic engagement culture among the Atiyeh brothers. Being involved in the community came to be seen as good way to balance the pressure of a career—Campbell's argument that Victor needed to "get out of the store" was reinforced by Atiyeh Brothers' push toward community

---

1957.

82 Campbell, "Atiyeh interview," 3.
83 Campbell, "Atiyeh interview," 1, 3.
84 Campbell, "Atiyeh interview," 1.

involvement to give back, and as a way to keep the brothers from being too immersed in the work in the business.[85]

Campbell later remembered a fishing trip to Astoria in 1957. "It was pouring rain and the fish weren't biting." Atiyeh, Campbell, and a third business acquaintance "sat in a motel room...on a dreary fall day ... Their discussion turned to the need for business people to get involved in government. 'We felt the free enterprise system government had more to do with how well we did in business or in our personal life than anything else,'" Campbell recounted. "Before the day was out Victor Atiyeh was a politician."[86]

Political Principles

Victor George Atiyeh was guided by a strong set of principles. He began to assemble them as he was growing up, and they were fully formed before he ran his first campaign in 1958. When people would ask Victor how he made tough political decisions, or how he survived the messy world of politics, he responded, "all you need is a set of principles and common sense."

His principles were clear to him in 1958, but he did allow that they evolved over time, just as one would expect as Atiyeh encountered the realities of legislating and being a governor.

1. The best government is one that is less involved in people's lives.[87]

2. The government that is closest to the people is best. Layers of government and bureaucracy needed strong justification for Atiyeh.

3. Democracy is not efficient, and that is a good thing.

---

85 David Atiyeh, "Atiyeh interview," 9.
86 Martin Rosenberg, "Race for Governor is Straub-Atiyeh Rematch: Election of Atiyeh Would Cap 20-year Career in Legislature," *Salem (OR) Statesman Journal*, 29 October 1978, 1F.
87 Victor Atiyeh, interviewed by Clark Hansen, "Tape 6, side 2," Oral history, recorded by Oregon Historical Society, Portland, OR, 11 December 1992. Transcript, 155–157, Atiyeh Collection, Pac. Univ. Archives.

4. People may want a public life and private life, but "you're one person." "If you've got a private life that is slippery, there's no way you can prevent yourself from being slippery in public." This was a good description of Victor himself. Ed's son David Atiyeh's impression of his uncle was that "he was just always the same." There was no difference between the way he was when David was growing up, or when David was going into business after he graduated from college, or when Victor was a legislator, or when he was governor. "He was just always the same person. There was just a tremendous sense of self and awareness."[88]

5. "We the people" means that we get the kind of government to which we are entitled. This also means that people have a responsibility to take part in civic life. Atiyeh would extend this to the idea that people ought to study issues and candidates before making voting choices.

6. There should be objective government policies for dealing with taxes and funding.[89] This made Atiyeh a self-avowed fiscal conservative. He wanted strong justifications for changes in taxes and funding, but if those justifications merited it, then he supported increases in both. The principle became an issue for Atiyeh when he proposed a tax surcharge in 1982 to balance a badly depleted budget and when the lottery was passed in 1984 and legislators wanted to use it for established programs.

7. Government should create incentives to change people's behaviors, not solely punishments.[90]

8. Never trade for votes or for something that violates closely held principles. Atiyeh always voted his conscience. He would research all the issues so that he often understood what he was

---

88 David Atiyeh, "Atiyeh interview," 6.
89 Victor Atiyeh, interviewed by Clark Hansen, "Tape 45," Oral history, recorded by Oregon Historical Society, Portland, OR, 9 July 1993. Transcript, 432, Atiyeh Collection, Pac. Univ. Archives.
90 Victor Atiyeh, interviewed by Clark Hansen, "Tape 9, side 1," Oral history, recorded by Oregon Historical Society, Portland, OR, 14 December 1992. Transcript, 236, Atiyeh Collection, Pac. Univ. Archives.

opposing better than proponents did, but he never traded for votes.⁹¹

*9. Was a policy proposal good for Oregon? Partisanship was irrelevant in Atiyeh's mind.*⁹²

10. Always govern without regard to reelection. In practical terms, this meant that Atiyeh was often a bit late to declare his intentions to run for an office or to run for reelection. This sometimes drove his staff a bit crazy.

Atiyeh respected that other people could have different principles. And if they used those principles to come to different conclusions that he did, Atiyeh had no problem with that. "It's those that don't have any set of principles or don't have any common sense, I don't have a great deal of respect for them."⁹³

---

91 Victor Atiyeh, interviewed by Clark Hansen, "Tape 22," Oral history, recorded by Oregon Historical Society, Portland, OR, 9 February 1993. Transcript, 651–652, Atiyeh Collection, Pac. Univ. Archives.
92 Victor Atiyeh, "Tape 22," 656.
93 Victor Atiyeh, "Tape 22," 660.

2 Legislating

Atiyeh served in the legislature for twenty years. He was one of the few legislators who read every bill that came before him, word for word, and sought to understand exactly what he was voting on. On various committees he dealt with issues of clarity in the sales of bread, selling state lands, and ethics rules. He was a participant in important bills like the Beach Bill, but he did not play a central role in their final form. This chapter will focus on those issues that were central to his governorship—taxes, land use, and leadership.

Atiyeh declared his candidacy for the Oregon House in March 1958, just before the filing deadline, a last-minute pattern he would stick to many times over the years to come. [94] His decision to run for public office came in the aftermath of revelations of corruption, crime, and vice in Portland that made national headlines.[95] Atiyeh remembered,

---

94 *Oregonian*, "Rug Dealer Seeks Office," 5 March 1958; *Oregon Statesman* (Salem) "Statewide List for Oregon Primary Told," 8 March 1958.

95 Jewel Lansing, *Portland: People, Politics, and Power 1851–2001*, (Corvallis, OR: Oregon State University Press), 367–368; Wallace Turner and William Lambert, "City, County Control Sought By Gamblers: Top Teamster Seeks Police Chief Ouster," *Oregonian*, 19 April 1956; Joseph A. Loftus, "Portland Called Vice-Ridden Now," *New York Times*, 9 March 1957.

My father-in-law said, "Why do you want to run for public office with all those crooks?" There was a bad image at that time. I thought well, I'm just going down there, and I'll do a good, honest job and work as hard as I can, [and…] raise the status of elected officials. There are things that I felt very keenly about. I thought that things were not running the way they should.[96]

With no strong issues driving him, he just wanted to make government work better. "I was going to straighten out all of state government in one session as a freshman legislator."[97] Quickly, he would learn to adopt the successful strategy he had employed when he took over the management of Atiyeh Brothers in 1944: "keep your ears open and your mouth shut."[98]

The 1958 campaign consisted of asking his friends for help, beginning to figure out campaign techniques based on what he had seen others do, a bit of innovation, and beginning to learn the issues that were important to his potential constituents. Campaigning, he learned, meant knocking on doors and talking to potential voters at gatherings across the county—House District 4 was a multiple-member district that covered all of Washington County. He had never seen lawn signs used in elections, but he thought it would be a good way to get his name out to voters. With his friend who was a painting contractor, "we got some boards cut up, and he painted them yellow, and then we cut a stencil. We were down there in his paint shop, a bunch of us, and we were stenciling 'Atiyeh for Representative.'"[99] Then Atiyeh learned how to find the right places to put up his innovative signs, and he began to meet voters as he knocked on doors and asked permission to put bright yellow signs on their property.

From his first campaign donation to his last, Atiyeh would be good at dialogue with donors, but he was never very good at

---

96 Victor Atiyeh, interviewed by Clark Hansen, "Tape 4," Oral history, recorded by Oregon Historical Society, Portland, OR, 4 December 1992. Transcript, 83, Atiyeh Collection, Pac. Univ.
97 Victor Atiyeh, "Tape 4," 84.
98 Victor Atiyeh, "Tape 4," 84.
99 Victor Atiyeh, "Tape 4," 81.

directly asking for specific amounts of money from those he did not know well. In that first campaign, Atiyeh figured out how to find influential support. Introducing himself to Henry Hagg, a dairy farmer in western Washington County after whom Hagg Lake is named, Atiyeh struck up a conversation. Only eventually did he say to Hagg, "You know, I'm running for the legislature. If you feel you can support me, I'd appreciate it."[100] This low-key approach did not get an immediate commitment, but financial support ultimately came through.

The Republican primary election in District 4 featured five candidates, including Republican incumbent Leon Davis, who was first elected in 1952. The night before the primary election, Atiyeh actually got a bit of political stage fright—"all of a sudden I had this terrible feeling, and I said to my wife, 'I might win. Then what do I do?'"[101]

He and Davis led the field and won spots in the general. Atiyeh got more votes than Davis (5,570 to 5,486), possibly due to the greater population concentration in eastern Washington County (where Atiyeh lived).[102] After he raised $217.50 and spent $138.70 in the 1958 general election,[103] Atiyeh and his Republican counterpart were victorious in District 4. This time Davis beat Atiyeh by about 300 votes (15,993 to 15,611), but each outdistanced their two Democratic rivals by more than 3,000 votes.[104] At campaign appearances during the 1958 election season, Atiyeh discovered that incumbents do not necessarily know the "right" answers. He also discovered that honest answers to questions, including "I don't know," were best.[105] He was applying his "eyes open" management style from his early days running Atiyeh Brothers to this new world of politicians, voters,

---

100 Victor Atiyeh, "Tape 4," 82.
101 Victor Atiyeh, "Tape 4," 82.
102 *Oregon Blue Book, 1959–1960*, 213; UP, "Nominees for House Listed," *Salem Oregon Statesman,* 18 May 1958.
103 Victor Atiyeh, "Tape 4," 84.
104 *Oregon Blue Book, 1959–1960*, 204; UP, "State Representative List," *Salem Oregon Statesman*, 6 November 1958.
105 Victor Atiyeh, "Tape 4," 82, 83.

and elections. He also ran into a local television station's political analyst, Tom McCall (then known as Lawson McCall), who was moderating a candidate event in Atiyeh's district.[106]

Atiyeh's first foray into a more formal public life was successful. He would continue to help lead Atiyeh Brothers for another twenty years, but he was on his way to becoming known as a politician, not a rug salesman and business owner.

Finding His Footing

The 35-year-old Atiyeh's first year in the legislature was part of a youth movement in Oregon politics. Governor Mark Hatfield was 36—and had served as Secretary of State for two years and been in the state legislature for six years before that. The Speaker of the House, Bob Duncan (D-Medford) was 38. The 1959 House members included fifteen (out of sixty members) under the age of 40, with the youngest being 28 years old.[107] Atiyeh recalled the jump from being a candidate to serving in the legislature as being like moving from grade school to high school. "You know, you're a big shot in grade school, and all of a sudden you're the smallest shot in high school."[108] He bonded with a group of four other first-time legislators—all Republicans and all staying at the same motel while they lived in Salem for the legislative session. Carl Fisher, F. F. "Monte" Montgomery, Pat Metke, and Doug Heider all shared a desire to make the legislature relevant, and to combat the feeling that there was corruption in Oregon politics. The group became known as the Young Turks, the name bestowed upon them to show their energetic activism in the House.[109] With the 1961 addition of newly elected Bob Smith, these six would stay close friends for years, and several of them would play major roles in Atiyeh's political life in the decades to come.

---

106 *Oregonian*, "Candidates Due at PTA: State, County Hopefuls Billed," 13 October 1958.
107 John Kerbow, Democrat from Klamath Falls, *Oregon Blue Book, 1959–1960*, (Salem, OR: Oregon Secretary of State, 1958), 31.
108 Victor Atiyeh, "Tape 4," 85.
109 Victor Atiyeh, "Tape 4," 86.

Atiyeh's relationship with Governor Hatfield was good from that first session on. They were the same age and had family about the same age. Atiyeh did not have much to do with the governor's office in 1959—"because I'm a freshman and because the Democrats were in the majority"[110]—but on a personal level Hatfield became an honorary member of the Young Turks. Atiyeh remembered, "I don't know whether he adopted us or we him, but it was a pretty good relationship."[111] Only on rare occasions would he and Hatfield disagree on issues.

Issues did not scare Atiyeh. He found himself relishing the details of legislation, and he found the complexity of meshing policy proposals with current policies an intriguing process to master. Atiyeh learned that his fellow legislators had a wide variety of reasons for voting as they did. He found that some would vote for or against measures simply based on how others in the legislature had come down on the issues.[112] Atiyeh used his logic and his principles to determine how he voted. And once he cast that vote, he "*never* went back and said, 'Gee, maybe I should have [voted the other way],' because I would pretty well think it through and come to a conclusion." Atiyeh's feeling from day one in elected office was, "I would just do what I thought was the thing to do. …I always figured if the people like what I'm doing, they'll reelect me, and if they don't, I'll go back in the rug business."[113]

Atiyeh was in the minority during his entire time in the legislature, but in that first 1959 session, he learned to do the homework, to learn the rules, and to figure out how to influence the majority while working on committees.[114] The culture of the

---

110 Victor Atiyeh, "Tape 5," 111.
111 Victor Atiyeh, "Tape 5," 110.
112 Victor Atiyeh, interviewed by Clark Hansen, "Tape 22," Oral history, recorded by Oregon Historical Society, Portland, OR, 9 February 1993. Transcript, 659, Atiyeh Collection, Pac. Univ.
113 Victor Atiyeh, "Tape 4," 81.
114 Victor Atiyeh, interviewed by Clark Hansen, "Tape 5," Oral history, recorded by Oregon Historical Society, Portland, OR, 12 December 1992. Transcript, 135–136, Atiyeh Collection, Pac. Univ.

legislature in the years that Atiyeh served was different than the more partisan legislatures that began in the late 1960s. It was common for members of the minority party to serve as chairs of committees. By Atiyeh's second session in the legislature in 1961, he served as the vice chair of the taxation committee.[115] In 1963 he was the chair of the Food and Dairying committee as well as vice chair of Rules and Resolutions and of the interim taxation committee.[116] Atiyeh's reputation for tax expertise went with him when he was elected to the Senate in 1964; he served as the vice chair of the Senate tax committee in 1965.[117] That non-partisan focus on expertise and relationships all would change in 1969 when fellow Young Turk Bob Smith became Speaker of the House and installed Republicans as the chairs of every committee, "[a]nd so of course when the Democrats took over, by that time it was institutionalized.... But still, seniority wasn't a major factor."[118]

Atiyeh was seen as an influencer in the legislature. Some of the attention was welcomed. Atiyeh's name was floated as a potential candidate for Congress and for secretary of state.[119] Some of the attention ended up being more embarrassing than anything else.

---

115 *Oregon Statesman* (Salem), "Democrats in Top Financial Policy Posts," 10 January 1961.

116 AP, "Republicans Head Three Committees," *Eugene (OR) Register-Guard)*, 14 January 1963; UPI, "House Committee Appointments Said to Be Step Ahead," *Medford (OR) Mail Tribune*, 15 January 1963; *Oregon Blue Book, 1965–1966*, (Salem, OR: Oregon Secretary of State, 1965), 35.

117 Harold E. Hughes, "Senate Receives Legislation to Increase Tax Court Muscle," *Oregonian*, 14 January 1965.

118 Atiyeh, "Tape 6, side 1," 149.

119 Marguerite Wright, "Statehouse Special," Column, *Medford (OR) Mail Tribune*, 26 April 1961; Zan Stark, "Hopefuls Keep Ears Turned to Howell Appling," *Medford (OR) Mail Tribune*, 25 December 1963; Don Scarborough, "Appling Will Not Seek Another Term, May Try for Governor," *Salem Oregon Statesman*, 28 December 1963. Mervin Shoemaker, "Ten Republicans Want Nomination to Succeed Norblad as 1st District Congressman," *Oregonian*, 25 September 1964; Mervin Shoemaker, "GOP Candidates Jockey Quietly for Nomination to House Seat," *Oregonian*, 23 September 1964; *Capital Press* (Salem, OR), "Walter Norblad," Editorial, September 1964, 1967 Session, scrapbook 1, Atiyeh Collection, Pac. Univ. *Oregonian*, "Wendell Wyatt, Astoria Lawyer, Wins GOP Nomination on Fifth Ballot by Committee," 27 September 1964.

There was an open bidding process to replace the carpet in the governor's reception room in the executive suite. Atiyeh Brothers won the contract and set out to weave the gold-colored carpet.[120] By the time the carpet was installed after the 1963 legislature adjourned the notoriety was not worth the contract.[121] Atiyeh felt guilty about the time he spent in Salem rather than running the business with his brothers. As a small business owner, he did "everything, ...sweeping the sidewalk, keeping the store clean. I swept the sidewalks...till I was elected governor."[122] But he was not there for the business on weekdays during legislative session

That first session was also one in which Atiyeh learned to try to balance the life of a legislator with that of a family man and that of a person with a business to run.

> That was very difficult on me because I realized that they were working and I was down in the legislature, and so I'd come home on a Friday after being down there all week, I'd go over to the Lloyd Center to work at night, because we were open nights at the Lloyd Center, I'd work all day Saturday, you know, and I'm away from my family, besides. ...So I had this guilty conscience....[123]

---

120 UPI, "Hatfield's Office to Get New Rug," *Salem Oregon Statesman*, 22 July 1961; UPI, "Hatfield's Office to Have New Rug," *Medford Mail Tribune*, 30 August 1961.

121 UPI, "Governor's Office Gets New Carpet: 'Round the State," *Eugene (OR) Register-Guard*, 8 June 1963. Atiyeh gubernatorial aide Denny Miles remembered that Atiyeh decided never again to get involved with high-profile business with the state after this incident. Denny Miles, interviewed by Jim Moore, "Atiyeh interview #3," Forest Grove, OR, 5 April 2016. Summary notes, 19.

122 Victor Atiyeh, interviewed by Clark Hansen, "Tape 3, side 1," Oral history, recorded by Oregon Historical Society, Portland, OR, 1 December 1992. Transcript, 65–66, Atiyeh Collection, Pac. Univ.

123 Victor Atiyeh, interviewed by Clark Hansen, "Tape 14," Oral history, recorded by Oregon Historical Society, Portland, OR, 19 January 1993. Transcript, 413, Atiyeh Collection, Pac. Univ.

His wife, Dolores, kept up her volunteering with the schools.[124] The Atiyeh children, Tom in the sixth grade and Suzanne in kindergarten, learned that their father was in Salem five days a week, and then he would be back at home for the weekends, but putting in time at the store in downtown Portland.[125] Suzanne's young impressions were that her father just disappeared. She learned to listen for his keys in the door when he came home from Salem each night. She asked her mother, "Where's dad?" Her mother replied, "He's in Salem." At that age, she just knew that her father was away.[126]

One highlight that still stands out for Tom Atiyeh as "way cool" was dressing up as pioneers with his father for the special Oregon Centennial legislative session held in Oregon City.[127] The pair appeared, dressed in their fringed shirts with tricorne hats, on the front page of the *Oregonian*, alongside a picture of Governor Hatfield in his frock coat taking the oath of office as Governor John Whiteaker (the state of Oregon's first governor).[128]

During spring break in 1961, Atiyeh's second legislative session, the Atiyeh family came to Salem to spend time with their husband and father. But, according to a legislative newsletter, "in that time he went back to Portland two evenings to work and had meetings all the other evenings."[129] With the kids and Dolores in Salem, Atiyeh saw them as much as he would have if they had stayed at home—not very much. Suzanne remembered doing her elementary school math homework just off the House floor

---

124 *Oregonian*, "PTA Serves Two Schools," 12 January 1959.
125 Edward Atiyeh, interviewed by Jim Moore, "Atiyeh interview #1," Raleigh Hills, OR, 18 October 2014. Summary notes, 1.
126 Suzanne Atiyeh, interviewed by Jim Moore, "Atiyeh Interview," Biography project, Portland, OR, 9 March 2018. Notes from phone interview, 1.
127 Tom Atiyeh, interviewed by Jim Moore, "Atiyeh interview," Sherwood, OR, 28 July 2015. Summary, 4.
128 Mervin Shoemaker, "Oregon Legislators Combine History and Hilarity at Oregon City: State Political Figures State 'Session' to Dramatize Centennial Year Events," *Oregonian*, 19 March 1959.
129 Mary Jane Dellenback, "Family Contributions to State Legislators Reviewed in Letter," Reprint of Legislative Newsletter, *Medford (OR) Mail Tribune*, 2 April 1961.

waiting for a legislative session to end.[130] Atiyeh never was comfortable with the time he took away from his family. He kept a one-panel cartoon showing a disheveled man returning to his house, a "Salem" sticker on his suitcase, while his children ran to their mother for protection. The tagline was, "It's only Daddy home from the legislature."[131]

Tax Expertise

From day one, Atiyeh was on the tax committee in the House. He felt he had a natural affinity for understanding tax issues because of his career in the retail rug business. Atiyeh always felt that there needed to be more legislators with small business experience. He observed that it was hard for the small businessperson to run for office because the only available times to campaign were at night and on the weekends. Atiyeh was always thankful that he had two brothers to run the business during the campaign season and when the legislature was in session.[132] On the committee, Atiyeh was willing to ask questions, unlike most other legislators, as he recalled. It "sort of developed" that taxes were not complicated; "it's simply a matter of who is going to pay the tax."[133]

Atiyeh's tax expertise grew quickly during his first legislative session. Before the session started, a national tax expert who had written reports about the Oregon tax system came and talked with legislators.[134] The expert, John Sly, would plant ideas in Atiyeh that he would come back to when he had his own major tax reform proposals as governor, twenty-four years later. Atiyeh found himself involved in hearings and policy ideas that got a lot of people very angry and frustrated. He soon was known as one of

---

130 Suzanne Atiyeh, "Atiyeh Interview."
131 "It's Only Daddy Home From the Legislature," Cartoon, n.d. 1963, 1963 Session, scrapbook 1, Atiyeh Collection, Pac. Univ.
132 Victor Atiyeh, "Atiyeh interview #1," 1.
133 Victor Atiyeh, "Atiyeh interview #1," 6.
134 Special, "Sly Tells Solons 'High Service' Means Higher Taxes," *Oregonian*, 11 January 1959.

the members of the tax committee who could explain complex matters clearly.

The House Committee on Taxation consisted of nine members: three Republicans and six Democrats, including fellow Young Turk Doug Heider (R-Marion County).[135] Chairing the committee was Clarence Barton, a Democrat from Coos County on the south coast, who served as Speaker two sessions later in 1963. Atiyeh learned from Barton the value of honest engagement with his political opponents. He recalled,

> He and I hit it off pretty well. Clarence Barton was generally mistrusted by the Republicans, but…I wasn't intimidated by him, nor he by me. Obviously, he thought less of me because I was a freshman, and he had been around, but I didn't mind standing up to him at all, and we spoke our minds pretty clearly. …If he told me something, I knew I could depend on it. So we had a good relationship, although we didn't always agree.[136]

Barton was acknowledged as the tax expert in the House. When Barton became Speaker in 1963, people started coming to Atiyeh as the tax expert.[137]

From his first session in the legislature to his last, in 1977–78, Atiyeh was in the middle of all tax discussions in Salem. In 1961 there was an overhaul in how to tax timber.[138] Governor Hatfield proposed a net receipts tax, a proposal that Atiyeh called "a 'milestone' in tax equity."[139]

---

135 *Oregon Statesman* (Salem), "House Members Assigned to 20 Boards by Duncan," 13 January 1959.

136 Victor Atiyeh, "Tape 4," 92–93: Barton had only been in the House for one term, first serving in 1957, Cecil L. Edwards, *Alphabetical List of Oregon's Legislators and Related Information: Provisional Government to Present*, (Salem, OR: Oregon Historic Services, Legislative Administration Committee, 1993), 5.

137 Victor Atiyeh, interviewed by Jim Moore, "Atiyeh interview #1," Raleigh Hills, OR, 19 December 2013. Summary notes, 7.

138 UPI, "Compromise Breaks Deadlock on Timber Tax: Decision Opens Way for Passage of Tax Reforms. House Committee Votes Approval," *Medford Mail Tribune*, 11 April 1961.

The concept of the net receipts tax was that individuals and businesses would figure out all their deductions on their taxes, and then a small additional tax would be assessed on the net income. Richard Munn, who began working for the Oregon Tax Commission in 1964, found it to be "really weird…—[Hatfield] wanted a second income tax."[140] In Munn's assessment, he thought that Hatfield was not entirely serious about the proposal. In a political system that would not support a sales tax, and in a system in which Hatfield felt he could not increase the income tax, and in a system in which the state government did not control the property tax, this net receipt idea showed that Governor Hatfield was actively trying to solve budgetary problems, but it was also a proposal that did not seem to have strong support. The net receipts idea would not become law, but Atiyeh would use many of its ideas when he proposed a similar tax after his landslide 1982 reelection to the governor's office. Munn, who was the Legislative Revenue officer in from 1974 to 1984, and then became Atiyeh's director of the Department of Revenue, applied the same analysis to Atiyeh's 1982 net receipts proposal as he did to Hatfield's idea twenty years earlier. Atiyeh "did not want to propose a sales tax, did not want to propose an increase in the income tax, and this [was] somewhat a backdoor increase in the income tax."[141] In Munn's view, Atiyeh knew it would not pass muster, but by proposing something he then put the onus on the Democratic leadership of the 1983 legislature to come up with some fiscal solutions of their own.

The net receipts tax was defeated in the legislature, but Atiyeh was asked by Hatfield to carry the proposal through the legislative process along with a cigarette tax. This highlighted Atiyeh's acknowledged expertise on taxes and his growing role as a leader in the House. When the cigarette tax also failed, the House Tax

---

139 UPI, "Net Receipts Tax Bill Debated by House Committee," *Medford Mail Tribune*, 31 January 1961.
140 Richard Munn, interviewed by Jim Moore, "Atiyeh Interview," Salem, OR, 9 June 2016. Summary notes, 9.
141 Munn, "Atiyeh Interview," 6.

Committee became the focus for the entire legislature. One observer noted that they had "the toughest job of the session." The Ways and Means Committee could not allocate funds to state spending priorities until the Tax Committee figured out how much money there would be in the coming budget.[142]

In late 1963 or early 1964, Atiyeh began to think about running for the Oregon Senate. In his oral history in the early 1990s, he was adamant that he "didn't have a path" toward a political career.[143] He "just took each step at a time." But after all the battles in the House, Atiyeh was drawn to the idea of the smaller Senate. "It's kind of nice to be in the Senate in the sense that in order to prevail you need sixteen votes. In the House you need thirty-one. Lobbying is a lot easier in the Senate to get sixteen rather than thirty-one."[144] It was a lot more appealing, Atiyeh admitted, to run for reelection every four years than every two.

Standing in Atiyeh's path was fellow Republican John Hare from Hillsboro. Hare had served for ten years, two in the House and then two four-year terms in the Senate. Atiyeh recalled that Hare "was pretty conservative, and I just really thought I'd like to get a different voice there in the Senate from Washington County."[145] But taking on a fellow Republican was not something that the party activists liked at all. Atiyeh remembered, "I did the unforgivable. I'm an incumbent Republican House member, he's an incumbent Republican Senate member, and for one incumbent to run against another, incidentally...vacating the House seat, you just didn't do those things."[146]

Atiyeh knew that the primary with Hare would be close, and he did not have a strong sense one way or the other how it would

---

142 Zan Stark, "House Tax Group Has Toughest Job of Current Session," Capital Memo column, *Medford (OR) Mail Tribune*, 18 April 1963.
143 Victor Atiyeh, interviewed by Clark Hansen, "Tape 8," Oral history, recorded by Oregon Historical Society, Portland, OR, 15 December 1992. Transcript, 199, Atiyeh Collection, Pac. Univ.
144 Victor Atiyeh, "Tape 8," 199.
145 Victor Atiyeh, "Tape 8," 198.
146 Victor Atiyeh, "Tape 8," 200.

turn out. Atiyeh had noticed a pattern in his six elections to date. "In every election…the very first [media] report that you heard [after the polls closed] was the one that prevailed, no matter what happened during the rest of the evening, even if there [were] just a few precincts [reporting]. At least that was with me," he recalled.[147] He went on:

> So on that night…they were giving some fragment reports, and the report was that John Hare was ahead. So I'm driving out to… Hillsboro [the county seat]…, and I'm thinking, …"Gee whiz, thank you, I enjoyed being in the legislature." You know, sort of a farewell going through my head. By the time I got there, that had changed, and I was ahead. But this was the only instance[148]

in which Atiyeh's gut instinct did not tell him the outcome of the election. It had been a hard fight, but Atiyeh won 53% to 47%, the ever more populous east side of the county supporting him, and the west side supporting Hare.[149]

Nationwide, the Republican Party had sustained huge losses in the 1964 elections. With Barry Goldwater as the Republican presidential nominee, Democrats made huge gains in almost all parts of the country.[150] Back in Oregon, however, Atiyeh was not expected to have any major problems against Democrat Thomas Roe, and he defeated him 58%–42%.[151] Oregon Republicans did well, due to the leadership of Bob Packwood, who worked with major donor Ernie Swigert and Howell Appling, then Oregon Secretary of State, to hand-pick candidates to take over the House of Representatives.[152] As a result, Vic Atiyeh joined the Oregon Senate, where Republicans were still the minority, and his

---

147 Victor Atiyeh, "Tape 8," 199.
148 Victor Atiyeh, "Tape 8," 199–200.
149 *Oregon Blue Book, 1965*, 213.
150 *New York Times*, "Mandate," 8 November 1964.
151 Harold E. Hughes, "Coalition Expected to Keep Control of Oregon State Senate," *Oregonian*, 18 October 1964; *Oregon Blue Book, 1965*, 222.
152 Paul W. Harvey, Jr., "GOP Controls House First Time in 8 Years," *Oregonian*, 5 November 1964.

Republican colleagues in the House took control of that side of the capitol.

One of the biggest tax issues was the perennial effort to make Oregon's tax system fairer. Without a sales tax, Oregon's local governments relied heavily on the property tax while the state government relied heavily on the income tax. There were other sources of income for both levels of government—licenses and fees being chief among them—but, by and large, property and income taxes were the biggest sources of government funding. Legislators in the 1960s and early 1970s explored providing relief to taxpayers on their income and property taxes in exchange for a sales tax of some kind. There were serious calls to limit property taxes from the mid-1960s on. A big issue was that property taxes had to be paid in cash, so people could end up with relatively valuable land while being cash-poor, as in the Great Depression.

The complexity came in figuring out which property would be taxed, and then in determining how to manage a tax levy that had been voted upon in a district. There were huge discrepancies in the properties on the tax rolls in different counties, exacerbated by the large number of foreclosures from the Great Depression and economic growth after World War II. This required the Oregon Tax Commission to reappraise property in all counties, a process that industries and other interests contested.[153] By the 1950s and 1960s this had resulted in a series of exemptions for different classes of property. The effect was a shift of the burden of the property tax system from big businesses with lots of land to homeowners and small businesses. The legislature tried to give property tax relief to those people whose taxes were going up too quickly, a group that contained many retirees on fixed incomes.

Over time, tax bases, which were only determined periodically, could become wildly out of line with their taxing districts. Without a credible baseline of property tax income to depend on, some districts could only fund themselves through annual levies

---

153 Munn, "Atiyeh Interview," 8.

approved by the voters. A levy could increase by up to 6% every year—this was designed to consider normal inflation and other costs (e.g., for personnel). However, by the late 1950s and early 1960s there was a huge problem with the six-percent growth limitation—the baby boom was in full swing. School districts in fast-growing parts of Oregon were finding that their costs—for new buildings, for new teachers, for new staff—were climbing much faster than 6% a year.

Atiyeh was working on solutions to the quickly growing property tax rates from 1965 on. There were proposals for ceilings on property taxes, lowering property taxes by raising other taxes, lowering capital gains taxes, and sales taxes. The only tax Atiyeh would not support was the sales tax. In 1969, the Republican-led House (Bob Smith was the Speaker) and Republican governor Tom McCall worked to refer a sales tax to Oregon voters. It lost 89% to 11%.[154]

National Politics Hits Home

In 1968, Atiyeh made his first jump into national issues. On a whim, he decided to run to be a delegate to the Republican national convention in Miami Beach.[155] Atiyeh was a Nixon supporter, along with thirty-two other legislators.[156] Oregon's May primary was a winner-take-all race, and Nixon won, so all Oregon's delegates would be for Nixon on the first two ballots at the convention. Atiyeh recalled that he had run across a list of the people vying to be statewide delegates, and he decided, "I think I'll run statewide just to see how it goes."[157] He and Dolores "began to plan our vacation, because, you know, I wasn't going to go to the convention. By George, I won, statewide."[158]

---

154 *Oregon Blue Book, 1971–1972*, (Salem, OR: Oregon Secretary of State, 1971), 260; B. Walth, *Fire at Eden's Gate*, 247.
155 *Oregonian*, "Solon Seeks Post," 15 March 1968.
156 *Oregonian*, "33 Solons Back Nixon," 30 March 1968.
157 Victor Atiyeh, "Tape 10," 271.
158 Victor Atiyeh, "Tape 10," 271; *Oregonian*, "Parley Delegations Ready to Organize," 6 July 1968.

The delegates met in early July to select leaders and decide which of them would sit on committees at the convention. Within a few days of being selected as a delegate, Oregon U.S. Representative Wendell Wyatt gave up his spot as Oregon's representative to the platform committee.[159] Led by delegation chair Mark Hatfield, the Oregon group elected Atiyeh to take Wyatt's spot. Atiyeh went to the convention a week early.[160] "I really lost a lot of sleep during that platform week. We went till late at night, and it was a long, tedious affair."[161] One of the biggest issues, of course, was Vietnam. The platform committee heard from former President Eisenhower about standing strong against communism with U.S. forces in Vietnam.[162] Atiyeh himself proposed a change to the platform—he proposed that young men ought to be subject to the draft for a single year, either at age 18 or after the completion of college. The goal was "to assure that our young men can be released from frustrating uncertainty."[163] Atiyeh would go public with this idea in February 1969.

The biggest issue for the Oregon delegation at the convention was whether Mark Hatfield would be selected as Nixon's vice president. But for Atiyeh, it was the platform committee that introduced him to big national political issues.

The issue of Israel and the Middle East came before the platform committee in a proposal to make Israel the favored recipient of advanced weapons—supersonic jets—"both for her protection and to help keep the peace of the area." The reason for this, according to the platform, was that "the Soviets persist in

---

159 *Oregonian*, "Wyatt Resigns Committee Job," 12 July 1968.
160 Victor Atiyeh, "Republican National Convention Day Planner, hand annotated," Republican National Convention, (1968), Atiyeh Collection, Pac. Univ.
161 Victor Atiyeh, "Tape 10," 271.
162 Harold Hughes, "Ike Urges GOP to Stand Firm About Vietnam: Republican Platform Committee Expected to Take Hard Line on War," *Oregonian*, 31 July 1968.
163 Victor Atiyeh, "Republican National Convention Platform Committee Notes," (Unpublished manuscript, 29–31 July 1968), Handwritten notes, Atiyeh Collection, Pac. Univ.

building an imbalance of military forces in this region."[164] Into these matters of geopolitics, Vic Atiyeh, proud Syrian American, stated his opinion before the Platform Committee. Years later, as Atiyeh talked with Syrian President Hafez al-Assad, Atiyeh told of his proposal to the committee to provide "American arms equally to the countries of the Middle East."[165] It got a bit tense. Atiyeh recounted to Assad that this "evoked a very angry response from Senator [Jacob] Javits [R-NY], which was so heated that the committee chairman Everett Dirkson had to apologize for Javits's behavior."[166] The *Lebanese-American Journal*, a national magazine, reported the events:

> State Senator Victor Atiyeh, an influential legislator from Oregon and a relative of the New York rug merchants, got up in executive session, informed sources disclosed, and tried to get his colleagues to drop the proviso on the U.S. supplying supersonic planes to Israel, but Javits made some comments repugnant to Atiyeh in front of the big committee (for which he later apologized), basing his argument on the premise that it was in the best interests of the U.S.[167]

Atiyeh came away from the convention knowing that he could hold his own with the national leaders of his party.

Introduction to Leadership

Vic Atiyeh was elected as Republican leader in the Senate in December 1970.[168] Atiyeh joined his Republican caucus in waiting during mid-December 1970 to see what the 16-member

---

164 *New York Times*, "Excerpts from Republican Platform," 5 August 1968.
165 "Oregon Governor Atiyeh's March 31 Meeting with Syria's President Hafiz Al-Assad," Department of State, U.S. Government, Confidential Telegram, (31 March 1984), 2, Atiyeh Collection, Pac. Univ.
166 "Atiyeh Conversation with Assad," 2.
167 "Says GOP Adopted Anti-Arab Stand in Platform," *Lebanese American Journal*, 15 August 1968, Atiyeh Collection, Pac. Univ.
168 Harold Hughes, "Atiyeh Wins GOP Vote," *Oregonian*, 9 December 1970.

Democratic caucus would decide for its own leadership slate. Atiyeh had the backing of fourteen Republicans—including himself—so it would be a contest to see which party could bring over the two votes needed to get to sixteen, the magic number to elect the President of the Senate. A coalition of a few conservative Democrats and the bulk of Republicans had led the Senate for most of the 1960s. An *Oregonian* editorial had high hopes that under Atiyeh's leadership, the Republicans would not go down the coalition road once again. Since Atiyeh had loudly and publicly decried the coalition, it seemed the time might be ripe for the leadership of the Senate to actually reflect the parties in power, not the cross-party mix of the coalition.[169] It was clear that the coalition was fraying at the edges, but there was pressure to use the coalition to elect an actual Republican as Senate President in case Governor McCall decided to run against Hatfield for the U.S. Senate in 1972. Under Oregon's succession laws at the time, the President of the Senate would become governor.[170]

The Republican caucus surprised everyone by not nominating Atiyeh. Instead, the group went with Lynn Newbry from Ashland.[171] "Neither Newbry nor Atiyeh would comment on how or why the switch took place except to state that the Republicans were united in their resolve to elect a Senate president this year," an *Oregonian* article explained,[172] but the maneuver looked like a transparent ploy to get the vote of Debbs Potts (D-Josephine County), a holdout who would not support anybody from the Portland area. Perhaps he would go for Newbry, a fellow southern Oregonian?

What happened in that caucus room? In the lead up to the caucus, since his selection as minority leader in December, Atiyeh had been the presumptive nominee for President. Atiyeh and the Democratic leader Berkeley "Bud" Lent had appeared in early

---

169 *Oregonian*, "New GOP Stance," Editorial, 10 December 1970.
170 Harold Hughes, "Demos: Work Harder; GOP: No Self-Destruct: Politicians Already Look to '72," Column, *Oregonian*, 8 November 1970.
171 Harry Bodine, "Deadlock Snags State Legislature: Senate GOP Switches Support to Newbry," *Oregonian*, 11 January 1971.
172 Bodine, "Deadlock Snags State Legislature."

January before a civic group in Portland with their different ideas about what was important in the upcoming session.[173] Atiyeh's candidacy was expected to finally put the coalition to rest.[174] Atiyeh recalled that "in the pre-session…[the caucus would] kind of go through the script, and we went through the script in which no one was [actually] selected, but I had been chosen."[175] But when it came time for the actual selection, Atiyeh's name was not even put to a vote. Atiyeh was surprised because he had actively campaigned for and won the minority leadership post. Reporter Henny Willis described Atiyeh's incredulity: "When the Republicans entered the full caucus room, Atiyeh looked like he'd been hit by an axe. Just having to come into the room, before the full Senate and the Capitol press corps, made his humiliation total."[176] The reports were that four of his fellow Republicans voted against him in the December leadership contest, but those kinds of splits happened all the time behind closed caucus doors.[177] When it came to the Presidency there was unity, but it was not behind Atiyeh.

Atiyeh attributed the move to his opposition to the coalition for the previous six years. He thought that his victory in the minority leader contest over Tony Yturri (Ontario), who was in favor of the coalition, offended pro-coalition members of the caucus.[178] Atiyeh admitted to Willis that "it was one of those times when I wished I could've been somewhere else, but I simply had to go into that room. It hurt and it hurt badly."[179] The way Atiyeh dealt with this setback was the same way he had dealt with adversity since he

---

173 *Oregonian*, "Lent, Atiyeh Differ in Sizing Up Key Matters Before Legislature," 7 January 1971.

174 *Oregonian*, "'Citizen Involvement' Expected to Play Key Role in Legislature: 'A Time of Hope and Fear…'," Editorial, 10 January 1971.

175 Victor Atiyeh, interviewed by Clark Hansen, "Tape 10," Oral history, recorded by Oregon Historical Society, Portland, OR, 23 December 1992. Transcript, 288, Atiyeh Collection, Pac. Univ.

176 Henny Willis, "A Senator With Dignity," Column, *Eugene (OR) Register-Guard*, January 1973, Atiyeh Collection, Pac. Univ.

177 Hughes, "Atiyeh Wins GOP Vote."

178 Atiyeh, "Tape 10," 288.

179 Willis, "A Senator With Dignity."

was in high school. He got back up, dusted himself off, and went forward with no recriminations for those on the other side. It was this same ability that Atiyeh used when he and his brothers disagreed about running the business—he and they would accept the decision one way or the other, and the three of them would share a car back to their neighborhood, get up the next day and move on.

The biggest environmental issue of the 1971 session was the Bottle Bill. It did not, however, go through Atiyeh's Environmental Affairs committee; it ended up in the Consumer Affairs Committee as it made its way through the Senate late in the session. Consideration of this bill ended up being a battle of principles for Atiyeh—should he go with the principle that the best government is the one that is less involved in people's lives? Or should he go with a policy proposal that he saw was good for Oregon? And, in between these two was a third principle: government should create incentives to change people's behaviors.

House Bill 1157, the Bottle Bill, was introduced in 1969 by Paul Hanneman (R-Cloverdale) after originating with Rich Chambers, an outdoorsman who thought bottles and cans should be returnable. McCall did not support it. The bill was back in 1971 with strong support from the governor and many interest groups.

The bill passed the House overwhelmingly, 54-6, in the second week in April. Its future in the Senate was not as certain.[180] When the Senate heard the bill on the floor in May, amendments were added and the measure, with Atiyeh's support, was sent back to the Consumer Affairs Committee. Sending a bill back to committee is usually a ploy to kill a measure.[181] Atiyeh argued that he voted to send the bill back to committee because he had

---

180 Harry Bodine, "Bottle Deposit Bill Wins House Vote: 5-Cent Returnable Beverage Containers Head for Predicted Tough Fight in Senate," *Oregonian*, 10 April 1971.
181 *Oregonian*, "Senate Shunts Bottle Measure Back to Consumer Committee," 22 May 1971.

noticed a problem in the way the bill defined some of its terms. "I was supportive of it. So having read the bill, I saw a defect"—there were issues with the implementation date of the bill and there was a provision that limited returns to twenty-four bottles or cans on a given day.[182] He was not the only one—a news story at the time noted that "[s]everal senators who spoke in favor of the move contended they wanted a better bill."[183] The definitions were fixed in committee, and the bill returned to the Senate for final passage just a few days later.[184] Atiyeh would face accusations that he had opposed the Bottle Bill in later statewide elections. He always pointed to his support for the final version to counter the charges.

Land Use Policies

The 1973 session would have several highlights.

Biggest among them, and the one to have the most impact on the lives of Oregonians, would be statewide land-use laws. Atiyeh would play a strong role in creating these laws in committee. The Senate Environment and Land Use Committee got its first detailed look at the land-use bill in the second week of the session. Senate bill (SB) 100 grew out of 1969's SB 10, a requirement that all counties must zone and plan their land by 1972. Governor McCall was on board with the bill. The bill's intention was to create something new in the United States, a meshing together of state-created land-use goals with local decision-making in meeting those goals. As a *New York Times* editorial put it, in a country that valued federalism—the multiple layers of government from the national level to states to cities and counties to school districts and the like—"the country can no long

---

182 Victor Atiyeh, interviewed by Clark Hansen, "Tape 12, side 1," Oral history, recorded by Oregon Historical Society, Portland, OR, 28 December 1992. Transcript, 321, Atiyeh Collection, Pacific University Archives, Forest Grove, OR; Harry Bodine, "Bottle Bill Passes Hurdle in Senate," *Oregonian*, 28 May 1971.

183 *Oregonian*, "Senate Shunts Bottle Measure."

184 Bodine, "Bottle Bill Passes Hurdle in Senate." Five Democrats and three Republicans voted No on the final bill.

afford to have decisions that vitally affect the well-being of the entire nation decided on whim and by the smallest units of local government."[185] The Oregon passage of SB 100 was the state-level effort to corral the "whims" of local governments for the good of the entire state of Oregon. The initial idea was to divide the state up into fourteen regional planning council districts. Atiyeh, a member of the committee since its first iteration as the Interim Public Health Committee in 1965, immediately focused on his area of expertise—taxes. He "wanted to know whether regional district councils dealing with planning would have taxing authority. He was told no."[186]

Oregon had actually been focused on land preservation issues for more than a decade. By the late 1950s it was clear that farmland was vulnerable to developers, especially farmland "on the fringes of growing urban areas."[187] Laws were passed that focused on property taxes—farmland would be taxed at a lower rate if rules were followed about what a farm actually was. This was a common tactic across the country as states faced the issue of a quickly growing post-war population and the desire of many of those new families to own their own homes. But Oregon put a different twist on the property-tax relief system: designated farming zones "had to be consistent with adopted [county] plans."[188] By 1967 there was an effort to classify the different soil types across the entire state to designate more clearly what ought to be considered agricultural land. The Willamette Valley, considered some of the most productive farmland in the country, was the area most threatened by suburban growth. There were findings by a planner for a mid-Willamette Valley council of governments "that the construction of Interstate 5 had paved over 1,500 acres of prime agricultural land" in the valley.[189]

---

185 *New York Times*, "Land Use—Or Giveaway?," Editorial, 10 July 1972.
186 *Oregonian*, "Senators Consider State Planning Bill," 19 January 1973.
187 Sy Adler, *Oregon Plans: The Making of an Unquiet Land-Use Revolution*, (Corvallis, OR: Oregon State University Press, 2012), 25.
188 Adler, *Oregon Plans*, 26.
189 Adler, *Oregon Plans*, 28.

Atiyeh was firmly in favor of land-use planning. He saw the reasons for it in the very neighborhood in which he had lived since 1947. He had watched the main road through the area, the Beaverton-Hillsdale Highway (Highway 10) change from "a two-lane mostly residential street [into] a four-lane commercial" line of strip malls. "There was a dairy farm across the street from where I was living," he recalled.[190] That became a Fred Meyer shopping center. What had been a neighborhood with "two Greek grocers, a service station, and a tavern" on the two-lane main road had become a neighborhood hemmed in by rows of car dealerships, fast food places, and furniture stores. As Atiyeh put it, "Anybody who lives in Raleigh Hills has got to be for land-use planning."[191]

It was clear to Atiyeh that land-use legislation needed to happen. He recalled that for him, two of his principles were in action as he considered the bill. First, would land-use laws be good for the people of Oregon? His answer was unequivocally, yes.[192] Second, could he make the hard decisions necessary to make the bill as good as he thought it could be, without worrying about his political future? Atiyeh answered yes to that as well. Atiyeh and two Democrats, John Burns and Mike Thorne, were the crucial swing votes in the committee. Atiyeh liked what SB 100 had to say about land-use rules, but the proposed system for deciding the rules was not "any good in my terms of what democracy is all about."[193] The idea of regional councils, known as Councils of Government (COGs), having jurisdiction was something that Atiyeh had real problems with. To him it was an unnecessary additional layer of government, and an unelected layer at that. Atiyeh, true to his principle that government closest to the people is best, "felt counties should be given the power to

---

190 Victor Atiyeh, "Tape 48," 508–509.
191 Victor Atiyeh, "Tape 48," 509.
192 Victor Atiyeh, "Tape 22," 656.
193 Victor Atiyeh, interviewed by Clark Hansen, "Tape 15, side 1," Oral history, recorded by Oregon Historical Society, Portland, OR, 19 January 1993. Transcript, 433, Atiyeh Collection, Pac. Univ.

review comprehensive plans which SB 100 now proposes to assign to regional councils."[194]

After a trip through an ad hoc committee, SB 100 changed. The role of regional governments was stripped out, the original idea for a five-person state lands commission (the Land Conservation and Development Commission, LCDC) was changed to a seven-person committee with at least one member from each of the four congressional districts and at least one member from Multnomah County, the most populous in the state. The biggest changes were in what types of land ought to be subject to special attention—so-called critical areas. Instead of precise measurements (e.g., within a quarter mile of a freeway interchange), the new designations gave more latitude to the LCDC to look at critical areas ("land adjacent to freeway interchanges," for example). Agriculture lands were now on the critical areas list. In addition, "public transportation facilities, public sewage systems, water supply systems, solid-waste disposal sites, energy generating and transmission facilities, and…public schools" were now firmly on the list.[195] In addition, lcdc could designate certain land uses as being of "statewide significance," for instance areas around park lands, the Oregon coast, and other natural areas.

A month later, the committee was ready to go to work on the actual bill as presented by the ad hoc group. The first day at it, after two hours of work (and some minor amendments being voted up or down), the committee was deadlocked on the role of regional governments. With four options before it, none of them could muster a majority of votes.[196] Eventually the bill made it through the committee with no provisions for regional governments. Atiyeh added provisions (supported by a majority of the committee) that lessened the intended power of LCDC—it would be sufficient for LCDC to simply review and comment

---

194 *Oregonian*, "Committee to Seek Land-Use Compromise," 14 February 1973.
195 Adler, *Oregon Plans*, 66–67.
196 Harry Bodine, "Senate Panel Divided Over Land-Use Issue," *Oregonian*, 14 March 1973.

"before planning and siting an activity of statewide concern."[197] He also advocated that appeals of an LCDC order could only be made by those "'adversely affected' or 'aggrieved' by that order."[198] This had the effect of radically reducing the power of citizen organizations and concerned individuals to challenge any LCDC decisions. Atiyeh was thinking like the lawyer he never got a chance to be—in order to file a suit or be party to an appeal, according to the law, a person must show some type of harm or direct effect. Atiyeh was holding the new land-use system to that same higher level of personal impact.

This new version of SB 100 made it out of committee, and it was passed in the Senate. The bill then passed the House on May 23 by a two-to-one margin with no changes and went to McCall for his signature.[199] By the end of June 1973, "only nineteen of the thirty-six Oregon counties had adopted both land-use plans and zoning ordinances" as directed by 1969's SB 10.[200] The counties would not finish the SB 10 process and the more stringent requirements of SB 100 and the LCDC until Governor Atiyeh pressured them to do so in the early 1980s.

The McCall Tax Plan

Vic Atiyeh's taxation expertise was put to the test by Governor McCall's second big tax reform effort after the 89%–11% defeat of the sales tax in 1969. In 1973 he was more popular, major progressive bills he had championed were admired across the state—the Beach Bill and the Bottle Bill—and he was working to get comprehensive land-use enacted into law, SB 100.[201]

The tax plan was a bit complex, but it would fund education in such a way that local property-tax payers were not feeling the

---

197 Adler, *Oregon Plans*, 72.
198 Adler, *Oregon Plans*, 73.
199 Harry Bodine, "Land-Use Planning Bill Approved," *Oregonian*, 24 May 1973.
200 Adler, *Oregon Plans*, 81.
201 For a broader context, both personal and political, see Walth, *Fire at Eden's Gate*, 362–368

pressure of constantly being asked to contribute more to local school systems. In its final form, the McCall Plan would remove school support from local property tax bills, shifting the state's contribution to K-12 education from about 30% to about 95%. The downside, for taxpayers, was that Oregon's income tax would increase by about 30%. However, most of that load would be put on higher-income earners, making Oregon's income tax one of the most progressive in the country. To make all this happen, there were two parts to the plan: a resolution calling for a constitutional amendment to limit property taxes; and a statute raising the income tax rate. Atiyeh was against such a huge raise in income tax rates and was also very concerned that the state's bigger share of the cost of K-12 education would mean that the state would be running school districts, a clear violation of his principle that government closest to the people is best.

The goal was to have the McCall Plan go before the voters in May 1973 "so that property tax reduction provisions in the bill [would] go into effect" in 1973.[202] Even as the bill worked its way through the Senate Revenue Committee after the House, where it had passed 43–16, people were counting noses in the Senate to see whether the McCall Plan could pass. Republican minority leader Atiyeh agreed with the Senate President, Democrat Jason Boe,[203] not to enforce party discipline on the bill: "the caucus will not attempt to dictate how individual senators vote on the measure when it reaches the Senate floor." But Republican McCall's tax plan was more supported by Democrats than by Republicans. It looked like ten to twelve Democrats (out of eighteen) supported the bill, but that was short of the sixteen needed to pass it. It would take several Republican senators supporting the bill to get it through.[204] The McCall Plan made it out of the Revenue

---

202 Doug Seymour, "Senate Revenue Committee Authorizes Use of Subpoena," *Oregonian*, 7 March 1973.
203 Harry Bodine, "Senate Leaders Coy on Tax Bill Support, Though Governor's Strategists Confident," Column, *Oregonian*, 9 March 1973.
204 *Oregonian*, "McCall Plan 'Foes' 'Undecided' on Vote," 15 March 1973.

Committee on March 17, a remarkably quick turnaround time, on a party-line vote (Democrats in favor).[205]

The bill came up before the full Senate on March 21. In what was described as "a hectic day of legislative activity," the bill was first defeated by all twelve Republicans and four Democrats, then reconsidered and passed with three Republicans voting for the measure.[206] Atiyeh recalled that he led the Republicans back into a caucus meeting after the initial defeat and argued that "the Republican senators should vote for it—but I didn't prevail."[207] Two of the Democrats in opposition "stressed the fear of possible loss of local control by their constituents" as the main reason they voted against the plan. The key to passage, however, was those three Republicans. Led by Atiyeh and joined by Hector Macpherson and C. R. Hoyt, their reasons for changing were pretty simple: they felt that the people of Oregon deserved to vote on such a momentous change in the tax system.[208]

The campaign was set. The people would vote on May 1, 1973, just six weeks away. There were debates and forums held across the state. The chief Yes campaigner was McCall himself. When McCall would appear in debates over the tax plan, Atiyeh was often the person who would appear with him to argue the opposition.[209] Atiyeh was noted by observers as the debater who "took the high road and shunned every opportunity to exploit the emotional side issues."[210] National interest in the McCall Plan seemed to arise because Oregon was building a reputation for new ways to think about pollution, beaches, bottles and the rest—the

---

205 Harry Bodine, "McCall Tax Plan Gains Approval of Senate Panel," *Oregonian*, 18 March 1973.
206 Doug Seymour, "School Finance Plan Approved by Senate," *Oregonian*, 22 March 1973.
207 Victor Atiyeh, "Tape 4," 108.
208 Harry Bodine, "News Analysis: Switch of Three GOP Votes Passes School Tax Plan," *Oregonian*, 22 March 1973.
209 Richard Munn, interviewed by Jim Moore, "Atiyeh Interview," Salem, OR, 9 June 2016. Summary notes, 10.
210 *Oregon Journal* (Portland), "There Is A Higher Road," Editorial, 23 April 1973, Atiyeh Collection, Pac. Univ.

Oregon Story.²¹¹ If the McCall Plan passed, it would put Oregon far ahead of any other state in taking responsibility for funding K-12 education.

Polling on the election showed the typical Oregon pattern on ballot measures. There was strong initial support, but as election day neared, polls showed an even race.²¹² On election day Oregon voters overwhelmingly defeated the McCall Plan by 59% to 41%.²¹³ Granted, it was a lot closer than the 1969 sales tax measure, but a three to two margin was a strong defeat. The only three counties to vote for the measure were Lane County (home of the University of Oregon), Benton County (home of Oregon State University), and Coos County (by some accounts, the county with the highest property taxes in the state).²¹⁴ McCall was crushed.²¹⁵ Richard Munn, of the Oregon Tax Commission observed that it was the results of this tax measure, and the active role that Atiyeh had played in defeating it, that led to Tom McCall's frosty relationship with Atiyeh for rest of McCall's life. Munn put it succinctly, "As a result, McCall would never endorse Atiyeh. It was a direct quid pro quo."²¹⁶

The legislature was still in session, so it cobbled together a variation of the McCall Plan. Voters rejected that 1974 ballot measure by 75% to 25%—anti–sales tax numbers.²¹⁷

McCall was furious with Atiyeh for actively campaigning against the McCall Plan. Later that May, both headed back to Washington, D.C., to take part in a panel discussion on land use and urban growth.²¹⁸ McCall was leading the panel in his role as

---

211   Evan Jenkins, "Oregon to Vote on School Taxes," *New York Times*, 29 April 1973.
212   Walth, *Fire at Eden's Gate*, 366, 367.
213   *Oregon Blue Book, 1975–1976.* (Salem, OR: Oregon Secretary of State, 1975), 251; Evan Jenkins, "Oregon Votes Heavily in Favor of Retaining the Local Property Tax to Finance the Public Schools," *New York Times*, 3 May 1973.
214   Todd Engdahl, "Reasons Vary for Tax Plan Loss," News Analysis, *Oregonian*, 3 May 1973.
215   Walth, *Fire at Eden's Gate*, 367–368. McCall even considered resigning as governor.
216   Munn, "Atiyeh Interview," 10.
217   *Oregon Blue Book, 1975*, 251.
218   AP, "Governor in Capital," *Oregonian*, 24 May 1973.

the governor of the state that had just passed one of the most far-reaching statewide land-use efforts in the country. He was seen as one of the leaders of the national conversation about responsible growth.[219] Atiyeh was on the panel at the behest of a national group of state legislators.[220] The panel was sponsored by the national Task Force on Land Use and Urban Growth, headed by Laurance Rockefeller.[221] The Task Force had just finished its report to the President Nixon which read, in part,

> There is a new mood in America. Increasingly, citizens are asking what urban growth will add to the quality of their lives. They are questioning the way relatively unconstrained piecemeal urbanization is changing their communities, and are rebelling against the traditional processes of government and the market place which they believe have inadequately guided development in the past.
>
> They are measuring new development proposals by the extent to which environmental criteria are satisfied.[222]

Oregon's bold excursion into statewide land-use rules, while too recent to make the report, was something that the Task Force wanted to hear about.

Atiyeh remembered the trip well. He and McCall traveled together to Washington, D.C., and they ate together the night before the panel. "Well," Atiyeh recalled, "he was stung by his loss on this school finance plan. He didn't take his losses very well....He said to me, 'Audrey [McCall's wife] said, 'Why are you going back with your worst enemy?'" He's telling me this.

---

219 David Bird, "Gov. McCall Seeks to Curb Oregon's Growth," *New York Times*, 7 May 1973.

220 Victor Atiyeh, "Tape 15, side 2," 446; Victor Atiyeh, "Tape 48," 515.

221 William K. Reilly, ed. *The Use of the Land: A Citizens' Policy Guide to Urban Growth. A Task Force Report Sponsored by The Rockefeller Brothers Fund*, (New York: Thomas Y. Crowell, 1973), 1.

222 Gladwin Hill, "Authority Over Land Use Is Termed a Public Right," *New York Times*, 20 May 1973; See Reilly, *Use of the Land*, 6 for the final version of this passage.

And it got a little embarrassing. There we were sitting in this fancy hotel, and he was fairly loud about chewing me out."[223] "Tom never forgave me....He was quite angry about losing, ... and he considered me [his]...number one enemy."[224]

Atiyeh ascribed McCall's dislike for him at this moment to McCall's personality. All of this was in line with Atiyeh's experiences with McCall. He recalled, "Tom was difficult in the sense that he would be...on or off; he would either hate me or, I wouldn't say like me, but didn't hate me. I always figured that was just Tom. So, he would do some things that were outrageous, and I'd say, 'That's Tom.'"[225]

McCall sent Atiyeh several personal notes during McCall's governorship. There were congratulations on being elected a Republican delegate to the 1968 national convention, a February 1969 handwritten P.S.—"You have been superb this session, as usual!"—just as Atiyeh was headed off with an Oregon contingent to meet with Nixon's new cabinet officers, and a delightful handwritten note (dated simply "Thursday") thanking "Delores and Victor" (note the misspelling of Dolores' name, a common problem) for having Tom and Audrey over for an "oft-postponed, but eminently worth waiting for" dinner with the Atiyeh family and some friends.[226] There seemed be a hint of nostalgia for occasional times in the late 1950s and early 1960s when McCall would come to dinner at the Atiyeh's home. Most relevant to Atiyeh's 1973 experience, however, was a note from McCall at the end of the very long session that hit upon their disagreements and their ability to work together.

---

223 Victor Atiyeh, "Tape 15, side 2," 446.
224 Victor Atiyeh, "Tape 15, side 2," 445; Atiyeh, "Atiyeh interview #2," 2.
225 Victor Atiyeh, "Atiyeh interview #2," 1.
226 Tom McCall, Typed note on governor's letterhead to Vic Atiyeh, "Congratulations on Delegate Victory," 25 June 1968, Atiyeh Collection, Pacific University Archives, Forest Grove, OR; Tom McCall, Typed note on governor's letterhead with handwritten PS to Vic Atiyeh, "Thank You for 1969 Session Work," 20 February 1969, Atiyeh Collection, Pacific University Archives, Forest Grove, OR; Tom McCall, Handwritten note on governor's letterhead to Vic Atiyeh, "Thank You for Dinner," Atiyeh Collection, Pac. Univ.

Dear Vic:

Your magnificent work in the Legislature was, again, a delight to behold. I almost fell off my chair when the Senate voted at first against my tax plan. But your point was made, and I am deeply appreciative that you delivered the needed votes, even it if was to no avail in the end.

Your efforts on that, the traffic safety bills and a host of other of our projects, and your singular cooperation and kindnesses will always be remembered. Thanks, Vic, very much.

Warmest personal regards,

Tom[227]

The Gubernatorial Primary

At some point, Atiyeh looked at McCall's governorship and said to himself, "Hell, I can do that job."[228] Republican Secretary of State Clay Myers was already in the gubernatorial race, but by the end of December 1973 Atiyeh pledged a positive campaign and officially announced his candidacy for the highest office in the state.[229] It would be a big change of political pace for the Washington County legislator.

From his position in the legislature, Atiyeh saw that McCall "just sort of took the bucket and dumped it upside down. There were still so many things that had to [be] or should be done," he thought "it had to be pulled together so it would work."[230] He remembered that the feeling that he should run "sort of gradually

---

227 Tom McCall, Typed note on governor's letterhead to Vic Atiyeh, "Thank You for 1973 Session," 13 July 1973, Atiyeh Collection, Pac. Univ.
228 Victor Atiyeh, "Atiyeh interview #4," 1.
229 Harry Bodine, "Race for Governor Off to Slow Start: Political Potpourri," *Oregonian*, 9 December 1973; *Oregonian*, "Atiyeh Pledges Effort to 'Positive' Campaign," 29 December 1973.
230 Victor Atiyeh, interviewed by Jim Moore, "Atiyeh interview #3," Raleigh Hills, OR, 26 March 2014. Summary notes, 7; Victor Atiyeh, interviewed by Clark Hansen, "Tape 25," Oral history, recorded by Oregon Historical Society, Portland, OR, 12 May 1993. Transcript, 712, Atiyeh Collection, Pac. Univ.

built up."[231] He knew that "we did some good things that were important and big," with McCall as governor, "but…the state had been shaken…and rattled and turned upside down, and I said, 'Okay, now's the time to kind of pull it all together and make it work like it should work.'"[232] Atiyeh was not thinking about who the competition was. He had been in the legislature for almost sixteen years; he knew the details of Oregon policy.

Atiyeh's first foray into statewide politics would be an education for him and for the electorate. For himself, he would discover that a statewide race was technically much more complex than simply making his legislative campaign bigger. He would have to write out speeches, get a driver, learn that he could not reach all voters in person, and master much about corners of the state far away from Portland and Washington County. The campaign would also be a lesson to him in issues over which he had no control—especially the national issue of Watergate. For Oregonians, they would meet a relatively obscure state legislator who they would eventually choose over a well-known statewide incumbent in the primary. But Atiyeh's relative obscurity, the shadow of Tom McCall's liberal years in the governor's office, and Watergate would send voters toward Atiyeh's fall opponent, leading to his only defeat as a candidate in his twenty-eight-year political career.

For years, Clay Myers had been talked about as McCall's heir apparent. Myers had been appointed by McCall to become secretary of state after McCall was elected governor in 1966. He had run for reelection twice, in 1968 and 1972, so he was familiar to voters, and he knew how to run a statewide campaign.

Once Atiyeh had begun to think seriously about running for the seat during the 1973 legislative session, he appeared before Republican groups to talk about the legislative session, as he had for years, but the tenor of the talks began to shift to the "basic

---

231 Victor Atiyeh, interviewed by Clark Hansen, "Tape 16," Oral history, recorded by Oregon Historical Society, Portland, OR, 22 January 1993. Transcript, 476, Atiyeh Collection, Pac. Univ.

232 Victor Atiyeh, "Tape 16," 476.

Republican philosophy and its past, present and future directions in Oregon."[233] He was sounding out his audiences to see how his ideas worked with Republican voters. But, as Atiyeh told a reporter in the fall of 1973, electoral "politics ain't my bag."[234] The reporter observed that "[c]ampaigning does not thrill him. In fact his wife Dolores is much better at it than he is."[235] Atiyeh seemed to relish the process of the first elections to the House, but the lack of competition made the Senate elections just an exercise he had to go through to continue his work in Salem. This attitude would have to change if Atiyeh was going to advance to statewide office.

Atiyeh was certain enough of his interest by late summer 1973 to commission an October 1973 poll assessing where he stood with voters.[236] According to the poll, he faced the traditional challenge before any legislator when running for statewide office: outside one's district, not many people know who the legislator is. Atiyeh had a bit of an advantage over others seeking to make this electoral leap because his last name was frequently in the Portland media market through advertisements for Atiyeh Brothers carpets. But he still faced an uphill battle. The initial findings of name recognition for potential gubernatorial candidates: Clay Myers 83% (and 90% among Republicans); Bob Straub 79% (82% among Democrats); Betty Roberts 53% (63% among Democrats); Jim Redden 44% (49% among Democrats); Victor Atiyeh 40% (50% among Republicans); Ed Westerdahl, aide to Governor McCall, 38% (42% among Republicans).[237] Even among registered voters, Atiyeh improved to just 46% from 40%. Given

---

233 Statesman News Service, "Benton GOP Bills Atiyeh," *Salem Oregon Statesman*, 19 August 1973.

234 Harry Bodine, "Atiyeh-Myers Primary Race Offers GOP Equal Time in the Gubernatorial Limelight: Choice is Philosophical," Analysis, *Oregonian*, 24 December 1973.

235 Bodine, "Atiyeh-Myers Primary Race."

236 Bardsley and Haslacher, "The Gubernatorial Potential of Vic Atiyeh," Public Opinion Research for Atiyeh Campaign, (October 1973), Atiyeh Collection, Pac. Univ.

237 Bardsley and Haslacher, "Gubernatorial Potential of Vic Atiyeh," S-2.

the margin of error, it was clear that more than half the electorate simply had no idea who he was. But there were some bright spots. Atiyeh had 60% recognition in the Portland metro area and 81% in his home area of Washington County; outside the Portland area his recognition dropped to 33%. Another bright spot was that most respondents identified him as a legislator (if they knew him) rather than a rug merchant (54% to 15%).[238] So the poll showed that he might have a political base out there on which to build a candidacy. But he would have to overcome the fact that his opponent would be Clay Myers, the most recognized of all the potential candidates.

Gerry Thompson, a Republican in Salem who would eventually become Atiyeh's chief of staff, recalled that "when Vic ran for office the first time, it made the Republicans pretty mad."[239]. She observed that "the old stalwarts" felt that Atiyeh had run out of turn, upsetting the plans that had been in place about who would run for which statewide office. This was exactly what Atiyeh had done in 1964 when he took on John Hare for the Oregon Senate seat from Washington County.

As the Atiyeh campaign put its polling together, they found out that Myers "had some very negative" ratings. Voters "knew him, but they weren't really all that hot about him or excited about him."[240] When Atiyeh was asked why he was running against Myers, he would say, "I'm not running against Clay, I'm running for me. He wants to be governor; I want to be governor. It's not that I don't want him to be governor, it's that I want me to be governor."[241]

Atiyeh himself did not share this negative assessment of Myers.[242] They had worked well when Atiyeh was in the Senate and Myers needed help getting legislation through in his role as

---

238 Bardsley and Haslacher, "Gubernatorial Potential of Vic Atiyeh," S-2, S-3.
239 Gerry Thompson, interviewed by Jim Moore, "Atiyeh Interview #3," Salem, OR, 19 January 2016. Summary notes, 8.
240 Victor Atiyeh, "Tape 16," 480; See Atiyeh, "Atiyeh interview #3," 2.
241 Victor Atiyeh, "Tape 16," 481.
242 Victor Atiyeh, "Atiyeh interview #3," 2.

secretary of state. When Atiyeh became governor, he and Myers had a good working relationship with Myers as state treasurer.

Of all the things that happened to Atiyeh in the 1974 race, one he rued the most was being identified as a conservative in media accounts of the race. Major issues in the race turned out to be the death penalty (Atiyeh was for bringing it back after a 10-year hiatus), lowering the drinking age to 19 (Atiyeh opposed this), and campaign spending (Atiyeh was much more successful raising money from the business community).[243] As the election neared, Atiyeh made it clear that he was "unalterably opposed to abortion used in lieu of contraceptives. Unwanted babies should be placed for adoption, not aborted."[244] In all of these, he was more conservative than Clay Myers. Atiyeh also was seeking to differentiate himself from the Republican legacy of Tom McCall, an avowedly liberal governor. Since Myers was seen as McCall's heir to the governor's seat, the contrast made Atiyeh appear to be more conservative than he viewed himself.

As Atiyeh recalled twenty years later, he found "it was a shock" to be labeled a conservative "in the sense that I had never been labeled, nor had I thought about a label."[245] In 2014, Atiyeh was much more to the point about his feelings when he was labeled a conservative. He recalled saying to himself, "Oh, shit!"[246]

Years later, Clay Myers was talking with Portland attorney Bill Campbell. Myers told Campbell that he had a great deal of respect

---

243 Charles E. Beggs, "Drinking-at-19 Heads for Spot on May Ballot," *Salem Oregon Statesman*, 28 June 1973; AP, "18-Year Olds Plan Splits Candidates," *Salem Oregon Statesman*, 20 April 1974; *Oregon Statesman* (Salem), "Vote Suggested on Restoring Death Penalty," 13 April 1974; Gordon Macpherson and Victor Atiyeh, "Restoring the Death Penalty," "The Legislature...A Minority View" Column, *Condon (OR) Globe-Times*, 19 April 1974.

244 AP, "Redden Endorsed by Portland Daily," *Salem Oregon Statesman*, 1 May 1974; Charles E. Beggs, "Who's He? Problem Battled by Atiyeh," *Salem Oregon Statesman*, 19 May 1974.

245 Victor Atiyeh, interviewed by Clark Hansen, "Tape 17," Oral history, recorded by Oregon Historical Society, Portland, OR, 25 January 1993. Transcript, 490, Atiyeh Collection, Pac. Univ.

246 Victor Atiyeh, "Atiyeh interview #3," 2.

for Atiyeh. Myers said, "People saw me as the progressive Republican, like Wayne Morse, and Vic as highly conservative. I never saw the man that way. That's why I worked for him after he beat me." Myers saw Atiyeh as the quieter of the two, but "a fundamental man of principle."[247]

As their gubernatorial campaigns got going, there was the matter of opening headquarters offices, organizing people across the state, and raising money. Clay Myers's Portland headquarters was next to the Governor Hotel. A photographer caught him working to remove the sign of the previous occupant of the space —Atiyeh Brothers Fine Carpets.[248]

In their first joint appearance, Atiyeh focused on what he perceived to be Myers' weak point—voters just did not see him as a strong leader for governor. He "said the next governor should be 'innovative but practical,' 'honest' and 'an advocate for the people,'" adding, "The issue is who is going to be the governor of Oregon and what kind of person will he be."[249] Myers stressed the continuity between his governorship and McCall's, pointing out that he would continue "the openness and accessibility" of the McCall administration.[250] One of the differences between the candidates was over the proposed Mt. Hood freeway. Atiyeh was for it, saying, "We do need one more freeway through this area, but this would be my last 'one more.'" Myers thought that there needed to be "better access through Southeast Portland, but not the original freeway plan." He felt that better mass transit and roads could solve the problem.[251] Atiyeh supported higher gas taxes for mass transit districts, but with the caveat that a ballot measure before voters in May 1974 not take away money that would otherwise go to cities and counties.[252]

---

247 Bill Campbell, interviewed by Jim Moore, "Atiyeh interview," Portland, OR, 9 April 2015. Summary notes, 8.
248 *Oregonian*, "Takeover," Photo caption, 14 March 1974.
249 Todd Engdahl, "Republican Hopefuls Field Tough Questions," *Oregonian*, 2 April 1974.
250 Engdahl, "Republican Hopefuls Field Tough Questions."
251 Engdahl, "Republican Hopefuls Field Tough Questions."
252 *Oregonian*, "Atiyeh Backs Mass Transit Gas Tax Help," 25 April 1974.

In the second week of April, the dynamic of the race changed. Myers, as secretary of state, fired Jack Thompson, the State Election Supervisor. The reason was Thompson's acceptance of material for the Voters' Pamphlet about a week after the deadline.[253] There were conflicting testimonies about what had happened, but it was enough for Myers to let Thompson go.[254] In light of the national Watergate scandal, there was speculation about the impact of the incident on Myers' candidacy.[255] Did it show corruption in the secretary of state's office? Did it show poor leadership by Myers in his elected position? Atiyeh asserted that he would not make an issue over the firing. He told a reporter, "I have too much respect for the political process we have established in Oregon to go for something like this as an issue in the campaign."[256] It came out that Myers himself had been involved in accepting another late filing for the Voters' Pamphlet in the 1972 election. Myers explained that in that case "he bent the Oregon election law...to resolve a conflict between two legal requirements and correct an error made by his own office."[257] Myers was forced to spend a lot of time at his own campaign appearances dealing with all these questions.[258]

The *Salem Capital Journal* came out for Atiyeh the second week in May. The endorsement noted that "Myers [had] been running for the governor's office almost from the day he was appointed...as secretary of state. ...And it has been widely

---

253 Harry Bodine, "Myers Dismisses Elections Official Jack Thompson," *Oregonian*, 11 April 1974.

254 Harry Bodine, "Testimony Conflicts in Report on Voters' Pamphlet Investigation," *Oregonian*, 11 April 1974.

255 Charles E. Beggs, "Myers Forced to Defensive as Election Drive in Jeopardy," Capitol Views column, *Salem Oregon Statesman*, 21 April 1974; Harry Bodine, "Firing of Elections Director Adds Spice to Coming Races: Impact to Follow...," Column, *Oregonian*, 14 April 1974; Todd Engdahl, "Chill Breeze of Scandal Cools Oregon Campaigns," *Oregonian*, 15 April 1974.

256 *Oregonian*, "Atiyeh Will Not Make Issue of Myers' Pamphlet Incident," 19 April 1974.

257 *Oregonian*, "Atiyeh Will Not Make Issue."

258 *Oregonian*, "Democrats Gather to Forge Platform," Political Potpourri column, 20 April 1974.

assumed that Myers would gain the Republican nomination without serious difficulty."[259] But the endorsement noted, as Atiyeh had learned as he traveled the state and talked with fellow Republicans, there was a "growing dismay among many Oregon Republican leaders over the prospect of a Myers administration in the Statehouse."[260] The endorsement characterized Myers as moderate to liberal and Atiyeh as conservative—someone who saw "government as the problem-solver of last resort," but "an active supporter of legislation for civil rights and environmental protection."[261] It was Atiyeh, "far more knowledgeable than Myers on most of the more complex issues of state government," who the newspaper recommended to Republican voters.[262]

McCall formally endorsed Myers on May 17, building on a clear set of messages that dated to the beginning of the campaign. McCall said, "I see Clay Myers as someone who will…seek to maintain Oregon's open, progressive system and work to keep this a quality state."[263] Two days later the *Salem Oregon Statesman* endorsed Atiyeh, noting that while he had to overcome a large name-familiarity gap, he was "not out selling himself, but what he stands for. If he were governor, we'd find ourselves respecting his decisions, even if we didn't always agree with them."[264]

On election day, May 28, 1974, Atiyeh beat Myers handily, 61% to 33%.[265] The front-page story in the *Oregonian* heralded a "GOP surprise" in Atiyeh's "landslide victory for the Republican

---

259 *Capital Journal* (Salem), "Atiyeh Over Clay Myers," Editorial, 9 May 1974, 1973–74 Interim Scrapbook, Atiyeh collection, Pacific University Archive, Forest Grove, OR.
260 *Capital Journal* (Salem), "Atiyeh Over Clay Myers."
261 *Capital Journal* (Salem), "Atiyeh Over Clay Myers."
262 *Capital Journal* (Salem), "Atiyeh Over Clay Myers."
263 AP, "McCall Gives Support to Myers in GOP Primary," *Oregon Statesman* (Salem), 18 May 1974.
264 *Oregon Statesman* (Salem), "Atiyeh Endorsed in Close Governor Race," Editorial, 19 May 1974.
265 *Oregon Blue Book, 1975–1976*, (Salem, OR: Oregon Secretary of State, 1975), 245.

gubernatorial nomination."[266] The *Oregon Statesman* headline across the top of the front page said "Atiyeh Upsets Myers."[267] Atiyeh's victory seemed to herald a new direction for the Oregon Republican party, with Atiyeh characterized by a reporter as "a conservative Republican and Portland businessman."[268]

Wearing his old television-analyst hat, McCall said, "It's the end of an era of progressive Republicanism. There've been 16 years of it, and it's gone."[269] He railed against the "Atiyeh wrecking crew," a reference to Atiyeh's leadership in defeating the 1973 McCall tax plan.[270]

A report noted that "Atiyeh, when told of McCall's remark…in the State Senate Wednesday, laughed."[271] He was probably thinking to himself, "That's just Tom being Tom." Behind the scenes, however, Atiyeh was not as sanguine about the comment. Bob Oliver, who worked in McCall's office at that point, recalled that Atiyeh was very upset and asked Oliver to come by Atiyeh's office—which at that point was next to the men's room on the second floor of the capitol.[272] Atiyeh asked Oliver if there was anything specific that made McCall angry—Oliver recalled that Atiyeh was "puzzled" about McCall's reaction. Oliver "frankly told him that it would be hard to finger any one particular thing. It was probably just the general feeling that you had been insufficiently supportive."[273]

---

266 Bodine, "Legislator Pulls GOP Surprise," *Oregonian*, 29 May 1974.
267 Paul W. Harvey, Jr., "Atiyeh Upsets Myers, Straub Leading Demos," *Salem Oregon Statesman*, 29 May 1974.
268 Wayne Thompson, "Myers Not Surprised at Atiyeh's 'Upset' Victory," *Oregonian*, 30 May 1974.
269 Todd Engdahl, "Atiyeh Victory Seen as Finish to an Era," *Oregonian*, 30 May 1974, 1973–74 Interim Scrapbook, Atiyeh collection, Pac. Univ. Archive.
270 Harry Bodine, "Straub, Atiyeh Runoff Seen as 'Clear Choice'," *Oregonian*, 30 May 1974.
271 Bodine, "Straub, Atiyeh Runoff Seen as 'Clear Choice'."
272 Bob Oliver, interviewed by Jim Moore, "Atiyeh interview," Salem, OR, 24 August 2015. Summary notes, 9.
273 Oliver, "Atiyeh interview," 9.

An early June editorial by the *Salem Oregon Statesman* wondered about McCall's ability to move voters. The May election had seen the defeat of five of the six state measures endorsed by McCall. It noted, "It doesn't take too long a memory to recall how the voters clobbered the McCall tax plan a year ago. McCall has great personal popularity, but his recent record shows that when asked to join the McCall endorsement bandwagon, Oregon voters may visit, but they don't stay."[274] That last dig at McCall's famous phrase about protecting Oregon from unplanned growth probably did not endear the paper to the governor.

Looking to the fall, an *Oregonian* editorial credited "Atiyeh's vigorous but low-keyed campaign statewide, strongly backed by conservative business leaders, [that] wiped out Myers' advantage of eight years of speech-making in communities throughout Oregon. Whether Atiyeh's style will appeal to Democrats, who have a 229,000-registration edge, is the essential question."[275]

The General Election

As the fall campaign got rolling there were problems faced by both nominees. The two were in debt after their primary races. Atiyeh was about $50,000 in the red; Straub owed a little less than $22,000.[276] The only statewide race in which candidates were not in debt was for the court of appeals. Atiyeh's response was clear to those who later worked with him on his statewide campaigns. Whatever would happen, those future campaigns would not go into debt.

Atiyeh quickly received the support of virtually every statewide and federal Republican officeholder. Only McCall held

---

274 *Oregon Statesman* (Salem), "McCall Offers Mixed Blessing,' Editorial, 3 June 1974.

275 *Oregonian*, "On to the November Wars," Editorial, 30 May 1974.

276 Ginny Burdick, "Oregon Primary Spending Leaves Candidates in Debt," *Salem (OR) Capital Journal*, 28 June 1974, 1973–74 Interim Scrapbook, Atiyeh collection, Pac. Univ. Archive; *Oregon Statesman* (Salem), "Atiyeh Outspends Myers by 2 to 1," 28 June 1974; Todd Engdahl, "Atiyeh's Campaign Debt Highest in State: Governor Hopefuls in Red," *Oregonian*, 28 June 1974; *Oregonian*, "Campaign Debt Figure Clarified," 29 June 1974.

out.[277] Hatfield, who was part of the "16 years of progressivism" that McCall had referenced as coming to an end with Atiyeh's victory, endorsed Atiyeh with enthusiasm. He said, "Personal integrity transcends any viewpoints on specific issues. I feel Victor Atiyeh has the capacity and intelligence in every way to be a great governor and will be a great governor. I believe the word progressive would not be at all foreign to Victor Atiyeh's administration."[278]

In July Atiyeh opened his campaign headquarters in downtown Portland; Straub's campaign took over Myers' spot in the old Atiyeh Brothers location just a few blocks away.[279] The Atiyeh campaign operation was simply a bigger version of the system he had in place to win his state senate races. His son Tom observed that the 1974 effort looked an awful lot like his father's legislative races but with "a lot more money."[280] While Atiyeh's legislative contests had not featured strong opposition candidates in years, he certainly faced strong and experienced opposition from Bob Straub. Atiyeh's co-chair was Marjorie Russell, the same person who had run his legislative campaigns. The campaign's secret weapon was its army of volunteers. Atiyeh knew he could not meet even a fraction of the voters in the general election, but he hoped that volunteers in counties across the state would make those connections for him. Their weapon of choice? The personal letter. Atiyeh's 1974 and 1978 gubernatorial campaigns would see thousands and thousands of these letters sent out to voters by volunteers. Gerry Thompson remembered that her husband Al, the Marion County Atiyeh chair, had about fifteen ladies who came in every day to write letters by hand.[281] At some point, Al got a message from campaign headquarters to stop writing letters, "they were out of money." Al said, "I can't tell those ladies to stop.

---

277 AP, "Fellow GOPs Support Atiyeh," *Salem Oregon Statesman*, 2 June 1974.
278 *Oregonian*, "Atiyeh Wins Praise of GOP Delegates," Political Potpourri column, 1 June 1974.
279 *Oregonian*, "Atiyeh Opens Office With Campaign Idea," 12 July 1974; *Oregonian*, "Straub and Atiyeh Launch Campaigns," 15 August 1974.
280 Tom Atiyeh, "Atiyeh interview," 4.
281 Thompson, "Atiyeh Interview #3," 8.

They think they're doing a great thing." Gerry decided, "Then we won't tell them to stop." They had boxes of letters that they quietly got rid of because they could not send them out. But they also created tremendous bonds to Atiyeh among those volunteers who thought they were instrumental to the campaign.

It was apparent that the volunteer-centered campaign had some organizational issues. Donna Campbell, Atiyeh's longtime friend from Washington High School and spouse of one of Atiyeh's closest friends, Jim Campbell, remembered working in the main office as a receptionist. "Everything was not good" in the organization of the office, "everything was a mess." She remembered telling Atiyeh, "You've got to go in the back room. Everything's a mess back there."[282] To his credit, in Campbell's eyes, Atiyeh did see the problems, learned from the experience, and got better as the campaign went on. Atiyeh's son Tom worked in the back rooms of all three of his father's gubernatorial campaigns, "which is where I like[d] to be." If things were disorganized, that was because "[i]t was all brand new to us."[283] Shirley Woodrow, with experience in several statewide races in Alaska, was asked to be Atiyeh's campaign manager in the late summer. She turned down the opportunity because she saw serious organizational issues.[284]

The first major moves of both campaigns took place in mid-August. Straub attacked Atiyeh's long voting record in the legislature, highlighting his support for the 1969 sales tax and opposition to the bottle bill.[285] Neither of these assertions were true. Atiyeh immediately responded by pointing out that he had supported the bottle bill, saying "I do not try to explain Bob Straub's stands on the issues, and I wish he would not try to

---

282 Donna Campbell, interviewed by Jim Moore, "Atiyeh interview," Raleigh Hills, OR, 26 June 2015. Summary notes, 1, Atiyeh project, Moore collection.
283 Atiyeh, "Atiyeh interview," 4.
284 Shirley Woodrow, "Atiyeh Interview," phone interview from Glenwood Springs, CO, 17 June 2015. Summary notes, 3.
285 AP, "Straub Hits Atiyeh's Vote Record," *Salem Oregon Statesman*, 16 August 1974; *Oregonian*, "Straub and Atiyeh Launch Campaigns."

explain mine—at least not until after he does his homework."[286] The bottle bill vote would continue to dog Atiyeh in the campaign. In September a campaign staffer said, "Vic can't understand why this thing on the bottle bill keeps coming up. He voted for the bill, and he has said that as governor he wouldn't want to see the bill tampered with."[287] There was agreement between the two candidates on land-use planning: they were in favor. But Straub liked the idea that state-level organizations should oversee Oregon's land-use system, while Atiyeh, true to his principles, argued that "the level of government 'closest to the people' be the planning agency."[288]

Then the political storm that was Watergate swept most other issues aside. After Richard Nixon resigned the presidency of the United States on August 8, 1974, Atiyeh was confident that the governance system had worked, and that people across the country would see that and know that the United States political system was strong. The Oregon Republican state convention took place just a few days later in Ashland. Atiyeh, in the keynote address to his fellow party members, told them, "History will show that this crisis has not weakened America; it has strengthened it. The walls have not come tumbling down. Anarchy does not prevail. Instead, out of tragedy has come triumph."[289] He was hoping, as Republicans had been hoping since the spring of 1973, that Watergate was a focus on Nixon himself, not something that voters would blame on the Republican party and its candidates. The early polling in August

---

286 AP, "Atiyeh Disputes Straub Charges," *Salem Oregon Statesman*, 17 August 1974.

287 Doug Yocom, "Atiyeh Says He Backed Bottle Bill," *Portland Oregon Journal*, September 1974, 1973–74 Interim Scrapbook, Atiyeh collection, Pac. Univ. Archive.

288 *Oregonian*, "Candidates Urge Fast Land-Use Decisions," Political Potpourri column, 21 August 1974; Frank Wetzel, "Straub and Atiyeh Talk of Land Use," *Salem Oregon Statesman*, 21 August 1974.

289 AP, "U.S. Strengthened by Nixon Quitting, State GOP Told," *Salem Oregon Statesman*, 11 August 1974.

had Straub ahead 40% to 30% (±4.1%), but with a sizable number of undecided voters, it looked like a wide-open race.[290]

Watergate kept playing a role as the campaigns moved into the two-month sprint of September and October, heading toward election day on November 5. On September 8, a Sunday, President Ford pardoned former-President Nixon "for all offenses against the United States which he...has committed or may have committed or taken part in during the period" of Nixon's presidency.[291] Speaking the next day, Atiyeh "applauded President Ford for pardoning" Nixon, saying, "I believe Nixon has already been punished more than necessary."[292] To another reporter, Atiyeh explained what he meant by "more than necessary." Nixon "probably has lost for life his status as a senior statesman, and has been personally castigated by those once considered his friends."[293] Atiyeh was always sure that Ford had done the right thing with the pardon. He was never sure how big an impact the pardon had on his own race, but when he saw his friends and former colleagues in the state legislature lose—southern Oregonian Republicans John Dellenback lost reelection to the US House and Lynn Newbry was defeated for reelection to the Oregon Senate—Atiyeh remembered that "there wasn't much that could stem the tide" of the Democratic gains.[294]

Atiyeh made a one-day trip back to Washington, D.C., for a photo op and discussion with President Ford, an opportunity the Ford White House afforded to several candidates across the country. Back at home, "Dolores said to me, 'Is that office really oval?' And I said, 'Gosh, I don't know...but,'" the rug merchant

---

290 AP, "Poll Shows Straub Has Early Lead," *Salem Oregon Statesman*, 20 August 1974.

291 Gerald Ford, "Granting Pardon to Richard Nixon," Office of the President, United States Government, Proclamation 4311, (8 September 1974).

292 Steve Metz, "Ford's Pardon Decision Draws Support of Atiyeh," *Portland Oregon Journal*, 10 September 1974, 1973–74 Interim Scrapbook, Atiyeh collection, Pacific University Archive, Forest Grove, OR.

293 *Oregonian*, "Pardon for Nixon Seen as Bringing Draft Amnesty Near," 10 September 1974.

294 Victor Atiyeh, "Atiyeh interview #3," 5.

replied, "I can tell you what the rug looks like."[295] The trip may have been a campaign stunt, but the visit was the beginning of a long relationship with Ford, something Atiyeh treasured. In October Atiyeh received a note from the president thanking Atiyeh "for your recent message sharing with me your views on the assistance the Federal Government may perform for the people of Oregon" and wishing him "Good luck on your campaign for Governor."[296]

Watergate and the unpopular pardon of Nixon defined how Straub approached the campaign. In Roseburg Straub connected Atiyeh to "the Nixon-Ford-Watergate economic policies." Atiyeh hit back.[297] He

> said he was sure Straub's remark was a slip of the tongue, "but Oregonians need to be certain of this. If it was not a slip of Bob's tongue to inject a reference to Watergate into the campaign for Oregon's governorship, then it would seem to constitute a reckless attack on Oregon's high minded public servants [and...] an irresponsible aggravation of the already widening gap in the confidence which people hold their government and their elective officials today across the land."[298]

Atiyeh's message to the voters was his "Action Plan." It called for streamlining state government, "more clearly defining responsibilities of local government to eliminate duplication of effort and cost," and welfare reform with a public service program.[299] The campaign was predictable as the partisan supporters for both sides lined up and took stands. Labor groups

---

295 Victor Atiyeh, "Tape 17," 506.
296 Jerry Ford, Letter on White House letterhead to Victor Atiyeh, "Thank You for Message," 23 October 1974, Atiyeh Collection, Pac. Univ.
297 *Oregonian*, "Straub Blasted," 4 October 1974.
298 AP, "Atiyeh Criticizes Straub, Hints at Court Decision," *Salem Oregon Statesman*, 4 October 1974.
299 Harry Bodine, "Victor Atiyeh: An 'Action Plan'," Analysis, *Oregonian*, 20 October 1974, D3.

endorsed Straub; Atiyeh did well with business groups.[300] Straub continued to hit at Atiyeh's legislative voting record, and Atiyeh continued to propose new ideas to make government more responsive.[301] Both candidates extolled the record of outgoing Governor McCall. They knew who the most popular politician in Oregon was, and they were attempting to transfer some of that popularity to their own candidacies.[302] Even though McCall had made it clear that he was more in favor of Straub, and even though some of his former aides were actively supporting Straub, McCall refused to officially endorse Straub.[303] In Atiyeh's mind, this was the implicit support of Straub he had feared when McCall did not immediately endorse him after the primary.

Both candidates positioned themselves to be seen as strong replacements for McCall. Straub's campaign theme was "Elect Another Leader." Atiyeh's was "Oregon's Next Great Governor." However, both candidates "take care to note they are not running to continue [McCall's] administration and point out where they differ with him."[304]

Straub's campaign was more confident—the candidate had run for statewide office many times before (two victories for State Treasurer, two defeats by McCall for the governorship), so his team knew how to run a campaign at this level. Straub observed that the differences between him and Atiyeh were huge. Atiyeh had a "narrow, restrictive attitude…he thinks government ought

---

300 AP, "Teamsters Union Endorses Straub" *Salem Oregon Statesman*, 14 September 1974; *Oregonian*, "Straub, Roberts Endorsed: Campaign Countdown," 13 September 1974; Robert E. Gangware, "Governor Candidates Tell AOI 'Productivity' Plans," *Salem Oregon Statesman*, 21 September 1974.

301 Harry Bodine, "Straub Rips Atiyeh Voting Record," *Oregonian*, 25 September 1974; Harry Bodine, "Atiyeh Action Plan Includes Office of Budget Productivity," *Oregonian*, 24 September 1974; Joe Frazier, "Atiyeh Proposes Office for Budget," *Salem Oregon Statesman*, 24 September 1974.

302 Harry Bodine, "Both Atiyeh, Straub Laudatory of Record of Retiring McCall," *Oregonian*, 21 September 1974.

303 *Oregon Statesman* (Salem), "Straub Gets Schmidt Aid," 28 September 1974; *Oregon Statesman* (Salem), "McCall Won't Back 1 Man for Governor," 25 September 1974.

304 *Oregonian*, "Both Admire McCall, But…," Column, 20 October 1974.

to stay out of things."[305] Straub believed strongly that government ought to be deeply "involved in solving social and economic problems," but he stressed his personal approach of being careful with every public dollar spent.[306] Straub was also clear that following in McCall's footsteps was fine, but that there would be changes. He would, for instance, work on making Oregon more attractive to tourists, and he noted that his rhetorical style was much different from the word-loving McCall's. "You'll be disappointed if you think I'll shine across the evening horizon like a rocket, because I'm not going to," he told Rotarians at one campaign stop.[307]

An issue that was particularly important was appealing to the votes of women. The Equal Rights Amendment had been passed by Congress in 1972 and was making its way through the states. The conversation about the role of women in public life was changing quickly. Since the 1970 gubernatorial election, seven new women had been elected to the Oregon House.[308] They joined stalwarts like Betty Roberts (D), serving in the Senate, and included people like Norma Paulus (R) and Vera Katz (D)—Paulus would secure election as Oregon's second female statewide winner in 1976 (Maurine Neuberger was elected to the U.S. Senate in 1960) and Katz would become speaker of the House and later three-term mayor of Portland. In the 1974 campaign Roberts was running for the US Senate. Atiyeh's campaign featured women in prominent roles. "The first person I turned to, when I decided to run for governor, was Marjorie Russell. She was the chairman for my last two Senate campaigns and is co-chairman of this one."[309] Six of his county campaign chairs were women, and the Coos County effort was led by women co-chairs. Straub pointed out "that he was the first state

---

305 Charles E. Beggs, "Straub Draws Battle Lines in Race for Oregon Governor," *Salem Oregon Statesman*, 28 October 1974.
306 Beggs, "Straub Draws Battle Lines."
307 Beggs, "Straub Draws Battle Lines."
308 *Oregon Blue Book, 1973–1974*, (Salem, OR: Oregon Secretary of State, 1973), 86–90.
309 *Oregonian*, "Political Candidates Air Views on Women," 11 October 1974.

constitutional officer to appoint a woman as his deputy" when he was treasurer.³¹⁰ Both candidates supported day care centers for working families.

At a candidate forum both gubernatorial candidates were asked, What's your view on the Commission for Women? Atiyeh recalled,

> Bob Straub answered first. ...I can't give you all the words, but he was doing the right thing. "[H]e thought that the Women's Commission was a great thing. And then he said, "And I'm going to have a man on my staff to see this happens." And I heard this. Now, wait a minute. You're going to have a *man* on your staff to see that this happens? After all these great words....³¹¹

Atiyeh did not point out the inherent sexism of Straub's response. He remembered, "Well, it was so patent to me. I said, 'Whoa, wait. Everybody's going to hear this.'"³¹² They did not. Atiyeh made a point to say that he would "have a woman on my staff take care of this," but the point was lost.³¹³ And, as Atiyeh observed, "Well, [the audience] still supported [Straub]" over Atiyeh.

Atiyeh's ads hit at Straub's plans to spend government money. "We Can't Afford Bob Straub as Governor" was the theme. One version highlighted the tough economic times and their impacts on everyday Oregonians. It began, "To everyone watching their savings dwindle, barely coping with skyrocketing taxes, and having trouble keeping their kids in tennis shoes...."³¹⁴ By the end of October, seeking to win the votes of disaffected Democrats and wavering Republicans, the Atiyeh ads stressed "You and Victor

---

310 *Oregonian*, "Political Candidates Air Views on Women."
311 Victor Atiyeh, "Tape 17," 510–511. Italics added.
312 Victor Atiyeh, "Tape 17," 511.
313 Victor Atiyeh, "Tape 17," 511.
314 *Oregon Statesman* (Salem), "We Can't Afford Bob Straub as Governor," Advertisement, 8 October 1974; *Oregonian*, "We Can't Afford Bob Straub as Governor," Advertisement, 8 October 1974.

Atiyeh Simply Have a Lot More in Common."³¹⁵ Straub's ads were straightforward—a vote for Straub was a vote to continue McCall's legacy. His slogan was "Elect Another Leader. This Time It Really Makes a Difference."³¹⁶

As the election grew near, it was clear that Atiyeh would have to depend on a big turnout, and lots of voters buying his argument that Straub was part of the economic problem, not the economic solution. Atiyeh knew he faced an uphill battle against a better-known opponent. He told one reporter,

> The question I've asked throughout this campaign is whether a guy like me can be elected governor. The thing that gets me...I read the editorials and some of the letters to the editors, and get the feeling that I'm the worst thing that could happen to Oregon.
>
> I've served 16 years in the legislature from Washington County. Is everybody in Washington County a dummy to elect me? Are the 144,000 Republicans who nominated me for governor dummies?³¹⁷

Atiyeh all but admitted that he would have a tough time winning, saying, "The success of my campaign depends strongly on Republican turnout. There's no other way to look at it."³¹⁸ Unsaid, there would have to be a near-collapse of Democratic turnout for Atiyeh to win—that huge voter registration edge for the Democrats was a big hurdle to overcome. Straub's campaign manager hoped to end any chance for Atiyeh by attracting "significant numbers of moderate Republican votes. 'I do expect a

---

315 *Oregon Statesman* (Salem), "You and Victor Atiyeh," Advertisement, 27 October 1974; *Oregonian*, "You and Victor Atiyeh," Advertisement, 27 October 1974; *Register-Guard* (Eugene), "You and Victor Atiyeh Simply Have a Lot More in Common," Advertisment, 27 October 1974.

316 *Oregon Statesman* (Salem), "Elect Another Leader: Bob Straub," Advertisement, 4 November 1974.

317 Charles E. Beggs, "Atiyeh Seeks Big GOP Turnout in Race for Oregon Governor," *Salem Oregon Statesman*, 26 October 1974. Ellipses in original.

318 Beggs, "Atiyeh Seeks Big GOP Turnout."

big crossover vote for Bob. I'm hoping for a good [pro-Straub] Republican vote.'"[319]

President Ford visited on November 1, 1974, to push for Republican candidates. He urged the Republican audience to "help elect a Congress that will 'bite the bullet' and deal with inflation and act responsibly on national security issues."[320] Governor McCall, making fun of his own more liberal views, called his presence on the stage with the president his "one day of the year to be a Republican." McCall "had long words of praise for" candidates running for the U.S. Senate and U.S. House. His "shortest introduction was for Victor Atiyeh" who McCall underwhelmingly described as "a man moving toward the midstream of politics…a worthy candidate of character and principle."[321]

Atiyeh himself "knew about two or three weeks before the campaign [ended]…that I wasn't going to win."[322] This was based on his long experience in elections, his 'gut feeling' that had served him so well before. Atiyeh felt bad for his volunteers. "They were so enthusiastic, and they worked so hard, and I let them down."[323]

Straub won going away.[324] Atiyeh's first loss at the ballot box after a string of twelve straight wins was not even close. Straub received almost 445,000 votes to Atiyeh's 325,000 votes, a victory of 57.7% to 42.1%.[325] In raw numbers, Straub's 120,000 vote victory was, at that time, the fourth-largest victory in Oregon history. In percentage terms (which considers population growth),

---

319 Harry Bodine and Todd Engdahl. "Straub, Atiyeh Campaign Teams Concentrate on 'Getting to the Voter' in Stretch Run Efforts," Column, *Oregonian*, 31 October 1974.
320 Todd Engdahl, "GOP Urged to Support Bullet Biters," *Oregonian*, 2 November 1974.
321 Engdahl, "GOP Urged to Support Bullet Biters." Ellipses in original.
322 Victor Atiyeh, "Atiyeh interview #3," 3.
323 Victor Atiyeh, "Atiyeh interview #3," 3.
324 AP, "Straub Wins Over Atiyeh For Governor," *Salem Oregon Statesman*, 6 November 1974; Harry Bodine, "Democrats Parlay Scandals Into Landslide: Straub Outpolls Atiyeh with 5-4 Margin," *Oregonian*, 6 November 1974.
325 *Oregon Blue Book, 1975*, 247.

his victory over Atiyeh was the eighth largest.[326] Accounts in 1974 noted that it was the largest victory since 1950. Atiyeh only won nine counties out of thirty-six, including Josephine and Klamath counties where the local papers had endorsed him, and not including his home Washington County.[327] Atiyeh was crushed. On election night "Atiyeh said he had expected a much closer race and seemed at a loss to explain the wide victory margin put together by Straub." Then, in an analysis that would drive his political future, "Atiyeh said he still believ[ed] he was in tune with Oregonians on major measures, 'but I just didn't get my message across.'"[328]

Shirley Woodrow saw this optimism in Atiyeh's supporters as well.[329] Atiyeh responded to this support after the contest was over. Woodrow observed that "he was filled with this euphoria" that people still wanted to help him even though he had lost. In Woodrow's estimation, after the loss, "people [knew] he was still there for them, he [was] still who he [was]. He was not a loser at all." Woodrow felt that Atiyeh's supporters thought it would just take Atiyeh a little longer to become governor.

It was an election for the Democrats in Oregon and across the country. Atiyeh was clear about the import of the victory, saying that Straub had "an unusual opportunity to carry out his wishes for state government. ...'The way is clear for him to accomplish these programs that he promised the voters.'"[330] Unsaid was that Atiyeh would be watching carefully to see how Straub did.

In the days after the election Atiyeh made the point that there had been good Republican candidates, but they had just been swept up in the anti-Watergate vote.[331] Some compared the results to the 1964 election when Barry Goldwater's presidential bid had

---

326 Jim Moore, "Gubernatorial Results in Oregon," 5, 6.
327 *Oregon Statesman* (Salem), "Straub-Atiyeh," County vote results, 7 November 1974.
328 John Guernsey, "Straub's Supporters Jubilant: 'Change Wanted'," *Oregonian*, 6 November 1974.
329 Woodrow, "Atiyeh interview," 3.
330 Harry Bodine, "Democrats Make Massive Gains in Elective Posts," *Oregonian*, 7 November 1974.

sunk Republicans across the country except for the Oregon House going Republican. The landscape looked ripe for Republican rebuilding. But what direction would it take? McCall Republicanism had been rebuffed in the primary. The new more moderate Republicans had been rebuffed in the general election. Who would step up to the lead the party in Oregon? With a presidential election swiftly approaching in 1976, it appeared that the new Republican choice would be between Ford moderates and the rising group of social and fiscal conservatives who were coalescing behind the governor of California whose two terms had just ended, Ronald Reagan.

One big thing had changed in Oregon. Vic Atiyeh, the candidate who seemed standoffish in crowds, who told a reporter at the beginning of the run for the governorship that he did not really like to campaign, had become a convert to talking with the people of Oregon. He recalled the 1974 campaign: "It was a grand experience, really, traveling Oregon, meeting people. ...The other thing [was] that I had seen other candidates lose, and they were devastated. I wasn't devastated. I was tired, but I said to myself, and I really believed it, that I know that I was where Oregonians were. Now I've traveled the state and talked to them, and I knew that I was where they were. They just didn't know it yet."[332] Atiyeh was "very comfortable that I was not out of step with Oregonians."[333]

Back in the Legislature

The federal government was also exercising its new programs developed under Nixon and continued by Ford. For state and local governments, one of the most powerful of these was revenue

---

331 Harry Bodine, "Stalwarts Say Republican Depression is Not Fatal, but a Major Upheaval Seems More Than Likely: Whither Goest the Elephant?" *Oregonian*, 24 November 1974.

332 Victor Atiyeh, "Tape 18, side 1," 515; see as well, Victor Atiyeh, interviewed by Clark Hansen, "Tape 53, side 2," Oral history, recorded by Oregon Historical Society, Portland, OR, 18 August 1993. Transcript, 660, Atiyeh Collection, Pac. Univ.

333 Victor Atiyeh, "Tape 18, side 1," 515.

sharing. President Ford wrote a letter to Atiyeh in April 1975 making the case for revenue sharing, a program he had helped create as the minority leader in the U.S. House.

> I am a strong believer in the Federal system of shared sovereignty which protects freedom of action and promotes creativity at all levels of government. This Federal system was designed to enable all Americans to be served by that level of government closest to them and best able to act in the public interest. In 1972, we made an historic decision to support and advance our Federal system with the passage of General Revenue Sharing.[334]

As the years went on, Atiyeh came to see more and more problems with federal revenue sharing. He recalled, "[R]evenue sharing means that you're going to give me back what I just sent you. I'd just as soon not send it in the first place."[335] If the best government was the one closest to the people, then why recycle tax dollars for local programs through the federal government? Why not let local and state government figure out the programs and the ways to pay for them? Atiyeh would be governor as revenue sharing and other Nixon-Ford–era national programs were quickly dismantled by President Reagan. It would be a wrenching time, with Oregon in a major recession, and Atiyeh would have some choice words for Reagan's budget people.

A new and ascendant Senate staffer got to know Atiyeh during this time. Senator Frank Roberts (D-Portland) had just been married. On the opening day of the session, the new spouse, Barbara Roberts, was at Frank Robert's desk on the floor—as the senator's aide—when Atiyeh walked over, put out his hand, and said, "You must be the new bride!" Barbara Roberts remembered it as being sincere and personal, and found him to be "as warm as

---

334 Gerald R. Ford, Letter on White House letterhead to Victor Atiyeh, "Revenue Sharing," 25 April 1975, 1973–74 Interim Scrapbook, Atiyeh collection, Pac. Univ.
335 Victor Atiyeh, interviewed by Clark Hansen, "Tape 37, side 1," Oral history, recorded by Oregon Historical Society, Portland, OR, 15 June 1993. Transcript, 184, Atiyeh Collection, Pac. Univ.

if he were my grandfather."[336] Frank Roberts served on the Revenue Committee with Atiyeh, and there were a lot of "technical bills that came to the floor," as Barbara Roberts remembered. Atiyeh was very good on the details. "It was something he understood as a businessman and a political leader."[337] She remembered a few times when Atiyeh would raise questions or issues on the floor of the Senate about revenue bills that Frank Roberts was carrying. "It was always an honorable exchange. It was never cranky or rude. They were both gentlemen, they were both articulate." Barbara Roberts was comfortable with Atiyeh from the beginning because her husband respected and liked him. Through knowing Atiyeh, she began to understand how the Senate really worked, skills that would come in handy when she was elected to the House in 1978, and later when she served as Secretary of State during Atiyeh's governorship, and even later when she became Oregon's governor in 1991, the first woman to hold the office.

For Atiyeh, the May 1976 primary was all about Gerald Ford. Atiyeh was probably one of the most active honorary chairs in Oregon presidential campaign history. Most honorary chairs show up at fundraisers and lend their prestige to important events while leaving the day-to-day campaigning to the state chair and whatever organization that person puts together. Atiyeh, who had loved visiting all parts of Oregon during his 1974 gubernatorial run, was right back at it. The Wednesday before the primary, Atiyeh "barnstormed" through Pendleton, Bend, Klamath Falls, Medford, and Roseburg.[338] Atiyeh was the face of the campaign talking about the amount of money raised in comparison to the Reagan campaign (Atiyeh thought they were about even, but the Reagan people said they had been outraised by about two to one), and prominently mentioned as one of the Ford "fund raiser 'captains'" to give Ford the best chance of winning the state.[339]

---

336 Barbara Roberts, interviewed by Jim Moore, "Atiyeh interview," Portland, OR, 23 February 2015. Summary notes, 2.
337 Roberts, "Atiyeh interview," 7.
338 *Oregonian*, "Voters Warned to Use Both Sides of Punchcards," 18 May 1976.

Until the end of Atiyeh's life, Ford remained his pick as the greatest president he had ever worked with or met. Atiyeh probably first met Ford in October 1973 when Ford came to Portland as the Vice President–designate after Agnew's resignation.[340] They had discovered they really liked each other during Atiyeh's quick visit to the White House in September 1974.[341] He recalled,

> Jerry Ford,…[was] a *great* president, in my mind one of the great presidents in our history. I don't think he'll ever go down [in history] that way, but in *my* mind [he was]. What he did after Nixon resigned, and he became president and pardoned Nixon, and…the turmoil the country was in, what he did in two-and-a-half years was incredible. Healing…. And what do people remember? He stumbles.[342]

Ford hit Oregon the Saturday before the primary with stops in Medford and Portland.[343] Reagan was in Pendleton the same day. Ford gave a standard stump speech in a sunny park in downtown Medford, then he spoke on foreign policy at Lewis and Clark College in Portland. He ended the day, flanked by Atiyeh and Republican former U.S. Representative Wendell Wyatt, at a reception for Ford campaign workers in downtown Portland.[344] At

---

339 Stan Federman, "Primary Candidates Find Money Scarce," Column, *Oregonian*, 10 May 1976; Wayne Thompson, "Small Group of Big Money Men Makes Oregon Go: Fund Raising for Politics—and Anything Else," Column, *Oregonian*, 16 May 1976.

340 "Gerald R. Ford, Vice-President Designate, Breakfast Briefing," Century Club, Portland, OR, 15 October 1973. Atiyeh Collection, Pac. Univ.

341 Jerry Ford, Letter on White House letterhead to Victor Atiyeh, "Thank You for Message," 23 October 1974, Atiyeh Collection, Pac. Univ.

342 Victor Atiyeh, interviewed by Clark Hansen, "Tape 17," Oral history, recorded by Oregon Historical Society, Portland, OR, 25 January 1993. Transcript, 494–495, Atiyeh Collection, Pac. Univ.

343 Ford's on-stage host in Medford was Republican Jackson County Commissioner Tam Moore, the author's father.

344 Jim Vincent, "Ford Woos Voters in Medford, Asks Oregonians for Mandate," Photographs, *Oregonian*, 23 May 1976.

the end, "despite outspending his opponent almost 3-to-1," Ford eked out a four percent margin of victory over Reagan. Out of Oregon's thirty Republican delegates to the national convention, sixteen would be committed to Ford, fourteen would be committed to Reagan.[345] The Oregon Reagan delegates were led by Bob Voy, but the leadership of the social conservatives was in the hands of Walter Huss. Huss would be a major player in Oregon Republican politics for the next few years. The stage was set for a fight for the soul of the Republican party not just in Oregon, but at the convention itself. Atiyeh would be in the middle of it. He served as one of the Ford campaign's whips at the Republican National Convention in Kansas City, Missouri. It was his job to count noses, line up support for Ford, and rush in to convince any wavering delegates. He reveled in the role.

On August 18, Gerald Ford beat Ronald Reagan in the floor vote to win the Republican nomination. Atiyeh was one of nineteen delegates accorded the honor to second Ford's nomination. With just twenty-five seconds, Atiyeh told the delegates and a national audience, "On July 4th, 1976, we began the first year of our third century. In the first year of our first century courageous leaders with an exciting commitment blessed this nation. That courage and that commitment is here tonight. Oregon wants a democracy in the year 2076 for her children's children. Oregon and the nation wants and needs Gerald Ford to be our Presidential leader into a certain future. I am honored, as is Oregon, to second the nomination of Gerald R. Ford for President of the United States."[346] Later, reflecting on his moment of fame, Atiyeh said, "Well, what can you say in half a minute?"[347]

---

345 Stan Federman, "Church Took Initiative from Carter in Tireless, Round-the-Clock Effort," Column, *Oregonian*, 27 May 1976; *Oregon Blue Book, 1977*, 262.

346 Raleigh E. Milton, *Official Report of the Proceedings of the Thirty-First Republican National Convention*, (Kansas City, MO: Republican National Committee, 1976), 407, Washington County Museum, Rock Creek, OR; Victor Atiyeh, "Oregon Delegates Share Experiences: 1976 Convention Not Unlike 1776," *Beaverton (OR) Valley Times/Aloha Times*, 26 August 1976, Atiyeh Collection, Pac. Univ.

347 Bill Keller, "16 Oregon Votes Help President's Victory," *Oregonian*, 19 August 1976.

By the end of the convention, the Ford-Dole ticket was ready to move forward. Now Atiyeh would turn his attention to the November election, with a special emphasis on winning Oregon for Ford. The fall campaign went as expected for Atiyeh's Senate seat. He ended up winning by another huge margin—about 70% to 30%—over his Democratic opponent with a campaign that played on his 1974 gubernatorial slogan–"Oregon's Next Great Governor"—by calling for voters to return "Oregon's Great State Senator" to office.[348] In meetings held the same week as the election, Atiyeh was unanimously selected the minority leader of the Senate for the fourth straight session. But, noting the numbers of each caucus (24 Democrats, 6 Republicans), Atiyeh said "Senate Republicans would be 'very vocal about things that haven't happened and probably won't happen in the next session.'"[349]

On a personal level, by 1977 Atiyeh was feeling that he had been in the legislature a long time. He had first run for office eighteen years earlier, and he had seen a lot of changes in almost two decades in the capitol. Atiyeh served longer than he thought he ever would, and he thought that there was no longer a need for people like him—older, more set in his ways on many policy stances—in the legislature anymore. But then he thought, no, they *do* need people like him; maybe not a whole legislature of them, but they need people like him. He was seeing that the legislature could get so mean at times that people would say, "Oh, just screw it."[350] So he threw himself into what would turn out to be his last legislative session as a member.

With Atiyeh's rising role in statewide politics and the pressures of being on so many Senate committees because of the tiny caucus, his time at Atiyeh Brothers was spent doing both rug

---

348 Paul Pintarich, "Washington County Rejects Pest Control, Recreation Funding," *Oregonian*, 4 November 1976; *Oregonian*, "Vic Atiyeh: Oregon's *Great* State Senator," Advertisement, November 1976.
349 Phil Cogswell, "Demos to Retain Lang as Speaker," *Oregonian*, 7 November 1976.
350 Victor Atiyeh, interviewed by Jim Moore, "Atiyeh interview #4," Raleigh Hills, OR, 3 June 2014. Summary notes, 2.

business and state business. One Atiyeh Brothers employee, Mike Brugato, was hired by Atiyeh in the early 1970s. He vividly remembered the job interview: "It was intimidating."[351] In the downtown store there was a main floor and a mezzanine. Atiyeh's office was in the far corner of the mezzanine. It was impossible to see his office from the main floor. "But," Brugato remembered, "you could see the smoke coming out of the office because he smoked pretty regularly, as did most of the employees." Atiyeh was dressed as "the typical Victor. White shirt, short sleeves." There was a circular Oregon emblem sewn on his shirt. Atiyeh sat behind his "big, huge desk" and Brugato sat across from him in a chair "shaking in my boots. I won't lie because he was a pretty intimidating fellow." Atiyeh talked about family, passion, and how important the business was to the whole family. Later in the interview, Atiyeh made it clear that if Brugato started going out on his own, buying and selling rugs on his own time without informing the company, there would be problems. "If we ever found that out, there would be no questions asked. You would just be history at Atiyeh Brothers."[352]

Brugato was hired. He recalled that by the mid-1970s Atiyeh used his Atiyeh Brothers office as an extension of his senate office. When Atiyeh came into the office, Brugato remembered, "I don't think he was ever off the phone. It was just one phone call after another; it was just unbelievable."[353] There were frequent visitors and guests who would come to the store to see Atiyeh. In Brugato's mind, "It was more of his private office" for his political career while he was in Portland.

The personal side of Atiyeh was apparent to those who worked in the Senate. Barbara Roberts sat at her husband Frank's desk on the floor. She got so she could recognize Atiyeh's laugh. "It wasn't loud, it was just distinctive," she recalled.[354] He would tell

---

351 Michael Brugato, interviewed by Jim Moore, "Atiyeh interview," Tigard, OR, 30 July 2015. Summary, 2.
352 Brugato, "Atiyeh interview," 2.
353 Brugato, "Atiyeh interview," 1.
354 Roberts, "Atiyeh interview," 7.

jokes and screw up the punchlines and then laugh at his own ineptness. She remembered "[h]e had so much fun telling it, and then it didn't matter." People would laugh at Atiyeh telling the joke, not necessarily the joke itself. And Atiyeh would laugh at himself.

The 1977 session ended in July without accomplishing any of the great deeds that had been almost commonplace from 1967 to 1973 (the McCall years). One lobbyist observed, "They didn't do much evil this time around, but they sure didn't pass much substance either."[355] *Oregonian* reporter Stan Federman wrote, "[T]he [school] 'safety net' completely dominated all legislation. Few bills came out of committee and those major enough to compete in publicity with the 'safety net' were kept well hidden."[356]

There was another reason, in Federman's estimation, for the anemic output of the legislature.

Many members were beginning to maneuver for the 1978 elections. Senate President Jason Boe, House minority leader Roger Martin, and Atiyeh were all mentioned as being interested in the 1978 gubernatorial race. Others in the Senate and the House were thinking about runs for other statewide offices. The next year would indeed be one in which competition for statewide elective office would dominate political life in Oregon. Victor Atiyeh and Roger Martin would be in the middle of it. And Tom McCall would finally make up his mind to run for an unprecedented third term as governor.

---

355 Stan Federman, "1977 Legislature Was Ensnarled by Political Ambitions," Column, *Oregonian*, 10 July 1977.
356 Federman, "1977 Legislature Was Ensnarled by Political Ambitions."

3 Running and governing

Movement for the 1978 primary began early.

There was Straub's performance—not seen as earth-shatteringly good—and the specter of former governor McCall out there. Would McCall attempt to be the first governor in Oregon history to win a third term? A February 1977 poll showed that "if a McCall-Straub election were held today, McCall would get 53 per cent statewide, and Straub would get 28 per cent."[357] On issues, the two were very similar, but Straub did not have a knack for picking quality people for his staff.[358] Straub did make an effort to counter his image in the public by being more forthcoming and fiery in his interviews with the media,[359] but his managerial weakness would leave an opening for either McCall or Atiyeh, both of whom were seen as better supervisors.

Meanwhile, Atiyeh was thinking, "I am a candidate that lost. It's going to be tougher for me to raise money. But," he

---

357 *Oregonian*, "Straub's Nemesis?' Editorial, 15 February 1977.
358 Victor Atiyeh, interviewed by Clark Hansen, "Tape 22," Oral history, recorded by Oregon Historical Society, Portland, OR, 9 February 1993. Transcript, 664, Atiyeh Collection, Pac. Univ. Archives
359 Charles K. Johnson, *Standing at the Water's Edge: Bob Straub's Battle for the Soul of Oregon*, (Corvallis, OR: Oregon State University Press, 2012), 243.

strategized, "I'll beat him with my volunteers."[360] Atiyeh, who had made connections across the state in 1974, kept those relationships going during the following years. He knew those volunteers would be there for him. Behind the scenes, Tom Atiyeh had conversations with Vic Atiyeh about the race. He saw that his father "felt really confident he could pull it off" and win the 1978 race against Straub.[361] The economy was an issue in the minds of voters, with inflation still high, so, in the way of politics, people would blame Straub for that. Straub did not look like an active governor, especially in comparison to his predecessor, Tom McCall. The timing just looked good for an Atiyeh run.

Roger Martin, the minority leader in the House, decided to make the run for the Republican gubernatorial nomination. In August Martin went on a big road trip in a motor home all around Oregon.[362] The Republican establishment looked at Martin and thought that he had the money, the experience, and the charisma, so he was the person to back in any Republican primary against Tom McCall. Secretary of State Norma Paulus refused to rule out a run, and McCall was telling a reporter that "pressure from his supporters is becoming so intense that 'I've never seen anything like it.'"[363] The fear among the core Republican supporters was that McCall would win the primary and then easily win the general election, and there would be another eight years of liberal Tom McCall.

Possibly to discourage Atiyeh from joining the race, Martin was working hard to increase his recognition around the state. In this sense, his problem was similar to Atiyeh's in 1974—people just did not know who the Lake Oswego legislator was. After two months of driving around southern and eastern Oregon in the late

---

360 Victor Atiyeh, "Tape 22," 665.
361 Tom Atiyeh, interviewed by Jim Moore, "Atiyeh interview," Sherwood, OR, 28 July 2015. Summary, 3.
362 Alice J. Porter, "Stalking a Hurt Straub: Early Starter Roger Martin Must Get His Party's Nomination First," *Portland, OR Willamette Week*, 9 August 1977.
363 Ed Mosey, "Martin, Atiyeh Eye 1978 Race," *Oregonian*, 6 August 1977; *Statesman Journal*, (Salem, OR), "Gubernatorial Possibilities Beginning to Fall Into Line," 6 August 1977.

summer of 1977, Martin's name recognition had about tripled, from 6% or 7% to 19%.[364] Not long after, on October 20, in two separate events just thirty minutes apart, Atiyeh and Martin announced their candidacies at Portland's Benson Hotel.[365] McCall had all the advantages by waiting to announce his plans— he could keep his job as a political analyst on television and radio, and he could make it "a hard winter for candidates whose plans depend on McCall" making up his mind.[366]

The big unanswered question was, how many McCall liberals were still left in the Republican party? Atiyeh's overwhelming defeat of Myers in the 1974 primary indicated there were not that many, but the 1976 primary suggested that there were still many moderate to liberal Republicans remaining as McCall-style Norma Paulus overwhelmed a conservative Republican foe in the secretary of state primary. Atiyeh created some distance from the label he detested: "I know I'm not a liberal, but I have real problems with the word 'conservative.' It's perceived to be way over on the right wing, but I'm not over there and don't want to be over there."[367] He stressed what he had felt in the aftermath of the 1974 loss, saying, "I honestly believe my viewpoints are in tune with most of the people of Oregon." As early as the end of the May 1978 primary, Atiyeh was being identified as a moderate by influential Eugene reporter Henny Willis.[368]

Atiyeh's campaign coordinator for the primary, and manager for the general election was Carol Whitney. Whitney recalled her own hiring as "a little strange."[369] In the midst of a divorce, she had been advised to talk to Atiyeh by the state Republican chair,

---

364 Stan Federman, "'Roger Who?' Optimistic in Bid for GOP Gubernatorial Nod," Column, *Oregonian*, 9 October 1977.

365 Stan Federman, "2 Legislators Enter Race for Governor," *Oregonian*, 21 October 1977; AP, "Republicans Toss Hats in Gubernatorial Ring," *Salem Oregon Statesman*, 21 October 1977.

366 *Oregon Statesman* (Salem, OR), "McCall Running True to Form," Editorial, 11 October 1977.

367 Henry Willis, "Atiyeh Isn't Awed by McCall," *Eugene Register-Guard*, 27 November 1977.

368 Henny Willis, "Atiyeh's Calmness Paid Off," Column, *Eugene (OR) Register-Guard*, 28 May 1978.

whom she met through her friend Mary Alice Ford, chair for Washington County. Whitney was told that Atiyeh would not be able to give her a job in the Senate Republican caucus office because he was running for office, "but maybe if you helped on his campaign a little he could give you some ideas."[370] She went to talk with Atiyeh, and Paul Newman, Atiyeh's campaign consultant, was there. She had an enjoyable conversation with both of them "A couple of days later they called and said, 'How would you like to run my campaign?'"[371] Whitney thought it would be fun, though she did not know anything about campaigning. She was hired "for almost no money; it was embarrassingly low." Newman then left and did not reappear until January 1978, so Whitney embarked on a crash course on learning what she ought to be doing. One of the people on the campaign steering committee asked where the campaign plan was. Whitney replied, "What's a campaign plan?"[372] When asked why he had hired Whitney, Atiyeh told an October 1978 interviewer, "I didn't want a political hack. I wanted someone who can organize people and keep things flowing without disruption. I wanted someone with a business background, even though this business is politics."[373]

Whitney would pick up another crucial player when Denny Miles was hired as the communications person. Miles recalled his first day on the job as "bizarre and . . . downright alarming."[374] The campaign staff had completely forgotten the deadline to get the candidate's statement in the Voters' Pamphlet. Miles joined in a rush effort late into the night to get the statement together "so it could be hand-carried to Salem by the deadline the very next

---

369 Carol Whitney, interviewed by Jim Moore, "Atiyeh interview," Bend, OR, 1 May 2015. Summary notes, 6.
370 Whitney, "Atiyeh interview," 6.
371 Whitney, "Atiyeh interview," 6.
372 Whitney, "Atiyeh interview," 7.
373 Wayne Thompson, "Women Prove Effective at 'Running' Vic Atiyeh," *Oregonian*, 16 October 1978.
374 Denny Miles, "Campaign Communications, 1978 Gubernatorial Campaign," (Unpublished manuscript), 1.

day."[375] Miles also helped to mold Atiyeh's image in the public's mind. "So, is it Vic or Victor?" Miles asked. The response: "My name is Victor." Miles pointed out that "Vic" was much better for political purposes, a point Atiyeh acknowledged. "But my really good friends call me Victor."[376]

Remaking Vic Atiyeh's image was a team effort, led by Carol Whitney. Out with the black raincoat; in with the white raincoat. Time to buy a new pair of glasses. A big, and ongoing, fight was waged over long-sleeved shirts. Atiyeh detested them, as he did throughout his life. When she found Atiyeh wearing a short-sleeved shirt, she threatened "If you do that again, I'm going to get together with Dolores and cut the cuffs off all your long sleeves and sew them inside your jacket" arms so the candidate would appear to be wearing full sleeves.[377] A few weeks later, the weather had warmed and Whitney wore a short-sleeved eyelet blouse to the office. Atiyeh sarcastically remarked, "I like that. I can't wear short sleeves and you're wearing a short sleeve shirt with holes in it." He could wear short sleeves, Whitney retorted, when he was not running for office.[378]

While Oregonians knew who Atiyeh was, with name recognition above 90%, he was not perceived as very interesting. At a campaign staff meeting at the Atiyeh home, those in attendance looked up on the wall and saw the framed 1944 invitation from the Green Bay Packers for Atiyeh to play professional football. Whitney was surprised. "Nobody knew that. He still hadn't mentioned that. Well, for God's sake!"[379] She told Atiyeh, "This is the kind of thing people need to know about you, Vic." He said he had never thought about mentioning it. For the campaign newsletter that she put out, staff member Sharon Page[380] then wrote a background article about Atiyeh that had all

---

375 Miles, "Campaign Communications, 1978 Gubernatorial Campaign," 1.
376 Denny Miles, interviewed by Jim Moore, "Atiyeh interview #3," Forest Grove, OR, 5 April 2016. Summary notes, 5.
377 Whitney, "Atiyeh interview," 6.
378 Whitney, "Atiyeh interview," 6.
379 Whitney, "Atiyeh interview," 2.
380 Whitney, "Atiyeh interview," 2.

these personal elements that nobody had ever heard of—the Packers contract, the uncertainty he dealt with when Richard and Ed Atiyeh had been POWs in World War II, and details about taking over the rug business at such a young age.

McCall finally made up his mind to enter the race on February 13, with the official announcement on February 14, the anniversary of Oregon's joining the union.[381] In a headline at the top of the front page, the *Oregonian* trumpeted his decision, "McCall Says He'll Run in Primary."[382] Two weeks later, at the end of February, Atiyeh and Martin were having to defend their decisions to stay in the race against the popular McCall. There were reports of "efforts of some party supporters to reduce the field."[383] Martin said, "there has been pressure within 'some prominent Oregon Republican circles for Vic and I to lock ourselves in a room, flip a coin, with one of us the candidate and the other honorary campaign chairman,'" and it seemed the pressure was coming "from party supporters who do not want McCall to be governor again."[384] The Republican National Committee saw McCall as being the inevitable candidate and wanted one of the other two candidates to drop out and not "rough" McCall "up in the primary."[385] A source close to McCall "said that McCall believes that he would have to spend only a modest amount in the primary because his name is widely familiar."[386] He clearly did not think that he would have the same problem that Clay Myers had in 1974 when Myers was outspent about two to one by Atiyeh and lost the race to Atiyeh by about

---

[381] Brent Walth, *Fire at Eden's Gate: Tom McCall and The Oregon Story*, (Portland, OR: Oregon Historical Society Press, 1994), 421.

[382] J. Richard Nokes, "McCall Says He'll Run in Primary," *Oregonian*, 14 February 1978.

[383] Phil Cogswell, "Martin, Atiyeh Plan to Stay Contenders," *Oregonian*, 28 February 1978; AP, "Martin Is Still Running for Governor," *Salem Oregon Statesman*, 28 February 1978.

[384] Cogswell, "Martin, Atiyeh Plan to Stay."

[385] Cogswell, "Martin, Atiyeh Plan to Stay."; Russell Sadler, "Martin Hangs Tough," In the Public Trough column, *Portland Willamette Week*, 7 March 1978.

[386] Nokes, "McCall Says He'll Run."

the same proportions among the Republican electorate.[387] By the middle of May, however, McCall would be criticizing his foes for outspending him, especially after a crucial poll showed that his lead was shrinking.[388]

Atiyeh responded to McCall's announcement by saying, "We had anticipated he (McCall) would come in. He's a good person, and many Oregonians have been pleased with the national attention he brought the state. But I find it interesting that he would plan to run against the person he effectively endorsed—Bob Straub—in the 1974 race. But he's in and he's welcome."[389] Watching behind the scenes of the campaign, Atiyeh's nephew Bob recalled that the reaction was more along the lines of "Holy shit!"[390] McCall's biographer characterized McCall's decision to run in the Republican primary instead of as an independent "inexplicable." McCall later "said he had done so out of loyalty to his" staunch Republican grandfather.[391]

All the talk of one of the candidates stepping aside finally reached an odd crescendo the first week in March. On March 7, Atiyeh and Martin attended a meeting, prompted by mutual friends who were afraid the two candidates would split the vote, allowing McCall to win.[392] The suggestion was made that the candidates "talk to some of the bigwigs in the Republican Party." This evolved into, "Would you be interested in having a panel sit down and decide which of you ought to drop out?" Atiyeh and Martin were ambivalent about this proposal,[393] but they decided to go through with the idea.

---

387 Harry Bodine, "Legislator Pulls GOP Surprise," *Oregonian*, 29 May 1974; *Oregon Statesman* (Salem), "Atiyeh Outspends Myers by 2 to 1," 28 June 1974.
388 Phil Cogswell, "Martin Won't Quit; McCall Attacks Spending by Foes," *Oregonian*, 18 May 1978.
389 Phil Cogswell, "Opponents Welcome McCall's Entry in Statewide Race," *Oregonian*, 14 February 1978. Parentheses in original.
390 Bob Atiyeh, "Atiyeh interview," West Linn, OR, 4 February 2015, summary 7.
391 Walth, *Fire at Eden's Gate*, 421.
392 Victor Atiyeh, "Tape 23," 670.
393 Martin, "Atiyeh interview," 6. Jack Faust recalled that the idea for the meeting originated with Martin and Atiyeh, not within the Republican party group.

The panel was made up of Howell Appling (former secretary of state), John Mason (Nixon's 1972 Oregon campaign manager), and Jack Faust (Republican activist and Portland attorney).[394] The meeting took place at a house in Woodburn Estates. The candidates appeared before the group, but the panel wanted the competing candidates to decide between themselves. Atiyeh and Martin were not having any of that. It was finally decided that the two would make their cases to the jury of three. Martin went first, talking about his travels around the state, the growth in support he was receiving, and the organization of his campaign. Atiyeh followed with an argument based on his political philosophy and how he was going to get things going in Oregon—elements that would receive top billing in Atiyeh's 1979 inaugural address, to which Jack Faust would contribute.

The panel decided Martin should stay in and Atiyeh should drop out. Faust recalled that "Vic wasn't organized at all," while Martin already had campaign chairs in every county.[395]

Inevitably, the meeting was leaked to the press. News reports quoted "a person close to both candidates" who "said the panel favored Martin because he is younger (43) than Atiyeh (55) and newer on the statewide political scene, therefore offering a better contrast to McCall. The panel reportedly also felt Martin's campaign was better organized."[396] Atiyeh argued at a press conference, "[W]ith my service to the state, with my record of accomplishments for Oregonians and with my acknowledged strength going into this election, it is totally ridiculous that anyone should consider my retiring from the campaign. It is appropriate," he went on, "that Roger Martin consider leaving the campaign. It is entirely appropriate that Tom McCall remove himself gracefully from the campaign. But Vic Atiyeh? Never."[397]

---

394 Jack Faust, interviewed by Jim Moore, "Atiyeh interview," Portland, OR, 15 April 2015. Summary notes, 1.
395 Faust, "Atiyeh interview," 1.
396 Phil Cogswell, "Panel Sees Martin Best McCall Foe," *Oregonian*, 10 March 1978. Parentheses in original.
397 Cogswell, "Panel Sees Martin Best."

Polls later in March showed McCall ahead with 54% to Atiyeh's 21% and Martin's 9%.[398] The Martin campaign's own polling showed that he was behind, but his name recognition had jumped from the single digits the previous summer to 60%. The same poll showed that McCall's name recognition was at 100% and Atiyeh's at 90%.[399] Atiyeh's campaign responded by pointing out that he was "just about where he expects to be." The McCall campaign emphasized the obvious: "[W]e're still way out in front."[400]

Three debates, set for late April and early May, would prove pivotal to the contest. As any frontrunner might, McCall had initially refused joint appearances with his opponents, saying "Why should I rent the hall, pull the crowd so that lesser known people can use me as a dart board?"[401] But, after a few critical editorials, he rather suddenly changed his mind.

Atiyeh's campaign staff worked hard to get the normally phlegmatic candidate to work on responses, techniques, and letting the personality that they knew come through for these important joint appearances. In a traffic jam ahead of one of the practice sessions, the campaign car was involved in a collision. The candidate was angry. After the practice, the campaign staff came out and asked Bob Atiyeh, the driver, "What did you do to Vic?" They loved it: he was fired up, and it showed.[402]

The Atiyeh preparation—practice debates, working on the wording of answers so they were succinct, learning to turn a question about one topic into something the candidate wanted to bring up to the audience—was the way of the future. Most major political debates follow this format to this day. McCall, on the other hand, was the veteran of public speaking and moving

---

398 AP, "McCall Favored," *Salem Oregon Statesman*, 22 March 1978; *Willamette Week* (Portland), "New Poll Shows Martin-McCall Gap Narrowing," 21 March 1978.
399 Ron Blankenbaker, "Political Excitement Takes a Week's Vacation: Politics '78," Analysis and Opinion, *Salem Oregon Statesman*, 26 March 1978, 1C.
400 Blankenbaker, "Political Excitement Takes a Week's Vacation," 4C.
401 Walth, *Fire at Eden's Gate*, 425 Brackets in original.
402 Bob Atiyeh, "Atiyeh interview," summary notes, 5.

audiences. "We had great confidence that it didn't matter what was thrown at McCall," his campaign manager Kim Skerrit recalled. "[H]e was better on his feet, and he was more colorful than either of those [other two] candidates, and we just thought his very presence would dominate. ...The other thing was, he knew the issues. All three of those guys knew the issues."[403]

The second debate, in Eugene, was seen as changing the tenor of the race. The format at this appearance was mainly questions and answers with brief statements. This played right into Atiyeh's hands. "Tom McCall blasted away at the administration of Gov. Bob Straub, Roger Martin blasted McCall and Victor Atiyeh talked about issues," was one characterization of the joint appearance.[404] Martin's opening line was, "I just want to be governor. I don't want to be king of the state of Oregon."[405] Martin remembered that McCall just exploded in anger. Martin and his campaign knew that this would be McCall's response. The audience was aghast; "I got booed," Martin recalled.[406] But this planted the seed of doubts about McCall's electability.

If McCall and Martin went after each other, then the Atiyeh people knew they could clearly position Atiyeh as the alternative to the two hotheads. Each time there was a debate, the campaign's own polling showed Atiyeh bumping up, closing the gap with McCall. The Atiyeh campaign liked to say that "they held Roger's coat while he went after Tom McCall."[407]

The crucial indication of a shift among voters was a poll splashed across the top of the *Oregonian* front page on Sunday

---

403 Kim Skerritt Duncan, interviewed by Jim Moore, "Atiyeh interview," Portland, OR, 22 December 2017. Summary notes, 6.
404 Ron Blankenbaker, "Martin Fires at McCall in 2nd Debate," *Salem (OR) Statesman Journal*, 29 April 1978.
405 Phil Cogswell, "Martin Rips 'Divine Right' of McCall," *Oregonian*, 29 April 1978; Henny Willis, "Martin Criticizs McCall at Debate," *Eugene (OR) Register-Guard*, 29 April 1978.
406 Martin, "Atiyeh interview," 7.
407 Miles, "Atiyeh interview #1," 13–14.

May 14: "Atiyeh Gains on McCall."[408] While McCall still had a "somewhat comfortable lead" over Atiyeh and Martin among registered Republicans, "among voters most likely to go to the polls on election day, there is a sharp shrinkage in the McCall vote with Atiyeh the primary beneficiary."[409] Called at home for comment, Atiyeh recalled that his "reaction was, 'Great! I've won.'"[410] He remembered a pause at the other end of the phone line.[411] He was quoted in the *Oregonian* story saying, "This is exactly what we had hoped would occur. …The most significant thing is that Tom is moving down and I am moving up. Movement is what it is all about. This poll is devastating to Tom and Roger because it shows them slipping. Mine is the only positive movement."[412]

The poll was the first formal indication that trends were going Atiyeh's way. Brent Walth, McCall's biographer, wrote, "McCall realized the campaign was over" when the poll results came in.[413] The former governor focused on the statistical dead heat among Republicans. "He could see that Atiyeh would soon pass him."[414] Martin remembered that after the *Oregonian* poll came out in the last two weeks of the election, he was driving with some of his campaign staff and one of them asked what he would do after the election. Martin answered, "Well, I think I'll be a lobbyist."[415] He stopped running television ads—a sign that he had run out of money and was not able to raise any more.[416]

On election night it quickly became clear in the early returns that Atiyeh would win. There was a bit of uncertainty because Multnomah, Oregon's most populous county by far, had a

---

408 J. Roy Bardsley, "Atiyeh Gains on McCall," *Oregonian*, 14 May 1978.
409 Bardsley, "Atiyeh Gains on McCall."
410 Victor Atiyeh, "Tape 23," 677.
411 Victor Atiyeh, "Atiyeh interview #3," 9.
412 Bardsley, "Atiyeh Gains on McCall."
413 Walth, *Fire at Eden's Gate*, 432.
414 Walth, *Fire at Eden's Gate*, 432.
415 Martin, "Atiyeh interview," 8.
416 Bob Baum, "'Longshot' Martin Says TV Cuts Don't Mean He'll Drop Out of Race," *Salem Oregon Statesman*, 18 May 1978; Cogswell, "Martin Won't Quit."

computer problem and did not report for hours. But when it did, it confirmed what the rest of the state's Republican voters had decided: Vic Atiyeh was the nominee for governor. Atiyeh won in thirty-three of Oregon's thirty-six counties. Even in Atiyeh's victory, the *Oregonian* headline focused on McCall—"Atiyeh Smashes McCall Comeback Bid"—across the top of the front page.[417] The *Statesman* ignored Roger Martin with "Atiyeh Takes Upset Win Over McCall."[418] And it was an upset—"the second gubernatorial primary in a row in which Atiyeh unexpectedly smashed the Republican frontrunner."[419]

Atiyeh also received a congratulatory call from Mark Hatfield. Atiyeh asked for Hatfield's advice: "'Mark, what do you do? I'm waiting for Tom McCall to call,' because it was clear that he was not going to win."[420] Hatfield did not have any advice, so Atiyeh, against the protocol that the defeated candidates either call or go to the winning candidate, went to the McCall headquarters at the Benson Hotel. At McCall headquarters, his campaign manager assumed that her candidate was going to talk to Atiyeh. Skerrit saw McCall was "stunned, he's hurt, he's angry, but he'll rise to the occasion. It never occurred to me that he wouldn't."[421] Atiyeh explained to a reporter that he went to McCall "because 'I have a great respect for Tom,' and he added that he would like McCall to be part of his administration. 'I don't intend to waste a talent like Tom McCall.'"[422] To himself, Atiyeh knew that "if I were to lose, it was like jumping out of a second-story window; for him to lose, it's like jumping off the Empire State Building."[423]

When Atiyeh got to the Benson, McCall was talking to reporters on live television. Atiyeh had wanted to talk to McCall

---

417 Phil Cogswell, "Atiyeh Smashes McCall Comeback Bid: Straub Wins Nod; '74 Rematch Seen," *Oregonian*, 24 May 1978.
418 Steve Graham, "Atiyeh Takes Upset Win Over McCall: McCall: Won't Endorse Atiyeh," *Salem Oregon Statesman*, 24 May 1978.
419 Cogswell, "Atiyeh Smashes McCall Comeback Bid."
420 Victor Atiyeh, "Tape 23," 679.
421 Duncan, "Atiyeh interview," 4–5.
422 *Oregonian*, "McCall Offers No Endorsement to 'Honorable Foe'," 25 May 1978.
423 Victor Atiyeh, "Tape 23," 679.

privately, but that only happened later in the evening. Phil Keisling, who was at the Benson, recalled that "Vic Atiyeh came over to shake Tom's hand. And McCall wouldn't do it."[424] In what was described as "a terse, brief exchange," McCall said, "I'm not going to bicker. You've apparently got the ability to get enough votes to win the Republican nomination, but you've only got 8 percent of the votes in the state."[425] As Atiyeh recalled, with the cameras running, "there's no escape."[426] Atiyeh "didn't want to embarrass Tom.... [McCall] was petulant as hell, and the media caught it."[427] In Roger Martin's estimation, McCall made an utter fool of himself on television that night.[428]

Atiyeh and McCall "left and went to his room—well, it's a good thing the media didn't catch the display in the room. He was really on his campaign manager, Kim Skerrit. ...Really on her case pretty bad. I had [state party chair] Steve Young with me—and he had Steve in tears."[429] Confirming that Young was weeping, Skerrit recalled, "No one knew what to say. There was no other personality in the room that had the clout and the stature to correct anything. ...I'm 28-years-old and competent mechanically, and understanding what needs to happen, but without a history with this man. None of the other staff had history with this man. He was wounded. He was a bull elephant, wounded."[430] Atiyeh was not hurt by McCall's tirade, saying to himself, "that's, unfortunately, Tom McCall, and...he'd calm down after—he wouldn't ever get over it, but...he would have his emotions a little more in check. ...But that was a rough night for him, and he was kind of swinging pretty wild at that point."[431]

---

424 Phil Keisling, interviewed by Jim Moore, "Atiyeh interview,' Portland, OR, 23 February 2015. Summary notes, 7.
425 Steve Graham, "Atiyeh Takes Upset Win Over McCall: McCall: Won't Endorse Atiyeh," *Salem Oregon Statesman*, 24 May 1978.
426 Victor Atiyeh, "Tape 23," 679.
427 Victor Atiyeh, interviewed by Jim Moore, "Atiyeh interview #2," Raleigh Hills, OR, 2 January 2014. Summary notes, 1.
428 Martin, "Atiyeh interview," 6.
429 Victor Atiyeh, "Tape 23," 679.
430 Duncan, "Atiyeh interview," 5.
431 Victor Atiyeh, "Tape 23," 680.

The day after the operatic events of election night, a news article published what McCall wrote to Atiyeh.

> My warmest congratulations to you for your hard-fought victory. The tenacity and integrity you've displayed throughout this campaign have been a credit to Oregon politics.
>
> Because my future plans may require journalistic objectivity, I am not free at this time to make any endorsements for the general election.
>
> Should you win in November, I know you will serve Oregon with competence and dedication. I wish you the best of luck in November. You have been an honorable foe and at all times a gentleman.[432]

The final results were Atiyeh 46%, McCall 34%, and Martin 17%.[433] It was a decisive victory. In a sign of problems for Governor Straub, he received 51% of the vote in the Democratic primary against a varied field of six competitors.[434] The 1978 Republican electorate acted, in the end, a lot like the 1974 electorate. Oregon was no longer a place for avowedly liberal Republicans to run for governor. But could Atiyeh win over enough of the Democrats dissatisfied with Straub?

The General Election

For Atiyeh the thematic outline of the general campaign was clear. Oregonians had "a chance to see Bob for four years, and here I am and there he is, and he's served as your governor, and I want to be your governor."[435] He knew that there was unhappiness with Straub's leadership, and Atiyeh meant to provide the

---

432 AP, "McCall to Atiyeh: You Are Credit to Politics. Election Aftermath," *Salem Oregon Statesman*, 25 May 1978; *Oregonian*, "McCall Offers No Endorsement."
433 *Oregon Blue Book, 1979*, 304.
434 *Oregon Blue Book, 1979*, 304.
435 Victor Atiyeh, interviewed by Clark Hansen, "Tape 24," Oral history, recorded by Oregon Historical Society, Portland, OR, 16 February 1993. Transcript, 698, Atiyeh Collection, Pac. Univ. Archives.

alternative for those who were disappointed with the way things had gone during Straub's term in office.

Greg Walden remembered Paul Newman saying, "Oregonians want oatmeal. And that's what we're going to serve them." In Walden's eulogy for Atiyeh in 2014, he recalled being somewhat taken aback. "No, there's nothing wrong with oatmeal…strong in fiber, high in protein, actually healthy for you…but it's not generally how one portrays a candidate. And yet, Vic was oatmeal. Darn good oatmeal. Competent. Effective. …A healthy choice for what Oregonians needed" as they faced hard choices about the future of the state.[436] Atiyeh himself remembered that Newman told him, "You're hokey. But maybe this is the year for hokey."[437]

Carol Whitney felt confident after the primary. Even though Straub was an incumbent, it did not feel like an impossible task to beat him. Whitney sought to build on the upset defeat of McCall with what she called the "bandwagon effect."[438] It started with billboards covering about 25% of Oregon, then the next wave ramped coverage up to 50%, and then it kept growing. This combined with the outreach to get more volunteers, reinforced voters' perceptions that a lot of their neighbors were joining the Atiyeh campaign. There were actually newspaper stories about all the people joining the campaign.

Atiyeh let Whitney make the plans for the campaign once they agreed on the big themes. The defining campaign issue arrived in the first week in June when California overwhelmingly passed Proposition 13, a radical rethinking of the property tax system in the state.[439] The California measure had many elements that tax reformers had been working toward in Oregon for years: reducing

---

436 Greg Walden, "Greg Walden Remembers Governor Vic Atiyeh at Public Memorial Service" (speech, Memorial Service in Oregon House Chambers, Salem, OR, 3 September 2014), Plus Media Solutions press release from Walden's D.C. office, 6 September. First two ellipses in original.
437 Victor Atiyeh, "Atiyeh interview #3," 6.
438 Whitney, "Atiyeh interview," 11–12.
439 Robert Fairbanks, "Prop. 13 Landslide: Prop. 13—More Battles Lie Ahead," *Los Angeles Times*, 7 June 1978.

property taxes and changing the way that property values were determined.[440] An active signature-gathering movement in Oregon sought to get a measure on the November 1978 ballot. The Oregon version, Measure 6, was "lifted verbatim from" Proposition 13, with the only minor difference being the 1.5% limitation instead of the 1% California limitation.[441]

Atiyeh and Straub both said, "the message from California's vote for a property tax limit [was] loud and clear and they [were] listening."[442] But neither of them supported the Oregon effort. Atiyeh, who had been in the middle of these tax discussions since the early 1960s, called for taxpayer relief. In the past, that had meant specific programs for homeowners and renters with limited incomes. Once the Oregon ballot measure qualified for the November election, Straub declared his opposition but said he would not campaign against it. In a more nuanced position, Atiyeh supported "'the concept' of the property tax limit" but also said he would not campaign for Measure 6.[443] Atiyeh, who had by and large opposed these attempts to limit the property tax unless there was some way to pay for services by local governments, seemed to have decided that it would be "'suicidal' to actively oppose the measure" because it would "probably bring out a bumper crop of voters," a more conservative electorate, that would support him in the governor's race.[444] Since the property tax went entirely to local governments, Atiyeh proposed some kind of sharing of the burden between state and local governments since Measure 6 would cause steep reductions in local services. His July proposal was to reduce state spending by

---

440 "What is Proposition 13?," California Property Tax Information, California Tax Data, http://www.californiataxdata.com.
441 *Oregon Statesman* (Salem), "Straub: Trip Showed Tax Disgust," 10 August 1978.
442 Jim Church, "Straub, Atiyeh Are Against Prop. 13 Here, But Call for More Relief for the Taxpayer," *Salem Oregon Statesman*, 8 June 1978.
443 Ron Blankenbaker, "Straub, Atiyeh Differ on Tax Limit Fate," *Salem Oregon Statesman*, 8 July 1978, 1A.
444 Blankenbaker, "Straub, Atiyeh Differ on Tax Limit Fate," 1A.

10% with the savings going to local governments and school districts to help their potentially strained budgets.[445]

August was a time for a response to Measure 6 Straub took "a three-day swing through seven western Oregon communities," and "was surprised at the depth of public discontent with taxes."[446] Atiyeh remembered hearing reports of this while he was campaigning in Roseburg. He said to himself, "What? After three and three-quarters years as governor he just discovered [people] were unhappy about property taxes?"[447] Straub was not clear on what his response would be, but the trip "convinced me that those of us in government who realize the pitfalls of Measure 6 have our work cut out. And I sincerely mean that. It's not just political ballyhoo."[448]

By the middle of August Straub's coalescing plan was to call a special session of the legislature to craft an alternative to Measure 6. Atiyeh was opposed to the possibility, calling it "nothing more than an attempt to use taxpayers' money to stop Ballot Measure 6."[449] Straub quickly shot back that Atiyeh still had not taken a stance for or against Measure 6, almost two months after it had made the ballot, adding, "I don't think Oregon needs that kind of leadership in the governor's office."[450] A few days after the announcement of the special session, Atiyeh finally came out with his own response to Measure 6. He neither supported nor opposed it, but he had an alternative. Atiyeh's version would keep the 1.5% limitation, but only apply it to residential property, not to business property. In addition, the taxable value of properties (as opposed to the market value) would be set from the market value in 1977, not 1976, as Measure 6 called for.[451] Atiyeh gave great

---

445 *Oregonian*, "Atiyeh Backs Aid if Tax Cut Passes," 15 July 1978.
446 *Oregon Statesman*, "Straub: Trip Showed Tax Disgust."
447 Victor Atiyeh, "Tape 24," 696.
448 *Oregon Statesman*, "Straub: Trip Showed Tax Disgust."
449 Phil Cogswell, "Straub, Atiyeh Clash Over Need for Session," *Oregonian*, 19 August 1978.
450 Cogswell, "Straub, Atiyeh Clash Over Need for Session."
451 Charles E. Beggs, "Atiyeh Proposes Tax Plan," *Salem Oregon Statesman*, 29 August 1978.

deference to the ideas behind Measure 6, calling it "the people's tax plan" because of the number of people who signed the petitions to get it on the ballot.[452]

In the special session, Straub called for the legislature "to produce a simple, easily understandable substitute" for the tax measure.[453] By all accounts, that did not happen. Atiyeh was firm that he would not support a quick solution to Measure 6 just so the governor would look better. He went into the session pushing his alternative, even though it had been rejected by the 21-member interim legislative committee he sat on. On Saturday September 9, the legislature reached agreement on its response to Measure 6. The plan was to create a 50% property tax reduction for residential property owners. After rejecting Atiyeh's plan again—by a single vote in the House—the legislature created Measure 11 to go on the November ballot. The move got the vote of Atiyeh, in a 24-6 vote in the Senate, who said "the 'decision of the Senate' results in 'the people now having a choice' in the general election."[454] Just two days later, Atiyeh, speaking before a Washington County audience, expressed "grave reservations" about Measure 11. He was awaiting more information about the fiscal impact on both taxpayers and local governments, but he stated, "I believe that what the Legislature gave to you (in Measure 11) is not what more than 200,000 people said when they put Ballot Measure 6 on the ballot."[455] Atiyeh put all his electoral chips on the table on September 14, coming out in favor of Measure 6 and opposing Measure 11, which he called a "shallow attempt to hoodwink the taxpayers of Oregon." His support of Measure 6 continued to be in deference to the 200,000

---

452 Phil Cogswell, "Atiyeh Likes '6' Goal, Suggests Changes," *Oregonian*, 29 August 1978.

453 Wayne Thompson, "Straub Calls for 'Simple' Tax Relief Plan," *Oregonian*, 6 September 1978; *Oregon Statesman* (Salem), "Legislature Didn't Meet Simplicity Test in No. 11," Editorial, 13 September 1978.

454 *Statesman Journal* (Salem), "Alternative for Measure 6 Is Approved," 10 September 1978, 1A.

455 Wayne Thompson, "Atiyeh Tells Doubts About Measure 11," *Oregonian*, 12 September 1978.

who petitioned to get it on the ballot. "They were pleading for tax relief," he said, "not a tax shift."[456]

Atiyeh's actions were a collision of his principles. On the side of supporting Measure 6, he constantly emphasized those 200,000 petitioners. This fit with his tenet that government that is closest to the people is best. What could be closer than citizens asking for a change in tax policy? It also fit with his principle that "we the people" means that we get the kind of government to which we are entitled. But, as he later concluded, he was violating, or coming close to violating his principle that he would never trade votes for something that violated his conscience. Atiyeh had opposed the various 1.5% limitations since they first appeared fifteen years earlier. He was also toying with his final principle to always govern without regard to reelection. This run for the governor's seat was not an actual reelection, but it was an election, and he admitted that he supported Measure 6 because it appealed to voters. Unsaid was whether he truly was in favor of the policy.

The impact of all this on the race? Atiyeh had what was characterized as "healthy lead over Straub" in a poll released on September 23.[457] Among those most likely to vote, Atiyeh had a clear advantage of 50% to 36%—with a 4.1% margin of error. The poll indicated that Atiyeh was holding on to Republicans, but also getting support from about one-third of Democrats. Straub's fear about the huge numbers of Democrats who had not supported him in the primary was coming true. With undecided at 14%, Straub would have to switch Atiyeh supporters rather than just rely on the relatively small number of undecideds to all come to his side. Along with the earlier poll showing Atiyeh leading in the Portland area and a newer poll showing even stronger support for Atiyeh in the Salem area, these results were almost exactly

---

456 Wayne Thompson, "Atiyeh Backs Measure 6, Scorns 11," *Oregonian*, 15 September 1978.

457 J. Roy Bardsley, "Atiyeh Grabs Healthy Lead Over Straub: GOP Challenger Tops Poll 47–38," *Oregonian*, 24 September 1978.

opposite of the findings in 1974 when Straub had defeated Atiyeh.[458] The election was far from won for Atiyeh, but he had the upper hand.

By this point, the Atiyeh campaign was delighted to see its candidate was no longer consistently referred to as "conservative." One observer described him as being "like the Oriental rugs he sells, …a study of intricate patterns, woven cautiously, if not conservatively, during a 20-year career in the Oregon Legislature."[459] The characterization was partly a deliberate strategy of the Atiyeh campaign, and partly it was because the Republican Party was moving farther to the right.

In Oregon this came to a head with the election of Walter Huss as the state party chair the first week in August. He and Atiyeh got into a very public fight almost as soon as Huss was elected. Huss told delegates to the Republican state convention that his goal was for "Republican candidates to be Christian."[460] While pointing out that his gubernatorial campaign was independent of the state Republican party apparatus, Atiyeh called on Huss to retract his remarks. "Many leaders of Oregon's Jewish community are serving key roles in my campaign. The Huss statement is an implied slur on these people and many other fine citizens both Jewish and non-Jewish."[461]

As the race went from October to November, it broke records to become "Oregon's first million-dollar race for political office," rivaling the U.S. Senatorial contests in 1966 and 1968.[462] Unlike

---

458 Howard Goodman, "Atiyeh Leads Straub in Salem, Poll Shows," *Salem (OR) Statesman Journal*, 24 September 1978; AP, "Polls Agree on Atiyeh Lead," *Salem Oregon Statesman*, 25 September 1978.

459 Wayne Thompson, "Vic Atiyeh, Bob Straub: A Contrast in Candidates," *Oregonian*, 1 October 1978, G1.

460 Ron Blankenbaker, "Atiyeh Claims Huss Slurred Non-Christians," *Salem Oregon Statesman*, 10 August 1978.

461 Blankenbaker, "Atiyeh Claims Huss Slurred Non-Christians."

462 Ron Blankenbaker, "Straub-Atiyeh Race is Costing a Million," *Salem Oregon Statesman*, 1 November 1978. Mark Hatfield beat Bob Duncan for US Senate in 1966; Bob Packwood edged out Wayne Morse in 1968.

the 1974 Straub-Atiyeh matchup, this race was unconstrained by campaign-finance rules that the Oregon Supreme Court had only recently struck down.

Atiyeh's 1978 campaign had as its secret weapon the huge number of volunteers who had worked to win the election in 1974, an estimated 10,000 people.[463] Information about each one of these volunteers was kept on an index card. As Atiyeh traveled around the state after 1974, he nurtured these relationships.

Atiyeh explained that he felt much more comfortable going into the 1978 campaign because "there was a much more solid base" of volunteers than in 1974.[464] In the 1978 campaign there was a big table just covered with these boxes of cards. The cards were filed alphabetically, with, according to Carol Whitney's instructions, "a notation at the bottom showing when [a volunteer] was contacted and what they will do."[465] *Oregonian* reporter Wayne Thompson skeptically asked about the cards. Thompson asked permission to take a small sampling of them to check out whether this volunteer army actually existed. He would not use his findings in a story, but he wanted to test the claim. Candidate Atiyeh told him, "Fine, take what you want."[466] Thompson called the contacts on the ten to twelve cards he had taken. He decided to test their active participation by asking if they went out on weekends to campaign, if they had a sign up, or if they made phone calls. He found that a large majority "were not only active volunteers, but they did all three things I asked about." Only one did just one thing, all the rest had done two activities and the majority had done all three. A couple of volunteers did not have signs up simply because they lived in apartments. And the sampling he took included volunteers from all over the state. The Atiyeh campaign became instantly credible to the reporter. Good to his word, Thompson did not directly use the card experiment in

---

463 Miles, "Atiyeh interview #1," 15.
464 Victor Atiyeh, "Atiyeh interview #3," 6.
465 Whitney, "View from the Winner's Circle," 8.
466 Wayne Thompson, interviewed by Jim Moore, "Atiyeh interview," Portland, OR, 2 April 2015. Summary notes 10.

his stories. At Thompson's retirement party years later, Atiyeh told the story: "I love other people to hear that I did that," Thompson recalled, "that I weighed [Atiyeh's] boast with the truth."[467]

The candidates' spouses, Dolores Atiyeh and Pat Straub, of course played very public roles in their husbands' campaigns. But behind the scenes women were the major players running the Atiyeh campaign. One story told of a caller to the Atiyeh campaign headquarters who "asked a secretary, 'Let me speak to the man in charge.' 'Sorry, sir, but there is no man in charge. The campaign manager is Carol Whitney.' 'Harold who?' the caller asked. 'Carol, as in woman,' the secretary replied."[468] The Atiyeh campaign had many women working in paid positions, and the bulk of the volunteers were women. Atiyeh also had women in important roles in 1974 (when he asked Shirley Woodrow to run his campaign), but there were a growing number of Republican women with political experience who had worked on Bob Packwood's statewide campaigns and Norma Paulus' successful run for Secretary of State in 1976. The Straub campaign was managed, for the second time, by Len Bergstein, but he was joined by women in the roles of press aide, campaign scheduling, volunteer coordinator, finance coordinator, office manager of the headquarters, and special-events coordinator.[469] As *Oregonian* reporter Wayne Thompson observed, "Women are…doing most of the work to elect a man to public office."[470]

The November 7 results brought victory for Atiyeh and surprises among the ballot measures. The surprises were that both Measures 6 and 11 failed. Oregon was not quite ready for its tax revolt. But in a race dominated by stances on property taxes, Atiyeh felt that his support for Measure 6 was crucial to his victory. He "insisted he had chosen the tax plan that the people

---

467 Wayne Thompson, "Atiyeh interview," 10.
468 Wayne Thompson, "Women Prove Effective."
469 Wayne Thompson, "Women Work Hard to Keep Straub Campaign Rolling," *Oregonian*, 17 October 1978.
470 Wayne Thompson, "Women Work Hard."

wanted and that it would help him in his bid for governor."[471] The next morning, Atiyeh hit on the realization that he had when he lost in 1974, saying "I think I won this time because I was speaking the way most Oregonians felt."[472]

Atiyeh defeated Straub by 89,000 votes, at that time the fifth-largest margin of victory in raw numbers in Oregon history. Atiyeh felt that his victory over Straub was more remarkable than his victory over McCall in the primary. In 1993 he reflected on the elections. "[T]o me the more significant thing was beating an incumbent governor. That's very difficult to do."[473] Straub ended up the campaign with a $30,000 deficit.[474] One of newly-sworn-in Governor Atiyeh's actions was to appear at the January 26, 1979, Straub Deficit Fundraiser in Portland.[475]

The morning after the election Atiyeh was at the campaign office bright and early, already moving forward. He had a phone call with Governor Straub during which Straub finally conceded, and the two talked about setting the transition in motion.[476] Atiyeh told well-wishers,

> I just want to savor this victory today. Just thinking about being governor really makes me excited and anxious. You have to understand that as a minority member of the Legislature for 20 years, I had to so often work through and around the controlling majority to establish the Victor Atiyeh identity. So often the real Victor Atiyeh never came through, but occasionally he did. But as governor, I now have an opportunity to bring my programs, philosophies and objectives above the surface. I want to tell you I'm really looking forward to leading this state to new directions.

---

471 Wayne Thompson, "Tax Issue Misfires for Straub," *Oregonian*, 8 November 1978.
472 Wayne Thompson, "Atiyeh Promises Spring Tax Relief, Jobs on Merits," *Oregonian*, 9 November 1978.
473 Victor Atiyeh, "Tape 25," 717.
474 AP, "Straub Campaign Debt Listed at $30,000," *Oregonian*, 7 December 1978.
475 "Monthly Diary Schedule, January 1979," Office of the Governor, State of Oregon, (1979), Atiyeh Collection, Pac. Univ. Archives.
476 "Atiyeh's Election as Governor, the Day After," Television News Story, Portland, OR, 8 November 1978. Embedded video, Atiyeh Collection, Pac. Univ. Archives.

I have programs I want to do, and I think they will fit the mood of Oregonians.[477]

Atiyeh made two personnel decisions that first day: to keep Glenna Hayden on as his personal secretary after years together in the Senate minority office and to hire Denny Miles as his gubernatorial press aide.

Atiyeh did say that he, who knew the many players in the state government bureaucracies from his long legislative experience, would not be radically changing the leadership of Oregon's many departments and divisions. He said, "True, it's safe to say that there are some agency directors I would want to replace and many who I feel would not be comfortable working for me. But I will sit down and talk with each one of the directors to find out just where or if they fit in before I make my moves."[478]

Transition Team

As governor-elect, Victor Atiyeh resigned his Oregon Senate seat, effective November 24, 1978.[479] For the first time since 1959, he had no official position in Oregon state government. But he had a state office and some nice state stationery paid for out of his transition funds.[480] He was now firmly in the executive branch, bringing his years of experience from the legislature with him to his new job, but changing his perspective to look at the entire state of Oregon instead of Washington County first. He was assuming office during a time when governors across the country were becoming more powerful, in many cases, but the power came to them because they were more expected to be administrators. The role of partisanship had diminished as

---

477 Wayne Thompson, "Atiyeh Promises Spring Tax Relief, Jobs on Merits."
478 Wayne Thompson, "Atiyeh Promises Spring Tax Relief, Jobs on Merits."
479 Victor Atiyeh, to Norma Paulus, "Senate Resignation," 24 November 1978, Atiyeh Collection, Pac. Univ. Archives.
480 "Stationery," Office of the Governor-elect, State of Oregon, (1978).

competence was seen as more important in the managerial model.[481] Two days after the election Atiyeh announced that his transition team would be led by Travis Cross and Lynn Newbry.[482] Straub had recommended that Atiyeh appoint two people to run the transition, one to deal with personnel and one to deal with general transitional issues.[483] Cross and Newbry had these qualities. Cross had deep ties to the Republican Party and deep experience in helping Oregon's government to function.[484] Newbry, son of a former secretary of state, had served with Atiyeh in the state senate for years. Atiyeh knew both well. At Straub's suggestion, Cross would be working with Straub's executive assistant, Bud Kramer, to learn how the Straub administration functioned.[485] To put together the policy proposals and ideas through the new budget that the new governor would advance when he took office in January, Newbry would work on the hand-off from the Straub administration budget with the director of the Executive Department.[486] Atiyeh wanted Newbry in charge of the budget because he had been the co-chair of the Ways and Means committee in the legislature.[487] Atiyeh knew the principles of the budget and a lot of details, but he had never been

---

[481] Thad L. Beyle and Robert Dalton, "Appointment Power: Does It Belong to the Governor?," in *Being Governor. The View from the Office*, eds. Thad L. Beyle and Lynn R. Muchmore, (Durham, NC: Duke University Press, 1983), 114.

[482] AP, "Lynn Newbry, Travis Cross to Aid in Atiyeh's Transition," *Salem Oregon Statesman*, 10 November 1978; Wayne Thompson, "Liaison With Straub Selected by Atiyeh," *Oregonian*, 10 November 1978; Charles E. Beggs, "Atiyeh Transition Rolls Along: Newbry and Cross at the Helm," *Salem Oregon Statesman*, 20 November 1978; Victor Atiyeh, interviewed by Jim Moore, "Atiyeh interview #1," Raleigh Hills, OR, 19 December 2013. Summary notes, 5.

[483] "Two Transition Staff Members Named by Governor-Elect," Office of the Governor-Elect, State of Oregon, News Release, (9 November 1978), Atiyeh Collection, Pac. Univ. Archives; Miles, "Atiyeh interview #3," 19.

[484] *Astorian*, "Top Rate Advisors," Editorial, 5 December 1978, Atiyeh Collection, Pac. Univ. Archives.

[485] "Two Transition Staff Members Named by Governor-Elect."

[486] "Two Transition Staff Members Named by Governor-Elect."

[487] Victor Atiyeh, interviewed by Clark Hansen, "Tape 25," Oral history, recorded by Oregon Historical Society, Portland, OR, 12 May 1993. Transcript, 714, Atiyeh Collection, Pac. Univ. Archives.

involved in putting together the entire budget; he had always stayed on the revenue side in his legislative work.

The most important job on Atiyeh's staff was executive assistant, later known as the chief of staff. Atiyeh approached the decision methodically, relying first on his years in retail at Atiyeh Brothers. The trick, as he saw it, was to hire people who could make decisions on their own so that customers' needs could be met. It was never just a matter of liking or not liking a candidate.[488] After considering even the mundane administrative mechanics of operating the office, his first choices for executive assistant were Lynn Newbry and Gerry Thompson, an insurance executive. Both turned the governor-elect down. Newbry was nearing retirement and did not want to change his plans; Thompson was in middle of an important project at Blue Cross/Blue Shield, where she was an executive.[489] After a meeting with Atiyeh in which she directly turned down the job, the governor-elect told Thompson he would be calling her in the next couple of years. When Thompson got home, her husband Al was appalled that she had turned down the offer, saying, "You never tell a governor, *no*." After those two passed on the job, "Well," Atiyeh said, "we went through a whole lot of names of people" to find the executive assistant.[490]

Former attorney general Lee Johnson's hiring as executive assistant was something of a surprise to those who knew him.[491] After serving two years in the House, Johnson was elected Oregon's Attorney General in 1968. He served two terms, then ran for an open seat on the Oregon State Appeals Court, a job he began in January 1977.[492] An *Oregonian* editorial referred to

---

488 Victor Atiyeh, interviewed by Jim Moore, "Atiyeh interview #4," Raleigh Hills, OR, 3 June 2014. Summary notes, 5.
489 Victor Atiyeh, "Tape 25," 725–726.
490 Victor Atiyeh, "Tape 25," 725.
491 *Oregonian*, "Lee Johnson Image Evolves as 'Hard Nose'," 2 March 1980, 1A, Atiyeh Collection, Pac. Univ. Archives; Sue Hill, "Johnson is Atiyeh's Top Aide: Judge and Ex–Attorney General," *Salem Oregon Statesman*, 7 December 1978.
492 "Midway Point," Office of the Governor-Elect, State of Oregon, News Release, (6 December 1978), Atiyeh Collection, Pac. Univ. Archives; *Oregon Statesman*

Johnson as raising "many quizzical eyebrows when he volunteered to 'defrock' himself to become...Atiyeh's executive assistant."[493] Johnson said he was "leaving the 'peaceful life' of the court because there [was] more action in the governor's operation."[494] Eventually, the same characteristics that made Johnson a successful statewide officeholder—being able to take charge of situations—would make his role as executive assistant and working with the governor problematic.

Once Johnson was hired in early December, the hiring process for the governor's staff moved away from Travis Cross and toward Johnson.[495] The major hires included Pat Amedeo, his chief aide for natural resources, Denny Miles, Glenna Hayden, Shirley Woodrow as appointments aide, and Bob Oliver as the governor's legal advisor. None of the hires in the governor's office were asked for their party registration—Amedeo and Oliver were Democrats.

Atiyeh wanted a system in which every major staff member had an individual relationship with the governor. Atiyeh hired people for their ability to formulate and carry out policy. Once those policies were in place, his core staff represented the governor himself in relations with other parts of the state and federal government.

During the transition, there was time for enjoying the notoriety of becoming a bit of a celebrity. During the election, *Oregonian* reporter Wayne Thompson had learned of Atiyeh's 1944 contract offer from the Green Bay Packers and wrote about it for the paper.[496] Packers coach Bart Starr saw the piece[497] and invited Atiyeh to come to Los Angeles to see the Packers take on the Los

---

(Salem), "Judicial Officials Sworn In: Redden's Oath Ad-libbed," 4 January 1977.
493 *Oregonian*, "'Defrocking' a Judge," Editorial, 11 December 1978.
494 "'Defrocking' a Judge."
495 Sandra McDonough, "Lee Johnson Appointed Executive Aide to Atiyeh," *Oregonian*, 7 December 1978.
496 Wayne Thompson, "Wink from Pros Deepened Atiyeh's Love for Football," *Oregonian*, 14 November 1978.
497 Wayne Thompson, "Atiyeh Gives Packers a Break; Refuses to Suit Up for Contest," *Oregonian*, 18 December 1978.

Angeles Rams for the last game of the season.[498] A quick, one-day trip was scheduled on a private aircraft.[499] Atiyeh, Republican donor Punch Green, reporter Thompson, and Denny Miles—the first three smoking like chimneys—flew south for the game.[500] Atiyeh, who was not awed by any of the politicians he met, whether American presidents or foreign leaders, was star-struck by Starr, according to Thompson. "He was like a little boy." The great quarterback of the 1960s was at the end of a mediocre coaching season, but Atiyeh did not care; he was talking with one of his team's football heroes. Starr kidded Atiyeh about playing in the game, saying "We've had some little injuries lately. Sure you wouldn't like to suit up? It's never too late, you know, to exercise that contract."[501]

Starr was a bit in awe as well. Someone who was something of a colleague, someone who had been offered a professional football contract, was now the governor of a state: "Here was the governor of a state, a former [almost] Packer, coming into the locker room."[502] According to Thompson, Starr and Atiyeh eventually got each other's autographs. The mutual admiration between the two men was quite apparent. However, Atiyeh's presence did not help the Packers—they lost to the Rams 31-14 "and were knocked out of the NFL playoffs."[503] In January 1979, a telegram from Starr arrived for Atiyeh informing the governor, "If you can tear yourself away from the governor's office, we hope to see you report to training camp July 15th. I'm sure we can come up with a better contract offer this time."[504] As Atiyeh would always point out, the colors of both the University of

---

498 Bart Starr, Letter to Victor Atiyeh, "Invitation to Green Bay Packers Game in Los Angeles," 7 December 1978, Atiyeh Collection, Pac. Univ. Archives.
499 "Green Bay Packers v. Los Angeles Rams," Governor-Elect, Transition Team, Game Day schedule, (17 December 1978), Atiyeh Collection, Pac. Univ. Archives; "Sports People," *Salem Oregon Statesman*, 15 December 1978.
500 Denny Miles, Phone call to Jim Moore, 9 April 2015; Denny Miles, Email to Jim Moore, "Remembering the Packers Game," 8 April 2015.
501 Wayne Thompson, "Atiyeh Gives Packers a Break."
502 Wayne Thompson, "Atiyeh interview," 4.
503 "Atiyeh Roots for Green Bay in LA—Didn't Do Any Good," *Salem Oregon Statesman*, 19 December 1978.

Oregon and the Green Bay Packers are yellow and green. They were his teams.

As of December 30, the items on the governor-elect's to-do list were mainly checked off.[505] His Portland house had been "completely wired for security/state police liaison" as had the Atiyeh family house near Mt. Hood (purchased by the Atiyeh brothers' parents and used by the three of them and their families). Atiyeh had resigned his business connections with Atiyeh Brothers.[506] In fact, Atiyeh Brothers made the decision while Atiyeh was in the Senate, and continued it while he was governor that it "would not accept or work with the state government in any way at all."[507] Key appointments had been made so that the handoff from the Straub administration to the Atiyeh administration would be relatively seamless. Yet friction was to come. The governor-elect's transition team gave Atiyeh one last word on the very dynamic executive assistant Lee Johnson in a memo on January 1, 1979:

> Lightning movement leaves trail of bodies and open mouths among immediate staff. Cannot be permitted to make eunuch of Denny or others like Shirley with identifiable responsibility. ... Frenetic pace and chain smoking portends danger. Greatest of potential, greatest of screwup potential. But of such is genius made.[508]

---

504 Bart Starr, Telegram to Victor Atiyeh, "Green Bay Packers Jersey," 25 January 1979, Atiyeh Collection, Pac. Univ. Archives.

505 "Program of Action for Governor-Elect in Loosely Priority Order," Office of the Governor-Elect, 30 December 1978. Atiyeh Collection, Pac. Univ. Archives.

506 Victor Atiyeh, to Atiyeh Bros. Board of Directors, "Letter of Resignation from Atiyeh Bros., effective 18 December 1978," 10 January 1979, Atiyeh Collection, Pac. Univ. Archives.

507 Edward Atiyeh, interviewed by Jim Moore, "Atiyeh interview #1," Raleigh Hills, OR, 18 October 2014. Summary notes, 3.

508 Transition, Travis Cross (unnamed) and Lynn Newbry (unnamed), "Memorandum," Office of the Governor-Elect, State of Oregon, Eyes-Only Memorandum to Governor-Elect Victor Atiyeh, (1 January 1979), 2, Atiyeh Collection, Pac. Univ. Archives.

Much of the coming conflict between Atiyeh and Johnson was foretold in these words. The "trail of bodies" and portent of "danger" would become clear to many, as well as Atiyeh, within the first weeks of his governorship.

It's Different Being Governor

In January 1979, Governor-Elect Vic Atiyeh wrote down the "Purpose of Administration," goals for his term as governor.[509]

> Eliminate duplication.
>
> Clarify dept. duties and objectives and authority.
>
> Establish goals for achievement.
>
> Open lines of communication w/state employees.
>
> Create unity of purpose w/in government.
>
> Achieve maximum use of tax dollar—minimum use of dollar in administration.
>
> Create governor's listening post.
>
> Create governor's council.

All these goals would be hard work. Some would be more attainable than others. He would be frustrated by "minimum use of dollar in administration." He planned to use the funding of the governor's office as a symbolic example. He would find a legislature that would not give him credit for his efforts and ideas about how to do this and would try to make life more difficult for him.

As with any governorship, there are many who take credit for the electoral victory, and many who feel they will be able to advance their own agendas through the person of the new governor. Atiyeh, the businessman Republican, would feel a great

---

[509] Vic Atiyeh, "Purpose of Administration (handwritten list)," Office of the Governor-Elect, State of Oregon, (January 1979), Memoranda and Reports, "Accomplishments," 1979, Atiyeh Collection, Pac. Univ. Archives.

deal of pressure from the Oregon business community to be *their* governor. He would push back, and sometimes push back hard. Atiyeh recalled a feeling of being "standoffish" with the business community members.[510] They supported him, but then they seemed to want to dictate how government would work through ad hoc advisory committees. Atiyeh did not need "blue-ribbon panels" to solve problems. He hired department heads to solve problems, and the new governor was not looking over the department heads' shoulders while they worked. As Atiyeh considered this tension over the years, he concluded that the business community "was not quite in charge as much as they thought they should be."[511]

All those business leaders had an open door to him, but they were angry because the governor did not necessarily carry out their agendas. Atiyeh, always the gentleman, would politely listen to them. He would also appease some of them by inviting them for brown-bag lunches. But, as Gerry Thompson noted, even though Atiyeh would listen very politely, a brown-bag lunch was a clear signal of lower status than a catered lunch with the governor. "The influentials—they misjudged him," Denny Miles said. "And they thought he was going to be easy to control. They didn't know the stubbornness factor."[512]

Atiyeh knew the influentials already. He had also received a memo about them from his transition team.[513] Powerful members of this group came to see Atiyeh's inner circle of staffers as problems. Atiyeh understood his close personal staff tried to protect him from issues that were unimportant. He pushed back:

[T]here's always that kind of perception thing. Palace guard. ... Lee Johnson or Pat Amedeo or Denny Miles. ...We talked about it. I did everything I could to avoid it from occurring. It does happen. But...it's a matter of them getting use[d] to me, too.

---

510 Victor Atiyeh, "Atiyeh interview #1," 6.
511 Victor Atiyeh, "Atiyeh interview #1," 6.
512 Miles, "Atiyeh interview #3," 12.
513 "Memorandum," Office of the Governor-Elect, State of Oregon, Unaddressed Memo to Vic Atiyeh, (ca. December 1978), Atiyeh Collection, Pac. Univ. Archives.

After a while, there wasn't the same protectiveness. They said, "Okay, that's the Governor, that's the way he is, that's what he's going to go out to do; he doesn't screw things up too badly when he's done. And just turn him loose."[514]

As long as he was conscious of the efforts to protect him, Atiyeh found he could make good decisions about when to deal with particular issues. He had seen Straub's staff control his activities, not letting "Bob be Bob."[515] With Atiyeh's long experience in the capitol, he knew that it was easy to become "trapped by the building; you have to be aware that you're being trapped"—or else one lost contact with the people and issues that are most important.[516]

One of Atiyeh's first confrontations with the Democratic legislature was his nomination of Kelly Woods to be the acting director of the Department of Energy. The senate turned down the nomination. The pressure to get the Woods nomination through was intense. It was Lee Johnson's first major test as executive assistant. Johnson used tactics that had "a few senators moaning and groaning that they hadn't felt so much pressure in years."[517] He was threatening gubernatorial vetoes of future bills if votes were not forthcoming for Woods, which Atiyeh denied.[518]

This began a pattern. The governor would admonish Johnson about running ahead of where the governor actually was on issues. Denny Miles remembered, "More than once, I was in a meeting where Lee and the Governor and I were there, maybe other people were there, and Lee would go, 'Governor! Governor! You've got to back me on this because I've already said it. And if you don't back me on this my credibility is going to be shot with

---

514 Victor Atiyeh, interviewed by Clark Hansen, "Tape 32," Oral history, recorded by Oregon Historical Society, Portland, OR, 7 June 1993. Transcript, 47, Atiyeh Collection, Pac. Univ. Archives.
515 Victor Atiyeh, "Tape 32," 48.
516 Victor Atiyeh, "Tape 32," 48.
517 Wayne Thompson, "Arm-Twisting Rumored in Battle Over Woods," Column, *Oregonian*, 26 February 1979.
518 Wayne Thompson, "Arm-Twisting Rumored."

the Democratic leadership.'"[519] Atiyeh would offer to explain to the legislative leadership that there had been miscommunication, always emphasizing that he remained the ultimate decision maker. After the tumultuous first sixty days as governor, it became clear to others that Atiyeh and Johnson did not work that well together.

It was Miles' job to take government position papers that were handed to him and send out press releases on the subject,[520] but that began to change when the governor, at Miles' urging, began having weekly media availabilities.

From the beginning of Atiyeh's term the media complained they were not getting enough access to the governor—a pretty standard gripe. Atiyeh asked his communications aide how to deal with the requests.[521] Miles suggested the media availability concept. It was not a press conference. The idea was that Atiyeh would be present to answer any questions that came up. It had never been done before, even by that master politician-journalist Tom McCall.

Reporters chafed at the term—and the governor began the first media availability on January 24, 1979, by telling the assembled group, "It's our intention of holding regular news conferences."[522] It would take a few months for the semantics to stop raising questions about what these events were. Within a few days, the nomenclature began spreading, with the House Minority Leader holding a media availability as well. The media availabilities took place every week that Atiyeh was in Salem.[523] For Atiyeh the distinction was that a press conference was what "*I* want to talk [about] to you, versus media availability, what do *you* want to talk about? Anything."[524] It became "one of the highlights of my week.

---

519   Miles, "Atiyeh interview #3," 21.
520   Miles, "Atiyeh interview #1," 3.
521   Miles, "Atiyeh interview #1," 9.
522   David Reyes, "Scribe Finds Men's Room But Rest of Day Rocky," Column, *Salem Oregon Statesman*, 25 January 1979.
523   Denny Miles, Email to Jim Moore, "Staff Access," 29 May 2017; Denny Miles, Email to Jim Moore, "Media Availabilities," 22 June 2017.
524   Victor Atiyeh, "Tape 28," 805. Italics are underlined by hand in Atiyeh's copy of the oral history.

I really looked forward to it."[525] The media also had access to the governor for individual stories. He remembered, "[I]f they wanted to follow up on something, or had their own [stories], they always had access to me. Always."[526]

When he left office, he was very honored to be given a certificate from the capitol press corps thanking him for his accessibility. As one of his "valued mementos," it hung on the wall of Atiyeh's office until he donated the certificate to Pacific University.

> Governor Vic Atiyeh
> Thanks for your accessibility.
> Best wishes for the future.
>
> FROM THE
> STATE CAPITOL PRESS CORPS
> SALEM, OREGON
> JANUARY 7, 1987

This presentation hung on ex-Governor Atiyeh's office wall, displayed with pride.

Cabinet Meetings

Having heard that his predecessor Bob Straub never brought agency heads into the office for regular conversations, Atiyeh

---

525 Victor Atiyeh, "Tape 32," 48; Victor Atiyeh, "Tape 28," 805.
526 Victor Atiyeh, "Tape 32," 49.

established weekly cabinet meetings, allowing him to keep on top of what was happening in state government but also to create an environment within which different state entities could learn from each other and transcend bureaucratic silos to solve problems together. Atiyeh wanted a more transparent system of government for those who worked in the various groups. The meetings were not secret, but neither were they open to the media or the public. The door was open to all statewide elected officials, the governor's staff could attend at any time, and the agency heads were required to be there.

Atiyeh had two goals from his point of view. "I don't want to be surprised by anything. If somebody asks me a question," he did not want to have to answer. "I didn't know that was going on. But number two, probably more important than anything, I realized that agencies were out doing their own thing without any cognizance or recognition of any other agency of state government."[527] The governor would often ask broad questions, as well as more detail-oriented questions, of the managers in the meetings. One of his favorites was "Why did you do it that way?"[528] He often knew that issues were arising because of managers' ways of approaching problems, so by asking this question he was "informing me, but also getting them to think about what they're doing."[529]

Jon Yunker, working in state finance, who attended the cabinet meetings, remembered the meetings had a relaxed atmosphere that encouraged openness. The group would sit around the conference table "and smoke their cigarettes or whatever."[530] The first person would "explain what had gone right and what had

---

527 Victor Atiyeh, "Tape 28," 799; Victor Atiyeh, "Tape 32," 64; Victor Atiyeh, "Tape 58, side 1," 5; Victor Atiyeh, interviewed by Clark Hansen, "Tape 62," Oral history, recorded by Oregon Historical Society, Portland, OR, 11 June 1998. Transcript, 17, Atiyeh Collection, Pac. Univ. Archives.
528 Victor Atiyeh, "Tape 32," 65.
529 Victor Atiyeh, "Tape 32," 65.
530 Jon Yunker, interviewed by Jim Moore, "Atiyeh interview," Salem, OR, 22 June 2015. Summary notes, 8.

gone wrong" in the previous week or with a particular issue. Atiyeh would listen, and if the issues were important, he would emphasize that he did not "want half the story, I need to understand exactly what happened." Yunker saw that within four or five minutes the governor would give an okay for whatever the next steps were needed, and they would go on to the next person. Yunker recalled that there were only about four or five directors who needed to talk to the governor every single week. The cabinet meetings thus became a good way for short reports and ideas to circulate among the rest of the managers and for the governor to comment on what was happening and possibly give new direction or support to initiatives and projects. If an issue was bigger than could be dealt with in the cabinet meetings, managers had follow-up meetings with Atiyeh. As Dan Simmons of Human Resources put it, Atiyeh "told you what to expect, he gave you feedback, he gave you the tools to do the job, and he got out of your way. …He was really good."[531] Recalling why he first ran for governor in 1974, Atiyeh saw the cabinet coordination as a way of "sorting out [these problems] that Tom McCall had dumped" out into the political world.[532]

Atiyeh knew that he was held responsible for state government during his term. He also knew he could not change things by himself. He made it clear to his agency and department heads, "You have to [reach goals] for me. I can't do them" alone.[533] Atiyeh was respected by state workers, so he remembered these conversations as "all very pleasant" and informational.[534] But the word was out. The governor was keeping tabs on how goals were, or were not, being met.

From 1985 on, newly elected Secretary of State, Barbara Roberts had a standing invitation from Atiyeh to join the meetings. She realized that he did not have to do that, but he

---

531 Dan Simmons, interviewed by Jim Moore, "Atiyeh interview," Salem, OR, 15 June 2015. Summary notes, 5.
532 Victor Atiyeh, "Tape 28," 800.
533 Victor Atiyeh, "Tape 28," 800.
534 Victor Atiyeh, "Tape 32," 67.

encouraged her to attend. She recalled, "It gave me an incredible insight into the workings of government." For two years she listened, quietly, "which is unusual for me," to what she referred to as "the guts of government."[535] Roberts compared her experience in the meetings to "a master's degree in government for two years." She saw different types of leadership among the agency heads, the diverse ways that they led their departments and reported what was happening. When she became governor, she found that sitting in on the meetings was "an incredible asset for me." Thinking about her attendance at the cabinet meetings, Roberts said, "Vic just handed me…a gift."[536]

New Staff Leadership

The clash in styles between Atiyeh and his executive assistant was too frustrating, and the governor saw that it was leading to some turmoil in his office. He found that Johnson eventually "drove me nuts. …I would go into his office and, 'God damn it, Lee, I'm the governor and you're not." Atiyeh never had "the certainty that my agenda was his agenda."[537] Atiyeh finally came to the decision that Lee Johnson needed to move on sometime in late 1980 or early 1981. He recalled, "If I couldn't work with somebody, I know myself that it wasn't going to get any better."[538] After Atiyeh asked Jack Faust to talk with Johnson about stepping down,[539] Johnson's resignation was announced in summer 1981. This indirect approach was not like Atiyeh's management of other personnel issues, but it reflected the problem he would have making hard decisions with those he knew well. Atiyeh had been unhappy with Johnson's attitude for almost two years. He finally admitted to himself that Johnson was not going to change, but even then, he needed an intermediary to deliver the bad news.

---

535 Barbara Roberts, interviewed by Jim Moore, "Atiyeh interview," Portland, OR, 23 February 2015. Summary notes, 1.
536 Roberts, "Atiyeh interview," 2.
537 Victor Atiyeh, "Atiyeh interview #3," 16.
538 Victor Atiyeh, "Atiyeh interview #3," 16.
539 Victor Atiyeh, "Atiyeh interview #3," 16; Miles, "Atiyeh interview #1," 10.

In July 1981, Johnson announced that he would leaving his job at some point soon. At the end of the busy 1981 legislative session, there were no firm dates about when he would depart, nor was there certainty about what he would do.[540] There had been an active attempt, through Mark Hatfield's office, to place Johnson at the head of the Bonneville Power Administration in the spring of 1981. But that position went to Peter Johnson of Boise, a nod to the chair of the Senate Energy Committee, James McClure of Idaho.[541] "Atiyeh said he was 'very disappointed.'"[542] Pat Amedeo was prominently mentioned as a possible successor in the executive assistant position, but she said, "I have mixed emotions about it. I haven't been offered the job and I really enjoy what I have been doing."[543] On July 20, the governor spent an hour with his staff to "clear the air on Lee's successor."[544] There were clearly those who currently worked for the governor who were maneuvering for the job.

That summer of 1981, Gerry Thompson received a telephone call from Atiyeh.[545] She knew very well what was coming. She had a long discussion with Atiyeh after-hours at his office about her coming on board as the executive assistant. Thompson's biggest fear was that she had always been on the periphery of politics—she had been active in Girls State when she was growing up—but politics was certainly not a career she wanted to

---

540 Sandra McDonough, "Lee Johnson Plans to Leave State Job," *Oregonian*, 18 July 1981.

541 Dulcy Mahar and Lynn Baker, *Power of the River: The Continuing Legacy of the Bonneville Power Administration in the Pacific Northwest*, (Washington, DC: Government Printing Office, 2012) PDF, 4–5; Don Bundy and Dick Johnston, "Idaho's Johnson Wins BPA Post; Atiyeh Unhappy," *Oregonian*, 29 April 1981.

542 Bundy and Johnston, "Idaho's Johnson Wins."; the governor was also talking to the Idaho press, "Atiyeh Daily Index-Card Schedule, April 30, 1981," Office of the Governor, State of Oregon, (30 April 1981), Interview: Ellen Marks, the Idaho Statesman re: Peter Johnson appmt, Atiyeh Collection, Pac. Univ. Archives.

543 McDonough, "Lee Johnson Plans."

544 "Atiyeh Daily Index-Card Schedule, July 20, 1981," Office of the Governor, State of Oregon, (20 July 1981), Staff (clear air on Lee's successor), Atiyeh Collection, Pac. Univ. Archives.

545 Gerry Thompson, interviewed by Jim Moore, "Atiyeh interview #1," Salem, OR, 16 September 2014. Summary notes, 15.

pursue. In the years since late 1978, she had a chance to think about working for the governor. She knew she needed to talk to Atiyeh about her view of the position itself. She knew she liked politics but was not absorbed by it. She had never worked in the legislature. Thompson recalled, "You've got to know the players. And that was my biggest concern. Yes, I was working in Portland, in a whole different area. But I was the biggest scaredy-cat when it came to knowing the players. Who really should be close to the governor, and who really shouldn't be, and who do I have to protect him from. I didn't know anything."[546] She emphasized to Atiyeh that he needed somebody who could "champion his causes and get them through." She told him that he needed someone with a powerful voice in the state. These and several other concerns, in her opinion, stood in the way of her being good at the job.

Atiyeh stopped her. "You can do all that. What I want is somebody who can be my alter ego, who I can trust when I'm out of state, or, for that matter, traveling in the state, who I know will carry out my agenda and not have a personal agenda. And you are the one for that."[547] Thompson told him that she did not think she could have been a good executive assistant in 1979. Atiyeh, however, "innately knew she could do it."[548] He characterized himself as very sensitive to the people he talked to, who they were, and how they might be able to do a particular job. For him it was not a matter of liking or not liking them, it was a matter of trusting his feelings about the personality and competence of the person. He knew he had not made a mistake in 1979 when he asked her to take the job.

Thompson said yes to the offer, "and we moved forward."[549]

Atiyeh and Thompson talked about what had not worked in the relationship with Lee Johnson. Thompson "understood perfectly." Atiyeh was the governor. It was the job of the staff to carry out

---

546 Gerry Thompson, interviewed by Jim Moore, "Atiyeh Interview #4," Salem, OR, 7 August 2017. Summary notes, 8.
547 Gerry Thompson, "Atiyeh interview #1," 15–16.
548 Victor Atiyeh, "Atiyeh interview #4," 5.
549 Gerry Thompson, "Atiyeh interview #1," 16.

the governor's agenda, not to lobby for favorite programs. Thompson discovered that one of the major parts of the job was to keep key assistants on task with that agenda. "It's not us who are governing," she told them, "it's he who is governing."[550]

Thompson's appointment was not anticipated by capitol watchers, just as Johnson's had not been anticipated in 1978. A newspaper story reported that Thompson's appointment "came as a surprise to staff members, state legislators, and to members of the Republican party," all of whom expected a political insider like Pat Amedeo, a current legislator, or Oregon's Public Utility Commissioner to get the nod.[551] Another report said that "her name never popped up in the gossip mill," and that the main response in the capitol was, "Who's she?"[552] Thompson, with understated accuracy, said "I am told that he (the governor) was looking for a strong administrator."[553]

The Open Office

Atiyeh prided himself on having an open door to his office. Unless he was in a meeting, it was common for people to be able to walk in and engage him in conversation. Gerry Thompson recalled that there was an unofficial priority list for getting through to the governor if he was busy.[554] Jim Campbell and Tom Galt, Atiyeh's friends from Washington High School, could always get through. They, especially Campbell, might call with a joke they found particularly funny that they wanted to share with their old friend.[555] Family could get in—as Atiyeh's son Tom remembered, "he was accessible. He was just busy" a lot in the

---

550 Gerry Thompson, "Atiyeh interview #1," 16.
551 Foster Church, "Atiyeh's Choice for Executive Aide Reflects Desire for Change," *Oregonian*, 6 September 1981.
552 Sue Hill, "Salem Woman Named Atiyeh's Top Assistant," *Salem (OR) Statesman-Journal*, 27 August 1981, 1A, 15A.
553 Church, "Atiyeh's Choice."
554 Gerry Thompson, "Atiyeh interview #1," 11.
555 Miles, "Atiyeh interview #3," 3; Miles to Moore, 29 May 2017.

job.[556] Grandchildren were especially welcomed by their grandfather the governor.

Any legislator who wanted to talk to the governor could always get through.[557] The legislators had never seen this behavior from a governor before, and Thompson observed that they respected Atiyeh for it. Thompson fielded a lot of skeptical questions about whether or not legislators would actually be able to see the governor—the door was equally open to Republicans and Democrats.

Every day he was available in Salem—usually at least one or two days a week—he held open houses.[558] "I would just walk out there in the ceremonial office" from 12:30 to 1:00, "and anybody that wanted to come in would come in."[559] Atiyeh loved the interaction. He recalled being asked, "'Are you the governor?' 'Yeah.' 'Are you *really* the governor?' 'Yeah.'"[560] He got a delighted letter from a Salem woman who had brought a family from Brazil to see the capitol. The family, "totally in awe," talked with the governor and posed for photos with him. The host wrote, "For you to see a common layman without being screened, let alone someone from another country was a shock, though a happy one."[561] Atiyeh loved talking with people from out of state who "can't believe that really this guy standing there is the governor."[562]

Atiyeh was also able to use the open house times to avoid one-on-one meetings with people he did not want to deal with. Shirley Woodrow remembered that Jerry Falwell, leader of the Moral Majority, wanted to talk with the governor. Through a series of

---

556 Tom Atiyeh, interviewed by Jim Moore, "Atiyeh interview," Sherwood, OR, 28 July 2015. Summary, 7.
557 Gerry Thompson, "Atiyeh interview #1," 11.
558 Based on looking at the governor's weekly schedules, Atiyeh Collection, Pacific University, Forest Grove, OR.
559 Victor Atiyeh, "Tape 28," 803.
560 Victor Atiyeh, "Tape 28," 803. Italicized word is underlined in original.
561 Joanne Bentley, Letter to Victor Atiyeh, "Brazilians Visit Atiyeh," 7 June 1980, Atiyeh Collection, Pac. Univ. Archives.
562 Victor Atiyeh, "Tape 62," 15.

phone calls, it became clear that Atiyeh "did not want to meet with him...but in the final analysis the governor said if Falwell came to the ceremonial office" during open house time, "the governor would acknowledge him. As a result, Falwell and about six aides arrived at the ceremonial office that day, and the governor shook hands with all of them."[563] No official meeting with Falwell, however.

In addition to set times for open access to the governor, and those knocks on his office door, Atiyeh was a regular in the capitol coffee shop. Barbara Roberts remembered "it was always exciting to see the governor walk into the coffee shop."[564] She saw him talk to reporters there, as well as engage in conversations with people who happened to be sitting nearby and visitors to the capitol. He maintained a special connection with Girl Scout and Boy Scout groups. Roberts observed that Atiyeh was not the type of governor who seemed to get entrenched behind closed doors. "He walked through the building with the comfort of a man who had lived in the house for a long time."[565]

Getting Underway

Governor-elect Vic Atiyeh knew what he wanted to accomplish as governor. There were a certain number of policies advanced by his predecessors he wanted to change, but by and large he wanted to guide Oregon as it implemented the actual policies of big ideas like land-use planning. As he had advocated in his campaign, especially when he talked about the property tax reform ideas in Measure 6, he wanted to give expression to what he called the "common voice of Oregon."[566] And he wanted the people of

---

563 Shirley Woodrow, "Notes for Atiyeh Interview," (Unpublished manuscript, 17 June 2015), 6–7; Shirley Woodrow, interviewed by Jim Moore, "Atiyeh interview," Phone interview, Glenwood Springs, CO, 17 June 2015. Summary notes, 7.
564 Roberts, "Atiyeh interview," 8.
565 Roberts, "Atiyeh interview," 9.
566 Victor Atiyeh, interviewed by Clark Hansen, "Tape 11," Oral history, recorded by Oregon Historical Society, Portland, OR, 28 December 1992. Transcript, 314, Atiyeh Collection, Pac. Univ. Archives.

Oregon to take up the responsibility to solve the problems they could, with or without government involvement.

His first official opportunity to make all this clear was his inaugural address, which he anticipated with excitement.[567] He recalled, "What I wanted to do was deal with the question philosophically. This is how you approach government; this is how you do things."[568] Although Atiyeh put together a speech-writing team to help him express his ideas, the process was incredibly streamlined. Jack Faust said, "We talked [for less than] 5 minutes about it; he wanted a theme of volunteerism. I wrote it, sent it to him for comment or conference. No comments, no conference. He gave it as it was, no changes. None."[569]

Recognizing that he was "only recently one of *you*," Atiyeh began the speech with a call to lawmakers: "I know how easy it is to view the legislative agenda as a kaleidoscope, tumbling fragments of varying shapes and colors, each bearing little or no relation to the other."[570] He asked colleagues in the chamber to hear "Oregonians talking," to hear all their "voices blend into one, a true common voice of the people of Oregon, expressing common concerns."[571] Alluding to his interpretation of the 200,000 people who had signed petitions for Measure 6, as well as the hundreds of thousands of Oregonians who voted for the property tax limitation measure, he declared that he heard Oregonian voices "rise to an anguished *scream* of anger, a cry of frustration at promises broken and government becoming more remote."[572] In a line that some of his closest advisors considered to reflect his core value, Atiyeh said, "The plain fact is that given the light to see the truth, our people will decide their destinies

---

567 Victor Atiyeh, "Tape 26," 744.
568 Victor Atiyeh, "Tape 26," 744.
569 Jack Faust, Email to Jim Moore, "Inaugural," 21 April 2015.
570 Victor Atiyeh, "First Inaugural Address, with annotations by Atiyeh" (speech, Joint Legislative Session, Salem, OR, 8 January 1979), 2, Atiyeh Collection, Pac. Univ. Archives. Italics underlined by Atiyeh; Victor Atiyeh, "Inaugural Address" (speech, Sixtieth Legislative Assembly, Salem, OR, 8 January 1979), Atiyeh Collection, Pac. Univ. Archives.
571 Victor Atiyeh, "First Inaugural Address," 2.
572 Victor Atiyeh, "First Inaugural Address," 3. Italics underlined in original.

better than any elite elected or not."⁵⁷³ Although he said "the responsibility rests with *us*" in Salem to realize the goals, to the citizens of Oregon he said, "Set us the task and we will choose the tools."⁵⁷⁴

Atiyeh pledged to lead by example in this as well. "This government will soon announce a policy which will *encourage* and *assist* state employees to participate in the volunteer efforts of their communities."⁵⁷⁵ He called upon Oregon's employers to do the same thing. "If all the people of Oregon can take to their hearts the age-old concept of volunteerism, we can reduce the need for government intervention and tax support, we can improve the quality of life in Oregon, and we will grow as a community."⁵⁷⁶

There was great interest among observers curious to see the working relationship between Atiyeh, the 20-year legislative veteran, but always in the minority, and the Democratic leadership in the House and the Senate. The Senate was not much of a mystery: Jason Boe was the Senate President once again, as he had been since 1973. He and Atiyeh knew each other well. The House side took a bit longer to come together. Rifts among the thirty-four Democrats prevented them from unifying behind a single candidate to lead them and become Speaker. Hardy Myers (D-Portland), who would eventually win the post, was the leader of the majority within the Democratic group of twenty-one, but there was "intense factionalization in the caucus."⁵⁷⁷ Myers recalled that he and Atiyeh were able to "fashion an easy personal working relationship."⁵⁷⁸ Even though they came from different

---

573 Victor Atiyeh, "First Inaugural Address," 4. Italics underlined by Atiyeh; Denny Miles, interviewed by Jim Moore, "Atiyeh interview #3," Forest Grove, OR, 5 April 2016. Summary notes, 3.

574 Victor Atiyeh, "First Inaugural Address," 5.

575 Victor Atiyeh, "First Inaugural Address," 9. Italics are underlined by Atiyeh.

576 Victor Atiyeh, "First Inaugural Address," 9–10.

577 Hardy Myers, interviewed by Jim Moore, "Atiyeh interview," Portland, OR, 19 February 2015. Summary notes, 1; *Oregonian*, "Democrats Still Stuck On The Speaker," 5 December 1978.

578 Meyers, "Atiyeh interview," 6.

parties, Myers said he "was able to develop a basically trusting relationship with Vic." They were both "what-you-see-is-what-you-get style politicians."[579] As they were both figuring out their new roles, Atiyeh quickly established a pattern of regular meetings with the legislative leadership.

The first concrete proposals of Atiyeh's administration came from the proposed budget. With inflation on his mind, the number-one goal for the new governor, as well as the legislative leadership from both parties, was to cut taxes. Atiyeh had been concerned about inflation since it emerged as an issue in the 1960s. In 1977 he had received an estimate from Oregon's Executive Department that Oregon's taxable income had grown $1.7 billion, creating an increase in tax revenue that accounted for most of the $175 million carried over from the 1975 budget. Atiyeh's thinking on the matter was shaped greatly by a 1975 report from the Legislative Revenue Office's Richard Munn pointing out how federal government spending and the market for government bonds could contribute to inflation and reduce "the private sector's purchasing power just as effectively as a tax."[580] So his 1979 budget was designed to slow the rate of growth of spending by the state government, and in doing so, to help slow down the effects of inflation by the largest single economic entity in the state (state government itself).

Building on his decades of work on taxes in the legislature, Atiyeh proposed a combination of over $700 million in tax relief including a property tax limitation, a new way to index "personal income tax rates so that cost-of-living pay raises will not drive individuals into higher tax brackets," and "a 22 percent one-time rebate of 1978 personal income taxes…as a means of returning the state general fund surplus."[581] The tax relief programs would be about 23 percent of the entire $3.1 billion general fund budget,

---

579 Meyers, "Atiyeh interview," 6.
580 Richard A. Munn, "Inflation," Legislative Revenue Office, State of Oregon, Research Report R-I No. 47-75, (18 July 1975), 5, Atiyeh Collection, Pac. Univ. Archives.
581 Phil Cogswell, "Tax Slash Tops Priorities," *Oregonian*, 7 January 1979.

lowering the effective budget to $2.67 billion.[582] More than $425 million would be returned to income-tax payers.

Tax relief would set up a replay of Measures 6 and 11 from the 1978 election. Although both measures had been defeated by voters, Atiyeh and the legislature ended up arguing that there needed to be tax relief because a large *minority* of Oregonians supported the two plans (Yes votes for Measure 6: 48.3%; Yes votes for Measure 11: 45%). With the momentum indicated by California's successful Proposition 13, there was fear that the minority of Oregonians in favor of major tax reform could become a majority if some new plan was not adopted.

The first focus for Atiyeh's tax plan—and for his budget—was the reform of the property tax. Starting with Atiyeh's old House committee, Revenue, the plan was to get the reforms through the legislature quickly, then refer the matter to an April 3, 1979, public vote so the changes could be implemented as soon as possible. The committee was holding lots of hearings, but there did not seem to be a coming-together of members to support Atiyeh's plan. At the end of January, after about three weeks of the session, Atiyeh was unconcerned with the pace of the committee—after all, he understood very well the committee's dynamics and what the issues were.[583] But there needed to be a final plan by the end of February to make the April 3 ballot, so Atiyeh gave a ten-day deadline, after which his office would use its campaign network to activate Oregonians to contact their legislators directly on the matter.

The Legislative Revenue Office testified before the House committee the first week in February that overall the Atiyeh plan would provide $443 million in tax relief, but lower taxes would occur in urban and suburban areas, while rural areas would see no change.[584] Just as Atiyeh's property tax proposal looked like it had died, a poll was published on February 11 that showed strong

---

582 Wayne Thompson, "Fiscal Conservatism Seen in Atiyeh Budget," *Oregonian*, 7 January 1979.

583 Suzanne Hill, "Atiyeh, Solons in Cat-Mouse Game Over Tax Plans," *Salem Oregon Statesman*, 1 February 1979.

support for the property tax limitation plan—71% for and 18% (±3.6%) against—among registered voters.[585] The polling took place before the Legislative Revenue Office findings, but with strong support across the state, across party lines, and across income brackets, it was clear that Oregonians saw the property tax as a big issue that they wanted to be fixed.

The poll results did not change the downward trajectory of the Atiyeh property tax plan in the legislature. The only discussion was how to move on. The House committee began hearing amendments that would keep Atiyeh's plan alive in name only and began to hear ideas for new tax relief plans as well.[586] The amendments to Atiyeh's plan drew support of just two Republicans and one Democrat on the nine-person committee. The committee moved to other options.[587] As one reporter put it, on February 22 "[t]he truce flag dropped and the guns came out... as a handful of Republican state senators declared war on the Democratic-controlled Legislature over the tax relief issue."[588] Six of the seven Senate Republicans (the caucus had grown by one after the 1978 election) backed "a petition drive to put Gov. Atiyeh's plan on the ballot."[589] Clearly, Atiyeh and the Senate Republicans looked at the overwhelming support in polling and decided that people would be receptive to a version of the Atiyeh plan.

By the end of February, the House Revenue Committee finally approved a three-bill tax plan to go to the floor—it was a version of the legislature's Measure 11 from the previous fall. The House

---

584 Phil Cogswell, "Atiyeh's Plan for Tax Relief Termed Varied," *Oregonian*, 7 February 1979.

585 J. Roy Bardsley, "Atiyeh Tax Plan Supported in Poll," *Oregonian*, 11 February 1979.

586 Phil Cogswell, "Changes Simplify Tax Relief Plan: Answer to Critics," *Oregonian*, 16 February 1979; Suzanne Hill, "Tax Cut Plan Still Hanging By a Thread," *Salem Oregon Statesman*, 16 February 1979.

587 Phil Cogswell, "House Panel Jettisons Atiyeh Tax Plan, Seeks Its Own," *Oregonian*, 17 February 1979.

588 Suzanne Hill, "GOP Plans Petition to Put Gov. Atiyeh's Tax Plan on Ballot," *Salem Oregon Statesman*, 23 February 1979.

589 Hill, "GOP Plans Petition."

passed its tax plan on March 15. With voting overwhelmingly in favor of the two income tax bills and one large bill that specified property tax relief, the plan drew criticism from the governor,[590] whose main concern was that there was no provision to lower property taxes. It was mainly a plan to send state money in various forms to those who had a harder time paying their property taxes. Atiyeh hinted at, but did not explicitly threaten, a veto of the plan. He was somewhat hindered because many House Republicans had voted for the bills, and the yes votes were well over the number required to override a veto.[591]

Oregon's revenues continued to increase. The economy was up, there was a change in the federal tax code that resulted in more money coming into the state's coffers, and inflation had raised the amount of money people were being paid. One reporter characterized the situation as "the state of Oregon...sheepishly counting an ever-growing amount of extra cash on hand."[592] Then, at the end of the month, tax relief was superseded by energy issues. The Three Mile Island nuclear facility in Pennsylvania had a horrific accident, putting lawmakers' attention on nuclear safety and the future of the proposed Pebble Springs nuclear plant to be built east of Bend.[593] Consequently, realistic Senate proposals for tax relief did not surface until the third week in April, well past the deadline to get anything to voters for the May 22 elections. After four weeks, the Senate Revenue Committee retained the 30% property tax reduction but had jettisoned the "one-time

---

590 Sue Hill, "House Passes $652 Million Tax Plan: Atiyeh Threatens to Veto Package if Not Modified," *Salem Oregon Statesman*, 16 March 1979; Phil Cogswell, "State Tax Relief Proposal Easily Approved by House," *Oregonian*, 16 March 1979.

591 Phil Cogswell, "Senate Bears Burden of Tax-Issue Decision," News Analysis, *Oregonian*, 16 March 1979.

592 Sue Hill, "Atiyeh Diverts Budget Surplus to Roads," *Salem Oregon Statesman*, 20 March 1979, 1A.

593 From Wire Service Reports, "Mishap to Affect Pebble Springs? Atiyeh Urges Hearings," *Eugene (OR) Register-Guard*, 30 March 1979, Atiyeh Collection, Pac. Univ. Archives; AP, "N-Safeguards: Atiyeh Wants Hearings Reopened," *Albany (OR) Democrat-Herald*, 30 March 1979, Atiyeh Collection, Pac. Univ. Archives; UPI, "News on Reactor Captures Attention at Oregon Capital," *Ashland (OR) Daily Tidings*, 31 March 1979, Atiyeh Collection, Pac. Univ. Archives.

rebate of the state surplus" in favor of "an automatic rebate of future state budget surpluses."[594] Atiyeh began talks with Senate President Boe and House Speaker Myers "in an effort to come up with a tax plan that can be approved by the Senate, the House and the governor."[595]

The first week in May, the Senate finally came up with its plan. The governor further complicated the negotiations by introducing a plan to "return all available tax relief funds to income taxpayers," thus avoiding what he saw as a flawed attempt to send the money to property taxpayers. Boe characterized Atiyeh's proposal as "'a parliamentary disaster' and a 'complex, awkward method of encouraging a conference committee'" that might be more amenable to the governor's ideas.[596] The full Senate rejected Atiyeh's plan 10–20.[597] The final Senate version, which passed with a veto-proof 20–10 margin, differed "technically but not conceptually" from the House version.[598]

The final bill contained the 30% property tax relief, more benefits for harrp recipients (the Homeowner and Renter Relief Program that helped low-income Oregonians pay their property taxes), an income tax rebate, and some state and local spending limits. It looked like overwhelming majorities in both chambers would support the bill, and on June 4 the three-bill package passed.[599] The governor immediately announced plans to launch a petition drive for an initiative to put his own plan before voters. In addition, a group from among those who backed 1978's Measure 6 introduced plans for a 1% property tax limit to appear before

---

594 AP, "Senate Panel Vetoes Lid on Home Assessments," *Salem Statesman Journal*, 21 April 1979, 8A; Phil Cogswell, "Weaker Tax Rebate OK'd By Committee," *Oregonian*, 24 April 1979.
595 Sandra McDonough, "Boe Promises Tax Limit Plan: On Residential Property," *Oregonian*, 28 April 1979.
596 Phil Cogswell, "Atiyeh Backs Plan Returning Relief Funds to Taxpayers," *Oregonian*, 4 May 1979.
597 Phil Cogswell, "Senate OKs $664 Million Tax Package," *Oregonian*, 5 May 1979.
598 Sue Hill, "Senate OKs Tax Relief Plan," *Salem Statesman Journal*, 5 May 1979.
599 Ron Blankenbaker, "New Tax Relief Package Should Be 'Veto-Proof'," Column, *Salem Oregon Statesman*, 1 June 1979; Sue Hill, "Legislature OKs Tax Relief Bill," *Salem Oregon Statesman*, 5 June 1979.

November 1980 voters.[600] Atiyeh declared that he would not veto the property-tax portion of the legislature's plan but would allow it to become law without his signature. He felt that the final plan's inability to limit future property tax increases was a mistake.[601] His claim that "he never really intended to use his veto power on the Legislature's tax relief package"[602] was viewed by some as a reaction to the veto-proof majority support in both houses. A week later, Speaker Myers and President Boe held their own signing ceremony for the property tax relief bill, "in lieu of the governor's signature and the accompanying fanfare of an official governor's bill signing ceremony," saying, "We felt a bill that returns $705 million [to taxpayers] really deserves some little ceremony."[603] Sixteen members of the legislature attended. On June 15 Atiyeh did sign both income-tax–relief bills.[604]

In May 1980, Oregonians voted 91% to 9% to continue the tax relief program.[605] Only five statewide measures before this had received higher support.[606]

Atiyeh's property tax plan did not get enough signatures to appear on the 1980 ballot. Proponents of the 1% property tax measure, conveniently given the name Measure 6 by the secretary of state's office, called in Howard Jarvis, the originator of

---

600 Hill, "Legislature OKs Tax Relief Bill," 8A.
601 Cogswell, "Conferees Draft State Tax Relief Package."; Phil Cogswell, "Legislature Votes $705 Million Tax Cut," *Oregonian*, 5 June 1979; *Oregonian*, "Atiyeh May Sign Tax Relief Measures by Friday," Legislative Notebook, 6 June 1979.
602 Ron Blankenbaker, "Monday's Tax Bill Vote Was Low-Key Excitement," Column, *Salem Oregon Statesman*, 5 June 1979.
603 Ron Blankenbaker, "Slow Day at Legislature Ho Hums: Tax Bill Signed With Little Fanfare," Column, *Salem Oregon Statesman*, 12 June 1979; *Oregonian*, "Solons Hold Bill-Signing," 12 June 1979.
604 Phil Cogswell, "$705 Million In Tax Relief Result of Six-Month Effort," *Oregonian*, 16 June 1979; AP, "Atiyeh Signs Tax-Relief Plan Without Fanfare," *Corvallis (OR) Gazette-Times*, 16 June 1979, Atiyeh Collection, Pac. Univ. Archives; UPI, "Atiyeh Signs Two Parts of Tax Bill," *Klamath Falls (OR) Herald and News*, 17 June 1979, Atiyeh Collection, Pac. Univ. Archives.
605 *Oregon Blue Book, 1981–1982*, (Salem, OR: Oregon Secretary of State, 1981), 334.
606 *Oregonian*, "Tax Revolt Express Passed by Politicians," Editorial, 26 May 1980.

California's Proposition 13 to rally voters just before the November 1980 election.[607] It did no good. The measure was defeated 64% to 36%.[608] There would be more efforts to limit property taxes, but recessions would dominate Oregon's tax and budget discussions for several years. Eventually, after property-tax initiative elections in 1982, 1984, and 1986, Measure 5 in 1990 would finally succeed in setting property tax limits, with a maximum rate of 1.5%, the level tax opponents had been predominantly calling for during the previous twenty-five years.

The longest-lasting artifact from the 1979 tax relief effort remains the so-called kicker. Its genesis was from Senate President Jason Boe, and it first appeared as part of Measure 11 put together by the legislative special session in September 1978.[609] A minor part of the proposals, the kicker was thrown into the mix to prevent inflation from artificially driving up state tax receipts, thus giving the government more money to spend than it had planned on. The concept was to create a permanent solution to tax surpluses—if they were over 2% of the projected tax income, then the entire surplus was to be returned to taxpayers. When Atiyeh became governor, it was apparent that there were hundreds of millions of dollars more than what the state needed for its programs. Atiyeh made the argument that much of this excess was simply because taxed wages had risen to match inflation. The surplus in tax collection did not mean that people were over-taxed. The rates did not change, there were no hidden taxes that took more from taxpayers. The surplus came from the difference between what it took to run government and the amount of tax the state brought in.

It was, and continues to be, a budgeting and forecasting artifact. The big debate about the money was always between those who argued that government would create new programs

---

607 *Statesman-Journal* (Salem), "You Win If 6 Wins," Advertisement, 3 November 1980.
608 *Oregon Blue Book, 1981*, 334.
609 Bill Grannell, Written questions and answers to Jim Moore, "Questions about the Kicker," 25 July 2017.

and spend every penny it got, regardless of the actual need for new programs, those who argued that extra income ought to be put away for the proverbial rainy day, or put into programs that were chronically underfunded, and those who called for the surplus to be returned to taxpayers.

Atiyeh was positive in 1993 about the kicker as he remembered when it occurred for the first time in 1985, to return the 2% overestimation of tax revenues: "This was good news as far as I was concerned."[610] He remained adamant that rainy day funds were just temptation for a legislature to spend more money. In 1998 he said, "I think it's a tragedy to [spend more money], I really do. [The budget funds can do] one of two things. You use it because it's essential to be used for state government, or, if you've got too much, you give it back to the taxpayer, because you start over in two years again, only two years away."[611] Reflecting on the ongoing debate in Oregon politics about the kicker versus creating a rainy day fund, Atiyeh mused at the time, "Apparently that's too simple an answer. Anyway, that's how I feel."[612] Since 1985, some form of kicker has been triggered in most of the passing biennia. Oregon voters put the kicker into the constitution in 2000 but sending checks directly to taxpayers was ended in 2011, saving over $1 million in postage and printing costs.[613] Over time, Atiyeh came to see the kicker become an entitlement, not a matter of good sense or generosity. In 2013, he said, "It loses the flavor" of what it meant in the late 1970s.[614]

A Welcoming Worldview

---

610 Victor Atiyeh, "Tape 47," 468.
611 Victor Atiyeh, interviewed by Clark Hansen, "Tape 63," Oral history, recorded by Oregon Historical Society, Portland, OR, 11 June 1998. Transcript, 10, Atiyeh Collection, Pac. Univ. Archives.
612 Victor Atiyeh, "Tape 63," 10.
613 Michelle Brence, "The 'Kicker': Oregon's Unique Law and How It's Changed," *Portland OregonLive*, 25 August 2015, http://www.oregonlive.com.
614 Victor Atiyeh, "Atiyeh interview #1," 9.

As governor, Atiyeh was in the position to act on some of his ideals, worldviews that dated back to his childhood. Growing up in northeast Portland, he had been in the middle of a virtual smorgasbord of people from many parts of the world. The young Arab American lived on a street with German Americans, Swedish Americans, Finnish American, Polish Americans, Japanese Americans and went to school with Black Americans and many other ethnic groups. And, in Atiyeh's thinking, none of these neighbors were Ethnic Americans; they were just plain old Americans. His election as governor had been celebrated by Arab Americans, and he had been on the cover of a Los Angeles monthly for Arab Americans.[615] But the governor, who never was viewed as an Arab by his constituents, was navigating volatile terrain in those days of the Iranian Revolution, higher gasoline prices, and his moves to create more state outreach to minority communities. And there was not even an acknowledgment of the distinctions between Iranian/Persian and Arab heritage.

Out of this came the Governor's Commission on Black Affairs and the Governor's Commission on Hispanic Affairs, both created by executive order in September 1980, after the legislature failed to establish them.[616] The 1983 legislature passed bills that provided money to hire directors for both commissions and gave them a more secure footing in state government—no subsequent governor could simply end the commission by executive order.[617] Both commissions continue their work to this day.[618]

While observing the governors who came before him, Atiyeh had decided that he would institute a new way to keep up with the concerns of Oregonians across the state. A big part of this was

---

615 "Victor Atiyeh: Governor of Oregon," Cover photo, *Los Angeles The News Circle: Monthly on Arab American Affairs*, January 1979, Atiyeh Collection, Pac. Univ. Archives.

616 *Oregon Blue Book, 1981*, 100; AP, "Minority Commissions Formed," *Salem (OR) Statesman-Journal*, 10 October 1980; George Rede, "Atiyeh to Form Commissions for Blacks, Spanish-Speaking," *Salem (OR) Statesman-Journal*, 5 September 1980.

617 AP, "Arbor Week Becomes Law," *Salem (OR) Statesman-Journal*, 4 June 1983; *Oregon Blue Book, 1985–1986*, (Salem, OR: Oregon Secretary of State, 1985), 127.

618 *Oregon Blue Book, 2017*, 33.

bolstering the ombudsman's office. His choice of former Salem NAACP chair Jackie Winters for the job had signaled that he wanted competence, as well as an office that women and minorities felt would take their concerns seriously.[619] When her appointment was announced, Winters was described as the "listening post for public complaints against government."[620] Under Atiyeh the ombudsman, later called the Citizens' Representative, had a wide set of responsibilities: investigate "any administrative action of any state agency" if there were complaints; "submit constructive criticism" to state agencies with ideas for changing procedures; "identifying patterns or clusters of problems"; work so that individuals have priority in state actions; help the governor to prioritize citizen concerns.[621] Winters pointed out in 2014 that it was rare before Atiyeh for the ombudsman to actually develop programs in response to findings out of that office. "With Vic, it was not only did you investigate to identify the problems, but then it was the next step."[622]

During the 1978 campaign, candidate Atiyeh announced that he would set up "informal 'listening posts'" across the state to meet "periodically on an informal basis to 'talk about things in their community.'"[623] The governor's staff would attend these gatherings and then report back to him the concerns from across the state. These statewide listening posts would connect to the governor through the office of the ombudsman. In Atiyeh's inaugural he promised to "establish listening posts in every county of the state, from the towns of Eastern Oregon to the

---

[619] Calvin O. L. Henry, "Winters Appointment as Ombudsman Pleasing," Column, *Salem (OR) Statesman Journal*, 24 December 1978.

[620] *Oregon Statesman* (Salem), "Atiyeh Selects New Administration Members," 14 December 1978.

[621] Georgena Carrow et al., "Citizens' Representative Final Report, 1979–1986," Office of the Governor, State of Oregon, (1986), Authority/Responsibilities: Authority, Atiyeh Collection, Pac. Univ. Archives.

[622] Dave Miller, Gerry Thompson, Jackie Winters, and Ted Kulongoski, "Oregon Remembers Former Governor Vic Atiyeh," Live interview, recorded by Think Out Loud, KOPB radio, Salem, OR, 3 September 2014. MP3, 4:00.

[623] *Oregon Statesman* (Salem), "Atiyeh to Set Up 'Listening Posts' If Elected," 12 October 1978.

districts of our cities, where people can gather together as often as they need to express their concerns to people who will talk directly to me. ...I will listen to all."[624]

Officially called the Listening Post Program, the idea was directly connected to Atiyeh's principle that government that is closest to the people is best. Within the ombudsman's office this was expressed as, "Government makes better decisions when it has the most information from the most people."[625] There were several formats over the eight years, with the Listening Post Program starting out as "tri-annual television presentation[s] discussing one or more major state issues of the day." Communities were polled for responses to the presentations with the results reported to the governor. A director from each county also made monthly reports to the governor on local concerns and issues. This system brought issues to the governor that he would otherwise have been unaware of, but it was not working as well as it could. Within two years, the program had grown so that there were fifty people designated as "Listening Post Representatives working in all 36 Oregon counties, representing 46 urban and rural communities."[626] These ears in the field wrote letters, placed

---

624 Victor Atiyeh, "Inaugural Address," 3.
625 Carrow, et al., "Citizens' Representative Final Report, 1979–1986," Special Programs: Listening Post.
626 Carrow, et al., "Citizens' Representative Final Report, 1979–1986," Special Programs: Listening Post; Denny Miles, "Son of Everything," Office of the Governor, State of Oregon, Executive Appointments; Lobby; Government; Congressional Delegation; Special Sessions; State Agency Heads; Toll-Free Numbers; Legislature; Standard Operating Procedures; State Agency Phone Lists, (1985), Affirmative Action and Labor Statistics, April 1981, 7, Atiyeh Collection, Pac. Univ. Archives.

telephone calls, and filed monthly reports from to keep the governor's office up to date on local issues.

The ombudsman's office became the headquarters of another program with lasting impact for the people of Oregon. In Atiyeh's first year, Congress changed the formula for food stamp eligibility. When the governor's office began fielding complaints about hunger, Atiyeh turned to his ombudsman, and said, "Jackie, we can't wait for Congress to correct this thing, we've got to do something right away."[627] By April 1979 Winters was formulating a solution.[628] From this problem came Oregon Food Share. The plan to make it all happen was Winters'. In a 2013 interview, Atiyeh said, "I get credit for it. Jackie did it. I keep telling them Jackie did that."[629]

Oregon Food Share launched on June 15, 1979, an expression of Atiyeh's belief that volunteerism was a crucial part of society and that the ombudsman's office would point to problems that he would otherwise not know about. The volunteer program was a way to finesse assistance from state agencies and from federal programs. Jackie Winters made it clear to those in attendance, "'The natural answer'—more state assistance—would not work because people would then receive less federal assistance."[630] As Congress was fixing the trouble it had caused in states across the country, Oregon Food Share "collected over 50,000 lbs of food for distribution."[631] Highlighting the program during the recession times, Atiyeh cited the "more than 6-million pounds of food and in excess of 60-thousand volunteer hours" donated to Oregon

---

627 Victor Atiyeh, interviewed by Clark Hansen, "Tape 58, side 2," Oral history, recorded by Oregon Historical Society, Portland, OR, 3 September 1993. Transcript, 29, Atiyeh Collection, Pac. Univ. Archives; See also, Victor Atiyeh, "Tape 62," 7.

628 Julie Tripp, "Food Drive Formulated to Offset Program Cuts," *Oregonian*, 5 June 1979.

629 Victor Atiyeh, interviewed by Pat Amedeo, "Arlington Club Oral History," Portland, OR, 10 September 2013, 53.

630 Dori Maynard, "Oregon Food Share Launched At Capitol," *Salem Statesman Journal*, 16 June 1979.

631 Georgena Carrow, "Ombudsman Report," Office of the Governor, State of Oregon, Summary report of 1979–1986, (1986), 7, Atiyeh Collection, Pac. Univ. Archives.

Food Share from July 1982 to June 1983.[632] By mid-1983, the organization had changed its name to the Oregon Food Bank, and it continues its work to this day.

The Accomplishments before the Storm

In an interview summing up Atiyeh's first year in office, the first line of the story was, "If it ain't broke, don't try to fix it."[633] Atiyeh's observation that his role was to make sense of all the policy ideas and laws from the McCall years was clearly referenced in the article.

"It was a year of evaluation and study as the governor and his staff decided what needed fixing and what didn't. It was a year in which the state developed a go-slow, hold-the-line approach to governing after two decades of rapid development and growing sophistication in government programs."[634]

Atiyeh, as a crucial part of the legislature during those times of great change, knew what he wanted to focus on. He was connected to the state agencies through their directors' participation in weekly cabinet meetings. Secretary of State Norma Paulus (R) observed, "He's making state government work better. One of the reasons you don't hear much about him is because things are working well on the inside. The internal workings of government are much better than when (former Gov. Bob) Straub was here."[635]

A first-year analysis by Jim Russell, on the governor's staff, remarked, "Agencies are working better together. For example, Agriculture and Economic Development have resolved

---

632 Victor Atiyeh, "State of the State Address for 1984" (speech, Eugene/Springfield Chambers of Commerce, Springfield, OR, 11 January 1984), 3, Atiyeh collection, Pac. Univ. Archives.
633 Sandra McDonough, "Atiyeh Calls First Year as Governor 'Successful' Term of Study," *Oregonian*, 2 March 1980.
634 McDonough, "Atiyeh Calls First Year."
635 McDonough, "Atiyeh Calls First Year." Parentheses in original.

difficulties relating to overlapping authority in international trade matters."[636]

Atiyeh's January 1980 State of the State address emphasized his work on gasoline shortages, creating a "budget to match the people's wishes," and the regional power bill.[637] He was especially proud of "the surplus returned to the taxpayers and the indexing of income the fight the effects of inflation—the *first* lowering of income taxes in my 20-year participation in government."[638]

It had been a year "as challenging and rewarding as I had anticipated; and, more productive than I had expected."[639] He also extolled the rise in volunteerism, as well as his work in affirmative action, "the outstanding…performance of our ombudsman office, and the high quality of your department heads."[640]

Democrats were not as happy with the governor, calling for more activism in dealing with issues like the energy crisis. Speaker Hardy Myers rued Atiyeh's effort to qualify a property-tax limitation measure for the November 1980 ballot after all the work the governor and the legislature had done to reach agreement on tax relief.

Myers said, "Given the strong bipartisan support for the legislative proposal, I wish he had been willing to say, 'This is a good job,' and let it go at that."[641] And those denizens of the capitol, the reporters, did not buy into the concept of the media

---

636 Jim Russell, "The Atiyeh Administration After One Year," Office of the Governor, State of Oregon, Memo to Governor Atiyeh, Denny Miles, Larry Sturholm, (21 December 1979), 1, Memoranda and Reports, "Accomplishments," 1979, Atiyeh Collection, Pac. Univ. Archives.
637 Vic Atiyeh, "State of the State Address, with hand annotations" (speech, Washington County Public Affairs Forum, Marika's Restaurant, Beaverton, Oregon, 7 January 1980), 17, Atiyeh Collection, Pac. Univ. Archives.
638 Victor Atiyeh, "State of the State, 1980," 17. Italicized word is underlined in original.
639 Victor Atiyeh, "State of the State, 1980," 1.
640 Victor Atiyeh, "State of the State, 1980," 15–16, 17.
641 McDonough, "Atiyeh Calls First Year."

availabilities, with some thinking "the governor's office is unduly closed and secretive. ...They think Denny Miles, the governor's press secretary, is overly protective and defensive about Atiyeh."[642]

All of these assessments, positive and negative, would be put to the test beginning in 1980 as recessions began to batter Oregon. Atiyeh, who was looking at a focus on natural resources and "studying the future of the state Land Conservation and Development Commission" during the 1981 legislative session, would be faced with budget shortfalls, special sessions, triage decisions about state agencies and activities, and uncertainty about what the economic future of the state would be.

It would turn out to be a very different governorship from the one that started in 1979.

---

642 McDonough, "Atiyeh Calls First Year."

4 Balancing resources

When Vic Atiyeh became Oregon's governor in January 1979, the nation was focused on the problems of energy and the economy—and on oil in particular.[643]

The United States had balanced its consumption, production, and import of oil very precariously. Between 1967 and 1973, the United States had gone from being a net exporter of oil to being a net importer.[644] Eventually the Organization of Petroleum Exporting Countries (OPEC) was able to push oil prices up by a factor of 8 between during the two oil crises of 1973–74 and 1978.[645] Oregon was on the sidelines of these world energy issues. Oregon also lacked any refineries; all petroleum products were imported, mainly from Seattle-area facilities. The only options available to Oregon officials were on the consumer side.

---

643 See Joseph S. Nye, Jr., "Energy Nightmares," *Foreign Policy* 40 (1980). Nye's contemporaneous discussion of the ways that the economics of oil and great power politics had collided gives a nice sense of the ways energy was understood in the late 1970s.

644 Daniel Yergin, The *Prize: The Epic Quest for Oil, Money, and Power*, (New York: Simon and Schuster, 1991), 567–568; Pacific Northwest Electric Power Planning and Conservation Act, Pub. L. No. 96-501, S.885, 16 United States Code Chapter 12H (1994 and Supp. 1 1995) (1980), 81–82.

645 Yergin, *Prize*, 688. The price went from $14.95 in 1978 to $25.10 in 1979, or $56.52 in 2015 dollars to $87.05 in 2015 dollars.

In the Pacific Northwest there was a second energy source centered on the Columbia River. The Pacific Northwest led the country in reliance on hydroelectric power. In a coincidence that drove home the importance of managing the region's energy, the 1973 oil crisis price rise was the same year that the Columbia River system had a low-water year—the price of Northwest-produced electric energy was higher as well.[646] As Oregon's new governor in 1979, Atiyeh would step into the management of this complex system, and he would push major reforms in how the states and power-producing entities dealt with each other.[647] At the same time, because all the major political decisions about the oil markets and production were out of his hands. he guided the state through a crisis that he could have no significant impact on.

Hydropower in the Pacific Northwest

Portland, Oregon, had been an early adopter of electricity. In 1889, the first long-distance transmission of electricity in the world connected a generating plant at Willamette Falls in Oregon City with Portland. A burgeoning hydropower industry quickly followed, its main source being the Columbia River system of dams. The hydropower system succeeded in bringing cheap power to the region, but there was a complex combination of ownership interests (U.S. Army Corps of Engineers, Federal Bureau of Reclamation, Federal Department of Interior—shifting to the Department of Energy, a federal entity to market the power, private electricity producers, private utility providers, federal, state, and local regulations) all reliant on a river system with a mind of its own. If the water flowed well after a good winter, all the stakeholders were happy. If there was a drought in any place

---

646 Dulcy Mahar and Lynn Baker, *Power of the River: The Continuing Legacy of the Bonneville Power Administration in the Pacific Northwest*, (Washington, DC: Government Printing Office, 2012) PDF, 33.

647 "Oil Shortages: Report to Governor Atiyeh," Department of Energy, State of Oregon, (18 May 1979), 14–20, Atiyeh Collection, Pac. Univ. Archives. This shows the Department of Energy's take on the international and market situation for petroleum products at the time. Atiyeh based his policy decision on this document.

in the system, the allocation of scarce resources raised all sorts of conflicts, as well as the price of electricity.

The first dam in the modern system was Bonneville, about sixty miles up the Columbia from Portland. The dam, and its promise of plentiful electricity, was fully supported by Portland's government and business groups to help bring new manufacturing concerns to the area. Its completion in 1937–38 was capped with congressional passage of the Bonneville Project Act of 1937. This created the interstate Bonneville Power Administration (BPA—the power marketing agency) and gave specific frameworks for the ways that power was to be allocated. "Preference in the sale or marketing of federal power" was to be given to "public and cooperative utilities" over private utilities.[648] As electric utilities came into being to serve the Northwest's growing population, a pattern developed. Oregon was home to privately owned utilities; Washington was home to government-owned and cooperative utilities. There were exceptions, of course, but the pattern showed two different political and economic cultures. By the time Atiyeh was becoming governor in the late 1970s, the allocation of power between private and public utilities was like "dividing up pieces of the pie."[649]

With all the population growth in the region, as well as the economic growth that came with companies locating to the Pacific Northwest for cheaper power rates, a limit began to be seen to the hydropower utopia. The region was coming to grips with the end of surplus power. By the 1960s and 1970s there were plans to build hydro-thermal power plants—either coal-fired or nuclear—to make up the difference between the Columbia's potential and the region's forecast needs.[650] The first nuclear-based power was generated by a new facility at the federal

---

648 Mahar and Baker, *Power of the River*, 6.
649 Wayne Thompson, interviewed by Jim Moore, "Atiyeh interview," Portland, OR, 2 April 2015. Summary notes, 5; *Gazette-Times* (Corvallis), Reslicing Bonneville's Pie," Editorial, 16 December 1978, Atiyeh Collection, Pac. Univ. Archives.
650 Mahar and Baker, *Power of the River*, 7.

Hanford Site in 1966.[651] The idea for building completely new nuclear plants first hit the media in 1967.[652] The dam system fed into the delivery infrastructure (wires) for the entire region. New nuclear plants could just plug into that system. At the same time, nuclear generation systems were seen as a way to remove the vulnerability of the hydro system from some future congressional whim. There were also plans for coal-fired plants, the first of which would be in Centralia, Washington, and in Wyoming.[653]

All this change in the Northwest power system amounted to a regional energy crisis a full three years before the first OPEC-centric petroleum energy crisis. As of 1970, the *Oregonian* was reporting a forecast for "[a] power crisis, beginning in the winter of 1971–72, and reaching a precarious imbalance during the winter of 1976–77."[654] Regional population growth, regional economic growth, and the proliferation of ways to use electricity left planners with a set of conundrums. The BPA preference ensured that public utilities got their cheaper power. But as the hydro system was no longer able to provide electricity to all its customers, private utilities found themselves having to buy power from more expensive sources and invest in the more expensive hydro-thermal plants.[655]

When he became governor in 1967, Tom McCall had been a staunch supporter of the nuclear option.[656] He was strongly in favor of the private utilities that provided power to most of

---

651 Michael Blumm, "The Northwest's Hydroelective Heritage: Prologue to the Pacific Northwest Power Planning and Conservation Act," *Washingnton Law Review* 58 (1982): 221, LexisNexis Academic.

652 Wayne Thompson, "Atomic Power to Relieve Strain on Columbia River, Insure Future Growth of Northwest," *Oregonian*, 26 February 1967; Wayne Thompson, "Multi-Million Dollar Nuclear Plants to Fill Power Gap," *Oregonian*, 27 February 1967; Wayne Thompson, "Pacific Northwest Ushers in Era of Nuclear Power During High-Voltage year of 1967," *Oregonian*, 1 January 1968.

653 Wayne Thompson, "Speedup of Two Power Plants Announced by Planning Council," *Oregonian*, 27 June 1970.

654 Wayne Thompson, "Is There Really a Power Shortage Coming?" Column, *Oregonian*, 12 July 1970.

655 Roy Hemmingway, Phone call to Jim Moore, "Power Questions," 1 March 2016.

656 Brent Walth, *Fire at Eden's Gate: Tom McCall and The Oregon Story*, (Portland, OR: Oregon Historical Society Press, 1994), 332–333.

Oregon. As it became clear that the region faced an energy shortage, McCall opposed building new dams on the Columbia River system. He created an Oregon Energy Council in September 1973 consisting of himself, the House Speaker, the Senate President, and the minority leaders of both houses—Vic Atiyeh occupied the Senate minority seat. McCall advocated for alternative forms of energy—solar and wind—but nuclear power was clearly the option that he felt could best meet the energy demands of the region. Atiyeh would follow the same guidelines when he was governor—although nuclear power would be ruled out by the Three Mile Island disaster in March 1979. The second regional nuclear power plant was the Trojan facility, located on the Columbia River about forty miles downriver from Portland. Built by the private Portland General Electric utility company (PGE), construction started in 1968 and the plant went online in 1976. It raised all sorts of issues as it was being built, including a shortage of qualified workers and engineers.[657]

Governor Bob Straub was very concerned because utility rates were going up rapidly in the mid-1970s. Private utilities were losing access to Bonneville power and having to invest in hydrothermal plants to meet demand, mainly in nuclear plants. At the end of April 1976, Straub announced the creation of a state power authority known as the Domestic and Rural Power Authority (DRPA), an idea resulting from research conducted by Oregon environmental lobbyist Roy Hemmingway working on a special project for the Public Utility Commissioner.[658] By the mid-1970s sixty percent of Washington State's power customers got the preferential rates because they were served by public utilities.

---

657 Wayne Thompson, "Scientist Sees Crisis Near in Nuclear Sites," *Oregonian*, 6 June 1968; Wayne Thompson, "Manpower Shortage in Nuclear Field Forces Utilities to Open Schools," *Oregonian*, 25 September 1969; Wayne Thompson, "Scientist Stresses Dangers, Others Back Trojan Plant," *Oregonian*, 3 July 1970.

658 Charles K. Johnson, *Standing at the Water's Edge: Bob Straub's Battle for the Soul or Oregon,* (Corvallis: Oregon State University Press, 2012), 238–239; Melinda S. Eden, "Straub to Propose State Buy Power Directly from BPA," *Oregonian*, 28 April 1976; Wayne Thompson, "Straub Unveils Power Agency Plan," *Oregonian*, 29 April 1976; Roy Hemmingway, interviewed by Jim Moore, "Atiyeh Interview," Portland, OR, 20 January 2016. Summary notes, 6.

Only twenty-five percent of Oregon's customers got that rate. DRPA was set up to buy from BPA at the public-utility preferential rate then resell the power to Oregon utilities at that lower rate. The estimate was that Oregon ratepayers would have their electrical bills cut in half by the new arrangement.[659] The formation of DRPA became part of a larger political game, a bargaining chip with Congress over the creation of regional control of the Pacific Northwest's energy resources. As a state senator, Atiyeh opposed DRPA, but not the idea behind it.[660] However, Atiyeh eventually voted for the bill when it came up at the end of the 1977 legislative session.[661] As he recalled in the early 1990s, "I don't think the state can do things better than private enterprise could."[662]

In early January 1979, governor-elect Atiyeh made it clear that he was going to propose ideas to explore non-hydro, non–hydrothermal energy options: solar, ocean power, wind, and wood waste. Atiyeh said, "I'm so concerned about energy that I'll be coming back with a new program" in addition to the programs that already existed.[663] Shortly after his inauguration, Atiyeh told a meeting of the Northwest Public Power Association that he was looking for a regional solution to the electrical power issues, and that he was going to work to make the Oregon Department of Energy meet the expectations he had for it when it was created in 1975. "I am not personally satisfied that the (Energy) department I helped create is matching my goals for it."[664] On March 16,

---

659 "Bill's Author Sees Lower-Cost Power," *Oregonian*, 2 December 1976.
660 Wayne Thompson, interviewed by Jim Moore, "Atiyeh interview," Portland, OR, 2 April 2015. Summary notes, 5; See William (WS) Sanderson, "First Year Summary," Department of Energy, State of Oregon, (19 December 1979), 1, Memoranda and Reports, "Accomplishments," 1979, Atiyeh Collection, Pac. Univ. Archives. This memo asserts that Senator Atiyeh supported DRPA in 1975.
661 Stan Federman, "Senate Vote Approves State Power Authority," *Oregonian*, 29 June 1977; *Oregonian*, "Power Measure Worries Utilities," 29 June 1977.
662 Victor Atiyeh, interviewed by Clark Hansen, "Tape 27, side 1," Oral history, recorded by Oregon Historical Society, Portland, OR, 20 May 1993. Transcript, 763, Atiyeh Collection, Pac. Univ. Archives.
663 John Hayes, "Atiyeh Plans More Later on Energy," *Salem Oregon Statesman*, 5 January 1979, Atiyeh Collection, Pac. Univ. Archives.

1979, Governor Atiyeh announced his "New Energy Directions for Oregon" in a speech and a report to the legislature:[665]

> Oregon has enormous and virtually untapped natural resources to which we *must* turn if we are to achieve a higher degree of energy independence.... [B]y the adoption of far-sighted and innovative public policy Oregon has the most effective and comprehensive residential energy conservation program of any state in the nation.[666]

What really caught the eye of capitol observers was the emphasis on renewables.[667] Not only was an alternative energy commission proposed, but there would also be emphases on using waste products from the wood industry, more information for businesses about energy conservation, and a special task force to "explore ways to reduce Oregon's demand for gasoline."[668]

There were a lot of ideas in the air, and Atiyeh was working to create a system to capture those ideas and test them out for Oregon's energy future.[669] Atiyeh ended the speech with a call for concrete action by the legislature. "Energy *conserved* costs *six times less* than new energy. Energy derived from unconventional

---

664 Paul Manley, "Atiyeh Wants 'Efficient, Compact' Energy Program," *Portland Oregon Journal*, 17 January 1979, Atiyeh Collection, Pac. Univ. Archives.

665 Victor Atiyeh, "Speech on New Energy Directions for Oregon to the Oregon Legislature" (speech, Oregon Joint Legislative Session, Salem, OR, 16 March 1979), Atiyeh Collection, Pac. Univ. Archives; Sanderson, "First Year Summary," 1; Victor Atiyeh, "New Energy Directions for Oregon: Report Presented to a Joint Session of the Oregon Legislature," Office of the Governor, State of Oregon, (16 March 1979), Atiyeh Collection, Pac. Univ. Archives.

666 Sanderson, "First Year Summary," 1. Italicized words are underlined in the original.

667 Jacqui Banaszynski, "Atiyeh Asks $10 Million for Energy," *Eugene (OR) Register-Guard*, 16 March 1979, Atiyeh Collection, Pac. Univ. Archives.

668 Banaszynski, "Atiyeh Asks $10 Million for Energy."

669 Norm Smith, "Must Not Close Door to Any Energy Resources," Norm's Notes, Legislative Report, *Tigard (OR) Times*, 9 May 1979, Atiyeh Collection, Pac. Univ. Archives; *News-Tribune* (Eugene), "And Now, Stream Power," Editorial, 4 April 1979, Atiyeh Collection, Pac. Univ. Archives.

fuels *displaces* conventional energy needed for other important uses."[670]

The legislative leadership thought the Atiyeh plan had a good chance of making it through the legislature.[671] The chairs of the Senate and House Environment and Energy Committees were not as optimistic. Ed Fadeley, the Senate chair, said that not only were the proposals the same as Bob Straub's, they did not go far enough,[672] calling Atiyeh's proposals "highpriced hype."[673] And Nancie Fadeley, the House chair, thought that Atiyeh's proposals would actually slow down implementation of workable plans.[674] The other big issue facing the legislature in 1979 was tax relief, but by the end of March, there were those wondering where tax relief had gone—it seemed like energy was dominating the work of the state government.[675] By the end of the 1979 session, more than twenty energy bills had been passed by the legislature.[676]

Hydropower continued to be the linchpin for the Pacific Northwest's electric energy needs. The winter of 1978–79 would be dry, and the rains in the fall of 1979 would be lighter than usual. The flow of water in the Columbia system was at its lowest level since 1924, more than a decade before the creation of the Bonneville power system.[677]

---

670 Atiyeh, "New Energy Directions for Oregon," 18. Yes, that ought to be "one-sixth the cost of new energy." Italics are underlined in the original speech.
671 Bob Baum, "Legislative Leaders Predict Passage of Conservation Plan," *Corvallis (OR) Gazette-Times*, 17 March 1979, Atiyeh Collection, Pac. Univ. Archives.
672 Steven Smith, "Energy Plan Fares Poorly," *Eugene (OR) Register-Guard*, 17 March 1979, Atiyeh Collection, Pac. Univ. Archives.
673 Timothy Kenny, "Fadely [sic] Blisters Gov. Atiyeh's Proposal as 'Highpriced Hype'," *Ontario (OR) Argus Observer*, 19 March 1979, Atiyeh Collection, Pac. Univ. Archives.
674 Smith, "Energy Plan Fares Poorly."
675 Jack Zimmerman, "Name of Salem Game—Energy, Not Taxes," *North Bend (OR) News*, 29 March 1979, Atiyeh Collection, Pac. Univ. Archives; Jack Zimmerman, "Trojan Still Anti-Nuke Target," *Canyonville (OR) Canyon Creek Current*, 29 March 1979, Atiyeh Collection, Pac. Univ. Archives.
676 "Energy Measures Approved by the 1979 Oregon Legislature," Department of Energy, State of Oregon, (1979), Atiyeh Collection, Pac. Univ. Archives.
677 Sanderson, "First Year Summary," 13.

The 1980 Northwest Power Planning and Conservation Act epitomized the region's efforts to balance policies and policy implementation among all the governing and power-community entities, and Atiyeh led the way. "I really would take credit for it," he has said. "I don't do that very often."[678] He thought of the Northwest region as a lake of energy potential: "the lake would be Oregon, Washington, Idaho, and western Montana, and you can't lower one part of the lake" without lowering the entire lake level.[679] With this analogy guiding him, he sought to get the other parts of the lake—the states—to come together behind a regional energy plan that Congress could approve.

The big question for Atiyeh was what one state could do considering the regional projected energy shortages and the national energy shortage, which had been made clear by the second oil crisis in 1978. The Trojan nuclear power plant was up and fitfully running, and the Washington Public Power Supply System (WPPSS) nuclear plant construction delays were getting more and more attention. Atiyeh knew a regional solution was the best outcome, but he also knew that he needed to take action to reduce electricity rates for Oregon consumers. As governor-elect, he testified before the U.S. House Subcommittee on Power and Energy on the nascent Northwest Power Planning and Conservation Act.[680] The bill had been introduced in August 1978 by Senator Henry "Scoop" Jackson and Representative Lloyd Meeds, both from the Washington State delegation.[681] Testifying before the U.S. House hearings at the Portland Auditorium on the Act on December 13, 1978, Atiyeh said,

---

678 Victor Atiyeh, "Tape 27, side 1," 764.
679 Victor Atiyeh, "Tape 27, side 1," 764.
680 Sanderson, "First Year Summary," 1–2; Steven Smith, "NW Power Bill Facing Trouble: National Plan Instead?" *Eugene (OR) Register-Guard*, 15 December 1978, Google News archive.
681 Bernard Goldhammer and Gus Norwood, *Columbia River Power for the People: A History of Policies of the Bonneville Power Administration*, (Portland: Department of Energy, Bonneville Power Administration, 1981), 262–263.

Activation of DRPA could be a unilateral solution to Oregon's quest for an equitable share of the region's power at an equitable price. However, I hope that we do not have to activate DRPA. What is needed is a statesmanlike approach wherein parochial interests are foregone in order to attain a regional solution that accommodates all interests.[682]

The bill died at the end of the 95th Congress, but it would be back.[683] In mid-January 1979, now–Governor Atiyeh told a meeting of public power utilities he was "prepared to implement DRPA if necessary…to help Oregonians get an equitable share of the region's federal hydropower at an equitable price." But, he added, "in this context, a unilateral action is not in the best interests of the Pacific Northwest as a region."[684]

In March 1979, Atiyeh was directly administering the Oregon Department of Energy himself because the Oregon Senate had refused to confirm his appointee, Kelly Woods. He began to use DRPA as a specific bargaining tool by activating the Authority—the first steps to implementing DRPA provisions.[685] Congress was working on the Northwest Power Planning Act. Atiyeh let it be known that he would not begin DRPA unless Congress failed to act. He was a bit reticent to institute DRPA because it "might 'spook the other governors' in the Northwest while each awaits the outcome of" Congress's work.[686]

---

682 Victor Atiyeh, "Testimony Before the Energy and Power Subcommittee Hearing on the Pacific Northwest Regional Energy and Power Conservation Bill," Office of the Governor-elect, State of Oregon, (13 December 1978), 2, Atiyeh Collection, Pac. Univ. Archives; Sanderson, "First Year Summary," 2.
683 Goldhammer and Norwood, *Columbia River Power for the People*, 263.
684 Sanderson, "First Year Summary," 2. First ellipses in original.
685 AP, "Atiyeh Plays Ace for Lower Rates: State Would Pass on Cheap Power," *La Grande (OR) Observer*, 13 March 1979, Atiyeh Collection, Pac. Univ. Archives; *Herald and News* (Klamath Falls), "Oregon Plays Trump in Fight Over Power," Editorial, 16 March 1979, Atiyeh Collection, Pac. Univ. Archives.
686 UPI, "Atiyeh Begins Power Authority," *Ontario (OR) Argus Observer*, 13 March 1979, Atiyeh Collection, Pac. Univ. Archives.

By April 1979, the four governors were publicly coming together to push for their ideas in the regional energy bill.[687] Governor Dixy Ray of Washington had been a tough sell: the bill as it was being written would be the end of nuclear in the Northwest because of its emphasis on cheaper conservation methods. But Atiyeh made a trip to Ray at the Washington capitol and convinced her personally to go along with the plans.[688] The bill was reintroduced in the Senate for the new Congress, and Senator Jackson was again leading the way. Ten days after Jackson's bill was reintroduced, the four governors announced their big idea for the bill, the Northwest Electrical Energy Planning Council. They asked Jackson to include the idea as an amendment to the larger bill.[689]

Several constituencies were interested in the bill. Public power wanted to continue the public power preference from BPA. Aluminum companies wanted new contracts from BPA. And "the states wanted a hand in planning and greater conservation," Roy Hemmingway recalled.[690] The coalition kept falling apart during this process, mainly because public power would get "nervous, and [congressional bill-writers would] have to go back and write new amendments to satisfy public power," as happened three or four times during the lobbying on the legislation.

In the summer of 1979 Atiyeh offered amendments to Jackson's bill "which made the conservation and renewable resources provisions of the bill more effective, and which assured greater state participation in the decision making process."[691] Atiyeh's amendments were incorporated almost word for word into the bill. The bill passed the Senate in August 1979, but it

---

687 Les Blumenthal, "NW Energy Bill Reintroduced," *Astoria (OR) Astorian*, 6 April 1979, Atiyeh Collection, Pac. Univ. Archives; AP, "Atiyeh: NW Energy Bill Depends on 4 Governors," *Albany (OR) Democrat-Herald*, 6 April 1979, Atiyeh Collection, Pac. Univ. Archives.
688 Hemmingway, "Atiyeh Interview," 3–4.
689 AP, "Four Northwest Governors Back Energy Council," *Astoria (OR) Astorian*, 16 April 1979, Atiyeh Collection, Pac. Univ. Archives.
690 Hemmingway, "Atiyeh Interview," 2.
691 Sanderson, "First Year Summary," 8.

faced a much tougher road in the House, where Jim Weaver (D-Eugene) had proposed a somewhat more aggressive bill.[692] Through this entire process, "in the event the bill does not pass in 1980, the Governor is prepared to activate... DRPA ..., which would qualify the state as a preference customer by establishing a state-run utility."[693]

Leading up to early fall hearings on the bill in Portland, in a show of bipartisan firepower, Atiyeh was joined by his predecessors Bob Straub and Tom McCall in public support of the bill.[694] Given that McCall's gubernatorial predecessor, Mark Hatfield, was a staunch supporter of the bill as a U.S. Senator, that was a clean sweep of living ex-governors.

But the power bill languished in the House. In November, Atiyeh "turned over his hole card" and began the process of implementing DRPA.[695] There was a sense that this would push along the process in Congress, but it would also give Oregon realistic alternatives if the House failed to act by the end of the congressional session in December 1980. The key problem appeared to be lack of support for the bill by public utilities.[696] That being the case, Atiyeh's invocation of DRPA would create the largest public utility of them all in the region.

---

692 Goldhammer and Norwood, *Columbia River Power for the People*, 263. Oregon Representative Al Ullman had introduced an identical version to Jackson's Senate bill in April 1979. Jim Weaver introduced his own version in May 1979. Eventually a decision was reached by the House leadership to put off the issue until 1980.

693 Sanderson, "First Year Summary," 8.

694 AP, "Atiyeh, McCall, Straub Back Regional Power Bill," *Eugene (OR) Register-Guard*, 7 September 1979, Atiyeh Collection, Pac. Univ. Archives.

695 UPI, "Governor Seeks Hearings on State Power Agency," *The Dalles (OR) Chronicle*, 3 November 1979, Atiyeh Collection, Pac. Univ. Archives; Wire Service Reports, "Governor Starts Work on DRPA: Agency Might Ensure Low-Cost Power Supply," *Eugene (OR) Register-Guard*, 3 November 1979, Atiyeh Collection, Pac. Univ. Archives; AP, "Atiyeh Orders Bid for Cheap Power," *Albany (OR) Democrat-Herald*, 3 November 1979, Atiyeh Collection, Pac. Univ. Archives; *Herald and News* (Klamath Falls), "Atiyeh Turns Over His Hole Card," Editorial, 7 November 1979, Atiyeh Collection, Pac. Univ. Archives.

696 *Democrat-Herald* (Albany, OR), "Get Ready for a Power Fight," Editorial, 5 November 1979, Atiyeh Collection, Pac. Univ. Archives; *Columbian* (Vancouver, WA), "BPA Could Use Conservation Boost Now," Editorial, 8 November 1979, Atiyeh Collection, Pac. Univ. Archives.

In mid-March 1980, the U.S. House once again took up the Power Act. Now known as "Son of Scoop," the House version had been rewritten by Al Swift (D-WA), a member of the Energy and Power subcommittee on the House Commerce committee.[697] The bill kept the same ideas that were in the Senate version—a regional council, an emphasis on energy conservation, and protections for the region's authority to run the system. But Swift's new version added some provisions as well. Representative John Dingell (D-MI), head of the subcommittee, acted on lobbying by Hemmingway, at Atiyeh's request, and the fish protection provisions were strengthened.[698] The manipulation of the rivers' flows to maximize this storage had a huge impact on the fish populations. It was not just a matter of dams being barriers to fish passage; it was the changing of the seasonal flows of the river. Various fish species, for instance, had evolved to take advantage of each spring's high, fast water flows to move young fish to the sea. Under the power management system, much of that spring flow was used to fill reservoirs for summer electricity needs. Between the early 1900s and the late 1970s, the number of fish in the Columbia diminished from fifteen to twenty million to two and half million.[699] The dam system got the bulk of the blame —estimates were that eighty to ninety percent of the human impact on the salmon runs was because of the dams.

The biggest change in the House bill, however, was in the makeup of the regional power council—Swift proposed a proportional membership instead of two members from each state and the BPA administrator. This did not sit well with Atiyeh and the governors of Idaho and Montana. And none of Swift's rewriting brought Jim Weaver over to the supporters' side. It was unclear what he might do to stop the bill, but momentum was

---

697 Dick Johnston, "'Son of Scoop' New Power Bill," *Oregonian*, 16 March 1980, Atiyeh collection, Pac. Univ. Archives; Dick Johnston, "Power Bill Alive as House Panel OKs 'New' Text," *Oregonian*, 13 March 1980, Atiyeh collection, Pac. Univ. Archives.

698 Hemmingway, "Atiyeh Interview," 3.

699 Lorraine Bodi, "The History and Legislative Background of the Northwest Power Act," *Environmental Law* 25, no. 2 (1995): 365. HeinOnline.

back with the pro–Regional Planning Act group. Even with the movement in the U.S. House, DRPA planning went on in Oregon.[700] By mid-summer there were projections that DRPA could lower utility costs by 20–50% for many consumers.[701] At the end of May, Atiyeh and former governor Straub wrote a letter to Jim Weaver calling for "swift action on the regional power bill" in the House.[702] Atiyeh and Straub were worried that if the bill was not passed in the congressional session it might take another five years before it could come up again. DRPA was a plan, but a poor one in comparison to the regional solution the Congress could create.

Weaver responded to the news from Oregon by publicly stating his opposition to the bill and vowing to fight it.[703] None too pleased, Atiyeh released a statement: "After supposedly supporting the Northwest regional power bill, the Oregon congressman has finally shown his true colors. He has turned his back on 80% of the electrical consumers of Oregon who seek lower electrical rates."[704] Weaver knew that the bill would make it out of committee, but he hoped to offer amendments on the floor of the House to rectify what he saw as major problems with the bill—overstatement of the energy problem in the Northwest and too much control in the hands of private utilities.[705]

As Oregon's chief lobbyist for the Act, Roy Hemmingway recalled that Weaver "basically tried to filibuster the bill in the

---

700 AP, "DRPA Hearings to Be Resumed in Mid-Summer," *Eugene (OR) Register-Guard*, 7 May 1980, Atiyeh Collection, Pac. Univ. Archives.

701 Dan Postrel, "Home Electric Bills in State Could Drop 20 to 50 Percent," *Salem (OR) Statesman Journal*, 11 July 1980, Atiyeh collection, Pac. Univ. Archives.

702 UPI, "Power Bill Concerns Atiyeh," *Portland Oregon Journal*, 29 May 1980, Atiyeh collection, Pac. Univ. Archives.

703 UPI, "Weaver Says He'll Work Against Power Bill; Atiyeh Responds With Scathing Statement," *Ashland (OR) Daily Tidings*, 25 June 1980, Atiyeh collection, Pac. Univ. Archives; UPI, "Weaver to Fight Power Bill," *Oregon City (OR) Enterprise-Courier*, 25 June 1980, Atiyeh collection, Pac. Univ. Archives; Dick Johnston, "Weaver's Power-Bill Fight Loses Ground," *Oregonian*, 25 June 1980, Atiyeh collection, Pac. Univ. Archives.

704 UPI, "Weaver Says He'll Work Against Power Bill"; UPI, "Weaver to Fight Power Bill."

705 Johnston, "Weaver's Power-Bill Fight Loses Ground."

House," introducing somewhere around 100 different amendments, many of them to be dealt with on the floor of the House. There was not much support for Weaver's position among his colleagues in the House, but Weaver was trying to delay the bill until the session expired at the end of 1980.[706] Weaver's tactics actually made him "persona non grata" with the House leadership. Speaker of the House Tip O'Neill kept assuring Hemmingway, "Don't worry, we're going to get this through." It took until after the 1980 election for that to happen, but it did.

The November 1980 passage of an Oregon initiative requiring voter approval for all nuclear plant licenses moved the energy discussion along in Oregon.[707] Atiyeh's new plans were based on the work of the Alternative Energy Development Commission, a temporary group that he created with the legislature. He proposed $144 million in energy programs to be taken up by the 1981 legislature.[708] The focus was on conservation programs, on changing consumer behavior through weatherization programs, and tax credits and energy project loans for small businesses and consumers. If Oregon could not build the power plants to create more electricity, then Atiyeh's program would guide Oregonians to use less energy, thus bringing supply and demand into better balance. The new director of the Department of Energy, Lynn Frank, said that the plan "could conserve or generate energy equal to 10 percent of expected growth in the state's non-transportation energy needs through the year 2000."[709] There were also proposals to explore other forms of energy—geothermal, wind, and solar were prominent.[710]

---

706 Hemmingway, "Atiyeh Interview," 1–2.
707 Measure 7, *Oregon Blue Book: Almanac and Fact Book, 2015–2016*, (Salem, OR: Oregon Secretary of State, 2015), 302.
708 George Rede, "Atiyeh's Energy Program Has a Little of Everything," *Salem (OR) Statesman Journal*, 21 November 1980, Atiyeh collection, Pac. Univ. Archives.
709 Rede, "Atiyeh's Energy Program Has a Little of Everything."
710 *Register-Guard* (Eugene, OR), "Plotting Oregon's Energy Future," Editorial, 15 November 1980, Atiyeh collection, Pac. Univ. Archives; *Herald and News* (Klamath Falls, OR), "Geothermal Potential Tallied," 11 November 1980, Atiyeh collection, Pac. Univ. Archives.

The Pacific Northwest Power Planning and Conservation Act finally passed the House on November 17, 1980, in a lame duck session after Reagan had defeated Carter for the presidency. The Senate quickly agreed two days later, and President Carter signed the bill into law on December 5.[711] The final version of the new law included "a requirement that bpa seek energy conservation first, renewable resources second, efficient power such as cogeneration third, and thermal power from oil, gas, or nuclear plants only if the others proved insufficient."[712] The emphasis on conservation as the dominant way to make the power system reach more customers was an unproven idea, but it was an idea that made sense in the energy world of the late 1970s. Looming over all this was the second oil crisis of 1978–1979, the jump in the price of gasoline, and how new types of cars that got better mileage were a solution that industry and consumers were buying into.

The second part of the law was the creation of the Northwest Electric Power and Conservation Council. Each of the four states in the region would have two members on the council appointed by the governors. The job of the council would be to draft "a power plan for the region as well as a fish and wildlife program."[713] The idea was to create an organization that could express the will of the four states and work with the federal government (especially BPA) to manage the region's power in the best possible way.

A big part of the regional act was making fisheries policies an explicit part of the management of the river system. The idea came out of Atiyeh's office from Hemmingway, was endorsed by Atiyeh, and championed by Dingell.[714] Before this, fish runs had always been a secondary concern in the management of the Columbia system for power.

---

711 Goldhammer and Norwood, *Columbia River Power for the People*, 305.
712 Mahar and Baker, *Power of the River*, 9.
713 Mahar and Baker, *Power of the River*, 10.
714 Victor Atiyeh, "Tape 27, side 1," 765–766; "Resource Management," Office of the Governor, State of Oregon, (May 1986), 1–2, "Accomplishments and Goals, 1979–1986," Atiyeh Collection, Pac. Univ. Archives.

Atiyeh's idea about how the Northwest Power and Conservation Council would bring the region's governments into the decisions about power issues and the shared management of the region's fish and wildlife came true. There have been lots of victories and defeats for the various stakeholders, but they have an agreed upon system to solve their differences, a system that Vic Atiyeh was instrumental in creating.

Energy Crises—Oil and Nuclear

Reviewing Atiyeh's first year in office, the Salem *Statesman Journal* editorial board was impressed with Atiyeh's success in pushing energy ideas, but it was because he had convinced gasoline distributors to voluntarily work to prevent the gas lines that had been so common in the 1973–74 oil crisis.[715] The governor himself agreed. After five months in office, Atiyeh listed his actions on the gasoline crisis among his most important accomplishments.[716]

The Atiyeh Plan, revealed in March 1979, had three phases. If Phase I did not help with the petroleum-product shortage, then Phase II would be implemented, and if that did not work, on to Phase III. Phase I was implemented in March 1979 and was the first statewide plan to be submitted to the federal Department of Energy.[717] The plan called for voluntary reductions in miles driven by Oregon drivers, and it also created a State Set-Aside program through the Department of Energy "to relieve spot shortages and to serve priority users through emergency allocations of gasoline and diesel from the set-aside" stores.[718] The voluntary reductions

---

715 Judy Van Rest, "Victor Atiyeh: Charting a Course for Oregon's Energy Future," Editorial, republished from *Salem Statesman Journal*, 6 January 1980, *First Monday*, March 1980, Atiyeh Collection, Pac. Univ. Archives.

716 "First Two Hundred Days of the Atiyeh Administration," Office of the Governor, State of Oregon, Annotated by Atiyeh, (July 1979), 2, Atiyeh Collection, Pac. Univ. Archives.

717 Sanderson, "First Year Summary," 3.

718 Lynn Frank, "Contingency Planning Briefing Paper," Memo to Governor Atiyeh, Department of Energy, State of Oregon, (14 November 1979), 2, Atiyeh Collection, Pac. Univ. Archives; *Outlook* (Gresham, OR), "Atiyeh: U.S. Has Itself to Blame for

worked: gasoline consumption was down over the previous year by anywhere from 4% to 8% month by month. During the high-demand summer driving season, usage was 6.6% lower than 1978, an amount that "more than cancels out demand growth."[719] The director of the Department of Energy attributed half of the reduction in vehicle fuel use to conservation, not just a slow-down in the economy.[720] Atiyeh made it clear in May 1979 that a repeat of the odd-even plan (phase II in the Atiyeh Plan) from the McCall era would not be necessary.[721] A similar phased approach was ready for the winter for heating oil and diesel.[722] The key to all this was voluntary participation.

But in June 1979 Atiyeh faced a blockade of many gas stations around Oregon by truckers. "They were concerned that they were not priority users in rationing of diesel fuels."[723] Atiyeh met with the truckers' representatives on June 14 and subsequently called Senator Hatfield. By June 18 there were hearings on Capitol Hill with truckers from all over the country. The issue was a federal one, but when it bubbled up in Oregon, Atiyeh was able to listen to the issues, figure out who could solve them in DC, and help get the process started. Natural resources aide Pat Amedeo wrote, "As a result of this request and I am sure, others, transportation was declared a priority user and was served as an emergency user."[724]

In July 1979, President Carter called for more energy production within the boundaries of the United States, especially

---

Energy Mess," 4 December 1979, Atiyeh Collection, Pac. Univ. Archives.
719 Frank, "Contingency Planning Briefing Paper," 2.
720 Lynn Frank, "Gasoline Conservation/National Standby Rationing Plan," Memo to Legislative Emergency Board, Department of Energy, State of Oregon, (21 December 1979), 4, Atiyeh Collection, Pac. Univ. Archives.
721 UPI, "Atiyeh: Odd-Even Plan Not Needed in Oregon—Found Okay by Most Governors," *Coos Bay (OR) World*, 31 May 1979, Atiyeh Collection, Pac. Univ. Archives.
722 Frank, "Contingency Planning Briefing Paper," 2–4.
723 Pat Amedeo, "First Year Report," Office of the Governor, State of Oregon, Memo to Denny Miles, Governor Atiyeh, Lee Johnson, Larry Sturholm, (17 December 1979), 4, Memoranda and Reports, "Accomplishments," 1979, Atiyeh Collection, Pac. Univ. Archives.
724 Amedeo, "First Year Report," 5.

heavy oil, natural gas, and nuclear power. The ten-year $140 billion investment in making the United States less dependent on foreign oil would be largely paid for by a windfall profits tax on oil companies.[725] Along with other Oregon political leaders, Atiyeh saw some things to like in the president's ideas, but the lack of details made him reticent to wholeheartedly embrace Carter's plans.[726] Carter's Secretary of Energy, Jim Schlesinger, noted in August 1979 that Atiyeh "exercised the states' discretionary relief authority" to limit the rise in price gas stations could charge at the pump.[727] Later that summer, Atiyeh filled his car with gasohol, one of the alternative fuels being touted to wean Americans off fossil fuels.[728] In January 1980, Atiyeh went one step further with alcohol-based fuel ideas. He had just returned from his second international trip as governor, this one to Costa Rica. He was impressed by the small power generating ideas he saw in the country. Atiyeh told a reporter that he would be open to small stills as part of an alternative energy plan, a way to bring the gasohol idea to a much more local level.[729]

Atiyeh met with President Carter and his advisors in November 1979 for a briefing on the impacts of the growing Iranian crisis and what it might mean to petroleum supplies.[730] Eleven days

---

725 Terence Smith, "President Urges $140 Billion to Ensure Energy Autonomy; Terms Nuclear Power Vital," *New York Times*, 17 July 1979.
726 UPI, "What Did State Leaders Think?" *Springfield (OR) News*, 17 July 1979, Atiyeh Collection, Pac. Univ. Archives.
727 Jim Schlesinger, "Memorandum for: The President; Weekly Activity Report, August 4–10 1979," Jimmy Carter Presidential Archives, United States Government, Office of the Staff Secretary, Presidential Files; Folder 8/14/79; Container 127, (10 August 1979). http://www.jimmycarterlibrary.gov.
728 AP, "Atiyeh Fills His Tank with 99.9-Cent Gasohol," *Pendleton East Oregonian*, 22 August 1979, Atiyeh Collection, Pac. Univ. Archives.
729 UPI, "Atiyeh Won't Rule Out Small Alcohol Stills," *Ashland (OR) Daily Tidings*, 29 January 1980, Atiyeh Collection, Pac. Univ. Archives.
730 Victor Atiyeh, "Handwritten Notes on White House Meetings on Iranian Oil Shortages," (15, 16 November 1979), Atiyeh Collection, Pac. Univ. Archives. Amedeo, "Atiyeh interview," 8; Jack Watson and Stu Eizenstat, "Memorandum for the President: Meeting with the Governors on Iranian Situation, November 16, 1979 1:00–1:30 p.m. East Room," Jimmy Carter Presidential Archives, United States Government, Office of Staff Secretary, Presidential Files, Folder 11/16/79 [2], Container 139, (15 November 1979). http://www.jimmycarterlibrary.gov.

earlier, on November 4, 1979, Iranian students stormed the U.S. Embassy in Tehran, taking hostages who would be held for 444 days, until the day that Ronald Reagan took the presidential oath of office in January 1981. The White House meeting stressed ideas that Atiyeh had advocated back in Oregon: if people drove fewer than three miles a day, that would be adequate conservation to avoid shortages; an enforced 55 mile-per-hour speed limit would save 100,000 barrels of oil per day; if governments saved 6–10% (with 50% compliance), that would save 60,000 barrels a day. Atiyeh's note to himself was, "Tell us what to save—let us do job."[731] His principle of the best government being the one closest to the people was guiding his thinking—each state could best decide for itself which conservation measures would be most effective. In an overview of the meeting, Atiyeh wrote,

> Management of Iranian oil cut-off shortage is within the relatively easy ability of this country. This situation, however, only sharply brings into focus the terrible exposure of this country by its dependence on foreign oil energy [for] gasoline or electricity....
>
> However, the administration seems only deeply committed to the necessary but short-term action of conservation and some conversion of oil-fired utilities to coal. There still does not seem to be any deep-seated determination to move as aggressively into other sources of energy—oil shale, coal & nuclear. Conservation *can* be accomplished by Americans—it *will not* solve the long-term problem, and each day we wait will make that solution one day further out into the future (we have already lost too many "one days").[732]

Atiyeh clearly saw a national government that was responding to energy as a crisis, not as a long-term issue that would require

---

731 Atiyeh, "Handwritten Notes on White House Meetings on Iranian Oil Shortages."
732 Atiyeh, "Handwritten Notes on White House Meetings on Iranian Oil Shortages." Italics are underlined in original. Minor changes made for syntax.

long-term planning and changes in the ways the energy markets functioned in the United States.

Nuclear energy was another one of the main energy issues in 1979. There were the struggles to get the Trojan plant on the Columbia River to perform up to standards—without long and costly shutdowns for repairs. There was a strong move to grant permission for a second Oregon nuclear-power facility, Pebble Springs. Then, on March 28, 1979, the Three Mile Island disaster in Pennsylvania put nuclear safety at the center of everyone's agenda.

Oregon's history with nuclear power had been fitful. PGE began building Trojan along the Columbia River in 1968. The same year, Eugene voters approved a $225 million bond for the Eugene Water and Electric Board to construct a nuclear power plant along the Oregon coast near Florence.[733] Two years later Eugene voters passed a four-year moratorium on any nuclear projects. At about the same time, a group of utilities began moving forward with the Pebble Springs project, to be located east of Bend in the high desert. In 1976 Oregon voters defeated a measure to further regulate the construction of nuclear power plants.[734] The defeat occurred partly because people were concerned about limiting options for future hydro-thermal plants in the region.[735] For his part, Atiyeh made it clear that he was going to explore the nuclear options thoroughly through his appointments of people who had expertise in nuclear power and who did not automatically rule out the plants.

The Three Mile Island disaster hit amid debate about adding Pebble Springs to the region's hydro-thermo mix, amid concerns

---

733 Joshua Binus, "EWEB Is On the Coast to Stay!," in *Oregon History Project*, (Portland, OR: Oregon Historical Society, 2004). http://oregonhistoryproject.org; Daniel Pope, "Anti-Nuclear Movement," in *Oregon Encyclopedia*, (Portland, OR: Oregon Historical Society). http://oregonencyclopedia.org.

734 *Oregon Blue Book, 1977–1978*, (Salem, OR: Oregon Secretary of State, 1977), 270.

735 *Oregonian*, "Vital Measures Recommended," Editorial, 1 November 1976; Steven Carter, "N-Power Backers Sip Champagne: Foes Stick to Coke," *Oregonian*, 3 November 1976.

about where to put nuclear waste, and amid larger discussions about the Northwest Power Plan and conservation. Atiyeh immediately called to reopen hearings on the safety of the Pebble Springs design.[736] A comparison of Three Mile Island's coolant system and the proposed Pebble Spring coolant system was on everybody's mind. Oregon's nuclear experts were "amazed" by the accident.[737] In April the Senate quickly passed a bill that called for a moratorium on any final decisions on Pebble Springs for at least a year, pending studies by the State Department of Energy.[738]

Atiyeh himself had the same ambivalence about nuclear power plants. In the early 1990s he recalled that "nuclear power plants are a good source of energy," but that the failure of the federal government to come up with nuclear waste disposal systems as well as the increased safety requirements for new plants after Three Mile Island just made nuclear energy an option that no longer made sense.[739] Atiyeh was also exasperated because the federal government preempted any state ideas on what to do with nuclear waste. Toward the end of Atiyeh's two terms in office, this irritation was very apparent in the dealings that Washington and Oregon had with federal agencies over issues at the Hanford Reservation.[740] In a 1986 letter to Mark Hatfield, Atiyeh made it

---

736 Wire Service Reports, "Mishap to Affect Pebble Springs? Atiyeh Urges Hearings," *Eugene (OR) Register-Guard*, 30 March 1979, Atiyeh Collection, Pac. Univ. Archives; AP, "N-Safeguards: Atiyeh Wants Hearings Reopened," *Albany (OR) Democrat-Herald*, 30 March 1979, Atiyeh Collection, Pac. Univ. Archives; UPI, "News on Reactor Captures Attention at Oregon Capital," *Ashland (OR) Daily Tidings*, 31 March 1979, Atiyeh Collection, Pac. Univ. Archives.

737 Ronald J. Schleyer, "Mishap 'Amazes' Nuclear Expert," *Corvallis (OR) Gazette-Times*, 2 April 1979, Atiyeh Collection, Pac. Univ. Archives.

738 UPI, "Three Ask for Poll on Pebble Springs," *Eugene (OR) Register-Guard*, 20 April 1979, Atiyeh Collection, Pac. Univ. Archives.

739 Victor Atiyeh, "Tape 28," 817.

740 See Lynn Frank, "Staff Update," Department of Energy, State of Oregon, Hanford Studies, (19 August 1985), Atiyeh Collection, Pac. Univ. Archives; Lynn Frank, "Washington Lawsuit on Hanford Repository," Department of Energy, State of Oregon, Memo to Governor Atiyeh and Pat Amedeo, (30 May 1986), Atiyeh Collection, Pac. Univ. Archives; "Atiyeh Daily Index-Card Schedule, June 2, 1986," Office of the Governor, State of Oregon, (2 June 1986), Lynn Frank, Pat & Gerry; regarding Hanford, Atiyeh Collection, Pac. Univ. Archives; "Oregon's Involvement in the Storage, Transport, and Disposal of High-Level Radioactive

clear that he had been "comfortable with the clear and detailed decision process mandated by Congress in 1982. But clearly, USDOE [Department of Energy] has played fast and loose with the rules."[741] The same day he wrote to Hatfield, the governor took the suggestions of chief of staff Gerry Thompson and announced that the state would most likely file suit over USDOE decisions to move Hanford up the list of possible nuclear-waste repositories.[742]

By the end of the 1979 legislative session, Atiyeh and the legislature had decided against a ban on nuclear power. But they agreed on a moratorium on issuing permission—a site certificate —to operate any new plants before November 1980.[743] The plans for Pebble Springs moved along. In September 1979 the process began to receive hearings before the Oregon Energy Facility

Wastes," Department of Energy, State of Oregon, (2 June 1986), Atiyeh Collection, Pac. Univ. Archives; Lynn Frank, "Hanford—Follow Up," Department of Energy, State of Oregon, Memo to Governor Atiyeh, Gerry Thompson, Pat Amedeo, (2 June 1986), Atiyeh Collection, Pac. Univ. Archives; see Victor Atiyeh, "Draft on Hanford Waste Decision," Office of the Governor, State of Oregon, (2 June 1986), Atiyeh Collection, Pac. Univ. Archives; Victor Atiyeh, Letter on Office of the Governor stationery to Ben Rusche, "Letter to Director, Office of Civilian Radioactive Waste Management, U.S. Department of Energy," 3 June 1986, Atiyeh Collection, Pac. Univ. Archives; "Atiyeh Daily Index-Card Schedule, June 6, 1986," Office of the Governor, State of Oregon, (6 June 1986), [Handwritten by staff] Lynn Frank, Bill Bary re: Hanford, Atiyeh Collection, Pac. Univ. Archives; "Atiyeh Daily Index-Card Schedule, August 11, 1986," Office of the Governor, State of Oregon, (11 August 1986), [Handwritten by staff] Lynn Frank, Gerry re: Hanford, Atiyeh Collection, Pac. Univ. Archives; Lynn Frank, "Transition," Department of Energy, State of Oregon, Memo to Governor Atiyeh, (31 October 1986), Atiyeh Collection, Pac. Univ. Archives.

741 Victor Atiyeh, "Letter on President Reagan's Hanford Decision," Office of the Governor, State of Oregon, Letter to Honorable Mark O. Hatfield, (3 June 1986), 2, Atiyeh Collection, Pac. Univ. Archives.

742 Victor Atiyeh, "Hanford, Governor Atiyeh Speaking Notes," Office of the Governor, State of Oregon, (3 June 1986), Atiyeh Collection, Pac. Univ. Archives; Gerry Thompson, "Hanford," Office of the Governor, State of Oregon, Memo to Governor Atiyeh, (30 May 1986), Atiyeh Collection, Pac. Univ. Archives.

743 Sanderson, "First Year Summary," 7; UPI, "Atiyeh Will Sign Bill Imposing Moratorium," *Springfield (OR) News*, 28 June 1979, Atiyeh Collection, Pac. Univ. Archives; Jacqui Banaszynski, "Atiyeh Gets Short N-Ban: 10 Years Cut to 16 Months," *Eugene (OR) Register-Guard*, 26 June 1979, Atiyeh Collection, Pac. Univ. Archives.

Siting Council. By December, most of the major issues of environmental and socioeconomic impact had been agreed to.[744] This was still early in the process to build the new plant.

In November, Atiyeh delivered an address to the Portland City Club that the final decision of the Energy Facility Siting Council would be "not merely a question of whether or not to go nuclear, but probably requires a choice between nuclear and coal."[745] Then the Trojan nuclear power plant exposed other shortcomings in the nuclear power system. In October 1979, Trojan shut down for a planned eight-day period to repair leaky pipes.[746] However, the eight days would eventually extend into the new year. By the beginning of December, there was something of a crisis in the PGE electrical generating system. Trojan was not coming back online, and PGE needed to start up its alternative generating plants to meet its needs. As PGE was constructing Trojan, it also built oil- and gas-fired plants to take over if Trojan was shut down. One of these was the Harborton plant in Linnton, the northwest corner of the city of Portland.[747] The Harborton generating plant had been built as a natural gas–fueled generating station in the early 1970s, but it had been given a conditional use permit because it put too many pollutants into the Portland airshed.[748] After much negotiation, (President Carter was skeptical of assertions by Oregon leaders), Trojan came back online in early January 1979.[749]

---

744 Sanderson, "First Year Summary," 10.
745 Sanderson, "First Year Summary," 11.
746 Sanderson, "First Year Summary," 10.
747 Ed Mosey, "Trojan Operates at Full Power: Gas, Oil Plants Shut," *Oregonian*, 3 January 1980.
748 *Oregonian*, "Schwab on Target,' Editorial, 3 December 1979.
749 Sandra McDonough and Ed Mosey, "Atiyeh Seeks OK for Harborton Use," *Oregonian*, 22 December 1979; Jack Watson, "Memorandum for the President: Oregon Energy Emergency Declaration," Jimmy Carter Presidential Archives, United States Government, Office of Staff Secretary, Presidental Files, Folder 12/28/79, Container 144, (26 December 1979). http://www.jimmycarterlibrary.gov, handwritten annotation by Carter; Ed Mosey, "Industry, Labor Groups Press for Restart of Trojan," *Oregonian*, 25 December 1979; Steve Jenning, "Carter Ties Harborton to Conservation Effort," *Oregonian*, 28 December 1979; Jenning, "Carter Ties Harborton to Conservation Effort"; Jimmy Carter, "Executive Order,"

The entire spectacle of Harborton and Trojan exposed major weaknesses in the regional energy system. Trojan's reputation for reliability, already suspect, took a big hit. And the gas- and oil-fired secondary power plants were shown to be severely deficient in light of decade-old environmental regulations from the state and the federal governments, as well as the new energy efficiency and conservation measures being asked for at the federal and state levels. One local columnist called Portland a "nuclear junkie" for its heavy reliance on Trojan.[750]

By early February 1980, Atiyeh was sounding much less pro-nuclear than he had earlier in his term. The Harborton incident, the unreliability of Trojan, the cost of building new nuclear power plants, and post–Three Mile Island concerns about safety had all moved him to a more skeptical position on nuclear power.[751] Atiyeh told PGE it "should defer building a power plant at Pebble Springs because it would take too long."[752]

Atiyeh took great pains to explain that he was "pro-energy."[753] The problem was simple: the projected energy needs of the region called for three more nuclear plants the size of Trojan or six more coal- or gas-fired plants the size of Boardman. Given public attitudes about nuclear plants, Atiyeh did not think that any more nuclear plants could be built; plus, there was the length of time it would take to build them. He was moving toward seeing energy conservation as *the* way out of the electrical power shortages

---

Jimmy Carter Presidential Archives, United States Government, Office of Staff Secretary, Presidential Files, Folder 12/28/79, Container 144, (December 1979). http://www.jimmycarterlibrary.gov; Don Bundy, "Board Approves Restarting Trojan," *Oregonian*, 30 December 1979; Mosey, "Trojan Operates at Full Power: Gas, Oil Plants Shut."

750 David Sarasohn, "Why Wasn't There a 'Welcome Back, Trojan' Party? Portland a 'Nuclear Junkie'," Column, *Oregonian*, 11 January 1980.

751 William Bebout, "Atiyeh Has Seen Light About Nuclear Plants," Column, *Salem Capital Journal*, 3 February 1980, Atiyeh Collection, Pac. Univ. Archives; *Oregon Journal* (Portland), "Atiyeh Favors PGE Security at Trojan," 7 February 1980, Atiyeh Collection, Pac. Univ. Archives.

752 AP, "Governor: He's Pro Energy," *Albany (OR) Democrat-Herald*, 7 February 1980, Atiyeh Collection, Pac. Univ. Archives.

753 AP, "Governor: He's Pro Energy."

looming in the next few years. The November 1980 elections proved to be the end of the line for more nuclear power in Oregon.[754] Oregon voters approved an initiative that called for any nuclear plant licensing to require voter approval and the existence of a nuclear waste disposal facility.[755]

Forestry

Oregon's reputation as a center of environmental issues was firmly established when Vic Atiyeh become governor in 1979. The Bottle Bill, the Beach Bill, statewide land-use planning, and some of the first successful efforts at pollution regulation systems in the country had given the state national stature at the forefront of approaches to how nature, human activity, and economic progress could come into some sort of balance. Atiyeh was not known as an environmentalist—as his predecessors Tom McCall and Bob Straub were—but he had been in the middle of most of the important policy discussions that created Oregon's environmental reputation over the years.

Atiyeh was an avid outdoorsman. Atiyeh planned fishing vacations, he fished to relax, he had friends with whom he would spend days at a time, cut off from the world, just fishing. As governor he incorporated as much fishing into his schedule as he could—usually with at least one trip to a private fishing camp along the Deschutes during the summer and several shorter outings for steelhead, trout, and salmon during the year.

Atiyeh was also a businessperson. He well understood that Oregon's natural resources were the linchpin of its economy, whether through timber harvest, commercial fishing, the qualities of soil and water that were the base of agriculture, as well as attracting people to remote parts of the state to hike, fish, and hunt. The further outside the Oregon's metropolitan areas, and the sparser the population, the higher the percentage of residents

---

754 *Register-Guard* (Eugene, OR), "Oregon Forecloses Its Nuclear Option," Editorial, 7 November 1980, Atiyeh collection, Pac. Univ. Archives.
755 *Oregon Blue Book, 1981*, 334.

employed in timber—approaching 100% of the manufacturing sector in several counties.[756] It would be the balancing act among the goals of conservation, economic development, and preservation that would define many of Atiyeh's ideas and policies about the environment and the use of natural resources.

As with much of Atiyeh's life as governor, he would be formulating policies not only with a Democratic legislature but within the larger context of federal government policies and consultations with neighboring states. The focus on environment and natural resources would take a backseat to simple economic survival from 1980 on. There would be other important issues that arose after that time, but the sheer size of the economic downturn and its impact on the people of Oregon and the state government dominated Atiyeh's political life for years.

Until the 1980s, Oregon's economy had been a forest economy. Especially since World War II, the economic purpose of the state was to provide wood to the booming American market. But the production of wood was a complex system of private companies, private lands, public lands, transportation systems, and workers. When Atiyeh became governor, there were indicators that change was coming—Weyerhaeuser, Crown Zellerbach, Boise Cascade, and Georgia-Pacific were in the process of shifting their ownership of timberlands to South.[757]

Oregon timber harvests in the 1920s yielded about 4 billion board feet annually; during the depths of the Depression that diminished to less than 2 billion board feet; the war took it to 7 billion board feet, and the post-war years saw generally 8–9 billion board feet harvested, with spikes to almost 10 billion board feet, and recessions back down to 7 billion board feet.[758]

---

756 *Oregon Blue Book, 1979–1980*, (Salem, OR: Oregon Secretary of State, 1979), 180–181.
757 Pamela G. Hollie, "Northwest Timbermen Go South," *New York Times*, 13 June 1979, D1.
758 William G. Loy et al., *Atlas of Oregon*, 2nd ed., (Eugene, OR: University of Oregon Press, 2001), 92.

Atiyeh's years in the legislature from 1959 to 1978 were during this boom. That was his baseline of understanding about how natural resources and Oregon's economy worked together.

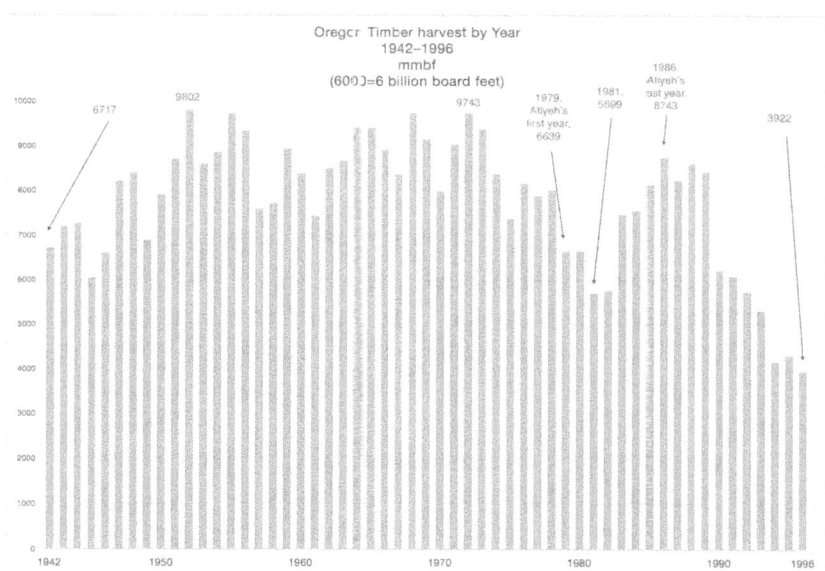

Annotated timber harvests, 1942-96. Andrews and Kutara, Oregon's Timber Harvests, 4-5.

As governor, Atiyeh played a major role in managing state lands through his constitutional seat on the Land Board, along with the secretary of state and the state treasurer.[759] For the management of all other land, he had the bully pulpit of the governor's seat, but all he could do was lobby for the goals he wanted. Between them, the US Interior Department's Bureau of

---

759 *Oregon Blue Book, 1979*, 54–55.

Land Management (BLM) and the US Department of Agriculture's Forest Service owned 50% of the land in Oregon, with the BLM land concentrated in the mountainous areas of the central and southern Coast Range and Cascades, and lots of land in the southeast of the state.[760] The U.S. Forest Service's territory was in the forests of the southern coast, almost the entire Cascade range, and in some of the forests in the northeast of Oregon. Forty-four percent of Oregon was in private hands, with 3% belonging to the state (mainly the Tillamook and Elliott State Forests, as well as land in south-central Oregon), and the remaining 3% in tribal lands as well as entities like National Wildlife Refuges.

Atiyeh's first state budget, for 1979–81, included funding to "improve the state's long-range timber supply through intensive forest management practices."[761] In December 1979, much of this was realized through an executive order "calling for coordination and development of a forest resources program for Oregon."[762] The process called for all state natural resource agencies "to divine and coordinate basic goals and policy objectives with regard to balanced multiple use forest resources" and identify "conflicts among goals and objectives, and recommendations of alternative goals and objectives that minimize conflict."[763]

Early in his administration, Atiyeh acted on an audit of the timber system conducted by Secretary of State Norma Paulus's office. Since the purpose of timber sales from state lands was to send money to the Common School Trust Fund and, thus, lower property taxes in local school districts, this all got caught up in the 1979 session's focus on property-tax relief. As a result of the

---

760 Loy, et al., *Atlas of Oregon*, 84.
761 "Transition Binder," Office of the Governor-elect, State of Oregon, (1978–79), Gary Wilhelms press release, January 4, 1979, 2, Atiyeh Collection, Pac. Univ. Archives.
762 Pat Amedeo, "First Year Report," Office of the Governor, State of Oregon, Memo to Denny Miles, Governor Atiyeh, Lee Johnson, Larry Sturholm, (17 December 1979), Memoranda and Reports, "Accomplishments," 1979, Atiyeh Collection, Pac. Univ. Archives.
763 Amedeo, "First Year Report," 2.

audit, there were changes in payment procedures for logs and the hiring of security for state lands. As the 1980 recession gathered strength, Atiyeh planned to push for more revenue from timber sales on state forest lands.[754] By November 1980, private timber lands in the Northwest were about out of old-growth forests. Change was going to hit the timber industry no matter what. The 1980–82 recession would simply add to the inevitable.

Atiyeh considered himself an environmentalist, especially because of his crucial work in forming the Department of Environmental Quality and Oregon's first-in-the-country environmental laws in the 1960s. Atiyeh carried on the Senate floor the 1967 law that, as he put it, said "the right to pollution does not exist," and he strongly supported air pollution and scenic easement legislation.[765] His governorship would pit his principle of doing the right thing for the people of Oregon against his principle of less government is better government. He discovered that the Reagan administration went too far toward the less-government side. Atiyeh needed to understand the new president's goals with respect to Oregon's largest landowners—the U.S. Forest Service and the BLM.

Atiyeh went into a meeting with Secretary of the Interior James Watt on September 11, 1981, with a list of items to talk about, ranging from land transfers to relations between the BLM and the state to wild horses and burros on public lands.[766] Watt would turn out to be a lightning rod for Reagan-era proposals encouraging economic activity on public lands.[767] His selection was very popular among big timber companies, as he was in favor of increasing harvests in the forests. The issue was, however, that

---

764 "Program Impact," State of Oregon, Hand marked by Atiyeh, (November 1980), 21, Atiyeh Collection, Pac. Univ. Archives.

765 Harold Hughes, "Tough Antipollution Laws Approved by State Senate," *Oregonian*, 27 April 1967.

766 Vic Atiyeh, "Subjects Discussed, Sec. Watt," Office of the Governor, State of Oregon, Handwritten notes of meeting with Interior Secretary James Watt, (11 September 1981), Atiyeh Collection, Pac. Univ. Archives.

767 Caroline Rand Herron and Michael Wright, "Much Ado About Secretary Watt," The Nation, *New York Times*, 23 August 1981, http://www.nytimes.com.

Congress had passed laws that "forced the federal land management agencies to take the multiple-use concept seriously on land that traditionally had been managed for single uses like timber cutting or grazing."[768]

By his own admission, Atiyeh "really objected to the federal—Washington, D.C.—management of Northwest timber. I really did."[769] He found that the federal government managed the resource only with an eye to the federal budget, not considering the impact of those decisions on the ground in timber country. Atiyeh was frustrated that income from federal timber sales did not go to the Forest Service or BLM to manage the resource—it instead went into the general funds of the U.S. budget where it could only be used for timber management if Congress appropriated the funds to do so.[770] It was partly because of this convoluted process of using the money from timber sales that Atiyeh entered into conflict with Reagan's director of the Office of Management and Budget, David Stockman.

As the recessions built, a growing number of companies found themselves unable to pay for federal timber contracts they had entered when the economy was in better shape. The high prices for the contracts reflected supply and demand, but inflation was a big driver as well.[771] Using his business experience, Atiyeh observed,

> The timber industry did use some bad judgment. In those days, if you got a public timber contract for harvesting, you had five years in which to harvest. That was the normal period of time. ... [A]t times when inflation was going up, someone could buy a timber sale today and pay too much for it. But the time it came to harvest, it was cheap.... So everybody was betting [on inflation].

---

768 Russell Sadler, "Timber Industry Happy With Interior Nominee," Column, *Oregonian*, 5 January 1981.
769 Victor Atiyeh, interviewed by Clark Hansen, "Tape 36, side 1," Oral history, recorded by Oregon Historical Society, Portland, OR, 15 June 1993. Transcript, 160, Atiyeh Collection, Pac. Univ. Archives.
770 Victor Atiyeh, "Tape 36, side 1,"160.
771 Amedeo, "Atiyeh interview," 4.

...Well, when the recession came along, all of a sudden here they were with $400 [per thousand board feet], $450, $500...that they had bid for, but now the price had gone down to $200. Actually, it even got under $100 at one point. And here they are with this contract[;...] clearly they're going to go out of business.[772]

Given the choice, Atiyeh was trying to save the employees of the mills that were in distress. He explained, "Are you worried about Joe Smith who owns the sawmill, or are you worried about the people who work for Joe Smith. ...I don't mind saving Joe Smith, if I can. ...I'm [really] trying to save the people who work for Joe Smith."[773]

Federal legislation written by Mark Hatfield and Idaho's James McClure (R) even proposed to "let holders of federal timber contracts turn back to the federal government 40 percent of the unharvested trees they agree[d] to buy."[774] In 1983, the low price of timber from the previous summer (a 10-year low) triggered bidding wars that tripled and quadrupled the price for trees harvested on Forest Service lands.[775] Since the timber could be harvested sometime in the next three years, there were fears that there could be "a possible repeat of 1978–80 when a bidding war inflated prices so much that purchasers were stuck with about 15 billion board feet of wood they could not afford to harvest during the wood products recession" of 1980–82.[776]

Pat Amedeo analyzed the situation by noting that large companies could probably fulfill their contracts with a slight loss to their economic health. They pushed for extensions of the contracts until the economy was better. But small companies had a much higher percentage of their total capital invested in these no-win contracts. They advocated for cancellation.[777] Timber industry representatives and the Oregon Department of Forestry

---

772 Victor Atiyeh, "Tape 36, side 1," 158.
773 Victor Atiyeh, "Tape 36, side 1," 165.
774 AP, "Timber Plan Worry Voiced," *Oregonian*, 8 May 1982.
775 Jim Kadera, "Panic Bidding Alarms Timber Concerns," *Oregonian*, 17 April 1983.
776 Kadera, "Panic Bidding Alarms Timber Concerns."
777 Amedeo, "Atiyeh interview," 4.

were constantly in the governor's office talking to Atiyeh.[778] Atiyeh proposed that the legislature allow the State Forester, Mike Miller, "authority to extend contracts for state timber held by private companies. He also want[ed] Miller to have authority to cut the price of state timber for companies that will harvest the trees this year," something of a cut-sooner discount to get cash into the system.[779] Atiyeh floated this idea just as the long January 1982 special session (one of three in that recession-scarred year) was getting started. The special session passed a timber relief plan.[780]

Through it all, Atiyeh was very concerned about making sure that the Department of Interior understood the western states' issues. Even though Watt was from Colorado, his background as an advocate for greater state control over federal lands did not necessarily deal with the concerns Atiyeh had, especially as the recessions bore down. Atiyeh found himself in agreement with Watt on certain things, for example, opposition to the growing power of what Atiyeh called "super-environmentalists." But Atiyeh found Watt's "super-Republican" opinions harder to take. Atiyeh recalled, "He said, 'What's good for the Republicans is good for the nation.' You know, I don't really agree with that, but that's the kind of guy he was."[781] Compared to the Carter administration, though, Atiyeh found it easier to work with Watt in the early days of the Reagan presidency.

The Reagan administration did come out with a timber contract relief plan in August 1983. Hatfield and Senator Howard Metzenbaum (D-OH) crafted a proposal that "would have provided relief primarily for small timber companies, allowing them to extend high-priced federal timber contracts without

---

778 Gerry Thompson, interviewed by Jim Moore, "Atiyeh interview #2," Salem, OR, 12 February 2015. Summary notes, 5.
779 Leslie L. Zaitz, "Atiyeh Seeks State Facelift: 'Miserable' Image," *Oregonian*, 19 January 1982.
780 AP, "Suit Filed to Cancel Oregon Timber Relief," *Oregonian*, 27 July 1983; George Rede, "Land Board Wins Attorney General Ruling: Key Decision on Forests," *Salem (OR) Statesman-Journal*, 12 February 1982.
781 Victor Atiyeh, "Tape 33, side 1," 81.

penalty." But the larger firms opposed the idea, and they successfully scuttled it.[782] Hatfield picked up the pieces and kept working on a timber relief bill. Atiyeh continued meeting with federal officials, state officials, and timber companies in 1984 about managing forests and reaching some kind of timber-relief solution.[783]

"A kind of hush has fallen over the forests and sawmills of the Pacific Northwest," one observer wrote during the summer of 1984, "as timber companies await a decision by Congress that would enable them to back out of deals they made with the Federal Government. ...Except for isolated pockets, Washington, Oregon and northern California have not benefited much from the recent resurgence of the nation's economy."[784] Atiyeh's office learned in August, through Vice President George Bush's staff, that the Office of Management and Budget and the Departments of Interior and Agriculture were "all strongly opposed to Hatfield's timber relief bill." It looked like there were votes to pass the bill, but the big question was whether Reagan would veto it. The Bush team told Gerry Thompson, "the unofficial information which must remain confidential...is that Interior and USDA strongly oppose a presidential veto on the basis that they do not believe there would be enough votes to sustain the veto."[785]

---

782 UPI, "Senate Defeats Hatfield's Timber Relief Measure," *Oregonian*, 12 November 1983.

783 "Atiyeh Daily Index-Card Schedule, January 5, 1984," Office of the Governor, State of Oregon, (5 January 1984), Bill Leavell, BLM; Jeff Sirmon, US Forest Service; Mike Miller; Pat [Amedeo], regarding forests on state lands, Atiyeh Collection, Pac. Univ. Archives; "Atiyeh Daily Index-Card Schedule, January 14, 1984," Office of the Governor, State of Oregon, (14 January 1984), 11:15 AM Informal Meeting: Bill Shields, VB, Willamette Industries; John Stevens, Roseburg Lumber; Aaron Jones, Jones Lumber; Max Petersen, chief, US Forestry; & Monte Montgomery [head of Association of Oregon Loggers]; 1:30 PM Meet: Max Petersen; Jeff Sirmon, reg. forester; John Hampton, Willamina Lumber; Stub [Stewart} & Monte [Montgomery], regarding forest service timber sale contracts (Pat [Amedeo] said you are up to speed on that issue), Atiyeh Collection, Pac. Univ. Archives.

784 Robert Lindsey, "Of Timber, Mexicans and Taxes," Western Journal, *New York Times*, 27 August 1984.

785 Gerry Thompson, "Conversation with Vice President's Office: Mid-East Briefing; Timber Relief; American State Bank," Memo, Gerry Thompson to Governor, 14

Finally, in September 1984, as the recession was beginning to end, but with the timber contracts coming due, timber relief legislation passed in Congress. This time the Senate vote was 94–2.[786] The House then duly passed the bill, and the Forest Service put together plans to implement the law. It was not perfect. It protected smaller companies from going out of business, but the timber management director for the Forest Service calculated that "more than a dozen larger publicly held companies…[would] probably turn back contracts on which they [were] capable of harvesting the timber."[787] The deal was that a sure $4 billion loss among small companies would be averted and turn into a $400 million loss in government revenue. The timber industry was pleased with it, but under no illusions that it would prevent many small companies from going out of business.[788]

In 1985, as the diminishing recession was leading to more construction activity, timber companies took another hit. They actually had an oversupply of lumber, which led to shutdowns and layoffs, just as if there had been a timber shortage.[789] What had changed? "Less use of wood in home construction and a surge of imports from Canada, Brazil and Venezuela," encouraged by favorable exchange rates.[790] Canadian timber policies had been a bone of contention for Pacific Northwest timber producers for years.[791] By 1985 a stronger dollar also meant that exported logs

---

August 1984, 1.

786 James C. Flanigan, "Senate Approves Timber Contract Relief Bill," *Oregonian*, 27 September 1984.

787 James C. Flanigan, "Forest Service Outlines Timetable for Timber Relief," *Oregonian*, 3 October 1984.

788 Staff, Wire Reports, "NW Timber Relief Bill Viewed as Not Enough," *Oregonian*, 27 September 1984.

789 Thomas C. Hayes, "The Timber Glut's Legacy," *New York Times*, 19 January 1985.

790 Hayes, "Timber Glut," 31.

791 "Atiyeh Daily Index-Card Schedule, October 20, 1981," Office of the Governor, State of Oregon, (20 October 1981), Interview: CBC-TV, …re: Canadian lumber import—Jerry McIntosh—Pat, too, Atiyeh Collection, Pac. Univ. Archives.

from the Northwest were more expensive to foreign buyers, so that part of the business was slowing down as well.[792]

Even though the timber industry was changing before the recessions, even though the recessions themselves remade much of the industry, it was the northern spotted owl and the Endangered Species Act that were blamed for the coming world of reduced timber harvests and a smaller timber industry. Atiyeh held an official meeting on the northern spotted owl in his last few months in office in October 1986.[793]

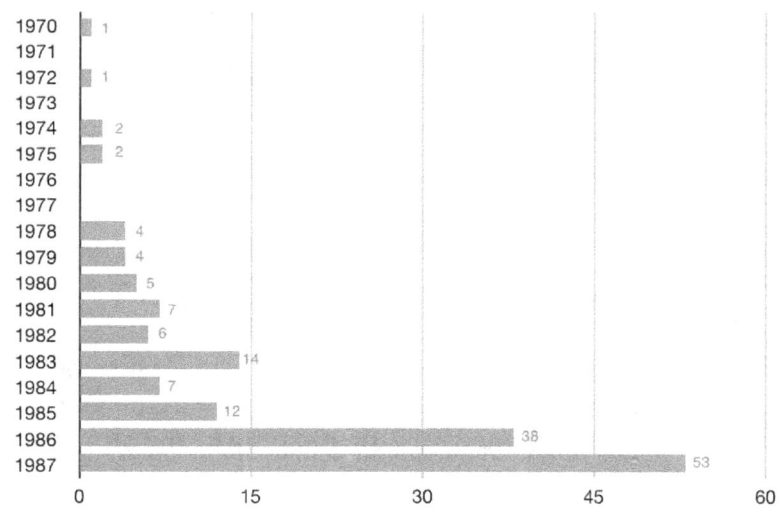

Oregonian articles mentioning "Northern Spotted Owl."

---

792 Nicholas D. Kristof, "Timber Towns Grow Silent," *New York Times*, 17 January 1986.

793 "Atiyeh Daily Index-Card Schedule, October 24, 1986," Office of the Governor, State of Oregon, (24 October 1986), Anna Hanus, Jon Yunker & Odie; regarding spotted owl, Atiyeh Collection, Pac. Univ. Archives; "Atiyeh Daily Index-Card Schedule, October 28, 1986," Office of the Governor, State of Oregon, (28 October 1986), Ann Hannus, Rollie Rousseau, Mike Weland, Jim Brown, Dave Stere, Martha Pagel, Tom Kennedy, Laila Cully, Jim Ross, Jim Knight & Bob; regarding spotted owl, Atiyeh Collection, Pac. Univ. Archives; "Governor's Schedule, 27 October–2 November 1986," Office of the Governor, State of Oregon, Confidential, (23 October 1986). 2, October 28, 1996, Atiyeh Collection, Pac. Univ. Archives.

The symbolic impact of the northern spotted owl's listing as an endangered species in 1990 would be understood by many in timber country to be what shut down the forests.[794] Another impact of the role of the northern spotted owl would be an acceleration of the change in political-party identities of voters in timber country. Timber country voters were on their way to becoming a solid Republican bloc.[795]

Looking back on it, Atiyeh said, "If…timber relief…hadn't passed, I don't know what would have happened."[796] He just imagined all those lost jobs, even more than the number of people shed by the timber industry during the recession.[797] The timber market by the mid-1980s was much more complex, with growing market pressure from the Canadians, competition that continues to this day.[798] Given the changes in the forests and the market that led large companies to begin leaving the state by 1979, it was most likely the case that no presidential administration could have come up with solutions that satisfied all the players. The timber industry was destined to shrink, recession or no, northern spotted owl or no.

Atiyeh in the 1990s did not see it that way. He told his oral historian "that if the timber industry weren't so beleaguered right now with the northern spotted owl and old growth and all kinds of things, then the economy of Oregon would be booming." The recessions had "really battered…the timber industry. …Had we not, however, expanded that [economic] base, we would be in

---

794 "Analysis of an Emerging Timber Supply Disruption," Forest Service, United States Department of Agriculture, FS-460, (June 1990), vii–x.
795 Peter Wong, interviewed by Jim Moore, "Atiyeh interview," Rock Creek, OR, 4 August 2015. Summary notes, 4.
796 Victor Atiyeh, interviewed by Clark Hansen, "Tape 62," Oral history, recorded by Oregon Historical Society, Portland, OR, 11 June 1998. Transcript, 23, Atiyeh Collection, Pac. Univ. Archives. Word order changed for syntax.
797 Victor Atiyeh, interviewed by Clark Hansen, "Tape 63," Oral history, recorded by Oregon Historical Society, Portland, OR, 11 June 1998. Transcript, 1, Atiyeh Collection, Pac. Univ. Archives.
798 Tom Kennedy, interviewed by Jim Moore, "Atiyeh Interview #1," Lake Oswego, OR, 18 January 2017. Summary notes, 1.

deep, deep trouble."[799] However, he found it hard to imagine what Oregon's economy would look like if timber was still the single largest economic sector in the state.[800]

Wilderness and Opal Creek

Oregon had 1.3 million acres designated as wilderness areas when Atiyeh took office.[801] The national Wilderness Act of 1964 created and defined the concept of wilderness in U.S. law, creating the National Wilderness Preservation System. Wilderness areas tended to be areas of scenic beauty, but "predominantly non-commercial forests or high-elevation areas of 'rock and ice'" that did not include the easily accessible low-elevation forests that had supplied Oregon's timber industry.[802] Any forest that happened to have wilderness protection was "typically in low productivity forest types, or in scattered, relatively small areas that were withdrawn from logging because of their steep slopes."[803] Thus, as one observer put it, "The wilderness areas don't do a good job of protecting biological diversity."[804]

Lands under the jurisdiction of the BLM were not part of the wilderness system, but a study was underway in the late 1970s

---

799 Victor Atiyeh, interviewed by Clark Hansen, "Tape 45," Oral history, recorded by Oregon Historical Society, Portland, OR, 9 July 1993. Transcript, 409, Atiyeh Collection, Pac. Univ. Archives; see also V. Atiyeh, "Tape 62," 20.

800 Victor Atiyeh, interviewed by Jim Moore, "Atiyeh interview #1," Raleigh Hills, OR, 19 December 2013. Summary notes, 4.

801 Amedeo, "First Year Report," 1.

802 Andy Kerr, *Oregon Wild: Endangered Forest Wilderness*, (Portland, OR: Oregon Natural Resources Council, 2004), 59.

803 Thomas A. Spies and Sally L. Duncan, "Searching for Old Growth," in *Old Growth in a New World: A Pacific Northwest Icon Reexamined*, eds. Thomas A. Spies and Sally L. Duncan, (Washington, DC: Island Press, 2009), 4; see also, K. Norman Johnson and Frederic J. Swanson, "Historical Context of Old-Growth Forests in the Pacific Northwest—Policy, Practice, and Competing Worldviews," in *Old Growth in a New World: A Pacific Northwest Icon Reexamined*, ed. Thomas A. Spies and Sally L. Duncan, (Washington, DC: Island Press, 2009), 15.

804 David Seideman, *Showdown at Opal Creek: The Battle for America's Last Wilderness*, (New York: Carroll and Graf Publishers, 1993), 28.

"for the purpose of assessing [BLM lands'] wilderness potential."[805] Part of this process was an inventory of public lands, the results of which would go to the president by June 1, 1980, for possible additions to the wilderness areas already in place.[806] This directive specified that the wilderness program was "not necessarily to preserve those areas having scenic grandeur, but rather to identify lands that have retained a large measure of their natural integrity—lands that offer the opportunity for solitude and introspection."[807] There could have been past human habitation; mention was made of ghost towns and "the ruts of the Oregon trail [that] can still be seen crossing some BLM lands."[808] Atiyeh was not happy that much of this potential wilderness land was locked up until a final determination was made about wilderness designations. He called on the Carter administration to release federal timberlands that had already been determined not to be future wilderness areas, arguing, "Now, let's not lock up everything else while we're studying it. Release all this. Let it be harvested, because we're not talking about" these areas as wilderness anymore.[809]

The Forest Service had started a study in 1977 called the Roadless Area Review and Evaluation, known as RARE II (the original RARE was in 1972; it satisfied no one). Roadless areas were not wilderness areas. The study was to determine how much of these roadless areas should be officially designated as wilderness. In Oregon, the conversation was about the balance between roadless areas on Forest Service land versus access to trees for harvest. At a September 1978 meeting in Roseburg,[810] a

---

805 "The National Wilderness Preservation System," *Congressional Digest* 61, no. 2 (1982): 291, EBSCO Publishing.

806 "The Wilderness Inventory: Alaska Lands Controversy," *Congressional Digest* 61, no. 2 (1982): 294, EBSCO Publishing.

807 "Wilderness Inventory," 294.

808 "Wilderness Inventory," 294.

809 Victor Atiyeh, interviewed by Clark Hansen, "Tape 30," Oral history, recorded by Oregon Historical Society, Portland, OR, 3 May 1993. Transcript, 25, Atiyeh Collection, Pac. Univ. Archives.

810 AP, "Oregon Wilderness Issue Draws 1,000 to Meeting," *Salem Oregon Statesman*, 22 September 1978.

crowd of 1000, mainly against the roadless idea in an area heavily dependent on the timber industry, heard from a prepared statement from Atiyeh's gubernatorial campaign that Atiyeh believed "we have enough wilderness in Oregon now and I do not support any more wilderness unless they are significant special areas." His statement added that "the forests should be available to all people, not just those who can hike or backpack into them."[811]

He strongly felt that "all remaining roadless areas under study should be opened to multiple use, except perhaps 'unique' areas that he [wasn't] already aware of."[812] He even went further in a campaign talk, calling for "the federal government to turn over the management of national forests in Oregon to the state Forestry Department." He explained, "I don't intend to rape national forest lands. I do intend to let local experienced foresters make decisions about Oregon trees, rather than leaving it up to Congress and the Office of Management and Budget [in the White House]."[813]

Governor Atiyeh did recommend 61,213 acres in Oregon be designated as wilderness areas on February 23, 1979. Although Mark Hatfield put it into bill form and introduced it in the U.S. Senate,[814] Hatfield neither supported nor opposed Atiyeh's proposal. The senator had filed another bill, the version he favored, that called for 451,000 Oregon acres to be designated as wilderness.[815] The eventual Senate bill passed in November 1979 with "506,000 acres in Oregon as wilderness areas and another 134,000 acres as a conservation area."[816] The U.S. House voted down the Senate plan, so the entire process had to be restarted. It

---

811 AP, "Oregon Wilderness Issue."
812 *Oregonian*, "Atiyeh Files RARE Challenge," Political Notebook, 17 October 1978.
813 Huntly Collins, "3 Candidates Offer Proposals to Improve Public Education," Political Notebook, *Oregonian*, 15 April 1978.
814 Wayne Thompson, "Atiyeh Proposes Huge Reduction in Wilderness" *Oregonian*, 4 March 1979; Amedeo, "First Year Report," 1; AP, "Carter Boosts U.S. Wilderness Acreage," *Salem Oregon Statesman*, 17 April 1979; "First Two Hundred Days of the Atiyeh Administration," 2.
815 Kerr, *Oregon Wild*, 58.

would be up to the 1981 Congress to come up with solutions. These would fail. Congress finally passed the Oregon Wilderness Act in June 1984, and there were 861,500 acres included.[817] This was almost fourteen times bigger than Atiyeh's 1979 recommendation and almost twice as big as the 1979 version that passed in the Senate but went nowhere in the House. Of course, it was no secret that Atiyeh had a personal interest in the legislation, too.

When Victor Atiyeh married Dolores Hewitt in July 1944, he married into a family that had worked mining claims on Opal Creek since the 1920s, an area in the Cascade foothills east of Salem and northwest of Mount Jefferson.[818] It was in an area of large old-growth trees that would be eyed by logging companies and workers in nearby Mill City and would become part of the Willamette National Forest. Tom Atiyeh loved going fishing with his dad up at the Hewitt grandparents' place on Opal Creek. The area was completely devoid of people. There were trout to be caught in water so clear that Tom and his father had to move carefully on the smooth rocks so as not to spook the fish they were trying to catch.[819]

Apparently Atiyeh's father-in-law, James Hewitt, also had a sawmill along the creek, but it was long gone by the time Atiyeh married Dolores in 1944. After Dolores's mother died in 1967, her father spent more time up on Opal Creek, building a flume to bring in water and "run the belt wheel for the electricity, and we'd have to patch up [the flume line] with tin cans."[820] Atiyeh would go up to the house, at a spot called Jawbone Flats, to work on

---

816 AP, "Wilderness Areas in Oregon Are Approved by the Senate," Around the Nation, *New York Times*, 27 November 1979.

817 Kerr, *Oregon Wild*, 60.

818 Victor Atiyeh, interviewed by Clark Hansen, "Tape 40, side 2," Oral history, recorded by Oregon Historical Society, Portland, OR, 28 June 1993. Transcript, 289, Atiyeh Collection, Pac. Univ. Archives.

819 Tom Atiyeh, interviewed by Jim Moore, "Atiyeh interview," Sherwood, OR, 28 July 2015. Summary, 9.

820 Victor Atiyeh, "Tape 40, side 2," 290. Brackets keep exact words, but placement changed for syntax.

maintenance and then "go fishing, and I'd shoot my muzzle-loaders and just have a nice vacation up there."[821]

Atiyeh worked with his father-in-law to organize all the little pieces of paper that signified claims, deals, and patents. Patents were for proven mining areas—they gave the holder of the patent private property rights on the surface as well as below ground. Atiyeh recalled that was "probably the best thing I ever did because he did pass away [in 1970], and everything was in his name."[822] Dolores inherited the whole conglomeration, and Atiyeh put in a little work to maintain the claims but "finally I was getting tired of it.... [I]t was just something I...wasn't that interested in...."[823] Eventually the claims (there were about 160 of them) were sold for $101,000, with a third going to Dolores and the other two-thirds to her two sisters. Apparently the last "$1000 paid for [James] Hewitt's baby grand piano."[824]

In the months before James Hewitt's death in December 1970, his grandson Tom and Tom's cousin, George Atiyeh (Richard's son), took over Jawbone Flats with the elder Hewitt's permission.[825] The two, along with another person living as a caretaker at the site, began scaring off interlopers with guns and knives. With opposition to the Vietnam War riding high, there were police intelligence reports that "'hippy types' [were] converting Jawbone Flats into a training base for urban guerrillas.[826] George Atiyeh saw himself as a protector of the spot, especially from logging companies that had been eyeing the area since 1964.[827]

---

821 Victor Atiyeh, "Tape 40, side 2," 290.
822 Victor Atiyeh, "Tape 40, side 2," 291.
823 Victor Atiyeh, "Tape 40, side 2," 291.
824 Victor Atiyeh, "Tape 40, side 2," 291; Atiyeh recalled $100,000, Seidman reported $101,000, Seideman, *Showdown at Opal Creek*, 171.
825 Seideman, *Showdown at Opal Creek*, 12; Zach Urness, "Timeline: The Fight for Opal Creek," *Salem (OR) Statesman Journal*, 24 September 2016, http://www.statesmanjournal.com.
826 Seideman, *Showdown at Opal Creek*, 13.
827 Seideman, *Showdown at Opal Creek*, 14.

By 1972, the Atiyeh cousins had organized themselves into the Shiny Rock Mining Company, President Tom Atiyeh, Vice President George Atiyeh. Shiny Rock was a subsidiary of the *Honolulu Advertiser* newspaper, part of the Persis Corporation in Hawaii.[828] It was to the Persis Corporation that Vic Atiyeh had sold the Hewitt claims in 1972.[829] The purpose of the purchase was "to move enough material to maintain mining claims under the General Mining Act of 1872, helping block U.S. Forest Service plans to log and build roads up Opal Creek."[830] Disputes arose with the administrators of the Willamette National Forest over the use of the land. The mining was legal, but there were questions about "who controls roads and bridges leading to them; whether a new water line will be allowed; and the number of residents at the mining camp."[831] A big concern was the decrepit bridge crossing Gold Creek. The Forest Service had condemned it as unsafe. Tom Atiyeh had plans to replace it with a covered bridge.[832] The entire area stretching from Opal Creek east into the Cascades was known as the Hidden Wilderness, a place that attracted "a great deal of attention from conservationists, loggers and miners alike."[833] It was "one of the last two…unexploited areas in the Cascades."[834]

In April 1981, Opal Creek became symbolic of a conflict between members of Oregon's congressional delegation. Jim

---

828 Chris Cowger, "Little North Fork Hangs on Impact Statement," *Salem (OR) Capital Journal*, 4 August 1975; Dan Postrel, "Valuable Copper May Be Hidden in Scenic Valley of North Fork," *Salem (OR) Statesman-Journal*, 8 December 1980.

829 Victor Atiyeh, interviewed by Clark Hansen, "Tape 61," Oral history, recorded by Oregon Historical Society, Portland, OR, 10 September 1993. Transcript, 88, Atiyeh Collection, Pac. Univ. Archives; Victor Atiyeh, interviewed by Clark Hansen, "Tape 64," Oral history, recorded by Oregon Historical Society, Portland, OR, 11 June 1998. Transcript, 35, Atiyeh Collection, Pac. Univ. Archives.

830 Zach Urness, "Timeline: The Fight for Opal Creek," *Salem (OR) Statesman Journal*, 24 September 2016.

831 Lewis H. Arends, Jr., "North Fork Mining Operation Facing Private Rights Battle," *Salem Oregon Statesman*, 28 June 1973.

832 Jerry Easterling, "There's a New Glow to an Old Mine," *Salem (OR) Capital Journal*, 4 June 1973.

833 Cowger, "Little North Fork Hangs on Impact Statement."

834 Cowger, "Little North Fork Hangs on Impact Statement."

Weaver (D-CD 4) favored the area becoming part of millions of acres of new wilderness in the state.[835] Denny Smith (R-CD 2) favored logging to bring jobs to areas hard hit by the 1980 recession. George Atiyeh opposed Smith's proposal, as did Representative Weaver and the city of Salem.[836]

When logging companies started looking carefully at the Opal Creek area, George Atiyeh led the fight to protect the trees. Vic Atiyeh, as governor, knew that this was something he needed to stay away from—the conflicts of interest were just too convoluted. He recalled, "I tried to stay out of that whole thing because…my wife's family, they were all involved, and I shouldn't be a party to anything that goes on. So I said, 'George, I'm going to stay out of it.'"[837] The governor remembered that George did not take 'no' for an answer from him. His nephew "kept trying to get me involved with it, and I said, 'No, George, I'm not going to do that.'" Pat Amedeo saw that the Opal Creek issue was the most difficult wilderness issue for the governor.[838] Vic Atiyeh made it clear to Amedeo that he wanted the area preserved, but the extensive human presence in the area—all those mining claims, the buildings around Jawbone Flats—did not seem to fit with the federal idea of wilderness areas.

As Atiyeh thought about the episode in 1993, he observed, "… [I]t had the smell of a potential scandal, and I didn't want to have anything to do with it. My wife would have been very sad about it. …[S]he didn't have particularly good feelings about the whole thing."[839] Bob Atiyeh, Ed's son, talked with his cousin George about all that happened. George was frustrated that his uncle was not standing up for him as George was being demonized by Republicans.[840]

---

835 Kerr, *Oregon Wild*, 58–59.
836 Norm Brewer, "Rep. Smith Urges Copter-Logging at Opal Creek," *Salem (OR) Statesman-Journal*, 13A; Dan Postrel, "Weaver Asks Opal Creek Delay," *Salem (OR) Statesman-Journal*, 12 August 1981; Urness, "Opal Creek Timeline."
837 Victor Atiyeh, "Tape 40, side 2," 292.
838 Amedeo, "Atiyeh interview," 2.
839 Victor Atiyeh, "Tape 40, side 2," 292.

In April 1984 rumors swirled that the governor had asked Senator Hatfield to include Opal Creek in Hatfield's wilderness proposal. Opal Creek had been in the first version of Hatfield's bill in 1982, but it had been removed.[841] While Atiyeh was traveling in the Middle East, Gerry Thompson wrote him a memo about the political storm brewing back in Oregon.

> Al Wilson from AOI [Associated Oregon Industries] called asking for a report on the Opal Creek area for the Wilderness Proposal. It was his information that you had notified Senator Hatfield asking that Opal Creek be made a part of his Wilderness Proposal.
>
> Governor, a terrible amount of concern has been coming in about the rumor of you making this request of Senator Hatfield. I believe Pat [Amedeo] probably visited with you upon her arrival in Israel. Obviously, AOI is also concerned, in fact somewhat angered. I refused to confirm or deny the subject with them until your return. I simply told them I had heard a similar rumor but had no confirmation of it.
>
> Al indicated to me that several timber company owners in the Opal Creek area are very angry and it would be my guess that AOI is preparing to cause a ruckus. Al also indicated to me that their information is that Hatfield will discuss the bill on the floor next week and they are preparing to do the mark up.[842]

The rumor was that "Atiyeh sent a telex from Syria...to... Hatfield...asking him to please include Opal Creek."[843] Years later, a story said that "at the same time, the governor discreetly informed the senator he would understand if he didn't help. That

---

840 Bob Atiyeh, interviewed by Jim Moore, "Atiyeh interview," West Linn, OR, 4 February 2015. Summary notes, 6.

841 Urness, "Opal Creek Timeline."

842 Gerry Thompson, "Daily Reports to Governor, Apr 1984," "Update to Governor," April 12, 1984.

843 Seideman, *Showdown at Opal Creek*, 278.

cooked it for the legislation" to create the Opal Creek Wilderness.[844]

The telex rumor was probably a fabrication by George Atiyeh. Pat Amedeo recalled that "the Governor's charismatic nephew, George Atiyeh, had taken it upon himself to tell people that the Governor supported inclusion of Opal Creek in the bill."[845] She clearly recalled briefing Atiyeh on "the firestorm at home on my arrival" in Israel to join the Middle East visit. Denny Miles, who was working hard coordinating the accompanying media on the Middle East trip also did not remember a telex being sent.[846] The most definitive word came from Tom Atiyeh, the governor's son, who was on the Egypt and Syria legs of the Middle East trip. Since he had been deeply involved in Opal Creek earlier, he is sure his father would have told him about such a telex. In addition, the author of the book about Opal Creek, *Showdown at Opal Creek*, never asked Tom about the telex.[847] Tom also recalled that the telex never came up on subsequent conversations with his father over the years.

Atiyeh came out publicly for the wilderness designation when he returned from the Middle East, but he was evasive about endorsing Hatfield's actual bill in the last week in April. During a phone interview on April 24 the governor said he had "recently asked Sen. Mark O. Hatfield…to include the Opal Creek area…as part of the Hidden Wilderness proposed in Hatfield's Oregon wilderness bill."[848] He explained, "I'm intimately familiar with it and the thought of a (timber) harvest taking place. It's a visual thing with me."[849] The next day at one of his regular media availabilities, Atiyeh explained that the 9,000 acres of the Opal Creek area were not as "important as settling the issue so other timberland can be freed up for commercial use." He was "more and more convinced that it is more important that the question be

---

844 Seideman, *Showdown at Opal Creek*, 278.
845 Pat Amedeo, Email to Jim Moore, "Telexes from Syria, I," 4 December 2017.
846 Denny Miles, Email to Jim Moore, "Telexes from Syria," 3 December 2017.
847 Tom Atiyeh, Email to Jim Moore, "Opal Creek," 4 December 2017.
848 Jim Kadera, "Atiyeh Wants Area Protected as Wilds," *Oregonian*, 25 April 1984.
849 Kadera, "Atiyeh Wants Area Protected." Parentheses in original.

settled rather than quibble about acreage."[850] The governor emphasized that "his family's mining interests in a portion of the Willamette National Forest have nothing to do with his recommendation that the area be protected by a federal wilderness designation."[851] An *Oregonian* editorial asked, "Has Gov. Vic Atiyeh undergone a conversion on the wilderness issue? It could be."[852] But in all this, Atiyeh avoided actually endorsing Hatfield's bill.[853] There was still uncertainty in the difference between his words and his actions.

As Atiyeh's natural resources aide saw all this unfold, Pat Amedeo came to feel, in retrospect, that Atiyeh "was not honest" with her about Opal Creek.[854] The family ties made the whole issue something that the governor should have publicly walked away from, in her opinion. The site itself did not meet the criteria for wilderness because of the active mining and human presence. She recalled that George was a charismatic and sincere advocate. He would meet with his uncle, the governor, and tell Amedeo that the governor had changed his mind. It appeared to Amedeo that the governor was probably hedging, saying one thing to George and another to her.

With George Atiyeh's growing celebrity as an environmental activist ("he was featured on multiple network newscasts and in the *New York Times*, *Washington Post*, and *Time magazine"*), environmentalist Andy Kerr said, "Opal Creek was ground zero. It became the center of the war" pitting loggers against preservationists.[855] By late 1983, the politicized George Atiyeh threw his hat into the ring to unseat the incumbent Oregon House

---

850 Don Jepsen, "Atiyeh Asks Solution to Wilderness Issue," *Oregonian*, 26 April 1984; "Governor's Schedule, 23–29 April 1984," Office of the Governor, State of Oregon, Confidential, (19 April 1984), 3: 10 a.m. Media briefing; 10:30 a.m. Gov. Atiyeh will hold media availability, Wednesday, April 25 Atiyeh Collection, Pac. Univ. Archives.

851 AP, "Atiyeh Calls Wilderness Issue Priority," *Salem (OR) Statesman-Journal*, 26 April 1984.

852 *Oregonian*, "Wilderness Gets New Fan," Editorial, 29 April 1984.

853 *Oregonian*, "Wilderness Gets New Fan."; Jepsen, "Atiyeh Asks Solution to Wilderness Issue."

854 Amedeo, "Atiyeh interview," 6.

member for district 38, a sprawling district encompassing parts of the Willamette Valley and reaching the crest of the Cascades, from the outskirts of Springfield in the south to Molalla in the north.[856] The incumbent was a Democrat. George Atiyeh filed as a Republican.[857] Regardless of the strength of George Atiyeh's platform, he was more of an environmentalist in 1984, and the Republican party of Ronald Reagan was going in a different direction. He was defeated in the primary by about a two to one margin.[858] This foray into elective politics was the only one by an Atiyeh, aside from the long career of George's uncle.

Resolution for Opal Creek did not happen until Mark Hatfield was preparing to leave the Senate. In March 1996, Hatfield filed a bill "to preserve almost 26,000 acres of pristine forest near Opal Creek from logging or mining."[859] In a crucial September 1996 meeting to avoid a government shutdown with the Speaker of the House, Newt Gingrich, the Majority Leader of the Senate, Trent Lott, and President Clinton's chief of staff, Leon Panetta, Hatfield stood his ground on Opal Creek. It had already been removed from the omnibus budget bill, but Hatfield brought it back up. He threatened to block the bill unless it contained the Opal Creek provisions. The other negotiators gave in.[860] The final bill passed and was signed into law on September 30, 1996, creating the 34,000-acre Opal Creek Wilderness and Scenic Recreation Area.[861]

---

855 Zach Urness, "George Atiyeh: Guardian of Opal Creek," *Salem (OR) Statesman Journal*, 26 September 2016, http://www.statesmanjournal.com.

856 *Oregon Blue Book, 1983–1984*, (Salem, OR: Oregon Secretary of State, 1983), 164.

857 *Statesman-Journal* (Salem), "Bennett, Opponent File," 16 December 1983.

858 Charles E. Beggs, "Demos Lose Two, Keep Two in State," *Salem (OR) Statesman-Journal*, 17 May 1984.

859 Theresa Novak, "Hatfield Defends Uncut Gem: He Unveils a Bill to Protect Almost 26,000 Acres of Opal Creek as Wilderness and Recreation Area," *Salem (OR) Statesman Journal*, 29 March 1996.

860 Zach Urness, "How Mark Hatfield, Unlikely Hero, Saved Opal Creek," *Salem (OR) Statesman Journal*, 24 September 2016, http://www.statesmanjournal.com.

861 Urness, "Opal Creek Timeline."; Scott Sonner, "Hatfield Leaves Senate With Dignity: Appropriations Bill; Senator Ensures Opal Creek Reserve as He Bade Farewell to Career," *Coos Bay (OR) World*, 1 October 1996.

Securing Public Access to The Deschutes

Saving the Deschutes River for public access was one of the high points of Atiyeh's time as governor. The details show a governor involved in the nitty gritty of making decisions, his role in bringing private and public resources to bear on a problem, and how Atiyeh's love of nature guided his understanding of solutions. *Oregonian* editorialist Wayne Thompson recalled that a lot of people were surprised at the environmental activism of the governor. When Atiyeh began to work to save the Deschutes, "heads turned. A lot of people were stunned he would go that far."[862] Atiyeh's environmentalism was not a surprise to others. *Oregonian* outdoors columnist Bill Monroe described the governor in 1982 as "partially political, completely non-radical and occasionally midstream…[on] environmental matters and tuned into the environmental movement important to many Oregonians."[863]

Atiyeh was very familiar with the Deschutes River. He had fished it for years, and he continued to do so when he became governor.[864] Atiyeh would sometimes fish at the private Deschutes Club, a 48-member group that owned fourteen miles of riverbank centered on an abandoned mining town upriver from Maupin.[865] The governor's aide and driver, Lon Holbrook, would drive the governor to the club, leave him there on his own with club members, and then come back to get him the next day.[866]

In the summer of 1980, the governor created the Deschutes River Scenic Waterway Advisory Task Force to look at management ideas for the lower stretches of the river. He

---

862 Wayne Thompson, interviewed by Jim Moore, "Atiyeh interview," Portland, OR, 2 April 2015. Summary notes, 3.
863 Bill Monroe, "Atiyeh Style Reflected in Outdoor View: Low-Key, Thoughtful, Mainstream," Column, *Oregonian*, 27 June 1982.
864 "Monthly Diary Schedule, June 1979," Office of the Governor, State of Oregon, (June 1979), June 2–3, Atiyeh Collection, Pac. Univ. Archives.
865 Bill Monroe, "Exclusive Club Has Stewardship Over Choice Stretch of River," *Oregonian*, 25 June 1982.
866 Lon Holbrook, interviewed by Jim Moore, "Atiyeh interview," Gladstone, OR, 6 June 2017. Summary notes, 16.

observed that the 100 miles of river from the Pelton Dam to the Columbia were "being placed under pressure by increased use."[867] By the end of 1981, outgoing executive assistant Lee Johnson reported that the task force's "proposals have been almost totally implemented."[868] From the work of the task force, Atiyeh proposed to the 1981 legislature "a boating user fee," designed "not to prevent people from using the river but to 'enhance the quality of the experience for everyone.'"[869] The legislature agreed.[870] The revenue from the passes was only to deal with the "vandalism, litter and fire" that had plagued the lower 100 miles because of so many people using the area.[871] There was a new "state park river ranger program" to enforce rules and keep the area cleaned up.[872] No fishing was allowed from any of the floating craft, so those wishing to do a little angling would need to head to the shore to cast their lines.[873]

Just as the new user-fee system was being implemented, another threat arose for the Deschutes. It was in facing this challenge that Atiyeh would, as Wayne Thompson put it, stun a lot of people with his environmental activism—but activism that would perfectly mesh with his principle that people ought to solve their own problems, with government playing a backup role. Douglas Robertson, an attorney for a commercial finance company, drafted a letter "asking for 200 applicants to chip in $7,500 each to purchase the [Deschutes] riverbanks from the mouth of the river" to fifteen miles upstream.[874] The riverbanks

---

867 *Oregonian*, "Deschutes Task Force Set," 12 July 1980.
868 Lee Johnson, "Swan Song," Office of the Governor, State of Oregon, Memo to Governor, (4 September 1981), 2, Atiyeh Collection, Pac. Univ. Archives.
869 AP, "Atiyeh Wants Boat Fee," *Salem (OR) Statesman-Journal*, 27 March 1981.
870 *Oregonian*, "Passes Start on Deschutes," 14 May 1982.
871 *Oregonian*, "Passes Start on Deschutes."
872 Denny Miles, "Legislative Package Summary," Governor's Office Communications, State of Oregon, Memo to Gov. Atiyeh, (2 August 1981), 3, Atiyeh Collection, Pac. Univ. Archives.
873 Bill Monroe, "Purchase Threat Used to Rescue Lower Deschutes," Column, *Oregonian*, 25 May 1982.
874 Monroe, "Purchase Threat Used to Rescue Lower Deschutes."; UPI, "Fight Is On for Deschutes," *Coos Bay (OR) World*, 26 May 1982.

would become "an exclusive fishing club. The access to the river for the public in that area would either be ended or sharply restricted."[875] Robertson argued that his effort seemed exclusionary in order "to catalyze some support for a public purchase."[876]

At the same time, a Portland publisher of a fishing newsletter, Frank Amato, was "leading the effort to find funds to purchase the [same] land for public use."[877] Both Robertson and Amato saw their plans as ways to control the hordes of people who floated the river. Amato was thinking that the federal government (Senator Hatfield (R) and Representative Les AuCoin (D-CD1) had been supportive of these ideas in the past) or the state government might purchase the land. Amato had talked with Atiyeh, describing the governor "as becoming 'glassy-eyed' when talking about the Deschutes."[878]

Coincidentally, a new group was formed in 1982, the Oregon Wildlife Heritage Foundation, with a goal to "develop food, water, and cover for fish and wildlife; preserve stream beds and acquire critically-needed fish habitat; and increase fish stocking activities and egg production."[879] Composed of Portland businesspeople who were outdoor enthusiasts, this group took a different direction than those who formed and joined the private Deschutes Club.[880] The new group wanted to help acquire land for the public. The Foundation was set up to take tax-deductible donations from the public, but it also counted many Oregon businesses as crucial partners.

The brand-new Oregon Wildlife Heritage Foundation found itself in a bit of a quandary. Its mission was to use private

---

875 Monroe, "Purchase Threat Used to Rescue Lower Deschutes."
876 Monroe, "Purchase Threat Used to Rescue Lower Deschutes."
877 Monroe, "Purchase Threat Used to Rescue Lower Deschutes."; UPI, "Fight Is On for Deschutes."
878 Monroe, "Purchase Threat Used to Rescue Lower Deschutes."
879 Blitz-Weinheard Brewery, "We're Giving Away $25,000 Worth of Prizes," Advertisement, *Oregonian*, 25 April 1982.
880 Don Black, "Saving the Deschutes: Campaign Strives to Keep River Open for Fishing by the Public," *Salem (OR) Statesman-Journal*, 14 November 1982, 1G.

donations to restore fishing opportunities, but a $1.5 million project to buy the land along the lower Deschutes was a big ask in the group's first few months.[881] The new board of directors met and decided to investigate the situation. By the last week in June, Atiyeh publicly jumped into the fray, saying he "will seek to preserve public recreational access to" the river.[882] Given the budget realities of the time (a second 1982 special legislative session had just taken place to cut state spending even more, and another special session would take place in early September), Atiyeh made it clear that "[i]t is not in the cards for the state to purchase the land outright. But we are interested in bringing the parties together to see if we can work out some kind of arrangement."[883]

That same week, the governor headed out to the Deschutes to see how the new permit system was working. A report from earlier in the spring described "smiling" boaters basking "in the sun,...but only after some gritted their teeth while buying river passes."[884] In a weekend of fishing, Atiyeh saw an estimated "1,000 men, women and children [float] by in rafts and drift boats."[885] Some made obscene gestures or mooned those fishing on the shore (it was clear that the people doing this had no idea the governor was the recipient of their actions), but most were "happy, smiling Oregonians and tourists getting the full benefits of one of the state's richest wild and scenic treasures."[886]

The governor formed a committee of state agency heads (Dave Talbot, director of State Parks headed the group; Pat Amedeo from Atiyeh's staff and Jack Donaldson, director of Fish and Wildlife, were on board) to work with "the Oregon Wildlife

---

881   Bill Monroe, "Battle Joined for Stretch of Deschutes," Column. *Oregonian*, 6 June 1982.
882   AP, "Atiyeh Pledges Work to Retain Access to River," *Salem (OR) Statesman-Journal*, 24 June 1982.
883   AP, "Atiyeh Pledges Work to Retain Access to River."
884   Andy McIvor, "Deschutes River Fee Has Boaters Upset," *Salem (OR) Statesman-Journal*, 2 May 1982.
885   Bill Monroe, "Atiyeh Views Shame, Hope in Human Use of Deschutes," *Oregonian*, 25 June 1982.
886   Monroe, "Atiyeh Views Shame, Hope."

Heritage Foundation to keep the land from being used for a private fishing club."[887] Atiyeh recalled that Talbot's leadership in the negotiations and the fundraising "was a marvelous thing."[888] As the movement to save the Deschutes gathered steam, donations to the Oregon Wildlife Heritage Foundation began to be encouraged in obituaries as ways to honor the life of a fishing enthusiast.[889] In August there was a meeting with the sellers of the Deschutes property. Private donations already amounted to $60,000, getting nearer to the $100,000 needed to meet the option price "to tie up the land for a few years until payments can be completed" to purchase the property outright.[890]

By mid-September 1982, it appeared that the agreements were moving forward. The state and the Wildlife Heritage Foundation would split the price, each paying about $750,000. The final price was estimated to be $1.5 million to $1.6 million.[891] A week later, the governor attended the event marking the successful negotiations.[892] The final price was $1.6 million, and the buyers had a one-year option to complete the sale. Atiyeh explained that the state's half would come from state agency budgets, while "the rest will come in the form of public donations in a fund-raising project spearheaded by the foundation."[893]

---

887 UPI, "Save the Deschutes," *Coos Bay (OR) World*, 2 July 1982.

888 Victor Atiyeh, interviewed by Clark Hansen, "Tape 58, side 2," Oral history, recorded by Oregon Historical Society, Portland, OR, 3 September 1993. Transcript, 30, Atiyeh Collection, Pac. Univ. Archives.

889 *Oregonian*, "Raymond G. Shay," Obituary, 18 July 1982; *Statesman-Journal* (Salem) "Thomas Neal Edwards," Obituary, 1 May 1983; *Oregonian*, "James J. Parker," Obituary, 3 March 1983.

890 Bill Monroe, "Rift Grows in NW Steelheaders Group," Column, *Oregonian*, 31 August 1982.

891 Bill Monroe, "State Officials Near Deschutes Riverbank Purchase," Column, *Oregonian*, 14 September 1982.

892 "Atiyeh Daily Index-Card Schedule, September 21, 1982," Office of the Governor, State of Oregon, (21 September 1982), Attend: Deschutes River Acquisition Event, Atiyeh Collection, Pac. Univ. Archives.

893 AP, "Wildlife Group Moves to Buy Riverfront Land," *Salem (OR) Statesman-Journal*, 23 September 1982.

The fundraising drive plan was led by the Oregon Wildlife Heritage Foundation.[894] The fundraising plan was sophisticated and ambitious. The governor met with Dave Talbot about the process the first week in February.[895] The first attempt at approving the state's role in the plan by the 1983 legislature did not go as smoothly, however. Legislators questioned whether the purchase would make the area more accessible to the public, especially since no new roads were planned along the banks of the river. Another legislator thought the value of the land was too high "and vowed to find out the value…on the tax rolls before making any decision on the plan."[896] Even with the doubt among some legislators, the newly re-elected Atiyeh was "confident… that the public purchase…will become a reality, and [was] working for legislative support of state departmental budgets committed to help pay the tab."[897]

On April 22, the public part of the campaign began. Atiyeh gave brief remarks at a breakfast meeting at the capitol, saying, "Those of us who really love the Deschutes know it is one of the real rarities in the world."[898] The legislature had still made no

---

894 Don Black, "Foundation Gives a Big Assist," *Salem (OR) Statesman-Journal*, 14 November 1982.

895 "Atiyeh Daily Index-Card Schedule, February 4, 1983," Office of the Governor, State of Oregon, (4 February 1983), [Handwritten by Atiyeh] Dave Talbot—Re: Deschutes River, Atiyeh Collection, Pac. Univ. Archives.

896 Bill Dixon, "Deschutes River Plan Gets Iffy Reception, but Backers Hopeful," *Salem (OR) Statesman-Journal*, 11 February 1983.

897 Bill Monroe, "Governor Lands First Steelhead," Column, *Oregonian*, 18 February 1983; Atiyeh also fished with KGW's Doug LaMear, "Atiyeh Daily Index-Card Schedule, December 28, 1984," Office of the Governor, State of Oregon, (28 December 1984), Fishing (Doug LaMear Show); No. Fork Nehalem River with Doug LaMear, Jim Teeny and Tom McAllister, Atiyeh Collection, Pac. Univ. Archives; "Atiyeh Daily Index-Card Schedule, August 6, 1986," Office of the Governor, State of Oregon, (6 August 1986), Fishing on Deschutes with Dudley Nelson, Doug LaMear & camera crew, Atiyeh Collection, Pac. Univ. Archives; "Atiyeh Daily Index-Card Schedule, August 7, 1986," Office of the Governor, State of Oregon, (7 August 1986), Fishing on Deschutes, Atiyeh Collection, Pac. Univ. Archives.

898 "Atiyeh Daily Index-Card Schedule, April 22, 1983," Office of the Governor, State of Oregon, (22 April 1983), Brief Remarks: Kickoff to announce start of statewide fund raising campaign for purchase of Deschutes River lands, Atiyeh Collection, Pac. Univ. Archives; "Governor's Schedule, 18–24 April 1983,' Office of the

final decision on the agency budgets to pay for the state's portion. Serious fundraising efforts ensued, including high-end sweepstakes. On July 27, it was announced that over $977,000 had been raised.[899] A surge of $167,000 came in during the last week of the drive, including $50,000 from former University of Oregon track coach and Nike co-founder Bill Bowerman (the son of 1910 Oregon governor Jay Bowerman). As the legislative session came to an end in July, money for the purchase was included in the State Parks and the Fish and Wildlife budgets, but it was "contingent on the success of the private fundraising effort."[900]

The money came through. In August, Atiyeh participated in a train tour of the lower Deschutes with the State Parks Advisory Committee to look over the new acquisition.[901] The actual handover took place in November with the Oregon Wildlife Heritage Foundation presenting the deed to the governor.[902] The final purchase was of the east bank going up the river eleven miles.

Atiyeh's 1984 State of the State address used the private fundraising to buy the Deschutes property as one of his examples of Oregonians who faced economic hardship but persevered because they were "an uncommon people."[903]

Governor, State of Oregon, Confidential, (14 April 1983), April 22, 4, Atiyeh Collection, Pac. Univ. Archives; "Campaign to Buy Stretch of Deschutes River Begins," *Salem (OR) Statesman-Journal*, 23 April 1983.

899 AP, "Deschutes Site Still Public After Successful Fund-Drive," *Salem (OR) Statesman-Journal*, 28 July 1983.

900 Alan Gustafson, "River Rescue: Outdoor Enthusiasts Bid to Save Deschutes Site for the Public," *Salem (OR) Statesman-Journal*, 15 July 1983.

901 "Governor's Schedule, 8–14 August 1983," August 10, 3.

902 "Governor's Schedule, 26 September–2 October 1983," Office of the Governor, State of Oregon, Confidential, (22 September 1983), September 26, 1, Atiyeh Collection, Pac. Univ. Archives; "Atiyeh Accepts Deed," *Coos Bay (OR) World*, 5 November 1983.

903 Victor Atiyeh, "State of the State Address for 1984" (speech, Eugene/Springfield Chambers of Commerce, Springfield, OR, 11 January 1984), 2, 3, Atiyeh collection, Pac. Univ. Archives.

By the summer of 1984, bids were being taken for a boat landing area at the mouth of the river. "The facility, to be called Heritage Landing, will be on the west bank across from the [new] Deschutes River State Recreation Area."[904]

Heritage Landing was dedicated at the end of July 1985 with Atiyeh in attendance.[905]

Heritage Landing, December 1985. Oregon Wildlife Heritage Foundation, Photo of commemorative sign for purchase of Deschutes River land, (December 1985), Atiyeh Collection, Pacific University Archives.

---

904 AP, "Boat Landing Bids Due," *Salem (OR) Statesman-Journal* 22 June 1984.
905 "Governor's Schedule, 29 July–4 August 1985," Office of the Governor, State of Oregon, Confidential, (25 July 1985), July 31, 3, Atiyeh Collection, Pac. Univ. Archives.

Then, in November 1984, the whole public process to raise money started up again. This time the available land began about where the earlier purchase ended, eleven miles up the river. It extended upriver about three miles to federal land. If successful, it would "result in a virtually contiguous strip of public ownership along the lower river's east bank for 42 miles."[906] Negotiations had been going between Fish and Wildlife and the owners since the end of the highly publicized 1983 purchase. Atiyeh had "personally" told Fish and Wildlife and the State Parks (the ever-dependable Dave Talbot) "to begin negotiations."[907] The Oregon Wildlife Heritage Foundation was initially reluctant to take on a project of this size so soon but was presently fully on board. Atiyeh met with the board in August 1984.[908] This time, the group "probably would not conduct a new full-blown public campaign" which might be perceived as "in poor taste on the heels of last year's pleas for money."[909] Atiyeh met with leaders of the group in November 1984 and May 1985 to talk about the purchase.[910]

---

906 Bill Monroe, "State Eyeing 2nd Deschutes Tract," *Oregonian*, 22 November 1984, *Oregonian* Historical Archives.

907 Monroe, "State Eyeing."

908 "Atiyeh Daily Index-Card Schedule, August 1, 1984," Office of the Governor, State of Oregon, (1 August 1984), Remarks: Wildlife Heritage Foundation Board of Directors' Mtg., Atiyeh Collection, Pac. Univ. Archives.

909 Monroe, "State Eyeing."

910 "Atiyeh Daily Index-Card Schedule, November 19, 1984, revised," Office of the Governor, State of Oregon, (19 November 1984), Roland Fisher & Mort Bishop, Ore. Wildlife Heritage Foundation; regarding decisions on Deschutes acquisition, Atiyeh Collection, Pac. Univ. Archives; "Atiyeh Daily Index-Card Schedule, May 22, 1985," Office of the Governor, State of Oregon, (22 May 1985), Mort Bishop, Ken & Joan Austin; regarding Deschutes River property, Atiyeh Collection, Pac. Univ. Archives.

The mix of money for this second $1.26 million opportunity ended up as $360,000 raised by the Wildlife Heritage Foundation, "$300,000 in federal funds and user fees administered by the state Parks and Recreation Division and $600,000 in federal funds administered by the state Fish and Wildlife Department."[911] The Burlington Northern railroad's foundation donated $50,000 in August 1985, in an announcement made by the governor.[912] Atiyeh again featured the private-public purchase of land along the Deschutes in his 1986 State of the State address, this time likening it to the creation of Oregon Food Share in 1979.[913] By February 1986, with considerably less fanfare than the 1983 effort, the property was in state hands.[914]

Atiyeh found the private-public nature of the Deschutes lands acquisitions to be quite satisfying. He was immensely grateful to those who donated money.[915] The whole process "was a wonderful thing [to] me. ...I was just so excited in seeing all this energy, and it was a good cause, and we acquired that" land for the people of Oregon.[916]

Sovereign Lands

Oregon had a long and troubling relationship with the Indian tribes who lived within its borders. A series of treaties in the 1850s between the U.S. government and the tribes consolidated the legal entities of reservations and tribal groups in the years before statehood. Within this context, Atiyeh built a very special relationship with the tribes of the Warm Springs Reservation.

---

911 AP, "Foundation Helps Buy Land," *Salem (OR) Statesman-Journal*, 2 August 1985.
912 AP, "Foundation Helps Buy Land."
913 Vic Atiyeh, "State of the State Address" (speech, Medford Rotary Club, Medford, OR, 31 January 1986), 15, Atiyeh Collection, Pac. Univ. Archives.
914 *Statesman-Journal* (Salem), "Deschutes Purchase," 20 February 1986.
915 Victor Atiyeh, interviewed by Clark Hansen, "Tape 57," Oral history, recorded by Oregon Historical Society, Portland, OR, 30 August 1993. Transcript, 756, Atiyeh Collection, Pac. Univ. Archives.
916 Victor Atiyeh, "Tape 58, side 2," 31.

The Warm Springs Reservation is the official home of the Confederated Tribes of the Warm Springs Reservation of Oregon.[917] There are three distinct tribes, the Warm Springs, the Wasco, and the Paiute. The Treaty of 1855, signed by the Warm Springs and Wasco leaders, created the 600,000-acre (almost 1000 square miles) reservation in exchange for surrendering 10 million acres to the U.S. government.[918] The Paiutes were moved to the reservation in 1879. In the 20th century, following the 1934 Indian Reorganization Act, the three tribes formed their unified government of the Confederated Tribes in 1938. While the Paiute had been primarily a hunting tribe, using lands that are now in Oregon, Idaho, Nevada, and Utah, the Warm Springs and Wasco were fishing tribes. The biggest change to their treaty-protected rights was the drowning of Celilo Falls on the Columbia River in 1957 following the completion of The Dalles Dam.

In the 1950s, in a move to encourage the assimilation of tribal members into the larger society, 109 tribes and bands were terminated, or lost their official status with the federal government. Sixty-two of these tribes and bands were in Oregon. "In 1975, the federal government recognized the failure of its termination policy and passed the Indian Self Determination and Education Assistance Act and, later, the Tribal Self-Governance Act."[919] During much of Atiyeh's time as governor, tribes in Oregon were regaining official recognition. He recalled attending the 1977 ceremony of the first Oregon tribe to be restored, and the second in the country, the Siletz.[920] From 1982 to 1986 four more tribes were restored to sovereign status—Cow Creek Band of the Umpqua, Confederated Tribes of Grand Ronde, Confederated

---

917 Brent Walth, "The People of Warm Springs," *Oregonian*, 7 December 2003, Atiyeh Collection, Pac. Univ. Archives.

918 "Treaty of the Tribes of Middle Oregon [Upper De Chutes Band of Walla-Wallas; Wyam or Lower De Chutes Band of Walla-Wallas; Tenino Band of Walla-Wallas; Dalles Band of Wascoes; Kigaltwalla Band of Wascoes; Dog River Band of Wascoes]," in *Laws and Treaties*, ed. Charles J. Kappler, vol. II, (Washington, DC: Government Printing Office, 1904). http://dc.library.okstate.edu.

919 *Oregon Blue Book: Almanac and Fact Book, 2017–2018*, (Salem, OR: Oregon Secretary of State, 2017), 218.

920 Victor Atiyeh, "Tape 27, side 1," 774; *Oregon Blue Book, 2017*, 218.

Tribes of Coos, Lower Umpqua and Siuslaw, and the Klamath tribes—with the Coquille following in 1989.[921] Atiyeh met with Umatilla tribal members during his visits to the Pendleton area, whether for the September Pendleton Round-Up or for other visits. Jill Thorne, a Pendleton-area resident, recalled that Atiyeh had a good relationship with Antone Minthorn of the Umatillas.[922] The governor visited the Paiute in Burns in 1986 and hosted representatives from the Yakama Nation to talk about fishing rights.[923] In September that year he was in Chiloquin for the Klamath Tribe Restoration Celebration.[924] In March and October the governor met with tribal leaders to discuss hunting and fishing issues.[925]

Atiyeh, in 1981, became the first governor to accept the Warm Springs tribes' invitation to attend the annual Pi-Ume-Sha celebrations held in June. According to Delvis Heath, the chief of the Warm Springs in 2014, Atiyeh continued attending the

---

921 *Oregon Blue Book, 2017*, 218.
922 Jill Thorne and Mike Thorne, interviewed by Jim Moore, "Atiyeh interview," Pendleton, OR, 23 June 2015. Summary notes, 2, Atiyeh project, Moore collection; "Atiyeh Daily Index-Card Schedule, September 5, 1986," Office of the Governor, State of Oregon, (5 September 1986), Dinner/Remarks: Black Hawk Powwow; Long House, Umatilla Indian Reservation; contact: Jay Minthorne, Atiyeh Collection, Pac. Univ. Archives.
923 "Atiyeh Daily Index-Card Schedule, April 25, 1986," Office of the Governor, State of Oregon, (25 April 1986), Meet: Burns Paiute Indians; Reservation Community Center, Burns; contact: Vernon Shake Spear, Atiyeh Collection, Pac. Univ. Archives; "Atiyeh Daily Index-Card Schedule, July 25, 1986," Office of the Governor, State of Oregon, (25 July 1986), Philip Olney, Leo Aleck, Johnny Jackson & David Sohappy of Yakima [sic] Indian Tribe; regarding fishing rights, Atiyeh Collection, Pac. Univ. Archives.
924 "Atiyeh Daily Index-Card Schedule, September 20, 1986," Office of the Governor, State of Oregon, (20 September 1986), Remarks: Klamath Tribe Restoration Celebration…, Chiloquin, Atiyeh Collection, Pac. Univ. Archives.
925 "Atiyeh Daily Index-Card Schedule, March 24, 1986," Office of the Governor, State of Oregon, (24 March 1986), Jim Weber, Tim Wapato & Rob Lothrup, Columbia River Tribal Fish Comsn; Katheryn Brigham & Jay Minthorn, Umatilla Tribe; Levi George, Yakima [sic] Tribe; Nathan Jim & Harold Culpus, Warm Springs Tribe; Pat, Atiyeh Collection, Pac. Univ. Archives; "Atiyeh Daily Index-Card Schedule, October 16, 1986," Office of the Governor, State of Oregon, (16 October 1986), 11 AM Rollie Rousseau; briefing on 2 p.m. meeting; 2 PM Grande Ronde Tribal Council; regarding hunting & fishing rights, Atiyeh Collection, Pac. Univ. Archives.

celebrations faithfully thereafter.[926] Atiyeh had already loved to fish on the Warm Springs reservation. His gubernatorial calendars show that these excursions were hardwired into his schedule from the beginning.[927] Clifford Jenkin, the Warm Springs Police Department Fish and Game officer in 1982, wrote a nice note to the governor after the 1982 Pi-Ume-Sha celebration. He and his wife "wish you much luck for re-election. But you are always welcome here even when you are no more Governor of Oregon. …P.S. You are a very skilled fisherman."[928] But his main tie to the Warm Springs was not the fish, it was Atiyeh's reaching out to all Oregon tribes to work with them as governmental equals—the sovereign Indian groups and the state of Oregon.

The governor began sovereign-to-sovereign relations between the tribes and the state government in 1982.[929] His schedule from 1985 shows a morning-long meeting with the reservation tribes one week in July followed by a morning-long meeting with non-reservation tribes the next week.[930] Both gatherings were followed

---

926 "State Memorial for the Honorable Vic Atiyeh," Memorial service, recorded by Oregon Legislative Media, Salem, OR, 3 September 2014. DVD, 1:42:20, Atiyeh project, Moore collection; "Monthly Diary Schedule, June 1981," Office of the Governor, State of Oregon, (1981), 6/26–27, Atiyeh Collection, Pac. Univ. Archives.

927 "Monthly Diary Schedule, August 1979," Office of the Governor, State of Oregon, (1979), 29–30 August, Atiyeh Collection, Pac. Univ. Archives; "Atiyeh Daily Index-Card Schedule, June 22, 1985," Office of the Governor, State of Oregon, (22 June 1985), 3 PM Leave For Fishing; 5 PM Cookout; More Fishing, Atiyeh Collection, Pac. Univ. Archives; "Atiyeh Daily Index-Card Schedule, June 23, 1985," Office of the Governor, State of Oregon, (23 June 1985), 8 AM Breakfast; Fishing; 2 PM Attend: Pi-Ume-Sha Celebration, Atiyeh Collection, Pac. Univ. Archives.

928 Clifford L. Jenkin, Letter to Victor Atiyeh, "Honor to Serve You," 15 July 1982, Atiyeh Collection, Pac. Univ. Archives.

929 Ted Kulongoski, interviewed by Jim Moore, "Atiyeh interview," Portland, OR, 30 March 2015. Summary notes, 11; "Atiyeh Daily Index-Card Schedule, March 28, 1981," Office of the Governor, State of Oregon, (28 March 1981), 9:00 Meet: Oregon Tribal Indian Leaders; 12:00 Lunch: Above at your home, Atiyeh Collection, Pac. Univ. Archives.

930 "Atiyeh Daily Index-Card Schedule, July 13, 1985," Office of the Governor, State of Oregon, (13 July 1985), 9:30 AM Tribal Leadership—conf. room. Buffet Lunch; Gov's home, Atiyeh Collection, Pac. Univ. Archives; "Atiyeh Daily Index-Card Schedule, July 20, 1985," Office of the Governor, State of Oregon, (20 July 1985),

by lunch at the governor's residence. This relationship continues with statutes mandating annual meetings between the state and the tribes as well as annual training "to state agency managers and employees who have regular communications with tribes on the legal status of the tribes, the legal rights of members of tribes and issues of concern to tribes."[931] A 1985 letter from the chair of the Warm Springs Tribal Council celebrated Atiyeh's role in showing "that people can work together to solve problems through the opportunities we allow ourselves."[932]

Atiyeh's connection to the Warm Springs tribe dated at least back to the early 1970s, culminating with his advocacy for the creation of the Legislative Commission on Indian Services, which came into effect in 1975.[933] Collaborating with Native American groups was so close to Atiyeh's heart that when he was elected governor, he said he "lamented" having to leave his position on that commission.[934] There is even some evidence that his work with Warm Springs went back to the 1960s. One of Atiyeh's close friends in the legislature was House member Sam Johnson (R-Redmond). In 1967, Representative Johnson and Senator Atiyeh served as the chair and vice chair, respectively of an interim committee on business climate.[935] Johnson had spent that spring not only representing his House district during the legislative session, but selling his Warm Springs Lumber Company and Jefferson Plywood machinery to the Confederated Tribes of the

---

9:30 AM Meet: Non-Reservation Indians—conf. room. Buffet Lunch; Gov's home, Atiyeh Collection, Pac. Univ. Archives.

931 "Training of State Agency Managers and Employees who Communicate with Tribes," State of Oregon, ORS 182.166, (2015). http://www.oregonlaws.org; "State Agencies to Develop and Implement Policy on Relationshiop with Tribes," State of Oregon, ORS 182.164, (2015). http://www.oregonlaws.org.

932 Zane Jackson, "Letter to Governor Victor Atiyeh," Tribal Council, Confederated Tribes of Warm Springs, Signed by Delbert Frank, Jr. for Zane Jackson, (11 July 1985), Atiyeh Collection, Pac. Univ. Archives.

933 Victor Atiyeh, interviewed by Clark Hansen, "Tape 19," Oral History, recorded by Oregon Historical Society, Portland, OR, 1 February 1993. Transcript, 573, Atiyeh Collection, Pac. Univ. Archives.

934 Victor Atiyeh, "Tape 19," 572.

935 "Group Elects Rep. Johnson," *Oregonian*, 26 August 1967.

Warm Springs Reservation.[936] The mill was located on the reservation; the machinery was located near Madras where Johnson's plywood plant had burned down in 1966. The new entity was to be known as the Warm Spring Forest Products Industry, and Johnson was to "be called on for executive help" as the operation got off the ground.[937] Because of the sovereign nature of the tribe, the deal took the approval of the Secretary of Interior, at that time Stewart Udall (whose nephew Gordon Smith —a Republican to his uncle's Democrat—would serve as U.S. Senator from Oregon from 1997 to 2009).[938] The expectation was the deal would create 250 jobs and bring in $1.5 million to $2 million a year for the tribe. By October 1967, a board of directors had been selected, and the company was moving forward.[939]

Phil Lang, Atiyeh's longtime colleague in the legislature in the 1960s and '70s, remembered how close Atiyeh and Johnson were. Lang did not know the precise nature of Atiyeh's and Johnson's relationship, but he saw that it was a strong one. In Lang's opinion, "It almost had to be Sam" who connected Atiyeh with the Warm Springs tribe. "Sam was very outspoken about the tribes."[940] Bruce Bishop, one of the first employees of what was then the State Legislative Research Office in 1973 (now the Office of Legislative Policy and Research), worked closely with Atiyeh to determine whether there should be a Legislative Commission on Indian Services, and he became its first executive secretary.[941] He too thought that Atiyeh's connection to the Warm

---

936 William Swing, "Confederated Tribes Find it Difficult to Start Mill Business," *Oregonian*, 26 February 1967.

937 AP, "Tribe to Buy Lumber Mill, Machinery," *Oregonian*, 14 April 1967.

938 Special, "Interior Secretary Approves Warm Springs Lumber Project," *Oregonian*, 11 May 1967.

939 *Oregonian*, "Indians Pick Mill Heads: Tribe Selects 7-Man Board," 4 October 1967; Lucille Jordan, "Work Moves Forward on Schedule on Warm Springs Lumber Complex," *Oregonian*, 26 October 1967.

940 Phil Lang, interviewed by Jim Moore, "Atiyeh interview," Portland, OR, 3 August 2015. Summary notes, 2.

941 Bruce Bishop, Email to Jim Moore, "Indian Commission Question," 11 January 2018; David Reyes, "Indians Say They Will Seek Role in Education Policies," *Salem (OR) Statesman Journal*, 30 April 1977.

Springs tribe came from Sam Johnson.[942] A fellow legislator at the time, Wally Carson, recalled, "Vic became the champion for the governance of the tribes, trying to get it so that they had a voice in their own government, but cooperated with our government."[943]

As Atiyeh was negotiating the delicate balance between commercial fishing interests, sports fisheries, and declining fish runs, the tribes played a vital role. He recalled it as very difficult situation.

> [Y]ou have to understand that they have a position that's a legitimate position. When there was a lot of fish, there were never these arguments because there was plenty for everybody. Basically, what took it way wasn't the commercial fishermen nor the sports fishermen nor the Indians. It was the dams.
>
> ...The arguments came about when we all of a sudden...were fighting over what's left.[944]

Atiyeh appreciated that the Warm Springs hosted a federal hatchery so the salmon returned up the Deschutes every year. He also had meetings with tribal representatives on fishing issues to talk about federal forest planning.[945]

One of Atiyeh's treasures was a lifetime fishing permit for the Warm Springs reservation. He smiled and recalled, "I understand they've only given out a couple of those in their history. [On the permit was] *Un kun kunga dumma,* ...'Let's go fishing.'"[946] Atiyeh would take the opportunity to use his fishing permit when

---

942 Bruce Bishop, Conversation to Jim Moore, "Discussion of the Tribes," 19 June 2015, Atiyeh project, Moore collection.

943 Wallace P. "Wally" Carson, interviewed by Jim Moore, "Atiyeh interview #2," Salem, OR, 9 June 2016. Summary notes, 1.

944 Victor Atiyeh, interviewed by Clark Hansen, "Tape 16," Oral history, recorded by Oregon Historical Society, Portland, OR, 22 January 1993. Transcript, 459, Atiyeh Collection, Pac. Univ. Archives.

945 "Governor's Schedule, 24–30 March 1986," Office of the Governor, State of Oregon, Confidential, (20 March 1986), March 24, Atiyeh Collection, Pac. Univ. Archives. Met with Jim Weber and Tim Wapato, Columbia River Tribal Fish Commisison; representatives of Umatill and Warm Springs Indian Tribes; and Pat Amedeo.

he went to Pi-Ume-Sha. Aide and driver Lon Holbrook recalled, "He was very, very close to Warm Springs, and he cherished going over there" every year.[947] Atiyeh would usually spend a full day fishing along the river. The tribe would bring in big trucks to feed all those out at the fishing hole. The governor would be there, as well as attorneys who represented the tribe, and many tribal members. One time as they were all fishing, a group floated down the river and started giving Atiyeh a hard time because he was a white man fishing on the Indian side of the river. Holbrook said a tribal policeman, "and that's a whole different breed of cat," with bandoliers and dark smudges under his eyes, pointed his M-16 at the rafters and said, "You better get the hell out of here." They swiftly rowed downstream. Holbrook just laughed.

Even more than twenty years after Atiyeh left office, the Warm Springs people honored him at the annual June Pi-Ume-Sha gathering. Oregon governor Kate Brown (2015–2023) attended in about 2011 and said "They treated him like he was the president of the United States . . . It was really extraordinary."[948] Brown first came to know Atiyeh as a first-term legislator in 1991 because she was appointed to serve on the Legislative Commission on Indian Services, a position she kept for her seventeen years in the legislature. Atiyeh was a regular at the Pi-Ume-Sha Treaty Days on the Warm Springs Reservation for over thirty years, attending his last just the month before his death in July 2014.[949]

---

946 Victor Atiyeh, interviewed by Clark Hansen, "Tape 56, side 1," Oral history, recorded by Oregon Historical Society, Portland, OR, 25 August 1993. Transcript, 726, Atiyeh Collection, Pac. Univ. Archives.
947 Holbrook, "Atiyeh interview," 15.
948 Kate Brown, interviewed by Jim Moore, "Atiyeh interview," Salem, OR, 2 September 2016. Summary notes, 7.
949 "Governor's Out Schedule, June 1981," Office of the Governor, State of Oregon, (1981), Atiyeh Collection, Pac. Univ. Archives; "Monthly Diary Schedule, June 1982," Office of the Governor, State of Oregon, (1982), Atiyeh Collection, Pac. Univ. Archives; "Governor's Out Schedule, June 1983," Office of the Governor, State of Oregon, (1983), Atiyeh Collection, Pac. Univ. Archives; "Governor's Out Schedule, June 1984," Office of the Governor, State of Oregon, (14 May 1984), Atiyeh Collection, Pac. Univ. Archives; "Governor's Out Schedule, June 1985," Office of the Governor, State of Oregon, (23 April 1985), Atiyeh Collection, Pac.

At the 2015 celebration, Atiyeh was posthumously honored by the tribe with his children and some of his grandchildren in attendance. A headdress that had been presented to Atiyeh by the Warm Springs tribes and made its way into the Pacific University library, home of the Atiyeh archive, was returned to the tribe in a special ceremony that June.[950]

The Columbia Gorge

From the beginning of his governorship in 1979, protection of the Columbia Gorge was an issue. The Gorge had long been important to the region with its natural features, unique animal and plant species, historical and cultural significance to the area's tribes for millennia and to the settlers since Lewis and Clark, and in more modern times, for the recreation and fishing industries.[951] It was also where federal control of the Columbia through the dam system and federal land ownership, and the states of Oregon and Washington came together with overlapping and sometimes contradictory political goals and systems. Efforts to protect parts of the Gorge dated back to 1910 when state parks were created on both sides of the river. Access features like the Columbia Gorge Scenic Highway, from 1914, encouraged tourism.

Atiyeh recalled such pleasures from when he was a boy and with his young family in the 1950s. In high school, in 1940, he had gone to a National High Y convention back east. He headed back to Oregon on the train, "and I woke up one morning, and I raised the shade of the train as we were coming down the Columbia River Gorge. And you know, it was just a very emotional feeling for me, and I remember that vividly. I

Univ. Archives; "Governor's Schedule, 17–23 June 1985," Office of the Governor, State of Oregon, Confidential, (13 June 1985), Atiyeh Collection, Pac. Univ. Archives; "Governor's Out Schedule, June 1986," Office of the Governor, State of Oregon, (1986), Atiyeh Collection, Pac. Univ. Archives; T. Kulongoski, "Atiyeh interview," 12.

950 Tom Atiyeh, "Atiyeh interview," 2.
951 Bowen Blair, Jr., "The Columbia River Gorge National Scenic Area: The Act, Its Genesis and Legislative History," *Environmental Law* 17 (1987): 869–871, LexisNexis Academic.

remember [as] a Sea Scout, sailing up the Columbia River...."[952] Atiyeh remembered driving with friends on parts of the Scenic Highway and saying to them that it was "important to preserve this, to make sure that my children and their children and their children's children are going to have the same beautiful view that I have." He said, "It was an emotional thing for me."[953]

Atiyeh worked behind the scenes to advance ideas to save and manage the area. His most influential role lasted several years: he got Washington's governors—Dixy Lee Ray (D) who was in office when Atiyeh started his term, and John Spellman (R), who took office in 1981—to agree to come together with him to work on the Gorge.

Year after year, Atiyeh faithfully and emphatically mentioned the Gorge in his January State of the State addresses: "Before I leave office as Governor of Oregon, I in turn want to see our unmatched Columbia River Gorge preserved and protected for future generations."[954] The politics was complex—there was Oregon's state government, Washington's state government, local governments throughout the Gorge, the congressional delegations of both states, and the possibility of management of the area by a federal agency. Atiyeh played a key role with the "Governors' Plan" put together with John Spellman in May 1983. This brought the heretofore absent Washington congressional delegation to the table. The final form of the Gorge bill took another three years, but it was finally passed with just seven weeks remaining in Atiyeh's term. In 1986 Ronald Reagan had a bill on his desk that would protect the Columbia Gorge. Mark Hatfield played the key role in lobbying Reagan to sign the bill, but Atiyeh also had some influence. Atiyeh was convinced that "President Reagan was going to veto the bill. ...That was not an unknown thing. I called

---

952 Victor Atiyeh, "Tape 45," 424.
953 Victor Atiyeh, "Tape 45," 424.
954 Victor Atiyeh, "Inaugural Address" (speech, Sixty-Second Legislative Assembly, House Chambers, Salem, OR, 10 January 1983), 6, Atiyeh Collection, Pac. Univ. Archives; Foster Church, "Atiyeh Urges Tax Reform at Inaugural," *Oregonian*, 11 January 1983.

the White House and talked to [Andrew Card], and I said…, 'Now, I haven't asked you for anything.' And he said to me, 'No, you haven't.' And I said to him, 'This I want. I do not want the president to veto this bill.'"[955] Reagan reluctantly signed the bill, writing, "While I am strongly opposed to Federal regulation of private land use planning, I am signing this bill because of the far-reaching support in both States for a solution to the long-standing problems related to management of the Columbia River Gorge."[956]

Atiyeh did not make his involvement very public at the time. There was a brief mention in a valedictory December 1986 *Oregonian* article that he had talked with the Reagan White House about signing the Gorge bill.[957] This discretion fit with his political personality. He recalled, "I still believe…that it's amazing what you can get done if you don't care who gets the credit. And sometimes I wish I could get the credit for some things, but the fact is that the important thing was to achieve it."[958] In the years since, the Columbia River Gorge National Scenic Area Act has been challenged in federal court—but has withstood the pressure. In 1992, the Ninth Circuit Court upheld the constitutionality of the nature of the compact between Oregon and Washington and the strong role of the federal government, finding that "the natural resources in the Gorge are protected by regional

---

955 Victor Atiyeh, "Tape 45," 423; Victor Atiyeh, interviewed by Jim Moore, "Atiyeh interview #2," Raleigh Hills, OR, 2 January 2014. Summary notes, 6–7. Atiyeh recalled talking to Jim Baker, but Baker had left the White House in 1985. Atiyeh was most likely speaking to Andrew Card, Special Assistant to the President and Director of Intergovernmental Affairs; for verification of Card's role, see Amedeo, "Atiyeh interview," 8; Atiyeh said in a 1986 interview that he called Reagan's Chief of Staff Don Regan about the Gorge, Alan Hayakawa, "Governor's Relationship with Legislature Stormy: Mixed Triumphs, Defeats Mark Tenure," *Oregonian*, 29 December 1986, B3.

956 Ronald Reagan, "Statement on Signing the Columbia River Gorge National Scenic Area Act," Ronald Reagan Presidential Archives, United States Government, (17 November 1986). http://www.reaganfoundation.org.

957 Alan Hayakawa, "Governor's Relationship with Legislature Stormy: Mixed Triumphs, Defeats Mark Tenure," *Oregonian*, 29 December 1986, B3.

958 Victor Atiyeh, interviewed by Clark Hansen, "Tape 50, side 2," Oral history, recorded by Oregon Historical Society, Portland, OR, 28 July 1993. Transcript, 580, Atiyeh Collection, Pac. Univ. Archives.

standards that transcend the prior law of Oregon and Washington."[959]

Atiyeh remembered talking to Nancy Russell, who had spearheaded efforts to protect the Gorge, warning her of being an environmental advocate in a world of compromise politics. He told her, "'Nancy, if you keep going like you're going, we're not going to have a bill at all.' And I like Nancy. I'm not picking on her. But…sometimes an over-enthusiasm, and you're making demands way out of your reach, and you just can't budge people that far." Atiyeh's more measured attitude was, "I wanted something that was going to do the job that was necessary to be done."[960] This clash in worldviews between the activists and the more circumspect politician played out at every turn in the process of securing the Gorge for the future.

When Vic Atiyeh was running for governor in 1978, his nephew Bob Atiyeh (Ed's son) was his driver during the primary election. They covered a lot of ground, and Bob got to know his uncle in a different way than he had before. Bob recalled talking with Vic about wilderness areas. Candidate Atiyeh was not a big fan of adding to already existing wilderness in Oregon. For Bob, even with his uncle's subsequent activism to save the Deschutes and strongly advocate for the Columbia Gorge, it was problematic that Vic never saw the need to add to wilderness acreage in the same way that the governor felt the need to protect the two rivers.[961]

Atiyeh served as governor as the state was changing from a natural resource–based economy to a service economy with more high-tech manufacturing. In this new world, for the state as a whole, natural resources are more valuable as assets to be enjoyed by visitors. But that has not changed the dreary economic reality for those who live in places that were formerly centered on

---

959 Lawrence Watters, "1992 Ninth Circuit Environmental Review: The Columbia Gorge National Scenic Area Act," *Environmental Law* 23 (1993): 1128, LexisNexis Academic.
960 Victor Atiyeh, "Tape 58, side 2," 28.
961 Bob Atiyeh, "Atiyeh interview," 8.

natural resource industries. In smaller cities across the state, there are lower incomes, populations that remain stable or even shrink, and frustration among residents who want to go back to the old days of seemingly limitless timber operations and fishing for the seemingly limitless salmon returning to Oregon's waters. Atiyeh was governor as that change was becoming clear.

5 Managing Crises

Unemployment in Oregon outpaced U.S. levels during every year of Atiyeh's terms as governor, usually by 1% to 3%.[962] As large timber companies moved out, wood products employment plummeted in every county in the state.[963]

If mills retooled or reopened, fewer people were needed to maintain the same output as before.[964]

Atiyeh, who had been dealing with timber issues since his first session in the legislature in 1959, observed there really was "no such animal as the timber industry. ...The small companies, they're interested in public timberland, and big companies don't care about public timberland, they've got their own. They're fractured all over the place. ...They fight each other."[965]

This fracturing was apparent in the many perspectives about the future of the industry among those who were engaged in it.

---

962 William G. Loy et al., *Atlas of Oregon*, 2nd ed., (Eugene, OR: University of Oregon, 2001), 67.
963 Loy, et al., *Atlas of Oregon*, 74–75.
964 For a discussion, see William S. Prudham, "Timber and Town: Post-War Federal Forest Policy, Industrial Organization, and Rural Change in Oregon's Illinois Valley," *Antipode* 30 (1998): 186, https://doi.org/10.1111/1467-8330.00073; See also, Jeff Barnard, interviewed by Jim Moore, "Atiyeh interview," Grants Pass, OR, 30 April 2015. Summary notes, no recording, 1.
965 Victor Atiyeh, interviewed by Clark Hansen, "Tape 5," Oral history, recorded by Oregon Historical Society, Portland, OR, 12 December 1992. Transcript, 133, Atiyeh Collection, Pac. Univ. Archives.

Portion of Oregon employment by sector	1970	1990	Change
Manufacturing	19%	14%	-5%
Service	17%	28%	+11%
Retail	15%	16%	+1%

Oregon employment by sector, 1970, 1990. Atiyeh's time in office (1979–87) would be a time of great change in employment patterns. Loy et al., Atlas of Oregon, 67.

It was difficult at the time to tell whether the changes in the timber industry were long-term or due to the ongoing national recessions.

The 1975 recession following the first oil crisis in 1973–74, and the confounding rise of inflation while the economy stagnated. This was the time of President Gerald Ford's Whip Inflation Now (win) buttons. It was also when economists coined the term *stagflation* to explain what their models had deemed impossible—a time of high inflation, high unemployment, and low economic growth.[966] By the late 1970s, the writing seemed to be on the wall that growth in the Northwest forest-industry sector was threatened by supply issues and transportation issues, not just by the ups and downs of the now-30-year-old post-war economy. Atiyeh saw that timber exports were a way to keep part of the industry going. Without exports, "sawmills would close. At least [with exports] they had some money coming in." He also realized that exports helped "the longshore industry."[967] It was all a matter of balancing unpleasant choices.

---

966 See, for example, Mark A. Lutz, "Stagflation as an Institutional Problem," *Journal of Economic Issues* 15, no. 3 (1981), EBSCO Business Source Premier.

967 Victor Atiyeh, interviewed by Clark Hansen, "Tape 34," Oral history, recorded by Oregon Historical Society, Portland, OR, 11 June 1993. Transcript, 110, Atiyeh Collection, Pac. Univ. Archives; see also, Victor Atiyeh, interviewed by Clark Hansen, "Tape 36, side 2," Oral history, recorded by Oregon Historical Society, Portland, OR, 17 June 1993. Transcript, 179, Atiyeh Collection, Pac. Univ. Archives.

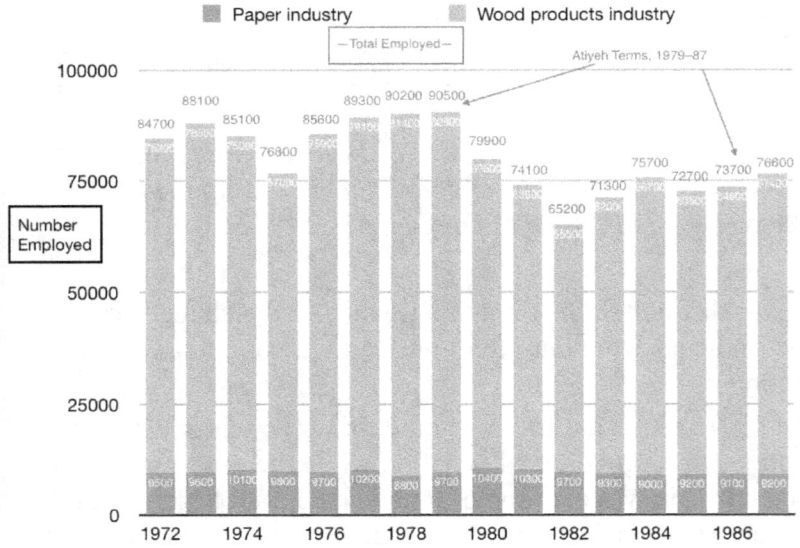

Lumber & Wood Products and Paper & Allied Products employment, 1972–87.

Inflation was also a major contributor to a phenomenon that Atiyeh had real problems with: Oregon's state budget ballooned during the high-inflation late 1960s and into the 1970s. The General Fund budget in 1967 was $567 million; by 1979 it was $2.885 billion, a more than five-fold increase.[968] Much of the growth in the budget was driven by new programs, and increased costs for policies, but a significant part of the growth went to higher monetary costs for worker salaries and costs for government work. With inflation, the extra money was needed just to keep real salaries and costs equivalent with previous years. One of Atiyeh's main goals in his first biennial budget in 1979 was to hold the growth of the budget in check to keep state spending from contributing to the country's inflationary spiral. It

---

968 *Oregon Blue Book, 1971,* 120; *Oregon Blue Book, 1981,* 186.

did not work. Oregon's budget was just too small a player in a national economic problem.

With the Federal Reserve raising interest rates and the prime rates going up for mortgages, the economic turmoil affected Oregon's employment rate dramatically. From 6.0% unemployment in 1978, the rate ticked up steadily, peaking at 11.5% in 1982 and then inching back down to 8.5% by Atiyeh's last year in office in 1986. Only in 1987 did unemployment return to pre-recession levels.[969] The entire process actually did break inflation (9.3% in January 1979, peaking at 15% in March 1980, back down to normal levels below 5% by 1983), but the cost was immense in states like Oregon.[970] Oregon had been forced to trade the potential uncertainty of high inflation for the absolute certainty that its economy had taken a major hit.

This combination of economic factors created a perfect storm for Oregon's economy and for Oregon's state budget. Fewer employed meant a reduction in the income tax, the number-one source of revenue for the state. Businesses retrenching or ceasing operation meant fewer workers as well as reductions in business taxes for the state.

The first warning sign came in August 1979. The 1979 legislative session adjourned on July 4 after not only balancing the budget but returning over $700 million to taxpayers in the form of property tax relief and income tax rebates. Just six weeks later, the Director of the Executive Department, Bob Smith, and Paul Egger, the economic consultant who made the predictions about state revenue, reported that "state income and corporate tax revenue…came in nearly $24 million under budget estimates." These two taxes together, accounting "for 80 percent of the state's revenues were much lower than the estimates used to build the

---

[969] *Oregon Blue Book, 1979*, 183; *Oregon Blue Book, 1981*, 201; *Oregon Blue Book, 1983*, 222; AP, "States' Rates High," *Oregonian*, 19 January 1983; *Oregon Blue Book, 1985*, 248; *Oregon Blue Book, 1987*, 254; *Oregon Blue Book, 1989*, 255.

[970] Tim McMahon, "Inflation in the 1980's," Historical Inflation Rate, Inflation Data, http://inflationdata.com, last modified 14 July 2017.

1979–81 state budget."[971]. Indicators that a recession was beginning had been evident during the session, but the legislature decided to return all those hundreds of millions of dollars to taxpayers anyway. In the spring of 1980, another warning sign: "State Revenue Department officials say there is a dramatic increase this spring in [the] number of taxpayers who aren't paying up."[972] Anecdotal evidence from phone calls to the tax collection office suggested that the recession was forcing "delinquent taxpayers…to put food on their tables first and worry about taxes later."[973]

Atiyeh announced the first projections of state revenue for the next biennium, 1981–83, in May 1980. The range of possibilities for revenue was between $3.4 billion and $3.7 billion; "spending projections range from $3.6 billion to $4.5 billion."[974] His explanation for the "projected budget squeeze" did not focus on the growing recession or on the high inflation rates of the 1970s; it focused on new programs created by the Democratic-led legislature along with governors McCall and Straub. One additional factor was also part of this projection—President Carter planned to end federal revenue sharing in his upcoming budget. That extra $52 million had been used for local school support in Oregon.[975] The state prediction clearly foresaw the end of the budget surpluses that had been the rule; the days of allocating hundreds of millions of dollars to property tax relief would be over. There were those in Salem looking longingly at the $705 million returned to taxpayers the previous year.

Announcing that the current 1979–81 budget faced a $65 million shortfall in May 1980, Atiyeh ordered an immediate 2%

---

971 Sue Hill, "State Tax Receipts $24 Million Short," *Salem Oregon Statesman*, 17 August 1979, 1A.
972 *Oregon Statesman* (Salem), "Many Sending in Tax Forms, But Say They Can't Pay Now," 18 April 1980, 1A.
973 *Oregon Statesman*, "Many Sending in Tax Forms," 10A.
974 AP, "Atiyeh Predicts Some Budget Belt-Tightening," *Salem (OR) Capital Journal*, 23 May 1980.
975 John Herbers, "States, Facing Revenue-Sharing Loss, Planning Cuts," *New York Times*, 4 August 1980.

cut in all agencies' budgets.[976] Then the bottom fell out of the 1979–81 budget as well. New projections showed that the current budget would come up $204 million short, the largest such shortfall in Oregon's history.[977] On July 3, 1980, after meeting with the legislative leadership for an hour, Atiyeh announced a special session for August 4.[978] This time Atiyeh did not blame the growth of government programs; he "blamed the economy for the worsening budget deficit. …[I]ncome tax revenues, which form the backbone of…the general fund…are dropping far below earlier projections."[979] Why were income tax revenues sagging? "With fewer people employed, tax collections dropped."[980]

What made the cuts seem even more onerous was that the fiscal biennium was more than halfway over. Instead of the $204 million being something along the line of a 10% reduction in a budget of more than $2 billion, it would be a reduction in a budget that was already more than halfway spent. Atiyeh asked many state agencies to come up with plans for 30% reductions in their spending for the rest of the biennium.[981] There were exceptions: Atiyeh rhetorically—but, as it would turn out, presciently—asked, "You don't think we're going to cut back the penitentiary budget by 30 percent, do you? Some agencies may be hardly cut; others may be cut more."[982]

The plan to meet the shortfall that the governor released on July 18 did not require huge numbers of public employees to lose

---

976 Sue Hill, "Special Session Called for Aug. 4: Lawmakers Must Erase Huge Deficit of $204 Million—Recession Blamed," *Salem (OR) Statesman-Journal*, 4 July 1980, 9A.

977 Don Jepsen, "Budget-Slashing Task Hazardous," Analysis, *Portland Oregon Journal*, 9 July 1980, Atiyeh Collection, Pac. Univ. Archives.

978 Victor Atiyeh, "Proclamation Calling Special Session," Office of the Governor, State of Oregon, (10 July 1980), Atiyeh Collection, Pac. Univ. Archives.

979 Hill, "Special Session Called for Aug. 4," 1A.

980 Hill, "Special Session Called for Aug. 4," 9A.

981 George Rede, "State Cuts: Blood-Letting in Major Programs Outlined if Agencies Must Make 30 pct. Reduction," *Salem (OR) Statesman-Journal*, 12 July 1980; Don Jepsen, "Atiyeh Orders State Agencies to Reduce Budgets 30%," *Portland Oregon Journal*, 9 July 1980, Atiyeh Collection, Pac. Univ. Archives.

982 Jepsen, "Budget-Slashing Task Hazardous."

their jobs. There would be reductions in state spending along with accelerations of the "payment of personal income and insurance taxes and stepping up efforts to collect delinquent taxes."[983] Oregon Legislative Revenue Officer Richard Munn had predicted to the legislative leadership that Atiyeh would propose the speedup of tax collections. The federal government was doing something similar at the time.[984] Atiyeh specifically protected basic school support, property tax relief, and he wanted to avoid new taxes. Atiyeh also created "a prudent person reserve of $45 million" because "it is essential to have this additional allowance because of the volatile state of the economy and the extreme difficulty of predicting future revenues."[985] But there was a sense that even this would not be enough.

In the August 1980 special session, Atiyeh got pretty much everything he asked for. There was an early attempt in the five-day session to reduce Atiyeh's $45 million prudent person fund by $8.9 million to use the money to offset cuts in education and welfare, but it died in a 7-7 committee vote in the Senate.[986] The $130 million in agency cuts and the changes in tax collections (worth $100 million) both breezed through their first floor votes. Atiyeh was pleased. Of the legislature, he said, "They faced the same torment and doubts as state agency heads did when they were looking for places to cut in the budget, and I think they did it in a very even-handed way."[987]

Atiyeh applied the lessons he had learned during his twenty years on the legislative Revenue committees. He knew that an

---

983 George Rede, "Atiyeh Plan Goes Easy on Layoffs," *Salem (OR) Statesman-Journal*, 19 July 1980, 1A.

984 Richard Munn, interviewed by Jim Moore, "Atiyeh Interview," Salem, OR, 9 June 2016. Summary notes, 4–5.

985 Vic Atiyeh, "Statement Calling Special Session," Office of the Governor, State of Oregon, (18 July 1980), 1, 7, Atiyeh Collection, Pac. Univ. Archives.

986 Sue Hill, "Sen. Fadeley Loses Bid to Use Reserve Funds to Help Ease Welfare, Education Cutbacks," *Salem (OR) Statesman-Journal*, 5 August 1980; Ron Blankenbaker, "Quick and Dirty Politics: Two Instances at Special Session," Column, *Salem (OR) Statesman-Journal*, 6 August 1980.

987 George Rede, "Boe Thinks Legislature Should Meet Every Year," *Salem (OR) Statesman-Journal*, 9 August 1980.

across-the-board cut was not feasible. Small departments would get hit much harder—a ten or fifteen percent cut might reduce the personnel to a level that made it impossible for the department to perform its duties. "But," he remembered in the early 1990s, "if we start dealing with Human Resources, that's a huge budget. Somewhere in there we can find some money that will take care of" the small departments and keep state government going.[988] The governor also felt confident about his ability to find those efficiencies and to create more equitable cuts to the budget "because of my twenty years in the legislature. I knew an awful lot about almost every agency of government. ...They call [the budget shortfall] a serious problem. It's a serious problem, but it's not one that can't be dealt with. ...Not painlessly...but it can be done."[989]

Atiyeh emphasized that governors should not "get mired down in the minutia" of which programs would be cut and by how much. "The object in mind is inflation at an unprecedented rate.... The object is almost a trillion dollars of deficit in the federal budget."[990] He emphasized that there was no way the Oregon budget could just absorb the federal cuts.

The governor testified before the House Revenue Committee in May 1981. Atiyeh listed the programs that would be hit hard by further cuts—schools, colleges and universities, state parks, eliminating corrections work camps, a huge reduction in state police personnel. Atiyeh ended his remarks with words he penned himself:

> No one can accuse me of being a spender—certainly this government is more under fiscal control than ever before. When I

---

988 Victor Atiyeh, interviewed by Clark Hansen, "Tape 20," Oral history, recorded by Oregon Historical Society, Portland, OR, 4 February 1993. Transcript, 597, Atiyeh Collection, Pac. Univ. Archives.
989 Atiyeh, "Tape 20," 597.
990 James Thompson et al., interviewed by Charlayne Hunter-Gault and Jim Lehrer, "Governors' Reaction to Reagan Plan," Live interview, recorded by MacNeil/Lehrer Report, Washington, DC, 23 February 1981. Transcript, 5, Atiyeh Collection, Pac. Univ. Archives.

say we have cut to the bone it is no cliché. I no more wish to raise revenue than do you. I get no personal joy in so doing—but I find the alternative even more distasteful.[991]

It was then that Atiyeh began to really look at solutions to Oregon's economic woes instead of primarily ways to balance an ever-decreasing budget. Gerry Thompson remembered a long lecture from Atiyeh in 1981 before he started campaigning for re-election, about Oregon's overdependence on timber and timber byproducts. The state was too dependent on agriculture. The fishing industry was being hit hard by the recession and declining fish runs. Oregon was not diversifying its economy, so the governor was asking where they needed to go next for economic development.[992] By November 1981, the governor was giving speeches on economic development as he talked to groups around the state.[993] Atiyeh himself understood his growing emphasis on diversifying Oregon's economy as a continuation of his plans to shift the attitude about Oregon, to move from McCall's "Visit but Don't Stay" motto to Atiyeh's "Oregon Is Open for Business."[994]

Prison Overcrowding and One Tough Call

In Oregon, as in many places across the country, the issue of overcrowding of prisons was deeply connected to budget realities, tough sentencing, and workplace issues for prison guards and workers. Governor Atiyeh had dealt with personnel issues at the prison since his first year in office.[995] He met with prison guards

---

991 Atiyeh, "Atiyeh to House Revenue Committee," 8. Handwritten by Atiyeh.
992 Gerry Thompson, interviewed by Jim Moore, "Atiyeh interview #2," Salem, OR, 12 February 2015. Summary notes, 5.
993 "Atiyeh Daily Index-Card Schedule, November 19, 1981," Office of the Governor, State of Oregon, (19 November 1981), Meet: Pendleton Chamber Committee re: economic development; Dinner & Speech Economic Improvement Council—Eugene, Atiyeh Collection, Pac. Univ. Archives.
994 Victor Atiyeh, interviewed by Jim Moore, "Atiyeh interview #1," Raleigh Hills, OR, 19 December 2013. Summary notes, 3.
995 "Atiyeh Daily Index-Card Schedule, September 25, 1979," Office of the Governor, State of Oregon, (25 September 1979), Kay Toran, Lee re: Correc. Div. problem,

in early January 1980 to talk about labor negotiations and prison conditions.[996] The guards told Atiyeh about life with 1500 inmates in a facility built for 1100. The governor was skeptical about building a new state prison, however, saying, "I think new regional jails are the way to go."[997]

The prison system continued to be a focus of concern. Inmates were escaping from minimum-security prisons, leading to a February 1980 proposal to build two 750-bed prisons, which flew in the face of a 1977 legislative decision to prioritize probation and rehabilitation.[998] By June 1980, non-security workers at the Oregon penitentiary had gone on strike—guards themselves were "prohibited by law from striking."[999] Seeing the strike coming, Atiyeh met with his executive assistant, Lee Johnson, Leo Hegstrom, the Director of the Department of Human Services, and Bob Watson, the Administrator of Corrections, in early June.[1000] The issue was the raises that prison workers had received compared to the negotiated raises of Oregon State Employees Association (OSEA) workers in 1979. Prison workers won a binding arbitration ruling that gave them similar raises and future increases tied to inflation. The state, under financial stress, appealed the decision.[1001]

At the end of January 1980, three Oregon penitentiary inmates had filed a lawsuit alleging that prison accommodations were so

---

Atiyeh Collection, Pac. Univ. Archives.
996 Sue Hill, "Guards Warn of 'Explosive Atmosphere' At Prison,'" *Salem Oregon Statesman*, 4 January 1980.
997 Hill, "Guards Warn of 'Explosive Atmosphere' At Prison."
998 Janet Evenson, "Panel Urges State Build Two 750-Bed Prisons," *Salem Oregon Statesman*, 20 February 1980.
999 Sue Hill, "Last Minute Talks on Prison Strike Planned," *Salem Oregon Statesman*, 13 June 1980; Linda Williams, "Prison Employees Call Strike," *Oregonian*, 17 June 1980.
1000 "Atiyeh Daily Index-Card Schedule, June 5, 1980," Office of the Governor, State of Oregon, (5 June 1980), Leo, Lee, Bob Watson re: corrections & what to do about population, Atiyeh Collection, Pac. Univ. Archives; "Atiyeh Daily Index-Card Schedule, June 13, 1980," Office of the Governor, State of Oregon, (13 June 1980), Leo Hegstrom, Bob Watson, Lee, re: strike plan; overcrowding, alternative to need for space for next biennium for population, Atiyeh Collection, Pac. Univ. Archives.
1001 Hill, "Last Minute Talks on Prison Strike Planned."

overcrowded and dirty that the conditions qualified as cruel and unusual punishment.[1002] Named after the lead plaintiff and the governor, the case *Capps v. Atiyeh* was decided by U.S. District Court Judge James Burns at the end of June. Burns found that the testimony before the court led to the "common sense" finding "that overcrowding leads to stress and in the setting of a penal institution, illness, disease, tension, resentment, bitterness, and ultimately violence and brutality."[1003] Burns found that the legislative idea of dealing with inmates at the local level was not adequate, if transferring prisoners occurred simply to relieve overcrowding. While he did not issue an injunction, Burns found prison conditions in Oregon unconstitutional based on his interpretation of the Eighth Amendment's ban on cruel and unusual punishment. The judge called for more facilities to be built and for the prison population to be reduced.[1004]

Later that night, June 27, 1980, rioting broke out at the Oregon State Penitentiary with prisoners taking a hostage, barricading themselves, guards shooting, six wounded inmates, and one in critical condition.[1005] The head of Oregon's prisons, Hoyt Cupp, issued a statement saying, "We believe this to be an isolated incident and in no way reflective of the general mood of the inmate population," stressing that the disturbance was not related to the overcrowding ruling or the strike of non-security workers at the penitentiary. Prison workers felt that was a gross misreading of the atmosphere inside the facility.[1006]

Atiyeh responded forcefully to the federal court ruling issued the day of the riot. He took Burns' findings to task for relying too heavily on the three inmates' testimonies and other people who,

---

1002 AP, "3 Prison Inmates Sue Over Conditions," *Salem Oregon Statesman*, 1 February 1980.

1003 Thomas Capps, et al., vs. Victor Atiyeh, 495 F. Supp. 802 (D. Ore. 1980), 7, Atiyeh Collection, Pac. Univ. Archives. Passage marked by Atiyeh.

1004 *Capps v. Atiyeh*, 27–28.

1005 Phil Manzano, "Cupp Orders Lockdown of State Prison: One Wounded Inmate Listed Critical After Hostage-Taking," *Salem (OR) Statesman Journal*, 29 June 1980, 1A.

1006 Manzano, "Cupp Orders Lockdown of State Prison," 9A.

by and large, had not actually visited Oregon's prisons to observe conditions. The governor also argued that the financial reality of the state constrained his actions. His argument was that the executive and legislative branches do a much better job making the hard decisions about the allocation of scarce resources than a single federal judge.[1007] To counter the ruling, former head of corrections in Utah and California Ray Procunier brought his comparative perspective to the case and found that Oregon's prison administration was "outstanding," and there was a solution that was "not as complicated and expensive as it appears at first."[1008] The governor studied alternatives, ranging from repurposing government-owned properties around the state (e.g., Camp Adair near Corvallis, a Coast Guard station at Winchester Bay) to moving inmates to the soon to be closed McNeil Island Federal Prison in Washington to changing the relationship between the state prison system and county jails to house more inmates in the counties.[1009]

Testifying in late July 1980 before the Oregon legislature's Joint Committee on Corrections, Atiyeh's executive assistant Lee Johnson said, "We fully agree that the crowded conditions at the institutions are not desirable and began actions to relieve those conditions several months ago. We vigorously disagree with the

---

1007 Vic Atiyeh, "Prison Conditions: Gov. Atiyeh Speaks Out," Speech to Oregon Newspaper Publishers Association, Welches, Oregon, *Salem (OR) Statesman-Journal*, 13 July 1980.

1008 R. K. Procunier, "Prison Overcrowding," American Correctional Association Former President, Former Director of Corrections Utah and California, Memo to Office of the Governor, (11 July 1980), Atiyeh Collection, Pac. Univ. Archives; "Atiyeh Daily Index-Card Schedule, July 11, 1980," Office of the Governor, State of Oregon, (11 July 1980), Ray Procunir [*sic*] (consultant) & Lee re Overcrowding Suit, Atiyeh Collection, Pac. Univ. Archives.

1009 Leo Hegstrom, "Copies of Reports on Prison Overcrowding Case," Department of Human Resources, State of Oregon, Memo to Governor Atiyeh, (14 July 1980), Atiyeh Collection, Pac. Univ. Archives; Hegstrom, "Copies of Reports on Prison Overcrowding Case," Watson to Hegstrom memo, "Availability of McNeil Island Prison," July 7, 1980; Watson to Hegstrom memo, "Examination of Alternatives for Prisoner Housing," July 11, 1980; Belleque to Watson memo, "Alternative Regional Facilities to Expand Corrections Division's Bed Capacity by Adding to County Facilities," July 11, 1980; AP, "Judge Outlines Prison Options," *Oregonian*, 21 September 1980.

judge's conclusions that such overcrowding constitutes cruel and unusual punishment."[1010] Johnson outlined the immediate actions to be taken to meet Burns' concerns.[1011] The main focus of Johnson's testimony, however, was the need to build more space, a process that was estimated to cost $120 million to be financed by selling state bonds.[1012] The August 1980 special session would go part way toward this with the authorization of $85 million in bond sales for a new facility, subject to approval by voters in November—the measure was defeated 47% to 53%.[1013]

Just days after hearing Atiyeh address the gathered union members, the AFL-CIO started a recall campaign against the governor based on his refusal to follow the arbitrators decision about prison-guard raises.[1014] As the August special session got going, the union leadership sent out instructions and materials to gather signatures for the recall effort.[1015] Two weeks later, the effort ended with the president of the AFL-CIO apologizing for any inconvenience.[1016] The recall movement had resulted in a meeting with Atiyeh at which it was clear that both sides disagreed on his refusal to accept the arbitration, but the union found that he had not asked "the Legislature to repeal the State's arbitration laws. He has stated he will continue to support all of

---

1010 Lee Johnson, "Oregon Prison Overcrowding," Office of the Governor, Testimony to Joint Committee on Corrections, (25 July 1980), 1, Atiyeh Collection, Pac. Univ. Archives.

1011 Johnson, "Oregon Prison Overcrowding," 2–3.

1012 Johnson, "Oregon Prison Overcrowding," 7; *Oregonian*, "Prison Bond Issue Proposed," 15 July 1980.

1013 *Oregon Blue Book, 1981*, 334; *Statesman-Journal* (Salem), "Legislature Does Its Job, Goes Home," 9 August 1980.

1014 Stan Federman, "AFL-CIO Supports Atiyeh Recall Move on Prison Pay Issue," *Oregonian*, 3 July 1980, Atiyeh Collection, Pac. Univ. Archives; Stan Federman, "Union Chief Stresses 'Bread, Butter' Issues," *Oregonian*, 1 July 1980.

1015 R. G. 'Bob' Kennedy, "Recall Governor Atiyeh," Oregon AFL-CIO, Memo to Oregon AFL-CIO Affiliates and Other Interested Parties, (5 August 1980), Atiyeh Collection, Pac. Univ. Archives.

1016 R. G. 'Bob' Kennedy, "Rescind Recall Governor Atiyeh," Oregon AFL-CIO, Memo to Affiliated Unions and Interested Parties, (20 August 1980), Atiyeh Collection, Pac. Univ. Archives.

the State's collective bargaining laws for public employees."[1017] He found the union "kept wanting a *quid pro quo*" on the arbitration issue, "and I just said, 'I don't do that.'" The union countered with "'We won't carry out the recall if you do what we want you to do.' As it ended up, we stayed where I [Atiyeh] was and they decided it wasn't worth the trouble, and they backed off."[1018]

The overcrowding issue and the search for solutions would go on for years. Republican Dave Frohnmayer was elected attorney general in 1980, leading to a reevaluation of Judge Burns' assessment under order of the Ninth Circuit Court of Appeals. Judge Burns announced his new findings on December 30, 1982. "Conditions in Oregon's prisons do not violate constitutional provisions against 'cruel and unusual punishment.'"[1019] State officials were "surprised and relieved."[1020] Burns found that overcrowding was an issue, but that condition did not, by itself, violate the U.S. Constitution.

Clearly, the 1983 legislative session would be the time to figure out some sort of solution that satisfied the federal court, the electorate, and the various political players in Salem. An idea was floated to convert the Eastern Oregon State Hospital into a prison. [1021] In the context of the national movement to shut down mental hospitals to stop warehousing the mentally ill, the hospital in Pendleton had long been on the list to close. Atiyeh met with decision makers and stakeholders. Pendleton residents split on their support for the idea, but it was the rapidity with which the proposal came into being and advanced through the system that

---

1017 Kennedy, "Rescind Recall Governor Atiyeh."
1018 Atiyeh, "Tape 32," 51. Italics in original.
1019 George Rede, "Judge Rejects Prisoner Claims on Overcrowding," *Salem (OR) Statesman-Journal*, 31 December 1982, 1A.
1020 Rede, "Judge Rejects Prisoner Claims on Overcrowding," 1A.
1021 Victor Atiyeh, interviewed by Clark Hansen, "Tape 38," Oral history, recorded by Oregon Historical Society, Portland, OR, 21 June 1993. Transcript, 215, Atiyeh Collection, Pac. Univ. Archives; Terry McDermott, "State Hospital at Pendleton Eyed as Prison Site," *Oregonian*, 29 April 1983.

caught many off guard.[1022] Salem legislators were adamant that Pendleton was the spot for the new prison. Most Oregon penal institutions were in Salem (with the exception of work camps and minimum-security facilities).

In Pendleton, it was not just an issue of providing for patients: the hospital was a major employer. State Senator Mike Thorne (D) in whose district the hospital sat, was part of a group of legislators who requested help from the governor in figuring how to balance jobs and services. Thorne recalled that Atiyeh was very responsive to hearing what local concerns were. "I credit him for providing some answers at a time when the activists were stridently in one camp, the defenders of the status quo were in the other."[1023] Atiyeh also helped solve the local issue about housing the newly independent mentally ill. Thorne saw him wade into this entire complex situation and create the context within which solutions were found. "So much of [Atiyeh's] management style was: understand the issue, understand the problem, try to do the right thing."[1024] In the last couple of weeks of the session (it would last until mid-July), the legislature passed the final bill to create the Pendleton prison. Funding came out of the general fund, so there would be no fruitless attempt to get voters to approve the sale of bonds. Oregon would have its first new prison in 25 years, with beds for 350 medium-security inmates.[1025]

In 1981, the fate of one inmate could have derailed Atiyeh's governorship. Duane Samples, a 1960s Stanford psychology major, had been sentenced to life in the Oregon State Penitentiary "after pleading guilty in 1975 to taking a 10-inch knife and slashing the bodies of two young women, killing one."[1026]

1022 Alan K. Ota, "Reaction Mixed on Hospital Conversion Plan: Panel's Hearing at Pendleton Draws 120," *Oregonian*, 11 May 1983.

1023 Mike Thorne, interviewed by Jim Moore, "Atiyeh interview," Pendleton, OR, 23 June 2015. Summary notes, 9.

1024 Thorne, "Atiyeh interview," 9.

1025 AP, "Converting State Hospital into Prison to Begin Soon," *Salem (OR) Statesman-Journal*, 29 July 1983.

1026 Linda Kramer, "Rehabilitated or Deranged? Duane Samples Remains in a Cell as Controversy Rages Around Him," *Eugene (OR) Register-Guard*, 27 August 1981.

Samples came to understand, and his friends and psychologists agreed, that "he was a victim of post-Vietnam delayed stress syndrome," now known as post-traumatic stress disorder (PTSD).[1027]

The governor's staff was aware of Samples: Denny Miles had met him on a facilities tour, and Samples had applied for a pardon during Atiyeh's first year in office. Atiyeh "thought about it at great length." To Atiyeh's mind,

> he really was a Jekyll and Hyde because the first part of his life he was very square, in dress and the things he did, his grooming, the whole bit. He was down in college in California, belonged to a fraternity.... Went to Vietnam as a lieutenant and experienced... some very traumatic instances. ...But then he comes home and he's 180 degrees the other way [opposite of a square]. ...So the case really was a matter of what they call the Vietnam Syndrome.[1028]

The crime was "heinous, ...it was not something you take very lightly."[1029] Atiyeh listened to the experts, many of whom thought Samples had worked through his PTSD.[1030] In November 1980, Atiyeh commuted Samples' sentence from life to twenty years. "Parole board officials said a good time release date on a 20-year sentence would be about 14 years," sometime in 1989.[1031] The governor went against the advice of most of his staff in issuing the clemency.

Atiyeh began to hear from people about his decision: he met with Oregon House member Fred Parkinson (R-Silverton) about

---

1027 Kramer, "Rehabilitated or Deranged?."
1028 Atiyeh, "Tape 36, side 2," 169–170.
1029 Atiyeh, "Tape 36, side 2," 170.
1030 "Atiyeh Daily Index-Card Schedule, September 29, 1980," Office of the Governor, State of Oregon, (29 September 1980), Dr. Davis & Dr. Dixon re: prisoner Duane Samples, Atiyeh Collection, Pac. Univ. Archives; "Atiyeh Daily Index-Card Schedule, October 6, 1980," Office of the Governor, State of Oregon, (6 October 1980), 1:00 Tania Samples re: husband (Duane); 1:30 Doris Bounds [Hermiston banker] re: Duane Samples, Atiyeh Collection, Pac. Univ. Archives.
1031 Kramer, "Rehabilitated or Deranged?."

concerns in his town, Silverton—the site of the murder.[1032] Marion County District Attorney Chris Van Dyke led the call for Atiyeh to reverse the decision. There was evidence that Samples had urges to murder before he went to Vietnam. After meeting with psychiatrists in late July,[1033] Atiyeh explained that he felt "'a personal sense of urgency' to complete the review of the Samples commutation."[1034] On August 20, Atiyeh learned that Samples committed an additional, and hitherto unknown, assault on a woman in 1971, four years before the murder.[1035] For the governor, this swayed the case. With the new evidence Atiyeh thought, "Wait a minute. This guy isn't nearly as rehabilitated as I thought he was. And he wasn't as truthful as he should have been during the time I was listening" and making the commutation decision.[1036] On September 3, 1981, Atiyeh rescinded Samples' commutation.

Immediately, Atiyeh's decision was questioned. As Foster Church at the *Oregonian* put it, "Gov. Vic Atiyeh could hardly have stumbled into a more complex, more potentially ruinous political and professional swamp than he did with his decision to investigate the case of convicted murderer Duane Samples, and ultimately commute Samples' sentence from life to 20 years."[1037] The story appeared in the *New York Times*. There were questions about the impacts of Samples' service in Vietnam versus Samples'

1032 "Atiyeh Daily Index-Card Schedule, January 28, 1981," Office of the Governor, State of Oregon, (28 January 1981), Rep. Parkinson re: Duane Samples in Silverton problem, Atiyeh Collection, Pac. Univ. Archives.

1033 "Atiyeh Daily Index-Card Schedule, July 29, 1981," Office of the Governor, State of Oregon, (29 July 1981), Kay Wood, Seidler, Lee—psychiatrist, Atiyeh Collection, Pac. Univ. Archives.

1034 Leslie L. Zaitz, "Veto Seen for Court Reform Bill," *Oregonian*, 7 August 1981.

1035 "Atiyeh Daily Index-Card Schedule, August 20, 1981," Office of the Governor, State of Oregon, (20 August 1981), Dr. Davis, Lee, re: Samples, Atiyeh Collection, Pac. Univ. Archives; Vic Atiyeh, "Statement by Gov. Vic Atiyeh on Duane Samples," Office of the Governor, State of Oregon, Recission of Commutation, (3 September 1981), 3, Atiyeh Collection, Pac. Univ. Archives.

1036 Atiyeh, "Tape 36, side 2," 171.

1037 Foster Church, "Original Samples Decision Based on Incomplete Information," Column, *Oregonian*, 7 September 1981.

apparent manipulation of "his combat experience to win commutation."[1038]

Atiyeh himself was "quite personally upset with some of the psychiatrists, some of whom backed off after having given their professional advice, and then you begin to lose some of your faith in their [professional] ability…to deal with" similar cases.[1039] He knew that dealing with the human personality and brain was an inexact science at best, "but they come down with such a great degree of certainty in one instance, and then finally back off a little bit." He found the episode to be part "of a very unhappy period of time."[1040]

The issue threatened to become something central to Atiyeh's 1982 re-election campaign. The governor's office was contacted in early 1982 by *60 Minutes*, the CBS news magazine. Mike Wallace, the legendary *60 Minutes* reporter, was on the story. Atiyeh was immediately alert to the political context, thinking, "This is now 1982, during the course of the election. When are they going to put it on the air? …Obviously we had no control, or we didn't even question. They were going to do what they were going to do."[1041] The governor's team decided on a strategy of making the never-scintillating public-speaker Atiyeh even more boring. Atiyeh explained that "if you don't want to get involved in something that's very controversial, don't be interesting."[1042] The goal was for the Wallace interview to take place, but for none of it to appear in the final story. The *60 Minutes* interview took place on February 10, 1982, and aired in February of the next year, well after the November election.[1043] Atiyeh never made the final cut.

1038 AP, "Convict Seeking Freedom Blames Vietnam for Slaying," *New York Times*, 13 September 1981.
1039 Atiyeh, "Tape 36, side 2," 171.
1040 Atiyeh, "Tape 36, side 2," 171.
1041 Atiyeh, "Tape 36, side 2," 171–172.
1042 Atiyeh, "Tape 36, side 2," 172.
1043 "Atiyeh Daily Index-Card Schedule, February 10, 1982," Office of the Governor, State of Oregon, (10 February 1982), Mike Wallace—60 Minutes, Atiyeh Collection, Pac. Univ. Archives.

Racial Harassment Legislation

Atiyeh articulated another criminal matter in his 1981 State of the State address. The governor wanted to make "the act of racial harassment a *crime* in Oregon—a *felony*, punishable by fine or imprisonment or both."[1044] Atiyeh told the assembled, "Citizens who 'do not want to get involved' only give courage to the lunatic fringe. *Never forget* that if this degradation is allowed to continue because we do nothing to *stop* it, the bell may toll for any one of us."[1045]

Some at the time thought of this conviction as surprising, but he had been following news of a series of disturbing incidents—some of which were splashed across the front page of the *Oregonian*, so not something hidden that legislators would not have heard of. Jackie Winters recalled that when Atiyeh heard about a 1979 cross burning, "he was as mad as I've ever seen him."[1046] In 1980 there had been racial threats against an African American family in Milwaukie, anti-Semitic bumper stickers posted in downtown Portland, and continuing verbal and physical abuse against a Ghanaian living in St. Helens.[1047] In November a man had gasoline poured over him "after a tirade of racial insults in a Salem bar."[1048]

Atiyeh began to study "the possibility of legislation to allow state agencies to participate in investigations of racial

---

[1044] Vic Atiyeh, "State of the State Address, hand annotated" (speech, 61st Legislative Assembly, Oregon House of Representative Chambers, State Capitol, Salem, Oregon, 12 January 1981), 12, Atiyeh Collection, Pac. Univ. Archives. Italics are underlined by Atiyeh in original.

[1045] Atiyeh, "State of the State, 1981," 13. Italics are underlined by Atiyeh in original.
[1046] "State Memorial for the Honorable Vic Atiyeh," Memorial service, recorded by Oregon Legislative Media, Salem, OR, 3 September 2014. DVD, 50:30.
[1047] Julie Tripp, "Racial Threats Plague Milwaukie-area Family," *Oregonian*, 17 August 1980; *Oregonian*, "Harassment Laid to Trio," 10 September 1980; *Oregonian*, "Mayor Urges Portlanders to Unite, Head Off Racism," 4 November 1980; Alan K. Ota, "Racial Harassment Incidents Increasing in Oregon," *Oregonian*, 21 December 1980.
[1048] Ota, "Racial Harassment Incidents."

harassment" in September 1980.[1049] It turned out that the State Police had no legal grounds to get involved in these cases, and there was no legal framework for the federal government, through the U.S. Attorney's office, to work with local law enforcement in dealing with racial harassment.[1050] In spring 1981 there were reports of a tiny neo-Nazi group in Portland (best estimates were that it had five members), and some ideas of plans to "unite other right-wing groups such as the Ku Klux Klan and the Posse Comitatus, and to start a right-wing newspaper."[1051] Atiyeh met with the state police in March 1981 about the Posse Comitatus, an anti-tax and anti-government group, and with a group of legislators and faith leaders about neo-Nazis in June. [1052] Also in June, Atiyeh gave a speech entitled "Bigotry, Incivility and the Responsibilities of Political Leadership" at a Forum on Bigotry at Western Oregon State College.[1053]

Atiyeh was personally offended by the acts of harassment. It went back to his childhood among the children of immigrants in Northeast Portland. "I hate bullies, I really do hate bullies, have since I was a kid. And I know that if you give them a little bit of slack they'll just keep going. You've got to call them [on their actions]. ...If you start trembling in their face, they just get... bolder all the time."[1054] In light of the 1980 events, he said,

---

1049 *Oregonian*, "Governor Wants State Law to Probe Racial Harassment," 19 September 1980.

1050 "Governor Wants State Law to Probe Racial Harassment."

1051 Tom Hallman, Jr., "Hijacker Turns to Neo-Nazi Cause," *Oregonian*, 29 March 1981.

1052 "Atiyeh Daily Index-Card Schedule, March 12, 1981," Office of the Governor, State of Oregon, (12 March 1981), Capt. Hollenback—Posse Comitatus, Atiyeh Collection, Pac. Univ. Archives; "Atiyeh Daily Index-Card Schedule, June 18, 1981," Office of the Governor, State of Oregon, (18 June 1981), Frank Shields; Aaron Hamlin; Rodney Page re: neo-naxism [sic] (there will be several other present, too—all from different denominations), Atiyeh Collection, Pac. Univ. Archives.

1053 "Atiyeh Daily Index Card, Jun 24, 1981," Lunch & Speech: WOSC Forum on Bigotry—"Bigotry, Incivility & the Responsbilities of Political Leadership".

1054 Victor Atiyeh, interviewed by Clark Hansen, "Tape 55," Oral history, recorded by Oregon Historical Society, Portland, OR, 25 August 1993. Transcript, 716, Atiyeh Collection, Pac. Univ. Archives.

"We've got to do something about that."[1055] He proposed making "any attempt by word or conduct to place someone in fear of his safety or damage of his property because of his race or religion" a "Class C felony punishable by up to five years in prison and a $2,500 fine."[1056]

The governor found the entire process to pass this law surprisingly difficult. He thought the bill would sail through because "Democrats controlled the legislature; 'they're for the little guy, they're for blacks and minorities' I thought." First-year House member Peter Courtney (D-Salem) carried the bill. It turned out to be a bumpy, but successful introduction to lawmaking in Salem for the person who would eventually set the record as the longest-serving Senate President and longest-serving legislator.[1057] The bill passed "at 1:30 in the morning on the last day of the session."[1058] Atiyeh recalled "really pounding hard and arguing with [Senators] Ruth McFarland [D-Gresham] and Ted Kulongoski [D-Junction City] in my office late at night to get that bill passed."[1059] McFarland, the only female member of the Senate, and Kulongoski wanted to add "harassment on the basis of sex" to the bill.[1060] Atiyeh "wanted [the bill] as clear as it could be; …just racial and religious harassment. …I didn't want to blur the message."[1061] His advocacy for the measure was characterized as "one of his more passionate actions."[1062]

The Economy Hits Bottom

1055 Atiyeh, "Tape 55," 716.
1056 *Daily Astorian*, "Stomp On It," Editorial, January 1981, Atiyeh Collection, Pac. Univ. Archives.
1057 Ron Blankenbaker, "Political Outlook for State's New Congressional District," Column, *Salem (OR) Statesman-Journal*, 9 August 1981.
1058 Atiyeh, "Tape 33, side 1," 78.
1059 Atiyeh, "Tape 55," 716.
1060 *Statesman-Journal* (Salem), "Legislature Passes Racial Harassment Bill," 2 August 1981; *Statesman-Journal* (Salem), "What the 1981 Legislature Did: End of the Session," 3 August 1981, 8A.
1061 Atiyeh, "Tape 55," 716.
1062 Foster Church, "Atiyeh Remains Moderate in Face of Fiscal Woes," *Oregonian*, 9 May 1982.

About three months after the end of the long 1981 legislative session, Atiyeh began to talk about the possibility of a special session to deal with revenue shortfalls, which by the end of October were projected in internal documents to reach almost $260 million.[1063] A publicly released draft economic forecast on November 9 "showed that the state's economy would be gloomier than expected in 1982 and 1983."[1064] Any Oregon economic recovery would not start until the second quarter of 1982, and it would be "very gradual."[1065] Atiyeh made it clear that he would not ask for more taxes: "We would have to cut budgets. There would be no alternative."[1066] Atiyeh directed state agencies on November 20 to prepare budget reductions of around 20% and on November 27 ordered a special session of the legislature—it would turn out to be the longest special session in Oregon's history. The budget shortfall reported in November was $250 million, far larger than even rumor had put it in the previous weeks, but right in line with the numbers Atiyeh had been told in late October.[1067]

One of Atiyeh's principles was to govern with no thought to re-election, but his own campaign was beginning as he called the January special session. In this case he had no choice—his constitutional duty was to work with the legislature to balance the budget, whatever it took. He also was very aware that all the members of the House and half the members of the Senate (except for those retiring from the legislature) were also up for election in 1982.

Atiyeh revealed his budget plan on January 4, 1982. His goal was refined to eliminating what was now a $239 million budget

---

1063 Gerry Thompson, "Handwritten Notes, Sep–Nov 1981, Apr–May 1982," Office of the Governor, State of Oregon, (24 September–25 November, 13 April–28 May 1981–1982), 56, Atiyeh Collection, Pac. Univ. Archives.
1064 Leslie L. Zaitz, "Atiyeh Considering Session on Deficit," *Oregonian*, 11 November 1981.
1065 Thompson, "24 Sep–25 Nov 1981; 13 Apr–28 May 1982 Handwritten notes," 56.
1066 Zaitz, "Atiyeh Considering Session on Deficit."
1067 Foster Church, "Atiyeh Orders Special Budget Session," *Oregonian*, 28 November 1981. Parentheses in original.

shortfall. As he had before in these situations, he met his goal through a combination of budget cuts and ideas that tinkered with the tax system to get more money into the state's coffers more quickly.[1068] But with all the cuts, some observers noted the lack of conviction that Atiyeh seemed to show as he laid out his plans. One journalist characterized Atiyeh's plan as being presented "with all the vigor of a high school student turning in an essay on Peru."[1069] The same Atiyeh who had vigorously pleaded with the legislature in the summer of 1981 to raise taxes instead of cutting programs, now presented the cuts as a symptom of "the times."[1070] This lack of impassioned leadership on all sides would contribute to the special session becoming the longest in history.

Atiyeh's January 18, 1982, state of the state message was bleak. "All is *not* well in Oregon," he began.[1071] It was not just the record unemployment (over 11% at the time), it was "thousands upon thousands of other Oregonians—presently working Oregonians—whose backs are now against the wall and who may be just one paycheck away from ruin and personal tragedy. ...We must not be in a position of pushing them over the edge."[1072] The governor explained that his budget cuts were based on his prioritization of the needs of Oregonians. Instead of across-the-board equal cuts, what he said some called a "fair share," he pushed for "a 'fair' response to the needs of all the people."[1073] In response to those who noted the difference between the tax-

---

1068 Sue Hill, "Atiyeh Delays Special Session a Week; Leaders Attack His Budget Proposals," *Salem (OR) Statesman-Journal*, 5 January 1982, 1A.

1069 Leslie L. Zaitz, "Atiyeh Cutbacks Lack Conviction," Analysis, *Oregonian*, 5 January 1982.

1070 Zaitz, "Atiyeh Cutbacks Lack Conviction."

1071 Vic Atiyeh, "State of the State Message" (speech, Special Session—61st Legislative Assembly, House Chambers, Salem, OR, 18 January 1982), 1, Atiyeh Collection, Pac. Univ. Archives. Italics underlined in original; "Joint Assembly in the House to Hear the Message of Governor Vic Atiyeh," Legislature, State of Oregon, Order for Ceremony, (18 January 1982), Atiyeh Collection, Pac. Univ. Archives.

1072 Atiyeh, "State of the State, 1982," 2.

1073 Atiyeh, "State of the State, 1982," 3.

raising Atiyeh of 1981 and the program-cutting Atiyeh of 1982, he responded clearly.

> Of course I have different recommendations today!
>
> Times have changed.
>
> The situation has worsened.
>
> Oregon's unemployment rate a year ago was 8.3 percent. Today it is 11.4 percent and rising.
>
> In 1981 we expected 240 million dollars more revenue than we expect today. Today more employed Oregonians are hard pressed to survive.
>
> The fever has risen and past remedies have not abated it. Now we must prescribe different and more distasteful remedies.[1074]

He emphasized that he would not "support a raid on the property tax relief fund." He considered that as raising taxes.[1075] He emphasized that the overall cuts were about 10% of the state budget, "this means that 90 percent remains to serve and protect our citizens."[1076] He also made it clear that there were many economic factors beyond Oregon's control, especially "federal fiscal policies" and "interest rates, which impact us most of all."[1077] These national factors contributed to the "27 percent!" unemployment rate in the forest products industry.[1078]

As the legislature got to work with its own not-quite-completed plan, Atiyeh laid down one more marker. "He would probably veto any attempt…to slash Oregon's property tax relief program."[1079] Legislators immediately figured out $63 million in cuts that they could agree on, $57 million short of the governor's

---

1074 Atiyeh, "State of the State, 1982," 4–5.
1075 Atiyeh, "State of the State, 1982," 5.
1076 Atiyeh, "State of the State, 1982," 6.
1077 Atiyeh, "State of the State, 1982," 7.
1078 Atiyeh, "State of the State, 1982," 9.
1079 Kathie Durbin, "Atiyeh Threatens Veto if Tax Relief Attacked," *Oregonian*, 19 January 1982.

proposal. At the end of the first week of the special session, there was still no movement, and week two ended the same as week one. In a possible sign of progress, however, the legislative leadership said it would meet with Atiyeh "to talk about a major revision in state property tax relief."[1080] More and more it looked like the governor was winning the battle over dealing with the budget shortfall. The legislature was in disarray.

When, on February 15, the total shortfall was reported to be over $330 million—$90 million higher than the number going into the special session—the tenor of negotiations changed. In his weekly cabinet meetings, the governor would usually respond to agency heads who said "Governor, we have this problem" by saying, "No. We have no problems. We have opportunities." But at about this point in the special session, one of the department directors came to him and said, "Governor, this is no longer an opportunity. We have big problems."[1081]

Two days after the legislature heard updated shortfall numbers, Atiyeh called for a one-year income tax increase by eliminating the personal exemption for taxpayers and their dependents. Although initially against a surtax, Atiyeh was also looking for a way to change the political conversation in Oregon from constantly focusing on the recession to beginning to focus on how Oregon could work its way out of the recession. Even with a larger shortfall and Atiyeh joining with most Democrats to call for a one-year income tax hike, the legislature still seemed no closer to adjournment.[1082]

Then on Saturday night February 27, by a one-vote margin, the House passed "a one-year, $75 million increase in state income taxes" already supported by the Senate. Instead of Atiyeh's proposal on exemptions, the legislative version actually raised the

---

1080 Sue Hill, "Budget Standoff Continues," *Salem (OR) Statesman-Journal*, 31 January 1982, 1A.

1081 Victor Atiyeh, interviewed by Jim Moore, "Atiyeh interview #4," Raleigh Hills, OR, 3 June 2014. Summary notes, 6.

1082 Sue Hill, "No Progress Made in Winding Up Session," *Salem (OR) Statesman-Journal*, 24 February 1982.

tax rate for a single year. And, if Congress followed through on its promise to lower federal income taxes, "taxpayers would notice no net decrease in their paychecks."[1083]

The special session finally ended at almost midnight on March 1. In the ever-colorful words of the *Salem Statesman-Journal*'s Sue Hill, the legislature "finally threw itself on the spear of compromise."[1084] The legislative form of the income-tax surcharge was part of the final package. After thirty-seven days, most legislators just wanted to get it done and go home. As legislators left Salem, there was an air of doom around them. They were almost certain that the new June 1982 revenue forecast would bring them back to Salem for yet another special session to balance the books.[1085]

The economic news in May continued to be unsettled. Inflation had taken a huge drop, but unemployment still hovered around 11%. Oregon's unemployment rate was among the worst six or seven state rates in the country, well above the 9.4% national rate, itself "the highest nationally in 40 years."[1086] The preliminary economic forecast was due on May 13, and on May 12 Atiyeh ordered state agencies to immediately cut spending.[1087] If the forecast shortfall came in at the low end of the broad preliminary estimated range of $30 million to $100 million, Atiyeh planned to handle it with new budgetary discretion approved by the attorney general. But if it was anywhere above that, and Atiyeh thought it was a 50-50 chance, he would call another special session.[1088] The state had already spent half its 1981–83 biennial budget, so any

---

1083 Sue Hill, "Legislature Approves Tax Increase: Property Tax Relief and Cigarette Tax Block Adjournment," *Salem (OR) Statesman-Journal*, 28 February 1982, 9A.
1084 Sue Hill, "Special Session is Over," *Salem (OR) Statesman-Journal*, 2 March 1982.
1085 Foster Church, "Economic Relief May Not Be Lasting," Analysis, *Oregonian*, 3 March 1982.
1086 Stan Federman, "State Reports Jobless Rate Dips to 11.3%," *Oregonian*, 12 May 1982.
1087 Leslie L. Zaitz, "New Budget Deficit Seen for Oregon," *Oregonian*, 13 May 1982.
1088 Sue Hill, "Atiyeh: 50-50 Chance of Special Session," *Salem (OR) Statesman-Journal*, 14 May 1982.

additional cuts would have to come from the remainder—and be much steeper.[1089]

The last week in May, the official projection came out. A $108 million shortfall would require a June special session. Atiyeh was clear that he did not want a repeat of the January-February train wreck. "I don't want any pride of authorship" on the final deal, he said, making it clear that the legislative leadership needed to work closely with him on a plan that all could approve relatively quickly.[1090] Atiyeh would not make any decision on the actual start date of the special session "until he works out a compromise plan with legislative leadership that would have a chance of passage."[1091] The governor's team met in the conference room, all rather morose because, as Denny Miles remembered, "We've got another revenue crisis." Somebody opened up the panel to the whiteboard, and on it was "the last [plan] we had just completed, with the little tweaks" from when they finalized the February proposal.[1092] The budget crises seemed to just keep coming.

On June 2, "convinced the skids are properly greased," the governor called the special session for June 14.[1093] He hoped "the advance work" would lead to "a 'very short session'—a week or less."[1094] And indeed, after the legislature opened the special session at 9:00 a.m. on the fourteenth, adjournment took place just over fourteen hours later, at 11:30 p.m. The final deficit number was $101 million. The solutions ranged from cuts to state aid to schools, cuts to property tax relief, to a mandatory 6% pay

---

1089 Leslie L. Zaitz, "Atiyeh, Top Legislators Brace for New Deficit," *Oregonian*, 14 May 1982.

1090 Sue Hill, "Atiyeh Expects Mid-June Special Session: $108 Million Deficit Means Spending Cuts or Tax Increases," *Salem (OR) Statesman-Journal*, 25 May 1982, 1A.

1091 Foster Church, "Revenues for State Fall Short," *Oregonian*, 25 May 1982.

1092 Denny Miles, interviewed by Jim Moore, "Atiyeh interview #3," Forest Grove, OR, 5 April 2016. Summary notes, 5..

1093 Sue Hill, "Atiyeh Calls a 'Very Short' Special Session for June 14," *Salem (OR) Statesman-Journal*, 3 June 1982.

1094 Hill, "Atiyeh Calls a 'Very Short' Special Session."

cut for most state employees.[1095] An unhappy side effect was that the reduction in property tax relief would mean that many Oregonians would have to pay an extra $300–$400 at the end of the year "to make up the difference between estimated and actual 1982–83 [property] taxes."[1096] Atiyeh was quite complimentary to the legislature for holding to the plan, especially the nature of the pay cuts, and finishing in a single day. "The people of Oregon have been well served by the result."[1097]

The SAIF Raid

The economy continued to dominate everything on Atiyeh's plate in the summer of 1982.

State workers represented by the Oregon Public Employees Union, one of eleven separate unions representing state workers, agreed to "a one-year pay freeze that would…save the state $10 million."[1098] Oregon's prison guards received layoff notices, "a formality terminating their jobs on a 40-hour week basis but offering them jobs back on a $37^1/_2$-hour week basis," the equivalent of a 6% wage reduction.[1099] In June the Salem Boise Cascade pulp and paper mill shuttered its doors, putting 341 employees out of work.[1100] There was a big national milestone as May saw "wholesale prices unchanged" from the month before, a strong indicator that inflation was tamed.[1101] At the same time, however, interest rates continued to climb. Oregon's unemployment rate dropped a bit to 11.1%, but the only good

---

1095 Sue Hill, "Special Session Over in One Day: Lawmakers Follow Script, Do Their Job and Go Home," *Salem (OR) Statesman-Journal*, 15 June 1982.
1096 George Rede, "Property Tax Bill Jolt Likely: House Payments Falling Short After State Cuts Tax Relief," *Salem (OR) Statesman-Journal*, 8 June 1982.
1097 Hill, "Special Session Over in One Day."
1098 *Statesman-Journal* (Salem), "OPEU, State Agree on Pay," 16 June 1982.
1099 Sue Hill, "Prison Guards Receive Layoff Notices With a Twist," *Salem (OR) Statesman-Journal*, 18 June 1982.
1100 Michael Arrieta-Walden, "Boise Cascade Closes Mill After Saturday's Shift," *Salem (OR) Statesman-Journal*, 20 June 1982.
1101 Lorraine Cichowski, "Economic Roundup: Wholesale Prices Unchanged for May," *Salem (OR) Statesman-Journal*, 12 June 1982.

news from the state Employment Division was to say, "If there is anything favorable in the May rate, it's that we may finally be at the bottom" of the recession.[1102] June and July were much the same, despite the bump usually expected with seasonal jobs in wood products and construction industries.[1103]

Governor Atiyeh let it be known in the first week of August that there would be another budget shortfall.[1104] His August 3 announcement to the press about the shortfall was not based on the computer model or his economic advisors. He was reacting to what he had seen as he traveled the state for his re-election campaign. Since the original 1981–83 budget had already been reduced twice, Atiyeh admitted that figuring out how to rebalance the smaller budget would be "complicated."[1105] The choices to balance the budget looked ever more bleak: end the rest of the property-tax relief; even more cuts to state agencies; add another surcharge to the income tax or raise tax rates.[1106] A third special session was announced on August 25, with the date of the session still to be decided from negotiations on solutions.[1107] The revenue shortfall was $87 million. The third special session in a year broke the previous record of two special sessions from 1933.[1108]

Then, on August 26, Atiyeh surprised everybody with a completely different plan.[1109] He proposed that $81 million of $87

1102 Stan Federman, "Oregon Jobless Rate Drops Slightly in May," *Oregonian*, 11 June 1982.
1103 Richard Read, "Economy Still Bumpy Despite Drop," *Oregonian*, 14 July 1982; Stan Federman, "Unemployment Down, but Gloom Persists," *Oregonian*, 12 August 1982.
1104 Sue Hill, "Atiyeh Warns of Budget Deficit, Is Iffy on Another Special Session," *Salem (OR) Statesman-Journal*, 4 August 1982; Leslie L. Zaitz, "Atiyeh Positive State Will Face Another Deficit," *Oregonian*, 4 August 1982.
1105 Zaitz, "Atiyeh Positive State Will Face Another Deficit."
1106 *Oregonian*, "Time for Prudence Eluded State," Editorial, 11 August 1982.
1107 Sue Hill, "Another Special Session on Its Way," *Salem (OR) Statesman-Journal*, 26 August 1982; Leslie L. Zaitz, "Atiyeh Begins Work on Budget Rescue," *Oregonian*, 26 August 1982.
1108 Douglas Heider and David Dietz, *Legislative Perspectives: A 150-Year History of the Oregon Legislatures from 1843–1993*, (Portland, OR: Oregon Historical Society, 1995), 126–128.

million be paid for out of the surplus in the State Accident Insurance Fund (SAIF).

The four party leaders of the House and the Senate, Hardy Myers (D) and Paul Hanneman (R) in the House along with Fred Heard (D) and Tony Meeker (R) in the Senate, got simultaneous phone calls from Atiyeh to come to his office for a meeting.[1110] They hurried in and sat at the long table. Atiyeh slowly walked in. Atiyeh did not say anything when he got there. He looked at each of them, then he walked over to the wood panels on the side of the room. Hanneman had never known that the panel were anything other than wall covering, but Atiyeh opened some of them up to show a board. On the board was written "SAIF $81." "Tony and I just about choked. If I'd had a denture, I would've swallowed it." Hanneman recalled that Heard and Myers did not say much. Meeker and Hanneman pointed out that those monies belonged to the employers who paid into the SAIF fund; they were not available to the legislature. "Vic said, 'I knew that you would ask that. Dave's right outside the door.'" Atiyeh walked over, opened the door, and asked attorney general Frohnmayer if it was okay to take the $81 million from the SAIF fund. Frohnmayer said, "I've researched that, and yes, we can." Atiyeh turned around and asked, "Do you want out of here, or do you want to stay here until Christmas?"

As one reporter put it, "The solution was so politically painless that legislative leaders rushed to embrace it."[1111] Legislator Norm Smith vividly recalled a House Republican caucus meeting "when Donna Zajonc [R-Salem], looking at [the] proposal from the governor's office, said, 'By golly, he had one more rabbit in the hat.'"[1112] The idea was that SAIF had overfunded its reserves, and,

---

1109 Sue Hill, "State May Crack SAIF to Pay Off Deficit," *Salem (OR) Statesman-Journal*, 27 August 1982; Leslie L. Zaitz, "Governor Spells Relief S-A-I-F," *Oregonian*, 27 August 1982.

1110 Paul Hanneman, interviewed by Jim Moore, "Atiyeh interview," Pacific City, OR, 22 July 2015. Summary notes, 15–16.

1111 Hill, "State May Crack SAIF to Pay Off Deficit."

1112 Norm Smith, interviewed by Jim Moore, "Atiyeh interview," Roseburg, OR, 28 April 2015. Summary notes, 9.

since SAIF was a quasi-independent part of state government, the state could use that money to meet the shortfall.

How did the governor come up with this extraordinary plan? Chief of Staff Gerry Thompson remembered the moment. Atiyeh was talking on the phone with his old friend Jim Campbell in August 1982. Thompson had been meeting with the governor on another matter, and it was her practice to step out of the office whenever he took a personal call.[1113] When he was done, he called Thompson in, "and tells me, 'I want you to go over to SAIF. I understand they've got far too much in reserve. You know about reserves and insurance companies [she was an insurance company executive in her non-government life], I want you to go over and see what you can find out.'"[1114] Jim Campbell, who was also in the insurance business, told Atiyeh that he "was convinced [SAIF] was ripping off employers, and we needed to get that money back, and this was the perfect time to do it." Thompson, who disagreed with this assessment, asked the governor to call Campbell in so the three of them could talk. "Vic said, 'That'd be a good idea, let's do that.'" In a 2017 interview, Thompson whispered, "It never happened."[1115] Thompson immediately objected to the SAIF idea. "It was my belief that the reserve money was for future and unknown liabilities, and if the reserves were too far beyond what was needed, [they] belonged to employers participating in SAIF, not to the state of Oregon to make up a deficit. Maybe it could be done as a loan to be paid back, but not outright."[1116] Atiyeh replied that all that might be true, but "if they're over-reserved" then the state could use the money.[1117]

Campbell did come in to talk with the governor without Thompson present. On August 25, Atiyeh's daily schedule index

---

1113 Gerry Thompson, Email to Jim Moore, "SAIF," 17 August 2017.
1114 Gerry Thompson, interviewed by Jim Moore, "Atiyeh Interview #4," Salem, OR, 7 August 2017. Summary notes, 3.
1115 Thompson, "Atiyeh Interview #4," 3.
1116 Thompson to Moore, 17 August 2017.
1117 Thompson, "Atiyeh Interview #4," 3.

cards note "Jim Campbell & an accountant, re: deficit."[1118] This was the day the special session was announced, the day before the SAIF raid was made public. The governor met with the two of them for forty-five minutes. There began a series of meetings among the governor's office, SAIF, the attorney general's office, and eventually the legislative leadership. All this lasted through much of the last few days of August 1982. Thompson went to SAIF and talked to the staff, mainly because she thought Atiyeh's old friend Monte Montgomery, who had been chair of the SAIF board until July 1982, would lie to her.[1119] She reported to Atiyeh that by current standards, SAIF's reserves were more than they needed. "He said, 'I think we're going to go in there and see if we can take some of that reserve to offset the budget deficit.'"

Atiyeh acknowledged that he took a big political chance with the SAIF idea. "What I actually did was respond as quickly as I could to the shortfall, because I knew I had a limited amount of time in which to save [with only ten months left in the 24-month 1981–83 biennium], and by the time I got to September, I had run the full gamut of cuts in revenue."[1120]

To nobody's surprise, "SAIF was adamantly opposed and fought us all the way," Thompson remembered.[1121] She herself took much of the heat. The governor was usually not at the meetings with SAIF leadership in the governor's conference room. It was almost always Thompson leading the meetings and facing down the opposition. After the determination by the attorney general's office that the move was legal, she finally had to tell SAIF's leaders, "This is what the governor wants. This is what we're going to do."[1122]

1118 "Atiyeh Daily Index-Card Schedule, August 25, 1982," Office of the Governor, State of Oregon, (25 August (revised) 1982), [SAIF Raid] Jim Campbell and an accountant, re: deficit, Atiyeh Collection, Pac. Univ. Archives.
1119 *Statesman-Journal* (Salem), "SAIF Chairman," Business & Professional Notebook, 25 July 1982.
1120 Atiyeh, "Tape 34," 123.
1121 Thompson to Moore, 17 August 2017.
1122 Thompson, "Atiyeh Interview #4," 3–4.

Atiyeh remembered "I had spent quite a bit of time, and I had talked to the attorney general's office [and the president of SAIF, Chuck Gill]..., and the theory behind what we were doing is that the state put in some money to begin SAIF. ...My contention was that the state was getting back some of the money we put in."[1123] The governor also saw that being a public entity, SAIF had saved millions in taxes it would have owed as a private company. In his mind, this led not only to the agency's surplus but to its practice of paying out dividends to employers. Atiyeh saw the dividends as evidence that SAIF had extra money in its accounts.

The special session opened on Friday September 3 at 10:00 in the morning. Atiyeh gave what was regarded by some as the best speech of his life. Atiyeh had been losing sleep over the issue and how to present it to the legislature. The night before the special session opened, after another look at the speech by the governor's staff, speechwriter David Olson was told to punch it up. Olson replied, "I'll be happy to. I *love* it when he does that."[1124] As Atiyeh prepared to deliver the address, Olson observed the governor was different from his usual self. Not only was the governor sleep deprived, Olson saw "the rare thing that almost never happened; he was very pissed off." He was angry at the pushback from his own party and from supporters who had backed him and were now criticizing him.[1125]

He listed the main reasons for Oregon's woes, and they were mainly the fault of the federal government and the Reagan administration:

Record-breaking federal deficits

Crippling high interest rates

A 180 degree *turnaround* in federal policy supports for housing

---

1123 Atiyeh, "Tape 36, side 1," 166–167.
1124 David Olson, interviewed by Jim Moore, "Atiyeh interview," Forest Grove, OR, 12 January 2016. Summary notes, 5. Italics reflect stressed word in original recording.
1125 Olson, "Atiyeh interview," 5.

Confusion and uncertainty in financial institutions and markets

Slashes in aid to state and local government.[1126]

Atiyeh took on the conservative Republicans who wanted to cut more from the budget. "There are those who say state government must tighten its belt. *Tighten… our… belt……?* …I become totally *frustrated* and *exasperated* when I am lectured by people knowledgeable enough to know what has *happened* in state government during the past three years [a direct reference to the SAIF board]. My friends, the 'belt' has never been tighter in the history of this state."[1127]

Then Atiyeh got to the heart of the matter. He had a solution; the legislature did not.

> It is *not* so easy to put forth any responsible alternative that is acceptable to the people of Oregon. To criticize this proposal without offering any alternatives shows a *gross* lack of leadership and courage. …You in this chamber…know that attacking and undermining…choices without proposing any acceptable alternatives is *wrong*.
>
> You *know* it is *wrong*.[1128]

The governor proceeded to justify the transfer of SAIF funds to the general fund: there would be no workers who lost benefits; the $81 million was not from employer premiums, it was from investment earnings; if saif had been privately held and required to pay taxes, it would have paid "over $85 million" to the state and federal governments from 1977 to 1981; none of this was

---

1126 Vic Atiyeh, "Message to 3rd Special Session, hand annotated by Atiyeh" (speech, Oregon 61st Legislative Assembly, House of Representatives Chamber, 3 September 1982), 1–2, Atiyeh Collection, Pac. Univ. Archives. Italics are underlined by Atiyeh in original.

1127 Atiyeh, "Message to 3rd Special Session," 4 Italics are underlined by Atiyeh in original. Ellipses in "Tighten our Belt?" are in original; Blankenbaker makes the connection between Atiyeh's frustration and the SAIF board explicit—see Ron Blankenbaker, "Atiyeh Has His Finest Hour," Column, *Salem (OR) Statesman-Journal*, 4 September 1982.

1128 Atiyeh, "Message to 3rd Special Session," 9. Italics are underlined by Atiyeh in original. The word "gross" was inserted by hand by Atiyeh in original.

done without consulting with the leadership team of SAIF.[1129] He did not mention that the entire leadership was adamantly against the proposal.

Atiyeh ended with a call to legislative arms. "I hope we can show the people of Oregon today that, for the *third time this year*, our state was eyeball to eyeball with the recession. And for the *third time this year*, Oregon did *not* blink."[1130]

David Olson thought it was the best speech he ever saw Atiyeh give. After the success of the speech, Olson recalled that Miles and Thompson decided that all they needed to do to get the governor to deliver better speeches was to deprive him of sleep. Olson saw the Speaker of the House stand before his colleagues later in the day and tell them, "Ladies and gentlemen, the governor has spoken. We all need to do our duties here. I know you've been concerned about all this, but the governor is as clear as I've ever heard him. This is what we need to do."[1131]

The last front page of the *Oregon Journal*, before it was absorbed by the *Oregonian*, featured "SAIF Way OK'd by Legislature."[1132] The main bill passed the House 35-22 and the Senate 16-12. Arguments from opponents featured variations on the word "immoral." Senator Frank Roberts (D-Portland) countered with "If you vote no on this bill, what are you willing to vote yes on?"[1133] Ted Kulongoski, who was engaged in the gubernatorial campaign against Atiyeh, recalled that the governor's staff was "working me pretty hard. And it wasn't to change my [no] vote, [they were] just saying, 'Don't say anything.'" He knew what the issues were, and for him "it was a tough call." The $81 million did, however, get the state out of a

---

1129 Atiyeh, "Message to 3rd Special Session," 10–11.
1130 Atiyeh, "Message to 3rd Special Session," 14. Italics are underlined by Atiyeh in original.
1131 Olson, "Atiyeh interview," 5.
1132 Jepsen and McDermott, "SAIF Way OK'd by Legislature."
1133 Leslie L. Zaitz and Foster Church, "Legislature OKs Plan to Assess SAIF Millions," *Oregonian*, 4 September 1982.

tough situation, from his point of view.[1134] Hardy Myers recalled the SAIF transfer—he hated it being referred to as the saif raid—as an example of Atiyeh being "quite flexible about revenue and taxation." When Atiyeh "put it out on the table one day, to our great surprise," the transfer solved a lot of problems for a legislature that was out of ideas on how to balance the budget.[1135]

The total shortfalls from 1980 to 1982 were $967 million, about 16% of the original budgets. There were those in the capitol who looked longingly at the $700 million given back to taxpayers by the 1979 legislature.

A note from a constituent. UGN was United Good Neighbors, an organization that folded into the United Way in the 1970s. Atiyeh Collection, Pacific University Archives.

1134 Ted Kulongoski, interviewed by Jim Moore, "Atiyeh interview," Portland, OR, 30 March 2015. Summary notes, 9.

1135 Hardy Myers, interviewed by Jim Moore, "Atiyeh interview," Portland, OR, 19 February 2015. Summary notes, 2.

Within two weeks, SAIF decided by a unanimous vote of its board to challenge the action in court.[1136] The SAIF legal saga contesting the legislature's actions would take years. The Oregon Supreme Court ruled in 1988 that the legislature had been wrong, but that the state did not need to pay back the money.[1137] In 1993 the Supreme Court ruled that the legislature was not only wrong, but *did* owe the money back.[1138] It took another eighteen months to figure out the interest owed, and in May 1996 an agreement was finally reached to repay $225 million in three installments, after the 1995 legislature had agreed to put the money in the budget.[1139] With eventual attorney fees, the total would be $245 million, more than three times the original $81 million from the raid.[1140] Kulongoski by then was Oregon's attorney general, in which position he signed off on the final SAIF settlement.[1141]

The SAIF raid in September 1982 exposed some issues with its board. During Atiyeh's governorship, the State Accident Insurance Fund had shifted from a state agency to a state-owned business in 1979, known as "quasi-public." The governor appointed its first board that year.[1142] Several of his closest friends and supporters—Monte Montgomery and Lynn Newbry among them, as well as Roy Livermore who would serve as Atiyeh's

---

1136 Don Jepsen, "SAIF Decides to Contest Diversion of Funds," *Oregonian*, 14 September 1982.

1137 Staff and Wire Reports, "Legislature Loses Case: Court: SAIF Money Shouldn't Have Been Used for Budget," *Salem (OR) Statesman-Journal*, 6 August 1988.

1138 Shawn Wirtz, "Workers' Comp Reform Proposed," *Salem (OR) Statesman Journal*, 12 April 1990; AP, "Appeals Court Rules SAIF Money Dispute is Class Action," *Salem (OR) Statesman Journal*, 10 December 1992; Dave Steves, "State Pays for Cracking SAIF," *Salem (OR) Statesman Journal*, 19 November 1993.

1139 Dan Bender, "Measures, Issues Will Affect Her Proposal," *Salem (OR) Statesman Journal*, 15 October 1994; *Statesman Journal* (Salem), "State, Businesses Sign SAIF Settlement," 24 May 1996.

1140 Craig Harris, "SAIF Case Lawyer Fees Cost State $20 Million," *Salem (OR) Statesman Journal*, 31 May 1997.

1141 Ted Kulongoski, interviewed by Jim Moore, "Atiyeh interview," Portland, OR, 30 March 2015. Summary notes, 9.

1142 Don Jepsen, "SAIF Corp. Created Amid Bitter State Battle to Insure Workers," *Oregonian*, 12 September 1982.

election treasurer in both 1978 and 1982—were named to the board. Progress was made in making SAIF more responsive to injured workers and to the businesses that paid workers' compensation insurance premiums to the corporation. By the summer of 1982, Livermore had been appointed chair of the SAIF board, replacing Montgomery. Vice chair was Newbry, who had served as the first board chair in 1979.[1143] Board members, all of whom strongly opposed the raid, made some sweeping claims as the SAIF raid was being debated about SAIF and it stewardship of insurance premiums that were clearly not true.[1144] This led to major investigations of SAIF and its operations.

In the process of investigating whether SAIF actually had the funds available to close the 1982 budget gap, the attorney general's office found that there were issues with the way money was managed at the quasi-public corporation. The initial findings were that board member Monte Montgomery had a special deal with SAIF to run an independent workers' compensation plan for the Associated Oregon Loggers (AOL), which Montgomery headed. This was a clear violation of Montgomery's board duties to manage SAIF—he was also running a competitor to SAIF. Montgomery was one of Atiyeh's closest friends. Thompson remembers vividly the day the news was broken to the governor. "The room was absolutely silent. [Atiyeh looked like he had a] totally different body. Head down, body limp, and he just sat there. And finally, he raised his head and said, 'That's not the Monte Montgomery I know.' [Thompson] said, 'We know that Governor, but you need to understand that this is real.' Head down.... For a man who showed very little emotion, he was devastated."[1145]

Secretary of State Norma Paulus' office already had a routine audit of SAIF in process as the SAIF raid was developing.[1146]

1143 *Statesman-Journal*, "SAIF Chairman."
1144 Blankenbaker, "Atiyeh Has His Finest Hour."
1145 Thompson, "Atiyeh interview #1," 9.
1146 "Atiyeh Daily Index-Card Schedule, September 14, 1982," Office of the Governor, State of Oregon, (14 September 1982), Norma Paulus re: SAIF, Atiyeh Collection, Pac. Univ. Archives.

Atiyeh appointed Lester Anderson as the governor's personal representative on the matter, making it clear to Anderson that the focus of the governor's investigation was the SAIF board and whether any of them "got 'sweetheart deals' on their workers' compensation rates."[1147] Although there were up to twenty allegations involving board members, when Anderson submitted his report in December 1982, he found "no apparent reason to pursue further any of the matters" he investigated, recommending "*no further action pertaining to Board members.*"[1148] Aided by the Criminal Justice division of the Oregon Department of Justice, Anderson found in each case that there was no criminal wrongdoing.[1149] As Atiyeh released the report to the public, he said it "vindicate[d] board members," but that "the Legislature needs to give board members clearer instructions on guiding SAIF's affairs."[1150]

The Anderson exoneration did not put an end to rumors, allegations, and uncertainty about SAIF. Monte Montgomery resigned from the SAIF board on March 1, 1983, "to form a competing insurance company" for AOL.[1151] Montgomery said the resignation was "to avoid the appearance of a conflict of interest." The governor's office had no inkling Montgomery was planning to leave the board. Atiyeh "was caught unaware," and there was no formal letter of resignation.[1152] When the governor met with Norma Paulus and her chief auditor on April 1, 1983, to talk

---

1147 AP, "Atiyeh Sets SAIF Probe Limitations," *Salem (OR) Statesman-Journal*, 28 September 1982; UPI, "Expedient Probe of SAIF Urged," *Oregonian*, 28 September 1982.

1148 Lester E. Anderson, "Report on Allegations about SAIF," personal representative Office of the Governor, State of Oregon, (3 December 1982), 4, Atiyeh Collection, Pac. Univ. Archives. Italics are underlined in original..

1149 Anderson, "SAIF report 1982," Letter from Department of Justice, Criminal Justice Division to Lester Anderson, November 24, 1982, 2.

1150 Bill Dixon, "Atiyeh Says Report Clears SAIF Board," *Salem (OR) Statesman-Journal*, 9 December 1982, 1A.

1151 George Rede, "SAIF Director Quits to Form Competing Firm," *Salem (OR) Statesman-Journal*, 3 March 1983; AP, "Governor Taps Pendleton Man," *Oregonian*, 17 August 1983.

1152 Rede, "SAIF Director Quits."

about their findings, Atiyeh learned that Montgomery's handling of funds actually resulted in lost earnings for SAIF.[1153]

The attorney general's office in April 1983 formed a task force to get to the bottom of Montgomery's dealings. In the attorney general's investigation of SAIF, questions had also arisen about where and how the governor got the idea for the $81 million SAIF raid in August 1982.

Thompson was more and more worried that Atiyeh's close relationship with the saif board members would lead to a scandal that would take years to untangle. She was confident the governor had nothing to do with SAIF's decisions (aside from appointing his friends to the board), but the nature of the SAIF raid—seeming to come out of nowhere and to solve an intractable budget situation—combined with the apparently nefarious doings of the SAIF board, especially Monte Montgomery, were clearly weaving together in people's minds. She knew that these two issues had to be separated. Atiyeh met with Frohnmayer and Thompson on August 23 to talk about SAIF, just five days after Thompson's memo to the governor.[1154] The governor was very conscious of the necessary separation as well, but for him it was a painful process because of the history of his friendship with Montgomery, dating back to the Young Turks in the 1959 legislature.

To add more pressure to the governor's understanding of what was happening at SAIF, he heard from SAIF officials on January 2, 1985, that there was going to be a reported loss at the corporation; a financial report in February 1985 revealed "that SAIF was suffering from a loss of $47 million in 1984."[1155] There

---

1153 "Atiyeh Daily Index-Card Schedule, April 1, 1983," Office of the Governor, State of Oregon, (1 April 1983), Norma Paulus & George Renner, re: SAIF Audit, Atiyeh Collection, Pac. Univ. Archives.
1154 "Atiyeh Daily Index Card, Aug 23, 1983."
1155 "Atiyeh Daily Index-Card Schedule, January 2, 1985," Office of the Governor, State of Oregon, (2 January 1985), Gary Raid, SAIF; Jo Driscoll & Gerry; subject: financial briefing, Atiyeh Collection, Pac. Univ. Archives; Thompson, "SAIF [1985]," memo to Governor, Office of the Governor, State of Oregon, 4 March 1985, 1, Atiyeh Collection, Pac. Univ. Archives; Michael Arrieta-Walden, "SAIF Lost $47 million in 1984, Report Says," *Salem (OR) Statesman Journal*, 23

was a distinct possibility that the quasi-public corporation could be insolvent by the end of 1985. Gerry Thompson informed the governor "it would appear that state government would be the responsible party" to bail out SAIF if it went under.[1156]

In August 1985, the whole thing came to a head. Former Deputy Attorney General Stan Long, by then in private practice in Eugene and acting as the independent investigator, sent a "personal and confidential, to be opened by addressee only" letter to Thompson in the governor's office.[1157] It contained the allegations uncovered by a criminal investigation by the Lane County district attorney, allegations that, as Long put it, "would make almost anyone blush."[1158] Montgomery engaged in low-level fraud with expense accounts and somewhat improbably rented himself a home in Eugene that he paid for with insurance company money. Thompson laid out to Atiyeh how Montgomery was planning to "weave you into [his] problems." Montgomery had said that Lee Johnson and the governor promised him the chairmanship on the new SAIF board.[1159]

Atiyeh thought Montgomery only began to understand the governor's role during a deposition of the governor. Montgomery was present and heard his old friend's words. "Well," Atiyeh remembered, "that kind of broke the ice in terms of him beginning to at least understand" that the two friends were on opposite sides of their understanding of the scandal.[1160] Atiyeh himself "really tried to divorce myself from [the details] as much as I could..., as if he were a stranger," to let the course of justice

---

February 1985, Atiyeh Collection, Pac. Univ. Archives.

1156 Thompson, "SAIF [1985]," 1.

1157 Stanton F. Long, "Personal and Confidential Letter to Gerry Thompson about Monte Montgomery," Swanson Harrang, Long and Watkinson Attorneys at Law, (8 August 1985), Atiyeh Collection, Pac. Univ. Archives.

1158 Long, "Personal and Confidential Letter."

1159 Gerry Thompson, "AOL/SAIF/Monte Montgomery," Office of the Governor, State of Oregon, Memo to Governor, (9 August 1985), 2, Atiyeh Collection, Pac. Univ. Archives.

1160 Victor Atiyeh, interviewed by Clark Hansen, "Tape 52," Oral history, recorded by Oregon Historical Society, Portland, OR, 10 August 1993. Transcript, 635, Atiyeh Collection, Pac. Univ. Archives.

flow wherever the facts took it.[1161] Indictments came through in the last week of January 1986. Montgomery would be found guilty and serve a short jail sentence. The shortcoming in SAIF's leadership would be addressed, but the long-term issue of creating a self-sustaining workers' compensation system would not be solved until the early 2000s.

The Election Matchup

There was really no question that Atiyeh would run for re-election. No Republican rivals had challenged him in his first term over his leadership, his policy proposals, or his responses to the economic crises. Even in the teeth of the recession, Atiyeh found that he and the legislature were working well together to deal with budget shortfalls and the economy.[1162] He decided to run for re-election because he felt strongly that it would be bad for Oregon if there was an interruption between his governorship and a new administration. Atiyeh knew that land-use planning was still a work in progress, property taxes remained a big issue, and job creation was a huge concern. He wanted to leverage relationships he had made overseas and in California to create jobs in Oregon.[1163]

The initial assumption in the Atiyeh campaign was that his opponent would be Neil Goldschmidt. Goldschmidt, who had been the popular mayor of Portland, then the U.S. Secretary of Transportation in the Carter administration, was working as a vice president for local athletic-shoe marketing giant Nike at the time. Another potential opponent was U.S. Representative Jim Weaver, who had fought against the Northwest Power Planning Bill in 1980 and ultimately incurred the wrath of Atiyeh, all the former Oregon governors, and his colleagues in Congress. Weaver would be an interesting opponent, but polls showed the Atiyeh side would be in a real fight if Goldschmidt entered the race.

1161 Atiyeh, "Tape 52," 636.
1162 Victor Atiyeh, interviewed by Jim Moore, "Atiyeh interview #3," Raleigh Hills, OR, 26 March 2014. Summary notes, 11.
1163 Atiyeh, "Atiyeh interview #3," 11.

Goldschmidt would have been Atiyeh's preference, too. It was, "I suppose, a matter of ego." Goldschmidt was the "up and coming Democrat, and he stood for a lot of things that I just didn't think were the right things."[1164] Atiyeh relished the thought of debating Goldschmidt on a whole host of issues. He also saw Goldschmidt as a politician who was good at expressing large ideas, but not so good at the details about how to accomplish goals. In Atiyeh's opinion, "Neil doesn't say much. He says it very well, but he doesn't say much. That kind of politician is not one that I am particularly favorable to."[1165] The two were not open enemies and were friendly to each other in their professional lives, but they did not agree on most of the major issues of the day. Alas, Goldschmidt made it official that he would not enter the race with a letter to the Oregon Democratic Party chair in November 1981.[1166] And Jim Weaver, who had never formally announced intentions to run, bowed out explicitly in mid-November.[1167]

On the Democratic side, Ted Kulongoski had served as a state legislator since 1975 (two House terms, appointed and then elected to the Senate by 1978), but more importantly, he had run against Bob Packwood for the U.S. Senate seat in 1980. Kulongoski handily won the 1980 statewide Democratic primary, then went on to lose to the incumbent senator 44% to 52%.[1168] In the process, Kulongoski was introduced to statewide voters, just as Atiyeh had been during his unsuccessful 1974 gubernatorial run.

Oregon's economy was hurting, and Kulongoski knew, as did everybody in the political game, that in a down economy voters tended to vote against incumbents. Taking on Atiyeh was a reasonable risk because political wisdom says that voters will

---

1164 Victor Atiyeh, interviewed by Clark Hansen, "Tape 35," Oral history, recorded by Oregon Historical Society, Portland, OR, 15 June 1993. Transcript, 128, Atiyeh Collection, Pac. Univ. Archives.

1165 Atiyeh, "Tape 55," 696.

1166 Henny Willis, "It's Probably Atiyeh vs. Clark," Column, *Eugene (OR) Register-Guard*, 29 November 1981.

1167 Willis, "It's Probably Atiyeh vs. Clark."

1168 *Oregon Blue Book, 1981*, 326–327.

blame the incumbent for economic hard times. As a Republican, Atiyeh had an extra problem to deal with along these lines. Ronald Reagan was president, and the president's party traditionally loses seats in Congress and governors in statehouses during the midterm election. Atiyeh worked to counter this tendency by blaming Reagan's fiscal policies in the recession for Oregon's down economy. In a speech to business leaders the day after the announcement of his re-election committee in September 1981, Atiyeh said that the federal government "should see to it that both the inflation rate and interest rates are lowered" so the business community could get investment and jobs flowing once again.[1169] This argument resonated with voters and made Kulongoski look a little absurd when he blamed Atiyeh's support for Reagan's policies as the reason Oregon's recession was so deep.

The way Atiyeh was characterized in the 1982 race was much different from the 1974 and 1978 races when, to his frustration, he was consistently called "conservative." Since 1978, however, especially with the election of Reagan to the White House, Atiyeh had come to represent the moderates in the political world. National columnist David Broder came out to Oregon to observe the primary, during which Atiyeh faced token opposition, including ultra-conservative challenger Walter Huss, a candidate almost guaranteed to make Atiyeh look moderate.[1170]

Broder highlighted that the quiet Atiyeh was confronting Reagan's fiscal policies head-on. Atiyeh wrote an open letter (sent simultaneously to Oregon's entire congressional delegation, to national Republican leaders, and to fifty-four governors of states and territories) to Reagan in March making the case that the interest rates that were crushing Oregon's economy were the results of the "villain" that "is your proposed budget deficit. I cannot allow this to happen without speaking out for those

---

1169 Martin Rosenberg, "Business Could Revive Economy, Atiyeh Says, " *Salem (OR) Statesman-Journal*, 26 September 1981.

1170 AP, "Walter Huss to Oppose Gov. Atiyeh," *Salem (OR) Statesman-Journal*, 7 March 1982.

162,100 Oregonians without work. ...We are now impatient, especially when the solution is so well known—a controlled federal deficit which would lead to lower interest rates."[1171] The president responded to Atiyeh's open letter within a day. After defending his programs, Reagan wrote, "When times are difficult it is easy to waiver [sic] and follow the politically expeditious path. I hope you will see your way clear to continue to support our efforts."[1172] Atiyeh did not get what he wanted from the Reagan administration. Director of the Office of Management and Budget David Stockman wrote to Atiyeh in mid-May: "You object to the impact of budget cuts on Oregon. An essential part of the Administration's progress is to reduce or eliminate unnecessary Federal programs, and at the same time give States and localities more control over the funds they receive. ...[I]t is simply not possible to cut the Federal budget without reducing the flow of funds to Oregon or any other State. ...We cannot have it both ways, nor can you."[1173] Stockman did not deal at all with Atiyeh's assertion that the record federal budget deficits were keeping interest rates higher than they otherwise would have been.

In early June, Atiyeh wrote to the president that the detailed response from David Stockman contained no good news for Oregon. "I must sadly report that little has changed in Oregon.... Unemployment has risen to 11.4 percent and 50,000 more Oregonians are out of work today than were out of work a year ago. Housing starts, so important to Oregon's economy, are at the lowest point since the early 1960's."[1174] Atiyeh made it clear that

---

1171 David Broder, "Sick Oregon Sends Message to Reagan," Column, *Oregonian*, 5 May 1982; Ronald Reagan, "Correspondence from Ronald Reagan," Office of the President, U.S. Government, Letters to Victor Atiyeh, (1980–1987), Letter from Victor Atiyeh to The Honorable Ronald Reagan, March 25, 1982, 1, 4, Atiyeh Collection, Pac. Univ. Archives.

1172 Reagan, "Correspondence from Ronald Reagan," Letter from Ron to Vic, May 6, 1982, 2.

1173 Reagan, "Correspondence from Ronald Reagan," Letter from David A. Stockman, Director to Honorable Victor Atiyeh, May 19, 1982, 3.

1174 Reagan, "Correspondence from Ronald Reagan," Letter from Victor Atiyeh, Governor to The Honorable Ronald Reagan, June 2, 1982, 1.

from his point of view, "Our suffering today is generated primarily from the fiscal and monetary policies on the national level."[1175]

The same day, Atiyeh wrote a less nuanced letter to David Stockman.

> I just read your letter to me in response to my message to our President. In reading your response I feel like someone poking a balloon and upon pulling back realizing nothing has change the shape from before. I also must tell you I resent the "kindly" lesson in budgetary science. I do not need it. And do not pat me on the head in a condescending way....
>
> Do not tell me how tough it is—Do not tell me what you inherited —Do not tell me how something cannot be done—Just tell me you know that an uncontrolled federal budget is holding up interest rates, that high interest rates are suffocating our economy, and that you will be in the vanguard to reduce the deficit. If you do not care for my ideas that is your choice, but at least I did not just carp and criticize....
>
> David, I have said it before and I will say it again—when the national economy cools off, Oregon gets pneumonia. We Oregonians are proud and loyal Americans but are we expected to contribute ourselves into oblivion? I certainly do not think so and feel no shame in fighting for them as vigorously as my knowledge and strength will take me.[1176]

Atiyeh was clearly differentiating himself from Reagan policies, and he was making his fight with the administration known to his constituents. Back in Oregon, Kulongoski was having none of it: "The Dear Abby syndrome, I call it. It doesn't fool anyone,

---

1175 Reagan, "Correspondence from Ronald Reagan," Letter from Victor Atiyeh, Governor to The Honorable Ronald Reagan, June 2, 1982, 1.
1176 Reagan, "Correspondence from Ronald Reagan," Victor Atiyeh, Governor to David Stockman, Director U.S. Office of Management and Budget, June 2, 1982.

especially as he didn't start writing until March when it became obvious he might be in trouble."[1177]

Especially in the legislature, Democrats were making the argument that Atiyeh was a "caretaker" governor, someone "incapable of the vision to steer Oregon through the unstable '80s."[1178] Atiyeh's "if it ain't broke, don't fix it" position on Oregon state agencies and policies was interpreted as being evidence of Atiyeh being a "nice, do-nothing guy incapable of the kind of leadership to inspire new solutions to the state's growing problems."[1179] Kulongoski would add to the slogan with "Well, now the state is broke and Atiyeh can't fix it."[1180] In fact Atiyeh suspected that within the Democratic caucus they probably discussed ways to mangle Atiyeh's anti-recession policies to make him more vulnerable in his re-election bid. But Atiyeh also knew that there were those within the caucus who felt that dealing with the economy was too important to politicize. He recalled, "To their credit they were working with the Republican governor while their guy was sitting in with them and running for election."[1181]

But early indications in 1982 from the January economic update by the Executive Department were that state income tax revenue would climb, possibly by "17 to 23 percent by the next two-year budget period, 1983–85."[1182] Atiyeh responded to the report by saying, "The figures confirm what I have been saying all along. There will be money next time around to plug in wherever the shoe pinches badly."[1183] If this were the case, Salem

---

1177 Muriel Dobbin, "Impact of Reagonomics Worries Ore. Governor," *Baltimore (MD) Sun*, 7 September 1982.

1178 Ron Blankenbaker, "Playing the Money Game," Column, *Salem (OR) Statesman-Journal*, 23 January 1982.

1179 Ron Blankenbaker, "Atiyeh Wins An Early Round," Column, *Salem (OR) Statesman-Journal*, 29 August 1982.

1180 Blankenbaker, "Atiyeh Wins An Early Round."

1181 Atiyeh, "Atiyeh interview #3," 11.

1182 Blankenbaker, "Playing the Money Game."; Sue Hill, "Forecast: Pleny of Money. Economic Update Shows Short Term for State Problems," *Salem (OR) Statesman-Journal*, 23 January 1982.

1183 Hill, "Forecast: Pleny of Money," 1B.

columnist Ron Blankenbaker noted that "Atiyeh will be in incredibly good re-election shape."[1184] From February on, the Atiyeh campaign focus was on "Economic Development showing results for Oregonians. ...Vic must be the coach bringing all related groups together."[1185] Atiyeh hired a new director the Department of Economic Development, Doug Carter, to work on cooperation between state government and the business community to put the now 165,000 unemployed back to work. It was clear that "the political future of Atiyeh...may well hinge on the success of new economic recovery efforts to be mounted by the department, Carter said."[1186]

To Change a Sign

As 1982 progressed Vic Atiyeh had shifted his thinking to growing Oregon's economy from simply preserving state services. He thought of one impediment to Oregon's growth that just rubbed him the wrong way. And he set his mind to change that obstacle.

As motorists drove up from California on Interstate 5, at the Oregon border in the Siskiyou Mountains there was a sign. It was made of redwood, and it proclaimed: "Welcome to Oregon. We Hope You Will Enjoy Your Visit."[1187] Atiyeh did not like the sign's message. It spoke of Tom McCall's Oregon and his joking welcome to 1971 convention delegates meeting in Portland: "We want you to visit our state again and again. But, for heaven's sake, don't move here to live."[1188] McCall was speaking during a time in which concerns for the environment and quality of life across

---

1184 Blankenbaker, "Playing the Money Game."
1185 Gerry Thompson, "Campaign Documents," Executive Campaign Committee, Re-Elect Governor Atiyeh Committee (1982), Atiyeh Collection, Pac. Univ. Archives. Re-Elect Governor Atiyeh Committee, Executive Committee Minutes, 2-24-82.
1186 Martin Rosenberg, "Economic Development Boss Says He'll Stress the Positive," *Salem (OR) Statesman-Journal*, 14 March 1982, 1J.
1187 Ron Barker, "Atiyeh Wants to Explode Tourist Myth," *Oregonian*, 6 May 1982.
1188 Barker, "Atiyeh Wants to Explode Tourist Myth."

much of the country were becoming central political questions. In Oregon these questions led to the creation of statewide land-use law, as well as some of the strictest environmental policies in the country. But the somewhat xenophobic message fostered by McCall had continued after that time. In 1982 it was reported, "State officials went shopping several years ago to woo new industries here. Oregon, the word came back, doesn't like newcomers."[1189]

Atiyeh said, "I just had gotten my fill of 'Aren't you the ones that want us to come visit but don't stay?' Or, during open house [at Atiyeh's office], 'Where are you folks from?' They'd pause, and 'Well, we're from California.' [They were] embarrassed by the fact that they're from California. ...That's not what Oregon's all about, that's not who we really are."[1190] Atiyeh appointed a Tourism Task Force to formulate new ways of attracting tourists and immigrants alike to the Beaver state.

But first, that sign had to go.

At one of the governor's May 1982 cabinet meetings with representatives from the Department of Transportation there was a copy of the *Medford Mail Tribune* with a picture of the Welcome sign. "That really triggered me. I said, 'I want to go down there and blow up that damn sign.' And they said, 'Yeah, yeah, okay, governor.' 'No! I want to put dynamite under that thing and blow it up.' They said, 'You can't do that governor.' 'Yes, I can. I want to blow that thing up.'"[1191]

Atiyeh left the meeting and walked into Denny Miles' office.[1192] He lit a cigarette and said, "Denny, you know that sign" at the California border? Miles did know that sign. "Well, we want to get a lot of coverage on that, don't we?" Miles agreed. "We're going to blow it up with dynamite." Miles thought it was

---

1189 Sue Hill, "Atiyeh Wants to Push State As a Great Place to Live," *Salem (OR) Statesman-Journal*, 5 May 1982.
1190 Atiyeh, "Tape 35," 144–145.
1191 Atiyeh, "Tape 35," 144.
1192 Denny Miles, interviewed by Jim Moore, "Atiyeh interview #1," Forest Grove, OR, 31 July 2014. Summary notes, 3–4.

a joke. "No! No! We're going to blow it up with dynamite!" Miles asked, "You remember the [exploding] whale?" The 1970 dynamiting of a dead whale on the beach had become a part of Oregon lore—and the video of the event is now considered to be the first viral video story in the world.[1193] Miles also thought of the location, just a few miles from the spot the DeAutremont brothers blew up a train during a 1923 robbery and killed several people.[1194] Miles argued to the governor, "This thing is just fraught with disaster." Atiyeh told him, "Look. Handle it." Atiyeh left for Portland.

As soon as Miles said to himself, "Oh, man," his phone rang. It was Gerry Thompson with a sharp, "Denny?! My office. Now." In her office were the superintendent of the State Police, the head of the Military Department, the head of Emergency Services, the head of the Department of Transportation, Bob Oliver—"all of the affected parties were there. And the first words out of her mouth were, 'You've got to talk the governor out of this.'" The arguments against blowing up the sign were practical—I-5 would have to be closed; the National Guard did not have access to the proper explosives; and there was the chance of a landslide heading down the mountainside toward the California hamlet of Hilt.

The news got the publicity. The *Wall Street Journal* sent a senior national correspondent to talk with the governor about "economic development & Oregon's image."[1195] But the scheme also handed Kulongoski an issue with which to pillory the governor: "Atiyeh's fantasy about blowing up the sign is a silly

---

1193 Paul Linnman, "Oregon's Exploding Whale," KATU television, 12 November 1970, YouTube Video; AP, "Thar She Blows: Whale is Blasted," *Salem Oregon Statesman*, 13 November 1970; AP, "Road Crews to Blow Up Whale Near Florence," *Salem Oregon Statesman*, 12 November 1970.

1194 *Mail Tribune* (Medford), "4 Killed S.P. Hold-Up in Siskiyous," 11 October 1923; Ron Blankenbaker, "Blow-Up in the Siskiyous," *Salem (OR) Statesman Journal*, 21 July 1982.

1195 "Atiyeh Daily Index-Card Schedule, May 28, 1982," Office of the Governor, State of Oregon, Ray Vicker, Sr. Natl. Correspondent, Wall Street Journal re: economic development & Oregon's image, (28 May 1982), Atiyeh Collection, Pac. Univ. Archives.

stunt born out of his shallow analysis of our economic problems." Not only that, Kulongoski also argued, Atiyeh's efforts to recruit business investments backfired: "Governor Atiyeh has done more than anyone else to contribute to Oregon's anti-business image by running around the country proclaiming it to be true."[1196]

By mid-May Atiyeh had agreed that the practical concerns with blowing up the redwood structure were insurmountable, so the sign—and all the welcome signs at the state's borders—would be repainted to say, "Welcome to Oregon."[1197] On July 21,[1198] the redwood sign was replaced with more durable aluminum. The new message would be unveiled at a ceremony along the freeway,[1199] giving Kulongoski the opportunity for one last dig: "Atiyeh was actually 'standing on the border waving bye-bye to all the people going out to find a job.'"[1200]

However, it was not the changing of the sign or the shots taken by Kulongoski that dominated the story of that July day. Former governor Tom McCall agreed to accompany Atiyeh to the brief ceremony. McCall's biographer wrote, "McCall was determined to come to this spot."[1201] Atiyeh gave his short speech, then McCall came forward when Atiyeh introduced him saying, "Governor McCall will now be the speaker at the funeral of his own prose."[1202] McCall took on Atiyeh, telling the assembled, "'There's been a lot of bad mouthing about 'Visit, but don't stay.' It's served its purpose. We were saying 'Visit, but don't stay' because Oregon, queen bee though she is, is not yet ready for the

---

[1196] Foster Church, "Kulongoski Attacks Atiyeh's 'Fantasy' Over Sign," *Oregonian*, 11 May 1982.

[1197] AP, "Atiyeh Puts Paint, Not TNT, to 'Unwelcome' Sign," *Oregonian*, 15 May 1982.

[1198] "Atiyeh Daily Index-Card Schedule, July 21, 1982," Office of the Governor, State of Oregon, Ceremony: Siskiyou Summit, (21 July 1982), Atiyeh Collection, Pac. Univ. Archives.

[1199] *Oregonian*, "Sign Remade," Photo caption, 22 July 1982.

[1200] Foster Church, "Democratic Chairman Rips GOP Policies," *Oregonian*, 22 July 1982.

[1201] Brent Walth, *Fire at Eden's Gate: Tom McCall and The Oregon Story*, (Portland, OR: Oregon Historical Society Press, 1994), 2.

[1202] Walth, *Fire at Eden's Gate*, 7.

swarm. I am simply saying that Oregon is demure and lovely, and it ought to play a little hard to get."[1203] Atiyeh was most likely saying to himself, "That's just Tom being Tom."

Tom McCall died in January 1983. In one remembrance of him, the trip to the border was used to illustrate how McCall's principles did not waver, even as the political and economic times moved on from his heyday in the late 1960s and early 1970s.[1204] For Atiyeh, the story became one of having his passions reined in by his staff and of giving McCall one last chance to roar in front of the television cameras.

The General Election

Atiyeh's re-election "campaign was designed to talk to Oregonians'...hope for the future. They want...a good stable government. They want somebody in government that really has the strength—and the compassion—to do the job they needed to be done" in the face of "the very depth of our recession, 12.6% unemployment."[1205] The strategy continued the message from the primary that Atiyeh had the knowledge and experience to govern during tough economic times. The focus in the general election would be on Kulongoski as being "too liberal for Oregon." The strong implication would be that this was not time for "radicalism."[1206] Atiyeh knew that "it was up to me to go out and sell that message." Longtime colleague and 1978 primary opponent Roger Martin noted that Atiyeh's personality really helped in the race. Atiyeh "was not a firebrand."[1207] Maybe the welcome sign episode helped breathe some life into Atiyeh's image. After one of the three fall 1982 debates with Kulongoski,

---

1203 Walth, *Fire at Eden's Gate*, 8.
1204 Charles E. Beggs, "McCall Unyielding in His Committment to Conservation," *Salem (OR) Statesman-Journal*, 9 January 1983.
1205 Atiyeh, "Tape 35," 131.
1206 Thompson, "Campaign 1982," Thompson handwritten notes, memo to Denny Miles, re: Paul Newman, 7-19-82.
1207 Roger Martin, interviewed by Jim Moore, "Atiyeh interview," Lake Oswego, OR, 23 April 2015. Summary notes, 13.

Atiyeh came out to his staff and somebody said to him, "Wow, they even said you had charisma!" He responded, "You should have told me! I didn't know they wanted charisma."[1208]

The Atiyeh campaign had been angling for Vice President George H. W. Bush to come campaign for Atiyeh since February.[1209] Reagan's unpopularity in Oregon made a visit by the president something to be avoided. His more moderate vice president would be a better bet.[1210] Bush had two tasks during his July visit: to help Atiyeh make the argument the economy was getting better and to raise money for Atiyeh and Oregon US Representative Denny Smith. He was successful on both counts. The Vice President "appeared to have disarmed a potentially hostile Gov. Atiyeh…with assurances of a recovering economy." Atiyeh agreed with the assessment, saying, "I am confident a turnaround has occurred and there has been some good news."[1211] When asked about Atiyeh's frustration with high-deficit spending, Bush "said the administration doesn't expect every Republican governor 'to march in lockstep.'"[1212] Bush left Atiyeh with a note —"Win–big."[1213]

Former President Gerald Ford stumped for Atiyeh in the second week of September. His main argument was that the Reagan administration had "made progress in reversing the sick

---

1208 Miles, "Atiyeh interview #1," 18.
1209 George H. W. Bush, "Hope We Can Help," Office of the Vice President, U.S. Government, Handwritten note, (2 February 1982), Atiyeh Collection, Pac. Univ. Archives; George Bush, to Sharon Page, "Letter from Vice President Bush to Sharon Page, Atiyeh's Campaign Staff, Regarding Scheduling," 2 February 1982, Atiyeh Collection, Pac. Univ. Archives.
1210 Denny Miles, "Elements of a Political Campaign," (Unpublished manuscript), 105.
1211 Foster Church, "From the Top, Bush Says 'Recession is Over'," *Oregonian*, 8 July 1982.
1212 AP, "Bush Visits Portland, Says Recession Is Over," *Salem (OR) Statesman-Journal*, 8 July 1982.
1213 George H. W. Bush, "Great Being With You," Office of the Vice President, U.S. Government, Handwritten note, (11 July 1982), Atiyeh Collection, Pac. Univ. Archives.

economy" inherited from the Carter administration.[1214] Ford backed Atiyeh's attack on the Reagan administration over timber policies, but the ex-president simultaneously supported Reagan's stance, saying "I think Gov. Atiyeh was exactly right in representing the people of Oregon. But that doesn't mean the federal government has to automatically respond."[1215] Atiyeh combined a successful fundraiser with Ford's visit.

The Atiyeh campaign put together ads that excoriated Kulongoski for his 1981 bill that would have required large companies to give advance notice before shutting down any manufacturing facilities. The bill was to protect workers, but it had been given the name of "plant closure bill" as it went through the legislative process. Speaking on September 6 in the heart of Kulongoski territory in Eugene, Atiyeh called his opponent a novice and hit on the plant closure bill as reinforcing "the anti-business image Oregon had."[1216] The implication was that Kulongoski's plan would lead to closed production plants, that "plant closure legislation is a 'dangerous scheme' and drives away jobs."[1217] As Kulongoski noted in a 2015 interview, "…this is why words matter greatly in politics."[1218] Roger Martin observed that the words had a lot of meaning because so many plants were closing at the time; it looked like Kulongoski was in favor of that. Martin's analysis: "They wrapped that around his neck."[1219]

Radio ads began in early September.[1220] Atiyeh ads called Kulongoski's policies dangerous, which created a backlash of Kulongoski supporters accusing Atiyeh of calling Kulongoski

---

1214 *Oregonian*, "Ford Stumps: GOP Credited with Reversal of Inherited Economic Woes," 11 September 1982.
1215 George Rede, "Ford Backs Atiyeh on Timber-Aid Fight," *Salem (OR) Statesman-Journal*, 11 September 1982.
1216 Henny Willis, "Atiyeh Launches Bid with Attack: He Calls Kulongoski 'Novice'," *Eugene (OR) Register-Guard*, 7 September 1982.
1217 Terry McDermott, "Atiyeh Radio Ads Hit by Kulongoski Aide," *Oregonian*, 8 September 1982.
1218 Kulongoski, "Atiyeh interview," 6.
1219 Martin, "Atiyeh interview," 13.
1220 McDermott, "Atiyeh Radio Ads Hit by Kulongoski Aide."

himself dangerous.[1221] Atiyeh thought long and hard about approving the "Kulongoski's ideas are dangerous" ads. "I never believed…that speaking about what is public record is dirty campaigning. That's public record. …Public record is not dirty. Reminding people of the public record…is fair game, not dirty."[1222]

The responses of each campaign to the other became a signature of the contest. Denny Miles, who had left the governor's office to become Atiyeh's campaign manager, was aware that a letter from Bob Packwood had gone out that actually did call Kulongoski dangerous. Miles knew of the letter because it had been "drafted by Gov. Atiyeh's campaign staff," then "read and approved by Packwood himself."[1223] Miles was mindful of the fire with which he was playing. He observed that it is very hard to win a campaign if there is nothing but bad said about an opponent. Voters need to be given a reason to vote for a candidate, not just reasons to vote against the opponents. But "If you don't bring out things that the voters don't like about someone, then you're only running half a campaign."[1224] Atiyeh made a point to highlight some of those things that voters might not like about Kulongoski by calling the Democrat's message about Atiyeh's lack of action in the face of the recession "a lie."[1225]

There was a response. Three Democratic legislative leaders immediately "accused Gov. Vic Atiyeh of conducting an advertising campaign based on 'falsehoods.'"[1226] Many people called the ads negative, "typical of the kind of advertising the

---

1221 Miles, "Atiyeh interview #1," 17.
1222 Atiyeh, "Tape 35," 143.
1223 AP, "Packwood Labels Kulonogoski 'Dangerous' in Atiyeh Letter," *Salem (OR) Statesman-Journal*, 15 September 1982; Foster Church, "Packwood Letter Calls Kulongoski 'Dangerous'," *Oregonian*, 14 September 1982.
1224 Miles, "Atiyeh interview #1," 18.
1225 Ron Blankenbaker, "The Experts Miss Something," Column, *Salem (OR) Statesman-Journal*, 29 June 1982.
1226 Terry McDermott, "Democrats Rap Atiyeh Radio Ads: Accusations Against Opponent Kulongosi Said Untrue," *Oregonian*, 9 September 1982.

Republicans have been doing since 1980."[1227] National columnist David Broder wrote about the new style of politics—"Get the opponent's name known first, and unfavorably. ...Rather than wait for Kulongoski to arrive with favorable information about himself, the governor filled the vacuum with his own version of Kulongoski's record."[1228] Observer Russ Dondero saw that Atiyeh was able to frame Kulongoski as "a labor goon. ...By the time the election was over, nobody would have voted for Ted Kulongoski, including his mother."[1229] Atiyeh accepted the criticism but disagreed with the premise. "If that's observed to be negative, I have to live with it. I can't change that. But to me it's public record. Public record…is perfectly legitimate. There are some obviously irritated by the fact that they liked [Kulongoski], they don't want to see anybody say anything that might be harmful to him. I can understand that."[1230]

Norm Smith (R-Tigard), serving in the House at the time, analyzed the Atiyeh campaign. It "was necessary, as it sometimes is in politics, to establish that the challenger is a risk, and is a dangerous person."[1231] Smith saw that Kulongoski and Atiyeh had very different styles for dealing with political challenges. There was the traditional businessperson Republican incumbent, and there was the liberal labor lawyer Democrat. Kulongoski's principles were different from Atiyeh's. Smith never saw Atiyeh personally being "vicious or mean," but when Atiyeh felt "somebody was just plain wrong, he'd say so." In Astoria, for example, "[a] longshoreman [asked] Atiyeh about Oregon's land-use planning laws, which were being challenged by a ballot measure. 'How about this LCDC, Vic. They're screwing us bad,' he [shouted]. Atiyeh [replied] with uncharacteristic sharpness: 'If

---

1227 McDermott, "Democrats Rap Atiyeh Radio Ads."
1228 David S. Broder, "What's In a Name? Plenty," Column, *Washington Post*, 20 October 1982; David S. Broder, "Atiyeh Follows Trend with Negative Ad Tactic," Column, *Oregonian*, 20 October 1982; Atiyeh, "Tape 35," 148.
1229 Russ Dondero, interviewed by Jim Moore, "Atiyeh interview," Forest Grove, OR, 13 August 2014. Summary notes. 4.
1230 Atiyeh, "Tape 35," 150.
1231 Smith, "Atiyeh interview," 7.

they vote land-use planning out, we are in a hell of a shape as far as economic development.'"[1232] Overall, Norm Smith saw that Atiyeh "was calmer in appearance than he must have been" in reality, because among those close to Atiyeh there was a sense that the election was going to be a tough, tough race. With the economy as bad as it was, the conventional wisdom was that voters wanted to make changes.[1233]

Kulongoski called for the "dangerous ad" to be pulled from radio stations. Miles was in Medford for the third debate when the news came that Kulongoski was going to hold a press conference on the "dangerous" ad. Miles was quite happy about this. He would get free publicity to explain the differences between calling Kulongoski's policies dangerous and calling Kulongoski himself dangerous. Miles was also able to make the final point that the plant closure proposal was actually a dangerous idea.[1234] It turned out that the ad was going to end anyway, but the Atiyeh campaign had to leave it on the air so as not to appear to respond to Kulongoski's demand.[1235] As Miles put it, "We loved it whenever he would complain about it, because we got to talk about it, and we didn't have to pay for it."[1236] Kulongoski tried to turn the words to his advantage, saying, "[I]f being concerned about Oregon's 150,000 jobless, its thousands of business bankruptcies and skyrocketing utility rates is dangerous, 'then I'm dangerous, and it's time Oregon's governor was dangerous.'"[1237]

This whole episode contributed to reporter Chuck Beggs' analysis that "Kulongoski imploded. Shot himself in the foot with the plant closure bill." The timing of the bill, when people were looking to attract businesses to Oregon, was "very poor."[1238] Kulongoski's response to Atiyeh's ads just made things worse.

1232 Foster Church, "Campaign Trail Reflects Atiyeh of Many Moods," *Oregonian*, 28 October 1982.
1233 Smith, "Atiyeh interview," 7.
1234 Miles, "Atiyeh interview #2," 5.
1235 Atiyeh, "Tape 35," 142.
1236 Miles, "Atiyeh interview #2," 6.
1237 AP, "Atiyeh and Kulongoski Tune Up: Debate No. 2 on Monday," *Salem (OR) Statesman-Journal*, 19 September 1982, 1A.

While public polls showed a dead heat, private polling showed Atiyeh with a 7–10% lead from mid-September on.[1239]

The bulk of the Atiyeh campaign ads, however, were not aimed at Kulongoski; they were designed to make it easy for voters to support Atiyeh. Miles wanted them to build on the sense of many Oregonians that they knew Vic Atiyeh, a sense reinforced by his frequent travels throughout the state. People had been in a room with him, they had actually talked with him, they had seen him come to their towns. "The ads simply reminded people about this guy who they already knew really well."[1240]

Atiyeh, in his analysis of the race in late September, said, "If you remove that issue of the economy, I don't think I would have a strong opponent."[1241] There was however, an issue that united Kulongoski and Atiyeh. Yet another property-tax limitation initiative was on the ballot, Measure 3. This one would "limit property taxes to 1.5 percent and roll back [property] values to 1979–80 levels."[1242] Both gubernatorial candidates opposed the measure. Just as the passage of California's Proposition 13 loomed over the 1978 election, the post–1978 reality of California's finances loomed over consideration of Measure 3— California's $7 billion 1978 surplus was gone, and "libraries, parks and roads have been hit hard."[1243] An ad opposing Measure 3 implored voters, "Whether you vote for Vic or Ted, ballot measure #3 would stop your man cold."[1244] Property taxes were

---

1238 Charles E. Beggs, interviewed by Jim Moore, "Atiyeh interview," Salem, OR, 12 March 2015. Summary notes, 3.

1239 Bardsley and Haslacher, "Politics—1982: An Evaluation," Public Opinion Research for Atiyeh Reelection Campaign, (1982), 2, Atiyeh collection, Pac. Univ. Archive.

1240 Miles, "Atiyeh interview #2," 7.

1241 Wallace Turner, "Gubernatorial Election in Oregon Expected to Focus on the Economy," *New York Times*, 28 September 1982.

1242 Don Campbell, "Oregon's 'Measure 3' Has Politicians Trembling," Column, *Binghamton (NY) Press and Sun-Bulletin*, 30 September 1982; Don Campbell, "Cutting Taxes in Oregon," *Honolulu (HI) Star-Bulletin*, 25 September 1982.

1243 Campbell, "Oregon's 'Measure 3' Has Politicians Trembling." Campbell, "Cutting Taxes in Oregon."

1244 Oregon Committee, "Whether You Vote for Vic or Ted, Ballot Measure #3 Would Stop Your Man Cold!," Advertisement, *Salem (OR) Statesman-Journal*, 31 October

not the defining issue of the 1982 gubernatorial campaign as they had been in 1978, but the drumbeat for property tax reform was still strong.

Atiyeh was running like a challenger, with lots of energy and a high number of appearances across the state, in addition to the heavy ad campaign. Atiyeh recalled pushing back against a classic incumbent strategy of simply appearing "gubernatorial." "I'm not going to sit here and do that. ...I'm going out. ...I'm going to take the risk, but I am certainly not going to sit back and...protect my lead."[1245] As Denny Miles observed, Atiyeh's natural inclination was *not* to run an "incumbent" race, but to actively engage with voters and his opponent.[1246]

On primary election night, Atiyeh had challenged Kulongoski to a series of debates. The campaign staff was against Atiyeh challenging Kulongoski so soon. They were not opposed to the debates, but they did not want to immediately give Kulongoski the opportunity to have them. He was the lesser-known opponent, so quickly elevating him to some parity with the governor seemed like a bad idea.[1247] But Atiyeh was firm, "I'd just had enough of this [debate scheduling] nonsense for all these years, and I wasn't going to be a party to it."[1248]

The power of television made debates crucial for any statewide campaign, and people still remembered the 1968 televised confrontation between Bob Packwood and Wayne Morse that was credited with Packwood's narrow defeat of the four-term U.S. Senator.[1249] Although Atiyeh thought people watched debates for "the same reason people go to auto races. They're all there to see

---

1982.
1245 Atiyeh, "Tape 35," 135.
1246 Denny Miles, Phone call to Jim Moore, "Comments on 'Running for Governor 1982' Chapter," 27 July 2017.
1247 Miles, "Atiyeh interview #2," 3.
1248 Atiyeh, "Tape 35," 134.
1249 Mason Drukman, *Wayne Morse: A Political Biography*, (Portland: Oregon Historical Society Press, 1997), 450–452; Smith, "Atiyeh interview," 7.

a big crash,"[1250] the debates were a good showplace for Atiyeh. The analysis after each debate never said that Atiyeh won, but Atiyeh deftly got Kulongoski to make points that Atiyeh wanted to pin on his challenger. Atiyeh's message in the debates was exactly what it was on the campaign trail. "To blame me for the recession that has hit Oregon is something Oregonians don't believe. I didn't create high interest rates; I didn't create a trillion-dollar (federal) deficit."[1251]

Public polling showed the race was even statewide, but an early October poll indicated that Atiyeh was ahead by 10 points (±6%) in the Portland area.[1252] Democrats had been able to count on big wins in Multnomah County in recent years. The Portland-area poll showed that Kulongoski might have some major problems connecting with the electorate.

Campaign manager Miles was very carefully managing the campaign's assets. He knew that the ideal campaign would be one that spent every dollar that came in. But he made what he acknowledged was a tactical and strategic error in late September that could have swung the election to Kulongoski. The plan was to raise a lot of money (it would end up being a record $1.2 million) so the Atiyeh campaign could hit the airwaves early with television advertisements and never go off the air until the day after the election. Miles's internal polls looked pretty good for Atiyeh, with about a 10% lead and a spike to 15% at the end of the month. The fundraising numbers were okay but could have been better. So, he decided to get ready for a final ad push in the last few weeks of the campaign by suspending campaign ads on television, which were expensive, and backfilling with less expensive ads on radio. Miles recalled his thinking: "And since

---

1250 George Rede, "Governor Debates: The Lure of Blood?" *Salem (OR) Statesman-Journal*, 9 September 1982.

1251 Don Campbell, "Oregon Gubernatorial Race Eyed Closely," *Ithaca (NY) Journal*, 24 September 1982. Parentheses in original.

1252 *Oregonian*, "Poll Shows Atiyeh Lead Over Kulongoski in City," 9 October 1982; *Oregonian*, "Governor, Kulongoski Race Even, " 7 October 1982.

it's before the real climax of the campaign, it shouldn't hurt us."[1253]

"It hurt immediately."[1254] The campaign's daily tracking polls showed diminishing support of Atiyeh and growing support for Kulongoski. What had been a fifteen-point advantage for Atiyeh in the third week in September was a statistical tie at the end of the first week in October. Miles learned that media strategy was more complex than simply buying time and placing ads when voters would see them. Television was a much stronger medium for reaching voters statewide than radio.[1255]

Fixing a mistake like this is difficult. Media buys are made in advance, so there is no way to just go buy advertising time for the next day on television stations. The campaign got back on the air, but on programs that aired after the late-night talk shows were done. But at least the campaign had television advertising. Miles did not know if the Kulongoski campaign had the same data that showed how the opinion poll numbers were converging.

He was sick to his stomach about what happened. "I had made the silliest mistake in the entire campaign. It was correctable, thank goodness, but it was stupid."[1256] This was Miles' mistake to make. He was in charge. Another lesson for Miles was that the expense of the daily tracking polls was worth it simply for being able to recognize the mistake and being able to correct it in time.[1257] "If we had not had tracking, the biggest mistake I made in the 1982 campaign could have lost it for us."[1258]

1253 Miles, "Atiyeh interview #2," 4.
1254 Miles, "Atiyeh interview #2," 4.
1255 Miles, "Atiyeh interview #2," 4.
1256 Miles, "Atiyeh interview #2," 4.
1257 Miles, "Atiyeh interview #2," 5.
1258 Miles, "Atiyeh interview #2," 16.

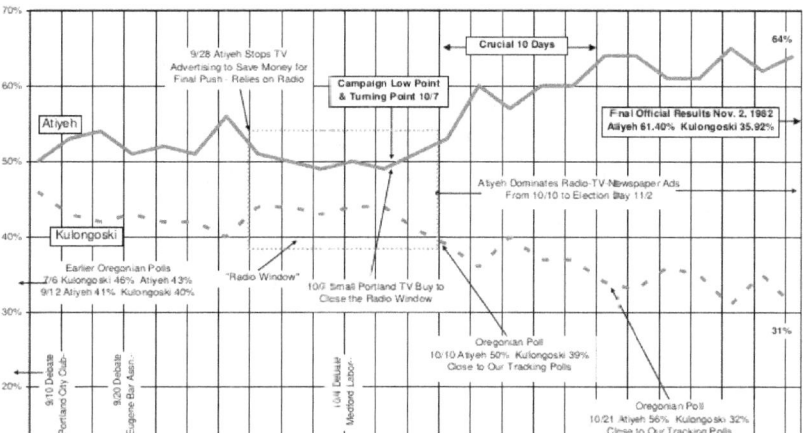

Denny Miles, "Atiyeh for Governor DMI Tracking Poll" (unpublished), private memoir.

As television ads reappeared and the Atiyeh campaign advertising dominance tactic kicked in, internal polling showed Atiyeh's lead growing to 15%, 20%, and heading toward 30% on good days. By mid-October, Atiyeh was moving ahead in public polls. Soon, another statewide poll indicated Atiyeh over Kulongoski by an almost unbelievable 24% (±4.9%).[1259] Ultimately, the Atiyeh campaign strategy for the last three weeks of the contest was to dominate advertising—to get the word out about the candidate and his ideas, and to deny the Kulongoski campaign media time it could buy for its own ads. The Kulongoski campaign seemed to be struggling with fundraising,

---

1259 J. Roy Bardsley, "Atiyeh's Poll Lead Widens," *Oregonian*, 27 October 1982.

so it could not get the good ad slots nailed down as far in advance as the Atiyeh campaign could.[1260]

Atiyeh was the happy political campaigner in 1982. He relished talking to people across the state, but he also knew this was his last campaign. Toward the end, however, he was physically worn down. Some of the travel days had been epic. The July day that Atiyeh presided over the changing of the Welcome to Oregon sign at the California border, he had started out in Salem, flown to Portland to pick up Tom McCall, flown to Medford, driven to the Siskiyou summit, flown back to Portland after a lunch in Ashland, dropped off McCall at the KATU television studios, dedicated a new bandstand at the zoo in Washington Park in Portland, then flown to Durkee in far eastern Oregon for a steak feed.[1261] That was at least a twelve-hour working day covering around 1000 miles, with six events or meetings.

The governor's driver Lon Holbrook recounted that in the last week of campaigning in late October they were scheduled to fly into La Grande from Bend.[1262] The weather was bad, so they ended up flying into Pendleton. Winter was getting an early start. Holbrook put in a hurried call to get a state police vehicle to the Pendleton airport for them. The car ended up being a detective's car (unmarked) that did not even have studs on the tires. They headed off from Pendleton on the snowy and icy freeway to La Grande for the campaign event. It was a long nerve-racking drive. They got about three hours of sleep in the motel in La Grande.[1263] The governor was sitting in the lobby the next morning as they were waiting for a state police trooper to come pick them up. "The governor was just exhausted. He looked at me and said,

---

1260 Miles, "Atiyeh interview #2," 6.
1261 "Atiyeh Daily Index Card, Jul 21, 1982."
1262 Lon Holbrook, interviewed by Jim Moore, "Atiyeh interview," Gladstone, OR, 6 June 2017. Summary notes, 14; "October 1982 schedule," 10/29. Participate: Forum. Eastern Ore. State College, La Grande.
1263 "Atiyeh Daily Index-Card Schedule, October 28, 1982," Office of the Governor, State of Oregon, Overnight: Pony Soldier Motel, La Grande, (28 October 1982), Atiyeh Collection, Pac. Univ. Archives.

'Lon, I don't know if I can get up.' I said, 'Governor, you made it this far, you're getting up. We're going clear to the bitter end.'" Atiyeh chuckled; Holbrook saw that he was kind of joking, and they got in the car and completed all the day's events. Holbrook knew that he himself was very tired. He appreciated that the governor must be even more exhausted, because he had to be on all the time giving speeches, talking to people, and looking like the energetic candidate. "I just had to worry about if he was okay, and the transportation."

The Atiyeh-Kulongoski battle was on national lists of hottest races.[1264] Oregon's daily newspapers were unanimous in endorsing Atiyeh.[1265] Part of this was because of the Atiyeh check list for every town the candidate visited—the local editorial board was always toward the top of that list. The endorsement numbers were a big change from the 1974 race—evenly split between Straub and Atiyeh—and the 1978 race in which Atiyeh was endorsed by ten of the eighteen dailies and Straub by eight. During the last days of the election, Kulongoski just could not get voters to put the plant closure idea out of their minds.

Atiyeh won a stunning victory. He beat Kulongoski 61% to 36%, at that time the sixth biggest percentage victory in Oregon history.[1266] In terms of actual votes, Atiyeh's 265,525 margin over Kulongoski was the largest victory in Oregon history up to that time, over 100,000 more votes than second place.[1267] Atiyeh won in every county of the state. His victory was characterized as "hefty," "easy," and "best in 20 years" in headlines.[1268]

1264 AP, "50 States Prepare to Vote," *Anniston (AL) Star*, 28 October 1982; AP, "These are the Hottest Races of the November Election," *Sioux Falls (SD) Argus-Leader*, 3 October 1982.

1265 AP, "Atiyeh Wins Backing of Daily Newspapers," *Salem (OR) Statesman-Journal*, 28 October 1982.

1266 Jim Moore, "Gubernatorial Results in Oregon," (Unpublished manuscript, 9 December 2018), Table, 6.

1267 Moore, "Gubernatorial Results in Oregon," 5.

1268 Foster Church, "Atiyeh Triumphs; Measures 3, 6 Falling Behind; Democrats Chalk Up Major Gains in U.S. House: Governor's Edge Best in 20 Years," *Oregonian*, 3 November 1982; Sue Hill, "Atiyeh's Hefty Victory Opens Way for Stronger Second Term," *Salem (OR) Statesman-Journal*, 3 November 1982;

Much to Kulongoski's chagrin, he became identified in news stories from then on as "Ted Kulongoski, who lost by the largest number of votes of any gubernatorial candidate in Oregon history."[1269] He thought this would be his place in Oregon history for the rest of his life, even after Kulongoski had served as Oregon's attorney general and was sitting on Oregon's supreme court. But in the 1998 election, John Kitzhaber defeated Bill Sizemore by over 383,000 votes, by far the largest numerical victory in Oregon history; in terms of percentage, it ranked number three. Kulongoski, who taught classes after his own two terms as governor were over in 2011, would tell his students, "You know, there is a political god."[1270]

The relationship between Ted Kulongoski and Vic Atiyeh took a long time to recover. Kulongoski always thought of Atiyeh as a gentleman, even during the political battle.[1271] Kulongoski said, "We both left the campaign somewhat bitter at each other. Not bitter in the sense that we'd never say anything to each other, but we just didn't have any desire to get together."[1272]

Years later, when Governor Kulongoski was working on workers' compensation reform, he saw former Governor Atiyeh, and they talked about the issue. Atiyeh encouraged Kulongoski, telling him, "It's a long time coming. Keep after it."[1273] Kulongoski reached out to Atiyeh on a couple of other issues as well, which began to bring them closer together.

They could eventually joke about their mutual 1982 election experience. The plant closure issue, the center of Atiyeh's campaign against Kulongoski, made them both smile. Kulongoski recounted, "Later in life we laughed at this. I said, 'Vic, you used

---

George Rede, "Atiyeh Wins Easily Over Kulongoski: Verne Duncan Tops Kendrick," *Salem (OR) Statesman-Journal*, 3 November 1982.

1269 Kulongoski, "Atiyeh interview," 8; Dave Miller et al., "Oregon Remembers Former Governor Vic Atiyeh," Live interview, recorded by Think Out Loud, KOPB radio, Salem, OR, 3 September 2014. MP3, 8:25.

1270 Kulongoski, "Atiyeh interview," 8.

1271 Miller, et al., "Oregon Remembers Former Governor Vic Atiyeh," 16:15.

1272 Kulongoski, "Atiyeh interview," 7–8.

1273 Kulongoski, "Atiyeh interview," 13.

to run around going like this [Kulongoski tapped his breast pocket],' 'I've got a list of companies!' I said, 'Vic! You never showed anybody that list!'"[1274]

With his record-breaking victory over Ted Kulongoski, Vic Atiyeh now had political capital—the backing of the electorate to push through policies upon which he had run his campaign. Atiyeh wanted to revisit tax reform, going back to ideas to straighten "out the property tax system by shifting the tax burden to the income tax."[1275] He also stressed the need to bolster Oregon's higher education system and the effort to "trumpet Oregon's open arms to newcomers, especially new industries."

Diversifying Oregon's economy would open the doors of Oregon to the world economy in ways not understood or anticipated at the time. Atiyeh would accelerate Oregon's stature in the high-tech industry, and he would lead a very public (but small) tax revolt that would revolutionize Oregon's economy.

And there was that group out in central Oregon wearing the reddish colors of the sun: the Rajneeshees. They would play an outsized role for the next three years.

1274 Kulongoski, "Atiyeh interview," 7.
1275 Hill, "Atiyeh's Hefty Victory Opens Way for Stronger Second Term."

6 Developing and taxing

Two days after Vic Atiyeh's second inauguration, state leaders gathered again in the House chambers at the state capitol to mourn the person against whom all subsequent governors would be measured.

Tom McCall was dead. The legislature suspended its regular activities—there was no decision on who would lead the Senate; the governor's call for tax reform was on hold; "the color and ceremony of the [legislature's] opening-day events were shadowed…by the death of…McCall."[1276]

Governor Atiyeh wrote his own speech for McCall's memorial. The lives of the two had been politically and personally intertwined since that candidate forum in 1958 when a young rug dealer first encountered the television news reporter and political analyst. In his remarks, Atiyeh spoke to McCall directly. "Tom, it is terribly hard not to feel sad, not to feel a little bit lonely—not to feel an agonizing sense of loss. But in the spirit of your wishes, I also feel grateful for your life, am very proud that you were a product of Oregon and that, because of you, we all share the enormous joy of what God has given us."[1277] The governor addressed the former governor to "answer a deep, nagging

---

[1276] Foster Church, "Atiyeh Urges Tax Reform at Inaugural," *Oregonian*, 11 January 1983.

concern you once expressed: '...Where is the glow of yesteryear? Wondering where the heroes went. ...Heroes are not giant statues.... They are people who say: This is my community, and it's my responsibility to make it better. ...I think we're gonna have to reassess what constitutes a hero.'" To his predecessor and those gathered to remember him, Atiyeh said, "Wonder no more, Tom—you have shown us what constitutes a genuine hero."[1278]

The years of the liberal Republicans in Oregon were already receding into the past. It was the time of the moderates, and, with the election of Ronald Reagan to the presidency, it was easy to see the future reclamation of the party by the true conservatives. Senators Hatfield and Packwood would continue to be liberal to moderate Republicans until they left office in the mid-1990s. In Salem, it was time for the moderate Republican Atiyeh to build on his predecessors' work and his own remarkable re-election victory. Atiyeh became governor in part to change the McCall-era perception of Oregon across the country and especially in the business community. As governor, he heard Tom McCall's "Visit but Don't Stay" mantra as far afield as Saudi Arabia.[1279] It was almost a personal affront to Atiyeh that this was what people associated with the state. As a replacement, he liked the idea that "Oregon Is Open for Business."[1280]

Atiyeh set about diversifying Oregon's economy during his first year as governor in 1979. He recalled that as he met with potential investors at the beginning of his time in office, he was competing against Washington, New Mexico, California, Arizona, and Colorado.[1281] By the time he left office in 1987, he saw that those states were now trying to compete with Oregon—Oregon

---

1277 Victor Atiyeh, "Handwritten Draft of McCall Eulogy" (speech, McCall Memorial Service, Salem, OR, 12 January 1983), Atiyeh Collection, Pac. Univ. Archives.

1278 Victor Atiyeh, "Statement by Governor Victor Atiyeh" (speech, McCall Memorial Service, Salem, OR, 12 January 1983), 1–2, Atiyeh Collection, Pac. Univ. Archives.

1279 Victor Atiyeh, interviewed by Jim Moore, "Atiyeh interview #1," Raleigh Hills, OR, 19 December 2013. Summary notes, 3.

1280 Atiyeh, "Atiyeh interview #1," 3.

1281 Atiyeh, "Atiyeh interview #1," 4.

had seized the high ground as a place for investment and job growth. Atiyeh knew that Oregon had good transportation systems, good power resources, and a good workforce. But its economy was too reliant on the timber industry. During his years in Salem, he saw that "when they cooled down the [national] economy, Oregon got pneumonia."[1282] The recessions from 1980 to 1983 indicated that cases of economic pneumonia could be fatal to small towns across the state. When Atiyeh prioritized economic growth and business recruitment from 1982 on, he was not working to replace timber; he was mainly seeking to diversify Oregon's economy, no matter what. As he recalled in 2013, if timber had remained the single industrial giant of Oregon's economy, "we'd look like West Virginia and its reliance on the coal industry."[1283]

To attract investment and to encourage Oregon businesses to grow, Atiyeh focused on two main areas in his first years in office. The first was Oregon's statewide land-use system. The second was making state government more responsive to investment through what he called "one-stop permit and licensing."[1284] It was these two sectors that would provide a foundation for much of the economic outreach that took place in the governor's second term, when he put his efforts into creating a more unified economic development system that added higher education and investment recruitment to the mix.

Since their inception in the late 1960s, Atiyeh had been involved in developing land-use planning laws and regulations, and he had actively campaigned against ballot measures in 1976 and 1978 that sought to either end or radically change the land-use laws on the books.[1285] As he became governor, he saw Oregon's land-use laws, especially 1973's SB 100, as a crucial

---

1282 Atiyeh, "Atiyeh interview #1," 4.
1283 Atiyeh, "Atiyeh interview #1," 4.
1284 Victor Atiyeh, interviewed by Clark Hansen, "Tape 39," Oral history, recorded by Oregon Historical Society, Portland, OR, 23 June 1993. Transcript, 254, Atiyeh Collection, Pac. Univ. Archives.
1285 *Oregon Blue Book, 1979–1980*, (Salem, OR: Oregon Secretary of State, 1979), 311.

part of the future of the state. But he also saw a system that he felt had not lived up to its potential. There were still too many local variations in interpretations of land-use law, and there did not seem to be a sense of urgency to fulfill some of the basic requirements of the law among counties around the state. Atiyeh's business sense told him that investment was more likely when there was certainty about the conditions within which capital could be put to work. Some of those conditions were out of the state's hands—inflation and interest rates, for example. Others were clearly under the state's control. In Oregon, with its statewide land-use laws, the ability of businesses to have a clear view about the future of the land upon which they might build was one of those controllable areas.

Oregon's unique land-use system was a balance among three major parts.[1286] The first was the creation of the Land Conservation and Development Commission (LCDC)—a seven-member commission appointed by the governor—and the Department of Land Conservation and Development, whose director was selected by LCDC. The second was that local governments—cities and counties—were required to create what were called comprehensive plans to address land-use issues in their jurisdictions. The state would then "acknowledge" the plans, and future growth would be guided by them. The third was the formulation of goals that local governments needed to address in the creation of their plans. There ended up being nineteen of them, but some goals were specific to geographic areas (like the coast), and not required to be part of comprehensive plans in other parts of the state.

From the start, Atiyeh made it plain that he wanted to head off another attempt at the ballot box to change Oregon's land-use laws. The governor-elect's emphasis was on making "the LCDC...more sensitive to local needs and citizen input into the

---

1286 See Sy Adler, *Oregon Plans: The Making of an Unquiet Land-Use Revolution*, (Corvallis, OR: Oregon State University Press, 2012).

land use process."[1287] Once the land-use system was working in a way that Atiyeh thought functioned well, after 1983, he would use it as recruiting tool. He recalled telling companies, "And besides, you can come to Oregon[.] …[I]f you pick a piece of property that you can build a plant on…you know what [is] going to happen around you. …You can go to California; you don't know what's going to happen to your next-door neighbor. You don't know what's going to happen in back of you. In Oregon, you know."[1288] Atiyeh recalled success with this pitch: "People liked that."[1289]

The major change Atiyeh had implemented in 1979 was the creation of the Land Use Board of Appeals (LUBA) to take land-use disputes "out of the contentious arena of LCDC into an area in which…the citizens thought they had some opportunity to have a review. …It's been sort of a pressure valve."[1290] Atiyeh thought of it as a system patterned after the tax courts, a place taxpayers could go to resolve conflicts with the Department of Revenue instead having to appeal a ruling "to the body that was assessing you."[1291] Atiyeh advisor and LCDC member Jack Faust recalled that LUBA worked very well to prevent people from being tied up for years in appeals over how to develop land.[1292] It would, however, be a number of years before LUBA reached its potential. In its first thirteen months, LUBA heard 212 cases; two years later, LUBA was averaging 100 cases a year.[1293] The Oregon

---

1287 "Transition Binder," Press release, Transition Office, November 22, 1978.
1288 Victor Atiyeh, interviewed by Clark Hansen, "Tape 33, side 1," Oral history, recorded by Oregon Historical Society, Portland, OR, 7 June 1993. Transcript, 77, Atiyeh Collection, Pac. Univ. Archives.
1289 Atiyeh, "Tape 33, side 1," 78; see also, Victor Atiyeh, interviewed by Clark Hansen, "Tape 48," Oral history, recorded by Oregon Historical Society, Portland, OR, 23 July 1993. Transcript, 510, Atiyeh Collection, Pac. Univ. Archives.
1290 Victor Atiyeh, interviewed by Clark Hansen, "Tape 63," Oral history, recorded by Oregon Historical Society, Portland, OR, 11 June 1998. Transcript, 23, Atiyeh Collection, Pac. Univ. Archives.
1291 Atiyeh, "Tape 30," 8.
1292 Jack Faust, interviewed by Jim Moore, "Atiyeh interview," Portland, OR, 15 April 2015. Summary notes, 2.
1293 *Oregon Blue Book, 1983–1984*, (Salem, OR: Oregon Secretary of State, 1983), 95.

courts kept refining what LUBA and LCDC could do. Getting the system going was an exercise in legal interpretations, of local governments chafing at the requirements to finish up their comprehensive plans, and then LUBA and LCDC figuring out their roles in enforcement of those plans.

The land-use system had good intentions, but it was complex for each county and city to figure out its plan. Atiyeh recalled that when a business wanted to develop a parcel of land during the time before the comprehensive plans were completed, "we almost had a moratorium on anything happening until the plan is acknowledged."[1294] In May 1982, just as his re-election campaign got started, Atiyeh appointed an eleven-member task force "to see how the state's land-use planning laws affect economic development."[1295] An *Oregonian* editorial lauded the effort, arguing, "Roadblocks to economic development tend to be in time and uncertainty rather than in local and state goals."[1296] There was a strong sense that there were ways to make the system more streamlined, but "most important, …the task force should encourage recalcitrant local officials to quit blaming the state for their own foot-dragging and get on with the planning…[that] economic development needs."[1297] After the first statewide land use law in 1969, counties were remarkably slow in completing their plans—only eleven out of thirty-six by March 1972.[1298] The main land-use law from 1973, SB100, set a 1978 deadline for cities and counties to complete plans. In 1981 it was reported that only 34% of local governments had comprehensive plans in place.[1299] By 1982, "five years after the first plan completion deadline, 22 cities and counties still [had] not submitted plans."[1300] Summarizing a March 1982 cabinet meeting for the

---

1294 Atiyeh, "Tape 37, side 1," 182.
1295 *Oregonian*, "Atiyeh's Land Use Task Force a Timely Idea," Editorial, 9 June 1982.
1296 *Oregonian*, "Atiyeh's Land Use Task Force a Timely Idea."
1297 *Oregonian*, "Atiyeh's Land Use Task Force a Timely Idea."
1298 Adler, *Oregon Plans*, 36.
1299 Adler, *Oregon Plans*, 221.
1300 John Hayes, "Friends, Foes Sense Ever-Shortening Fuse on Land-Use Time Bomb," Analysis, *Oregonian*, 20 June 1982, E3.

governor, Gerry Thompson wrote that "Columbia County is still indicating their lack of willingness to participate in the land use planning process. Jim Ross [LCDC director] will be meeting with the county commissioners personally."[1301]

By mid-July of Atiyeh's re-election year, another element of complexity had been added to the hearings. Ballot measure 6, to repeal the statewide land-use laws, qualified for the November 1982 ballot. There was a sense that whatever the final report of the task force was, it would be the alternative that voters would use to help decide their stances on the measure.[1302] Critics argued that the problem was LCDC and LUBA. Those in favor of land-use laws agreed that the entire process of submitting plans and appealing decisions needed to be simplified, possibly by creating "a new land-use court, together with laws allowing only one appeal."[1303]

The recommendations were clear: to reduce the time in the process, "one state hearing and one appeal by right."[1304] The task force also recommended that LUBA end in 1983 (when its initial mandate would end) and that a Land Use Court be formed with more power to "grant such legal and equitable relief as it deems necessary."[1305] The task force recommended setting a deadline of January 1, 1984, for completion of comprehensive plans and the acknowledgment from LCDC that the plans were valid.[1306] Given the economic disaster that was Oregon in 1982, there was a strong recommendation that economic development be given as much emphasis as conservation and preservation.[1307]

1301 Gerry Thompson, "Daily Reports to the Governor," Office of the Governor, State of Oregon, (April 1982), Memo to Governor Atiyeh, "Cabinet Meeting, Friday, March 26, 1982," 1, Atiyeh Collection, Pac. Univ. Archives.

1302 John Hayes, "Hansell's Report Expected to Influence the Reshaping of Land-Use Policies," Analysis, *Oregonian*, 19 September 1982.

1303 John Hayes, "Land-Use Planning Criticized, Praised," *Oregonian*, 11 August 1982.

1304 "Governor's Task Force on Land Use in Oregon," Report to Governor Vic Atiyeh, September 1982, 11, Atiyeh Collection, Pac. Univ. Archives.

1305 "Governor's Task Force on Land Use in Oregon," 11.

1306 "Governor's Task Force on Land Use in Oregon," 12.

1307 "Governor's Task Force on Land Use in Oregon," 16.

In the plans he laid out for changing the land-use laws in December 1982,[1308] Atiyeh adopted most of the task force's recommendations, especially ways to speed up the process. The governor highlighted land-use reform in his second inaugural address, emphasizing that Oregon voters had given the legislature another chance when they voted down Measure 6 and "did not overwhelm us with rage and rejection."[1309] LUBA survived the 1983 legislative session, with more clarity about the terms of its members (four years) and a requirement that those who served be members of the Oregon State Bar.[1310]

LUBA continues to this day with those 1983 revisions to its original charter.[1311] Outgoing LCDC director Ross wrote in 1986 that he was "proud that after ten years we have finally approved the plans of all 277 cities and counties."[1312]

Notice began to be taken by the mid-1980s around the country that Oregon's land-use system was contributing to the turnaround of the state's economy.[1313] A California magazine article marveled that "the state with the green dream, with the most restrictive land-use laws in the nation" had not, according to Oregon Director of the Department of Economic Development John Anderson, lost "one competition [for high tech investment] to anyone in the nation in the last six months. Since last May [1984],

---

1308 Foster Church, "GOP Asked to Study Tax Plan: Atiyeh Outlines Forestry, Land-Use Changes," *Oregonian*, 12 December 1982; "Atiyeh Daily Index-Card Schedule, December 13, 1982," Office of the Governor, State of Oregon, (13 December 1982), Meet: re: land use legislation, Atiyeh Collection, Pac. Univ. Archives.

1309 Victor Atiyeh, "Inaugural Address" (speech, Sixty-Second Legislative Assembly, House Chambers, Salem, OR, 10 January 1983), 2, Atiyeh Collection, Pac. Univ. Archives.

1310 *Oregon Blue Book, 1985–1986*, (Salem, OR: Oregon Secretary of State, 1985), 107.

1311 *Oregon Blue Book: Almanac and Fact Book, 2017–2018*, (Salem, OR: Oregon Secretary of State, 2017), 68.

1312 James F. Ross, "Resignation letter," Department of Land Conservation and Development, State of Oregon, Letter to Neil Goldschmidt, Governor-Elect (10 December 1986), Atiyeh Collection, Pac. Univ. Archives.

1313 UPI, "Oregon Credits Land-Use Plan with Economic Growth," *Dallas (TX) Times Herald*, 14 April 1985, Atiyeh Collection, Pac. Univ. Archives.

we've had eleven major announcements of new plants by companies brand new to the state, or of very substantial expansions by companies already located here."[1314] Atiyeh was highlighting Oregon's land-use laws specifically to lure investment to the state. At November 1985 meetings with the Japan Optics Laboratory and Toshiba in Japan, he stressed, "there will be no changes in the rules of doing business in Oregon with respect to land use planning [or] reimposition of [the] unitary [tax]."[1315] The promise of 1973's SB 100 was fulfilled because Atiyeh made it happen.

Land use policies gave Atiyeh an advantage not only in attracting businesses to the state but also in guiding local governments to make decisions that were better for Oregonians' quality of life and their economic well-being. Washington County had many "plant sites" amid what a *Hillsboro Argus* editorial called "the campus-like environment" of the high-tech corridor along the Sunset Highway.[1316] Metro, the regional government that Atiyeh had opposed from its inception (and that voters had supported overwhelmingly) decided to locate a garbage collection facility in the heart of the area.[1317] "Atiyeh was upset—as he had a right to be—when he learned of the vote" because there seemed to be no consideration about what a garbage center would do to the recruitment efforts to bring more high-tech companies to the area. And, the editorial noted, "his words were backed by letters from high-tech firms."[1318] The governor appointed a task force to figure out how to balance the need for a solid waste transfer

---

1314 Bob Simmons, "Environmental Protections Help Attract Business to Oregon: Glamour Spot for High-Tech Development," *California Journal*, January 1985, 11, Atiyeh Collection, Pac. Univ. Archives.

1315 "Governor's Fall Mission to Japan—Meeting Sheet," Office of the Governor, State of Oregon, (9–19 November 1985), Japan Electron Optics Laboratories; Toshiba Corporation, Atiyeh Collection, Pac. Univ. Archives.

1316 *Argus* (Hillsboro, OR), "Shows True Colors," Editorial, 15 April 1986, Atiyeh Collection, Pac. Univ. Archives.

1317 Harry Bodine, "Sunset Highway Site Wins Vote for Transfer Station," *Oregonian*, 17 January 1986.

1318 *Argus*, "Shows True Colors."

station and economic growth potential in the area.[1319] Washington county's land-use plan, sanctioned by the state, was crucial to preventing the transfer station from being in that spot. Today there are a high school, several light industrial businesses, and two iconic Oregon food processing companies (Beaverton Foods and Resers) in the area where the waste would have piled up.

Congressman Earl Blumenauer, who served on the crucial legislative committees in the Oregon House in the 1970s when the land-use system was created, and who had been an advocate for planning and preparation for future growth, came to think of Atiyeh's work to goad local governments into finishing their comprehensive plans as "one of the untold stories" of the Oregon system, "where Vic Atiyeh rode to the rescue." Blumenauer said, "I just profoundly respected Vic as governor stepping out for something that wasn't his baby and that he had some skepticism [of]. But he made it possible for [the statewide land-use system] to survive."[1320] A liberal Democrat, Blumenauer found Atiyeh's actions on land-use to be evidence that "Governor Atiyeh was different than minority leader Atiyeh."[1321]

Atiyeh also had his eyes on one-stop permitting for a long time. In his first run for governor in 1974, he had called for "one-stop sources of information about land use planning" as part of his plan to make SB 100 responsive to the needs of farmers and city planners as well as for the people of Oregon at large.[1322] When Atiyeh entered the governor's office in 1979, he set to work to implement the plan. By 1981 there was a one-stop permit center within the Executive Department "to assist individuals in dealing with the entire array of state permits and licenses that are required to operate a business."[1323] There had been many complaints that it took state government too long to respond to

---

1319 Harry Bodine, "Atiyeh Enters Waste Tranfer Site Fray," Analysis, *Oregonian*, 20 February 1986.
1320 Earl Blumenauer, interviewed by Jim Moore, "Atiyeh interview," Portland, OR, 8 June 2015. Summry notes, 9.
1321 Blumenauer, "Atiyeh interview." 7–8.
1322 Frank Wetzel, "Straub and Atiyeh Talk of Land Use," *Salem Oregon Statesman*, 21 August 1974.

economic problems as they arose during the downturn. There were too many agencies that had to approve too many actions—it was just too complex.

In Atiyeh's second term, though, there came to be a truly streamlined system. The 1983 legislature created new permitting rules for developers, but now through the Department of Economic Development.[1324] When the governor found prospects to invest in Oregon, he was able to refer them to the Economic Development Action Council to help figure out everything that needed to happen. Gerry Thompson remembered Atiyeh's attitude was, "If they know I, the governor, am paying attention, and I am interested, that gets us ten steps ahead of" all the other states seeking economic investment.[1325] Atiyeh recalled the usefulness of the Action Council went beyond just one-stop permitting: "when we had prospects we would sit with the prospect" and work to get them to Oregon. He saw this as part of "laying the groundwork for the diversification which I wanted to accomplish as governor."[1326] All natural resource agencies—LCDC, Energy, Forestry—were asked to also streamline the permit process to encourage economic development.[1327]

In a 1986 summary of state economic development written for Gerry Thompson, the Economic Development Action Council was described as demonstrating "to businesses that [they] no longer must take a 'back seat' to other priorities of the state. When necessary, Governor Atiyeh has made himself available to business representatives, at their convenience, to personally discuss their concerns."[1328] This, combined with the ability of the Action Council to "be convened on short notice to explain

---

1323 Laila Cully, "An Analysis of Recent Economic Accomplishments," Research Division Department of Revenue, State of Oregon, Memo to John N. Groupe, (2 November 1981), 11, Atiyeh Collection, Pac. Univ. Archives.

1324 *Statesman-Journal* (Salem), "A Quick Look at What the Legislature Did," 17 July 1983.

1325 Gerry Thompson, interviewed by by Jim Moore, "Atiyeh interview #2," Salem, OR, 12 February 2015. Summary notes, 6.

1326 Atiyeh, "Tape 39," 254.

1327 Thompson, "Atiyeh interview #2," 15.

specific regulations, help overcome particular obstacles, and, in general, to educate businesses on doing business in Oregon," turned out to be the key to encouraging investment in the state, but at the same time protecting what was special about Oregon by pointing out the advantages to land-use laws, environmental laws, and quality of life.[1329] The Action Council was the key player for investors looking at Oregon. Thompson recalled, "It gave anybody interested in Oregon, no matter how small or how big, instant and authoritative access to state government."[1330]

Economic Development

Atiyeh had ideas for improving economic development in Oregon from the day he became governor. Like one-stop permitting, some of his business ideas were easy to implement but took a while to get going. Others were a matter of reconfiguring current programs like the Department of Economic Development. And still other reforms came as Atiyeh pushed to move responsibility for state tourism from the Highway Department to the Department of Economic Development. He felt strongly that tourism should be one of the major economic sectors in the state, not just an adjunct to the state highway system's planning goals. And Atiyeh would work hard to bring Oregon's public higher education institutions more clearly into the equation for economic development.

Atiyeh convened a meeting in 1982 at which all state agencies that could have impact on economic development were encouraged to help the economy grow. The governor made it clear that he expected each agency to ease the way for business investment. Change was happening in Oregon's economy, but it was slow and often hard to see. During the depths of the 1982

1328 Economic Development Action Council, "Summary of Economic Development During Atiyeh Administration," Office of the Governor, State of Oregon, Summary for Gerry Thompson, (Summer 1986), 14, Atiyeh Collection, Pac. Univ. Archives.
1329 Economic Development Action Council, "Summary of Economic Development," 14.
1330 Thompson, "Atiyeh interview #2," 8.

recession, Gerry Thompson was on a drive with her husband when he stopped the car and said, "Look at that."[1331] She really did not notice anything until he pointed to an actual construction site in front of them. That was an amazing sight in those months. Atiyeh's goal was to marshal state resources so that those tiny shoots of economic growth would begin to grow across the state. When voters approved a state lottery in 1984, an effort Atiyeh opposed, he worked diligently with state senator Mike Thorne to ensure that all lottery profits went to foster economic recovery and expansion.

During Atiyeh's first term, the Economic Development Commission had not functioned well. Atiyeh met with Phil Bladine of the Commission in January 1981 to talk about "Economic Development Commission problems."[1332] Thompson, who began working for the governor in September 1981, saw "a bunch of egos" all vying for privileges and advantages against each other. Atiyeh worked to clean that up with new appointments to the commission, the group with the power to hire and fire the Director of the Department of Economic Development.[1333] However, even though the commission had the power to hire and fire on paper, this was one of several commissions where Atiyeh made it known that the governor was totally in control.

Atiyeh had been part of the legislature when the Department of Economic Development was created in 1973. He had been unhappy with the way that the department had been run ever since. The goals of the department were lofty: "balanced economic growth and development for the state" through maintaining and improving "existing industries"; diversification through "high technology, nonpolluting industries"; expansion of international trade; "to expand the economy while preserving the state's environmental quality"; and assisting "lagging areas" to

---

1331 Thompson, "Atiyeh interview #2," 10.
1332 "Atiyeh Daily Index-Card Schedule, January 23, 1981," Office of the Governor, State of Oregon, (23 January 1981), Phil Bladine re: Economic Development Commission problems, Atiyeh Collection, Pac. Univ. Archives.
1333 Thompson, "Atiyeh interview #2," 12.

become equal with the rest of the state. An overall target was to "reduce unemployment to levels below the national average and to increase the per capita income of the state to levels equal to the national average."[1334] The reality was somewhat different. The department provided technical assistance to communities, but one recipient "liken[ed] the department's program to a 'traveling road show' featuring speakers who tell community leaders what they can or can't do in economic development in their areas." The department's assistance was characterized as "no expertise" and "no follow-up."[1335] Atiyeh wanted to change this perceived reality.

The economic development problems in Oregon in 1979 were very different from what Atiyeh would encounter for the next seven years of his time in office. The economy was growing, some of it fueled by inflation, and the issues centered on guiding this growth. Between 1970 and 1978, Oregon's population increased by 18%.[1336] Josephine County in southern Oregon was the fastest growing county in the state, with central Oregon's Deschutes County rivaling it. Portland's Multnomah County had decreased in population, but simply because people were flocking to the suburbs in Clackamas and Washington counties. People were moving to Oregon for the quality of life, not for "industrial and business expansion," according to the Department of Economic Development's director, John Groupe.[1337] Many of those immigrants found that the Oregon land-use laws were not what they expected when they envisioned a future for themselves. This group saw the more stringent state laws as an attack to be parried—legally, economically, and politically.

In the early years of his governorship, Atiyeh was personally contacting large businesses about Oregon investments, and he welcomed trade missions to Oregon.[1338] There was funding given to plans to raise "large freshwater Malaysian shrimp in warm

---

1334 *Oregon Blue Book, 1979*, 38.
1335 Robert Olmos, "Communities Receive Help from Port: Free Advice," *Oregonian*, 15 January 1979.
1336 Linda Williams, "Rapid Growth Adding Tension to Oregon Life," *Oregonian*, 28 October 1979.
1337 Williams, "Rapid Growth Adding Tension to Oregon Life."

geothermal waters in Klamath County," an inventory of "gravel and allied rock resources in the Willamette valley" in light of "comprehensive land-use plans... being developed that could put future constraints on mining of this mineral resource," and ongoing "determination of costs to business of government regulation in Oregon."[1339] In a sign of how Atiyeh's cabinet system was encouraging agencies to work better together, "Agriculture and Economic Development...resolved difficulties relating to overlapping authority in international trade matters."[1340] In November 1979 an 18-page advertisement "dubbed 'The Oregon Story'" appeared in *Forbes* magazine. No taxpayer dollars were used—"the state [got] one page free for every two pages of paid ads" from participating Oregon companies—but the main message was Governor Atiyeh's mantra, "Oregon: Open for Business."[1341]

Atiyeh's main push for development in early 1981 was to improve "the image of Oregon in the national business community and...[to speed] the process by which permits are granted for business and industrial projects."[1342] The governor wanted to "wash away [Oregon's] 'miserable image' in industry.... 'We need to do many responsible and dramatic things to help persuade industry both in-state and out-of-state that our purpose is serious.'"[1343] The focus, however, was the industrial bond program—the primary method by which the Economic Development Department attracted business.

1338 Jim Russell, "The Atiyeh Administration After One Year," Office of the Governor, State of Oregon, Memo to Governor Atiyeh, Denny Miles, Larry Sturholm, (21 December 1979), 2, Memoranda and Reports, "Accomplishments," 1979, Atiyeh Collection, Pac. Univ. Archives.
1339 Russell, "Atiyeh Administration After One Year," 2–3.
1340 Russell, "Atiyeh Administration After One Year," 1.
1341 Don Bundy, "Ads Tout Oregon in New Approach," Column, *Oregonian*, 11 December 1979.
1342 Foster Church, "Atiyeh Program Warms Up to Business: Development Pushed," *Oregonian*, 19 January 1981.
1343 Leslie L. Zaitz, "Atiyeh Seeks State Facelift: 'Miserable' Image," *Oregonian*, 19 January 1982.

The idea for industrial development revenue bonds had started in 1975. About forty other states had similar programs.[1344] In what was called "smokestack chasing," the idea was the bonds would "be a vehicle for pulling rural and small-town Oregon out of its overdependence on a couple of basic industries."[1345] The state would sell the bonds, the money would go to the project, secured "by the revenues and assets of the company borrowing the development money."[1346] No taxpayer money was involved, and trustees of the bonds were usually banks. By 1980, nobody had ever measured the business impact of the bonds. A complaint was lodged with a member of the Economic Development Commission that "some electronics plants, whose expansion and development had been financed through Department of Economic Development Revenue bonds, were not providing the jobs promised."[1347] The Commission asked for an investigation.

In 1980 Atiyeh created a Bonded Debt Advisory Council, the focus of which was supposed to be other bonding programs, for instance those that funded "the popular veterans' home loan programs."[1348] When the Council considered the industrial bonds, its first unofficial opinion was that the state should get out of that particular bond business. Voting for the abolition of the program: Atiyeh's executive assistant, Lee Johnson. Opposing the end of the program: Oregon's treasurer, Clay Myers, still a statewide elected officer after his defeat by Atiyeh in the 1974 Republican gubernatorial primary.[1349] By the end of February 1981, the Bonded Debt Advisory Council criticized the bond program, but did not quite call for its demise. Blaming unclear objectives for the program dating to its creation by the legislature in 1975, the

---

1344 Tom Brennan, "Pros, Cons of Industrial Revenue Bond Plan Examined," *Oregonian*, 5 April 1981.
1345 Brennan, "Pros, Cons of Industrial Revenue Bond."
1346 *Statesman-Journal* (Salem), "Industrial Development Chief Defends Program," 11 December 1980.
1347 Bob Olmos, "Do Revenue Bonds Produce State Jobs? Firms Get Money, No Followup," *Oregonian*, 27 February 1980.
1348 George Rede, "Advisory Panel Wants Oregon Out of Bonding Program," *Salem (OR) Statesman-Journal*, 24 January 1981.
1349 Rede, "Advisory Panel Wants."

suggestion was that "the 1981 Legislature consider a list of recommendations by the Congressional Budget Office to curb bond financing abuse nationally."[1350] There was a shift from using bonds to attract business to touting Oregon's overall openness to investment.

By the end of 1981, the Economic Development Commission got around to Atiyeh's call to change the image of the state. Commissioner Jason Boe, former president of the Oregon senate, was in full agreement, saying, "What started out as a joke by [Tom McCall] has really taken root throughout the country. (People) are completely swayed by that damnable joke."[1351] The Commission would "work with the 700-member Portland Advertising Federation in raising funds for a study aimed at attracting new business and industry to the state."[1352] Money, however, was in short supply as the recession deepened. A $100,000 request to get the program going yielded a $12,000 allocation from the Legislature's Emergency Board. As one observer noted, "That the board finally approved giving the department even $12,000 at a time when other agencies are girding for agonizing cuts was in itself a symbolic act" of support for the concept.[1353] There was a great deal of skepticism from at least one member of the legislature. Representative Vera Katz (D-Portland) said, "Stealing jobs from other states doesn't make sense."[1354] It would be this attitude that would dog Atiyeh when he hit the road to drum up investments to help Oregon's economy from 1983 on.

By the end of 1981, the governor made a pivot in his economic focus. Even though the economy was worsening—and unknown

---

1350 George Rede, "Task Force Criticizes Bond Program," *Salem (OR) Statesman-Journal*, 26 February 1981.
1351 Bob Olmos, "State Seeks Business Lure," *Oregonian*, 9 December 1981. Parentheses in original.
1352 Olmos, "State Seeks Business Lure."
1353 Foster Church, "Development Debate Due," Column, *Oregonian*, 13 December 1981.
1354 Sue Hill, "E Board Draws Line on Funding Requests," *Salem (OR) Statesman-Journal*, 4 December 1981.

to him at the time, there would be three special legislative sessions in 1982 to balance the ever-decreasing budget—he changed his role from primarily budget triage to economic recruitment. The shift in Atiyeh's mindset took place relatively quickly. The change in state policy would take longer, especially given the tough economic times. Gerry Thompson saw a governor who "was desperate to save our state and make sure people weren't standing in food lines."[1355] Partly through the Oregon Food Bank, there were no food lines. But Thompson remembered, "I think Vic was hurting. That's the best way I can say it, that he was actually hurting."[1356]

"Frankly, the bad economy drove us to do good things," Thompson said.[1357] The governor's eventual decision was to become Oregon's salesperson-in-chief. According to Thompson, Atiyeh determined that he had to create confidence for businesses to either expand in Oregon or to start up in Oregon. He knew he could do this by being the frontman for the state's economy. After all, he concluded, if the governor himself was available on a person-to-person basis for potential investors, that sent a message that Oregon was serious about changing its economy.[1358] It was this idea that became the driving force behind Atiyeh's economic development efforts in his second term.

Atiyeh's idea for a strong marketing campaign to let the world know that Oregon was open for business came together in October 1982. The plan was for a "multi-pronged" approach to promote "'continuity' and cooperation among state and local agencies, establish a new, professional advertising campaign to lure out-of-state employers and increase international trade development efforts."[1359] In addition, Atiyeh announced plans to move Oregon's "tourism promotion effort from the Department of

---

1355 Gerry Thompson, interviewed by Jim Moore, "Atiyeh Interview #4," Salem, OR, 7 August 2017. Summary notes, 4.
1356 Thompson, "Atiyeh Interview #4," 4.
1357 Thompson, "Atiyeh interview #2," 5.
1358 Thompson, "Atiyeh interview #2," 16.
1359 Steve Jenning, "Oregon to Undertake Advertising Campaign: Atiyeh Hopes to Stretch Dollars for Development," *Oregonian*, 2 October 1982.

Transportation to the Department of Economic Development."[1360] Gerry Thompson made the case that moving tourism to Economic Development would allow the state to "get a lot more mileage with our dollar [...by integrating] tourist promotion with general economic development."[1361] The deep recession was clearly encouraging policy makers to look for more effective and efficient ways to jump-start parts of Oregon's economy. Just as Atiyeh had made moves to have a more hands-on role with the Department of Economic Development, Thompson said that tourism promotion would benefit from the same change. "We know we want it closer to the governor," but with a role for some version of an advisory council.[1362] Thompson, though, understood tourism was just a part of what needed to be a much larger economic development effort.[1363]

There were short trips by the governor to try to attract more investment in Oregon. Just a month after his November 1982 re-election, Atiyeh spent the day in Palo Alto, California, talking with executives at Hewlett-Packard about their plans for their Oregon operations.[1364] He would meet with Hewlett-Packard officials at the company's Corvallis location and again in Palo Alto in January 1983 as well.[1365] But these initial efforts were nothing compared to the systematic process that would develop within the next twelve months. Outlines of monthly activities in 1983 for the Department of Economic Development showed

---

[1360] Don Jepsen, "Posturing, Personalities Complicate Promotion Issue," Analysis, *Oregonian*, 1 October 1982.

[1361] Jepsen, "Posturing, Personalities Complicate Promotion Issue."

[1362] Jepsen, "Posturing, Personalities Complicate Promotion Issue."

[1363] Gerry Thompson, interviewed by Jim Moore, "Atiyeh interview #1," Salem, OR, 16 September 2014. Summary notes, 7.

[1364] "Atiyeh Daily Index-Card Schedule, December 7, 1982," Office of the Governor, State of Oregon, (7 December 1982), Meet: Wiche, Hewlett Packard, Palo Alto, Atiyeh Collection, Pac. Univ. Archives.

[1365] "Atiyeh Daily Index-Card Schedule, January 7, 1983," Office of the Governor, State of Oregon, (7 January 1983), Hewlett-Packard Meetings, Palo Alto, Atiyeh Collection, Pac. Univ. Archives; "Atiyeh Daily Index-Card Schedule, January 6, 1983," Office of the Governor, State of Oregon, (6 January 1983), Hewlett-Packard Office, Corvallis, Atiyeh Collection, Pac. Univ. Archives.

conferences, small-business-loan initiatives, and promotions with major companies like Nike.[1366] International outreach was also very active. Doug Carter, who replaced Groupe at the Department of Economic Development, and Gerry Thompson went to Taiwan to represent Oregon at the USA–Republic of China Conference. A trade mission to Japan and Hong Kong was just coming to an end; a joint Economic Development and Department of Agriculture mission to Canada would take place the second week in May; and World Trade Week would be celebrated with "a major promotional activity in Coos Bay," home of a large timber-centric port.[1367]

Atiyeh was not focused just on the out of state and international trade missions. He was looking at forest products and agriculture, traveling the state to encourage people. He felt it was his job to reassure Oregonians that the economy would grow again, and prosperity would return. Thompson remembered him saying to her, "Why does everybody keep talking negative? Everything in the media is about how bad it is. ...It's a self-fulfilling prophecy, Gerry. You've got to get people more positive."[1368] Thompson remembered quietly rolling her eyes at the Pollyanna-like governor. But Atiyeh was sincere about helping people to think in a different way about the economy.

Oregon's reputation had changed from "Visit but Don't Stay." The state was increasingly seen as a fast-growing high-tech center. Articles in the *Washington Post* and the *New York Times* extolled the change from timber country to entering the global high-tech market.[1369] But former timber centers had nothing to

---

[1366] "Things Currently Happening in Economic Development," State of Oregon, (21 April 1983), Atiyeh Collection, Pac. Univ. Archives.

[1367] "Atiyeh Daily Index-Card Schedule, June 15, 1983," Office of the Governor, State of Oregon, (15 June 1983), Bruce Laird, Chm., Port of Coos Bay Comsn.; Frank Martin, Gen. Mgr. of Port; Doug Mauharin, Weyerhaeuser; Doc Stevenson, County Comsnr.; John Mohr, Port of Coos Bay; Jim Whetty, Ore. Public Ports Assn.; Gerry; Doug Carter & Fred Miller, re: update on Coos Bay projects (conf. room), Atiyeh Collection, Pac. Univ. Archives.

[1368] Thompson, "Atiyeh interview #2," 9.

[1369] Nicholas D. Kristof, "Every Region Gets Into the Technology Act," The Market, *New York Times*, 24 March 1985, Atiyeh Collection, Pac. Univ. Archives;

replace the high-paying jobs from the mills. Oregon's economy was referred to as "the two-state economy" because of the differences between high-tech centric Washington County's growth and population centers in other parts of the state "such as Eugene and Medford, where the book never quite closed on the recession."[1370] Where the economic growth was happening, more economic activity was spawned. Japanese automaker Toyota, familiar with Portland because it was a major port of entry for its cars to U.S. markets, persuaded a California truck conversion firm to open an operation in Portland.[1371] The president of the firm reported "that there had never been one negative note from [the Portland Chamber of Commerce and the Oregon Economic Development Department] in Oregon. It's a clear signal that the bureaucratic process can—and does—work."[1372] Within six months, the Portland outpost was leading the company in output and profit.

Atiyeh kept working as the state's salesman. He would fly to the Bay Area to talk with the leaders of high-tech companies, both American and Japanese.[1373] The Department of Economic Development put together data and marketing materials touting the "Oregon advantage."[1374] From business taxes (lower than Washington and California because of no sales tax) to wage rates and worker productivity to energy costs and the availability of

---

Washington Post, "A New Trail Takes Oregon to High Tech," 24 February 1985, Atiyeh Collection, Pac. Univ. Archives.

1370 Michael A. Anderson, "Diversification Top State Priority," *Portland (OR) Daily Journal of Commerce*, 7 January 1985, Atiyeh Collection, Pac. Univ. Archives.

1371 Brian Cour, "NW Firm Sees No Limit in Conversions," *Oregonian*, 20 March 1986, Atiyeh Collection, Pac. Univ. Archives.

1372 Cour, "NW Firm Sees No Limit in Conversions."

1373 "Atiyeh Daily Index-Card Schedule, March 14, 1985," Office of the Governor, State of Oregon, (14 March 1985), Meet: Charles Sporck, pres. & CEO; National Semiconductor, Atiyeh Collection, Pac. Univ. Archives.

1374 "Oregon Advantage: Industry Cost Comparison of the Pacific Coast States," Economic Development Department, State of Oregon, (September 1986), Atiyeh Collection, Pac. Univ. Archives; marketing materials derived from "Industry Cost Comparison of the Pacific Coast States," Business Development Division Industrial Property Section, Economic Development Department, State of Oregon, (July 1986), Atiyeh Collection, Pac. Univ. Archives.

industrial property, Oregon was clearly open for business investment.¹³⁷⁵ The business of grants and loans to encourage community development continued apace, too. In 1986 alone, forty-nine cities and counties received grants for rental housing rehabilitation, nineteen cities, counties and port districts received grants and loan for special public works projects, creating somewhere around 29,000 jobs, all of this using more than $7 million from the new lottery to add to state funding for projects.¹³⁷⁶

The film industry had really taken off, with movie makers spending $41 million in the state between 1968 and 1979.¹³⁷⁷ Oregon was one of first states in the late 1960s with an outreach program to filmmakers. Big movies shot in Oregon during this time included *Paint Your Wagon*, *Sometimes a Great Notion*, *One Flew Over the Cuckoo's Nest*, *The Great Northfield Minnesota Raid*, *Animal House*, and *Rooster Cogburn*. The nighttime soap opera *Knots Landing* would be filmed at Salishan on the Oregon coast in the 1980s, with Atiyeh himself visiting the set by helicopter.¹³⁷⁸ Several other feature-length films used Oregon locations, including *The Goonies*, *Short Circuit*, and *Benji the Hunted*. The executive director of the Newport Chamber of Commerce worked hard to build on the success of *Knots Landing*. By 1986 "ten film or television projects [had] been made [nearby], and eight more [were] pending."¹³⁷⁹ The word was out about Oregon locations and movie expertise, and it tickled Gerry Thompson to hear Atiyeh say, "We've got to reach out to that Hollywood crowd."¹³⁸⁰

1375 "Oregon Advantage," 1.
1376 Robert Montgomery, "Developing Oregon: Community Development Programs 1983–1986," Intergovernmental Relations Division, State of Oregon, (October 1986), Atiyeh Collection, Pac. Univ. Archives.
1377 Linda Kramer, "Aide Washes Away Film-Makers' Fears of Oregon Rain," *Oregonian*, 7 October 1979.
1378 Helen L. Mershon, "Japanese Diplomate Gets Royal Treatment: Red Carpet Rolled Out for Knots Landing," *Oregonian*, 19 August 1984, Living 2.
1379 Ron Cowan, "Oregon Will Co-Star with Benji," *Salem (OR) Statesman-Journal*, 30 May 1986; UPI, "Film Targets Oregon," *Bend (OR) Bulletin*, 7 May 1986.
1380 Thompson, "Atiyeh interview #2," 9.

Visibility on screen helped with tourism, a sector that Atiyeh thought could really help diversify the economy in much of the state. When Atiyeh became governor, about $400,000 a year was dedicated to promoting tourism. When he left, the amount was $2.3 million and there was a request to double that amount heading to the 1987 legislature.[1381] Atiyeh recalled how narrow Oregon's economic base was when he became governor with "timber, agriculture, and to some degree, although struggling, tourism," which he also referred to as "half tourism."[1382] As the long 1982 special session began, Atiyeh insisted that the budget "retain $2.3 million he said was necessary to promote the state for business and tourism development."[1383] The governor clearly put tourism on an equal footing with other economic development programs. In his 1982 State of the State message, Atiyeh called "tourism…one of the few *exciting* spots in our economy in 1981. Given that the economy of many other states likely will improve at a rate faster than our own, we should build on and intensify this bright opportunity."[1384] There were hopes in the spring of 1982 that hard-hit parts of Oregon—the natural resource–dependent coast was called out for special mention—would be able to count on tourism to replace some of the jobs that evaporated with the collapse of the timber industry.[1385]

Atiyeh insisted that tourism be one of the sectors included in all the international trade trips. Thompson called the result

---

[1381] Thompson, "Atiyeh interview #2," 8; Economic Development Action Council, "Summary of Economic Development," 11; Julie Tripp, "Tourism Division to Ask State to Double Budget Allocation," *Oregonian*, 21 October 1986.

[1382] Victor Atiyeh, interviewed by Clark Hansen, "Tape 45," Oral history, recorded by Oregon Historical Society, Portland, OR, 9 July 1993. Transcript, 408, Atiyeh Collection, Pac. Univ. Archives; Atiyeh, "Tape 62," 20.

[1383] AP, "Governor Says Oregon Is in Economic Crisis," *New York Times*, 19 January 1982, ProQuest.

[1384] Atiyeh, "State of the State, 1982," 14. Italics: "bright" was crossed out and "exciting" was written in by Atiyeh.

[1385] Kathie Durbin and Huntly Collins, "Oregon's Recession Leaves Workers on Ragged Edge: Sorrowful Spring—the Unemployed," *Oregonian*, 18 April 1982; Foster Church, "Fiscal Evangelist Stimulates Hardy Souls: In Coos County," Analysis, *Oregonian*, 22 March 1981.

"incredible."[1386] As Atiyeh began to make more and more international trips, he learned that tourism was a major player in east Asian economies. South Korea's 1984 "major fields of foreign investment [were] chemicals (19.2 percent), tourism and hotels (16.2 percent), electric and electronics (13.0 percent)" followed by textiles, machinery, petroleum, and steel.[1387] South Korea was the United States' eleventh largest market for exports in 1979 (the latest data available for Atiyeh's 1984 trip), up from fifteenth in 1975. It was the second most important economy in Asia, after Japan,[1388] for the United States at the time. And tourism was a huge part of its international footprint. On trips to Japan, the governor made particular arrangements to talk with the editors of travel publications, taking care to highlight "those unique 'events' in Oregon which are difficult to duplicate elsewhere: Mt. Hood Jazz Festival; Portland Marathon; Ashland Shakespearean [*sic*] Festival," and several others.[1389]

At the annual Governor's Tourism Conference in October 1986, Atiyeh was happy to report the results of outreach to tourists during the year. Travelers to Expo '86 in Vancouver, B.C. "spent an average of four days in Oregon," clearly making the sector stronger and justifying the tourism budget for the year.[1390] Atiyeh was always proud that, at a time when budgets were being cut, "I increased the Department of Economic Development budget. I made the request, the legislature passed it."[1391]

Tax Reform, 1982–1985

1386 Thompson, "Atiyeh interview #2," 8.
1387 "Travel Binder: Governor Atiyeh's Trade Mission to Taiwan and Korea," Office of the Governor, State of Oregon, (1–13 May 1984), U.S. Department of Commerce, "Marketing in Korea," Overseas Business Reports, OBR 80-22, July 1980, 20, Atiyeh Collection, Pac. Univ. Archives.
1388 "Travel Binder," U.S. Department of Commerce, "Marketing in Korea," Overseas Business Reports, OBR 80-22, July 1980, 2.
1389 "Fall Mission to Japan—Meeting Sheet," Meeting sheet, Travel Times magazine, November 18, 1985.
1390 Tripp, "Tourism Division to Ask State to Double Budget Allocation."
1391 Atiyeh, "Tape 62," 20.

When Atiyeh first ran for office in 1958, Oregon's eternal conversation about tax reform was in full cry. Governor Robert Holmes had commissioned a 1958 report by a national tax expert, John Sly, that called for a broader system of taxation.[1392] Among the items Sly recommended, a cigarette tax, an annual tax on automobiles, and a possible sales tax. The absence of a sales tax is one of the main reasons that tax reform is a constant in Oregon politics. Without a sales tax, the state is even more susceptible to the ups and downs of an economy that changes due to national and international factors. Oregonians have always been looking for ways to share the tax burden more equitably, while at the same time ensuring governments' ability to deliver services. The sales tax seems to be bitterly fought by everybody in Oregon politics—unless they suddenly see the sales tax as the salvation for what ails the system. Atiyeh remembered that Sly reasoned that the sales tax was not truly regressive if the benefits of the tax would provide more to low-income Oregonians than they paid in sales tax.[1393] The impact of the Sly report was such that the sales tax always seemed to be on the table during Hatfield's time as governor (1959–1967) and Atiyeh's time in the Oregon House and his first term in the state Senate, even if it was not the first choice of legislators.

Atiyeh prided himself on being one of the few legislators who actually read the Department of Revenue's annual report.[1394] He started this practice in his first term in the House. He learned that the sources of taxes relied heavily on the huge number of middle-class taxpayers. His reading of the situation was that if the top taxpayers were assessed 100% of their income, it still would not

---

1392 *Oregon Statesman* (Salem), "Sly Asks New Tax, Cost Curb," 14 December 1958; *Oregon Statesman* (Salem), "Broader Tax Structure For Oregon Minus New Spending Advised by Sly," 14 December 1958.

1393 Victor Atiyeh, interviewed by Clark Hansen, "Tape 45," Oral history, recorded by Oregon Historical Society, Portland, OR, 9 July 1993. Transcript, 436, Atiyeh Collection, Pac. Univ. Archives.

1394 Victor Atiyeh, interviewed by Clark Hansen, "Tape 4," Oral history, recorded by Oregon Historical Society, Portland, OR, 4 December 1992. Transcript, 91, Atiyeh Collection, Pac. Univ. Archives.

come close to funding state programs and agencies that were considered vital. A fair tax system had to engage with middle class taxpayers.[1395] But from 1959 to 1984, he opposed every sales tax idea that came up. His personal understanding of the tax made him an opponent of every plan.[1396]

In 1983, Governor Atiyeh had a distinct take on the sales tax. He called it a hidden tax, something that he would avoid in general. "I really believe people ought to know the tax they pay," Atiyeh told a reporter.[1397] Atiyeh's reasoning was that the sales tax cost consumers "pennies at a time. It doesn't really hurt. You don't know, really, how much" sales tax is paid in a year.[1398] For him the tax was hidden not because people did not know they were paying it—"they didn't like the…nickels and dimes and pennies and stuff like that"—but because "they really didn't know how much tax they paid" overall.[1399] The ideal tax would be visible and the amount paid would be clear to the taxpayer. It was philosophical for Atiyeh: "As long as a tax is perceived to be onerous,… people will keep the pressure on the elected officials from spending" too much.[1400]

As an employee at Atiyeh Brothers, Victor would have observed a major shift away from "hidden taxation": the advent of pay-as-you-go income taxes, put in place to pay for World War II. As withholding became the norm, Atiyeh would have seen the difference in the size of his paycheck as the changeover occurred. And as the new owner/manager in the summer of 1944, he would have a behind the scenes view of how deductions worked as he met payrolls at the business. As Atiyeh thought about the income tax fifty years later, he was in favor of it because "at least once a

---

1395 Atiyeh, "Tape 4," 91.
1396 Denny Miles, Email to Jim Moore, "Principles," 23 July 2015.
1397 Terry McDermott, "Atiyeh to Keep Hands Off Any Sales Tax Campaign," *Oregonian*, 19 January 1983.
1398 Victor Atiyeh, interviewed by Clark Hansen, "Tape 5," Oral history, recorded by Oregon Historical Society, Portland, OR, 12 December 1992. Transcript, 120, Atiyeh Collection, Pac. Univ. Archives.
1399 Atiyeh, "Tape 5," 120.
1400 Atiyeh, "Tape 5," 120.

year, somebody knew how much they were paying in income taxes" as the withholding totals were used to file taxes.[1401] While much of the country considered the pay-as-you-go plan a way to hide taxes (because employees get used to their net pay amount), Atiyeh strongly felt just the opposite was true.

As soon as Atiyeh won re-election in 1982, the words "sales tax" were already in the air.[1402] Much of this was Atiyeh's own doing and the response to his plans. At the beginning of December 1982, he released his proposed 1983–85 budget, and its main feature was a 1% net receipts and gross receipts tax, a form of income tax. Characterized as "a fairly daring piece of work for a governor who only a few months before had said he would not raise taxes," the net receipts idea resurrected a policy that Governor Mark Hatfield had pushed twenty years earlier.[1403] The idea of the tax plan was two types of taxes—businesses would pay a 1% net receipts tax, and individual taxpayers would pay a 1% gross receipts tax. The tax was expected to raise $650 million over the biennium—$613 million from individual taxpayers and $37 million from businesses.[1404] Businesses would pay much less because of allowable deductions already in place. The "net" of the net receipts tax referred to business income *after* those deductions. The "gross" in the gross receipts version for individuals meant that the 1% would be taken *before* any deductions from total income. This was the main reason for the huge difference in the amounts both groups would pay. There was initial support from both the Democratic and Republican

---

1401 Atiyeh, "Tape 5," 120.
1402 For Atiyeh's musing on the constant attraction of the sales tax, see Victor Atiyeh, interviewed by Clark Hansen, "Tape 38," Oral history, recorded by Oregon Historical Society, Portland, OR, 21 June 1993. Transcript, 217–218, Atiyeh Collection, Pac. Univ. Archives.
1403 Foster Church, "Atiyeh's Unexpected Budget Surprises Even Harshest Critics," Analysis, *Oregonian*, 2 December 1982; Atiyeh, "Tape 5," 116–119.
1404 Terry McDermott, "Individuals to Shoulder 1% Tax Plan," *Oregonian*, 3 December 1982. $650 million in 1983 is the equivalent of $1.56 billion in 2015.

leadership in the legislature. The governor held meetings to discuss his tax plan.[1405]

The major players in the business community, however, were strongly opposed to the business-centric net receipts proposal. There were fears that cyclical industries (agriculture, logging, home building) would be hit hard by the tax. There were also fears among retailers that taking hundreds of millions of dollars out of taxpayers' pockets with an additional tax would mean that there would be hundreds of millions of dollars missing in potential retail sales. Some business leaders were calling for a sales tax instead, to spread the tax burden evenly among businesses and individuals.[1406]

The 1983 legislative session opened with Atiyeh's net/gross receipts idea as the only major way forward toward tax reform. Atiyeh said he would not stand in the way of other efforts, but that he would stick with his tax concept.[1407] The editor of the *Daily Astorian* noted that Atiyeh's "twin mandates" of not having to run for election ever again and winning by such a large margin could free Atiyeh from more mundane political concerns—he could be very creative. By January 1983, however, it was reported that Atiyeh's proposal had "met heavy criticism from inside and outside the Legislature and particularly from the Oregon business community."[1408]

Notwithstanding the disparagement of Atiyeh's plan, it looked like the 1983 legislature would be the one to finally come up with meaningful tax reform that was supported by the major players, and tax reform that had a chance to pass muster with the voters.[1409] The tax committee held extensive hearings on Atiyeh's gross and net receipts proposal from January into February 1983,

---

1405 "Atiyeh Daily Index-Card Schedule, December 22, 1982," Office of the Governor, State of Oregon, (22 December 1982), Jack McIsaac & Gerry re: Gov's tax program, Atiyeh Collection, Pac. Univ. Archives.
1406 Steve Jenning, "Business, Bank Leaders Fear Atiyeh Tax Plan," *Oregonian*, 3 December 1982.
1407 McDermott, "Atiyeh to Keep Hands Off Any Sales Tax Campaign."
1408 Foster Church, "Money Top Issue Facing Solons," *Oregonian*, 9 January 1983.
1409 *Oregonian*, "Let the Tax Action Begin," Editorial, 28 January 1983.

but it quickly became clear that there was no major support for the idea among members of the legislature, and there was active opposition from most of the groups that testified before the committee. The proposed tax died due to neglect with no one strongly advocating for the idea.

Atiyeh continued to believe that the gross and net receipts tax was the way to go after he left office. In 1993 he laughed because "I picked the wrong term. AOI [the main business group] didn't like it."[1410] He was convinced that if he had called his idea a flat tax, there would have been more support for it.[1411] In December 1982, as Atiyeh first proposed the net receipts tax, it was characterized as a flat tax by the national *Bond Buyer*.[1412] As Ted Kulongoski learned with the Plant Closure bill, interpretation is often simply in the name of an idea.

Amid all this, national data about the states showed that only Oregon and Hawaii experienced a drop in state revenue in 1982. The rest of the country was coming out of the recession, but these two states were still feeling its effects in their tax income. About half of the revenues received by all the states in the country came from sales taxes and gross receipts taxes.[1413] Oregon had neither. As consumers started to spend more after the recession, Oregon had no way to take advantage of that spending to feed revenues into state and local government programs.

Tax reform was still alive in the session, but it focused on property tax relief. Even that, however, proved too much to accomplish.[1414] Atiyeh made it clear to the legislative leadership that if they did not solve this problem, he would call them back into special session. "I was trying to work very hard with them in coming up with…a method of property tax relief. I had insisted

---

1410 Atiyeh, "Tape 38," 216.
1411 Atiyeh, "Tape 38," 216.
1412 Special Report, "Ore. Governor Seeks Flat Tax on All Income," *New York Bond Buyer*, 8 December 1982.
1413 David Whitney, "Oregon's '82 Tax Revenues Plummet," *Oregonian*, 12 March 1983.
1414 Foster Church, "Adjournment Likely—Minus Property Tax Relief," *Oregonian*, 15 July 1983.

that we do something like that, and we just kept going. And to make a long story short, they didn't..., and I called them back."[1415] The governor called a special session for the middle of September.

Atiyeh opened the special session with a speech that highlighted what everybody in the capitol already knew: none had "seen *so much* frustration, so much *confusion*, so much *anger* and so much emotional energy as during that *exhausting* regular session."[1416] "Indeed," the governor said, "if the pioneers has had as much trouble charting *their* course for the Oregon Territory as this legislature had in charting *its* course for property tax relief, the Oregon Trail might have ended up somewhere in Wyoming."[1417]

The core negotiating group attempting to reach some sort of outcome was Atiyeh and the leadership of both houses. By day seventeen of the special session, tempers were running high. The Senate approved an Atiyeh compromise plan only because Ed Fadeley was faced with being stripped of the Senate Presidency if he did not allow a vote—it passed 16-14. [1418] Gerry Thompson recalled that Fadeley "was the problem. Always! Always!"[1419] On a whiteboard, Atiyeh had drawn one of his doodles, two railroad tracks coming together that would not meet because they were offset from each other. "This was his way of illustrating that they weren't meeting. He had to bring the railroad track together." Then the governor drew another doodle and called it "the Golden Spike." Every time they all came in for a meeting, they had to

---

1415 Victor Atiyeh, interviewed by Clark Hansen, "Tape 39," Oral history, recorded by Oregon Historical Society, Portland, OR, 23 June 1993. Transcript, 241, Atiyeh Collection, Pac. Univ. Archives; Phil Cogswell, "Lapse in Lawmaking Leaves Property Tax Relief Unsolved," Column, *Oregonian*, 17 July 1983.

1416 Victor Atiyeh, "Speech, Hand Annotated by Atiyeh" (speech, Special Session of the 62nd Legislative Assembly, Salem, OR, 14 September 1983), 1, Atiyeh Collection, Pac. Univ. Archives. Italics underlined by hand by Atiyeh.

1417 Atiyeh, "Speech to 1983 Special Session," 2. Italics underlined by hand by Atiyeh.

1418 Sue Hill, "Senate OKs Sales Tax Compromise," *Salem (OR) Statesman-Journal*, 1 October 1983.

1419 Thompson, "Atiyeh interview #1," 12.

look at the whiteboard where this doodle just sat there. Thompson knew that Atiyeh had done this for psychological effect.

Finally, after twenty-one days, a solution was patched together.[1420] It involved votes by all 602 Oregon cities, towns, counties, and school districts to support a 4% sales tax plan. Observers at the time attributed the baroque nature of the proposal as a way for Fadeley to send the proposal to voters and avoid blame for the measure, a sort of "poison pill."[1421] The odd grand bargain was eventually shut down by the courts as unconstitutional.[1422] Fadeley was opposed to all sales taxes. This would become very clear in the coming months. Atiyeh was coming around to the idea that a solid economic action plan would probably have to be accompanied by tax reform, and that would entail a sales tax proposal. If a sales tax proposal were to succeed it would need broad support—from the business community, unions, education, and the all-important voters across the state. In late September 1983, in the middle of the 21-day special session, Atiyeh, writing in doggerel, channeled his inner Dr. Seuss as he considered the sales tax.

> Some legislators want a sales tax.
>
> Some do not want a sales tax.
>
> Some want a sales tax with baubles to make it shine better.
>
> Some do not want baubles to make it shine.
>
> Some—for any of the reasons above—want a spending limit.
>
> Some do not want a spending limit.
>
> Some want a non-limit limit on gov. spending.

[1420] Foster Church, "Legislators Hand Tax Reform Back to Oregon Voters," *Oregonian*, 5 October 1983.

[1421] Russell Sadler, "Palace Coup Saves Tax Reform Package," Column, *Oregonian*, 3 October 1983, 3; Peter Wong, interviewed by Jim Moore, "Atiyeh interview," Rock Creek, OR, 4 August 2015. Summary notes.

[1422] John Hayes, "Court Strikes Down Oregon Sales Tax Proposal," *Oregonian*, 2 February 1984.

Some want a strong limit on gov. spending.

Some say they want a sales tax but really do not.

Some say they do not want a sales tax but really do.

Some do not want anything.

Some want a 1½% limitation [on property taxes].

Some want to control the growth of property taxes.

Some do not want any kind of control.

—Etc.—Etc.—Etc.[1423]

After writing all these possibilities, Atiyeh wrote what he thought was true: "The people want…control of property taxes; There are people who want a[n] opportunity to vote on a sales tax with assurances that the sales tax will truly lift the burden of property taxes; Most people do not want the destructive 1½% limitation and want a reason to put it to sleep."[1424] The governor was clearly wrestling not only with the idea of the sales tax but also about the strategy of getting the tax through the legislature and approved by a vote of the people. Ultimately, he said, "I worked on the sales tax, very diligently, personally, although up to this point in time I opposed it. Because my thought was, well, you know, we might have one someday, and if we're ever going to have one, I'd just as soon it be a good one."[1425]

Atiyeh's main focus was on the growing problem of the property tax, which hit people with fixed incomes particularly hard. That inequity was the problem to be dealt with, not necessarily the overall amount of tax revenue local governments would receive, although he was alarmed by how quickly government spending had grown in the 1970s and early 1980s.[1426]

1423 Vic Atiyeh, "Thoughts on a Sales Tax," (Unpublished manuscript, 30 September 1983), Handwritten thoughts on the sales tax, Atiyeh collection, Pacific University Archive, Forest Grove, OR.
1424 Atiyeh, "Thoughts on a Sales Tax."
1425 Atiyeh, "Tape 45," 435.
1426 Atiyeh, "Tape 30," 23.

Still, he never did buy one of the key arguments against a sales tax: that it was regressive. He looked at the sales tax as part of the total tax burden any one person would bear. For Atiyeh, the sales tax was aimed at those in the middle, the vast majority of taxpayers. And for that group, the sales tax was equitable.

In fact, in 1982, Oregon was right in the middle of the U.S. states in a ranking of state and local taxes, at #25.[1427] Since Atiyeh's advocacy for the sales tax was to keep the total tax burden the same, but rearrange how it was paid (among property, income, and sales taxes), he saw no major regressive qualities in the sales tax proposal. As he remembered in 1993, "I don't want to use the word neutral, because it isn't—but basically we're going to come out pretty even."[1428]

Atiyeh felt the tax plan idea could work with voters because it was not just a tax plan, but a way to balance the taxes paid by Oregonians, and a way to remove the uncertainty from something that Oregonians valued—the education system. Chief of Staff Thompson vividly recalled Atiyeh's words to her: "Okay, I will propose a sales tax as long as it includes my terms. I doubt it will pass, but if my business friends and political friends want it so badly, I can try for them. I have nothing to lose because I have no other political intention and it gives me an opportunity, so that, if it should pass, it will have built-in safeguards."[1429] He had requirements that would have to be met: "the rate of tax had to be set in the constitution; it had to offset (not add to) taxes currently [in place]. He insisted that all [political] leaders—Republican and Democrat—had to support the proposal [and] actively engage in campaigning for it."[1430] Atiyeh's leadership principle, first developed when led the Senate Republican caucus to vote for issues that that he did not necessarily support, was guiding him. He needed to go counter to his personal principles to lead the

---

1427 "State and Local Taxes—an Uneven Burden," Chart, 1982, Atiyeh Collection, Pac. Univ. Archives. Gerry Thompson kept this chart in her files.
1428 Atiyeh, "Tape 46," 439.
1429 Gerry Thompson to Jim Moore, "Atiyeh Question," email, 13 July 2016.
1430 Thompson to Moore, 13 July 2016.

people looking for solutions in ways he would not otherwise have chosen.

It became apparent that the right kind of packaging of Atiyeh's ideas for education reform and tax reform would put him in the driver's seat in Oregon politics, making it clear to everybody that he was the leader who mattered in the state, and that he was guiding Oregon to a better future. A brainstorming session in May 1984 led to a set of priority action issues: a) unitary tax reform; b) sales tax; c) tax reform tied to fix education funding; d) crime; and e) getting the legislature on board.[1431] Immediately after the brainstorming session, Governor Atiyeh decided to call a special legislative session for the end of July or beginning of August to repeal the unitary tax. A reporter at the time was hearing from the business community that it felt the unitary tax should be broken off from the "continuing soap opera" of the sales tax.[1432] The unitary tax repeal would be successfully achieved in just a few months. The larger question of education reform and tax reform would take much longer to work out.

The summer of 1984 was filled with research by the governor's staff to figure out what the proposals ought to be, as well as to begin efforts to bring the policies to fruition. Atiyeh made the decision to seriously evaluate the sales tax idea during this time, but only if it met "his criteria: locked into [the] constitution; [to] fund education; no local government sales tax [options]."[1433]

Governor Atiyeh delivered a speech on November 26, 1984, that defined his ideas for systematic reform of Oregon's tax system, defined the ways that Oregon paid for public education, and defined how this would help the diversification of Oregon's economy away from the timber industry.[1434] Called the Oregon

---

1431 Thompson, "Second Term 1982."; Thompson, "May 26 Vote Totals," 3.
1432 Wong, "Atiyeh interview," 3.
1433 Thompson, "Second Term 1982."; See Atiyeh thoughts on the importance of locking in changes in the constitution, Atiyeh, "Tape 46," 441.
1434 Atiyeh, "Oregon Plan." The plan is capitalized when used by Atiyeh after early November 1984. Responses to the plan did not bother with acknowledging the acronym.

Plan (**O**regon: **R**eliable **E**ducation for **G**reater **O**pportunity Now),[1435] it was the first public step in a complex set of policy proposals to fundamentally rethink Oregon's relationship to taxpayers and the educational outcomes Oregon's citizens expected.

After decades of opposing a sales tax, Vic Atiyeh was calling for one: "a statewide sales tax of 5 percent."[1436] The sales tax would be written into the constitution, which meant that the people of Oregon would vote on it, and it would be dedicated to education funding for k-12 schools and community colleges. Atiyeh's analysis was that property taxes would be cut by 40% since the portion of the property tax that went to fund local education would no longer be needed. The plan was also designed to conclude the never-ending property tax battles, something that had dogged Atiyeh's governorship since taking office in 1979. "And we must forever eliminate the perching vulture of the one-and-a-half percent limitation that has exhausted and divided Oregonians while consuming the otherwise constructive time, financial resources and talents of our citizens."[1437]

The tax ideas were relatively clear. But Atiyeh also was serious about using tax reform to institutionalize his actions to diversify Oregon's economy. The basic idea was that Oregonians were investing in K-12 education, but that the best students were going elsewhere for college, and a huge number of them never returned to the state to work. He found this to be a bad investment. Community colleges had proven their worth in creating opportunities for students to learn skills with immediate application in local Oregon economies. But Atiyeh went further. He wanted to "redirect existing general-fund revenues to enhance higher education" with three "modern, academic-industrial research centers" at Oregon's three major public universities.[1438] The University of Oregon would be the home of a new center for

---

1435 Thompson, "Second Term 1982."
1436 Atiyeh, "Oregon Plan," 4.
1437 Atiyeh, "Oregon Plan," 5.
1438 Atiyeh, "Oregon Plan," 7.

biological and advanced sciences, Oregon State would gain a center for electrical and computer engineering, and Portland State would host something close to Atiyeh's heart and his policies, a center focusing on international trade and business.[1439]

Atiyeh always saw higher education as a crucial part of economic development. The concept was straightforward—strong higher education led to spin-off businesses (as in Silicon Valley) and an accomplished workforce which led to business investment and job creation. During Atiyeh's political life, he had seen higher education as a greater or lesser priority of Oregon's governors. He recalled, "[I]t was Mark Hatfield that really kind of took higher education to a higher plateau, and, then, through the terms of Tom McCall and Bob Straub, it was just there. It would get whatever percentage increases were coming along, but never really moved it to another plateau."[1440] Atiyeh had been involved in rethinking Oregon's education system in the early 1970s so that there would be a continuity from elementary school to high school to college.[1441] This 1972 plan was coupled with tax reform to pay for it (reducing the pressure on the property tax), and it never went anywhere. There was another effort in 1970 to merge the Department of Education and the Department of Higher Education under what was referred to as a "superboard," but Atiyeh opposed that because "the interests of higher education and primary and secondary, by and large, were different."[1442] When people in Oregon talk about education politics, they talk about k-12. Higher education is an afterthought.

1439 Atiyeh, "Oregon Plan," 7.
1440 Victor Atiyeh, interviewed by Clark Hansen, "Tape 5," Oral history, recorded by Oregon Historical Society, Portland, OR, 12 December 1992. Transcript, 127, Atiyeh Collection, Pac. Univ. Archives; Verne Duncan, interviewed by Jim Moore, "Atiyeh interview," Milwaukie, OR, 12 August 2014. Summary notes, 3.
1441 Victor Atiyeh, interviewed by Clark Hansen, "Tape 14," Oral history, recorded by Oregon Historical Society, Portland, OR, 19 January 1993. Transcript, 415–416, Atiyeh Collection, Pac. Univ. Archives.
1442 Victor Atiyeh, interviewed by Clark Hansen, "Tape 8," Oral history, recorded by Oregon Historical Society, Portland, OR, 15 December 1992. Transcript, 220–221, Atiyeh Collection, Pac. Univ. Archives; Paul W. Harvey, Jr., "Oregon Urged to Restructure College Setup: Plan Ties 2, 4-year Schools to Single Board of Regents," *Oregonian*, 23 July 1970.

Beginning in 1982, Atiyeh had begun to fight to keep higher education budgets from being cut in the face of the three special sessions to deal with the recession-spawned revenue shortfalls. He thought strategically. Higher education needed to be part of the diversified economy that Atiyeh envisioned. In 1985, his idea was that Oregon's three major universities, through the creations of "centers of excellence," would become the basis of something similar to the uc Berkeley–Stanford connection that had created Silicon Valley in the San Francisco Bay Area.[1443] Chancellor Bob Davis was enthusiastic about the idea. This would, as deputy director of the Executive Department Jon Yunker observed, create opportunities and an educated workforce that would create jobs throughout the state.[1444]

How complex would this reform process be?[1445] It would require a new law on the role of the state in K-12 education, to be called the Basic Education Act of 1985. There would be a Community College Act, along with a set of funding packages from the general fund to "update and modernize [the] state system" of higher education. To pay for all this, there was the constitutional amendment to establish the 5% sales tax dedicated to education. And then there would be many "statutory elements" to implement the sales tax, as well as get all the reform packages through the legislature. The plan set up Atiyeh's work for his final two years in office—he would seek to institutionalize change that he felt would make Oregon more competitive in the global economy, would make it more likely that investment would come to Oregon, and would relieve both taxpayers and business of the uncertainty of Oregon's rickety tax system.

One way that Atiyeh began to approach the problem could be seen in successive drafts of the "Oregon Plan" speech. In the first

---

1443 Phil Manzano, "Higher Education Wins Big Budget Increase," *Oregonian*, 23 June 1985.

1444 Jon Yunker, interviewed by Jim Moore, "Atiyeh interview," Salem, OR, 22 June 2015. Summary notes, 3.

1445 Gerry Thompson, "Notes on Education and Tax Reform," (Unpublished manuscript, ca. October 1984), Typed and notated outline, Atiyeh collection, Pac. Univ. Archives. All these proposed laws and changes come from this document.

draft, the sales tax was in the first paragraph.[1446] A week later, the sales tax made its entrance one-third of the way into the draft.[1447] In the final speech, the sales tax first appeared halfway through the eight-page script.[1448] Clearly the idea was to extol the benefits of reform, then to address the ways to pay for that reform at the end. The headlines the day after the speech, however, focused on the payment plan: "Atiyeh Asks for 5% Sales Tax to Aid Schools" said the top headline on the *Oregonian* front page.[1449] The details of education reform and how the sales tax would help reduce other taxes were buried on page B2.[1450] And both stories had the word "tax" in their headlines.

The sales tax had been the preference of Republican legislators for years, but there was a sense that the Democratic majority could bring the sales tax to the voters and get it passed. With John Kitzhaber as the new Senate President, and Democrat Vera Katz becoming the Speaker of the House, the sales tax was being talked about as a real possibility.

Atiyeh felt strongly that a sales tax, coupled with a 45% reduction in property taxes, strict limits on the growth of property taxes, and the higher number of jobs that would be created by investing in the education system was the best route to a more stable economic future for Oregon. To those who wanted to simply cut property taxes (the supporters of Measure 3 in 1982 and Measure 2 in 1984), Atiyeh replied that

> 1. Imposing a Draconian tax limitation on local government could set back Oregon's economy by generations.

1446 Larry Pierce, "An Education Plan for Oregon's Future (draft)" 19 September 1984), Atiyeh collection, Pac. Univ. Archives.

1447 Pierce, "Briefing Packet for Governor's Eduction Reform Plan," Education Initiative Speech.

1448 Atiyeh, "Oregon Plan."

1449 Don Jepsen, "Atiyeh Asks for 5% Sales Tax to Aid Schools," *Oregonian*, 27 November 1984.

1450 Kathie Durbin and Phil Manzano, "State Education Officials Pleased with Atiyeh Sales Tax Plan," *Oregonian*, 27 November 1984; Jeff Mapes, "Atiyeh Tax Plan Welcomed, But Cautiously," *Oregonian*, 27 November 1984.

2. To generate 800-million dollars from an increased income tax, the upper bracket would rise to more than 16 percent.

3. This leaves the sales tax as the sole remaining generator of new revenue.[1451]

As expected, the path to the legislature's approval was tortuous, but success was finally achieved on April 19, 1985.[1452] A 5% sales tax would go out to voters. Most of Atiyeh's ideas were in the plan—goods would be taxed, but not services; there would be exemptions for groceries, drugs, and purchases by schools and churches; local property taxes would be reduced by an estimated 35%; income taxes would be reduced by an average of about 10%; there were limitations on how fast school property tax bases could grow (maximum 3% a year); and state spending growth was limited to the pace of Oregon residents' income growth. Finally, a series of breakthroughs moved the sales tax to approval in little more than a week, with a process afterward to resolve differences between the house and senate versions.

The sales tax was now set for a September vote of the people as Measure 1, the only item on the ballot. Would the very public legislative wrangling over the package help voters to understand the entire concept? Or would voters respond as they always had in Oregon when offered a sales tax—with a resounding "no"? A poll taken in May was bad news for the sales tax proponents: Against: 58%; For: 40%; Undecided: 2%.[1453]

Pressing forward, Atiyeh's biggest gamble was on getting the labor unions to either support the measure or stay neutral on it. In 1985 organized labor certainly favored Democratic programs and candidates with financial donations, but its biggest power was to move voters to cast ballots one way or the other. Atiyeh wanted

---

1451 Atiyeh, "Atiyeh Talking Points on Tax and Education," 7.
1452 Foster Church, "Voters to Decide Fate of 5 Percent Sales Tax," *Oregonian*, 20 April 1985.
1453 *Oregonian*, "Sales Tax Foes Outnumber Fans, Poll Indicates," 26 May 1985; Foster Church, "Time Short for Backers of State Sales Tax," Column, *Oregonian*, 2 June 1985.

labor to be anything but opposed to the sales tax plan.[1454] The governor met with representatives of the firefighters union in his office to try to get unions on board.[1455]

Then the Measure 1 campaign mailing came out.

It was a comic book.[1456]

The idea behind it was to make a complex series of policy changes clear to voters. The sales tax was not just a sales tax, according to this argument. It was the necessary step that would lead to lower property taxes, more stable school funding, higher educational achievement, and economic growth. The pro–sales tax campaign knew that it had been complicated to get this ungainly set of proposals through the Oregon legislature where members were supposed to devote their time to understanding these things. Oregon voters needed to know how it all fit together as well.

1454 Don Jepsen, "Atiyeh to Seek Labor Support for Sales Tax," *Oregonian*, 24 July 1985; Stan Federmar, "AFL-CIO Election Spurs Paucity of Hot Contests," *Oregonian*, 31 July 1985.

1455 "Atiyeh Daily Index-Card Schedule, August 12, 1985," Office of the Governor, State of Oregon, (12 August 1985), Ray Barnwell, Carl Below & Tom Whelan, Firefighters' Union; regarding sales tax, Atiyeh Collection, Pac. Univ. Archives.

1456 People for a Better Oregon, "Oregon's Balanced Tax Plan: Ballot Measure #1," Portland, OR, 1985. Atiyeh collection, Pac. Univ. Archives; Foster Church, "New Comic Book Argues for Sales Tax," *Oregonian*, 27 July 1985; Foster Church, "Sales Tax Mailing Draws Fire," *Oregonian*, 2 August 1985.

It was a comic book. Atiyeh Collection, Pacific University Archives.

The opposition made fun of the comic book, accusing it of speaking to Oregon voters as if they were children. Columnists had a field day parsing the campaign message wrapped in comic-book stylings.[1457] It was not clear that the outreach had the desired

---

1457 Jonathan Nicholas, "Comic Effect," Column, *Oregonian*, 7 August 1985.

effect with the electorate.[1458] One observer recalled that educating the voters in a humorous way was a good idea, but it backfired in this case.[1459]

Atiyeh remained optimistic.[1460] Then the AFL-CIO had its meeting in Coos Bay.[1461] Atiyeh attended in person and gave a talk that was characterized as spirited, well-argued, and the kind of speech that would get supporters jumping to go out to win the battle. The response in the hall was polite applause at best, and silence from many of the delegates. The vote on the floor was to oppose the sales tax, a process that seemed to be hurried through before the public employee unions could fully participate in the process. Since leaders of public employee unions were generally seen to be in favor of putting state and local government finances on a stronger footing, this maneuver was seen as a blow to the sales tax campaign. The union delegates needed a two-thirds vote for any stance on the measure. Atiyeh was hoping that the motion to oppose Measure 1 would not reach that threshold. It got 77% of the vote, 10% higher than needed. Atiyeh's attempt to at least neutralize labor had failed.

There was a big push around Labor Day to educate voters for the September 17 vote,[1462] but the election outcome had never

---

1458 Foster Church, "Tax 'Comic' Read, Not Always Liked," *Oregonian*, 18 August 1985. Atiyeh, "Tape 45," 433; Then reporter, later legislator and secretary of state, Phil Keisling recalled "I actually did not think it was a problem, but it got roundly criticized because it was" a comic book, Phil Keisling, "Atiyeh interview," Portland, OR, 23 February 2015. Summary notes, 3.

1459 Tony Van Vliet, "Atiyeh interview," Corvallis, OR, 11 March 2015. Summary notes, 6.

1460 Don Jepsen, "Atiyeh Still Hopeful on Tax," *Oregonian*, 20 August 1985.

1461 Jeff Mapes, "Disregarding Atiyeh, AFL-CIO Opposes Tax," *Oregonian*, 24 August 1985; "Atiyeh Daily Index-Card Schedule, August 21, 1985," Office of the Governor, State of Oregon, (21 August 1985), Arrive in Coos Bay; met by Sgt. Dougherty (May have dinner with labor leaders), Atiyeh Collection, Pac. Univ. Archives.

1462 "Atiyeh Daily Index-Card Schedule, September 3, 1985," Office of the Governor, State of Oregon, (3 September 1985), Participate: People for a Better Oregon Press Conference; Salon A, Marriott Hotel, Portland; Arrive Klamath Falls…(Balanced Tax people have told press they will have few minutes to ask questions at the airport); Speech: Klamath Falls Chamber; Elks Club, Atiyeh Collection, Pac. Univ. Archives; "Atiyeh Daily Index-Card Schedule, September 5, 1985," Office of the

really been in doubt. The only thing that was misestimated in the run-up to election day was the margin of victory for the No side. It was not a 3:2 defeat as the polling had suggested, it was 4:1 in the final tally.[1463] Atiyeh's "election gut" told him that the measure would fail. "I wasn't surprised it failed. I was surprised it failed by that margin."[1464]

Still seeing the need for a stable tax base for education, the governor pushed one more tax reform to go before the voters. The idea was "to create new, more flexible tax bases for Oregon's 306 school districts."[1465] But the effort was a failure, gathering less than a third of the signatures necessary to get it on the November 1986 ballot. Atiyeh blamed the Oregon Education Association (OEA) for the failure of the sales tax and the complex messaging around it. Atiyeh and OEA leadership met on Atiyeh's proposal for months in 1985 but could not come to agreement on the final version. The OEA's own tax reform plan went before voters in November 1986. It called for a sales tax, but with 80% guaranteed to alleviate local property taxes dedicated to schools, as well as a 20% cut in the income tax.[1466] It failed by the same percentage as Atiyeh's plan—22% yes to 78% no. Another proposal on the same ballot that called for property tax relief and the possibility of a future sales tax only through citizen initiative failed 37% to 63%.

A stronger reason for the defeat was probably what reporter Peter Wong observed. The political time for the sales tax was in 1983 or 1984, not in 1985. Fadeley's delay tactics, as baroque as they were, successfully postponed the actual vote of the people to

---

Governor, State of Oregon, (5 September 1985), Interview: Trish Nyworth, Channel 12; regarding sales tax—cere. office (15 min.), Atiyeh Collection, Pac. Univ. Archives.

1463 Foster Church, "Voters Defeat Sales Tax Measure 4–1," *Oregonian*, 18 September 1985; Jeff Mapes, "Tax Backers Dismayed; Foes Rejoice," *Oregonian*, 18 September 1985.

1464 Atiyeh, "Tape 46," 458.

1465 Alan K. Ota, "Atiyeh Gets Blame for Failure of School Financing Proposal," Analysis, *Oregonian*, 9 July 1986.

1466 *Oregonian*, "Voters' Guide: The Year of the Measure," Special Pullout Section, *Oregonian*, 2 November 1986.

a different political context and time. The recessions were ebbing from people's memories, local schools no longer faced imminent closure, and political focus that state budget shortfalls and increasing unemployment figures had created in 1983 and 1984 was dissipating.

After the defeat of Atiyeh's grand tax reform plan, Atiyeh "dried up a lot on big tax issues," Richard Munn, then the Director of the Department of Revenue, said.[1467] In Munn's estimation a big reason for this was because Atiyeh had been on the Revenue Committees for twenty years in the legislature and had seen all those other plans come through and not amount to much—voters would not approve them. Atiyeh recognized this reality: "I can't see where the people are going to pass a sales tax in Oregon. I don't see any future in it. They still don't believe there's a real problem, generally, out there."[1468]

No sales tax plan since 1993 has made it beyond the hearings stage in the legislature. Whenever a sales tax seems to be feasible, polling quickly shows that Oregonians have grown no fonder of the idea. John Kitzhaber, who ascended to the presidency of the Oregon Senate based, partially, on his support for a sales tax in 1984, was going to make tax reform the signature issue of his unprecedented fourth term as governor in 2014. But polling showed that Oregonians were no more likely to pass something that looked like a sales tax in 2015 than they had been in any previous elections.[1469]

Despite the defeat of the sales tax in 1985, the centers of excellence he envisioned for the state's universities had been built.[1470] However, by the end of 1987 and Bud Davis' resignation

---

1467 Richard Munn, "Atiyeh Interview," Salem, OR, 9 June 2016. Summary notes, 7.
1468 Atiyeh, "Tape 63," 15.
1469 Russell Sadler, "Various Pro-Sales Tax Strategies Simmer," Column, *Oregonian*, 13 February 1984; Terry McDermott, "Kitzhaber Foresees Tax Plan Changes," *Eugene (OR) Register-Guard*, 19 December 1984; Laura Gunderson, "John Kitzhaber Turns Attention to Challenges Ahead with Education, Tax Reform, and Chance of Kicker," *Portland OregonLive*, 8 November 2014, http://www.oregonlive.com; Van Vliet, "Atiyeh interview," 6.
1470 *Oregonian*, "OSU Building Project Slated," 24 July 1986.

as chancellor, the centers lost their champion and folded back into the regular operations of each university.[1471] But the investment in infrastructure, faculty salaries, and an advanced technology center in Hillsboro did create a university system that was more clearly supportive of economic development in the state.

Higher education was poised to move to a different level in Oregon, in terms of its abilities to produce research, to mesh with economic development, and to attract strong students. However, the reconfiguration of the overall Oregon education budget after the passage of Measure 5 in 1990, and the challenges of new recessions and budget constraints from the 1990s on, left a public university system still treated more as an accessory than a central part of Oregon's plans for its economic future. At best, higher education is seen by the business and political communities as a place to train workers and the home of sports teams to cheer for. Hopes are dormant of sparking some kind of Silicon Valley–light. New businesses spin off from old businesses in Oregon; they do not tend to come from the institutions of higher education.

The Other Issues for a Governor

Aside from the big reform efforts, the 1985 legislative session was known for the number of vetoes by the governor and for being the shortest session in ten years, ending as summer began on June 21.[1472] The length was attributed to the ways the new Speaker of the House, Vera Katz, and the new President of the Senate, John Kitzhaber, worked together so that the fights between the two house were fewer and of a lower intensity than they had been in earlier sessions. Known as Kitz and Katz, the two would dominate the legislature for the next six years. Atiyeh vetoed thirty-two bills in 1985, down from his high of forty in 1983. An *Oregonian* editorial argued that "he has used his veto

---

1471 Dan Hortsch, "Davis' Record Will Be Hard Act to Follow," *Oregonian*, 30 December 1987.

1472 Douglas Heider and David Dietz, *Legislative Perspectives: A 150-Year History of the Oregon Legislatures from 1843–1993*, (Portland, OR: Oregon Historical Society, 1995), 198.

power sparingly, given the overproductive nature of a liberal-leaning Legislature that tends to turn out impractical cures for a variety of social ills."[1473]

Atiyeh's legislative priorities and principles were primarily derived from his own personal principles. From watching Atiyeh use the veto over four legislative sessions, however, Denny Miles thought there were three different classifications.[1474] The first of these was to veto any bill that Atiyeh considered technically flawed. In Miles' recollection, none of these vetoes were overridden. An example of this was a 1985 bill on pay and classification reform for state workers. Atiyeh wrote in his veto message, "I regret having to veto this legislation because I support its intent."[1475]

The middle category was Atiyeh acting as the super-legislator, knowing that his vote was most important because he could stop a bill with the veto. These vetoes occurred when Atiyeh opposed a bill—Miles saw more of these vetoes overridden by the legislature than those from the other two categories. Atiyeh's veto of a measure aimed at dealing with jail overcrowding was one of these. Atiyeh wrote, "I cannot approve a legislative procedure for release of prisoners on grounds that the threat they pose to the public safety is not as great as some other prisoners."[1476] The governor also pointed out that the voters had rejected measures to pay for more state correctional capacity.

The third category was the "serious major philosophical benchmark kinds of issues." Atiyeh would fight to keep the legislature from overriding these—they were laws that struck at one or more of his core principles. A few of these vetoes were

---

1473 *Oregonian*, "Vetoes Make Sense," Editorial, 20 July 1985, Atiyeh Collection, Pac. Univ. Archives.
1474 Denny Miles, "Atiyeh interview #1," Forest Grove, OR, 31 July 2014. Summary notes, 3.
1475 "Governor Responses to Bills,' Office of the Governor, State of Oregon, 'Allowed to Become Law' Without Signature; 'Comments' on Signed Bills; 'Partially-Signed' Bills; Vetoed Bills, (1985), Senate Bill 59 veto letter, July 15, 1985, Atiyeh Collection, Pac. Univ. Archives.
1476 "Governor Responses to Bills,' Senate Bill 83 veto letter, July 15, 1985.

indeed overridden, including divestiture initiatives focused on South Africa's apartheid system that Atiyeh considered well-meaning but onerous. These violated Atiyeh's principles that the best government is one that is less involved in people's lives and that layers of government and bureaucracy got in the way of a government that was closest to the people. For similar reasons, Atiyeh vetoed a bill that would have created a legal path for college students who believed they had been discriminated against. Atiyeh wrote the "bill has the characteristics of a 'fifth-wheel on the coach' ...[because] adequate remedies, including ultimate resort to the federal courts, already exist to handle claims which would be enhanced by this measure."[1477] The bill would create too many government layers.

Throughout his second term, other official work continued apace. Although the constitution makes it clear that there should be elections for state judges, in reality judges were, and are, primarily appointed by the governor. Judges resigned in the middle of their terms, the open seats were filled by gubernatorial appointment, and the new judges then ran as incumbents in the next election. It is a system that is comfortable for those within it, and it gives governors a great deal of power to mold the judiciary. Atiyeh sought to expand this prerogative in the judicial reforms advocated by Speaker Hardy Myers in 1981. Atiyeh wanted the governor to explicitly select the Chief Justice of the Oregon Supreme Court. Myers did not. A vote of the people put an end to that extension of gubernatorial power.

Atiyeh took his role as selector-of-judges seriously. Atiyeh recalled his method of choosing judges. For him, there were a variety of reasons to appoint somebody as a judge. "It would all vary, but [party] registration had nothing to do with how" he decided on his picks.[1478] In this he was consistent with the ways that he hired people for his personal staff and considered other

---

1477 "Vetoes Make Sense," Senate Bill 413 veto letter, July 15, 1985.
1478 Victor Atiyeh, interviewed by Clark Hansen, "Tape 7," Oral history, recorded by Oregon Historical Society, Portland, OR, 11 December 1992. Transcript, 189, Atiyeh Collection, Pac. Univ. Archives.

appointments to state agencies, boards, and commissions. When Atiyeh first became governor, he looked over Bob Straub's personnel appointment forms. He remembered "in the list of questions was 'How are you registered?' and I was very offended by that. Very."[1479] Even though Atiyeh made a point to use up Straub's stationery to save money before new Atiyeh-specific gubernatorial stationery was printed ("just typed [Straub's name] out and typed my name in"), he ordered new personnel forms printed right away, just to get rid of that question. [1480]

Of all the judges Atiyeh appointed, it was the first appointment in 1982 that got all the attention. For the first time since Oregon's statehood, a woman was selected to sit on the Oregon Supreme Court. Betty Roberts had served with Atiyeh in the Senate—she a Portland liberal and he a business-owning Republican. He had served on committees with her, and he recalled "philosophical differences of opinion, but I did respect [her] very much."[1481] Atiyeh's appointment aide, Shirley Woodrow, saw that it was clear that Atiyeh wanted to appoint a woman to the Supreme Court. Woodrow observed that Atiyeh "just wanted the best person for the job," and for that particular appointment "he really wanted a woman."[1482] Roberts put some pressure on Atiyeh by announcing that she would be running for an open seat in 1982 no matter what.

On December 17, 1981, Governor Atiyeh announced that Betty Roberts was his choice to serve on the Oregon Supreme Court.[1483]

1479 Atiyeh, "Tape 7," 190.

1480 Victor Atiyeh, interviewed by Clark Hansen, "Tape 55," Oral history, recorded by Oregon Historical Society, Portland, OR, 25 August 1993. Transcript, 698, Atiyeh Collection, Pac. Univ. Archives.

1481 Victor Atiyeh, interviewed by Clark Hansen, "Tape 11," Oral history, recorded by Oregon Historical Society, Portland, OR, 28 December 1992. Transcript, 297, Atiyeh Collection, Pac. Univ. Archives.

1482 Shirley Woodrow, interviewed by Jim Moore, "Atiyeh interview," Phone interview, recorded by Jim Moore, Glenwood Springs, CO, 17 June 2015. Summary notes, 4.

1483 Janet Evenson, "Woman Is Appointed to State High Court," *Salem (OR) Statesman-Journal*, 18 December 1981; Linda Kramer, "Roberts Named to Supreme Court," *Oregonian*, 18 December 1981.

Atiyeh made it clear to reporters that "he believed the appointment of the first woman to the state Supreme Court was significant, but he said, 'The day will come, I hope, when it is not as big a deal as it is now.'"[1484] Roberts, who was plainly thrilled, "apologized for her excitement. 'I just learned about it not very many minutes ago.'"[1485] A Salem editorial a few days later, said, "It's about time" a woman served on the Oregon Supreme Court. Noting that with "Oregon voters' love affair with the Roberts name in the past, she would almost assuredly have been elected," the editorial applauded Atiyeh's choice, even though it "probably was recognition of reality by the governor."[1486] After four years on the bench, Roberts resigned from the Supreme Court in 1986. She decided it was time to take a step back from the very public life she had led for over two decades.[1487] She wrote the governor, telling him that she was "deeply grateful to you for the opportunity you gave me to serve on the court. It has been challenging and an experience to treasure," and she came to see Atiyeh in his office shortly thereafter.[1488] As one lawyer noted of Roberts, "In the relatively short span of four years on the state supreme court, she took a major role in developing an independent body of state law affecting individual rights."[1489] Susan Graber would be the next woman to serve on Oregon's Supreme Court, beginning in 1990.[1490] By 2021, five of the seven

---

1484 Kramer, "Roberts Named to Supreme Court."

1485 Evenson, "Woman Is Appointed to State High Court," 14A.

1486 *Statesman-Journal* (Salem), "Woman on the Court: It's About Time," Editorial, 19 December 1981.

1487 Betty Roberts and Gail Wells, *With Grit and By Grace: Breaking Trails in Politics and Law. A Memoir*, (Corvallis, OR: Oregon State University Press, 2008), 249–254.

1488 Betty Roberts, "Thank You," Supreme Court, State of Oregon, Handwritten letter to Vic, (10 January 1986), Atiyeh Collection, Pac. Univ. Archives; "Atiyeh Daily Index-Card Schedule, February 5, 1986," Office of the Governor, State of Oregon, (5 February 1986), Judge Betty Roberts, Atiyeh Collection, Pac. Univ. Archives.

1489 Ronald K. Collins, "Roberts Leaves Big Shoes for Gillette to Step Into," Column, *Oregonian*, 20 March 1986.

1490 *Oregon Blue Book, 1991–1992*, (Salem, OR: Oregon Secretary of State, 1991), 127.

justices were women, the Chief Justice was a woman, and of the thirteen members of the Court of Appeals, five were women.[1491]

Throughout his time as governor, Atiyeh was active in regional and national politics, both by obligation and by choice. One of the hallmarks of his 1982 re-election campaign was his direct opposition to the Reagan administration's stances on dealing with interest rates, inflation, precipitous changes to the funding of state programs from the federal government, and the perceived political tone deafness of Reagan's budget director, David Stockman. It was clear that the governor was supportive of Reagan as a fellow Republican, but he had big problems with the impact of Reagan's policies on Oregon. Since Atiyeh was the vice-chair of the Republican Governor's Association and scheduled to become chair in 1984, his hesitation to support Reagan carried some weight. In early March 1983, Atiyeh was meeting with the Republican Governors Association in Washington, D.C., and then heading back home on March 4.[1492] He planned to arrive at 3:25 and meet his granddaughter Meagan for the 6:30 ice show in Portland.[1493] But then he got an offer he could not refuse. President Reagan was in California. He offered Atiyeh a ride in Air Force One from San Francisco to Klamath Falls' Kingsley Field on March 5. The governor's schedule quickly changed.

Atiyeh's 3x5 daily schedule card (tucked in his shirt pocket) became his worksheet.[1494] He had phone numbers and contact names to confirm the departure of Air Force One, times to be ready for the presidential motorcade to drive out onto the San

---

1491 *Oregon Blue Book: Almanac and Fact Book 2021–2022*, (Salem, OR: Oregon Secretary of State, 2021), 85–87.
1492 "Atiyeh Daily Index-Card Schedule, March 1, 1983," Office of the Governor, State of Oregon, (1 March 1983), Atiyeh Collection, Pac. Univ. Archives.
1493 "Atiyeh Daily Index-Card Schedule, March 4, 1983," Office of the Governor, State of Oregon, (4 March 1983), [Handwritten by Atiyeh] Call & Confirm Air Force #1 Departure, Atiyeh Collection, Pac. Univ. Archives.
1494 "Atiyeh Daily Index-Card Schedule, March 5, 1983," Office of the Governor, State of Oregon, (5 March 1983), [Handwritten by Atiyeh] Minute by minute schedule of travel with President Reagan, San Francisco to Klamath Falls, Atiyeh Collection, Pac. Univ. Archives.

Francisco tarmac to deliver the presidential party to the plane, arrangements for Lon Holbrook to take an accompanying National Guard plane, and five-minute slots for the schedules of visiting Klamath Falls businesses and meeting with local leaders.[1495] The actual flight would only be about 50 minutes, but access to the president and his staff was priceless. At some point, Atiyeh wrote the whole schedule out on a legal pad, including the instructions to "wear Ore. pin—Calif. trooper, Officer Jack Briar, looking for pin to recognize you."[1496] At the end of the Klamath Falls visit, Atiyeh headed back to Salem in a National Guard aircraft, while Air Force One, with Oregon's Senator Mark Hatfield and U.S. Representative Denny Smith, headed back to Andrews Air Force Base just outside of Washington, D.C. Atiyeh kept the official program of the trip—complete with seating schematics of Air Force One, maps of the presidential visits, and Ronald Reagan's signature on the cover.[1497] Atiyeh recalled, "We pirated everything we got our hands on—…stationery and some matches."[1498] When he switched to the National Guard C-131 for the flight back to Salem, he kidded with the crew, saying, "Now I'm on Air Guard One." The crew made up an Air Guard One matchbook from a pack of matches from a Holiday Inn. Atiyeh treasured it.[1499]

In comparison with Atiyeh's lackluster support for Reagan in 1980—and meeting the presidential candidate among many in a reception line at the Portland airport—Atiyeh played a much

---

1495 Ronald Reagan, "Remarks and Question-and-Answer Session with Representatives of the Western Forest Products Coalition in Klamath Falls, Oregon," Ronald Reagan Presidential Archives, United States Government, (5 March 1983). http://www.reaganfoundation.org.

1496 Vic Atiyeh, "Handwritten Schedule of Atiyeh's Part in Reagan Visit," Office of the Governor, State of Oregon, (4–5 March 1983), Atiyeh Collection, Pac. Univ. Archives.

1497 "The Trip of the President to Oregon," White House, U.S. Government, Schedule signed by Ronald Reagan, (5 March 1983), Atiyeh Collection, Pac. Univ. Archives.

1498 Victor Atiyeh, interviewed by Clark Hansen, "Tape 37, side 2," Oral history, recorded by Oregon Historical Society, Portland, OR, 21 June 1993. Transcript, 198, Atiyeh Collection, Pac. Univ. Archives.

1499 Atiyeh, "Tape 37, side 2," 199.

bigger role in 1984. The highlight of the campaign was another ride on Air Force One, this time an October 22 flight from San Diego to Medford, and then Medford to Portland.[1500] And this time, Dolores came along for the ride. Atiyeh was in charge of introducing Reagan with a short speech at the Medford airport stopover, and then he rode in the presidential limousine with Reagan from the Portland Air Base to downtown Portland and rode back to the airport the next day in the limousine with the president and Senator Paul Laxalt (R-NV), Reagan's campaign chair.[1501] At an October 23 rally at the University of Portland, Atiyeh once again delivered the introductory speech. This was the election in which Reagan's age was something of an issue. Just two days before, in Kansas City, Reagan, with tongue planted firmly in cheek, said in a debate with Walter Mondale that he would not make an issue of his "opponent's youth and inexperience."[1502] Atiyeh's introduction ended with, "Ladies and gentlemen, I am proud to present to you the man who restored our faith in ourselves—a mature and experienced President of the United States, Ronald Reagan."[1503] After Reagan's election in November, Atiyeh explained that "his position had shifted from a desire that Carter not be re-elected to active and strong support for Reagan. He said he became more comfortable with Reagan the more that he was around him, and that George Bush's vice-presidential candidacy made the job of supporting Reagan 'very easy.'"[1504]

1500 "Atiyeh Daily Index-Card Schedule, October 22, 1984," Office of the Governor, State of Oregon, (22 October 1984), Atiyeh Collection, Pac. Univ. Archives; "Atiyeh Daily Index-Card Schedule, October 22, 1984, updated," Office of the Governor, State of Oregon, (22 October 1984), Atiyeh Collection, Pac. Univ. Archives; Ronald Reagan, "Remarks at a Reagan-Bush Rally in Medford, Oregon," Ronald Reagan Presidential Archives, United States Government, (22 October 1984). http://www.reaganfoundation.org.
1501 "Atiyeh Daily Index-Card Schedule, October 23, 1984," Office of the Governor, State of Oregon, (23 October 1984), Atiyeh Collection, Pac. Univ. Archives.
1502 Hedrick Smith, "Aftermath of Debate," *New York Times*, 24 October 1984.
1503 "Atiyeh Daily Index Card, Oct 23, 1984," Introduction.
1504 Jim Hill, "Atiyeh Pleased at Outcome," *Oregonian*, 5 November 1980.

Atiyeh found Bush to be somebody he could work with, " a very down-to-earth kind of guy."[1505] When Atiyeh was in D.C., Bush would meet with him in private.[1506] Atiyeh found him "less reserved than Ronald Reagan, much less reserved, and I'm more comfortable around people like that, just personality-wise, forget philosophy."[1507] Gerry Thompson was of the opinion that the only reason Atiyeh was able to even get in the door of the White House was because of George Bush: "We were treated well at the White House. But with Ronald Reagan, if we had not had Bush, I don't think we would've ever been in there. Bush opened the door, and we spent a lot of time in Bush's office. But never with Ronald Reagan."[1508]

At the 1984 Republican National Convention, Atiyeh had three roles: chair of the Republican National Governors Association, floor leader, and Oregon delegate. Atiyeh's role at the convention certainly did not compare to his positions on the platform committee in the 1960s and 1970s, nor to his central role in delivering the nomination to Gerald Ford in 1976. The Republican who had been characterized as a moderate in the 1960s, tagged as a conservative in the 1970s, and then seen the party shift right with the rise of Reagan, was described as coming "home to mainstream Republican Party politics Tuesday morning at the Republican National Convention, surprising some who thought he had strayed."[1509] The 1984 convention was a celebration of Reagan conservatism. Even Barry Goldwater made a featured appearance. When asked about the "strongly conservative Republican platform," Atiyeh said it "did not bother

---

1505 Victor Atiyeh, interviewed by Clark Hansen, "Tape 31," Oral history, recorded by Oregon Historical Society, Portland, OR, 3 June 1993. Transcript, 36, Atiyeh Collection, Pac. Univ. Archives.

1506 "Atiyeh Daily Index-Card Schedule, December 10, 1985," Office of the Governor, State of Oregon, (10 December 1985), Breakfast with Vice Pres. Bush…(Gov. only), Atiyeh Collection, Pac. Univ. Archives.

1507 Atiyeh, "Tape 31," 36–37.

1508 Thompson, "Atiyeh Interview #4," 9–10.

1509 Foster Church, "Atiyeh Praises Reagan, Blasts Demos," *Oregonian*, 22 August 1984.

him. He denied that the convention as a whole had a conservative tone."[1510] Atiyeh's Republican identity was secure, but the party was transforming, and he seemed to be on the losing side of national changes in the ideology and goals of Ronald Reagan's Republican America.

Atiyeh had been an active member of three governors associations, attending his first meetings when he was governor-elect. The National Governors Association (NGA), the Republican Governors Association (RGA), and the Western Governors' Association (WGA) played different roles in his political life. The NGA was Atiyeh's least favorite. As Atiyeh put it, "There's so many meetings in my life, …what's the use of all these things?"[1511] He found lots of passive listening was involved, and those who were speaking "were posturing. …Not an awful lot comes of it." Atiyeh noted that the NGA meetings were generally nonpartisan, so the posturing was just one of the "pitfalls of all these big shot governors with their own egos."[1512]

In the middle of Atiyeh's two terms, the NGA did something he found useful—it explored how government could be more efficient in the face of the cutbacks from the Reagan administration and the recession. "Governors sent their stuff, and it was all published. …That's the kind of thing, incidentally, that I would go for, instead of all this cosmetic stuff that was going on."[1513] Atiyeh recalled that Oregon got three or four good ideas into the final product—the benefit of having to cut programs and balance budgets from 1980 to 1983. Reagan's Director of Budget and Management, Jim Miller (who succeeded David Stockman), "he took some of those things pretty seriously."[1514] As a governor, "that's the best you can do" to influence the president's budgeting

---

1510 Church, "Atiyeh Praises Reagan, Blasts Demos."
1511 Atiyeh, "Tape 30," 19.
1512 Atiyeh, "Tape 33, side 1," 83; for a litany of reasons why Atiyeh thought NGA meetings were a waste, see Atiyeh, "Tape 55," 707.
1513 Atiyeh, "Tape 30," 19.
1514 Victor Atiyeh, interviewed by Clark Hansen, "Tape 54," Oral history, recorded by Oregon Historical Society, Portland, OR, 18 August 1993. Transcript, 677, Atiyeh Collection, Pac. Univ. Archives.

policies. Atiyeh talked with President Reagan in February 1986 about federal spending, but "talking to the President about something like that is not the way to accomplish anything." Atiyeh knew that Reagan was not going to "call up the Office of Management and Budget to say, 'Vic was just here, and he wants me to cut here, and go do it.'"[1515]

It was, however, through the NGA that Atiyeh made crucial connections with cabinet officers who were important to Oregon. Just a month after Ronald Reagan took office, Atiyeh was at a February 1981 NGA meeting at which he talked with the new Secretary of the Interior James Watt.[1516] It was because of opportunities for personal connections that Atiyeh attended all the D.C. NGA meetings. "That was a big deal. You get to go to the White House. That was a big deal for me."[1517] At the Washington, D.C., NGA meeting there was always a dinner at the White House. Atiyeh always enjoyed the dinners and meeting cabinet officers and ambassadors. One of the few useful parts of the NGA, from Atiyeh's point of view, aside from gaining access to key federal government players, was his membership on the Committee of International Trade and Foreign Relations.[1518] It was under these auspices that Atiyeh led a small group of governors to Japan in 1986, playing to his strength in making connections between the United States' and Japan's economic players and governing officials.[1519]

The governors organization closest to his political heart was the Western Governors Association. Membership was not just the western states (a line from North Dakota to Texas and all states to the west), but included the American territories of Guam,

---

1515 Atiyeh, "Tape 54," 676.
1516 Atiyeh, "Tape 33, side 1," 80–81.
1517 Atiyeh, "Tape 54," 692.
1518 Atiyeh, "Tape 55," 708.
1519 "National Governors Association Delegation Itinerary," Liberal Democratic Party, (27 September 1986), Atiyeh Collection, Pac. Univ. Archives; Vic Atiyeh, "Columns about Oregon's International Trade," Office of the Governor, State of Oregon, (1984–86), Press release, Sept. 11, 1986, Atiyeh Collection, Pac. Univ. Archives.

Northern Mariana Islands, and American Samoa. The governors talked about water rights, federal timberland, and wilderness designations. At both the WGA and the Republican Governors Association, what Atiyeh liked best were the sessions at which only the governors were present. That never happened at NGA meetings. Atiyeh just wanted to be able to "talk to my fellow governors," to be able to ask, "What are you doing?" in the face of all the common issues governors faced. Atiyeh's call for more group meetings of governors-only was a way to reduce the power relationships that are often magnified when staffers are present and get to the commonalities of holding this particular office.

Atiyeh also played a role as one of the faces of the National Rifle Association (NRA). He appeared in magazine advertisements in the "I'm the NRA" campaign by the gun-owners' interest group.[1520] Atiyeh said, "[T]he ad of course was the way I feel." He described it as a "campaign by the [NRA] that said, 'Hey, all these [gun owners] aren't crazies, you know. There's some pretty good people here.'"[1521] Atiyeh's membership in the NRA was the norm for many Oregon politicians up until the 1990s. Democrat or Republican, they pretty much all had their NRA cards. It was only as the NRA began to advocate for gun policies beyond those that guaranteed sportspeople the right to use guns and for citizens to reasonably protect themselves that the NRA became mainly the province of Republicans. Famously, Atiyeh's political friend George Herbert Walker Bush resigned from the NRA in May 1995 after the executive vice president of the organization "attack[ed]...federal agents as 'jack-booted thugs,'... a vicious slander on good people."[1522] Atiyeh kept his

---

[1520] "'I'm the NRA': NRA Advertisement Featuring Atiyeh, a Member," Advertisement, *Smithsonian*, April 1984, Atiyeh collection, Pac. Univ. Archives; "Monthly Diary Schedule, May 1982," Office of the Governor, State of Oregon, (1982), Photo Session: National Rifle Association, 5/15, Atiyeh Collection, Pac. Univ. Archives.

[1521] Victor Atiyeh, interviewed by Clark Hansen, "Tape 35," Oral history, recorded by Oregon Historical Society, Portland, OR, 15 June 1993. Transcript, 146, Atiyeh Collection, Pac. Univ. Archives.

[1522] George Bush, "Letter of Resignation Sent by Bush to Rifle Association," Transcript, *New York Times*, 11 May 1995, http://www.nytimes.com; Jon Meacham,

membership until his death. But he was very aware that the nra's message was shifting over time.

The governor addressed the organization at its national meetings in 1983, highlighting three "great traditions of the nra…: *history*, *service*, and an *unshakeable* commitment to *basic principles*."[1523] The history was precisely what excited Atiyeh about gun collecting, being able to possess and use an object that could "*transport our imagination* to the wellspring of our beginning—to the *brilliant* reasoning that led to our form of government."[1524]

Atiyeh found that from his position as governor he could be an important voice in the national conversation about guns. His attitude was that the gun culture was like Prohibition, "there's going to be an underground. If somebody wants a gun, they're going to get a gun." He explained, "I'm not a purist in terms of the NRA; …all the things that they oppose I don't necessarily oppose, and I think sometimes they go a little bit too far. But, basically, I think they're really on the right side."[1525]

Atiyeh's his biggest role in the gun world, however, was not being a governor and an NRA member, it was attending gun shows back in Oregon on many of his free weekends. If there was a gun show within a hundred miles of Salem, the governor would be there.

Another national role for Atiyeh was as one of the vanguard of Arab Americans elected to office. He was a regular at Arab embassies when he was back in D.C., and in February 1983 he attended a reception of the National Association of Arab

---

Destiny and Power: The American Odyssey of George Herbert Walker Bush, (New York: Random House, 2015), 544.

1523 Vic Atiyeh, "Speech" (speech, National Rifle Association, 1983 Annual Meeting, Phoenix Hilton Hotel, Phoenix, AZ, 8 May 1983), 1, Atiyeh Collection, Pac. Univ. Archives. Italics underlined by hand by Atiyeh; "Atiyeh Daily Index-Card Schedule, May 8, 1983," Office of the Governor, State of Oregon, (8 May 1983), Keynote Speech: NRA Members' Banquet, Atiyeh Collection, Pac. Univ. Archives.

1524 Atiyeh, "NRA Speech, 1983," 3. Italics underlined by hand by Atiyeh.

1525 Atiyeh, "Tape 64," 40.

Americans Board of Directors.[1526] By 1984 he and New Hampshire's Governor John Sununu (R), elected in 1982, were joined by two U.S. senators and three members of the House.[1527] From this group, Sununu would serve as chief of staff to President George H.W. Bush and Senator George Mitchell (D-ME) would serve as Senate Majority Leader and lead negotiator in ending the conflicts in Northern Ireland. All of the elected Arab Americans at the time had at least one Lebanese parent or grandparent, with some Palestinians and Syrians in the mix. Echoing the experience of Atiyeh's father, the diehard Republican, "the majority of Arabs are said to support the Republican party" with drives to register Arab Americans in Dearborn, Michigan, and that first stop in America for all Atiyehs, Allentown, Pennsylvania.[1528] In 1985 Atiyeh and Sununu were honored at a banquet in Washington, D.C. as the trailblazers among elected Arab Americans.[1529]

The Limitations of Home Life

Vic and Dolores Atiyeh lived on Winter Street in Salem during the eight years of Atiyeh's time in office in the same house Tom and Audrey McCall rented from the state when he was governor. It was a bit of a trial for both of them. When they moved in, Atiyeh described the place as "pretty badly run down" with needed fixes and painting to make it presentable.[1530] Atiyeh recalled that Oregonians' perceptions were that he, as governor, would have a mansion and a household staff. The reality was, "I

1526 "Atiyeh Daily Index-Card Schedule, February 26, 1983," Office of the Governor, State of Oregon, (26 February 1983), [Handwritten by staff] Reception of Nat. Assn. of Arab Americans Bd. of Directors and Arab Ambassadors, D.C., Atiyeh Collection, Pac. Univ. Archives.

1527 New York Times, "Arab-Americans Take an Increased Political Role," 4 November 1984.

1528 New York Times, "Arab-Americans Take an Increased Political Role."

1529 "Atiyeh Daily Index-Card Schedule, February 25, 1985," Office of the Governor, State of Oregon, (25 February 1985), NAAA Banquet honoring Govs. Atiyeh & Sununu, Atiyeh Collection, Pac. Univ. Archives.

1530 Victor Atiyeh, interviewed by Clark Hansen, "Tape 25," Oral history, recorded by Oregon Historical Society, Portland, OR, 12 May 1993. Transcript, 714, Atiyeh Collection, Pac. Univ. Archives.

had nothing. I rented from the state, we brought our own furniture down, our own silver down, our own dishes down, and Dolores did the cooking."[1531]

The home was not large, so entertaining the legislature (e.g., at open houses) required shifts.[1532] Dolores Atiyeh did all the work for these events, with one helper—often the teenage child of a friend—in the back while Dolores put out all the food and then acted as the hostess for the visitors.[1533] For big occasions, the food would be catered, but it was Dolores who set everything up. Atiyeh remembered that Dolores made cookies for many a gathering. He thought "she was very good at it, very good. ...She did it quietly, and went ahead and did it," but it "was tough work."[1534] Norm Smith (R-Tigard), who began his years in the House as Atiyeh became governor, remembered the legislators being invited over to the governor's residence. Dolores greeted everybody at the door. The governor would be inside "holding court." Smith asked Dolores if the new carpeting was from Atiyeh Brothers. She quickly responded, "Oh, heavens no. The state of Oregon can't afford that."[1535]

The legislature provided a $1,000 a month living allowance as a supplement to the governor's salary. This number had been set in the McCall years and never adjusted for inflation. It was cut back to $500 a month by 1982.[1536] Renting the house from the state was fine, but the rent was raised at least twice while he was

---

1531 Victor Atiyeh, interviewed by Clark Hansen, "Tape 60," Oral history, recorded by Oregon Historical Society, Portland, OR, 10 September 1993. Transcript, 80, Atiyeh Collection, Pac. Univ. Archives.

1532 Denny Miles, "Atiyeh interview #3," Forest Grove, OR, 5 April 2016. Summary notes, 28.

1533 Thompson, "Atiyeh interview #1," 17.

1534 Victor Atiyeh, interviewed by Clark Hansen, "Tape 26," Oral history, recorded by Oregon Historical Society, Portland, OR, 20 May 1993. Transcript, 741, Atiyeh Collection, Pac. Univ. Archives.

1535 Norm Smith, interviewed by Jim Moore, "Atiyeh interview," Roseburg, OR, 28 April 2015. Summary notes, 2.

1536 Sue Hill, "Oregon Governor Ranks 65th on State's Payroll," *Salem (OR) Statesman-Journal*, 4 July 1982, 6A, Atiyeh Collection, Pac. Univ. Archives.

there—as he and other state workers were taking pay cuts—and major issues with the house continued.[1537]

Gerry Thompson created a folder for "Project Pad," the ideas and negotiations to create an official governor's residence in Salem. The first letter in it, from December 1981, came from newly ex–executive assistant Lee Johnson about such a place. However, the person who talked with Atiyeh about the idea had "the impression you are not overly enthusiastic about the project," and Johnson pointed out "that some of the [1982 re-election] campaign people believe it would be a political liability" to push for something like an executive mansion.[1538] In 1983, discussion got more serious with talk of a grant from the Georgia-Pacific Foundation to pay for one-third of the cost of a Governor's mansion, up to $1 million, as long as "a significant amount of Oregon produced forest products [are used] in both the external and internal design."[1539] The G-P proposal involved not using any taxpayer money at all, but the creation of a foundation to solicit funds for the project.[1540] State Senator Bill McCoy (D-Portland) submitted a bill to authorize the construction of an executive residence.[1541] Atiyeh supported the McCoy bill, saying that while he would not personally benefit from the future residence, "It's important for the prestige of the state that there be a governor's residence." It did not have "to be an ostentatious 'mansion' like some other states provide for their governors, but simply a home that befits the office of governor."[1542]

1537 Miles, "Atiyeh interview #1," 11.

1538 "Project Pad: Documents Relating to Governor's Residence Proposals," Office of the Governor, State of Oregon, (1981–85), Letter from Lee Johnson to Governor Victor Atiyeh, December 1, 1981 Atiyeh Collection, Pac. Univ. Archives.

1539 "Project Pad," Letter from Bob Floweree, G-P Chair and CEO to Vic, February 1, 1983.

1540 "Project Pad," Letter from Robert E. Floweree to Governor Victor Atiyeh, April 28, 1983.

1541 "Project Pad," Senate Bill 604, 1983 Regular Session.

1542 "House Votes to Block Further Dam Construction," Legislative Notebook column, *Oregonian*, 20 May 1983; Victor Atiyeh, interviewed by Clark Hansen, "Tape 40, side 1," Oral history, recorded by Oregon Historical Society, Portland, OR, 23 June 1993. Transcript, 268–269, Atiyeh Collection, Pac. Univ. Archives.

By October 1983 there were various moves to sell a home in Salem to the state for use as the Governor's Official Residence and other groups got into the "design a home for the governor" game.[1543] In January 1984 Atiyeh held a flurry of meetings about the project.[1544] The same conversation was going on fifteen months later.[1545] Jon Yunker from the Executive Department felt that Atiyeh was working toward the creation of an executive residence because there was the assumption that Republican Attorney General Dave Frohnmayer would move in at some point as governor.[1546] Frohnmayer would miss out on that chance when he was defeated in 1990 by Barbara Roberts. By the end of Atiyeh's time in office, the project had not moved anywhere.

During the Goldschmidt administration, all the moving parts quickly came together and Mahonia Hall became the governor's official residence. It was the same house that been offered in 1983 —and in the 1950s.[1547] Goldschmidt and his family moved in at the beginning of December 1987, eleven months after he had taken office.[1548] On April 1, 1988, a committee of former governors Hatfield, Straub, and Atiyeh selected the name Mahonia Hall for the new residence from among submissions from school kids across the state in a contest that elicited almost

---

1543 "Project Pad," Letter from Trey Anderson, McKay High School Teacher, and students, to Honorable Victor Atiyeh, October 4, 1983; Memo from Gerry Thompson to Governor, "Project Pad," October 11, 1983.

1544 "Atiyeh Daily Index-Card Schedule, January 24, 1984," Office of the Governor, State of Oregon, (24 January 1984), Gerry Frank, regarding Project PAD (at your request), Atiyeh Collection, Pac. Univ. Archives; "Atiyeh Daily Index-Card Schedule, January 26, 1984," Office of the Governor, State of Oregon, (26 January 1984), 11 AM Norma Paulus, regarding Project PAD; 2 PM Tom Vaughan, regarding Project PAD; 3 PM Sen. Day, regarding Project PAD; 4 PM Warne Nunn, regarding Project PAD, Atiyeh Collection, Pac. Univ. Archives.

1545 "Project Pad," Confidential memo from Bob Oliver to Dolores Atiyeh, "Project Pad," April 15, 1985.

1546 Yunker, "Atiyeh interview," 5.

1547 Michele Matassa, "Leaders Choose Governor's Home," *Salem (OR) Statesman-Journal*, 11 August 1987; Ron Blankenbaker, "Governor Has Air Farce: Goldschmidt's Free Flights," Column, *Salem (OR) Statesman-Journal*, 1 March 1988.

1548 Alan Gustafson, "Governor Moves into Salem Mansion," *Salem (OR) Statesman-Journal*, 7 December 1987.

1400 entries. The winning middle schooler pointed out that Mahonia was "part of the Latin name of the Oregon grape, which is the state's flower."[1549]

For all its limitations, the Winter Street house was home from January 1979 to January 1987. When the governor was ill, it was there that he would convalesce. In 1985, that convalescence took on a bigger, but secret, meaning. On January 14 of that year, Governor Atiyeh gave his final address to the opening of a legislative session.[1550] Unbeknownst to anybody except his wife, his closest staff, and new Secretary of State Barbara Roberts, Atiyeh had spent the night before in a hospital. What only his wife and aides knew was that he was being treated for what most of his staff thought was an assassination attempt by the Rajneeshees.

[1549] Michele Matassa, "Governor's Mansion Gets Name," *Salem (OR) Statesman-Journal*, 2 April 1988.

[1550] "Joint Sesssion: The Sixty-Third Legislative Assembly of Oregon," Legislature, State of Oregon, Program, (14 January 1985), Atiyeh Collection, Pac. Univ. Archives.

7 Coping with Rajneeshees

One of Atiyeh's greatest challenges came in the form of an infamous sect that played an outsize role in Oregon history.

From August 1981 to November 1985 the Rajneeshees would challenge state laws on elections, land-use, and education and undertake many criminal activities though the court cases would last for years after the main players had left the state. The governor's focus on pressuring local governments to implement Oregon's land-use laws would turn out to play a crucial role that nobody could have foreseen.

This chapter is a sweep through the four-year Rajneeshee story from Atiyeh's point of view. He was always in charge, always informed, and always working closely with chief of staff Gerry Thompson, the governor's direct deputy for this episode. At the governor's direction, all Rajneeshee matters channeled through either Atiyeh or Thompson. The backbone of this account is interviews and documents from both main players.

In January 2014 Atiyeh was clear that the Rajneeshees were one of the two major challenges of his time as governor. "It was a tough time," he said. "I didn't need a recession and the Bhagwan all at the same time."

1981—Land-Use Challenges

On July 10, 1981, the purchase of the 64,000-acre Big Muddy Ranch, a few miles outside the town of Antelope in central Oregon, population 40, was announced. The new owners disclosed that they would employ around fifty workers in a new farming community. The buyers were Rajneeshees, followers of Bhagwan Mohan Shree Rajneesh, an Indian religious leader relocating to the United States.[1551]

The Rajneesh were led by the Bhagwan Shree Rajneesh, but the face and voice of the group was his chief deputy, Ma Anand Sheela. Known as Sheela, her strong personality and ability to step forward when the media was near made her the group's main player in the minds of outsiders.

The location turned out to be rather ideal; the ranch was isolated, the eventual layout of the town of Rajneeshpuram was constructed in such a way that the Bhagwan could spend time by himself in meditation, and the community could control access to the town itself.[1552] Ironically, the ranch was not well suited to agriculture. It was "on land that had been overused so much that it did not have enough nutrients in the soil to grow [crops] and not enough natural vegetation to make cattle ranching profitable."[1553] The Rajneeshees announced that they would form a small farming community, nonetheless. Unknowingly, the Rajneeshees' plan put them right in the middle of Oregon's land-use laws designed to protect agricultural land and guide the growth of all cities and towns in the state.

Compared to India, the United States offered a freedom that the Rajneeshees hoped would protect the group from government

---

[1551] Bill Driver and Ariana Boffey, "Chronology of the Rajneesh Cult," in *The Rajneesh Chronicles: The True Story of the Cult That Unleashed the First Act of Bioterrorism on U.S. Soil*, ed. Win McCormack, (Portland, OR: Tin House Books, 2010), 13; Gerry Thompson, "Rajneesh Timeline, 1981–1986 Governor and Staff Involvement," Office of the Governor, State of Oregon, (2006), July 10, 1981, Atiyeh Collection, Pac. Univ. Archives.

[1552] Scotta Callister, James Long and Leslie L. Zaitz, "Sheela's Brother Figures in Acquisition of Ranch," For Love and Money series, *Oregonian*, 6 July 1985, A9.

[1553] Thompson, "Rajneesh Timeline, 1981–1986," July 10, 1981.

interference.[1554] As the situation developed, Governor Atiyeh felt very strongly that the Rajneeshees considered themselves a religion. Atiyeh received many letters from Oregonians about the Rajneeshees, dating from these first months. He responded to all of them, telling the letter writers to try to be tolerant. He replied to one letter, "Regardless of the religious beliefs or practices of this group, they are entitled to every right afforded under our Constitution."[1555] He saw it as his job as governor to ensure that the processes of the state were fairly applied to everybody. The governor and his staff felt they "had to carefully follow the law so they wouldn't be charged with violating [the Rajneeshees'] ... civil rights."[1556]

In August 1981, the new owners received permission from the Wasco County government to locate fifty-four mobile homes on the property. Each one would hold fourteen people, many more people than the original fifty proposed farmers.[1557] What had initially been proposed as a farm began to look like it would be a town that needed to plan for its future according to land-use laws. This raised concerns with 1000 Friends of Oregon, the watchdog group formed to defend Oregon's statewide land-use laws.[1558] 1000 Friends used Oregon's land-use laws to challenge Wasco County's permission to develop land at the Big Muddy.

It was during the fall of 1981 that the Rajneeshees first came to the attention of Governor Atiyeh's office. At one of the weekly staff meetings, Bob Montgomery, the governor's staffer in charge of working with local governments, said, "By the way, a bunch of foreigners from India are making plans to settle at the Big Muddy

---

1554 Callister, Long and Zaitz, "Crowding, Hostility," A7.

1555 Les Zaitz, "Thwarted Rajneeshee Leaders Attack Enemies, Neighbors with Poison," Part 2 of 5, *Portland OregonLive*, 14 April 2011, http://www.oregonlive.com.

1556 Bob Oliver, interviewed by Jim Moore, "Atiyeh interview," Salem, OR, 24 August 2015. Summary notes, 4.

1557 Scotta Callister, James Long and Leslie L. Zaitz, "Rajneeshees Falter in Face of Opposition," For Love and Money series, *Oregonian*, 30 June 1985, A11; Driver and Boffey, "Rajneesh Chronology," 13; Thompson, "Rajneesh Timeline, 1981–1986," August 1981.

1558 Driver and Boffey, "Rajneesh Chronology," 13.

ranch."[1559] There was kind of a collective shrug among those at the meeting. Notes from a November 27 cabinet meeting indicate that the governor brought up "Antelope" and that Pat Amedeo, the governor's natural resources aide, should investigate the issue.[1560] At this early stage, the land-use issue was the top concern with the Rajneeshees.

The nearest town to the ranch, Antelope, was within its own urban growth boundary (UGB) area, so there could be a variety of developments within the town that could not take place on the Big Muddy Ranch, which was outside the UGB.[1561] By October 1981 the Rajneeshees had purchased "several properties in Antelope to use for extra housing and had asked the city council for a permit to build a printing plant and an office complex large enough for a hundred workers."[1562] Several Rajneeshee adherents moved into Antelope to work in the new businesses. In effect, this move into Antelope was forced by 1000 Friends of Oregon and that group's arguments about what could and could not be built on the Big Muddy.[1563]

At the same time, the Rajneeshees decided that the ranch itself should be incorporated as a city, thus allowing the kind of development they envisioned. In early November 1981 the Wasco County government approved the plan for an incorporation election to take place in May 1982. The new city of Rajneeshpuram was duly created after a decisive win on May 18,

---

1559 Oliver, "Atiyeh interview," 6.
1560 Gerry Thompson, "Handwritten Notes, Sep–Nov 1981, Apr–May 1982," Office of the Governor, State of Oregon, (24 September–25 November, 13 April–28 May 1981–1982), 75, Atiyeh Collection, Pac. Univ. Archives; Gerry Thompson, "Daily Reports to the Governor," Office of the Governor, State of Oregon, (November 1981), Atiyeh Collection, Pac. Univ. Archives
1561 Antelope was about 20 miles from the ranch, but it could easily take an hour or more to make the trip across some very rough dirt roads.
1562 Frances FitzGerald, "Rajneeshpuram II," A Reporter at Large, *New Yorker*, 29 September 1986, 83, http://archives.newyorker.com.
1563 FitzGerald, "Rajneeshpuram II," 83.

1982.[1564] Its mayor was Krishna Deva, known to one and all as KD, formerly David Knapp from California.

Bob Davis, an old associate of the governor's legal assistant Bob Oliver, had been hired as the Rajneeshees' lobbyist. "The Bobs" had worked together in Governor Tom McCall's office. Davis invited the governor to a meeting at a restaurant in Salem to hear the plans the Rajneeshees had for their new land in the desert. The governor, "of course, was too busy to come."[1565] Bob Oliver went in his place, meeting Ma Anand Sheela and Prem Jayananda, Sheela's husband. Oliver heard about plans, saw a slide show, and was asked to convey the group's intentions to the governor. Oliver found the Rajneeshees were pleasant enough to deal with in person, "almost ingratiating, [but] the whole thing had a funny smell."[1566]

1982—Communities Collide

David Sarasohn, then a reporter and editorial writer for the *Oregonian*, remembered that the Rajneeshees initially appeared as an offbeat group. The Rajneeshees were outsiders whose adherents dressed in shades of red and led very different lives from most Oregonians, but they were "generally cheerful and not dangerous."[1567] And they came to a rural area and put a lot of money into it, something that resounded in an Oregon reeling from the recession. All this was an interesting story for journalists. Well-educated and affluent people from all over the

---

1564 Bob Oliver, "Rajneeshpuram, May 19," Office of the Governor, State of Oregon, Memo to Governor Atiyeh, (19 May 1982), Atiyeh Collection, Pac. Univ. Archives; Scotta Callister, James Long and Leslie L. Zaitz, "Guru's Orange City Opens Door to Development," For Love and Money series, *Oregonian*, 8 July 1985, A1.

1565 Oliver, "Atiyeh interview," 6. The "too busy to attend" spiel was what Oliver used when he talked to most groups. It could either mean that Atiyeh's schedule was full or that Atiyeh did not want to talk with the group. Or both. In the case of the Rajneeshees, the governor did not want to talk to the group.

1566 Oliver, "Atiyeh interview," 6.

1567 David Sarasohn, interviewed by Jim Moore, "Atiyeh interview," Portland, OR, 17 February 2015. Summary notes, 3.

world streamed to the Big Muddy ranch and began to change the way things worked in nearby Antelope.

Thompson recalled that Atiyeh "really put stress on [the State Police]." He told them, "We've really got to have ears to the ground" on what was going on out at the ranch. He told them to try to get inside the ranch. And the state police did.[1568]

Thompson stressed that the state police were central to the governor's plans and actions dealing with the Rajneeshees over the next years. "The state police didn't get a lot of credit," she remembered, but "I've got to tell you that they were our soul through the whole thing. ...They were solid as a rock. ...They were more solid for us than anybody was."[1569] There would be conflicts with other state and federal agencies, but the governor continued to rely on the state police as his number-one agency the entire time.

Statewide elected officials—governor, attorney general, secretary of state, superintendent of public instruction—were getting letters and phone calls about the Rajneeshees.[1570] The Rajneeshees wanted copies of those letters. A decision was made to block out the names and addresses of the correspondents. Copies were made and the Rajneeshees were charged for them.

1568 Gerry Thompson, interviewed by Jim Moore, "Atiyeh Interview #3," Salem, OR, 19 January 2016. Summary notes, 14.

1569 Gerry Thompson, interviewed by Jim Moore, "Atiyeh Interview #5," Salem, OR, 8 August 2017. Summary notes, 2.

1570 Glenna Hayden, "Conversation with Barbara Bailey, Wasco County Planning Commission," Office of the Governor, State of Oregon, Memo to Governor, (17 March 1982), Atiyeh Collection, Pac. Univ. Archives; Victor Atiyeh, Citizens for God and Country letter and Governor response to Anne Neamon, "Support Constitution," 11 March 1983, Atiyeh Collection, Pac. Univ. Archives; There was no gubernatorial response to the racist notes, Laura Bentley, Racist Threat Letter to Oregon Governor's Office, "Concerned Oregonians of Wasco County," 25 September 1984, Atiyeh Collection, Pac. Univ. Archives; Susan P. Graber, Letter to Oregon Governor to Victor Atiyeh, "Impressed," 22 October 1984, Atiyeh Collection, Pac. Univ. Archives; Victor Atiyeh, Office of the Governor letter to Patricia I. Dela, "Legal Power," 25 October 1984, Atiyeh Collection, Pac. Univ. Archives; Victor Atiyeh, Office of the Governor letter and response to Ron Brown, "Avoiding Intemperate Actions," 25 October 1984, Atiyeh Collection, Pac. Univ. Archives.

There was a feeling that if the Rajneeshees had forced the issue then the names of the letter writers would have to be disclosed.[1571]

Very quickly the governor's office learned, through State Police intelligence resources, that there were a lot of sincere believers among the sannyasins at Rajneeshpuram. At the same time people in Antelope who were worried about the influx of newcomers were calling the governor's office. Atiyeh's security officer, Lon Holbrook, would get a lot of these calls.[1572] He remembered, "They didn't have anybody to talk to. They were desperately looking for help." He emphasized to the callers that the governor was working very hard on the issues, but there were no more details than that.

By early 1982 the governor was giving definite direction to state employees.[1573] Agency heads were instructed to treat Rajneeshees like any other citizens; they were to "[a]pply laws in [a] fair manner [and] monitor and report…concerns" to Gerry Thompson.[1574]

Atiyeh's designated representatives in dealing with the group were Bob Oliver, the governor's legal assistant, and Gerry Thompson, his chief of staff.[1575] Thompson was given the leadership role. It was her job to "coordinate all reporting and activities regarding the Rajneeshees from the state level."[1576] Competence and confidentiality would be paramount: "Most of which had to be done quietly, not publicly."[1577]

[1571] Verne Duncan, interviewed by Jim Moore, "Atiyeh interview," Milwaukie, OR, 12 August 2014. Summary notes, 5.

[1572] Lon Holbrook, interviewed by Jim Moore, "Atiyeh interview," Gladstone, OR, 6 June 2017. Summary notes, 11.

[1573] Gerry Thompson, "Chronology of Rajneeshees to November 1984," Office of the Governor, State of Oregon, (1984), Atiyeh Collection, Pac. Univ. Archives.

[1574] Thompson, "Chronology of Rajneeshees to November 1984."

[1575] Oliver, "Atiyeh interview," 5.

[1576] Thompson, "Rajneesh Timeline, 1981–1986," 1982.

[1577] Thompson, "Atiyeh Interview #3," 1.

Atiyeh's management style "was always based on complete trust in those who worked for him, delegation with result tracking, and management according to his principles."[1578]

> The Governor was very much involved every step of the way, but in keeping with his belief, he never wanted direct involvement with any Rajneeshee—Bhagwan, Sheela or whoever. He correctly believed they wanted his attention, and the minute he gave [it] to them they would use it for supposed power on their behalf....

He was the ultimate decision maker and negotiator by proxy.[1579]

The Rajneeshees quickly became a subject at the weekly meetings with state agency directors. These meetings sometimes got intense. "That was a zoo for a while," Jon Yunker, Deputy Director of the Executive Department, remembered. It seemed to Yunker that nobody knew how to deal with the Rajneeshees at the beginning.[1580]

The Rajneeshees were being covered in the local and national media as a group with new ideas working to make the Oregon desert bloom. Oliver warned that this could fuel a public relations issue. During a March 1982 interview on a Redmond radio station, Atiyeh expressed his personal opinion that the Rajneeshees should leave. He explained his stance by saying, "I'm provincial. I admit it. I was born and raised in Oregon, and, of course, my loyalty is to Oregonians."[1581] The son of Syrian immigrants had to do some explaining that he was not against the Rajneeshees because of their status as "not truly residents of the state. 'If that is the way it was read, I am sorry. Oregonians are made up of people from all over the world. My sympathies are

---

1578 Gerry Thompson, Email to Jim Moore, "Our Last Meeting," 21 January 2016.
1579 Thompson to Moore, 21 January 2016.
1580 Jon Yunker, interviewed by Jim Moore, "Atiyeh interview," Salem, OR, 22 June 2015. Summary notes, 8, Atiyeh project, Moore collection.
1581 Foster Church, "Atiyeh Picks Antelopers Over Interlopers," *Oregonian*, 13 March 1982.

with those residents who are concerned with Rajneesh. They are concerned with a tidal wave of people into a community that has been quiet and peaceful for many years.'"[1582] A letter from a Houston petroleum executive caught Oliver's eye. The executive wrote to the governor,

> I was shocked to read the inflammatory statements attributed to you concerning the Rajneesh development near Antelope. These statements are the kind I would expect from the Grand Dragon of the Ku Klux Klan, not the Governor of one of our United States. ...The Governor of a state must not promote bigotry and intolerance nor may he use his office to determine who lives in his state based on his perception of their philosophy, religion or culture.[1583]

Oliver noted that "several letters such as this have come in in recent weeks from individuals and firms who have had business with the Bhagwan's followers. They are troublesome."[1584] Oliver feared a wave of national public opinion could inflame the situation in Oregon.

1000 Friends of Oregon's land-use challenge to Rajneeshpuram was working its way through the system in the spring of 1982, but the leadership of the nonprofit thought they found a shortcut to invalidate Wasco County's decisions. The group discovered that a Wasco County commissioner (they are titled as judges), Rick Cantrell, one of the officials who had approved the incorporation vote for the Big Muddy ranch to become Rajneeshpuram, had also entered into a September 1981 deal to sell cattle to the Rajneeshees. The group demanded that

---

1582 Church, "Atiyeh Picks Antelopers Over Interlopers."
1583 A. W. Dugan, Letter from President of A. W. Dugan Petroleum Investments to Victor Atiyeh, "Concern about Bigotry and Intolerance," 21 April 1982, Atiyeh Collection, Pac. Univ. Archives.
1584 Bob Oliver, "A.W. Dugan's Letter," Office of the Governor, State of Oregon, Memo to Gerry Thompson, (29 April 1982), Atiyeh Collection, Pac. Univ. Archives.

the governor investigate the claims in early March 1982.[1585] The State Ethics Commission had already received a complaint about Cantrell's actions in February.[1586] Upon deeper investigation, it became abundantly clear that the cattle deal had involved normal amounts of money, had not been an ongoing activity between Cantrell and the Rajneeshees, and was simply a business deal among ranchers in the area.[1587]

For a while there was a sense among some that the good people of Antelope were just small-minded small-town people.[1588] Sarasohn wrote about the whole phenomenon in the summer of 1982 for *Oregon Magazine*. He found locals who were encountering something "they had never imagined."[1589] In the spring of 1982, the few citizens of Antelope "decided that the only way to save their town from the Rajneeshee building projects was to disincorporate it."[1590] Given a quirk in Oregon election law —any Oregon resident could vote in a city election if that person showed "an intent to reside" in the city—a lot of new voters appeared, mainly people who had been residing on the Big

---

1585 Henry R. Richmond, Letter from 1000 Friends of Oregon to Victor Atiyeh, "Request for Investigation Under ORS 180.070 of Sale of Cattle from Wasco County Judge Rick Cantrell to Agents of Bhagwan Shree Rajneesh," 5 March 1982, Atiyeh Collection, Pac. Univ. Archives; Mark J. Greenfield, Staff Attorney, "Rajneesh Cattle Sale," 1000 Friends of Oregon, Memo to Henry R. Richmond, Executive Director, (5 March 1982), Atiyeh Collection, Pac. Univ. Archives.

1586 Scotta Callister, "Rajneesh Debate Runs from Freedom to Goals," *Oregonian*, 9 February 1982; Leslie L. Zaitz, "Panel Sees Possible Ethics Violation by Wasco Official," *Oregonian*, 25 February 1982.

1587 James M. Habberstad, Attorney letter to Governor to Victor Atiyeh, "Response to Request for Investigation Concerning Wasco County Judge Rick Cantrell," 17 March 1982, Atiyeh Collection, Pac. Univ. Archives; "Records of Madras Auction Yard," Evidence of Cantrell Cattle Sales, (23 September 1981), Atiyeh Collection, Pac. Univ. Archives.

1588 Sarasohn, "Atiyeh interview," 3.

1589 David Sarasohn, "Sagebrush Gothic: Antelope's Last Stand. The Town's Desparate Bid to Disincorporate Ends in Failure," in *The Rajneesh Chronicles: The True Story of the Cult That Unleased the First Act of Bioterrorism on U.S. Soil*, ed. Win McCormack, (Portland, OR: Tin House Books, 2010); reprint, *Oregon Magazine*, May 1982.

1590 Bob Oliver, "The Dalles Meeting, March 23," Office of the Governor, State of Oregon, Memo to Governor Atiyeh, (23 March 1982), 2, Atiyeh Collection, Pac. Univ. Archives; FitzGerald, "Rajneeshpuram II," 83.

Muddy Ranch, and the effort to disincorporate was defeated in an April 1982 election.[1591] The concerns about the voting process were so strong that Oregon's Secretary of State (the official who oversees elections in the state), Norma Paulus, came out to personally supervise the proceedings.[1592]

The concerns in the governor's office in April 1982 were that either side might do something rash in Antelope that could inflame the situation. The "Governor's concern is that tempers, especially those of the Antelope residents and surrounding farmers, could elevate and they might decide to take matters into their own hands.... Rajneeshees seem to enjoy pestering and harassing the Antelope citizens. Antelope residents are threatening to have a 'shoot out' or 'blow up' or 'burn' down the ranch."[1593]

To try to establish a dialogue and possible solutions between the groups in April 1982, Jefferson County District Attorney Mike Sullivan invited the federal mediation services.[1594] Some of the local people "had said, in fact, that they might do bad things."[1595] The idea was to have a dialogue to anticipate some of the feelings between the Rajneeshees and their neighbors in Jefferson and Wasco counties—but Thompson made it clear that "no rep from Gov's staff" would take part in these meetings.[1596]

A report that April from the U.S. Department of Justice Community Relations Service (crs) "rated the situation at 'tension level 4' on a scale that would rate a riot as a 5."[1597] The report

---

1591 Scotta Callister, James Long and Leslie L. Zaitz, "Threads of Paranoia Infiltrate Ranch as Rajneeshees Cast Security Net," For Love and Money series, *Oregonian*, 10 July 1985, A6.

1592 FitzGerald, "Rajneeshpuram II," 83.

1593 Thompson, "Rajneesh Timeline, 1981–1986," month of April 1982.

1594 Michael Sullivan, interviewed by Jim Moore, "Atiyeh interview," Phone interview, recorded by Jim Moore, Bend, OR, 8 September 2015. Summary notes, 7.

1595 Sullivan, "Atiyeh interview," 7.

1596 Bob Oliver, "Antelope/Rajneesh Puram Mediation," Office of the Governor, State of Oregon, Memo to Governor Atiyeh, (26 April 1982), Atiyeh Collection, Pac. Univ. Archives.

1597 Callister, Long and Zaitz, "Threads of Paranoia," A6. The Community Relations Service works to calm community conflicts based on a variety of characteristics

went on to warn about local residents' reactions to the Rajneeshees and the role that state and local governments might play. "The overt response by state and local officials to Rajneesh concerns may be perceived by Central Oregon inhabitants as a consensus to suppress Rajneesh efforts by violence."[1598] A memo from an April 20 meeting with a Wasco County commissioner, the district attorney, and the sheriff, as well as the Oregon State police described "the situation over there [as…] very explosive and [it] could blow at any time." There was a strong recommendation conveyed by federal mediator John Mathis to those in attendance that "the Governor should come out with a statement…that law and order will be enforced in that area at all times."[1599] The recommendation continued that such a statement "would have a great effect on the citizens of Antelope" where there was a fear that people in Antelope might retaliate against the Rajneeshees by making "something drastic happen."[1600] Jefferson County DA Sullivan remembered that the tensions were very high among the local people and the Rajneeshees.

After CRS-led meetings on April 27 and 28 with Antelope residents and Rajneeshees, Bob Davis, the lobbyist for the Rajneeshees

> said he has never perceived such an intensity of hatred as that exhibited at the meeting by older [Antelope] residents.… After the meeting a rancher approached him wearing a necklace made of 30-caliber bullets…and asked, "Are you Davis?" Davis says when he acknowledged his identity, the man asked further, "Let me see your gun." Replying that he had no weapon, Davis was told, "You son of a bitch, if you ever show your face in this part of the country again, you damn well better have a big gun." Davis

---

among which are religion and national origin.
1598 Callister, Long and Zaitz, "Threads of Paranoia," A6.
1599 Kathleen Harbaugh, "Telephone Call from John Mathis re Rajneesh-Antelope Situation," Office of the Governor, State of Oregon, Memo to Paul Phillips, (21 April 1982), Atiyeh Collection, Pac. Univ. Archives.
1600 Harbaugh, "Telephone Call from John Mathis re Rajneesh-Antelope Situation."

said a number of older residents within earshot applauded these remarks and said, "Give it to him!"[1601]

The analysis of the meeting by the governor's legal assistant, Oliver, said that the governor should not be actively involved in the discussions, but such an active role might be advisable in the future. Gerry Thompson had a handwritten response to this idea:

> No—no public statement. They are desperate to get Gov's attention. When the time is right and productive, perhaps. Furthermore, Bob, no one from Gov's ofc should be visiting the ranch or make an appearance in Antelope. LET'S DISCUSS.[1602]

Among those at the meeting there was a sense that "many of the older residents in the area appear to be proceeding under the assumption that the Governor will condone any action taken to clear out the newcomers."[1603]

Bill Gary, Oregon's Solicitor General, remembered that in 1982 "[i]t became apparent...that we had a significant risk of conflict. Armed conflict—people firing guns. Because you had a very armed Rajneeshee Peace Force, and you had farmers and ranchers who were not happy having these folks in town."[1604] Gary became very concerned that the relationships among the Rajneeshees and the local residents "needed to be handled with some care, because it could get away from us."

Feelings about the Rajneeshees were split. The locals were tired of them, but there was "continued support from businesses in Oregon from whom major purchases are being made by the Rajneeshees. They believe the Rajneeshees and their buying is a big boost to Oregon's failing economy. They ask the Governor

---

1601 Bob Oliver, "Bhagwan, April 29," Office of the Governor, State of Oregon, Memo to Gerry Thompson, (29 April 1982), Atiyeh Collection, Pac. Univ. Archives.
1602 Oliver, "Bhagwan, April 29."
1603 Oliver, "Bhagwan, April 29."
1604 Bill Gary, interviewed by Jim Moore, "Atiyeh interview," Portland, OR, 14 June 2016. Summary notes, 6.

[to] leave the Rajneeshees alone and let them proceed with their plans."[1605] As late as August 1984 this divide continued. Speaking to Oregon's mayors, director of the Oregon Department of Economic Development John Anderson responded to a question from Rajneeshpuram mayor KD about "what sort of economic development Gov. Vic Atiyeh was achieving by efforts to oust the [Rajneeshees]…from their new Wasco County community. Anderson declined to speak on behalf of Atiyeh, but said, 'You are an economic force, there is no question about it. I am happy you are.'"[1606] Anderson's comments illustrate the pro-business support for the group, but they also show how closely held any information about the governor's response to the Rajneeshees was. The head of a major state agency had no idea what Atiyeh was up to.

The situation calmed a bit in the next six months. A CRS report in October 1982 "said that although community tensions continued to grow, 'overt violence is not anticipated.'"[1607] Jefferson County DA Sullivan believed most people felt that the local governments in the state of Oregon were doing what needed to be done to try to ease the tensions. So, after the friction between the parties in the spring of 1982, "many of the people backed off. That doesn't mean that there weren't really hard feelings, and I'm not suggesting that the folks who lived [nearby] weren't very, very concerned as they certainly have the right to be. But we were concerned that there not be any unnecessary violence, and we were trying to make sure that that did not occur."[1608]

The registered voters of the Big Muddy voted on May 18, by a vote of 154–0, to incorporate themselves as the city of

---

1605 Thompson, "Rajneesh Timeline, 1981–1986," month of May 1982.
1606 Jeff Barnard, "Economic Development Officer Praises Repeal of Unitary Tax," *Oregonian*, 18 August 1984.
1607 Callister, Long and Zaitz, "Threads of Paranoia," A6.
1608 Michael Sullivan, interviewed by Jim Moore, "Atiyeh interview," Phone interview, recorded by Jim Moore, Bend, OR, 8 September 2015. Summary notes, 7.

Rajneeshpuram.[1609] That November, local elections saw Rajneeshee candidates take over the Antelope city council. New voters were people who had moved there to work in Rajneeshee businesses, as well as those who moved there and registered to vote against the disincorporation effort in April. An observer from an Oregon university saw the outcome as tragic, and laid the blame at the feet of Governor Vic Atiyeh. "The disaster might have been averted if there had been any coherent political power in the state..., a governor as popular as the late Tom McCall... might have imposed a compromise settlement that seemed fair to all."[1610] This fight for Antelope had raised the visibility of the Rajneeshees across the region, alienating "a good many state legislators" and set the county leaders in Wasco and Jefferson counties against the group.[1611] As the Rajneeshee issue grew, others shared the perception that Governor Atiyeh was not on top of things. When people read or heard news about the state of Oregon dealing with the Rajneeshees, it was about Norma Paulus and the elections.[1612] This perception was exactly what Atiyeh wanted, but there began to be questions and political costs: where was the governor?

Atiyeh was watching proceedings very carefully. But he realized that "[a]ctually [the Rajneeshees] were working at the margin of the law. They didn't step over. They tried to step over and actually were in the courts because of it, but they kept pushing the law as far as they could push it."[1613] Unless the group actually broke laws, the state's job was to ensure that all the players were treated equally by the laws on the books.[1614]

By October 1981 the Portland office of the federal Immigration and Naturalization Service (INS) was directed to begin

---

1609 Oliver, "Rajneeshpuram, May 19."
1610 FitzGerald, "Rajneeshpuram II," 84.
1611 FitzGerald, "Rajneeshpuram II," 89.
1612 Sarasohn, "Atiyeh interview," 3.
1613 Victor Atiyeh, interviewed by Clark Hansen, "Tape 49," Oral history, recorded by Oregon Historical Society, Portland, OR, 24 July 1993. Transcript, 546, Atiyeh Collection, Pac. Univ. Archives.
1614 Atiyeh, "Tape 49," 550.

investigations into reports of immigration fraud. In addition, there was a request in November 1981 for the Bhagwan to be granted permanent residency as a religious worker.[1615] The American Consul in Bombay (now Mumbai), India, sent an extensive report on the Bhagwan and his followers to the Portland INS office in January 1982. It looked like the Bhagwan began dismantling the Pune ashram in anticipation of his move to the United States, rather than having to leave suddenly for treatment of his health problems. That would mean that he lied on his visa application.[1616]

Behind the scenes, another political challenge to the Rajneeshees had been raised. In May 1982 Oregon's senior U.S. Senator, Mark Hatfield, had contacted the INS with concerns about the Rajneeshees, which he called a cult, "endangering the way of life for a small agricultural town in Oregon, as well as constituting a threat to public safety."[1617] Hatfield "was very concerned" about the Rajneeshees, according to his chief of staff, Gerry Frank. "And they hated him." The Rajneeshees regularly attacked Hatfield with words and actions. "It was a very unpleasant relationship."[1618]

It was not clear whether the Hatfield communication had any impact on INS actions, but by the winter of 1982–83 the INS denied the Bhagwan's permanent-residency request and denied that he was a religious worker.[1619] This was made even more interesting because the INS would not provide complete evidence for either ruling (a single one-page statement from a U.S. consular official in Bombay was missing)[1620]—so the Rajneeshee lawyers challenged the findings and received a somewhat favorable

---

1615 Scotta Callister, James Long and Leslie L. Zaitz, "Rajneesh's Uncertain Health Improves En Route to Oregon," For Love and Money series, *Oregonian*, 5 July 1985, A13.
1616 American Consul in Bombay, "Report on Rajneesh Activity in India," Department of State, U.S. Government, Telegram to INS District Director: Portland, (January 1982), Atiyeh Collection, Pac. Univ. Archives. Each paragraph in the telegram was numbered in the original.
1617 FitzGerald, "Rajneeshpuram II," 89.
1618 Gerry Frank, interviewed by Jim Moore, "Atiyeh interview," Salem, OR, 17 August 2015. Summary notes, 3.
1619 FitzGerald, "Rajneeshpuram II," 89.

outcome in December 1983. The Bhagwan would not receive a green card, but he was officially considered a religious worker as of February 1984.[1621] All these challenges from the INS spooked the Rajneeshee leadership. In November 1982 "an expected Immigration raid prompted a full-scale exodus from the ranch."[1622] Some of the Rajneeshees with immigration problems were transported as far away as San Francisco to avoid being anywhere near the ranch when the raid was supposed to happen.

The summer of 1982 also saw the beginning of the armed Rajneeshees who eventually amassed a considerable armory. The First Annual World Celebration that summer found the Rajneeshees hiring a private force of armed guards, the Project Centurion security workers.[1623] Bob Oliver and State Police Major Doyle Watson briefed Atiyeh on the proceedings by showing him slides of the changes at the ranch to prepare for the four-day festival.[1624] Wasco County had insisted that the Rajneeshees were responsible for providing security at the festival itself. In a meeting with sheriffs from Wasco and Jefferson Counties, the head of Rajneeshee security, and Centurion, the Oregon State Police worked on coordinating the patrols of nearby roads for the arrival of an expected three to four thousand people for the festival. At this meeting Centurion was revealed as the low bidder for the Rajneeshee security contract, a company led by a person with "no experience in crowd control and...more geared for building and personal security."[1625] That fall a decision was made

---

[1620] Scotta Callister, James Long and Leslie L. Zaitz, "Influx of Rajneeshees Catches Immigration Service Napping," For Love and Money series, *Oregonian*, 19 July 1985, B4.

[1621] FitzGerald, "Rajneeshpuram II," 89; Scotta Callister, James Long and Leslie L. Zaitz, "Immigration Woes Plague Rajneeshees," For Love and Money series, *Oregonian*, 18 July 1985, A12.

[1622] Callister, Long and Zaitz, "Immigration Woes," A1.

[1623] Callister, Long and Zaitz, "Threads of Paranoia," A6.

[1624] "Atiyeh Daily Index-Card Schedule, July 14, 1982," Office of the Governor, State of Oregon, Maj. Doyle Watson; Bob O. re: view slides of Muddy Ranch, (14 July 1982), Atiyeh Collection, Pac. Univ. Archives.

[1625] K. L. Lamkin, Letter from Bend State Police office to Superintendent of Oregon State Police to John C. Williams, "Rajneesh Festival," 13 May 1982, Atiyeh

to create the Rajneeshpuram Peace Force, the town's own police officers.[1626] The reasons for establishing the Peace Force were twofold: it took too long for Jefferson or Wasco County deputies to get to the town, and there was a sense of threat from the neighbors out in the desert.

At the end of the year, the Rajneeshees had a falling out with Bob Harvey, the person who had been managing the ranch portion of the property for them and who had been an intermediary as the group learned how to navigate local and state laws. Partly from the sense of betrayal engendered by the break with Harvey, a January 9, 1983, Coordinators' meeting considered and accepted the use of violence. The Coordinators were the de facto government of the Rajneeshees—separate from the municipal government that ran Rajneeshpuram, although many people played roles in both groups. The Coordinators agreed that "if we find someone cheating us we have to set a precedent that we don't stand for this and this may mean being brutal." The Peace Force would carry out that mission.[1627]

1983—Tensions Erupt

The town of Rajneeshpuram, the renamed Big Muddy Ranch, had grown from a few dozen inhabitants in 1981 to over a thousand by 1983. A comprehensive plan for growth put together by Rajneeshpuram leaders foresaw a population of 3,700 sometime between 1983 and 1995.[1628] The quick growth was not what the Rajneeshees expected in 1981, but it had happened, and the town, like all towns in Oregon was subject to state land-use laws and was planning for its future. The main goal was for Rajneeshpuram to become a center for education, both religious

---

Collection, Pac. Univ. Archives.

1626 Scotta Callister, James Long and Leslie L. Zaitz, "Rajneeshees Establish Security Forces, Large Armory," For Love and Money series, *Oregonian*, 9 July 1985, A1.

1627 "Last Week's Catastrophe; Peace Force," Coordinators' Meeting, Rajneesh Leadership, (9 January 1983), Atiyeh Collection, Pac. Univ. Archives.

1628 FitzGerald, "Rajneeshpuram I," 71; In March 1982 the projection was for 3000–4000 people by the year 2000, Oliver, "The Dalles Meeting, March 23," 2.

and general[1629]—something like the new Epcot Center in Florida, an intentional city that would serve as an ideal and a model for people from all walks of life.[1630]

As Oregonians tried to figure out the Rajneeshees, a reporter in 1983 found "an extraordinary variety of opinion, crisscrossing political lines."[1631] There were people who saw the Rajneeshees in the heroic pioneer mold that had built Oregon in the mythic times of the nineteenth century. Others saw the Rajneeshees as a cult and the Bhagwan as possessed by the Devil.[1632] Some found them to be "a laughable gathering of aging sixties dropouts," while others thought the Rajneeshees were the latest in a long history of outsiders who had made Oregon the place it was by the 1980s.[1633] Gerry Thompson continued to hear from Oregon businesspeople about the Rajneeshees. They wanted her "to be sure the Governor does not interfere because the 'Rajneeshees are good for our economy.'"[1634] The Rajneeshees' immediate neighbors in Wasco County remained almost uniformly skeptical or hostile to the group.[1635]

In the summer of 1983, the annual religious festival at Rajneeshpuram attracted 15,000 people, each of whom paid for the experience, and many of them stayed afterward for classes there, paying tuition to do so. The festival was also on the radar of federal officials—the U.S. State Department and the INS received a letter about the 1983 religious festival from the governor's legal counsel, Bob Oliver, that noted that "Governor Atiyeh expressed neither approval nor disapproval of the [previous] event in 1982" and that all local and state laws were being followed.[1636] Clearly,

---

1629 FitzGerald, "Rajneeshpuram I," 71.
1630 FitzGerald, "Rajneeshpuram I," 71.
1631 FitzGerald, "Rajneeshpuram I," 48.
1632 FitzGerald, "Rajneeshpuram I," 54.
1633 FitzGerald, "Rajneeshpuram I," 48.
1634 Thompson, "Rajneesh Timeline, 1981–1986," month of August 1983.
1635 FitzGerald, "Rajneeshpuram I," 48–49.
1636 Robert W. Oliver, Letter from Assistant to Governor to Marvin Groensweg, Visa Office, US Department of State, "Festival Concerns," 1 April 1983, Atiyeh Collection, Pac. Univ. Archives.

as the immigration investigations moved forward, the INS was concerned about a huge influx of international visitors to the festival and what they would do when the festival ended.

"Tense," Jefferson County district attorney Mike Sullivan emphasized, "just doesn't give the environment a good description."[1637] Sullivan was trying to keep the peace and make sure nobody got hurt. This is typically a job for the police, but in a small community the district attorney is on the front line for this type of situation, albeit without carrying a gun. Law enforcement in the local area would turn to him whenever situations involving the Rajneeshees occurred.[1638] In one instance, an incident involving aggressive pushing between Rajneeshees and a state trooper ended up in Sullivan's office. Sheela was there to argue, very loudly, the Rajneeshee case. Sullivan had to impose order, telling Sheela, "You don't get to speak until you raise your hand, until I recognize you."[1639]

Sometime in late 1982 or early 1983, the governor's office had been dealing with a leak to the press about dealing with Rajneeshee issues. Denny Miles, the communication director who oversaw plugging the leak, came to Gerry Thompson and said, "You know, I think we ought to be sweeping our office" for bugging devices.[1640] Thompson recalled that there were members of the Rajneeshees all over the Capitol building all the time. She responded, "Denny; not necessary." Miles pressed the issue. The governor and Thompson talked about it, and the governor decided that if they could get somebody to sweep the office, they should sweep. No bugs were ever found, but regular checks were made until Rajneeshee communities collapsed. By the end of the saga, not only was Atiyeh's office in Salem was being scanned for electronic listening devices, top state officials would go to the governor's residence on Winter Street whenever they discussed

---

1637 Sullivan, "Atiyeh interview," 3.
1638 Sullivan, "Atiyeh interview," 3.
1639 Sullivan, "Atiyeh interview," 3.
1640 Thompson, "Atiyeh Interview #3," 9.

the Rajneeshees.[1641] There was never hard evidence that the governor's offices were bugged, but they took no chances. All the governor's staffers were speaking in code when they used telephones outside their offices. [1642] Other statewide offices were checked for listening devices as well. [1643]

Atiyeh and Sheela did actually meet on one occasion.[1644] On June 23, 1983, both were present at an appreciation breakfast for the Greater Portland Convention and Visitors Association at Memorial Coliseum in Portland, where the governor gave a speech.[1645] The next day, with a picture of the two shaking hands, a front-page story ran in the Rajneeshees' newspaper with the headline, "Governor Finally Accepts Sheela's Invitation to Visit Rajneeshpuram."[1646] Atiyeh kept a copy of the newspaper, adding a 2011 note that said, "This is her version of what she thought I said—I never did visit the ranch or negotiate with her."[1647]

The presence of Rajneeshees in the capitol building became a big issue for Atiyeh only twice. Groups of Rajneeshees, including Sheela, came to the governor's ceremonial office. Lon Holbrook had four state troopers in the room. He did not frisk the visitors or do anything else out of the ordinary aside from having more uniformed state police on hand.[1648] The members of the Rajneeshee delegations were not hostile at either event. Away

---

1641 Denny Miles, interviewed by Jim Moore, "Atiyeh interview #1," Forest Grove, OR, 31 July 2014. Summary notes, 7.

1642 Oliver, "Atiyeh interview," 7.

1643 Verne Duncan, Conversation about Atiyeh findings to Jim Moore, "Conversation," 16 July 2015.

1644 Victor Atiyeh, interviewed by Pat Amedeo, "Arlington Club Oral History," Oral history, recorded by Arlington Club, Portland, OR, 10 September 2013. Transcript, 24, Atiyeh Collection, Pac. Univ. Archives; Gerry Thompson, Email to Jim Moore, "Clarification Question," 1 January 2018. Second set of ellipses in original.

1645 "Governor's Schedule, 20–26 June 1983," Office of the Governor, State of Oregon, Confidential, (16 June 1983), June 23, Atiyeh Collection, Pac. Univ. Archives.

1646 *Rajneesh Times* (Rajneeshpuram, OR), "Governor Finally Accepts Sheela's Invitation to Visit Rajneeshpuram," 24 June 1983, Atiyeh Collection, Pac. Univ. Archives.

1647 Victor Atiyeh, "This is Her Version," Victor Atiyeh and Company, Handwritten note, (21 April 2011).

from the capitol there was some concern that Rajneeshees might pull some kind of stunt when the governor was present. Holbrook noted, however, that security for the governor was difficult at these events because all the Rajneeshees would have to do was not wear red; there would be no way security would know they were even there.[1649] Thompson said that the governor's instruction were that the Rajneeshees "were treated like any other civilian except for gaining access to the Gov."[1650] She did, however, find it interesting that she and Atiyeh frequently had lunch in the capitol coffee shop—"I don't ever remember them bothering the Gov there."[1651]

By September 1983 the Land Use Board of Appeals "ruled that Rajneeshpuram's incorporation was invalid because county officials had not properly considered the effects of creating a new urban center."[1652] The Rajneeshees challenged this finding in court, but the original threat to the validity of Rajneeshpuram seemed to be winning in the Oregon legal system. In May 1983, Atiyeh and Gerry Thompson consulted with Attorney General Dave Frohnmayer about the legality of the creation of Rajneeshpuram because the main organization behind the city had registered as a religious organization. Since there was no separation of church and state, the three felt that there could be a legal challenge to the incorporation.[1653] In fall 1983 Frohnmayer challenged the incorporation of the city based on "the unique and pervasive interrelationship" among the public entities of the city and the private religious entities that owned and operated the

---

1648 Lon Holbrook, interviewed by Jim Moore, "Atiyeh interview," Gladstone, OR, 6 June 2017. Summary notes, 12.
1649 Holbrook, "Atiyeh interview," 12.
1650 Thompson to Moore, 1 January 2018.
1651 Thompson to Moore, 1 January 2018.
1652 Callister, Long and Zaitz, "Guru's Orange City," A7.
1653 Thompson, "Rajneesh Timeline, 1981–1986," May 1982. The timeline clearly says May 1982, and later says that Atiyeh and Frohnmayer agreed to challenge the city September and October 1982. But the letter from the governor is dated October 1983, as is the opinion itself; Dave Frohnmayer, "Opinion on Legality of Rajneeshpuram," Department of Justice, 8148, (6 October 1983), Atiyeh archive, Pacific University, Forest Grove, OR.

entire town.[1654] City records obtained by reporters for the *Oregonian* showed that the "city plowed its income into Rajneeshee businesses, primarily the commune," a religious entity.[1655]

Atiyeh read the opinion and, "under the authority vested in me by the constitution and laws of this state, I request that you institute appropriate legal proceedings in the name of the State of Oregon to have these issues finally decided by our judicial system."[1656] The next day the governor received a telegram from the Rajneeshees deploring "that you have joined in Attorney General Frohnmayer's actions against our community without any prior investigation into the facts of the situation." The telegram went on, "We are simply trying to build our community. We would be able to do that if the bigot [*sic*], religious zealots and political opportunists in this state would leave us alone."[1657] A few days after this, Atiyeh's legal counsel received a "cordial" phone call at home from a Rajneeshee leader about the same issues.[1658]

Newly appointed Deputy Attorney General Bill Gary put in a lot of work on the opinion. In his mind, it was clear that Rajneeshpuram was not a legal city because the government and institutions that ran it were entirely religious, as well as the facts that the city denied free access to its public streets, limited who could live within the city limits, and was owned by a single entity.[1659] But what if the Rajneeshees argued that they were indeed a religious institution, gave up on their attempt to become a city, and asserted their right to be out on the ranch under the free

---

1654 Callister, Long and Zaitz, "Guru's Orange City," A7.
1655 Callister, Long and Zaitz, "Guru's Orange City," A7.
1656 Victor Atiyeh, Office of the Governor letter directing Attorney General Dave Frohnmayer, "Legality of Rajneeshpuram," 13 October 1983, Atiyeh Collection, Pac. Univ. Archives.
1657 Na Yoga Didya, Telegram to Vic Atiyeh, "We Are Dismayed," 14 October 1983, Atiyeh Collection, Pac. Univ. Archives.
1658 Bob Oliver, "Jayananda's Call," Office of the Governor, State of Oregon, Memo to Rajneesh File, (19 October 1983), Atiyeh Collection, Pac. Univ. Archives.
1659 Frohnmayer, "Opinion on Legality of Rajneeshpuram," 1–5.

exercise clause as a church and religious center?[1560] Could this religious entity be exempted from the land-use law that required the Rajneeshees to be a city? As the case unfolded in court, these issues were never resolved. The collapse of the Rajneeshee experiment occurred very shortly after the final 1985 legal ruling, a ruling that upheld Frohnmayer's opinion.

That fall, in September 1983, the Rajneeshees took over the public school district in Antelope. There had been a conversation for about a year between the Rajneeshees and the non-Rajneeshee ranch families who composed the school district, along with various plans, votes by the school board on ideas, and votes by the district's voters on tax levies. The Rajneeshees wanted their own public school; the local people wanted their school-age students go to school locally instead of commuting 30–50 miles to the next-nearest elementary schools. But if the children did have to travel, then the local families wanted the Rajneeshee-dominated Antelope school district picking up the bill for transportation and tuition to attend a neighboring school district.[1661] The issue was resolved in the Rajneeshees' favor by mid-October—they refused to pay the tuition and transportation costs they had agreed to in an earlier version of the deal.[1662] A reporter, looking at the situation, marveled at the open use of power by the Rajneeshees. "The Rajneeshee [*sic*] had reneged on an agreement and taken over the school in a bare-knuckle power play, causing their neighbors maximum hardship."[1663]

State Superintendent of Public Instruction Verne Duncan was in the middle of the education discussions.[1664] State support for the Antelope schools was about $50,000 a year. Looking at the number of $80,000 Rolls-Royces that the Bhagwan was buying,

---

1660 Gary, "Atiyeh interview," 3–4.

1661 FitzGerald, "Rajneeshpuram II," 86–87.

1662 Jeanie Senior, "Antelope School Work Continues as County Seeks to Freeze Funds," *Oregonian*, 9 October 1983; Kathie Durbin, "Duncan Releases School Support to Rajneeshees," *Oregonian*, 22 October 1983.

1663 FitzGerald, "Rajneeshpuram II," 88.

1664 Verne Duncan, interviewed by Jim Moore, "Atiyeh interview," Milwaukie, OR, 12 August 2014. Summary notes, 4–5.

Duncan thought control of the public schools was not a money issue. Duncan concluded that the Rajneeshees wanted state approval so that they would be seen as credible in the political community. However, if there was no state approval, then they were the oppressed party in their own worldview. In effect they had a private school system, but they really craved that state approval. If they had gone totally private, then Duncan's reason for playing a role in the community would be very diminished, focused on rules about basic education requirements rather than issues of separation of church and state and state funding for the district.

Duncan ruled on church-state issues in the schools.[1665] For instance, he ruled that people could not wear any decoration with the Bhagwan's picture on it in the classroom. He realized, however, that he clearly could not outlaw teachers from wearing the color red.[1666] A key issue was whether there was public access to the public school. Duncan went to Rajneeshpuram and found, among other things, a newly painted sign that said "public access" directing anybody in town to the school.

During the 1981–1983 period another side to the Rajneeshees was emerging. Sheela was hiding illegal acts from the authorities in any way she could. Most of the initial problems were focused on the number of people on the ranch and violations of the land-use agreements with Wasco County under state law. There were also big issues of immigration fraud.[1667] A intelligence bulletin from the INS in April 1983 suggested that "95% of the marriages between citizens and alien members of this organization are phony."[1668] There were even Rajneeshee-sponsored elocution

---

1665 Verne A. Duncan, "Statement Regarding Report of Fact-Finding Team Visit to Antelope School District," Department of Education, State of Oregon, (21 October 1983), Atiyeh Collection, Pac. Univ. Archives.
1666 Jeanie Senior, "Red Gets OK From Antelope School Board," *Oregonian*, 21 March 1984.
1667 FitzGerald, "Rajneeshpuram II," 113–114.
1668 Callister, Long and Zaitz, "Immigration Woes," A12.

lessons to train foreign accents to sound more mainstream American to deceive immigration agents.[1669]

With all this hidden activity, Sheela also began to fear that some of those closest to her would betray her. A solution to this came through the Rajneeshee medical officer, Ma Anand Puja. Puja and Sheela had been close since the sect's days in India. Puja drugged and poisoned those who Sheela felt threatened the order of the commune.[1670] Puja created a secret laboratory in one of the canyons on the ranch. There she experimented with a variety of pathogens—bacteria and viruses.[1671] The general practice of using tranquilizers to control people probably dated back to the sect's time in India. There were rumors and stories about this practice in March 1983, but in October 1983 an allegation came to the governor's office "that Sheela is 'keeping the Bhagwan Shree Rajneesh in a drug-induced stupor.'"[1672] Not only did this raise the question about the use of drugs to control people, but it also called the leadership of the Rajneeshees into question.

In February 1983, an incident took place that would not take on major importance until September 1985. Mike Sullivan suddenly got very ill. "There were a number of doctors that didn't expect me to recover. I was that sick."[1673] When he became ill, the Jefferson County district attorney was seen at home by Dr. Bud Beemer, then transported by ambulance to the hospital in Madras. Then he was sent on to St. Charles Hospital in Bend. Among the doctors who saw Sullivan "was a Rajneeshee doctor, a very well-educated man, and, at that point, he said, 'Could this be poisoning?'" The doctors who were there dismissed it out of hand because they just did not think anybody would be poisoning an

---

1669 Callister, Long and Zaitz, "Threads of Paranoia," A6–A7.
1670 FitzGerald, "Rajneeshpuram II," 114.
1671 Zaitz, "Thwarted Rajneeshee Leaders Attack Enemies, Neighbors with Poison."
1672 Bob Oliver, "Rajneesh, October 19," Office of the Governor, State of Oregon, Memo to Gerry Thompson, (19 October 1983), Atiyeh Collection, Pac. Univ. Archives; Duane A. Pankratz and John C. Williams, "Report Regarding Rajneesh Organization," Department of State Police, State of Oregon, (18 October 1983), Atiyeh Collection, Pac. Univ. Archives.
1673 Sullivan, "Atiyeh interview," 5.

elected official in Oregon. Sullivan barely recovered "by the skin of my teeth" after being pumped full of forty liters of fluids to save his life. His illness was diagnosed as pneumococcal pneumonia. He did not care what they called it, but as the father of young children he was really worried about whether he would make it. "I do want to emphasize that it was nip and tuck about whether I would survive or not."[1674]

The relatively open commune at Rajneeshpuram was becoming more closed by the fall of 1983. Partly in response to threats from outsiders (a person with several bombs had been staying in the Rajneeshees' Portland hotel when one exploded and caused a fire —the other bombs exploded about an hour later),[1675] and partly as an assertion of power by those in control of the commune, visitors to Rajneeshpuram were met by uniformed Peace Force officers and issued plastic visitors bracelets, while the residents of Rajneeshpuram were leading more regimented lives. Bob Atiyeh, the governor's nephew, and his wife stopped in at the ranch in the summer of 1983 after the Portland bombing. He vividly remembered the armed guards and the paranoia among the Rajneeshees. At Christmas 1983 Bob mentioned to his uncle Vic that he and his wife had been to the ranch, and Bob suggested that the governor should go out to see what was going on. Vic told Bob, "The Rajneeshees are bad, bad news for Oregon. I can't tell you what I know, but they're bad."[1676]

The governor asked the State Police "to develop partnership, as best possible, with law enforcement at [the] ranch and to coordinate closely with local law enforcement agencies in Wasco and Jefferson counties."[1677] There were rumors reaching the governor's office that drug trafficking and drug use were becoming more prevalent on the ranch.

1674 Sullivan, "Atiyeh interview," 5.
1675 Thompson, "Rajneesh Timeline, 1981–1986," July 29, 1983; Rolla J. Crick and Jeanie Senior, "The Hotel Bombing: Rajneeshees Tighten Security, Decry Violence," *Oregonian*, 30 July 1983.
1676 Bob Atiyeh, interviewed by Jim Moore, "Atiyeh interview," West Linn, OR, 4 February 2015. Summary notes, 7.
1677 Thompson, "Rajneesh Timeline, 1981–1986," month of October 1983.

The implication of the attorney general's October 1983 opinion that "[t]he incorporation of Rajneeshpuram as an Oregon city is in violation of state and federal guarantees of separation of church and state"[1678] became clearer in mid-November. The state of Oregon decided that the town could not use state funds. Payments that went to other towns in Oregon for police, especially for the 911 system, were withheld based on Frohnmayer's ruling.

KD, the mayor of Rajneeshpuram, was up in arms.[1679] He pointed out that the relevant statute on withholding funds from incorporated areas stated that this could happen "only 'if the court or (administrative) agency determines that incorporation is invalid.'"[1680] The state was withholding the monies based solely in the attorney general's opinion. The state agency in charge of disbursing the monies sought an explanation from the attorney general.[1681] The money was not forthcoming to Rajneeshpuram.

The attorney general was acting in his role as the attorney for the state. The advice that the attorney general gave the governor, as the chief executive of the state, about funding for Rajneeshpuram was quite clear. Bill Gary remembered the advice.

> It was our view that the Constitution was pretty clear [and that] the religion clauses of the Oregon Constitution [were] actually much more specific than the United States Constitution. Particularly on the establishment clause side. ...Our advice was that the city was unconstitutional, that they are not entitled to share revenue. If we have our client give them a check, we are advising our client to violate that constitutional provision.... Our

---

1678 Frohnmayer, "Opinion on Legality of Rajneeshpuram," press release.
1679 Krishna Deva, Rajneeshpuram mayoral letter to Neal R. Fisher, Oregon Executive Department, "State-Shared Revenues," 14 November 1983, Atiyeh Collection, Pac. Univ. Archives.
1680 Deva to Fisher, 14 November 1983. Parentheses in original letter.
1681 Neal R. Fisher, Executive Department letter to Attorney General Dave Frohnmayer, "Withholding Distribution of State Funds," 14 November 1983, Atiyeh Collection, Pac. Univ. Archives; Neal R. Fisher, Executive Department letter to Mayor of Rajneeshpuram Krishna Deva, "Withheld Monies," 15 November 1983, Atiyeh Collection, Pac. Univ. Archives.

view was, they [the Rajneeshees] are free to go to the court and ask the court to order us to write a check.[1682]

The Rajneeshees never took this path, in Gary's memory.

Toward the end of 1983 and the beginning of 1984, KD and Gerry Thompson began to have confidential conversations, usually by phone. KD was not an informant at this time, but he was reaching out as he saw the pathologies of the Rajneeshee community begin to become larger. Thompson remembered, "I quickly realized that there was something in KD that was making him be very honest and forthright. I realized that it was perhaps because things were starting to crumble, and he knew. He was a smart man, and he knew it was [crumbling], but he had to contend with Sheela."[1683] She considered KD "an offhanded informant."[1684] They had not arrived at the point where Thompson was trying to build trust with KD or KD was trying to build trust with Thompson—this took place late in 1984. "But for some reason he had decided he could talk to me, and I don't know why."

1984—Plans and Counterplans

As tensions grew between the Rajneeshees and the various groups in Oregon, talk among the Rajneeshee leaders turned to ideas of violence to protect themselves and their towns. By the summer of 1984, it became clear that the Peace Force had put together an arsenal of semi-automatic weapons, rifles, and handguns.[1685] There were attempts to buy automatic weapons, but "the federal Bureau of Alcohol, Tobacco, and Firearms [ATF] had prevented the sales from going through—at least, when they tried to buy them legally."[1686] In 1984 the ATF specifically rejected an application to buy weapons because "we have been informed that

---

1682 Gary, "Atiyeh interview," 5.
1683 Thompson, "Atiyeh Interview #3," 1.
1684 Thompson, "Atiyeh Interview #3," 11–12.
1685 Callister, Long and Zaitz, "Rajneeshees Establish Security Forces," A10.
1686 FitzGerald, "Rajneeshpuram II," 96.

the State of Oregon does not recognize Rajneeshpuram as a political subdivision or agency of the state."[1687] The issue of whether the town was recognized as legitimate at that time was in the courts—the ATF was supporting Frohnmayer's assertion that his ruling in fall 1983 was enough to derecognize Rajneeshpuram as a city. Other federal agencies took the same approach.[1688]

Rajneeshpuram had a trained police force (its members were trained at the Oregon police academy, just like police officers in any part of Oregon), but there were now 150 Rajneeshee armed security guards and two helicopter teams to protect the area.[1689] There were also alarming statistics: Rajneeshpuram had many more police officers per capita than any other town in Oregon; and the ammunition budget in 1984 began to approach that of the Portland city police force—a much larger organization.[1690]

There were fears that the group could be moving toward violence with its neighbors, or even a Jonestown-style mass suicide. The most common stories indicated that the Rajneeshees were acting like survivalists—getting ready to live off the land in any way that worked.[1691] Atiyeh's legal aide responded to a caller's concerns about "why the Rajneesh are allowed to carry automatic weapons."[1692] Bob Oliver pointed out that, according to Oregon law, police forces were free to carry automatic weapons, even though very few other Oregon law enforcement groups did so. Interestingly, Oliver rested his argument on the legality of Rajneeshpuram—"Pending the outcome of litigation now before the courts as the to the legality of Rajneeshpuram's incorporation, that community does have a peace force consisting of persons

---

1687 Callister, Long and Zaitz, "Rajneeshees Establish Security Forces," A10.
1688 See William F. Gary, Letter from Oregon Deputy Attorney General to John G. Keane, Director, Bureau of Census, U.S. Department of Commerce, "City of Rajneeshpuram," 20 November 1984, Atiyeh Collection, Pac. Univ. Archives. Keane asked about federal revenue sharing money. Gary advised him of the AG's opinion that Rajneeshpuram was not a duly constituted city.
1689 FitzGerald, "Rajneeshpuram II," 96.
1690 Callister, Long and Zaitz, "Rajneeshees Establish Security Forces," A10.
1691 FitzGerald, "Rajneeshpuram II," 96–98.
1692 Robert W. Oliver, Letter from Governor's legal counsel to Robert Fisher, "Automatic Weapons," 10 July 1984, Atiyeh Collection, Pac. Univ. Archives.

who have been certified as trained police officers."[1693] Oliver saw the possession of weapons as different from the state's policy not to send money to the city of Rajneeshpuram. The federal and state constitutions are clear that state money may not be used for a religious institution. But "you have to go through a lot of inferences" to argue that a religious institution is not allowed to possess whatever legal weapons it may choose.[1694] However, since the argument (granted, not in a legal brief or opinion, but in a letter to a citizen) was about automatic weapons that were *not* allowed to regular citizens but were only allowed to a duly constituted city's police force, some questions remain.

At about this time, Atiyeh began to insist on cooperation among the various federal, state, and local agencies.[1695] There was a normal tendency among law enforcement agencies to say that investigations were under the jurisdiction of one agency or another. Atiyeh told them to end the turf wars and focus on the issue at hand.

Achieving the governor's goal of cooperation among the different agencies, however, was an ongoing task. Tensions between the Oregon State Police and the Oregon office of the attorney general—some just a function of different goals and means and some of it simple turf wars—bubbled up to the level of the governor on April 18, 1984. That day, the governor held a meeting with State Police Superintendent John Williams, Bob Oliver, and Gerry Thompson "regarding problems between State Police and AG's office."[1696] Thompson recalled that the issues between the state agencies were "perhaps more intense than [what] we experienced with the Feds. I would classify both as

---

1693 Oliver to Fisher, 10 July 1984.
1694 Oliver, "Atiyeh interview," 4.
1695 Thompson recalls this enforced cooperation as dating to Fall 1984, Thompson, "Chronology of Rajneeshees to November 1984."
1696 "Atiyeh Daily Index-Card Schedule, April 18, 1984," Office of the Governor, State of Oregon, (18 April 1984), Supt. Williams, Bob O. & Gerry, regarding problems between State Police and AG's office, Atiyeh Collection, Pac. Univ. Archives.

'turf wars.'"[1697] The state police had been designated by Atiyeh in early 1982 as

> the ears and the eyes on the ground inside the ranch and outside; in central Oregon, The Dalles, and the Portland area. They worked with the Salvation Army and other organizations. And they had undercover personnel on the ranch that were invaluable. When the AG sent in his own investigative men, Gov made it clear who was in charge and that all things must be coordinated with OSP. In a very short time it became clear the AG's personnel preferred not to coordinate and began to interfere with some of the critical relationships that had been developed with key Rajneeshees, including my own source[, KD].[1698]

Even with these almost inevitable tensions, Atiyeh and Frohnmayer were very aware that they had different roles. Each had been elected to statewide office by a vote of the people, so each had an electoral responsibility to the voters and constitutional job to do. The governor was responsible for public policy, and the attorney general was responsible for legal policy, "and that's a really blurry line," according to Bill Gary. But it was a guideline for the actions that both offices took. Gary recalled, "I think I learned a lot about how attorneys ought to interact with their clients by watching Dave and Vic in their respective roles. Both were very respectful of the other's authority."[1699]

At the center of the collaborative effort was Gerry Thompson. Different law enforcement agencies were "all living in my office, and we're plotting, and we're planning and coordinating, and we couldn't talk about it."[1700] By late 1983 to early 1984 the federal agencies began to become more involved—agencies in addition to the INS investigation that had been going on since 1981.

1697 Gerry Thompson, Email to Jim Moore, "Another Biography Question," 22 December 2017.
1698 Thompson to Moore, 22 December 2017.
1699 Gary, "Atiyeh interview," 4.
1700 Gerry Thompson, interviewed by Jim Moore, "Atiyeh interview #1," Salem, OR, 16 September 2014. Summary notes, 2.

Thompson recalled that the federal government was not interested until this point.[1701] On September 26, 1984, Thompson had a meeting—at the attorney general's office conference room in the Justice Building to avoid the many prying eyes in the capitol building—with all the different law enforcement agencies.[1702] The coordination came about because Thompson went to the governor to talk with him about all the players involved as well as their varying degrees of secretiveness. She told him,

> "First we had the politicals involved who always wanted to get their political bent out there to make them look good. Secondly we had the different federal agencies who also wanted to [look good]." Horrible! [Thompson said in 2014.] …Finally I went to the governor and I said, "Governor, I'm going to slam my fist on my desk. …They won't coordinate." He said, "Go for it." And I did. I slammed my fist on the desk and…said, "You *will* sit here and coordinate with me and we *will* have a conference call every day and each one of you *will* give a report with the other ones on the line."[1703]

Thompson insisted that all the agencies were to keep her informed so there was not duplication of effort or stepping on each other's toes as they performed their particular parts of the investigation.[1704] What Thompson got was a daily update about what was happening. "We weren't instructing the feds what to do, but we needed to know."[1705] It was also a way Thompson used to keep the governor informed about what was happening.

1701 Thompson, "Atiyeh Interview #3," 14.
1702 Thompson, "Rajneesh Timeline, 1981–1986," September 26, 1984; FitzGerald, "Rajneeshpuram II," 100. Fitzgerald reported that the Attorney General called the meeting. It was Thompson. Gerry Thompson, "Briefing by Oregon State Police: Rajneesh—Williams, Pankratz, Lamkin, Thompson, Oliver," Office of the Governor, State of Oregon, Memo to Governor, (25 September 1984), Atiyeh Collection, Pac. Univ. Archives.
1703 Thompson, "Atiyeh interview #1," 2. Italics are vocally stressed in the interview.
1704 Thompson, "Atiyeh Interview #3," 14.
1705 Thompson, "Atiyeh Interview #3," 15.

The coordinating meeting was held the last week in September.[1706] Concerns at the meeting came from all directions. Secretary of State Norma Paulus not only focused on the influx of new voters to Wasco County: she was also worried that Oregon's new vote-by-mail system (for local elections) might be used in some unforeseen way.[1707] The Federal ATF representative talked about the rumors of the Rajneeshee arsenal vs. certainty about what the group might have purchased.[1708] Both the Oregon Military Department (the National Guard) and the State Police assured the group that "THEY WOULD BE READY TO ACT SHOULD the Governor declare a state of emergency."[1709] Both could have a task force on the scene within three hours. Federal INS, DEA, and IRS representatives shared that they had been the recipient of a lot of rumors, but, aside from specific INS cases, there was no confirmation of any of them.[1710] The FBI felt its hands were tied "because they have no legal justification for investigation." The agency was concerned about who might be among the street people flooding into Rajneeshpuram, but were waiting for "leads from those leaving the ranch."[1711] The US Department of Justice was focused on drug trafficking, but, "like many of the others, [it was] unable to penetrate the ranch and [was] continually looking for a high level defector."[1712]

Thompson's main focus during this time was to "[k]eep the people of the state of Oregon safe and secure, and calm us down, and get over it. That's the goal. Don't let the rednecks get out of

---

1706 Attendees (all signed in by hand): Gerry Thompson, representing the governor; Dave Frohnmayer, attorney general; Norma Paulus, secretary of state; head the state police; head of the Oregon military department; Jefferson County district attorney Mike Sullivan; FBI; IRS; ATF; Oregon's US attorney; US Customs; DEA; INS. Source: Gerry Thompson, "Confidential: Federal/State/Local Agency Meeting," Office of the Governor, State of Oregon (26 September 1984), last page, photocopy of handwritten attendance list, Atiyeh Collection, Pac. Univ. Archives.
1707 Thompson, "Confidential: Federal/State/Local Agency Meeting," 1.
1708 Thompson, "Confidential: Federal/State/Local Agency Meeting," 3.
1709 Thompson, "Confidential: Federal/State/Local Agency Meeting," 3. Capitalized in original.
1710 Thompson, "Confidential: Federal/State/Local Agency Meeting," 4.
1711 Thompson, "Confidential: Federal/State/Local Agency Meeting," 5.
1712 Thompson, "Confidential: Federal/State/Local Agency Meeting," 5.

control, and don't let the Rajneeshees get out of control and protect the people in Antelope. It's simple. So, let's all talk to each other."¹⁷¹³ Thompson remembers that "it was tough." Atiyeh was working seven days a week; Thompson was working seven days a week. In the normal course of their long working days, "No matter where we went [the governor and I] were hooked to each other [with multiple communication links]. I called them my umbilical cords. Because we didn't know what was coming down at us." The communications link was used even more frequently than usual during this time. But the coordinated meetings were the key. Atiyeh recalled, "This was a pretty well-coordinated effort. Probably one of the few times in which the city, county, state, and federal government all worked together. Usually it's a frustrating thing, they don't always work together."¹⁷¹⁴

About this time, Bill Gary remembered, "We began to have twice-daily telephone calls. On the call there was Gerry Thompson, Governor Atiyeh, Dave [Frohnmayer], me, Charlie Turner, the US Attorney, and the head of the Oregon State Police [John Williams]. Calls would often last for no more than five minutes. It was just to touch base; anybody have anything they need to report. …[T]he level of concern was so great for quite a number of months that it seemed, from where I sat, pretty all-consuming."¹⁷¹⁵ He recalled 1984 and 1985 as "a pretty heavy-duty time."¹⁷¹⁶

In August 1984, the Rajneeshees had announced plans to gather the homeless from cities across the country and bring them to share "the abundance" of Rajneeshpuram in a program called Share-a-Home.¹⁷¹⁷ One Rajneeshee later told investigators she

---

1713 Thompson, "Atiyeh interview #1," 3.
1714 Victor Atiyeh, interviewed by Clark Hansen, "Tape 50, side 1," Oral history, recorded by Oregon Historical Society, Portland, OR, 24 July 1993. Transcript, 555, Atiyeh Collection, Pac. Univ. Archives.
1715 Gary, "Atiyeh interview," 6.
1716 Gary, "Atiyeh interview," 6.
1717 Thompson, "Chronology of Rajneeshees to November 1984."; FitzGerald, "Rajneeshpuram II," 98–100. Thompson, "Rajneesh Timeline, 1981–1986," month of April 1984. Thompson has this listed in April, but it is clear that first evidence

first heard of the idea that summer after overhearing a conversation, in July or August, between Puja and Sheela about "how they were going to win the November election."[1718] Intelligence sources inside Rajneeshpuram informed the governor's office that the program "is to aid political takeover of Wasco County. They inform us that the effort is to gain control of the upcoming elections to take over Wasco County government."[1719] "As the homeless rolled onto the ranch in the late summer of 1984, they were obliged to register to vote" by their Rajneeshee hosts.[1720] They were expected to vote for candidates backed by the Rajneeshees in upcoming county elections. Oregon's attorney general proposed some kind of task force, including members of his office and the secretary of state's office to quickly deal with any legal issues or public safety issues that might arise in the November elections.[1721]

Oregon's state police on the scene reported the influx of new people, the planning for a "man camp" housing 1,500 people in Antelope, and Rajneeshee interest in purchasing land in Idaho to create a man camp for 6,700 people.[1722] The population of Antelope in October 1984 was estimated to be eighty Rajneeshees and thirteen non-Rajneeshees.[1723] Multiplying the population by fifteen times with the man camp would be a big step for the tiny

---

was not until later in the summer of 1984.

1718 "Interview of Ma Ava," State Police, State of Oregon, (15 October 1985), 2, Atiyeh Collection, Pac. Univ. Archives.

1719 Thompson, "Rajneesh Timeline, 1981–1986," month of April 1984. Same issue with April notation in Thompson notes, but August being the real date.

1720 Les Zaitz, "Rajneeshee Leaders Take Revenge on The Dalles with Poison, Homeless," Part 3 of 5, *Portland OregonLive*, 14 April 2011, http://www.oregonlive.com.

1721 Dave Frohnmayer, Letter from Oregon Attorney General to Gerry Thompson, "Confidential Letter, Voting Issues," 19 September 1984, Atiyeh Collection, Pac. Univ. Archives.

1722 "Events of the Day: Rajneeshpuram–Antelope," State Police, State of Oregon, (6 September, 7 September 1984), Atiyeh Collection, Pac. Univ. Archives; See "Aerial Photographs of Man Camp Outside Antelope, Oregon," Oregon State Police, State of Oregon, (1 November 1984), Atiyeh Collection, Pac. Univ. Archives. There is a collection of buildings under construction that looks like it would increase the population of adjacent Antelope from a few dozen to the advertised 1500.

community. Gerry Thompson reported to the governor that the total population on October 8 of Rajneeshpuram was 7,000, with 3,500 street people among that number.[1724]

A quick calculation showed that Wasco County's voter registration was about 13,000—based on these numbers, the Rajneeshee plan to carry the 1984 elections could actually work.[1725] On that same date, Thompson heard from Michael Stoops, of Portland's Baloney Joe's—a homeless shelter—that street people at his establishment were reporting that the Rajneeshees were dumping their population of street people at night, kicking them out of Rajneeshpuram by delivering them to various towns in Oregon.[1726].

From here to the end of the saga in late 1985, the Rajneeshees were part of Atiyeh's regular pattern of weekly concerns. Thompson broke it down:

1. Weekly, and toward the end, daily briefing memos reporting all that occurred and the next steps to be taken.

2. Periodic briefing by state agencies and federal agencies.

3. Weekly, and toward the end, daily, briefings by the Oregon State Police and the military.

4. Agency discussions at weekly cabinet meetings.

5. Daily conversations between the Governor and me.[1727]

1723 "Rajneesh—insert in 26 September 1984 meeting material," Office of the Governor, State of Oregon, (26 September 1984), Atiyeh Collection, Pac. Univ. Archives.

1724 Gerry Thompson, "Rajneesh Update, October 10," Office of the Governor, State of Oregon, Memo to Governor, (10 October 1984), Atiyeh Collection, Pac. Univ. Archives.

1725 Thompson, "Rajneesh Timeline, 1981–1986," Summer 1984.

1726 Gerry Thompson, "Handwritten Notes on Rajneeshee Issues," Office of the Governor, State of Oregon, (1 October–12 October 1984), 8 October 1984, Atiyeh Collection, Pac. Univ. Archives.

1727 Thompson to Moore, 21 January 2016.

On September 11, 1984, the State Police made a request to establish a substation at the Bauman Ranch near Rajneeshpuram. There was word that the ranchers themselves were organizing and forming groups to protect themselves and their property.[1728] Thompson's recommendation was that the substation be jointly staffed by state and local law enforcement. Governor Atiyeh agreed, directing Thompson to get the State Police to quietly work with the Oregon National Guard to identify potential command posts, should the worst happen.[1729] A task force was developing mutual enforcement plans to coordinate any law enforcement actions that might be needed. There was pressure from state lawmakers for the State Police to have a much more aggressive presence in the area—for instance, intervening within Rajneeshpuram when a matter occurred involving a non-Rajneeshee.[1730] Thompson characterized the mood among some state legislators as "absolute panic."[1731]

During this same time, the poisonings of outsiders by Rajneeshees started (not including the poisoning of Michael Sullivan in February 1983). Three Wasco County commissioners visited Rajneeshpuram on August 29, 1984, and accepted glasses of water from Sheela as they changed a flat tire. One of the three became deathly ill, the other was slightly ill, and the third experienced no effects.[1732] In mid-September, hundreds of people in The Dalles, the largest city in Wasco County, were sickened by salmonella poisoning after eating at salad bars throughout the city.[1733] People believed that the Rajneeshees had deliberately poisoned the victims. Later it was learned that the mass poisoning

---

1728 Thompson, "Rajneesh Timeline, 1981–1986," September 11, 1984.
1729 Thompson, "Rajneesh Timeline, 1981–1986," September 15, 1984.
1730 K. L. Lamkin, "Meeting with Concerned Legislators," Oregon State Police, State of Oregon, Memo to John C. Williams, (18 September 1984), 2, Atiyeh Collection, Pac. Univ. Archives.
1731 Gerry Thompson, "Rajneesh, 17 Sep 1984," Office of the Governor, State of Oregon, Memo to Governor, (17 September 1984), 3, Atiyeh Collection, Pac. Univ. Archives.
1732 Zaitz, "Rajneeshee Leaders Take Revenge."
1733 FitzGerald, "Rajneeshpuram II," 100; Zaitz, "Rajneeshee Leaders Take Revenge."

"was merely a test run for Election Day, when Sheela's minions were to poison the entire water system of The Dalles."[1734]

Rajneeshee responsibility for the poisonings "was still an open question," and it was very difficult to prove any of these suspicions.[1735] By the end of September, an invoice verifying an order for *Salmonella typhi*—the parasite that causes Typhoid fever—by the Rajneeshee lab had been discovered, as well as evidence of a quick-freeze dryer for "use in the bio-lab (presumable for the development of viral cultures)."[1736] The evidence strongly pointed to deliberate poisonings by the Rajneeshees.

During all of this, the Rajneeshees were still bargaining with the governor's staff. At a meeting in Bob Oliver's office with Jayananda and Sheela, Jayananda asked, "What would the governor think if we agreed to give up Antelope [and keep our] hands off the Wasco County Commission?"[1737] Oliver told them that he was not optimistic that the governor would go for such a deal. In fact, when Oliver delivered the message to Atiyeh, Oliver's advice was, "Don't do it." Oliver duly delivered the message back to the Rajneeshees that the governor would not agree to any deals at all.[1738] John Mathis, the federal mediator, was also pressing for a meeting between the governor and the Rajneeshee leadership. Thompson, in full agreement with Oliver, was dead set against it.[1739] Atiyeh met with Mathis twice in October 1984, but the governor stuck with his position that he would not make any deals with the group, nor would he meet any of its members.[1740]

1734 FitzGerald, "Rajneeshpuram II," 116.
1735 Oliver, "Atiyeh interview," 7.
1736 Thompson, "Rajneesh Timeline, 1981–1986," September 25, 1984; Thompson, "Rajneesh Timeline, 1981–1986," September 1984.
1737 Oliver, "Atiyeh interview," 5.
1738 Oliver, "Atiyeh interview," 5.
1739 Gerry Thompson, "Rajneesh Briefing Session, September 27," Office of the Governor, State of Oregon, Memo to Governor, (27 September 1984), 3, Atiyeh Collection, Pac. Univ. Archives.

Governor Atiyeh directed the Oregon Military Department to prepare for any eventuality. The planning for Operation Serenity was completed on October 12 and forwarded by Gerry Thompson to the governor and Bob Oliver with a handwritten note: "Gov, Bob—Review military plan for action if called to duty by Gov. CONFIDENTIAL! Not for release to ANYONE Feds or State."[1741] This secret National Guard plan was never implemented. However, an appendix was added in the first week in November 1984 for a plan to deal with the homeless exodus from Rajneeshpuram.[1742] Nine months later, in late summer 1985, the establishment of communications capabilities linking the desert of central Oregon with the governor's office, was based on ideas outlined in the Operation Serenity plan.

A central part of the media coverage of the Rajneeshees was elections. Secretary of State Norma Paulus was the leading Oregon official dealing with the group on election issues—she became the face of state government in the public's mind as the Rajneeshee saga continued. By playing that role, Paulus earned herself a place on a Rajneeshee hit list (that became public knowledge in the fall of 1985), as well as some concerns from people in central Oregon. On October 5, 1984, Paulus announced plans to monitor voter registration in Wasco County, but she said the details would not be released until the following week.[1743] Town meetings in Albany and The Dalles highlighted the

---

1740 "Atiyeh Daily Index-Card Schedule, October 11, 1984, revised," Office of the Governor, State of Oregon, (11 October 1984), John Mathis, Bob Lamb, Gerry [Thompson] & Bob [Oliver], Atiyeh Collection, Pac. Univ. Archives; "Atiyeh Daily Index-Card Schedule, October 24, 1984," Office of the Governor, State of Oregon, (24 October 1984), John Mathis, Bob Lamb & Gerry [Thompson]; regarding Rajneeshees, Atiyeh Collection, Pac. Univ. Archives.

1741 "Operation Plan No. 01-84 (Operation Serenity)," State Area Command (STARC) Oregon Military Department, State of Oregon, (12 October 1984), Atiyeh Collection, Pac. Univ. Archives. Capitalization in original.

1742 "OPlan 01-184, Operation Serenity, Draft: Annex J (Disaster Relief)—Draft," State Area Command (STARC) Oregon Military Department, State of Oregon, (6 November 1984), Atiyeh Collection, Pac. Univ. Archives.

1743 Staff and Wire Service Reports, 'Rajneeshees Stir Elections Concerns: Wasco Voter Registration Monitoring Set," *Oregonian*, 6 October 1984.

Rajneeshee voting plan and called for citizen action.[1744] Paulus's reticence to provide details, the spectacle of angry anti-Rajneeshee Oregonians, accusations that Governor Atiyeh had called those angry Oregonians "vigilantes," and Democratic congressional candidate Larryann Willis's call for federal monitoring of Wasco County's elections combined to add fuel to the fire for those living with the Rajneeshees as neighbors.

On October 7, 1984, an attorney working with 1000 Friends of Oregon, Ed Sullivan, had a phone conversation with Gerry Thompson that centered on the influx of homeless people to the ranch (on the Wasco County side of the border). Thompson told him, "[E]ach street person will be sent back to their home and we will be sure it happens. Those who want to stay to vote can do so as long as they are legally registered. If legal[,] they are entitled to vote." Ed Sullivan asked "that we get Norma Paulus to calm down her actions. She is causing unrest. If Norma would calm herself and her words, Rajneeshees would calm down."[1745]

On October 9, 1984, John Mathis, the federal mediator, asked for a meeting with Governor Atiyeh in order the settle the unrest.[1746] Sheela and KD told Mathis they wanted to meet with Gerry Thompson two days later on October 11. Mathis expressed concerns to Thompson about stability within the Rajneeshee leadership. He was fearful that a large number of street people and members of the Rajneeshees, would be "jumping" on buses and saturating towns across the state. The meeting would be to get Atiyeh's endorsement of three Rajneeshee goals: to be left alone; to adjust the Bhagwan's immigration status to resident alien; and to resolve the land-use issues surrounding Rajneeshpuram. Mathis told Thompson that KD and Sheela would "present to Gov what

---

1744 Staff and Wire Service Reports, "Rajneeshees Stir Elections Concerns"; "Daily Report Summaries on Rajneeshee Activities," 15

1745 Thompson, "Rajneesh Timeline, 1981–1986," October 7, 1984.

1746 Thompson, "Handwritten Notes on Rajneeshee Situation," 9 October 1984. A note in Thompson's Rajneesh Chronology notes "Federal Mediator spending lots of time with Rajneeshee leadership. Continually bringing their requests (demands) to Gov's office," Thompson, "Chronology of Rajneeshees to November 1984," October 9, 1984; Thompson, "Rajneesh Timeline, 1981–1986."

is needed to peacefully co-exist."[1747] Mathis's take on the offer was that it was a realization that the situation was "very explosive" and the Rajneeshees were "[l]ooking for a way to get out."[1748] On the day of the scheduled meeting, Atiyeh and Thompson met at 1:30 p.m. with Mathis and Robert Lamb, Mathis's boss from the Community Relations Service in Seattle.[1749]

The governor went over the state's bargaining position and the "principles" from Sheela on October 11, as relayed to his office by Mathis and Lamb.[1750]

> Sheela principle #1: Bhagwan to become a resident alien.
>
> Atiyeh response: "he has never involved himself in immigration matters since he has been Governor and will not get involved for the Rajneesh."
>
> Sheela principle #2: "Governor instruct LCDC to review the one remaining goal issue for the land use plan."
>
> Atiyeh response: "Will review."
>
> Sheela principle #3: Resolve church-state issue between Rajneeshees and state attorneys.
>
> Atiyeh response: "Will look at it. This issue is currently before the federal courts and the question is separation of powers."
>
> Sheela principle #4: Governor needs to urge that the Rajneeshees be treated the same as any other Oregon residents.
>
> Atiyeh response: "This is up to the Rajneeshees to resolve. Only the Rajneeshees can accomplish this request by taking pressure off citizens of Oregon."

1747 Thompson, "Handwritten Notes on Rajneeshee Situation," 9 October 1984.
1748 Thompson, "Handwritten Notes on Rajneeshee Situation," 9 October 1984.
1749 Gerry Thompson, "Handwritten Notes on Meeting with Mathis, Lamb, and Governor," Office of the Governor, State of Oregon, (11 October 1984), John Mathis, Bob Lamb, Gerry [Thompson] & Bob [Oliver], Atiyeh Collection, Pac. Univ. Archives; "Atiyeh Daily Index Card, Oct 11, 1984, rev.."
1750 Gerry Thompson, "Rajneesh Update, October 15," Office of the Governor, State of Oregon, Memo to Governor, (15 October 1984), Atiyeh Collection, Pac. Univ. Archives. Paraphrases and quotations of this meeting are from this memo.

Sheela principle #5: Support for 15-mile paved road from the ranch to the county road.

Atiyeh response: Not a realistic request due to geography and cost to the county.

The October 11 meeting never took place. Sheela and KD had heard that there were 800 National Guard troops on maneuvers on the streets of Salem in full military gear to incite a confrontation. That evening Thompson explained to KD that there were only 863 total members of the Oregon Guard in the entire state, that there were only sixteen members on standby in the Salem area, ten more nearby who were out of uniform, and about thirty total Guard members in the greater Salem area. There was also an armory with rifles for 1500–2000 soldiers, but reality suggested that Sheela and KD had heard incorrectly.[1751] The events of the day showed the pressure that was ratcheting up among the Rajneeshees, as well as Mathis's desire to bring about some concessions from the governor.

While Thompson had convened the September 26 coordination meeting to be sure that the state knew what all the different government agencies were up to, she still had a feeling that the federal government through mediator John Mathis was more on the side of the Rajneeshees than the state of Oregon.

But late on a mid-October evening, about a week after the failed October 11 date, Sheela and KD, along with one of Sheela's confidantes in the dirty tricks unit, finally met with Atiyeh's chief of staff, Gerry Thompson, at a state office building in Portland.[1752] Thompson recalled that night.[1753] "Up to this point I'd been

---

[1751] Thompson, "Handwritten Notes on Meeting with Mathis, Lamb, and Governor."
[1752] Les Zaitz, "Rajneeshee Leaders See Enemies Everywhere as Questions Compound," Part 4 of 5, *Portland OregonLive*, 14 April 2011, http://www.oregonlive.com.
[1753] Best guess is October 16. October 11 was the date Sheela and KD did not show up for the meeting. By October 20, KD was definitely an informant for Thompson, the night of the "dump" of street people. Thompson's notes for October 16 specifically mention "KD meeting today" along with clear points about immigration, city/state relations, land use, road improvements, and voting—the same agenda/principles passed along to Atiyeh and Thompson by Mathis and Lamb as being from Sheela

meeting with KD. KD's been pleading with us to meet with Sheela. Finally, he calls me in panic and says, 'Gerry, please promise me we'll sit down and talk. Things are really getting bad.'" Thompson asked under what circumstances they would meet. KD told her that the Rajneeshees wanted to get an airplane and fly her over to the ranch. Thompson refused. "The state police would not ever have allowed that to happen. At that point they were protecting me, and they said, 'You go over there, and who knows what's going to happen.'" KD proposed that they come pick Thompson up and meet at the Rajneeshee hotel in Portland. That was also not acceptable. Thompson said, "I've got to tell you, KD, I'm not going to meet you in any of your facilities." KD countered that the Rajneeshees would not meet in the governor's office. That was okay with Thompson. She offered to find a neutral place. But she would need to know who KD was bringing to the meeting.

Thompson emphasized to KD, "Understand that if we have a meeting, that it will be under the strict rules that I set, nobody else's."

The night of the meeting with Sheela was dark and rainy.[1754] "It was so undercover, it tickles me even to this day," Thompson remembered. "[State Police Superintendent John Williams, Oregon Military Department Adjutant General Richard Miller, and a driver] pick me up underneath the Capitol building and then we go up on the main street in front of the Capitol building." Thompson was not too sure about this; she wondered what this was all about. "And this seedy looking, gruff [man]…walks up to this unmarked police car (I'm not sure who's driving us, but General Miller's sitting in the front, John Williams is on the passenger side in the back, and I'm in the back). John Williams

---

on October 11. By October 17 Thompson told the state police "that KD had called her frequently all day, related he was 'sitting on a bomb.'" Circumstantial evidence, but October 16 could be the date—and both KD and Sheela were in Salem earlier that day to attend Bob Davis' funeral. The weather October 15–17 was foggy and cool at night. Thompson, "Atiyeh Interview #3," 10–11.

[1754] Zaitz's article reports a Fall 1984 meeting, Zaitz, "Rajneeshee Leaders See Enemies."

rolled his window down, and this guy talks to John Williams, like, 'You got a cigarette?' John Williams, who doesn't smoke at all, hands him the cigarette, and they say something, and [he] rolls the window back up, and we go." Thompson asked what this was all about. It was one of their "undercover people from Rajneeshpuram giving John a last-minute report about what they had found."

"I mean we really did have great insight, thanks to the state police. The state police never got the credit they deserved. Anyway, that was message passing," Thompson laughed as she told the story.

They met in the Public Service building in Portland. It was late enough at night that there was nothing going on anywhere around the building. Thompson's group got there early. Sheela and KD and two or three others walked in. "We greeted everybody friendly, on very friendly terms. We sat down. I remember sitting behind a desk. John's sitting to my left. I thank Sheela for being willing to meet, but I tell her that her temper tantrums have caused her a lot of problems and there can be no temper tantrums tonight. 'Sheela, I will not tolerate any of your foul language. The first time it happens, that's the end; I'm closing the meeting down, it's all over.'"

"Well, I can't even remember exactly how fast it happened, but rather fast, and she started calling me a [Thompson makes a garbled bleeping noise] because I wouldn't give her her first demand. I literally did slam my fist down [Thompson slams her fist on the table in the interview] and said, 'Meeting's over, Sheela! Sorry. Out. We're done!'"

"Well her temper went. She jumped up out of that chair…, and they walked out into the hall. KD, I still have that vision vivid in my mind—he's walked out—but he comes back in, and he leans around the door, and he says, 'Gerry, promise me you'll keep talking. Please, promise me. We really need you to keep talking.' I said, 'You and I will talk later.' That was the end of it." From that moment onward (beginning with phone calls the next day), KD became an informant for Thompson.

"Driving home, I am feeling [*pffft*]. I remember saying to John, 'I'm not sure I did the right thing.' And John's not saying much. I may have blown this. But in the back of my mind...I'm saying to myself—I made it clear to her, and I had, that we would not accept threats, because any threat she wanted to throw our way, we were ready to handle. And those were the governor's instructions. He always said, 'Gerry, make it clear to them that no matter what they threaten we can handle anything they throw our way.' And that's what I said in the preface of the meeting. So, I kept reminding myself, 'Okay, there's nothing we can give them.' The main three issues: the land-use issue—the city [Rajneeshpuram]—the immigration issue, and they wanted the Bhagwan to become a citizen of the United States. And all three of them, I can't do it. I don't care if I want to. I can't do it."

In Thompson's opinion that was the turning point for the Rajneeshees. "I really do." "Don't get me wrong. I'm not saying I [caused the corner to be turned], but the fact that I shut it down made it clear we were not going to discuss anymore, that I showed a little bit of anger; I think Sheela went home, scared, and decided, 'We're hurting.'"[1755] An intelligence report the governor's office received a few days later reinforced this sense. In the days leading up to the meeting with Thompson, an informant told of phone calls with Sheela that ranged between revengeful anger ("They would not sit by and watch their organization be destroyed") and feeling that "she had made a terrible mistake" bringing in the street people.[1756] If Sheela was showing this much stress before the meeting, the complete collapse of the talks would certainly have exacerbated the pressure Sheela felt.

[1755] Thompson, "Atiyeh Interview #3," 1; brackets indicate 2017 toning down of Thompson's role in causation, Thompson, "Atiyeh Interview #5," 2.

[1756] John P. McCafferty, "Officer's Report: Intelligence Information," Oregon State Police, State of Oregon, (19 October 1984), 1, Atiyeh Collection, Pac. Univ. Archives.

Atiyeh agreed that this October meeting with Sheela was the pivotal event that led the Rajneeshee leadership to consider leaving Oregon. Atiyeh thought that when the Rajneeshees figured out that there would be no trades with the Atiyeh administration that this was the time the Bhagwan began thinking about leaving.[1757]

KD became the crucial Rajneeshee informant for Gerry Thompson.[1758] "He and I got on the telephone, and we had a long conversation." Thompson told KD, "I will help you in any way I can, but you understand that the paramount issues, neither the governor nor I can bend on. But I will help you in any way." Thompson sensed that there was trouble brewing within the Rajneeshee leadership. "I sensed that you're running out of money, I sensed that things were beginning to crumble," along with the street people problem. "I said, 'I'd really like it if we could work together.' And he said, I can remember him saying very clearly, 'Beloved Gerry, I will always trust you, and I want you to always trust me. And if we work together as partners, we can get through this.' That's just indelibly inscribed in my mind."

KD "tipped us off on everything" from then on.[1759] KD would call Thompson at all hours of the night. "But that was okay. He was trying to show that he was willing. I think he was afraid. I think he saw it coming down; I think he lost faith in Sheela."

Bill Gary, still Deputy Attorney General, remembered feeling that the Rajneeshees were undergoing some changes in the ways they were thinking about their relations with Oregon. From his point of view (not knowing of the secret meeting between Sheela and Thompson), he felt it was because of the pressure of the church-state issue and the attorney general's opinion against the existence of the town of Rajneeshpuram. "We had some pretty

---

1757 Victor Atiyeh, interviewed by Jim Moore, "Atiyeh interview #2," Raleigh Hills, OR, 2 January 2014. Summary notes, 3. Thompson did not know the governor agreed with her 1984 assessment of the timing of her showdown with Sheela until Thompson was interviewed for this book project and the author showed her the governor's words.
1758 Thompson, "Atiyeh Interview #3," 12.
1759 Thompson, "Atiyeh Interview #3," 12.

high-level settlement talks with the Rajneeshees around this time."[1760] At one meeting Gary held in the Governor's conference room with KD, Prem Niren—who was the group's chief lawyer—and Jayananda, the Rajneeshees were trying to find a way that would satisfy the state so that the Rajneeshees could continue to exist as a commune and not violate the establishment clause. Gary had never had a face-to-face meeting with Niren before, but they had seen each other once in court. At this meeting, pleasantries were exchanged, and then Niren and Jayananda asked what they needed to do to satisfy the state. Gary told them, "'You have to really, truly, actually give up control of the government.' And there was a long silence. Jayananda said, 'That can never happen.' And that was the end of the discussion."

Things were coming to a head with the scheme to register the formerly homeless residents of Rajneeshpuram to support Rajneeshee candidates for the Wasco County commission in the November 1984 elections. This broke out into the open after weeks of rumor in early October. At 8:30 a.m. on October 10, word reached the governor's office that "several bus loads [were] on way to Wasco County to register" as voters.[1761] The county clerk shuttered the office.

That same day, Secretary of State Paulus suspended regular registration of new voters in the county and instituted "a special hearing process" set up in The Dalles (Wasco County's seat) to judge whether the new voters had the intent to continue to live in Wasco County.[1762] Oregon Deputy Attorney General Gary was of the opinion that Paulus's plan "has real problems. Federal law provides that you cannot treat persons seeking to vote any more stringently than existing voters." He told Gerry Thompson, "Norma [is] not accepting the information very well."[1763] In a very public way, Sheela agreed with Gary's assessment:

1760 Gary, "Atiyeh interview," 2.
1761 Thompson, "Handwritten Notes on Rajneeshee Situation," 10 October 1984.
1762 FitzGerald, "Rajneeshpuram I," 100.
1763 Thompson, "Rajneesh Timeline, 1981–1986," October 12, 1984.

Sheela complained that it would mean a 200-mile round trip for those from Rajneeshpuram who want to register to vote. "Why should they (Rajneeshees and street people) go there when they can register people in Rajneeshpuram?" Sheela asked. "They should make it convenient and possible for people to vote." "Elections are for people," Sheela said, "they are not for Comrade Paulus's comfort. I do not live in the USSR, I live in America."[1764]

Paulus heard a very different message from former chief judge of the Oregon Court of Appeals, Herb Schwab. She recalled that "people were relieved that someone had stood up and said, 'This is it.'" Schwab "told her, 'Norma, you could be elected queen today.'"[1765]

The October 23 voter registration hearings in The Dalles were something of an anticlimax. There were 315 potential voters there, but only fifteen of them were from Rajneeshpuram. By the 2:15 pm end of the hearings, "three hundred non-Rajneesh were afforded hearings and none rejected. Fifteen Rajneesh were examined, with two rejections."[1766] When election day actually arrived on November 6, Rajneeshee voters seemed to vote only for municipal candidates in Rajneeshpuram, leaving the county commission candidates to be decided by the non-Rajneeshpuram voters in the county.

The Rajneeshee Share-a-Home program reached a crisis point on October 20, just days before the anticlimactic voter registration hearings. The pressure had been building for weeks. As the homeless turned up in Portland on their way to Rajneeshpuram, the local shelters noticed an uptick in those needing services. Portland mayor-elect Bud Clark expressed concerns that "the homeless now settling at Rajneeshpuram would eventually move to Portland, placing an additional burden on already strained

---

1764 Don Jepsen and Roberta Ulrich, "State to Hire Lawyers for Wasco Voter Registration," *Oregonian*, 13 October 1984. Parentheses in original.
1765 Norma Paulus, Gail Wells and Pat McCord Amacher, *The Only Woman in the Room: The Norma Paulus Story*, ed. Melody Rose, Women and Politics in the Pacific Northwest, (Corvallis, OR: Oregon State University Press, 2017), 168.
1766 "Daily Report Summaries on Rajneeshee Activities," October 28, 1984.

resources."[1767] By the end of September there were reports of grim conditions for the Share-a-Home participants in Rajneeshpuram, raising further fears that many of the new arrivals would leave the ranch for Oregon cities and towns.[1768]

Meetings in the governor's office were underway to figure out what to do about the street people who had been invited to Rajneeshpuram but were now beginning to leave the Rajneeshee community. On September 25, 1984, there was a meeting of top Oregon department heads, along with the Superintendent of the State Police and Bob Oliver, the governor's legal assistant, that concluded that the big problem was money. That same morning Jefferson County DA Sullivan told the State Police that the Rajneeshees would "no longer pay for the return of street people to their original place of residence as was promised in the recruitment."[1769] The State of Oregon simply had no funds available to help people with bus tickets, housing, or anything else. The State Police had limited funds, but not much.[1770] Those attending the meeting were afraid that the situation was moving from a political problem to a potential violence problem.[1771] As a result of this meeting, Oregon's Adult and Family Services swung into action with ideas about how to deal with the influx of homeless from the Share-a-Home program.[1772] Homeless agencies in Portland made an appeal for help to house the expected influx of people from Rajneeshpuram.[1773]

1767 John Painter, Jr., "Burnside Fears Influx of Homeless, Clark Says," *Oregonian*, 14 September 1984.
1768 Phil Manzano, "Rajneeshees' Guests Cite Armed-Camp Conditions," *Oregonian*, 27 September 1984; Jeanie Senior and Phil Manzano, "Exodus Stirs New Tensions in C. Oregon," *Oregonian*, 29 September 1984.
1769 "Daily Report Summaries on Rajneeshee Activities," 10.
1770 Thompson, "Handwritten Notes on Rajneeshee Situation," 25 September 1984.
1771 Thompson, "Briefing by Oregon State Police: Rajneesh—Williams, Pankratz, Lamkin, Thompson, Oliver."
1772 Keith Putnam, "Briefing Paper—Rajneesh Street People," Adult and Family Services Division, State of Oregon, Memo to Leo Hegstrom, Dave Fiskum, (25 September 1984), Atiyeh Collection, Pac. Univ. Archives.
1773 Nelson Pickett, "Fund for Stranded Proposed," *Oregonian*, 10 October 1984; Janet Christ, "Agencies Seek Help to House Influx of Homeless to Portland," *Oregonian*, 12 October 1984.

State government, even with a lack of funds to pay for transporting the street people, inventoried its capabilities. Transportation was a key problem, so bus lines were contacted, schedules were studied, and plans were made. Bill Bebout, in the office of Oregon's Public Utility Commissioner, worked on getting cut rates from the bus companies.[1774] Trailways Bus Lines revised its schedule as of October 1 to add more buses among Northwest cities. Specific state contingency plans alerted private social service groups throughout the state and ensured that the National Guard could be mobilized, "within a few hours" to "feed anywhere from 1,200 to 1,500 individuals." But the biggest problem the state still faced was a shortage of funds to pay for transportation of the street people back to their places of origin. "We have been unable to identify any existing appropriation of state monies which lawfully could be used to provide this transportation—other than through allocation by the Emergency Board."[1775]

Tension grew. Would there be a big dump of homeless? Or would they continue to trickle out as they decided that Rajneeshpuram was not for them? By October 19 there were unconfirmed reports of buses of homeless heading to Eugene, Medford, and Portland.[1776] On October 19, twenty former Share-a-Home people left Portland by bus with tickets paid for by the Salvation Army from "its growing pot of contributions to finance travel for homeless people who have visited" Rajneeshpuram.[1777] Clearly the plea for donations was beginning to work.

October 20, however, saw the day the governor's staff had dreaded. That evening, the dump started in earnest. Gerry

---

1774 "Record of Transportation Capabilities," Office of the Governor, State of Oregon, (October 1984), Atiyeh Collection, Pac. Univ. Archives.

1775 Bob Oliver, "'Dumping' Contingency Plans," Office of the Governor, State of Oregon, Memo to Governor Atiyeh, (18 October 1984), 2, Atiyeh Collection, Pac. Univ. Archives.

1776 Gerry Thompson, "Rajneesh-Related Activities," Office of the Governor, State of Oregon, (19 October 1984), Atiyeh Collection, Pac. Univ. Archives.

1777 Dan Hortsch and Roberta Ulrich, "Score from Rajneeshpuram Head Home by Bus," *Oregonian*, 20 October 1984.

Thompson was at home that Saturday evening. In his new role as informant, KD had warned Thompson that the dumping might occur that night. Thompson had a personal line to the governor, a police radio, and whatever was needed so that she was on top of what was happening. Her husband, Al, sat at the kitchen table with her and wrote down everything as it was happening. "It was scary." Pat Amedeo was tracking down bus lines. Bob Oliver was providing legal advice. Denny Miles had to be informed in the event the media found out. And the governor was informed of everything. "It was a busy time."[1778]

From 9:00 that Saturday night until shortly after midnight on Monday morning, about twenty-seven hours, information flowed to Thompson, her husband Al kept notes, actions were coordinated with the Salvation Army in The Dalles, with Deputy Attorney General Bill Gary, with the state police, with state and local school officials (to open gyms to house overflows from other shelters). Bob Oliver was patched in to many of the calls. Governor Atiyeh was updated throughout the weekend. And the relationship between Thompson and her new informant, KD, was put to the test.[1779]

The days following the dumping weekend saw a lot of action from the state. Atiyeh had a meeting about the situation on October 25 and October 30.[1780] Salvation Army Lieutenant Wes Trueblood reported on what had happened. The governor responded with a four-page letter detailing what Trueblood had done. "Thank you again, Lieutenant Trueblood," Atiyeh wrote. "Your efforts are very much appreciated, and I thank you for having responded so quickly and so well. You can be assured of

---

1778 Thompson, "Atiyeh Interview #3," 3.
1779 Gerry Thompson, "Timeline of 'Dumping' of Street People," Office of the Governor, State of Oregon, (20 October 1984), Atiyeh Collection, Pac. Univ. Archives.
1780 "Atiyeh Daily Index-Card Schedule, October 25, 1984," Office of the Governor, State of Oregon, (25 October 1984), Laura Bentley, Myrtle Flanan or Margaret Hill & Gerry [Thompson]; regarding Rajneeshees, Atiyeh Collection, Pac. Univ. Archives; "Atiyeh Daily Index-Card Schedule, October 30, 1984," Office of the Governor, State of Oregon, (30 October 1984), Bill Dixon, Margaret & Phil Hill; regarding Rajneeshees, Atiyeh Collection, Pac. Univ. Archives.

my continuing support for your efforts."[1781] Reports came from the media and from the state police about ongoing departures from Rajneeshpuram.[1782] Sheela announced on October 29 that only a few more people would be leaving Rajneeshpuram, "in other words the dumping is just about over," Gerry Thompson conveyed to Atiyeh.[1783]

Back on the ranch, the State Police maintained two types of presence—one very open, and the other secret to everybody. The open presence was a 24/7 manned State Police outpost right in Rajneeshpuram. There was very little that got by the eyes of these officers as they worked with the Rajneeshpuram Peace Force. The covert presence was through the infiltration of undercover officers, like the "gruff" person who had approached the car the night Gerry Thompson and John Williams went to meet with Sheela. With all the tensions during October 1984, Williams wrote to the Chief of the Rajneeshee Peace Force to emphasize that trust and openness were goals that both sides needed to continue to cultivate.[1784] This seemed even more important with a report from the State Police that the Rajneeshees had purchased over 110,000 pounds of blasting powder and over 220 cases of dynamite between March and October 1984. Combined with confirmed reports of twenty semi-automatic weapons on the ranch and almost 44,000 rounds of ammunition, this was beginning to

---

1781 Victor Atiyeh, Governor to Wes Trueblood, Salvation Army, The Dalles, "Review of 'Evaluation of October 20–21 Operation Homeless' Paper," 30 October 1984, Atiyeh Collection, Pac. Univ. Archives.

1782 Duane A. Pankratz, "Departures," State Police, State of Oregon, Memo to Bob Oliver, (26 October 1984), Atiyeh Collection, Pac. Univ. Archives; Jeanie Senior, "More Leave Rajneeshpuram After 'Participation' Talk," *Oregonian*, 23 October 1984; Jeanie Senior, "'Non-Participation' Cited as Rajneesh Homeless Ejected," *Oregonian*, 22 October 1984.

1783 Gerry Thompson, "Info Relayed by Telephone to Governor," Office of the Governor, State of Oregon, (29 October 1984), Atiyeh Collection, Pac. Univ. Archives.

1784 John C. Williams, Letter from Superintendent of Oregon State Police to Ma Deva Barkha, Chief of Police, Rajneeshpuram, "Trust Between OSP and Rajneeshpuram Peace Force," 1 November 1984, Atiyeh Collection, Pac. Univ. Archives.

look like either a very well-armed road construction crew or something that could be much more dangerous.[1785]

The governor appointed a liaison between his office and those who provided services to the homeless in Portland. Dave Fiskum had worked in state government and the governor's office, taking over for Denny Miles as communications director in 1982 when Miles ran the governor's re-election campaign. He would now serve as the governor's liaison "for the Homeless Evicted by the Rajneesh" with responsibilities including communications, assisting the Salvation Army, collecting information for the governor and other officials, and to "prepare final community impact reports for the Governor and local community."[1786]

There was other fallout. Deputy Attorney General Bill Gary met with federal mediator John Mathis. "Mathis was candid—admitted he was too close to the situation and is now trying to get out of it."[1787] This began to make sense out of the cryptic communication between Mathis and Bob Oliver reported on October 1—about "the federal government's 'disengagement' from this problem."[1788] Mathis told Gary that the Community Relations Service "has deviated from usual practices and [was] re-examining their involvement." He continued that the Rajneeshees were ready to bargain away the Share-a-Home program "and get the street people out of here. AG told Mathis, 'No trade.'"[1789]

The money issue continued to bedevil the governor. How to pay for the bus tickets so the homeless could return to the places they had been when the Rajneeshees enticed them to come to

---

1785 "Explosives," State Police, State of Oregon, (1 November 1984), Atiyeh Collection, Pac. Univ. Archives.
1786 Gerry Thompson, "Position: Governor's Special Community Liaison for the Homeless Evicted by the Rajneesh: For David Fiskum," Office of the Governor, State of Oregon, (26 October 1984), Atiyeh Collection, Pac. Univ. Archives.
1787 Thompson, "Rajneesh Update. October 29," 3.
1788 Bob Oliver, "John Mathis," Office of the Governor, State of Oregon, Memo to Gerry Thompson, (1 October 1984), Atiyeh Collection, Pac. Univ. Archives.
1789 Thompson, "Rajneesh Update. October 29," 3.

central Oregon?[1790] The governor's office hit upon asking for help from two of the large charitable foundations in Oregon. Atiyeh sent letters to the head of the United Way of the Columbia Willamette and the director of the Oregon Community Foundation.[1791] Ned Look at the Oregon Community Foundation was able to help raise money which was funneled to the Salvation Army to help pay for bus tickets. By the third week in November the Salvation Army reported that it had raised $56,000 for its efforts, including $5000 from Ned Look (anonymously), and $20,000 from Ecumenical Ministries of Oregon.[1792] None of this was ever public.[1793]

A report by the State Police in early December counted around 1900 homeless people departures from Rajneeshpuram since October 20. The estimate was that about 1400 were left in Rajneeshpuram but estimates by departing street people put the number as low as 300.[1794]

The governor's office had weekly meetings on the Rajneeshee situation, following the pattern of the weekly meetings among the state agency directors. Meetings were more frequent when specific issues came up. Atiyeh and Gerry Thompson were very careful who they invited to those meetings. They did not want too

---

1790 Jerry Bieberle, "Resources for Homeless in Portland," State Community Services, State of Oregon, Memo to Leo Hegstrom, (2 November 1984), Atiyeh Collection, Pac. Univ. Archives.

1791 Victor Atiyeh, Letter on Office of Governor letterhead to Edward H. Look, Executive Director of Oregon Community Foundation, "Fundraising Request, OCF," 5 November 1984, Atiyeh Collection, Pac. Univ. Archives; Victor Atiyeh, Letter on Office of Governor letterhead to Daniel Regis, Chairman of the Board, United Way of the Columbia Willamette, "Fundraising Request, United Way," 5 November 1984, Atiyeh Collection, Pac. Univ. Archives; Dave Fiskum, "Fundraising Connections," Office of the Governor, State of Oregon, Memo to Gerry T., (5 November 1984), Atiyeh Collection, Pac. Univ. Archives.

1792 Dave Fiskum, "Salvation Army," Office of the Governor, State of Oregon, Phone message, (21 November 1984), Atiyeh Collection, Pac. Univ. Archives. "Groups to Aid Homeless," *Oregonian*, 22 November 1984.

1793 Victor Atiyeh, interviewed by Jim Moore, "Atiyeh interview #4," Raleigh Hills, OR, 3 June 2014. Summary notes, 8.

1794 Duane A. Pankratz, "Street People Departures, December 5," Department of State Police, State of Oregon, Memo to Bob Oliver, (5 December 1984), Atiyeh Collection, Pac. Univ. Archives.

many people because of the problem of leaks. Crucial to the process was keeping the identity of KD, the key informant, absolutely secret.[1795] Dave Frohnmayer was at the meetings when legal matters were in play. There were the FBI, the US attorney; there was a huge list of people and agencies involved. There were land-use issues; there were health issues. If there was a specific issue involving the state, then only the relevant people were brought in to deal with that. For instance, Norma Paulus "was monitoring the election process in Wasco County," so she would only be at meetings that dealt with elections. But state government people did not come to the meetings as a rule. They were just given specific tasks to work on.[1796]

Recalling the secrecy, Atiyeh shared: "[W]e had to limit who knew what it was that we were doing. Too many leaky boats."[1797]

State	Local government	Federal	Other
Governor*	Antelope City attorney	FBI*	1000 Friends of Oregon
Attorney General*	Jefferson County District*	Federal Mediator	Baloney Joe's, Portland
Secretary of State*	Jefferson County Sheriff	IRS*	Guardian Angels,
	The Dalles city attorney	ATF*	West Coast
State Police*	Wasco County Clerk	US Attorney, Portland office*	Guardian Angels, International leadership
Military Department*	Wasco County Commission	US Customs*	
	Wasco County District Attorney	US Dept. of Justice, Seattle office	
State Legislators from district	Wasco County Emergency Services	US Drug Enforcement Agency (DEA)*	
	Wasco County	US	

1795 Thompson, "Atiyeh interview #2," 4.
1796 Thompson, "Atiyeh interview #2," 3–4.
1797 Atiyeh, "Tape 50, side 1," 557.

	Sheriff	Immigration and Naturalization service (INS)*	
Commerce			
Department of Environ-mental Quality			
Department of Justice*			
Education			
Energy			
Fire Marshall			
Health Division, Department of Human Services			
Intergovernmental Relations, Executive Department			
Land Conservation and Development Commission (LCDC)			
Public Utilities Commission			
State Health Planning and Development Agency (SHPDA)			
Transportation			

A list of the agencies involved. Asterisks show agencies specifically in attendance at the September 26 coordination meeting.

Thinking about this compartmentalization in 2017, Thompson did not think that it was a strategic intention to limit the roles of other statewide officials, "we just wanted to keep it clean. We wanted to know who was doing what, for what" reason.[1798] Atiyeh and Thompson were acutely aware of the constitutional roles of the other officeholders, "and that was part of our reasoning," Thompson said. The governor told her, "I've got my duties for what I've been elected [to do], but I" have a broader mandate than

---

1798 Thompson, "Atiyeh Interview #5," 3.

the others.[1799] Atiyeh continued, "We don't instruct them what to do. They've got their own bailiwicks."

The costs of breaking the secrecy seemed to be huge. On Christmas Day 1984, Gerry Thompson recalled, "We are 99% certain that they tried to set my house on fire." Thompson's family celebrated with Christmas Eve and Christmas dinner. As she was setting the table for Christmas dinner, she looked out the window and "these plants, mind you, it's Christmastime and it's cold and it's wet outside, and these plants were charred.... They've been burned. They were pretty much certain that was Rajneeshees. They started putting security on my house."[1800]

1985—Crisis and Composure

A potentially catastrophic incident shook those close to the governor in January 1985. The night before Atiyeh's final regular legislative session was to start, he was invited to say a few words at a dinner. During the course of the dinner he got sick. "Really sick." He got up, said a few words, and left. He went home, but "finally went to the hospital, emergency ward, and my doctor, Dr. Bill Drips, ...came. This was at night. They gave me a shot to take care of my dizziness. They began to monitor it because it had the signs of a heart attack, and you know, monitor and check all of that out. I stayed in the hospital all that night, being monitored all the time."[1801] He was dizzy, he was nauseous, "it just came on."[1802] Denny Miles, Dolores Atiyeh, and Gerry Thompson all thought the Rajneeshees had something to do with it. Lon Holbrook, the governor's security, did not make any connection between Atiyeh's sudden illness and the Rajneeshees—he just focused on getting the governor to the hospital and making sure

---

1799 Thompson, "Atiyeh Interview #3," 3.
1800 Thompson, "Atiyeh Interview #3," 9.
1801 Victor Atiyeh, interviewed by Clark Hansen, "Tape 45," Oral history, recorded by Oregon Historical Society, Portland, OR, 9 July 1993. Transcript, 427–428, Atiyeh Collection, Pac. Univ. Archives.
1802 Atiyeh, "Atiyeh interview #4," 7; Robert Jones, interviewed by Jim Moore, "Atiyeh interview," Portland, OR, 21 July 2015. Summary notes, 2.

there was a state trooper with him all night.[1803] Holbrook was totally unaware of the suppositions of others that the Rajneeshees might have been involved. Atiyeh was given shots and he was able to get up and go to the legislature the next morning. He was anxious because this was his last chance to speak at the opening of a new legislative session.[1804] Atiyeh got clearance from Drips to deliver his speech: "I got there and made my speech, and again, nobody really knew this ever happened to me. I don't know today what it was, and Bill Drips doesn't know, but really it was a terrible feeling. I haven't felt anything like that before or since."[1805]

Newly sworn-in Oregon Secretary of State Barbara Roberts vividly remembered the incident. "I got a call from Gerry one night. 'Madame Secretary, I just wanted you to know that they took Governor Atiyeh to the hospital.' There was a second sentence, but by then I was on the floor. ...It scared the hell out of me."[1806] It was a stark reminder that in Oregon the Secretary of State is the successor to the governor.

Communication between the Rajneeshees and the state was sporadic in early 1985. When KD would not tell the State Police when there was another group of street people heading away from the ranch on buses, the State Police would stop every vehicle to check. At one point in early January 1985, "KD 'stupidly' arranged a demonstration of the use of weapons possessed by the Peace Force and its reserve" in front of about fourteen reporters with their attendant cameras.[1807] The idea was to show how

---

1803 Holbrook, "Atiyeh interview," 12.
1804 Miles, "Atiyeh interview #1," 7.
1805 Atiyeh, "Tape 45," 428.
1806 Barbara Roberts, interviewed by Jim Moore, "Atiyeh interview," Portland, OR, 23 February 2015. Summary notes, 1.
1807 Bob Oliver, "Rajneesh, January 4," Office of the Governor, State of Oregon, Memo to Gerry Thompson, (4 January 1985), Atiyeh Collection, Pac. Univ. Archives. Quotation is from John Mathis report to Oliver; Duane A. Pankratz, "Phone Message," Office of the Governor, State of Oregon, (4 January 1985), Atiyeh Collection, Pac. Univ. Archives. Jeanie Senior, "Rajneeshees Demonstrate Gun Skills," *Oregonian*, 5 January 1985.

prepared the group was to manage the expected thousands of attendees for the 1985 summer religious festival.

By the end of June it was clear that the footprint of the Rajneeshees had "shrunk dramatically."[1808] In Portland the Rajneeshee businesses had closed, and the moneymaking machine that had supported the movement showed signs of serious problems. At about the same time, the Rajneeshees initiated a series of public information requests from the state government—calendars and notes that had been taken during meetings, mainly—trying to build a case that there had been a conspiracy against the group from the governor on down.[1809] Sheela compiled a hit list of enemies in June 1985. The U.S. Attorney in Oregon, Charles Turner, Oregon's Attorney General, Dave Frohnmayer, Secretary of State Norma Paulus, Jefferson County District Attorney Michael Sullivan, the *Oregonian*'s investigative reporter Les Zaitz, other local officials and several people in the Rajneeshee community were all targeted.[1810]

In September of 1983 Les Zaitz of the *Oregonian* had informed the governor's office that he and some colleagues were about to launch an investigation of all things Rajneeshee.[1811] The twenty-part series was scheduled to begin running in the paper at the end of June 1985, which it eventually did. Knowing this was coming up, Sheela asked KD to go "case" Zaitz's office at the *Oregonian* in April or May 1985. He did so, knowing that another Rajneeshee was living in Portland with the specific task of "trying to get into the *Oregonian* building and destroy the files on the Rajneesh," possibly by running magnets over the electronic files.[1812] The plot was never fully carried out, but it showed the descent

---

1808 Callister, Long and Zaitz, "Rajneeshees Falter," A10.
1809 "Rajneeshee Public Records Requests, Legal Correspondence," Rajneesh Legal Services Corporation, City of Rajneeshpuram; State of Oregon, (25 June–10 September 1985), Atiyeh Collection, Pac. Univ. Archives.
1810 FitzGerald, "Rajneeshpuram II," 119; Atiyeh, "Tape 50, side 1," 559.
1811 Bob Oliver, "Les Zeitz' [sic] Investigation," Office of the Governor, State of Oregon, Memo to Rajneesh File, (9 September 1983), Atiyeh Collection, Pac. Univ. Archives.
1812 Krishna (K.D.) Deva, "Deposition: Burglary/The *Oregonian* Newspaper,' FBI State Police, INS, State of Oregon, U.S. Government, (29 October–5 November

into fear and lashing out that characterized the last year of the group in Oregon.

That summer the INS investigation was seen as the biggest threat to the commune.[1813] And there were several hearings before the Oregon Supreme Court dealing mainly with the land-use arguments. There was a "sub rosa" invitation to all the Supreme Court law clerks to go out to Rajneeshpuram. Some of them actually went. The Chief Justice, Ed Peterson, was very angry—it was a tremendous conflict of interest to go visit a group that had a case before the court like that. Robert Jones, an associate justice, wondered at the judgment of these supposedly bright young lawyers working as clerks in the court.[1814]

The intelligence available to the governor was comprehensive. They could tell where the Bhagwan was at any given time—on federal property, on private property, driving in one of his Rolls-Royces—and the same went for the other leaders of the Rajneeshees.[1815] By the end, Atiyeh's security person, Lon Holbrook, thought there were about twenty state police detectives in Rajneeshpuram itself.[1816] Holbrook knew there was concern for their safety if the whole Rajneeshee enterprise disintegrated.

Throughout 1985, Atiyeh always carried with him, usually in his inside coat pocket, an unsigned declaration of martial law for Jefferson and Wasco Counties.[1817] There was a ready room back at the capitol for the governor in which all possibilities were planned for, just like they planned for disasters and incidents at the Trojan nuclear power plant.[1818]

Richard Miller, the Adjutant General of the Oregon Military Department was told that the governor was carrying the state of

---

1985), Atiyeh Collection, Pac. Univ. Archives.
1813 Callister, Long and Zaitz, "Immigration Woes," A1.
1814 Jones, "Atiyeh interview," 2.
1815 Miles, "Atiyeh interview #1," 6.
1816 Holbrook, "Atiyeh interview," 11.
1817 "Unsigned Rajneesh Proclamation," Office of the Governor, State of Oregon, (1985), Atiyeh Collection, Pac. Univ. Archives.
1818 Miles, "Atiyeh interview #1," 6.

emergency declaration and the martial law declaration in his pocket. Thompson recalled, "I remember we were sitting and talking with General Miller. And the governor said, 'You know, we're getting close to the point when any little thing could cause havoc. Is there any way you could find a possibility to be in the area?' 'Oh yeah. We could just have maneuvers over there. We've got to do training all the time' And that's exactly what they did. That's how quickly that happened." Atiyeh ordered the Oregon National Guard out on maneuvers about ten miles north of the Rajneeshee communities, and stretching south to "property overlooking the ranch," in mid-September 1985, complete with helicopters, personnel carriers, and live ammunition.[1819] "We were very quiet about all that," recalled Thompson.[1820] Atiyeh was pleased because if the Guard was in training, then the federal government actually picked up the tab.[1821] The National Guard stayed in place, on maneuvers, and only began to pull back on October 2, 1985.[1822]

On September 16, 1985, the commune announced that Sheela and several other leaders had left Rajneeshpuram for Europe.[1823] That day, and in the days that followed, the departed group was accused, by the Bhagwan himself, who remained in Oregon, of attempting to poison the Bhagwan and his close companions, poisoning the water system for The Dalles, poisoning the Jefferson County DA, "of robbing and setting fire to the Wasco County planning office," several other poisonings of people in the county, and "quite possibly…the salmonella outbreak in The Dalles."[1824] It was a stunning turnaround in the Rajneeshees' view of themselves. All of this just confirmed, however, the view of many Oregonians that something bad was happening up at the

---

1819 Atiyeh, "Atiyeh interview #2," 4; Miles, "Atiyeh interview #1," 6; Thompson, "Rajneesh Timeline, 1981–1986," September 1984.
1820 Thompson, "Atiyeh Interview #3," 8.
1821 Atiyeh, "Atiyeh interview #4," 8.
1822 Thompson, "Rajneesh Timeline, 1981–1986," October 2, 1985.
1823 Robert Madsen, "Events of the Day: Leaders have left," State Police, State of Oregon, (16 September 1985), Atiyeh Collection, Pac. Univ. Archives.
1824 FitzGerald, "Rajneeshpuram II," 108.

ranch. And it turned out that the allegations were true.[1825] It was only then that Mike Sullivan realized he might have been a victim of the Rajneeshees with his life-threatening illness in February 1983.[1826]

Officers from various federal, state, and local law-enforcement groups swarmed the ranch, along with journalists of all stripes. There was not much initial evidence of the allegations, but investigators were shown a state-of-the-art system of electronic eavesdropping and wiretapping that covered most of the buildings and rooms in Rajneeshpuram.[1827] This sophisticated eavesdropping system had apparently begun in 1984. Sheela had bugged the Bhagwan's compound to keep track of those she felt challenged her authority.[1828] On September 20 and 21, 1985, the Oregon State Police and the FBI discovered extensive wiretap and hidden microphones in the Rajneesh Hotel in Portland. Thirteen microphones were removed from the ceilings of four rooms. The next day more microphones were removed from Rajneeshpuram buildings, and an extra one was found in the group's Portland restaurant.[1829]

Madras, in Jefferson County, was used as a staging area for all the different federal, state, and local law enforcement groups as they went into Rajneeshpuram and Rajneesh (the former Antelope) to execute the search warrants. One of these groups was a special team from the FBI. Mike Sullivan got a call at work from a person who lived in Madras. "We just saw about twelve guys running by, and they don't look like the kind of people hanging around Madras. They've got tiny, tiny little waists, and their shoulders look like they play football in the NFL." Sullivan told this person, "Well I can't tell you what they're doing, but I don't want you to bother them.... Let me just assure you they're

---

1825 Zaitz, "25 Years After Rajneeshee Commune."
1826 Sullivan, "Atiyeh interview," 5. *Oregonian*, "Police Try to Unsnarl Tangle of Rajneesh Charges," 18 September 1985.
1827 FitzGerald, "Rajneeshpuram II," 108.
1828 Zaitz, "25 Years After Rajneeshee Commune."
1829 Mervin H. Baker, "Officer's Report," State Police, State of Oregon, (24 September 1985), Atiyeh Collection, Pac. Univ. Archives.

there because they need to be here. And that's all you need to know, and I'd appreciate it if you didn't speak to anybody else about your observations."[1830]

In October 1985 a federal grand jury indicted the Bhagwan, Sheela, and a six others with "a conspiracy to evade the immigration laws."[1831] That weekend two Lear jets transporting the Bhagwan and his close aides flew from the ranch and hopscotched across the country.[1832] Atiyeh was in Taiwan on a trade mission when the Bhagwan was preparing to flee; the governor would be in Damascus when word of the Bhagwan's arrest reached him—and Sheela's arrest would occur in Germany on the same day. On this October trip, Atiyeh talked in code to Thompson back in Salem because they were worried the Rajneeshees had tapped the state's phones. "Later he tells me, 'I thought I knew what you were telling me, but I wasn't positive.'"[1833] Thompson knew that he understood what was going on, that they were moving in for the arrest of Sheela in Germany.

The federal government knew exactly where the Bhagwan was at every minute and probably how much fuel he had in his jet. Gerry Thompson followed the October 27 flight of his jet in great detail.

> GT is monitoring all activity by private telephone line—in direct contact with FAA. Reports to Governor every few minutes [in Damascus on his foreign trip]. We know if Bhagwan's plane flies south we can apprehend him before he leaves the United States because plane will have to stop for refueling. If plane goes north, we will lose opportunity to apprehend and arrest. Plane would not have to refuel until out of the United States.

1830 Sullivan, "Atiyeh interview," 10.
1831 Charles H. Turner and Robert C. Weaver, Confidential Letter from U.S. Attorney to Governor accompanying sealed indictment of Bhagwan Shree Rajneesh, Ma Anand Sheela, et al. to Vic Atiyeh. "Sealed Indictment," 23 October 1985, Atiyeh Collection, Pac. Univ. Archives; FitzGerald, "Rajneeshpuram II," 110.
1832 FitzGerald, "Rajneeshpuram II," 110–111.
1833 Thompson, "Atiyeh interview #3," 6.

FAA monitors flight for us. The flight takes the southern route.[1834]

In Charlotte, North Carolina, where arrangements had been made for another chartered jet to make the hop to Bermuda, federal agents arrested the Bhagwan, "with six of his disciples, and also a gun, fifty-eight thousand dollars in cash, and a box containing thirty-five jewel-encrusted watches and bracelets."[1835] Always updating her boss, Thompson sent a detailed memo to Atiyeh on October 31 about the nearly simultaneous arrests of Sheela and Puja in Germany on October 28 and the Bhagwan in North Carolina.[1836] Upon his return to Portland after two weeks in Taiwan and Damascus, Atiyeh was asked, as Thompson had predicted, about the Rajneeshee saga, not about what he accomplished on his trip. He emphasized that the legal system was working well, and that Oregon had planned for just the eventualities that led to both sets of arrests.[1837]

The state's Rajneeshpuram task force continued its daily reports on activities at all the areas where the Rajneeshees were active. Reports continued to come in to the governor's office about plea deals over criminal charges, figuring out who was now in charge of the Rajneeshee operations in Oregon, and resolving tax issues with Wasco County.[1838]

At the end of October, KD was telling all he knew about the Rajneeshee operation. He verified all kinds of information: 500–600 illegal marriages to evade INS rules, assassination lists, false immigration documents dating back to July 1981, and the use of

---

1834 Thompson, "Rajneesh Timeline, 1981–1986," October 27, 1985.
1835 FitzGerald, "Rajneeshpuram II," 111.
1836 Gerry Thompson, "Important and Urgent," Office of the Governor, State of Oregon, Memorandum to Governor, (31 October 1985), Atiyeh Collection, Pac. Univ. Archives.
1837 *Oregonian*, "Governor Says Arrests Well-Planned," 2 November 1985.
1838 Thompson, "Handwritten Notes on Rajneeshee Situation," 22 Nov, 25 Nov, 26 Nov, 27 Nov 1985. "Summary of Daily Reports, 2–29 December," State Police, State of Oregon, (2 December–29 December 1985), Atiyeh Collection, Pac. Univ. Archives.

sophisticated computer and eavesdropping systems.[1839] KD confirmed all the allegations the Bhagwan had made when Sheela's group fled in mid-September. Atiyeh was kept informed of all the legal happenings in meetings with Dave Frohnmayer, Bill Gary, and State Police Superintendent Williams.[1840] By the middle of November, the Bhagwan had cut a deal with federal prosecutors back in Portland, receiving $400,000 in fines, a suspended ten-year prison term, and agreeing to leave the United States and stay away for at least five years. That same day he flew out of the country never to return.[1841]

Within weeks in the autumn of 1985, the commune fell apart and disbanded.

By 1986 a series of criminal cases and lawsuits had dispersed the assets of the movement, and its leaders were either in prison or expelled from the United States.[1842] Atiyeh had his last scheduled meeting on the group in January 1986, with Dave Frohnmayer and Gerry Thompson.[1843] The Bhagwan lived until 1990, dying in Pune, India, where his movement had become so strong in the 1970s and 1980s.[1844] In 1989 the Bhagwan changed his name to Osho—there are still hundreds of Osho meditation centers around the world.

1839 Marlen G. Hein, "Interview of Krishna Deva," State Police, State of Oregon, (1 November 1985), Atiyeh Collection, Pac. Univ. Archives.
1840 "Atiyeh Daily Index-Card Schedule, November 5, 1985," Office of the Governor, State of Oregon, (5 November 1985), [Handwritten by staff] Dave Frohnmayer, Bill Gary, Atiyeh Collection, Pac. Univ. Archives; "Atiyeh Daily Index-Card Schedule, November 25, 1985," Office of the Governor, State of Oregon, (25 November 1985), [Handwritten by Atiyeh] John Williams/Frohnmayer, Atiyeh Collection, Pac. Univ. Archives.
1841 FitzGerald, "Rajneeshpuram II," 112.
1842 Charles H. Turner and Dave Frohnmayer, "Joint Statement by United States Attorney Charles H. Turner and Oregon Attorney General Dave Frohnmayer," U.S. Attorney; Oregon Attorney General, (31 January 1986), Atiyeh Collection, Pac. Univ. Archives.
1843 "Atiyeh Daily Index-Card Schedule, January 8, 1986," Office of the Governor, State of Oregon, (8 January 1986), Dave Frohnmayer and Gerry; regarding Rajneesh, Atiyeh Collection, Pac. Univ. Archives.
1844 Driver and Boffey, "Rajneesh Chronology," 35.

As for the challenges to the legitimacy of the town of Rajneeshpuram, in July 1985 the Oregon Supreme Court ruled that Wasco County had followed land-use laws when it allowed the incorporation vote in 1981. But the court sent back to the Land Use Board of Appeals questions about whether County Commissioner Rick Cantrell had a conflict of interest because of the cattle sale, and whether there was a complete study of the impact of development on agricultural land.[1845] The Oregon Court of Appeals, in August 1986, held that Cantrell did have a conflict of interest, so the original Wasco County approval was invalid.[1846] This was a win for 1000 Friends of Oregon—but on the procedural side, not on the land-use side. In a final ruling in 1987, the Oregon Supreme Court ruled that there was no "apparent" or actual bias in Cantrell's private and public actions.[1847] And in December 1985 a U.S. District Judge ruled in favor of Dave Frohnmayer's opinion that Rajneeshpuram could not be incorporated because it violated the separation of church and state.[1848]

The problem the Rajneeshees faced may have been their own leadership's unwillingness to compromise with the government on election and church-state issues. This is the intriguing argument laid out by historian Carl Abbott in a 2015 *Oregon Historical Quarterly* article.[1849] Unlike the Mormons in 19th century Utah, who faced "an advancing federal force of three thousand," the Rajneeshees faced "a state elections official" and would not accede to government requirements.[1850] The LDS

[1845] Driver and Boffey, "Rajneesh Chronology," 25.
[1846] Driver and Boffey, "Rajneesh Chronology," 31.
[1847] Allen L. Johnson, "Letters: Response to Abbott article on Rajneeshees," *Oregon Historical Quarterly* 117, no. 4 (2016), https://doi.org.10.5403/oregonhistq.117.4.0666.
[1848] Driver and Boffey, "Rajneesh Chronology," 28.
[1849] Carl Abbott, "Revisiting Rajneeshpuram: Oregon's Largest Utopian Community as Western History," *Oregon Historical Quarterly* 116, no. 4 (2015), https://doi.org.10.5403/oregonhistq.116.4.0414.
[1850] Abbott, "Revisiting Rajneeshpuram," 443.

leadership gave up the governorship of Utah in exchange "for tacit religious tolerance that lasted for a generation."[1851]

A big difference between the two cases, however, was that Utah's laws were created with the large Mormon population in mind (in fact, the laws were created by legislatures full of Mormons). The Rajneeshees, on the other hand, thought they had purchased a piece of empty land far away from intervening governments. Instead, they had purchased a piece of land in the only state in the country with statewide land-use laws, laws that quickly entangled the new group and contributed to the embittered relations between the Rajneeshees, the state, and the independent land-use watchdogs like 1000 Friends of Oregon.

In 2016, an eerily similar situation would develop as anti–Federal land advocates occupied Malheur National Wildlife Refuge buildings in southeast Oregon for over forty days. The group, basing its ideals on an interpretation of Mormon theology, demanded local control of the federal lands.[1852] It was very apparent that they, just like the Rajneeshees, had no idea that Oregon's land use laws would severely limit what could be done with the land if it did revert to the state. The *Oregonian* reporter coordinating coverage of the 2016 standoff was Les Zaitz, the same reporter who was on Sheela's hit list back in 1985.[1853]

"The reason that so many people have forgotten about this episode so quickly," in Mike Sullivan's opinion, "is that we had a government at that point that worked well together and did the right thing and handled the situation according to law and observed people's rights during the process." From the perspective of someone poisoned by the Rajneeshees, Sullivan

---

1851 Abbott, "Revisiting Rajneeshpuram," 443.
1852 Carli Brousseau, "Oregon Standoff: What Does Mormonism Have to Do with the U.S. Constitution?" *Portland OregonLive*, 16 February 2016, http://www.oregonlive.com.
1853 Mark Katches, "Oregon Standoff: The *Oregonian/OregonLive* Newsroom Produced 356 Stories During Occupation," Editor's Notebook, *Portland OregonLive*, 26 February 2016, http://www.oregonlive.com.

felt that "we were fortunate to have Governor Atiyeh as the head of our state at the time that this occurred."[1854]

Summed up his own part in the affair, Atiyeh said,

> [T]here was a lot of misunderstanding about my role and what I was doing. I was protecting Oregonians, but we had to do it in a very silent sense, you know. It was not a public sense. And… politicians were free [to act] in any direction they wanted. They didn't have the responsibility that I had, at least that I felt that I had. Here as I say I'm trying to keep it calm and they're stirring the pot. And I know it was [a] good political thing to do to stir the pot, politically for them. But it certainly wasn't a responsible thing to do. But you just persist in doing what you think is the right thing to do. I suppose that's where a good grounding in what your belief in the system of government is, a real test, you know, you really get tested. One thing is to say you believe it and the other is to get tested to see if you believe it. I didn't really consider it a test, I mean, to me it was just one of those things and there was no question that we were going to do what our democracy called for.[1855]

1854 Sullivan, "Atiyeh interview," 1–2.
1855 Atiyeh, "Tape 50, side 1," 563.

8 Building relationships

Vic Atiyeh was not the first Oregon governor to travel to other countries in search of economic partners. Nor was he the last. But Atiyeh made these trips more consistently, and seemingly with more enthusiasm, than any other governor before or since. For him, the reasoning was simple: he applied his salesman's logic from decades in retail business.

He knew the key to long-term success in building ties between Oregon and foreign companies and governments was the personal relationships that could only be built with face-to-face meetings and socializing. Atiyeh paid a political cost for the trips—when he returned to Oregon many people would ask what he had brought back from a specific trade mission, and Atiyeh would explain that the missions were about establishing relationships and making connections; they were about proving that Oregon was a good place to invest. Atiyeh's chief of staff, Gerry Thompson, recalled that the questioning in the media and by some economists was "unmerciful" as they questioned the cost-benefit analysis of the trade trips.[1856]

[1856] Gerry Thompson, interviewed by Jim Moore, "Atiyeh interview #1," Salem, OR, 16 September 2014. Summary notes, 6–7.

During Atiyeh's first term, he made two trips, about the norm for Oregon governors. He spent three of those first years struggling to figure out Oregon's ailing economy and how to get it back up and smoothly running. Beyond Oregon's overdependence on timber and timber byproducts, Atiyeh pointed out that the state was too dependent on agriculture, and that the fishing industry had been hit hard by the recession and declining fish runs. This was the way Atiyeh's first term in office ended—it was basically economic triage.[1857] In contrast, during his second term, he traveled abroad nine times. All these journeys were directly tied to his goal of bringing jobs and investments to Oregon.

Atiyeh was one of many U.S. governors to actively pursue international investment, especially in his second term. But he was always slightly ahead of governors in other states. By midway through his second term, in about 1984–85, Atiyeh would run into governors on his travels who always told him that he had been there first, or most often, in making connections with other countries. Atiyeh recalled the governor of Missouri, Kit Bond (R) arriving at Atiyeh's Tokyo hotel right after Oregon's September 1984 announcement that Fujitsu would open a factory. Bond called out, "Hey, leave something for me!"[1858] Bond had just been told by Epson executives that "his state would have to stand in line behind Oregon" for future investment.[1859]

The role of governors had changed in the 1950s and 1960s as state governments grew: governors were expected to be managers of the growing state bureaucracies.[1860] In negotiating the ever more complex relations with the federal government, governors acquired the skills and expectations to also deal with foreign

---

1857 Thompson, "Atiyeh interview #2," 6.
1858 Victor Atiyeh, interviewed by Jim Moore, "Atiyeh interview #1," Raleigh Hills, OR, 19 December 2013. Summary notes, 2.
1859 Sue Hill, "Mae Yih Takes Limelight as Mission Reaches China," *Salem (OR) Statesman Journal*, 19 September 1984, Atiyeh Collection, Pac. Univ. Archives.
1860 Samuel Lucas McMillian, "Subnational Foreign Policy Actors: How and Why Governors Participate in U.S. Foreign Policy," *Foreign Policy Analysis* 4, no. 3 (2008): 229, https://doi.org.10.1111/j.1743-8594.2008.00068.x.

countries. Beginning with Mark Hatfield, Oregon's governors began to make overseas trips to find trade opportunities. Hatfield visited Japan, West Germany, and France in two trips in 1964 and 1965.[1861] The first Japanese trade mission to the west coast stopped in Portland in 1966.[1862] Tom McCall made trips to east Asia in 1968 and 1972, even getting a tour of the Taiwanese Presidential Palace from Madame Chiang Kai-shek.[1863] Atiyeh himself had been a member of an eight-person Oregon delegation that visited the Philippines in June 1974 just days after Atiyeh won the Republican gubernatorial primary, and just hours after a typhoon hit the delegation's destination of Luzon.[1864] Bob Straub visited Japan with Washington Governor Dan Evans (R) in 1975 with a heavy focus on timber trade.[1865] Straub was deeply involved in planning a 1978 trip to China, a trip that would have been a coordinated effort among the governors of Washington, Idaho, and Oregon. But Dixy Lee Ray, Washington's governor, objected to the China venture, stressing that Taiwan was a long-trusted trading partner and that a China trip would upset ongoing commercial ties.[1866] The China trip was officially canceled in the

---

1861 AP, "Hatfields Meet Japan Royalty," *Oregonian*, 18 November 1964; Gerry Pratt, "Hatfield Tells Japan of Two-Party Need: Making the Dollar," *Oregonian*, 26 November 1964; AP, "W. German Parliament Greets Hatfield, State Trade Mission," *Oregonian*, 2 December 1965; AP, "Hatfield Eyes New Meetings," *Oregonian*, 8 December 1965; *Oregonian* "Hatfield Lauds Members of German Trade Mission," 12 January 1966.

1862 *Oregonian*, "Japanese Trade Mission Schedules Portland Visit," 16 February 1966; *Oregonian*, "Visiting Japanese Trade Mission Seeks Close Culture, Economic Ties," 15 March 1966.

1863 AP, "McCall Visits South Korea: Trade Mission Makes Rounds," *Oregonian*, 26 November 1968; AP, "Trade Group Eyes Talks: Oregon Mission Arrives in Japan," *Oregonian*, 16 November 1968; Leverett Richards, "China Line to Study Portland Flights," *Oregonian*, 10 December 1968; AP, "McCall to Head Tour of Far East," *Oregonian*, 8 January 1972; *Oregonian*, "Oregon Women Taste Lavish 10-Course Chinese Dinner on Far Eastern Trade Mission," 17 February 1972; Edmund Ames and Muriel Ames, "Taiwan's Cities Decay While Industry Booms: From Disaster, New Growth," *Oregonian*, 14 December 1972.

1864 *Oregonian*, "Oregon Group Avoids Typhoon," 13 June 1974.

1865 *Oregonian*, "State Lumber Purchase Seen," 7 October 1975; *Oregonian*, "Straub Bills Japan Trip," 31 July 1975.

1866 Donald J. Sorensen, "Oregon Trade Mission to China Said Possible," *Oregonian*, 20 December 1977; *Oregonian*, "Oregon Slates China Mission: Washington

summer of 1978 because Evans and Straub could not "get final authorization from the Chinese for technical seminars and trade discussions."[1867]

Atiyeh, and other subnational leaders, were stepping into the international role because they needed to engage their economies with the world, regardless of what the US government might or might not be up to. This was part of a new understanding of global politics called complex interdependence.[1868] It was not just the high politics of diplomacy among countries that was important, it was all those international relationships among lower-level actors that really made the world work. Atiyeh's move toward a more intensive engagement with other countries as he sought foreign direct investment in Oregon was indicative of the times

Laying Groundwork in Early Trips

Atiyeh started thinking of international concerns soon after taking office. He pushed an emphasis on language training in Oregon schools, creating the Governor's Commission on Foreign Languages and International Studies, seeing a need to get Oregon students up to speed in a rapidly globalizing world.[1869] When the commission released its final report in 1982, it confirmed Atiyeh's observations that Oregonians did not, as a whole, really grasp the broader world that they lived in.[1870] The solutions the commission proposed centered on education, but the timing of the final report

---

Governor Objects," 29 April 1978.

1867 *Oregonian*, "Straub Drops Summer Trip to China," 27 June 1978.

1868 See Robert O. Keohane and Joseph S. Nye, *Power and Interdependence: World Politics in Transition*, (Boston: Little, Brown, 1977).

1869 Atiyeh, "Tape 52," 633; Richard Colby, "Teachers Seek Way to Enrich Foreign Studies," *Oregonian*, 2 February 1980; Huntly Collins, "State Panel on Global Studies Asked: Educators Ready Plan," *Oregonian*, 11 February 1980; "Final Report," Oregon Governor's Commission on Foreign Language and International Studies, State of Oregon, (August 1982), Atiyeh Collection, Pac. Univ. Archives.

1870 "Final Report."

put it in the middle of Oregon's worst recession since the Great Depression. There was no new money for many of the proposals.

Atiyeh's first international trip as governor would be to east Asia in October 1979, beginning in Japan and finishing in Taiwan, with a few days in South Korea in the middle. This first delegation was heavy on government participants, and a bit light on Oregon businesses. With relatively little fanfare, the delegation headed off.[1871] The eleven members accompanying Atiyeh was headed up by Jason Boe (D-Reedsport), the President of the Oregon Senate, and included five people representing the Port of Portland, one person from the state's Department of Economic Development, two people affiliated with the Department of Agriculture, the publisher of the *Daily Astorian*, and the director of Coos Bay's Western Bank.[1872] Atiyeh was well aware that Japanese companies had been in Oregon for years before he became governor, noting that there had even been a Bank of Tokyo branch in Portland.[1873] However, he started out on his first trip working to recruit more business to Oregon, particularly Japanese investment that would work with Oregon's export economy.

And, as it turned out, Japanese companies liked the Port of Portland's location so much they had begun to use it as a major place to export Japanese goods (like cars), which could then be sent to bigger U.S. markets via rail or trucking. The delegation's meetings in Japan centered around the big Japanese shipping lines so crucial to the Port of Portland's role, as well as some of the major shippers—Toyota Motors (which had made the Port of Portland its main shipping destination in the United States), the Honda Motor Company, and representatives of the U.S. Western

---

1871 AP, "Atiyeh Begins Visit," *Oregonian*, 30 September 1979.
1872 "Asian Trip: State of Oregon–Port of Portland Delegation Schedule and Itinerary," Office of the Governor, State of Oregon, (28 September–11 October 1979), 1, Atiyeh Collection, Pac. Univ. Archives.
1873 Victor Atiyeh, interviewed by Clark Hansen, "Tape 40, side 2," Oral history, recorded by Oregon Historical Society, 28 June 1993. Transcript, 283, Atiyeh Collection, Pac. Univ. Archives.

Wheat Association.[1874] This was also Oregon's first official meeting with the Japanese Keidanren, "described," according to the governor's itinerary, "as the most prestigious association of top management in Japan."[1875] There would also be a meeting with the powerful Ministry of International Trade and Industry, MITI, a major player in Japan's transition into an economic powerhouse during the 1960s, '70s, and '80s.[1876] At the end of this leg of the trip, Atiyeh announced, "Personally, I'm delighted.... We've no firm offers yet, but we will have."[1877] There was, however, a bit of learning about how the two economic systems worked. Atiyeh noted that the Japanese companies were not rushing to invest in Oregon; they wanted to understand "things like environmental laws, our tax structure and the situation with regard to labor relations."[1878]

Then it was on to South Korea for more meetings with shipping lines, wheat customers, and potential customers for shipping automobiles through the Port of Portland.[1879] South Korean delegations had visited the United States a few months earlier, making a stop in Seattle, but skipping Portland, in what was described as "a buying spree" of business deals.[1880] Oregon was clearly a bit behind in the Pacific Northwest economic sweepstakes with east Asia. Atiyeh hoped that South Korea and Oregon could continue to grow together, saying, "Our current trading partners—and our potential customers in the Orient—are nations which have undergone a dramatic change in recent years. Economic trends in nations such as Korea, Japan and Taiwan and others in the Orient have created new markets. Beneficial trade

---

1874 "Asian Trip Schedule and Itinerary," 4, 5, 6.
1875 "Asian Trip Schedule and Itinerary," 4.
1876 "Asian Trip Schedule and Itinerary."; see Chalmers Johnson, *MITI and the Japanese Miracle: The Growth of Industrial Policy, 1925–1975*, (Stanford, CA: Stanford University Press, 1982).
1877 AP, "Oregon Governor 'Delighted' Over Trade Talks," *Tokyo (Japan) Asahi Evening News*, 2 October 1979, Atiyeh Collection, Pac. Univ. Archives; AP, "Atiyeh Enthused," *Oregonian*, 2 October 1979.
1878 AP, "Oregon Governor 'Delighted'"; AP, "Atiyeh Enthused."
1879 "Asian Trip Schedule and Itinerary," 8–10.
1880 AP, "Seattle to Court Korean Traders: Billions at Stake," *Oregonian*, 1 April 1979.

with these nations has shown great promise for Oregon."[1881] As a result of connections made on this trip, the Oregon-Korea Economic Cooperation Committee was created in 1980. South Korea would become a very important economic partner with Oregon in the years to come with 1982 being designated the "Year of Korea" in the state.[1882]

The last stop on the trip, Taiwan, was a more complex political environment for the Oregon delegation because the Carter administration had been sending signals in 1978 that it might diplomatically recognize the People's Republic of China (PRC).[1883] In Oregon as in many other places, Republicans tended to be on the pro-Taiwan side of the question. This was Vic Atiyeh's stance. As governor, Atiyeh would make statements about Oregon's respect for the free-market system and call for more openness by mainland China. But Atiyeh always knew that there was only so much he could do to advance these ideas.

In mid-December 1978, as Atiyeh was deep in transition plans to become Oregon's governor in January 1979, Carter did announce that the United States had officially recognized the PRC. When Oregon's delegation arrived in Taipei, the capital of Taiwan, the visit coincided with the celebration of Taiwan's National Day, on October 10, called the Double Tenth holiday (10/10). Atiyeh showed that his natural gift for diplomacy was at work. He told a reporter, "We deliberately focused on Taiwan, deliberately avoided visiting the People's Republic of China, which is being wooed by other Oregon groups. We came here

---

1881 *Korean Herald* (Seoul), "Oregon Realizes Korea's Potential: Gov. Atiyeh on Visit," 5 October 1979, Atiyeh Collection, Pac. Univ. Archives; Ahn Young-sop, "State of Oregon Seeks Closer Ties with ROK: Visiting Governor," *Seoul Korean Herald*, 5 October 1979, Atiyeh Collection, Pac. Univ. Archives.

1882 "Atiyeh Daily Index-Card Schedule, February 26, 1982," Office of the Governor, State of Oregon, Special Signing: 'Year of Korea', (26 February 1982), Atiyeh Collection, Pac. Univ. Archives; 'Atiyeh Daily Index-Card Schedule, April 30, 1982," Office of the Governor, State of Oregon, Chang Sohn re: Ore./Korea Trade, (30 April 1982), Atiyeh Collection, Pac. Univ. Archives.

1883 James Reston, "Inching Toward China," *New York Times*, 14 June 1978.

primarily to thank the government and people of Taiwan for their business and their staunch friendship over the past 30 years."[1884]

This first trip would come to be understood by Atiyeh as the beginning of a long process. The trips from January 1979 to March 1987 (when Atiyeh accompanied the new governor, Neil Goldschmidt, on his first visit to Japan) were a process of "continually pushing, moving forward, to diversify the economy of the state, and it [was] something I would tell you was extraordinarily successful. [In 1979] we had as our base agriculture and wood products, timber, and about half tourism. When I left, we had the wood products, agriculture, full-blown tourism, high-tech, and international trade."[1885]

Cultural Diplomacy

From 1981 on, the Jewish community in Portland had approached Atiyeh about making a trip to Israel.[1886] Atiyeh recalled that he would always tell them, "I'd like to do that," but he would add, "You know, if I ever do that I'm going to have to go to Syria," his father's home country.[1887] As Atiyeh began to focus on the potential for economic connections with different parts of the world, he began to think about the Middle East as a possible destination. No Oregon governor had traveled to the region, but there were several Oregon companies—wood products businesses and electrical generation companies—doing business

---

[1884] Leverett Richards, "Taiwan Heads Woo Atiyeh to Promote More Trade," *Oregonian*, 11 October 1979.

[1885] Victor Atiyeh, interviewed by Clark Hansen, "Tape 44," Oral history, recorded by Oregon Historical Society, 7 July 1993. Transcript, 407, Atiyeh Collection, Pac. Univ. Archives.

[1886] "Atiyeh Daily Index-Card Schedule, April 28, 1981," Office of the Governor, State of Oregon, (28 April 1981), Paul Romain, Denny re: Israel trip, Atiyeh Collection, Pac. Univ. Archives; "Atiyeh Daily Index-Card Schedule, May 28, 1981," Office of the Governor, State of Oregon, (28 May 1981), Paul Romaine Hershel Tanzer re: Israel/Syria trip, Atiyeh Collection, Pac. Univ. Archives.

[1887] Victor Atiyeh, interviewed by Clark Hansen, "Tape 41," Oral history, recorded by Oregon Historical Society, 28 June 1993. Transcript, 311–312, Atiyeh Collection, Pac. Univ. Archives.

there. Atiyeh added it all up, and finally said to himself and his staff, "Okay, that's not a bad idea. Let's do that."[1388] And so his eventual 1984 trip was put in motion. The Oregon delegation visited Saudi Arabia, Egypt, Syria, and ended in Israel.

The visit had a personal rather than political quality to it. There was no great hope that Oregon would have a strong trade relationship with Syria and Lebanon. Atiyeh was the first American governor of Arab descent, but an Arab American identity was not part of Atiyeh's political persona—in contrast with, for instance, the role Irish Catholicism played in Kennedy family campaigns. For journalist Mike Donahue, who accompanied the governor on most of the trip, the visit was not "Arab" per se, "it was like someone going to visit their home in another country."[1889] *Oregonian* writer David Sarasohn had a similar take on the personal nature of this trip.[1890] The trips had to do with building ties between the Arab countries and the United States in general, not just Oregon. And, in Sarasohn's eyes, for Atiyeh it was a very personal trip.

Atiyeh's delegation visited Jeddah, Jubail, and Riyadh in Saudi Arabia in March 1984. His job, as it was on all the international trips, was to open doors for the Oregon delegation as they sought to make business contacts. He loved the role of chief salesman. It was not his responsibility to close deals but to get people together. He told the members of the delegation, "If you want me to make calls with you, I'll be glad to do that." His understanding of his role was that the governor was "always doing ceremonial things. But I was willing to go talk to [the business] prospects. …I was always for them and their business, and so I was lending the prestige of the governor's office. And I enjoyed it. Being a businessman, I did enjoy it."[1891]

1888 Atiyeh, "Tape 41," 312.
1889 Mike Donahue, interviewed by Jim Moore, "Atiyeh interview," Portland, OR, 2 February 2015. Summary notes, 4–5.
1890 David Sarasohn, interviewed by Jim Moore, "Atiyeh interview," Portland, OR, 17 February 2015. Summary notes, 7.
1891 Atiyeh, "Tape 41," 314.

Atiyeh's Arab heritage was mainly tied to familiar family foods and his parents' Syrian friends, so he was unexpectedly overcome as he stepped out of the plane at the airport in Jeddah, Saudi Arabia:[1892] "[A]ll of a sudden I got this huge emotional feeling[;] ...it surprised me. ...I hadn't thought, 'Oh boy, ...I'm going back to my roots.' ...I never thought about it, [and then] I just couldn't hardly wait to get down on the ground. And I'm in Saudi Arabia; I'm not in Syria yet."[1893] Atiyeh visited a rug factory in Jeddah. The rug salesman turned governor compared the techniques used in the factory with the types of rugs he had sold over the decades at Atiyeh Brothers.[1894] The delegation toured desert wheat farming, including a project carried out by a representative of Oregon's growers. There were Oregonians working in Saudi Arabia—as journalists or in agriculture, and there were Hood River pears to be found (on sale) in the Jeddah Safeway.[1895] Of course the pears were obvious because Atiyeh was appearing at a scheduled "promotion for Northwest fruits."[1896]

As the delegation headed to Egypt, the economic landscape was very different. While the Saudis were spending their oil

---

[1892] "Mid-East Itinerary: Tuesday, March 13 through Monday, April 16, 1984," Office of the Governor, State of Oregon, (1984), 3, Atiyeh Collection, Pac. Univ. Archives.

[1893] Atiyeh, "Tape 41," 313.

[1894] Mike Donahue, "Rug Factory," News story, recorded by KOIN television, Jeddah, Saudi Arabia, 6 April 1984. Transcript, Atiyeh Collection, Pac. Univ. Archives; Stan Wilson, "Rug Factory," News story, recorded by KATU television, Portland, OR, 27 March 1984. Transcript, Atiyeh Collection, Pac. Univ. Archives; Mike Donahue, "Saudi Manufacturing and Goods," News story, recorded by KOIN television, Jeddah, Saudi Arabia, 6 April 1984. MOV file, Atiyeh Collection, Pac. Univ. Archives.

[1895] Mark Sanchez, "Oregonian in Arabia," News story, recorded by KOIN television, Jeddah, Saudi Arabia, 2 April 1984. Transcript, Atiyeh Collection, Pac. Univ. Archives; Mark Sanchez, "Americans in Arabia," News story, recorded by KOIN television, Jeddah, Saudi Arabia, 5 April 1984. Transcript, Atiyeh Collection, Pac. Univ. Archives; Lisa Stark, "Jeddah Safeway," News story, recorded by KATU television, Jeddah, Saudi Arabia, 27 March 1984. Transcript, Atiyeh Collection, Pac. Univ. Archives; Mike Donahue, "Pears from Oregon," News story, recorded by KOIN television, Jeddah, Saudi Arabia, 3 April 1984. Transcript, Atiyeh Collection, Pac. Univ. Archives.

[1896] "Mid-East Itinerary," Wednesday, March 21.

wealth on infrastructure, buildings, and beginning to prepare for a post-oil world, Egypt "was having financial troubles," in Atiyeh's memory.[1897] Atiyeh had been to Costa Rica, a developing country, in 1980, but his visit there focused on meetings with government officials and visits to tourist spots. Egypt was his introduction to the poverty of much of the world. He recalled, "I was in the Ramses Hilton, a very fine room, very western, first-rate, first class. And I'm on a high floor and I'm looking down out of the window at some of the most poor—I mean, just terrible housing. Right out of my window, out of this fancy hotel I'm in, and all of the poverty and terrible living that's right around me."[1898] The shift from a socialist economy under Nasser, the 1981 assassination of Nasser's successor, Anwar Sadat, and the relatively new presidency of Hosni Mubarak made Egypt a different environment for Oregon investment.

Atiyeh did get a meeting with President Mubarak. He and his cousin, Sami Kahl—who also served as an Arabic interpreter on the trip—talked directly with Mubarak. The scheduled fifteen-minute meeting continued for over an hour.

The only hitch was the gift Atiyeh attempted to give the Egyptian president. As knives were considered very popular among Arab and other Middle Easter leaders, the governor brought along knives made by Gerber, an Oregon company.[1899] The knives were kept in myrtlewood boxes and engraved. One of Mubarak's staff members came in with the box containing the knife and opened it up; the president thanked Atiyeh, and then the box was closed and promptly taken away. Nobody in Atiyeh's entourage was anywhere near Mubarak when this took place. Given that Mubarak's predecessor, Anwar Sadat, had been assassinated just three years earlier by his own bodyguards, this reticence to have weapons in close vicinity to the president made

---

1897 Atiyeh, "Tape 41," 315.
1898 Atiyeh, "Tape 41," 318.
1899 Gerber is now owned by a Finnish company, Fiskars. William G. Loy et al., *Atlas of Oregon*, 2nd ed., (Eugene, OR: University of Oregon Press, 2001), 81.

a lot of sense. The Oregonians did not even try to bestow a knife as a gift to Assad in Syria.[1900]

As Atiyeh headed to reporters outside following his talk with Mubarak, a U.S. embassy official could be seen gesturing intently and making some distinct points with Atiyeh. Reporters had the sense that Atiyeh was being told that the "very frank" discussions with Mubarak needed to be kept under wraps in Atiyeh's conversation with the press.[1901]

For Atiyeh, the trip to Syria was both business and a family reunion. But he knew very well that Syria was in the middle of a tense region and was playing a role in the disintegration of Lebanon (in the middle of a civil war that lasted from 1975 to 1990), as well as the ongoing confrontation with Israel. There were hostages, among them Americans, being held in Lebanon. Atiyeh made his chief of staff, Gerry Thompson, sign a "no hostage-negotiation" pledge to use if he was kidnapped.[1902] Thompson said she could not sign such a document, but the governor insisted. And he made it clear to Thompson that she could not allow Dolores to negotiate either. The pledge was signed. Dolores Atiyeh knew nothing of this, nor did Denny Miles nor Lon Holbrook, Atiyeh's staffers who accompanied him on the entire Middle East trip. Miles found out about the pledge after Atiyeh had left office.[1903]

Just getting permission to go to Syria had been difficult. Regardless of Atiyeh's family ties to the country and the region, high politics had intruded on his plans to mix business and pleasure. In February 1984, the Syrian government made it clear that it did not want Atiyeh to leave Syria and continue to Israel. Saudi Arabia and Syria both boycotted Israel and companies

---

1900 Miles, "Atiyeh interview #2," 9.
1901 Mike Donahue, "Journey to Amar: Egypt," News stories, recorded by KOIN television, Cairo, Egypt, March 1984. MOV file, Atiyeh Collection, Pac. Univ. Archives.
1902 Thompson, "Atiyeh interview #1," 10; Bob Atiyeh, interviewed by Jim Moore, "Atiyeh interview," West Linn, OR, 4 February 2015. Summary notes, 8.
1903 Denny Miles, interviewed by Jim Moore, "Atiyeh interview #3," Forest Grove, OR, 5 April 2016. Summary notes, 4; Holbrook, "Atiyeh interview," 7.

doing business with Israel; this was not an issue with Egypt because of the 1978 Camp David Accords and peace treaty. In early February the governor's first cousin, Sam Joseph 'Sami' Kahl paid a visit to the Syrian embassy… with Douglas V. Frengle, manager of the international trade division of the [Oregon] Department of Economic Development.

> …According to Kahl, Syrian officials, including Ambassador Rafic Jouejati, told him that Atiyeh would "stab them in the back" by going to Israel because the Syrians planned a "red carpet welcome" for the governor.[1904]

As of March 2, it looked like the Syria visit would not take place, but the governor asked the State Department to step in; a written invitation from Syria duly appeared by mail.[1905]

When Atiyeh arrived in Damascus, there truly was no big greeting. "Two apologetic Syrian foreign ministry officials… stood on a nearly deserted runway at the Damascus International Airport."[1906] The explanation was that the Syrians had been given the wrong time for the arrival of the flight from Cairo, but one observer noted that "the foul-up may have solved the dilemma" of Atiyeh's embarrassing upcoming trip to Israel: "It prevented a big welcome, and it meant no television or print pictures of his arrival in the Syrian press."[1907] Indeed, after Atiyeh arrived, he and his party were "treated royally. In a richly furnished airport room, [Atiyeh] was greeted by [the…] governor of the city of Damascus."[1908]

One of the first places Atiyeh was taken to was a "martyred village" on the Syrian side of the Golan Heights.[1909] It was an opportunity for Syrians to narrate the history: that Israel had

---

1904 Alan K. Ota, "It Took Plenty of Political Grease, Clout to Open Syria's Door for Atiyeh Visit," *Oregonian*, 27 March 1984.
1905 Ota, "Plenty of Political Grease."
1906 Alan K. Ota, "Syrians Cite Mix-Up When Atiyeh Arrives at Deserted Airport," *Oregonian*, 27 March 1984.
1907 Ota, "Syrians Cite Mix-Up."
1908 Ota, "Syrians Cite Mix-Up."

destroyed the village of Qunaytirah. Naturally, Israel had its own take on events, which was told to Atiyeh a week later when Israeli guides took him to a different vantage point above the same village. They explained "that the Syrians destroyed the village" in a plan to rebuild the city after the war, something like war-zone urban renewal.[1910] Years later, Atiyeh talked with Henry Kissinger about what he knew of the situation surrounding Qunaytirah. Atiyeh remembered that "his was a rather abrupt response. ...'Oh,' he says, 'Israel destroyed that village,' and he said it was a very stupid thing to do."[1911]

Because he needed to be back in Damascus to speak with Assad on Monday, Atiyeh ultimately was only able to visit his father's home village of Amar overnight, Saturday to Sunday. This was a disappointment, but he strongly felt that it was very important for him to speak with Assad.

The drive to Amar was about two and a half hours. Accompanied by Oregon newspaper reporters and television crews from Portland and Eugene, the group headed off in a convoy.[1912] Tom Atiyeh was in the lead car because he knew the route to the family village. He took them up around the castle and along the roads around the area, the scenic route.[1913]

Atiyeh got a message from the governor of Homs, the district that included Amar—and the name of the dominant city—to stop by his home for a courtesy visit. But there was not time to fit this in with the potential of waning daylight. As they approached the city of Homs, the entourage stopped, and Atiyeh joined the district leader in his government Mercedes as they continued into Amar.[1914] Taking in the interior of the car and making small talk,

---

1909 Alan K. Ota, "Atiyeh Visits Ruins of Town: Syrians Blame Wreckage on Israelis," *Oregonian*, 28 March 1984.
1910 Atiyeh, "Tape 42," 325.
1911 Atiyeh, "Tape 42," 326.
1912 Atiyeh, "Tape 42," 348; Alan K. Ota, "Talks Show Atiyeh Gulf Between U.S., Syrian Views," *Oregonian*, 1 April 1984.
1913 Tom Atiyeh, "Atiyeh interview," Sherwood, OR, 28 July 2015, Summary notes, 6.
1914 Atiyeh, "Tape 42," 348–349.

Atiyeh the gun collector commented on an unusual leather covering for a pistol that the governor of Homs had. The Syrian official immediately offered it to Atiyeh, who refused it.[1915] When they arrived at Amar, all seemed forgotten, but the next day as the Atiyeh party returned to Damascus, they all stopped at the governor's home in Homs, "[a]nd there he formally presented me with his pistol."[1916] It became a bit of an issue for the staff, but ultimately the gun, and a sword as well, made it back to Salem via a reluctant State Department, with final delivery by UPS.[1917] Atiyeh recalled that aide Lon Holbrook told him, "I'm glad you didn't admire that machine gun."[1918] That would have been one gift too many.

As Atiyeh and his wife Dolores entered Amar that Sunday afternoon, they walked up its narrow streets of cobblestone, filled with people.[1919] One report said that all 500 of Amar's inhabitants were there "to give a dramatic and joyous welcome...."[1920] Young women and girls presented the couple with flowers. A band of Girl and Boy Scouts played music—clearly homework had been done on Atiyeh and his personal connection to the Scouts.[1921] The crowd ululated, rosewater was sprinkled from somewhere above them, Atiyeh recalled, "and there was a sign of both President Assad and myself, 'Welcome Home.' And we got up to my dad's [then Atiyeh's cousin's] home."[1922] Atiyeh knew there would be a welcome to his father's village, but this "was just marvelous."[1923]

1915 Atiyeh, "Tape 42," 349.

1916 Atiyeh, "Tape 42," 349.

1917 Holbrook, "Atiyeh interview," 6–7.

1918 Victor Atiyeh, interviewed by Pat Amedeo, "Arlington Club Oral History," Oral history, recorded by Arlington Club, Portland, OR, 10 September 2013. Transcript, 32, Atiyeh Collection, Pac. Univ. Archives.

1919 Atiyeh, "Tape 42," 350; Victor Atiyeh, interviewed by Clark Hansen, "Tape 43, side 1," Oral history, recorded by Oregon Historical Society, 30 June 1993. Transcript, 351, Atiyeh Collection, Pac. Univ. Archives.

1920 UPI, "Syrians Greet Atiyeh Warmly," *Medford (OR) Mail Tribune*, 1 April 1984, Atiyeh Collection, Pac. Univ. Archives.

1921 Donahue, "Journey to Amar: Syria."

1922 Atiyeh, "Tape 43, side 1," 351.

1923 Atiyeh, "Tape 43, side 1," 352.

Dolores carried a bouquet of flowers. Atiyeh was "smiling ear to ear bigger than I've ever seen him smile before," remembered Mike Donahue.[1924] They were led up the hill to meet the mayor and receive municipal gifts. The Atiyehs found themselves surrounded by "cousins, second and third or fourth cousins, I don't know.... A little old lady came up. She...remembered when we were there when I was six years old. This old lady."[1925] That evening it was "Gypsies playing drums and flute, Gypsy women dancing, food, drinking—a whirlwind."[1926] "What an afternoon and evening," Atiyeh remembered.[1927] Donahue said they went on into the night with dancing and drinking and having a great time. "They declared him the Greatest Governor in the United States."[1928]

Early the next morning, Atiyeh and Dolores woke up to a quiet house. They walked out of their bedroom into the central courtyard to get to the bathroom. "But I had to walk by this living room, and all the security was in there. These Syrians, they were sleeping. That's where they slept." As the Atiyehs quietly passed, "Well, they woke up. ...Next thing you know the village [was] awake, and I never did get my quiet visit."[1929] Before the Atiyeh contingent returned to Damascus that Sunday morning, they ascended and explored the Crusader castle, the Krak des Chevaliers. KOIN television's Donahue and photographer Dale Birkholz recalled "falling over stone walls trying to get shots and stay ahead of them coming up the hill."[1930] As Atiyeh was walking along a street with arches letting in the light, "That's what it is that I remember. ...I remember [the arches] from as a six-year-old."[1931]

1924 Donahue, "Atiyeh interview," 4.
1925 Atiyeh, "Tape 43, side 1," 352.
1926 Atiyeh, "Tape 43, side 1," 352. Handwritten insert by Atiyeh to replace spot where the recording tape broke. He added, "Too bad it is lost."
1927 Atiyeh, "Tape 43, side 1," 352.
1928 Donahue, "Atiyeh interview," 4.
1929 Atiyeh, "Tape 43, side 1," 352–353.
1930 Donahue, "Atiyeh interview," 4.
1931 Atiyeh, "Tape 43, side 1," 353.

Atiyeh left Amar feeling closer to his roots. And, since much of the trip was chronicled by Oregon television stations, he heard from all sorts of Oregonians that seeing his reception in the village had rekindled their sense "that they were going home to their roots—Sweden, or France, or Italy—like they had gone home."[1932] Atiyeh himself felt "a little bit closer" to his heritage. He recalled, "It becomes real, everything that I imagined or tried to put in my memory, now it's real; I can see it, I know what the buildings look like, I know what the village looks like. ...Now you've got the real feel of it."[1933]

Atiyeh got his meeting with President Assad that Sunday afternoon, March 31. Atiyeh opened the meeting as he had the one with Mubarak in Egypt, declaring that he "was a devout American," even though he was just one generation removed from being Syrian. Atiyeh recalled that "Assad's reply was even more enthusiastic than ever Mubarak.... 'Good, that's really all we expect that's wonderful, that's the way it ought to be.'" Atiyeh delivered the message from Washington about opening up communications between the two countries. Assad "said, 'That's fine. But if we sit down with the U.S., we sit at the table with the U.S., and Israel is on one side and we're on the other.'"[1934]

Atiyeh proposed to Assad that a way to bring about more understanding between Syria and the United States would be for more state delegations to visit, with business ideas and opportunities to create economic ties.[1935] Atiyeh noted that as the head of the Republican Governor's Conference, he would write to his fellow Republican governors to suggest the idea. Assad directed his aide to take up the idea, possibly with invitations to American states to come from the Syrian Minister of the Economy. Atiyeh also pointed out that one reason his visit was

---

1932 Atiyeh, "Tape 43, side 1," 353.
1933 Atiyeh, "Tape 43, side 1," 356.
1934 Atiyeh, "Tape 42," 327; "Oregon Governor Atiyeh's March 31 Meeting with Syria's President Hafiz Al-Assad," Department of State, U.S. Government, Confidential Telegram, (31 March 1984), 3, Atiyeh Collection. Pac. Univ. Archives.
1935 "Atiyeh Conversation with Assad," 1–2.

showing the world a different side of Syria was because he was accompanied by journalists from Oregon who were sending back stories and their own observations.[1936]

These proposals were classic complex interdependence ideas. Atiyeh knew that multiple layers of relationships between Syria and the United States could move both countries to different understandings of each other. Atiyeh then brought up, "on my own—I'm delivering my message—about the hostages" being held in Lebanon by Shia groups.[1937] Atiyeh knew that Syria had been involved in the release of one hostage, "and I thanked [Assad] for that" and encouraged Syria to help with the other hostages. "And that went along quite well."[1938]

The conversation turned to terrorism. Atiyeh was well aware of the concept of state-sponsored terrorism, and that Libya, Iran, and Syria were often mentioned as playing that role. After this talk, however, Atiyeh "came away…with the notion that Assad himself did not actively promote terrorism. But I still [in 1993] have that little bit of doubt that he probably was aware it was going on and sort of looked the other way. …I wasn't completely relieved of my own particular views on that subject that he [or the government] was not directly…involved in promoting terrorism."[1939] In a news account of the Assad conversation, Atiyeh "said Assad was 'warm personally and a very gentle person.' He discounted reports that Assad and his regime [had] been brutally repressive. 'The people of Syria have great affection for the president,' Atiyeh said. 'If he's bad and oppressive, then the people wouldn't have this affection for him.'"[1940]

Atiyeh later told his nephew Bob about meeting Assad. Bob Atiyeh pressed his uncle on the reports of Assad's brutality toward his fellow Syrians. There had been a 1982 uprising against Assad's regime in the city of Hama, a city just north of Homs and

---

1936 "Atiyeh Conversation with Assad," 2.
1937 Atiyeh, "Tape 42," 328.
1938 Atiyeh, "Tape 42," 328.
1939 Atiyeh, "Tape 42," 329.
1940 Alan K. Ota, "Syrians Doubt U.S. Policy Goals," *Oregonian*, 1 April 1984.

about an hour and a half drive from the Atiyeh hometown of Amar. Thousands were killed by the Syrian military in putting down this revolt.[1941] Atiyeh told his nephew that Assad had said, "There were some bad people in that town, I gave people weapons, and they took care of the problem."[1942] Bob Atiyeh was never convinced that his uncle knew the enormity of the violence of the Assad regime within its own borders.[1943]

The entire conversation with Assad lasted for about ninety minutes. The two would meet again in 1985, and then once more for a two-and-a-half hour talk after Atiyeh left office. Atiyeh had a strong sense during this first visit "that President Assad had this dream of a United Arab World."[1944] Atiyeh, due to his own family and cultural dynamics, did not understand how this would work. "I know, having been around these people, that we argue with each other. ...That's the typical Arab, you know. We argue with each other, within our families, they argue within Syria, they argue within Saudi [Arabia], they argue wherever...."[1945] On Atiyeh's second visit with Assad in 1985, Atiyeh "sense[d] that... was no longer a vision of his."[1946] The Lebanese Civil War lasted for about fifteen years. Atiyeh realized that sectarian (religious) identities were dominant in Syria and Lebanon, unlike the United States where he felt that he was an American first who happened to be Episcopalian.[1947]

The Israel leg of the trip was partly professional—Atiyeh would meet the Israeli prime minister and other government officials—but the trade mission was over. Atiyeh was joined by his wife, Dolores (who had also been in Syria) and Portland

---

1941 *New York Times*, "Syria Pulls a Tiger's Tail," 14 February 1982; John Kifner, "Assad Said to Be in Control Despite Rebel Uprising," *New York Times*, 14 February 1982; Basma Atassi, "Breaking the Silence Over Hama Atrocities," *Al-Jazeera*, 2 February 2012, http://www.aljazeera.com.

1942 Bob Atiyeh, "Atiyeh interview," 6.

1943 Bob Atiyeh, "Atiyeh interview," 6.

1944 Atiyeh, "Tape 42," 331–332.

1945 Atiyeh, "Tape 42," 332.

1946 Atiyeh, "Tape 42," 332.

1947 Victor Atiyeh, interviewed by Jim Moore, "Atiyeh interview #2," Raleigh Hills, OR, 2 January 2014. Summary notes, 5–6.

friends, including Jim and Donna Campbell. This part of the trip was triggered by his conversations with Oregon's Jewish community about visiting Israel. Their tour was a set itinerary that the country used for important guests.

Atiyeh met with Prime Minister Yitzhak Shamir.[1948] The meeting made a bit of national news because Shamir complained about the US refusal to move its embassy from Tel Aviv to Jerusalem.[1949] The official statement from the prime minister's office also noted "that Atiyeh 'is of Arab origin,'" an obvious swipe at Atiyeh's claim to be "just an American."[1950] Atiyeh did not step into this particular minefield with the Israeli press—Jerusalem was a divided city whose legal status was not clear to most countries of the world. However, he had been quite clear that he thought moving the embassy was a mistake when he talked with the Syrian press just a few days earlier. Until that issue was resolved among Israelis, Palestinians, and Jordanians (at that point), the international embassies stayed in the more cosmopolitan, and indisputably Israeli, city of Tel Aviv.

After visits to the Holocaust Museum,[1951] the Dead Sea (the sensation of which he considered "terrible"),[1952] Masada, and the Sea of Galilee, Atiyeh finally came to believe that the Israelis wanted "to embrace sadness. "[T]het want to grasp the terrible things, and they want to make sure" Israelis never forget. "Maybe that's their culture," Atiyeh mused. "It just seems a tragic thing to do instead of thinking about the good things."[1953] On the third

---

1948 AP, "Atiyeh to Meet Shamir," *Albany (OR) Democrat-Herald*, 4 April 1984, Atiyeh Collection, Pac. Univ. Archives; AP, "Atiyeh Talks in Jerusalem," *Pendleton East Oregonian*, 4 April 1984, Atiyeh Collection, Pac. Univ. Archives; UPI, "Atiyeh, Israel's Leader Meet," *Eugene (OR) Register-Guard*, 6 April 1984, Atiyeh Collection, Pac. Univ. Archives.

1949 David K. Shipler, "Shamir Urges U.S. to Move Embassy," *Oregonian*, 6 April 1984; David K. Shipler, "Shamir, After Meeting an Arab-American, Deplores Embassy Site," *New York Times*, 6 April 1984; Atiyeh, "Tape 41," 320.

1950 Shipler, "Shamir Urges U.S. to Move Embassy."

1951 AP, "Atiyeh in Israel," Photo and caption, *Albany (OR) Democrat-Herald*, 3 April 1984, Atiyeh Collection, Pac. Univ. Archives.

1952 Atiyeh, "Tape 43, side 2," 368.

1953 Atiyeh, "Tape 43, side 2," 368.

night in Israel, as the party was resting, Atiyeh told Dolores, "... [N]ow we're at the Sea of Galilee, and where the Sermon on the Mount is, and all of these ruins and some that had been restored, and all of this was just marvelous. I said to her, 'You know, I really don't care where the barbed wire is and where they shot up the Syrians or the Egyptians.' But you see, that was all part of their ...spiel."[1954]

There were constant reminders, some from the scripts of the tour guide, some from conversations with people, about the Palestinians who had been displaced after Israel's birth in 1948. To Atiyeh, the ways that his guide spoke of how well the Palestinians were taken care of "smacked of" the way Americans had talked about taking care of slaves.[1955] Atiyeh felt that he was getting just one side of the modern story from the Israelis, whereas he felt that he had encountered more openness of thought and more respect for differing views in his conversations in Egypt and Syria.

Atiyeh did leave Israel with a strong sense of the permanence of the state, and of how its view of the region was different from the other countries that he had visited. He strongly supported Israel's right to exist, but he wanted to the see the United States play a more neutral role in the region. He recalled that he would tell his "hotheaded friends, ...'No wait a minute. Israel isn't going anywhere. Israel is there. ...If there's any danger to Israel, the United States is going to jump in. ... Now, how do we get peace in the Middle East?'"[1956] His diplomatic approach was received differently in Israel, too. Atiyeh made it clear to all the national leaders he met that he was an American first, and secondly somebody of Arab descent:

> My conversation started out, 'I want you to know that I'm a devout American.' ...I wanted to position myself, so that I'm not pro this or anything, the only pro thing I am [is] pro-American.

1954 Atiyeh, "Tape 43, side 2," 367.
1955 Atiyeh, "Tape 43, side 2," 369.
1956 Atiyeh, "Tape 43, side 2," 375.

Mubarak's and Assad's reactions were identical. They said, 'Wonderful. Can't ask for anything more than that. You know, whatever's best for the country, that's fine.' I said the same thing to Shamir [Israel's prime minister]. I got no reaction at all.[1957]

When Atiyeh returned to the United States, he contacted the State Department to report on his meetings with the Egyptian, Syrian, and Israeli leaders. The Reagan administration brushed him off. He was frustrated by the experience—"I know mine isn't the only view, but just let's plug in my view" to the overall U.S. understanding of the leaders in the region.[1958] Friend Jack Faust recalled that Atiyeh told him he "was very offended" that he never heard back from the Reagan White House.[1959] Atiyeh finally did meet with National Security Advisor Robert "Bud" McFarlane in Texas at the 1984 Republican Convention. Atiyeh had talked to Vice President George H. W. Bush "and told him, 'I've got something to say' to him." Bush acknowledged Atiyeh's question from Air Force Two in August 1984,[1960] and his intervention directly led to Atiyeh's meeting with McFarlane,[1961] where Atiyeh said, "When I left I heard that Syria wasn't interested in peace [from the NSC and State Department briefings]. I've come home to tell you that I think Israel's not interested in peace. As long as there's a continual threat to Israel, the U.S. will continue to send them money, and they're very dependent on the money that America sends. And if that threat's taken away, we really have no

---

1957 Atiyeh, "Tape 41," 316–317.
1958 Atiyeh, "Tape 41," 317.
1959 Jack Faust, interviewed by Jim Moore, "Atiyeh interview," Portland, OR, 15 April 2015. Summary notes, 6–7.
1960 George H. W. Bush, "Check on Syrian Trip," Office of the Vice President, U.S. Government, Typewritten note, (8 August 1984), Atiyeh Collection, Pac. Univ. Archives.
1961 Gerry Thompson, "Conversation with Vice President's Office: Mid-East Briefing; Timber Relief; American State Bank," Office of the Governor, Memo to Governor, (14 August 1984), Atiyeh Collection, Pac. Univ. Archives; "Atiyeh Daily Index-Card Schedule, August 22, 1984," Office of the Governor, State of Oregon, (22 August 1984), Meet: Robert C. "Bud" McFarlane, asst. to pres. & head of National Security Council; Gov's suite, Hyatt Regency, Atiyeh Collection, Pac. Univ. Archives.

reason to continue to send a lot of money, and I don't think they really want peace."[1962]

As the trip came to an end, the first results were in from the business contacts made by Oregon's delegation. The Saudis were interested in fruit trees, there were possibilities for wheat to be sold in Syria (but politics and the ability to pay for products were big stumbling blocks), and Atiyeh was confident there would be "definite prospects" for other deals.[1963] In a speech to the Oregon Public Ports Association at the end of April 1984, the governor emphasized that Saudi interest had been piqued by the Oregon delegation's visit. He told the group, "Already Egypt is our No. 5 trading partner, almost exclusively because of wheat purchases, but we have identified Saudi Arabia as a major prospect."[1964] Atiyeh was also looking beyond Oregon's trade in agricultural products to "processed foods, manufactured goods and electronics" both in the Middle East and in east Asia.[1965]

Atiyeh remembered that those on the trade mission felt the entire trip was a big success. It was Atiyeh's job as governor to "open those kinds of doors." He recalled that the business delegation was "ecstatic. We met more cabinet heads in one day than they would probably [meet] in two years."[1966] In the early 1990s Atiyeh observed that Saudi Arabia had not developed into a major trading partner for Oregon, with the exception of a couple of companies, but that Egypt had become an even bigger consumer of Oregon wheat. To him, it was the groundwork of those personal meetings in the mid-1980s that had started the relationships that led to the increased wheat trade.[1967]

1962 Atiyeh, "Tape 41," 317.
1963 AP, "Saudis Interested," *Oregonian*, 4 April 1984; Patricia Moir, "Politics, Poverty Hamper Syrian Wheat Talks," *Pendleton East Oregonian*, 7 April 1984, Atiyeh Collection, Pac. Univ. Archives; Don Jepsen, "Atiyeh Calls Mission to Mideast a Winner," *Oregonian*, 17 April 1984.
1964 AP, "Governor Lists Middle East Trip's Benefits," *Grants Pass (OR) Daily Courier*, 28 April 1984, Atiyeh Collection, Pac. Univ. Archives.
1965 AP, "Governor Lists Middle East Trip's Benefits."
1966 Atiyeh, "Tape 44," 382.
1967 Atiyeh, "Tape 44," 382.

Repealing the Unitary Tax

Atiyeh's international travel refocused on Asia—that was where the capital was to invest in Oregon. Mere weeks after Israel, a May 1984 trip to Taiwan and South Korea would be another with a high degree of diplomatic balancing. Atiyeh left with the intention to create a sister-state relationship with Taiwan, in effect threading the diplomatic needle between official US policy that the People's Republic was the true China and the lingering support for the Republic of China as the true China. Atiyeh was doing this because of his own beliefs and longtime support for Taiwan, but also because Taiwan was a major trade partner for Oregon.

There were also hopes that Taiwan would begin to use the Port of Portland as a shipping point for the export of U.S. coal to the island. Atiyeh carried a letter to that effect from U.S. Senator Mark Hatfield, who was then chair "of the Senate Appropriations Committee, which would rule on military aid to Taiwan."[1968] Clearly, the entire trip was a great illustration of complex interdependence—the high politics of U.S recognition of the PRC and derecognition of the ROC, the congressional politics of Hatfield seeming to hold up ROC military aid in order to get economic benefits for his state, the state to state politics of economic ties and sister relations among Taiwan, Oregon, and Fujian province in the PRC, and the business connections to be made by the Oregon delegation.

On Monday May 7, Atiyeh told his Salem office that there had been a delay in signing the sister-state agreement with Taiwan, ultimately because he wanted to take care with Oregon's gestures toward mainland China. Atiyeh told reporters upon his return to Oregon a week later that "the agreement was not formalized because the country is in political transition. 'We'll have to wait,' he said about the agreement, adding, 'It's going to happen.'"[1969] He took guidance from the US Department of State, ensuring that

---

1968 Eric Goranson, "Delegation Leaves for S. Korea, Taiwan, Hoping to Spur Trade," *Oregonian*, 2 May 1984.

any agreement was within the 1972 Shanghai Communiqué's language that said that US entities could deal with Taiwan in any way they wanted as long as they did not call it the Republic of China. The document that Atiyeh negotiated did not have those offending words. At the banquet to sign the Taiwan agreement there were lots of television cameras, lots of lights, and a lot of people. The document that Atiyeh saw before him had been changed so that Taiwan was identified as the Republic of China. Reconstructing events later, Portland-based Chinese law expert Bill Campbell put it this way: "Atiyeh, under the lights and under the cameras said, 'Ah, there's just one small change. I'll sign it privately tomorrow.'"[1970] And then those gathered drank toasts to the new relationship. In his oral history in the 1990s, Atiyeh emphasized that the Taiwanese government "kept saying they want ROC [in the document], and I said, 'Gee, I can't do that.'"[1971]

It was this sharp-eyed last-minute diplomacy of Atiyeh's that changed his, and Oregon's, stature in the eyes of the mainland Chinese. The PRC noticed what Atiyeh had done. In September the Oregon delegation was treated extremely well in both Beijing and in Fujian Province because of who Atiyeh was and the diplomacy that he had shown earlier in the year in Taiwan.

South Korea was much more important to Oregon's economy than Taiwan, and the visit was less politically fraught. Total trade in 1983 was almost $600 million. Just as with Taiwan, the bulk of that number (a little less than half) was the shipment of unmilled wheat from Oregon to South Korea.[1972] Where the 1979 trip had focused on shipping and wheat, the May 1984 delegation showed the maturation of the relationship between South Korea and Oregon, and highlighted the concerns about trade barriers

---

1969 Phil Manzano, "Atiyeh Back from Taiwan: Contacts Hailed; Sister-State Pact Fails," *Oregonian*, 14 May 1984.
1970 Bill Campbell, interviewed by Jim Moore, "Atiyeh interview," Portland, OR, 9 April 2015. Summary notes, 2.
1971 Atiyeh, "Tape 44," 388.
1972 "Travel Binder," Korea.

between the U.S. and South Korea slowing down that trade.[1973] The Oregon group consisted of CH2M Hill looking to expand its water and general civil engineering presence, Jeld-Wen looking for markets for its doors and windows, Thermo Industries and its energy-saving insulation products, as well as shipping interests from the Port of Astoria, shipping companies, and the ever-present Oregon Wheat Growers League. A Korean-language brochure introduced all the major Oregon players to their potential customers.[1974] The Korean part of this trip was quite important to Oregon's economy, as it was focused on expanding economic ties beyond simply trade, including cooperation on technology issues.[1975]

A year before, Frank Ivancie, the mayor of Portland, had appeared before the Oregon legislature's Joint Committee on Trade and Economic Development. The May 1983 hearing was supposed to focus on how Oregon could engage more comprehensively with Japan's quickly growing economy, especially in technology and electronics. Ivancie and Atiyeh had just returned from a trade delegation to Japan; after years of negotiation, the Portland International Airport was again connected directly to Asia with United Airlines' nonstop service between Portland and Tokyo. The first flight was a symbolic gesture to emphasize the ties between Oregon and Japan, as well as open the door to more connections between the two. Governor Atiyeh and Mayor Ivancie stayed in Japan for the better part of a week making connections with Japanese government officials and businesses. The days were filled with meetings with wheat

---

1973 "The State of Oregon Trade Mission to Korea," U.S. Information Service, U.S. Government, Press Release 84–08, (4 May 1984), Atiyeh Collection, Pac. Univ. Archives; *Korea Herald* (Seoul), "Oregon Governor Aims to Tie State Closer on 2nd Visit to Korea," 13 May 1984, Atiyeh Collection, Pac. Univ. Archives; *Korea Herald* (Seoul), "ISCK President Hosts Party for Oregon Trade Mission," 12 May 1984, Atiyeh Collection, Pac. Univ. Archives.

1974 "State of Oregon Governor's Trade Mission to Republic of Korea, May 8–12, 1984, Seoul, Korea [Korean language]," U.S. Trade Center, Oregon Economic Development Department, (1984), Atiyeh Collection, Pac. Univ. Archives.

1975 *Register-Guard* (Eugene), "Governor in S. Korea for Talks," 10 May 1984, Atiyeh Collection, Pac. Univ. Archives.

associations (Oregon wheat was a mainstay in Japanese noodle production), lunch with Honda Motor Company executives, and talks with shipping lines."[1976]

On Atiyeh's return to Oregon after his 1983 Japan trip an announcement was made that he and Japan's ambassador to the United States would keynote a day-long conference about Japanese trade with Oregon just a few days later.[1977] That April 19 conference, sponsored by the Oregon Department of Agriculture and the Japan Economic Institute of America, focused on food products. But there was also talk about trade in manufactured goods and tourism. Thinking like the retailer that he was, Atiyeh called on Oregon businesses to go beyond the contacts with Japan that occurred during trade fairs and delegation visits: "we can't get their business unless we knock on their doors more frequently."[1978] An editorial in the *Oregonian* just a few days later urged the Oregon legislature to provide funds to continue its outreach to international partners, noting that while thirty-three states were "courting economic recovery with high technology" efforts, Oregon's "advantage as a beachhead on the Pacific Rim" was a reality that ought to be built upon.[1979] Within a year it would become very apparent that Atiyeh was going after both—high tech would be actively courted, and international trade would be the linchpin to make it happen.

Atiyeh was benefiting from a change in Japanese investment policies. Japanese firms had an incentive to build plants in the United States. As trade relations with the US grew more fractious during the Reagan years, any Japanese facilities located within the United States would be within the tariff boundaries and other barriers that might be erected by the US government. Atiyeh thus had something to bargain with aside from what Oregon itself had

---

1976 "Atiyeh Daily Index Cards, Apr 5–12, 1983, " Office of the Governor, State of Oregon, Saturday, April 9; Sunday, April 10.
1977 *Oregonian*, "Japanese Ambassador, Atiyeh to Speak at Trade Conference," 13 April 1983.
1978 Julie Tripp, "Japan Open to Oregon Goods: Ambassador Sees Myths Hampering Trade," *Oregonian*, 20 April 1983.
1979 *Oregonian*, "Build Oregon's Pacific Rim Trade," Editorial, 22 April 1983.

to offer—he could offer a tariff-free haven for any Japanese manufacturing if it located within the United States. Atiyeh knew that if he could get Japanese companies to build in Oregon, it would lead to more factories and investment and to the hiring of more Oregonians.[1980] The large Japanese companies at the time were "establishing facilities in America and Western Europe" that required "relatively low-skilled labor."[1981] It would be Atiyeh's challenge to convince Japanese companies that building manufacturing facilities in Oregon would be even more beneficial because Oregon's workforce could handle the highly technical high-skilled tasks needed to create more sophisticated products. Other countries were figuring out how to make these types of bargains, distinguishing "between direct investments in their nations which merely create new jobs and those which also increase the quality of their labor force."[1982] Atiyeh's bargaining chip in these talks would be the already extant high tech businesses surrounding Tektronix and the growing presence of Intel manufacturing facilities in Washington County.

But the message that the Oregon legislative committee heard again and again from Ivancie and the representatives of the business community in May 1983 was that Oregon's unitary tax was keeping Japanese companies from investing in the state.[1983] Virtually all states in the U.S. have a corporate income tax. By the middle of the twentieth century states realized there was a growing issue with taxing corporations. Corporations had entities in several states, and some had entities outside of the country. How should the tax systems of each state respond? A relatively simple method was *separate accounting*—each corporate entity in different states was taxed as if it was a unique business. But this began to run into problems as all these different parts of a single company were, in effect, buying and selling parts and materials

---

1980 Atiyeh, "Atiyeh interview #1," 4.
1981 Robert Reich, "Beyond Free Trade," *Foreign Affairs* 61, no. 4 (Spring 1983): 802.
1982 Reich, "Beyond Free Trade," 803.
1983 Foster Church, "Tax Rate Called Obstacle to Foreign Trade," *Oregonian*, 3 May 1983.

from other parts of the same company for state tax purposes.[1984] To simplify this complexity, many states began to tax corporations as a *unitary business*. To make this work, states simply multiplied the total taxable income of a company by the proportion of that company that existed in each state. Companies that argued they were being taxed twice under the scheme lost their arguments in the federal courts.

Atiyeh had a meeting on the unitary tax with Robyn Godwin, director of the Oregon Department of Revenue, and Atiyeh's chief of staff Gerry Thompson on May 27, 1983.[1985] Thompson "was having talks with some of the Japanese businessmen…not CEOs…and the unitary tax was continually raised as an issue."[1986] The meeting "was to get a better understanding from the Governor to see if he would be amenable to change or repeal." She "had been having many conversations" with Japanese companies, and Thompson "did not want to walk potential investors in Oregon down the wrong path, especially the Japanese, or put the Governor in a position he couldn't support."[1987] She discovered that the unitary tax brought in an estimated $20 million to the biennial budget, around 1% of the resources available to the state's general fund.[1988] This was about 10% of the total taxes brought in by businesses.

Japan had another concern with the unitary tax. It was not just that it was perceived as unfair and double-taxation, it was that Japan was, as Atiyeh put it, "very secretive. They don't want to open their books to anybody. And in order to make that determination, we have to go look at their books."[1989] It was not just Japan. The governments of Canada, the United Kingdom, the

---

1984 Alan J. Auerbach, review of McLure, ed., *The State Corporation Income Tax: Issues in Worldwide Unitary Combination*, 1984, *Journal of Economic Literature* 23, no. 3 (1985): 1224–1225.

1985 "Atiyeh Daily Index-Card Schedule, May 27, 1983," Office of the Governor, State of Oregon, (27 May 1983), [Handwritten by staff] Robin Godwyn [sic]; Gerry re: unitary tax, Atiyeh Collection, Pac. Univ. Archives.

1986 Gerry Thompson to Jim Moore, "Unitary Tax," Email, 15 August 2017. Ellipses in original

1987 Thompson to Moore, 15 August 2017.

1988 *Oregonian*, "Unitary Tax Called a Roadblock," 7 June 1983.

Netherlands, and the European Economic Community (EEC) had all asked for the unitary tax to be repealed in the United States.[1990] Atiyeh was well aware of this wider interest, recalling, "...[V]ery quietly in the wings was England. England hated our unitary tax, but they kind of let Japan be the leaders in this thing."[1991]

The Oregon Legislature's Joint Committee on Trade and Economic Development eventually decided to allow a five-year moratorium on the unitary tax for companies that came to Oregon.[1992] The five-year moratorium was seen as an experiment of sorts to decide whether to continue the tax.[1993] The bill got caught up in a larger discussion of the sales tax and did not make it out of the 1983 legislative session.[1994]

In July 1983, the unitary tax sprang into the news in Oregon with the decision by Japan's Mitsubishi, along with U.S. partner Westinghouse, to locate a high-tech factory in North Carolina instead of Oregon. The president of the US subsidiary of Mitsubishi said, "[The unitary tax] was one of the factors, a material factor. Especially in our case, we are very nervous about that."[1995] Oregon had gone all out to get the plant. Atiyeh and

---

1989 Victor Atiyeh, interviewed by Clark Hansen, "Tape 40, side 1," Oral history, recorded by Oregon Historical Society, 23 June 1993. Transcript, 278, Atiyeh Collection, Pac. Univ. Archives.

1990 Special to the New York Times, "Unitary Tax is Critized," *New York Times*, 16 August 1983; Reuters,"Unitary Tax Opposed," *New York Times*, 20 September 1983; Philip T. Kaplan, "The Unitary Tax Debate, the United States Supreme Court, and Some Plain English," *Journal of Corporate Taxation* 10, no. 4 (1984): 296–298.

1991 Victor Atiyeh, interviewed by Clark Hansen, "Tape 62," Oral history, recorded by Oregon Historical Society, 11 June 1998. Transcript, 20, Atiyeh Collection, Pac. Univ. Archives.

1992 *Oregonian*, "Unitary Tax Called a Roadblock."

1993 *Willamette Week* (Portland), "A Message to Japan," Editorial, 7 June 1983.

1994 "Atiyeh Daily Index-Card Schedule, April 28, 1983," Office of the Governor, State of Oregon, (28 April 1983), Rep. Zajonc, Robyn Godwin & Gerry, re: unitary tax proposal, Atiyeh Collection, Pac. Univ. Archives; "Atiyeh Daily Index-Card Schedule, April 29, 1983," Office of the Governor, State of Oregon, (29 April 1983), Robyn Godwin, Rep. Zajonc & Gerry, re: unitary tax proposal, Atiyeh Collection, Pac. Univ. Archives.

1995 Steve Jenning, "Unitary Tax Cited in Mitsubishi Decision Not to Locate in Oregon," *Oregonian*, 19 July 1983.

several of his department heads had met directly with Mitsubishi to make the case for a Salem site. This was the first time in the 30-year history of the tax in Oregon that a company had cited the unitary tax as a reason for not locating to the state. An analysis done after the decision showed that Oregon had fared well with "quality of life, the labor situation, and cultural amenities."[1996] According to the report, the Japanese "winced at the state's unitary tax," but Mitsubishi had stated that the tax was *not* the ultimate reason for the decision to locate in North Carolina. The unitary tax was still caught up in the ongoing, and much larger, discussion about balancing Oregon's tax system with a sales tax. But because of the Mitsubishi decision, the unitary tax became part of the public conversation.[1997]

For Atiyeh, the conversation was part of his broader concern with ensuring that Oregon was open for business. Beginning with his efforts to finish up the land-use system's implementation in the early years of his administration and continuing through his ever-increasing trips outside of Oregon to recruit investment in Oregon jobs, Atiyeh was beginning to see the unitary tax as an impediment in the minds of investors. An October 1983 visit to Oregon by a national group of site consultants—people who worked with large companies as they decided where to locate new plants—illustrated the problem that Oregon faced. There was a national perception that dated back to Tom McCall's "Visit but Don't Stay" motto from the early 1970s. One of the consultants told of hearing about Oregon's "anti-growth reputation" among companies in the eastern United States.[1998] Atiyeh reached out to this group directly as it toured the Portland area. Seeing an effort to coordinate land-use permitting, public agency processing of building requests, and the discussion about changing the unitary

---

1996 *Willamette Week* (Portland), "Why We Lost Mitsubishi," Editorial, 13 September 1983; A Coopers & Lybrand study for Illinois found that perceptions seemed to be driving opposition to the tax rather than economic factors, Kaplan, "Unitary Tax Debate," 284, ff. 5.

1997 Steve Jenning, "Labor, Business Square Off on Sales Tax," *Oregonian*, 8 October 1983.

1998 Steve Jenning, "Site Consultants Get In-Depth Look at City," *Oregonian*, 15 October 1983.

tax, the group was impressed. The consultant said, "I can't wait to get a chance to test you guys to see if you can deliver."[1999]

Back in Washington, D.C., the Reagan administration formed an advisory panel, the Working Group on Worldwide Unitary Taxation, headed by Treasury Secretary Donald Regan. In December 1983 early word from the group was in favor of keeping the unitary tax system.[2000] By August 1984 the panel had failed to come to a consensus on national policy, but the unitary tax was on the table in the states.[2001] Japan was also learning that that a single U.S. law on the unitary tax would be a long time coming. Atiyeh observed that the Japanese were discovering the "laboratories of democracy" concept—that individual states could try out policy ideas that might later be adopted by Congress. "The Japanese were unsuccessful" at changing the tax, Atiyeh recalled, "until the light went on in their heads, and they said, 'Wait a minute. The place where we can get that done is in the states.' And all of a sudden things started to happen."[2002]

In 1984, Atiyeh directed the Oregon Department of Revenue to figure out a way to get rid of the unitary tax. Atiyeh's own idea was to use an idea called "the water's edge."[2003] This system taxed companies on their U.S. operations, not their global operations, thus treating them the same as companies whose locations were spread among several states. Atiyeh recalled his direction to the Revenue people: "'Here, this is what we're going to do. I want to take the federal taxable income, and I want to apply Oregon rates to it.' That way we were uniform with everybody: small business, big business, didn't make any difference. And if they had a

---

1999 Jenning, "Site Consultants."
2000 AP, "'Unitary' Tax Study by U.S.," *New York Times*, 7 December 1983.
2001 *Oregonian*, "The Nation," 1 August 1984; AP, "Regan Says U.S. May Seek Unitary Tax Curb," *New York Times*, 1 August 1984.
2002 Victor Atiyeh, interviewed by Clark Hansen, "Tape 30," Oral history, recorded by Oregon Historical Society, 3 May 1993. Transcript, 21, Atiyeh Collection, Pac. Univ. Archives.
2003 Auerbach: 1225; "Atiyeh Daily Index-Card Schedule, January 27, 1984," Office of the Governor, State of Oregon, (27 January 1984), Rich Munn, John Anderson, Gerry, Bob, Denny, Jim, regarding unitary tax, Atiyeh Collection, Pac. Univ. Archives.

problem with the unitary system of taxation, it wasn't with Oregon, it had to be at the federal level. We removed it from us."[2004]

Richard Munn, then the new director of the Department of Revenue, observed "that Atiyeh as a political animal understood the huge amount of concern among business, especially international business," over the unitary tax.[2005] Munn recalled meeting about the unitary tax with a Japanese company in his office. "They wanted to explain exactly how their business worked, because they were sure that if you knew exactly how the business worked you would not apply unitary to them."[2006] That tight corporate secrecy that Atiyeh had noted was breaking down as the frustration over the unitary method gripped the Japanese negotiators. Japanese electronics company NEC decided to build a fiber optics plant in Hillsboro in May 1984. The governor's office stepped up to take credit for recruiting the company because NEC was given a five-year exemption from the unitary tax based on a "new company clause," formulated and endorsed by a legal memo from Elizabeth Stockdale, the Department of Justice tax expert.[2007]

The unitary tax became the subject of political conversations across the state. Munn was beginning to hear from state senators about other companies that wanted the same deal that NEC had received. There was growing opposition to the repeal as well, mainly based on the fear of lost tax revenue.[2008] Aside from the revenue issues of repealing the unitary tax, there were concerns that Oregon was bowing to pressure from big business. *Oregonian* editorial board member David Sarasohn saw this as a demand from the Japanese if they were to invest in Oregon.[2009] At the end of May the governor changed his mind on the timeline to

---

2004 Atiyeh, "Tape 40, side 1," 279
2005 Richard Munn, "Atiyeh Interview," Salem, OR, 9 June 2016, Summary notes, 6.
2006 Munn, "Atiyeh Interview," 6–7.
2007 Richard Munn, Summary of phone conversation to Jim Moore, "Unitary Tax details," 10 June 2016.
2008 Steve Myers, "Union Chief Urges Caution on Unitary Tax," *Medford (OR) Mail Tribune*, May 1984, Atiyeh collection, Pac. Univ. Archives.

repeal the unitary tax. It was no longer seen as part of a larger tax reform discussion; it was seen as an impediment to investment in Oregon all by itself. A May 31, 1984, news article noted "the governor also said he had made his decision on what to do about the unitary tax but wants to circulate his proposal before making a public announcement."[2010]

What had he decided? Immediate repeal of the unitary tax was not part of the original plan. But during negotiations with NEC it became clear that the unitary tax had to be changed.[2011] After the governor and his chief of staff spent an afternoon with Dr. Ko Muroga, the president and CEO of NEC, and Satoshi Nakaichi, the secretary of NEC America, it became clear to Gerry Thompson that the Japanese aversion to the unitary tax was an impediment to future Japanese investment in the state. On the drive back to Salem after a non-NEC-related dinner in Portland, she told the governor her opinion that repealing the unitary tax would guarantee two new Japanese plants, with revenues more than offsetting the losses from the repeal.[2012] Atiyeh immediately responded with, "'Nope. Can't repeal any taxes, not at a time like this.' He was adamant." She let the matter go for a while and sat in silence, but before they arrived in Salem, she broached the topic again. "'Governor, would you consider it?' 'No. No,' [Atiyeh told her]. I mean he was adamant." Thompson went home and spoke to her husband about the situation, telling him "I don't know how to move [the governor]. ...I just know it's the right thing to do." Her persistence paid off with a decision the next day.

2009 David Sarasohn, interviewed by Jim Moore, "Atiyeh interview," Portland, OR, 17 February 2015. Summary notes, 2.

2010 *Oregonian*, "Japanese Businessmen to Visit Oregon Sites," 31 May 1984.

2011 Gerry Thompson, interviewed by Jim Moore, "Atiyeh interview #2," Salem, OR, 12 February 2015. Summary notes, 8.

2012 Gerry Thompson, interviewed by Jim Moore, "Atiyeh Interview #4," Salem, OR, 7 August 2017. Summary notes, 13; This conversation was initially off the record. However, Thompson gave permission for it to be used to highlight the role of the chief of staff to bring all arguments to the governor, Gerry Thompson, Phone call to Jim Moore, "Talking to the Governor," 10 October 2017.

In the office, "about mid-morning..., [Atiyeh] called me in, and he said, 'Go ahead; get ready; do it.'"[2013]

The unitary tax was a small tax, but, as Thompson had realized and the governor came to agree with, it was a symbolic tax whose immediate repeal could lead to big and necessary changes in Oregon's economy. When the repeal happened, Atiyeh found it one of the most satisfying political events of his life. He got there because his chief of staff would not give up in the face of her boss's 'No.'

The decision to call a special session to repeal the unitary tax was tough for Atiyeh, and there was resistance from Oregon legislative leadership.[2014] Democrats would be in the position of voting to give tax breaks to large corporations in an election year. Republicans feared that the Democrats would use the vote to pummel Republican candidates in the fall. But Atiyeh held fast. He argued that it was an election year for all candidates, so the electoral costs would not favor one party over another. In June, Atiyeh gave a speech that called for the end of the unitary tax in order to bring in outside investment and "eliminat[e] Oregon's dependence on the cyclical forest products industry."[2015] Media coverage reported that business leaders and legislators generally approved of the idea of repealing the unitary tax but there was no consensus about whether or not a special session should be called to deal with the issue.[2016]

Atiyeh was doing his homework behind the scenes. On an article about the unitary tax in the June 25 *Fortune* magazine,[2017] he highlighted the clause "Multinationals will keep the pressure on" as Japanese delegations visited the United States. Atiyeh's last highlight was about those delegations: "They'll visit four

---

2013 Thompson, "Atiyeh Interview #4," 13.
2014 Atiyeh, "Tape 40, side 1," 280.
2015 Eric Goranson, "Unitary Tax Death Urged by Atiyeh," *Oregonian*, 21 June 1984.
2016 *Oregonian*, "Unitary Tax Repeal Generally Favored," 21 June 1984.
2017 Peter W. Bernstein, "A Taxing War on Sticky-Fingered States: A Major Checkpoint in Choosing Plant Locations is Whether the State of Your Choice Practices Something Called Unitary Taxation," *Fortune*, 25 June 1984, Atiyeh Collection, Pac. Univ. Archives.

states with worldwide unitary tax laws—and more than a dozen without. The message is clear." At that same time the *Oregonian* came out with an editorial entitled "Scrap Unitary Tax Now."[2018] The editorial writers decided that there was no time to waste in order to send what they called a "crisp signal to multinational corporations" that Oregon was open for investment. The same editorial board, two months earlier, had called for the end of the unitary tax, but, at that point, doing so during the 1985 legislature would be fine.[2019] There was a growing sense of urgency about a special session.

The public discussion of the unitary tax had changed in June. Instead of being about tax breaks, the discussion was about economic development. Atiyeh appeared before the Revenue Committee to testify that he would take care of the $20 million hit to the budget when he presented his 1985 budget the next January.[2020] A report from the state economist estimated that the lost tax revenue would indeed be in the $20 million range, an amount that would require about 10,000 jobs to make up, through a combination of income and property tax revenues.[2021]

There was some international diplomacy occurring during this time. Atiyeh had a very strong relationship with the Japanese players, especially Sony's chairman and chair of the Keidanren Committee on International Investment and Technology Exchange, Akio Morita. The Keidanren was the Japanese Federation of Economic Organizations, a group that played a major role in the blending of Japanese government and private business interests to create Japan's huge economy. Morita offered to do what he could to help with the repeal of the unitary tax. Atiyeh knew that an open campaign for repeal by a well-known Japanese figure like Morita would muddy the waters in the

---

2018 *Oregonian*, "Scrap Unitary Tax Now," Editorial, 23 June 1984.
2019 *Oregonian*, "Rid State of Unitary Tax," Editorial, 29 April 1984.
2020 Atiyeh, "Tape 40, side 1," 280–281.
2021 Chang M. Sohn and Ronald A. Oliveira, "Revision of July 2 Unitary Tax Impact Memo," State Economist, Memo to Governor Atiyeh, Robert Smith, Jon Yunker, (9 July 1984), Atiyeh collection, Pac. Univ. Archives.

arguments Atiyeh wanted to make. If people were raising concerns about the repeal being a tax break for big corporations, Atiyeh could just imagine what those same people would say about tax breaks for big *foreign* corporations. Atiyeh asked Morita to stay out of the legislative fight, and Morita agreed.[2022] Atiyeh also talked in mid-June about an upcoming Morita-led Keidanren visit and its aftermath with the Japanese Consul General in Oregon.[2023] It is entirely possible that the diplomatic niceties of the special session were discussed at that time.

On Monday July 30, 1984, the Oregon legislature met for the special session. Atiyeh opened the session calling the repeal of the unitary tax "an issue of extraordinary importance for the future of our State and…the future of its citizens."[2024] He emphasized that "[w]orking Oregonians are my bottom line."[2025] For Atiyeh, the repeal of the unitary tax was not about short-term economic growth, it was a way to tell the world that Oregon was open for business. With an oblique swipe at the McCall legacy of "visit but don't stay," Atiyeh said that "[s]ince 1979, we have distanced Oregon from an image that we do not care about business investment…, that we want to be left alone in the wilds of the Oregon Country."[2026] He spoke of the hard work of navigating through a deep recession while simultaneously reconfiguring Oregon's government and tax systems so that Oregon would not just return to the timber-dependent economy of pre-1980, but would become a part of a larger global economy with new businesses creating jobs in the state. In classic speech style—grouping ideas in threes[2027]—Atiyeh asserted, "Oregon is interested in maintaining" current companies. "Oregon is

---

2022 Denny Miles, Email to Jim Moore, "Unitary Tax Repeal Discussion," 22 June 2015, Atiyeh Collection, Pac. Univ. Archives; "Reminder about Morita," Office of the Governor, State of Oregon, Hotel contacts, (12 June 1984), Atiyeh Collection, Pac. Univ. Archives.
2023 "Atiyeh Daily Index-Card Schedule, June 15, 1984," Office of the Governor, State of Oregon, (15 June 1984), Con. Gen. Kamoshida, Mr. Kawagishi & John Anderson; regarding Keidanren, Atiyeh Collection, Pac. Univ. Archives.
2024 Atiyeh, "Speech on Unitary Method," 1.
2025 Atiyeh, "Speech on Unitary Method," 1.
2026 Atiyeh, "Speech on Unitary Method," 1.

interested in investment of U.S.-based companies whose international presence causes to them to spurn Oregon because of our tax laws." And "Oregon is interested in foreign-based companies that usually will not even consider investment... because of our use of the unitary method."[2028]

In nine hours of concentrated work, the bill passed the House 53-6 and the Senate 27-3. Those in favor cited economic development. Those few opposed cited tax breaks for wealthy companies.[2029] As soon as the legislature repealed the unitary tax, news of the change "quickly reached foreign countries including Japan and Great Britain."[2030] Atiyeh vividly recalled phoning Morita: "Called him up. I was most anxious because I wanted to make sure when they wrote that [Keidanren] report that the fact that we repealed the unitary tax was in it. Got him off the golf course in Japan and said, 'We did it. We repealed it.'"[2031] When he got off the phone, he told Gerry Thompson, "Now they really trust me."[2032] Morita also immediately sent a letter of congratulations to Atiyeh.[2033]

Atiyeh signed the unitary tax bill into law on August 15, 1984.[2034] During the international trade mission to Japan and China later that year in September, Atiyeh was able to personally deliver the news of the repeal to representatives from Nissan and

---

2027 The use of the phrase makes this an epinome, Ward Farnsworth, *Classical English Rhetoric*, (Boston, MA: David R. Godine Publisher, 2011), 10–12.
2028 Atiyeh, "Speech on Unitary Method," 3.
2029 Jeff Mapes, "Legislature Votes to Jettison Unitary Tax Law: 'Border Tax' Repeal Also Wins Approval," *Oregonian*, 31 July 1984.
2030 Jeff Mapes, "McFarland Gives Tax Steamroller Green Light," *Oregonian*, 31 July 1984; Charles E. Beggs, "Tax Death Flashes Over Globe," *Oregonian*, 1 August 1984; Mapes, "Legislature Votes to Jettison."
2031 Atiyeh, "Tape 40, side 1," 281–282.
2032 Thompson, "Atiyeh Interview #4," 13.
2033 Akio Morita, to Victor Atiyeh, "Letter from Akio Morita to Atiyeh Thanking Him for the Repeal of Unitary Taxation," 30 July 1984, Atiyeh collection, Pac. Univ. Archives.
2034 "Atiyeh Daily Index-Card Schedule, August 15, 1984," Office of the Governor, State of Oregon, (15 August 1984), Signing Ceremony: Unitary Method Bill—Gerry has the bill, Atiyeh Collection, Pac. Univ. Archives.

Mitsubishi.[2035] The Japan leg of the trip was "triumphal."[2036] Oregon was the first U.S. state to be invited to address a meeting of the Keidanren.[2037] Oregon was really open for international business. Atiyeh credited it to the repeal. "Now, Oregon got quite a bit of notoriety worldwide. I mentioned England, for example, and European countries including Japan now, because we were the first state to do it. You know, if we had been the second or third or fourth, it wouldn't have been a particularly big deal."[2038]

By the end of 1984, Fujitsu America, Fujitsu Microelectronics, and Epson announced plans to invest in Oregon. West German Wacker Siltronic announced it would build a huge plant as well.[2039] Atiyeh talked about the new investments in a November meeting with the state's crucial department heads.[2040] The repeal of the unitary tax was well on its way to attracting the 10,000 jobs that would counter the lost state revenue—by the end of 1984 there was $370 million of new investment in Oregon and the lost taxes were more than offset.[2041]

Visiting Asia, Post–Unitary Tax

The repeal of the unitary tax was political, but it also fit in with the times. Americans realized that the United States economy was changing and that there was a need to pay a lot more attention to global economics. In a reversal of the postwar years when the United States was courted by countries around the world to build factories and put people to work in those countries, the United

---

2035 Steven Carter, "Atiyeh Tells Nissan, Mitsubishi Officials of Unitary Tax repeal," *Oregonian*, 11 September 1984, Atiyeh Collection, Pac. Univ. Archives.
2036 Campbell, "Atiyeh interview," Summary notes, 1.
2037 Steven Carter, "Oregon's Virtures (sic) Outlined to Japanese Executives," *Oregonian*, 15 September 1984, Atiyeh Collection, Pac. Univ. Archives.
2038 Atiyeh, "Tape 40, side 1," 282.
2039 Nicholas D. Kristof, "Investment in Oregon Spurred by Tax Repeal," *New York Times*, 17 December 1984.
2040 "Atiyeh Daily Index-Card Schedule, November 7, 1984," Office of the Governor, State of Oregon, (7 November 1984), Fred Fergson, Dallas Hurston, Jim Joyce, Rich Munn & Gerry; regarding unitary tax, Atiyeh Collection. Pac. Univ. Archives.
2041 Thompson, "Atiyeh interview #2," 17.

States would have to become a place that sought to attract foreign companies that wanted to come build factories here.[2042] On Atiyeh's September 1984 trip to Japan, China, and Hong Kong, trade—which had been the focus of earlier international discussions—was important, but it was more important to attract actual factories and businesses to Oregon. The governor wanted more opportunities to put people to work. The original meeting list for Japan had twenty or twenty-five appointments. Given the challenges of transportation in crowded Tokyo and the fact that Oregon was a relatively unknown player in Japan, that number was considered pretty good for such a trip. Atiyeh looked at the list "and he said, 'Well, this isn't enough meetings.'"[2043] At the governor's directive, the number of meetings was essentially doubled, to more than forty.

Atiyeh prioritized sources of investment by geographic location: for him California led the way, followed by Japan, then Taiwan and South Korea were next on the list.[2044] Just before his trip to Asia, Atiyeh flew to Santa Clara, California, to talk with a company that was "considering coming to Oregon." The sudden trip was consistent with Atiyeh's sales role, Denny Miles observed: "The governor, being a salesman, believes that the No. 1 salesman in the state should be the one involved in attempting to close the sale."[2045] There were no immediate results, but Atiyeh was out there recruiting.[2046] The end of the unitary method of taxation would be about the only major concession to be made by state recruiters to get new companies into Oregon's economy. If companies were going to come to Oregon, they needed to agree to

---

2042 Sarasohn, "Atiyeh interview," 3.
2043 Tom Kennedy, interviewed by Jim Moore, "Atiyeh Interview #1," Lake Oswego, OR, 18 January 2017. Summary notes, 7.
2044 Victor Atiyeh, interviewed by Jim Moore, "Atiyeh interview #1," Raleigh Hills, OR, 19 December 2013. Summary notes, 3.
2045 AP, "Atiyeh Flies to Silicon Valley to Meet Firm Heads," *Grants Pass (OR) Daily Courier*, 4 September 1984, Atiyeh Collection, Pac. Univ. Archives.
2046 AP, "No Results on Atiyeh Trip to Silicon Valley," *Roseburg (OR) News-Review*, 7 September 1984, Atiyeh Collection, Pac. Univ. Archives.

live with Oregon's laws on land use, environmental, and labor. Atiyeh saw all of these as positives for recruiting.

On September 7 the delegation headed off. The first wave of thirty-two Oregonians was primarily businesspeople seeking ties with Japan—industries, agriculture producers, engineering firms, as well as a group working "to advertise the state as a good location to build manufacturing plants."[2047] In the new post–unitary tax era, this was the first of Atiyeh's international trade missions "with a heavy focus on encouraging foreign investment in Oregon" instead of simply increasing trade.[2048] About a week later, another wave would head out from Oregon with a focus on tourism.[2049] And then, while some stayed in Japan or came home, and others went to China, a third group would join the Oregon entourage as it made its way to China in mid-September.

Atiyeh had meetings with large Japanese companies to tell them about the repeal of Oregon's unitary method of taxation.[2050] He noted that Florida and California had not changed their tax laws, implying that Oregon was friendly to international investment and open for business. The personal touch seemed to be paying off for Atiyeh as he built personal relationships with Japanese business and government leaders. In a meeting with the vice-chair of Mitsubishi, the company that had publicly stated it had chosen North Carolina over Oregon in 1983 because of the unitary tax, Atiyeh stressed Oregon's investment climate after the repeal of the tax.[2051]

2047 AP, "Atiyeh Arrives in Japan," *Roseburg (OR) News-Review*, 9 September 1984, Atiyeh Collection, Pac. Univ. Archives.

2048 Steven Carter, "Oregon Delegation Arrives for Tokyo Trade Talks," *Oregonian*, 9 September 1984; AP, "Atiyeh Arrives in Japan."; UPI, "Atiyeh Expects Japan Trip to Be Fruitful," *Ashland (OR) Daily Tidings*, 10 September 1984, Atiyeh Collection, Pac. Univ. Archives

2049 Carter, "Trade Mission Delegates."

2050 Carter, "Atiyeh Tells Nissan, Mitsubishi Officials of Unitary Tax repeal"; UPI, "Mansfield, Atiyeh Confer," *Ashland (OR) Daily Tidings*, 11 September 1984, Atiyeh Collection, Pac. Univ. Archives.

2051 "Atiyeh Daily Index-Card Schedule, September 20, 1983," Office of the Governor, State of Oregon, (20 September 1983), Dinner: Con. Gen. of Japan (please see memo in folder re Mr. Yamaguchi, pres. of Mitsubishi), Atiyeh Collection, Pac. Univ. Archives; "Atiyeh Daily Index-Card Schedule, August 12—

Along with secrecy over business negotiations, the cross-cultural issues involved in trying to understand what was going on behind the scenes in Japan were immense. Sue Hill of the *Salem Statesman Journal* wrote, "Separating boon from boondoggle on Gov. Vic Atiyeh's current trade mission here is as difficult as separating honesty from politeness in traditional Japanese [ambiguity]."[2052] A Japanese reporter from one of Japan's most important newspapers began an interview with Atiyeh "by saying: 'You are the most important governor in Japan,'" in Hill's telling.

US Ambassador to Japan Mike Mansfield did not pull many punches talking about the Oregon visit to Japan. "Oregon has been a self-satisfied state for too long, letting its neighbors to the south and north get the jump on it. Now I see you waking up to the possibilities and looking outward."[2053] Mansfield told a reporter that "he knows of no state that isn't pursuing trade with Japan." In fact, Atiyeh was one of three governors in Tokyo during this time.[2054] Missouri's Kit Bond (R) had been told that Oregon took precedence in dealing with the Epson corporation because of the groundwork laid during previous visits. Oklahoma Democrat George "Nigh complained to Atiyeh, 'You're stealing all the headlines here.'"[2055] Mansfield pointed out, however, that Oregon was doing the right thing, even if the state was somewhat late to the process of moving beyond simple trade talks and into the possibilities of investment. He pointed out that "the Japanese welcome all the wooing...because they figure the more Japan invests in the United States, the more Americans will have a

---

Revised, 1983," Office of the Governor, State of Oregon, (12 August 1983), John Lobdell, Robyn Godwin, & Geo. Webber, regarding Mitsubishi, Atiyeh Collection, Pac. Univ. Archives; "Atiyeh Daily Index-Card Schedule, December 14, 1983," Office of the Governor, State of Oregon, (14 December 1983), Pat, regarding Mitsubishi, Atiyeh Collection, Pac. Univ. Archives.

2052 Sue Hill, "Trade Mission Work Filled with Frustration," *Salem (OR) Statesman Journal*, 12 September 1984, 1A, Atiyeh Collection, Pac. Univ. Archives. Ambiguity was spelled abiguity in the original.

2053 AP, "Barb Aimed at Oregon Discovery," *Oregonian*, 15 September 1984.

2054 AP, "Barb Aimed."

2055 Sue Hill, "Mae Yih Takes Limelight as Mission Reaches China," *Salem (OR) Statesman Journal*, 19 September 1984, Atiyeh Collection, Pac. Univ. Archives.

positive image of Japan." Given Japan's reliance on exports, Mansfield saw a concern that "a negative image [of Japan] will result in trade barriers against Japanese goods."[2056]

Atiyeh realized that Oregon needed a permanent presence in Japan. It needed a state of Oregon trade office.

The trade office idea came from Atiyeh's "retail days," as he recalled.

> I realize that if you're trying to get people in Japan to do business—first of all to find out where Oregon is, and second to do business with them—you can't do it on a hit-and-run deal; go there for two or three days and come home and expect anything to happen. Because as a rug man, the people we did business with were salesmen that would call on us…routinely. We'd get to know them.
>
> So I knew that, and I said, "Okay, we've got to have some kind of continuing presence." Even when the governor goes—and he obviously can't go there for six or seven months[—]…we still have a continuing presence."[2057]

The first occupant of Oregon's new Tokyo trade office, opened during the September 1984 visit, was David Lutjen, a six-foot four-inch trade expert known affectionately in Japan as "the bearded barbarian."[2058] While the Port of Portland had operated an office in Japan since 1962, and the Oregon Wheat Growers League had operated an office in Tokyo since 1958 (along with one in New Delhi), the new state office was for the wider issues of investment, tourism, and trade all together.[2059] One big

---

2056 AP, "Barb Aimed."

2057 Victor Atiyeh, interviewed by Clark Hansen, "Tape 39," Oral history, recorded by Oregon Historical Society, 23 June 1993. Transcript, 252–253, Atiyeh Collection, Pac. Univ. Archives.

2058 Kennedy, "Atiyeh Interview #1," 7.

2059 Lawrence Barber, "Shippers Remember '62 for Action on Columbia Channel," *Oregonian*, 31 December 1962; "Final Report," Oregon Governor's Commission on Foreign Language and International Studies, State of Oregon, (August 1982), 54, Atiyeh Collection, Pac. Univ. Archives.

advantage Oregon had, compared to other states, was a good deal on its actual office. In Tokyo, a huge deposit was required by rental companies for office space; $80,000 was not uncommon.[2060] Oregon, however, did not have to put down the deposit. Its Tokyo landlord was "the Mitsubishi Group, a major investor in the new Pacwest Center building in Portland. Oregon's [deposit] was waived as part of the negotiations that led to the company's investment in the bank building."[2061]

Overall, the fall 1984 Oregon visit was a success. Morita, the chair of Sony and an important leader in the Keidanren, told Japanese and Oregonians at a reception, "I say to you that Oregon is the most suitable state for Japanese investments," in the context of the change in the unitary tax.[2062] Oregon officially opened its trade office in Tokyo, with a "focus on selling Oregon goods in Japan, attracting Japanese capital to Oregon and pitching the state as a tourist destination."[2063] Attorney Bill Campbell's impression was that the Japanese industrial sector felt respected because of the unitary tax repeal. The delegation was treated royally, in his memory.[2064]

One recurring theme during this trip was the Japanese television show, *From Oregon With Love*.[2065] Understood as part of the effort to entice Japanese tourists to spend time and money in Oregon, the plot was something of a soap opera involving a Japanese boy who lived in Oregon.

The show was the brainchild of a Portland employee of the Azumano travel agency, Kiyoshi Nakamura.[2066] He ran an Oregon

---

2060 Steven Carter, "With Trade Office, Oregon Joins Battle for Japanese Investment, Tourism," *Oregonian*, 16 September 1984, B1. That is about $180,000 in 2016.

2061 Carter, "With Trade Office," B6.

2062 Steven Carter, "Oregonians Put on Party for Big Names in Japan Industry," *Oregonian*, 13 September 1984, Atiyeh Collection, Pac. Univ. Archives.

2063 Carter, "Oregonians Put on Party."

2064 Campbell, "Atiyeh interview," 1.

2065 Carter, "Oregonians Put on Party"; AP, "TV Program Set in Oregon," *Pendleton East Oregonian*, 17 September 1984, Atiyeh Collection, Pac. Univ. Archives.

2066 Kennedy, "Atiyeh Interview #1," 10; George I. Azumano, "Resignation letter," Oregon Tourism Council, State of Oregon, Azumano Travel Services stationery,

summer-stay program for Japanese students. One time when he was in Japan, he saw a show on Japanese television about a father with two children who moved from Tokyo to the wilderness of Japan's northern islands. He wondered if a similar show could be set in Oregon. He got a meeting with the producer of the Japanese show, Toshio Nakamura, and pitched the idea.[2067] Back in Portland he talked to Tom Kennedy, then at the Greater Portland Convention and Visitors Association (GPCVA), and said, "they're going to send a person to explore the idea. …We need to see what we can do to welcome them, to show them around, and it would be nice to get an audience with the governor."[2068] Producer Nakamura and the governor met on July 1, 1983.[2069] Atiyeh loved the idea, and the wheels were in motion.[2070]

Hisashi Hieda, who became the Chairman and CEO of Fuji Television, recalled the genesis of the television show in a letter of condolence after Atiyeh's death in 2014. "31 years ago in 1983, I received a personal letter from Governor Atiyeh. That letter triggered me to make the decision to commence a TV drama series production overseas, which those in the TV industry back then considered an adventurous business decision."[2071] That business decision eventually contributed to an International Emmy Founders Award in 1999. And at that ceremony, it was former governor, and still close friend, Victor Atiyeh, who helped

---

(18 December 1986). Atiyeh Collection, Pac. Univ. Archives.

2067 Kennedy, "Atiyeh Interview #1," 10; T. Nakamura is listed as the producer for a 1986 meeting with Atiyeh. "Governor's Fall Mission to Japan—1986: Meeting Sheet," Office of the Governor, State of Oregon, (October 1986), Fuji Broadcasting Network, October 3, 1986, Atiyeh Collection, Pac. Univ. Archives; Atiyeh, "Tape 44," 398.

2068 Kennedy, "Atiyeh Interview #1," 10.

2069 "Atiyeh Daily Index-Card Schedule, July 1, 1983," Office of the Governor, State of Oregon, (1 July 1983), Mr. Toshio Nakamura, Fuji Telecasting Co., Ltd., Japan, Atiyeh Collection, Pac. Univ. Archives.

2070 This was also the first time Kennedy met the governor. Kennedy, "Atiyeh Interview #1," 10.

2071 Hisashi Hieda, Condolence Letter from Fuji Television to Victor Atiyeh, "To Victor Atiyeh, a Great Friend Who I Had the Utmost Respect For," 3 September 2014, Atiyeh Collection, Pac. Univ. Archives.

Hieda prepare before his speech to those assembled for the ceremony.

Filming for the second season took place in June 1985.[2072] Atiyeh went to watch some of the work near Lake Billy Chinook just before he went to the Pi-Ume-Sha celebration on the Warm Springs Reservation.[2073] The show made a return to Oregon in April 1986 to begin a sequel.[2074] Atiyeh welcomed the group upon its arrival at the Portland airport, and then the cast and crew were whisked to Portland's iconic "Portlandia" statue for a formal welcome by Portland mayor Bud Clark. When that season of *From Oregon With Love* aired in summer 1986, it "captured an 18% viewer share in Japan."[2075]

After the success in Japan, the Oregon delegation moved on to the potential markets in China. The China leg of the trip turned out to be a diplomatic success, and the beginning of important economic and cultural ties between Oregon and Fujian Province. But there were also clear differences in the assumptions that both the Oregon delegation and its Chinese hosts had about the other. One that would take several years to iron out was simply the relative size of Oregon and Fujian. Oregon was twice the physical size of Fujian, about 97,000 square miles to about 47,000 square miles. But Oregon's 1984 population was about 2.7 million compared to Fujian's estimate 26 million.[2076] To the Chinese, Oregon seemed to be a large empty place—learning what economic ties could be between the two would take some time.

2072 "Atiyeh Daily Index-Card Schedule, June 4, 1985," Office of the Governor, State of Oregon, (4 June 1985), Welcome: Fuji Telecasting Crew; Participate: News Conference with Fuji Telecasting, Portland International Airport, Atiyeh Collection, Pac. Univ. Archives.

2073 "Atiyeh Daily Index-Card Schedule, June 21, 1985," Office of the Governor, State of Oregon, (21 June 1985), 1 PM View: Fuji TV fliming; Mt. View Hospital, Madras…; 1:45 PM Receive Plaque (naming viewpoint): Fuji TV; near Billy Chinook Lake, Atiyeh Collection, Pac. Univ. Archives.

2074 "TV Cast Due Limo Fanfare," *Oregonian*, 12 April 1986.

2075 "Governor's Fall Mission to Japan—1986: Meeting Sheet," October 3, 1986.

2076 Steven Carter, "Sister State Enjoys Special Status to Promote Development," *Oregonian*, 26 September 1984, *Oregonian* Historical Archives; *Oregon Blue Book, 1985–1986*, (Salem, OR: Oregon Secretary of State, 1985), 6.

To the Oregonians, Fujian was millions of customers—but learning about what those customers (and the government) really wanted and learning about the pervasive individual-level poverty of China would also take some time.

Atiyeh met with the premier of China, Zhao Ziyang, the number two person in China after Communist Party Chair Deng Xiaoping,[2077] their second meeting, but the first in China.[2078] Their September encounter took place in a beautiful room filled with purple lights and lasted for almost an hour. Atiyeh was the only one of the twenty-six Oregonians to speak.[2079] Zhao was very familiar with the proposed Taiwan-Oregon sister-state agreement, but the focus of the talks was Oregon's relationship with Fujian province. In fact, Zhao did not raise the Taiwan agreement as an issue in the talks.[2080] Zhao had given his blessing to both of Oregon's sister-state proposals, an explicit one with Fujian, and a tacit one with Taiwan.[2081] Atiyeh's basic steadiness, his deftness knowing that he was in some sense involved in the high politics between the United States and China, was an incredible performance, according to those who saw him in action. Bill Campbell had the sense that Atiyeh was aware he should be himself through and through.[2082] Campbell was convinced that the

---

2077 AP, "Atiyeh to Meet With Zhao," *Astoria (OR) Daily Astorian*, 21 September 1984, Atiyeh Collection, Pac. Univ. Archives; UPI, "Atiyeh Shrugs Off Snags in China Trip," *Coos Bay (OR) World*, 21 September 1984, Atiyeh Collection, Pac. Univ. Archives; Steven Carter, "Oregon's Trade Mission Strikes Snafu in China," *Oregonian*, 21 September 1984.

2078 "Atiyeh Daily Index-Card Schedule, January 13, 1984," Office of the Governor, State of Oregon, (13 January 1984), 6:30 PM Social Hour: St. Francis reception honoring Premier Zhao Ziyang; 7:30 PM Dinner honoring Premier, Atiyeh Collection, Pac. Univ. Archives; "Atiyeh's Monthly Diary," Office of the Governor, State of Oregon, (January 1984), January 13.

2079 Steven Carter, "Chinese Premier Receives Delegates," *Oregonian*, 23 September 1984, *Oregonian* Historical Archives; AP, "Governor in China," Photo and caption, *Oregonian*, 23 September 1984, Atiyeh Collection, Pac. Univ. Archives.

2080 AP, "Governor in China."

2081 UPI, "Governor's Visit With Premier Brings Up Thorny Taiwan Topic," *Ashland (OR) Daily Tidings*, 24 September 1984, Atiyeh Collection, Pac. Univ. Archives; UPI, "Chinese Don't Object to Sister Cities," *Ontario (OR) Daily Argus Observer*, 24 September 1984, Atiyeh Collection, Pac. Univ. Archives.

2082 Campbell, "Atiyeh interview," 3.

reason for Atiyeh's high-level reception was Atiyeh's astute reaction to the incorrectly written Taiwan-Oregon agreement the previous spring. And eventually, in a separate trip in 1985, Atiyeh found a way to finalize the sister-state agreement with Taiwan.

The entire Oregon delegation then flew from Beijing to Fuzhou, the capital of Fujian Province. The Fujian trip involved some visits to industrial sites, but the main work was negotiating the Fujian-Oregon sister-state/sister-province protocol. During the negotiations, led on the Oregon side by Blake Hering, it became clear that Fujian governor Hu Ping actually had the authority to order actions in the industrial sector.[2083] As Campbell understood it, the Chinese thought of Oregon as a political unit just like Fujian. A moment of understanding occurred when the Chinese finally understood that Atiyeh, as governor, did not have the authority to simply order industrial companies to do certain things.[2084] Campbell saw that among the Chinese there was a dawning realization that this amazing event had taken place (the signing of the protocols), but they were not dealing with people who could deliver what the Chinese thought ought to be delivered.[2085] Atiyeh and Hu signed the general agreement, which included trade protocols and promises, on September 24. Hu, toasting Atiyeh with champagne, said, "May the flower of friendship be as beautiful as your Douglas fir and as everlasting as our banyan tree." Atiyeh replied, "I hope you will feel we have left some of Oregon in your hearts."[2086]

2083 Campbell, "Atiyeh interview," 3.
2084 Campbell, "Atiyeh interview," 3.
2085 Campbell, "Atiyeh interview," 4.
2086 Steven Carter, "Oregon, Fujian Leaders Sign Friendship Link," *Oregonian*, 26 September 1984.

Governors Atiyeh and Hu sign sister state/province agreement, September 24, 1984. Atiyeh Collection, Pacific University Archives.

When Atiyeh returned to Oregon he was quite happy with the trip. In the context of all his travel in 1984, he said, "No governor in any other state has done what the Oregon governor has done" by visiting so many countries and making so many connections for economic ties.[2087] At almost the same time Atiyeh returned from Asia, NEC announced plans to double its operation in Hillsboro, explicitly citing "the elimination of the unitary tax" and noting that "Oregon certainly will become an attractive place for other Japanese companies."[2088] When NEC opened its doors in 1986, the NEC representative made it explicit that it was Atiyeh

---

[2087] Eric Goranson, "Excited Atiyeh Returns from Far East Mission," *Oregonian*, 28 September 1984, Atiyeh Collection, Pac. Univ. Archives.

[2088] Steve Jenning, "NEC to Double Initial Operation in Hillsboro," *Oregonian*, 29 September 1984.

who was the crucial player in NEC's decision to invest more in Oregon—the governor "shows concern that the company is being treated fairly and that the State lives up to its commitments," whether that was the repeal of the unitary tax or pushing through road improvements around the facility,[2089]

After all these international trips and the repeal of the unitary method of taxation, Oregon was beginning to get some national acclaim for its economic outreach in 1984. The Silicon Forest's two trees (Tektronix and Intel) had begun to create new seedlings in spinoff companies; they were now joined by international companies that were also growing into productive parts of the Oregon economy. Oregon was on the national and international map as being open for business.

With the rush of new business deals that accompanied the end of the unitary tax behind him, Atiyeh's subsequent trips were focused on maintaining Oregon's visibility, ensuring that Oregonians could get access to the people they needed to see in other countries, and working on recruiting more economic connections. Atiyeh knew, with about eighteen months left in his term, that much of what he would accomplish would come to fruition after he left office. But as Oregon's governor–sales representative, he knew that it was his job to close the deals that would pay off years into the future.

There were 1985 negotiations for an RCA-Sharp plant in the Portland area, but the final decision was to locate just across the Columbia in Camas, Washington. Atiyeh was happy about the addition to the Portland-area high tech community, but behind the scenes he was "madder than hell" that Washington had won out in the competition, recalling that he said, "'Baloney!' I'm not the governor of Washington, I'm the governor of Oregon. I get no satisfaction that it's 'in the area.'" Oregon did win the Seiko/Epson factory, to be located in the Silicon Forest. The governor was deeply involved with negotiations, even down to

---

[2089] "Honoring Vic Atiyeh," NEC America, (24 November 1986), 1, Atiyeh Collection, Pac. Univ. Archives.

the level of contributing to the decision making on new street construction in Washington County. Atiyeh's trips to Japan led to a close relationship with U.S. Ambassador Mike Mansfield, and that led to more open doors among Japanese companies for Oregon representatives.

In the governor's last few months in office, he was still traveling to Japan to work on deals for more investment in Oregon and to introduce some of his fellow governors to the Japanese way of doing business.

From left, U.S. Ambassador Mike Mansfield, Atiyeh, Kennedy, Dave Lutjen, embassy staffers, all having coffee. Kennedy reported that it was not great coffee.... Atiyeh Collection, Pacific University Archives.

Trader Vic

It was during the post–unitary-tax flurry of travels that Atiyeh came to be commonly referred to as Trader Vic. The nickname started out as a criticism of his travels, but it ended up as a label that he embraced. Even in a news story about Atiyeh's death in 2014, with no irony at all, he was identified as "the first state leader to court Asian business, earning him the name 'Trader Vic' and laying the groundwork for a modern Oregon economy that relies heavily on international trade."[2090]

The first week of September 1984, *Salem Statesman Journal* columnist Ron Blankenbaker used the name. Blankenbaker was skeptical about Atiyeh's arguments for change in state tax policy to promote economic growth. Blankenbaker argued that "there seems to be no end to the anti-business boogiemen in the governor's collection of economic development myths."[2091] At the end of the column, Blankenbaker wrote, "And who knows, maybe Atiyeh—or 'Trader Vic,' as a friend of mine calls him—can pick up some contributions" against a looming ballot measure on his trip to China.

Blankenbaker's friend was Chuck Beggs, an AP reporter and former *Statesman* reporter, who recalled "I coined that, I think. I'll take credit for that. Ron Blankenbaker, …he was a good friend of mine, he wrote biting columns about everybody. He called Vic, eventually, Governor Gulliver because of these trade missions he went off on. Ron would poke fun at him. …I said, 'Yeah, a good name for him would be Trader Vic.' 'Oh!' [responded Blankenbaker]. And that's where it started, I think."[2092] But while some journalists—and especially

---

2090 Jeff Mapes, "Republican Vic Atiyeh, Who Guided Oregon Through Economic Upheaval, Dies at 91," *Portland OregonLive*, 20 July 2014. Given the trips to the Far East by Hatfield, McCall, and Straub, Atiyeh was clearly not the first governor to court Asian business.

2091 Ron Blankenbaker, "The Governor as Salesman," Column, *Salem (OR) Statesman Journal*, 5 September 1984.

2092 Charles E. Beggs, interviewed by Jim Moore, "Atiyeh interview," Salem, OR, 12 March 2015. Summary notes, 5.

Blankenbaker—looked askance at Atiyeh's travels, Beggs remembered that overall, the public seemed to think it was a good to develop trade to diversify the economy; "That was pretty plain."[2093]

However, as with all good stories, there are skeptics about this version, and Atiyeh's communications aide Denny Miles remains one.[2094] Gerry Thompson's recollection is that the nickname came from critics in the legislature.[2095] Giving some credence to the Miles-Thompson recollections was a story in the Salem paper two days before Blankenbaker's column. The Labor Day "Capital Life" column was about a celebration of the twenty-five years of judging chocolate cakes by Gerry Frank at the Oregon State Fair. Frank, who was Senator Hatfield's administrative assistant (and the cake contest started when Hatfield was governor), was surprised by a group of dignitaries, a few musicians, Mark and Antoinette Hatfield, and Vic Atiyeh. Atiyeh was identified as have "been dubbed 'Trader Vic' for his frequent trade missions to the Far East."[2096]

Nationally syndicated columnist Richard Reeves used the term in December 1985: "'Trader Vic' is a nickname that Gov. Victor Atiyeh of Oregon has picked up in the process of making regular overseas trade missions."[2097] David Sarasohn, the *Oregonian* editorial writer, recalled that it was clear that Oregon needed some kind of "different economic future" after the crushing 1982 recession. East Asia was clearly the place to look for that future.[2098] As national columnist Reeves noted, while Atiyeh was the first governor to go to East Asia on regular visits, it became

---

2093 Beggs, "Atiyeh interview," 5.
2094 Miles, "Atiyeh interview #3," 4.
2095 Gerry Thompson, interviewed by Jim Moore, "Atiyeh interview #2," Salem, OR, 12 February 2015. Summary notes, 8.
2096 Gloria Bledsoe, "Group Pays Tribute to State Fair's Chocolate Cake Judge," Capital Life column, *Salem (OR) Statesman Journal*, 3 September 1984.
2097 Richard Reeves, "Trader Vic's Visits Prove Profitable," Column, *Oregonian*, 26 December 1985, Atiyeh Collection, Pac. Univ. Archives.
2098 Sarasohn, "Atiyeh interview," Summary notes, 7.

the norm for governors all over the country to go off on trade trips.

Trader Vic saw an international opportunity much closer to home during his last year in office. Vancouver, British Columbia, had been selected in the early 1980s to host a world's fair in 1986. In March 1984, Atiyeh was approached "by two Expo 86 officials who visited Gov. Vic Atiyeh to urge him to have the state participate" in the event.[2099] At the end of April, Atiyeh announced that Oregon would take part in "the only worldwide exposition scheduled in the Pacific Rim through the year 2000[,...]expected to draw 15 million visitors."[2100] Atiyeh wanted a shot at the exposure that Oregon could get with all those people passing through the Expo grounds. It may be that he recalled what the Lewis and Clark Exposition of 1905 had done for Atiyeh Brothers, sparking tremendous growth in the business because of its award-winning displays. And the Expo would bring people to displays of Oregon's products, instead of Oregon delegations traveling the world to convince those in other countries to invest in the state.

The big emphasis within Oregon was capturing those tourists as they headed north on I-5, but money was also spent to entice travelers who would wend their ways north along the coast and through central Oregon.[2101] There was some grumbling in Oregon about the cost of the Expo pavilion. The issue became a minor part of the 1986 gubernatorial primary elections. Democratic frontrunner Neil Goldschmidt observed, "Isn't it ironic that this summer, Californians will get in their cars, barrel through Oregon, pull off I-5 only once to buy gas and use a bathroom near Eugene, and then arrive at Expo 86 in Canada to find a $2 million Oregon pavilion to tell them about the state that they just drove through without bothering to stop in?"[2102] But Goldschmidt's

---

2099 *Oregonian*, "Tall Ships Due in '86," 6 March 1984.
2100 AP, "Oregon to Participate in Expo 86," *Oregonian*, 1 May 1984.
2101 UPI, "NW States Hope to Cash In On Expo 86 Tourist Trade," *Oregonian*, 3 January 1986.

voice was lost amid growing excitement about the Oregon presence at the Expo.

The pavilion turned Tom McCall's "Visit, But Don't Stay" mantra from the 1960s and 1970s on its head. Visitors would be greeted with "Oregon—You're More Than Welcome" as they entered a building promoting business and tourism in the state.[2103] Eighty Oregon ambassadors told visitors about the state.[2104] To open the pavilion, a relay of Oregonians ran 2000 miles across the state and on to British Columbia, arriving on the first of May to cheers.[2105] On May 24, the entire Expo celebrated Oregon Day featuring the world's largest strawberry shortcake, big enough for 10,000 dessert aficionados—and "10,000 miniature Oregon flags were placed in all McDonald's hamburgers sold on the exposition grounds" that day.[2106]

After Expo 86 concluded in October, Atiyeh spoke to the annual Governor's Tourism Conference. He told those assembled that "nearly 3 million people, nearly twice the predicted number, toured the Oregon exhibit. ...A survey of pavilion visitors showed that 80 percent of respondents were planning to return to visit Oregon within five years."[2107] To put the data in perspective, the final report of the Expo chair to Atiyeh noted that 300,000 more

---

2102 Correspondent and Wire Service Reports, "Goldschmidt Pushes Tourism to Top of Economic Agenda," *Oregonian*, 1 February 1986.

2103 Gail Curtis, "Oregon's Time Tunnel," *Oregonian—Northwest Magazine Special Section*, 2 March 1986, 12.

2104 *Oregonian*, "Diversity of Oregon Highlighted," 1 May 1986.

2105 Julie Tripp, "Expo Relay Arrives to Hoist Flag and Flagon," *Oregonian*, 1 May 1986.

2106 Phil Hunt, "Oregon Takes Daylong Bow at Expo 86," *Oregonian*, 23 May 1986; Oregon Expo 86 Committee, "A Report on the Participation of the State of Oregon in the 1986 World Exposition, Vancouver, B.C., Canada," State of Oregon, Salem, OR, 1986, 40, Atiyeh Collection, Pac. Univ. Archives; "Atiyeh Daily Index-Card Schedule, May 24, 1986," Office of the Governor, State of Oregon, (24 May 1986), Cut Lebanon Shortcake in front of Pavilion (Mrs. Atiyeh and Rep. VanLeeuwen will participate; Gov. available to media), Atiyeh Collection, Pac. Univ. Archives.

2107 Julie Tripp, "Tourism Division to Ask State to Double Budget Allocation," *Oregonian*, 21 October 1986; for official statistics see Oregon Expo 86 Committee, "Expo '86 Report," 3–6.

people visited the Oregon pavilion than actually lived in Oregon.[2108] The efforts to get visitors to stop in Oregon on the way to British Columbia resulted in a 17 percent increase in visits to Oregon's border centers, and Atiyeh told the Tourism Conference, visitors "spent an average of four days in Oregon... dispelling the myth that many of the Expo travelers drove straight through the state."[2109] Atiyeh recalled that the World's Fair "turned out to be extraordinarily successful. ...Very good for Oregon."[2110]

The first Portland-Tokyo Delta flight in March 1987 carried Oregon's new governor, Neil Goldschmidt, and a delegation to Japan, echoing the first direct United Airlines flight that Atiyeh had flown on in 1983. Goldschmidt was something of "a reluctant traveler" to continue the frenetic international pace of his predecessor, but former Governor Atiyeh was there to hand off the relationships Atiyeh had built in his years of travel.[2111] Goldschmidt had been asked to make the trip "by businessmen and legislative leaders, and he believed it was important to demonstrate 'continuity' in the state's leadership. 'This will be a passing-of-the-torch trip. It had to happen at some point. I'm very pleased Gov. Atiyeh will come."[2112] Goldschmidt's reluctance came from the fact that he was in the middle of his first legislative session as governor. He observed that "the trip's timing was not the 'best in the world,'" but he noted, "There's never going to be a right time for this trip."[2113]

In the fast-paced world of international investments, ideas and policies had shifted in just the two months that Atiyeh was out of office. Alan Ota, the *Oregonian* reporter who had traveled so

---

2108 Julie Tripp, "Oregon's Expo Deli Still Whets Visitors' Appetites," *Oregonian*, 5 January 1987.
2109 Tripp, "Tourism Division to Ask State to Double Budget Allocation."
2110 Atiyeh, "Tape 44," 403.
2111 *Oregonian*, "Goldschmidt Calls Japan Trip 'Passing of Torch'," Capital Notebook analysis, 28 February 1987.
2112 *Oregonian*, "Goldschmidt Calls Japan Trip."
2113 Alan Ota, "Off to Japan, Goldschmidt Says He's 'Reluctant Traveler'," *Oregonian*, 1 March 1987.

much with Atiyeh, wrote that then-candidate Goldschmidt was a skeptic "of the benefits to be gained by traveling abroad in search of industry and trade" in contrast to Atiyeh's frequent efforts to do just that. During the 1986 campaign, Goldschmidt and his Republican opponent Norma Paulus had vied with each other over changes they would make to Atiyeh's economic development plans. Paulus emphasized she would "take care of business in the state and not travel outside of Oregon in her first years in office"—Goldschmidt said he would "focus his travels inside the state."[2114] Ota noted that "Goldschmidt said he would make more trips if asked by his staff, but he did not sound like a man who was planning to make frequent journeys abroad. 'I don't think that's what drives us,' he said. 'I think it's what we do in our local communities.'"[2115]

Atiyeh recalled that for him "[i]t was pretty much...a desire that I had that there be no interruption. That we have a change of governor, but I wanted to make sure that...our relations...with Japan would continue uninterrupted."[2116]

Relying on his knowledge of Japanese culture and his personal ties with the people they met, Atiyeh upended normal protocol by asking to go first in meetings. He recalled, "[t]hat would not be typical. The governor would go first. I said, 'Let me go first, and then I will introduce you.' That would be my way of passing it on."[2117] The Japanese were somewhat surprised that Atiyeh, a Republican, was going to such great lengths to help his successor, a Democrat. Atiyeh recalled, "They said, 'How come you're doing this?' I said...that my interest was in continuing the relationship. ...So they understood that part of it. Maybe it reinforced it a little."[2118]

2114 Ota, "Off to Japan."
2115 Ota, "Off to Japan."
2116 Victor Atiyeh, interviewed by Clark Hansen, "Tape 60," Oral history, recorded by Oregon Historical Society, 10 September 1993. Transcript, 51, Atiyeh Collection, Pac. Univ. Archives.
2117 Atiyeh, "Tape 60," 51.
2118 Atiyeh, "Tape 60," 52.

When Vic Atiyeh left office in January 1987, Oregon was in a strong position for international trade, especially with northeast Asia. As Phil Keisling a journalist at the time, but headed toward becoming Oregon's Secretary of State in the 1990s, saw it, Atiyeh understood that things had changed and Oregon could no longer "coast on its reputation" for innovative legislation and ideas.[2119] Keisling suspected Atiyeh's international perspective might have come from the rug business, but whatever it was, Atiyeh pushed state companies and state government to reach out to the global community. But Oregon was not the only state to seek economic ties with the world. In fact, Atiyeh was leading a wave of international interest that would profoundly change all the states in the country.

By the time Atiyeh left office in 1987, he had made eleven international trips with twenty-four different Oregon missions (each country visit was considered a separate mission), more than doubling the cumulative Oregon total of gubernatorial international trips before 1979. Between 1980 and 1986, seven years of Atiyeh's eight years as governor, foreign assets in the United States grew from $544 billion to $1.434 trillion.[2120] From 1984 on, Atiyeh was actively seeking to grab as much of that direct investment as he could. Spurred on by the demise of the unitary tax, Oregon's negotiating position was relatively strong during this amazing period of foreign investment. In the last years of the Straub administration, 11% of Oregon's manufacturing jobs were tied to international trade. When Atiyeh left office, that percentage had increased by more than half.

Ted Kulongoski, Oregon's governor from 2003 to 2011, observed that of course there was international trade before Atiyeh. But, he said, "The fact is that Vic was out there plowing this ground long before anybody else was." Kulongoski added,

---

2119 Phil Keisling, interviewed by Jim Moore, "Atiyeh interview," Portland, OR, 23 February 2015. Summary notes, 3.

2120 Earl H. Fry, *The Expanding Role of State and Local Governments in U.S. Foreign Affairs*, (New York: Council on Foreign Relations Press, 1998), 33. Dollars are constant in 1996 value.

"All the rest of us since then actually followed in his footsteps. I don't care if it was Neil [Goldschmidt], Barbara [Roberts], John [Kitzhaber], and my guess is that Kate [Brown] will do the same thing. We have all cultivated that trade issue."[2121]

Vic Atiyeh's vision was to understand this and take the initiative when his state needed it the most, in the wake of the devastating 1982 recession.

2121 Ted Kulongoski, "Atiyeh Interview," Portland, OR, 30 March 2015, Summary notes 2.

9 Moving on

Although Vic Atiyeh kept pushing to bring more investment to Oregon and sell the state to its citizens and the world up until the moment he left office, at a certain point in a two-term governor's life, the words "lame duck" begin to emerge in conversation. Atiyeh had seen this happen to his predecessors, governors Hatfield and McCall. It began to happen to him in 1986.

Atiyeh's state of the state address in January 1986 already had a valedictory tone. He dwelt on the continuity of history from the spirit of the pioneers in the 1840s to the people who had made it through the worst recession since the Great Depression, people who "*still* have that toughness of spirit which fights back against adversity."[2122] Atiyeh told the Medford audience that natural resources were still an important part of Oregon's economy, as they had been for the pioneers, but, "no longer isolated, Oregon has become an integral part of the *world* community."[2123] The

---

2122 Vic Atiyeh, "State of the State Address" (speech, Medford Rotary Club, Medford, OR, 31 January 1986), 2, Atiyeh Collection, Pac. Univ. Archives. Italics underlined by Atiyeh's hand.
2123 Vic Atiyeh, "State of the State, 1986," 3. Italics underlined by Atiyeh's hand.

programs the governor had championed in the face of government budget cuts and business closings were still working their magic. Lakeview millworkers' jobs were saved because the state, with lottery dollars, purchased a "rail line to keep those mills running." The same thing happened in Tillamook, saving 550 jobs between the two sites.[2124] Research programs through Oregon State University were working on strains of wheat that would be more attractive to the world market.[2125] The ground was being broken for centers of excellence at universities in Eugene, Corvallis, and Portland. Red tape had been reduced, with business licenses now requiring the completion of a four-page Commerce Department form instead of the twenty-seven pages over eight documents that had been required before.[2126] Atiyeh extolled the increase in voluntarism, harking back to his inaugural address, "the formation of the *first* statewide food bank in the *nation*," and the private purchase of the banks of the lower Deschutes to guarantee public access to the river.[2127]

Unsaid was the disappointment he felt that major education and tax reform had failed in 1985, and that the property tax system was still seen as onerous and unfair by so many Oregonians. Atiyeh had spent years of his political life, dating back to the early 1960s, trying to enact solutions to these problems. He had pushed for change during both his terms in office. Now he was done with those kinds of big policy proposals.

The governor did, however, have "blue and gold…*bumper sticker*[s] expressing the *strong emotional* feelings we have for our *wonderfully unique state*" available for the address's audience to "share *your* pride in being citizens of *this* great state by displaying [them] on your car[s]."[2128]

2124 Vic Atiyeh, "State of the State, 1986," 6; Tom Kennedy, interviewed by Jim Moore, "Atiyeh Interview #1," Lake Oswego, OR, 18 January 2017. Summary notes, 6.
2125 Vic Atiyeh, "State of the State, 1986," 8.
2126 Vic Atiyeh, "State of the State, 1986," 10.
2127 Vic Atiyeh, "State of the State, 1986," 14–15. Italics underlined by Atiyeh's hand.
2128 Vic Atiyeh, "State of the State, 1986," 25. Italics underlined by Atiyeh's hand.

I'M PROUD TO BE AN OREGONIAN

The Bumper Sticker. "I'm Proud to Be an Oregonian," Office of the Governor, State of Oregon, Bumper Sticker, (31 January 1986), Atiyeh Collection, Pacific University Archives.

In April of his final year in office, Atiyeh's to-do list included twenty-two items listed in a letter from Gerry Thompson. Many of the items were focused on completing tasks that had already been started—responses to studies of ports, railroad issues, U.S. Forest Service management proposals, resolution to a shortfall in the Department of Human Resources—but there were also activities to move Oregon forward—trade missions, "Department of Commerce final phase of developing one-stop permit office," protecting the Columbia Gorge.[2129] The governor was looking toward the end of his time in office, but he was also working for Oregon's future in his last months on the job.

The governor's office was also closely following the gubernatorial political campaigns moving toward the May 20 primary election. Particular attention was given to Norma Paulus' campaign, she being the presumptive Republican nominee. The 1986 gubernatorial election was already going strong by the summer of 1985. Neil Goldschmidt—Nike executive, former mayor of Portland, former U.S. Secretary of Transportation—was the presumptive nominee of the Democrats. Norma Paulus— former legislator, former Secretary of State, and second woman

---

2129 Gerry Thompson, "Daily Reports to the Governor," Office of the Governor, State of Oregon, (April 1986), Letter from Gerry Thompon to William Love, April 15, 1986, 2–3, Atiyeh Collection, Pac. Univ. Archives.

elected to statewide office in Oregon—was considered to have a lock on the Republican nomination. The state saw its political future with them, not with the incumbent governor.

Paulus' campaign met with Atiyeh, his 1982 campaign manager, Denny Miles, and Gerry Thompson on January 16, 1986, at the governor's Winter Street house.[2130] Instead of asking for Atiyeh's advice, the Paulus team simply presented a campaign plan. Much of the tension between the Paulus campaign and Atiyeh was visible to outside observers. In March 1986, one analyst observed that "Paulus has been vague about the degree to which she wants Atiyeh involved in her campaign. She does not lock him out, but she has given no signs that she wants him to participate."[2131] Paulus had been an important, but very independent, part of Atiyeh's time as governor. That independence led to wariness on the part of Atiyeh's staff. In an October 1981 meeting to talk about how the governor's official office and his re-election campaign would operate in their separate ways, Gerry Thompson wrote, "Norma Paulus—care, feed and handle carefully."[2132]

[2130] "Atiyeh Daily Index-Card Schedule, January 16, 1986," Office of the Governor, State of Oregon, (16 January 1986), Norma Paulus, Steve Wirn, Ron Saxton, Bill Love, Jim Houlden, Gerry & Denny; Gov's residence, Atiyeh Collection, Pac. Univ. Archives.

[2131] Foster Church, "Atiyeh's Anger May Carry Him Into Paulus Campaign," Column, *Oregonian*, 23 March 1986.

[2132] Gerry Thompson, "Handwritten Notes, Sep–Nov 1981, Apr–May 1982," Office of the Governor, State of Oregon, (24 September–25 November, 13 April–28 May 1981–1982), 10-21-81, 43, Atiyeh Collection, Pac. Univ. Archives.

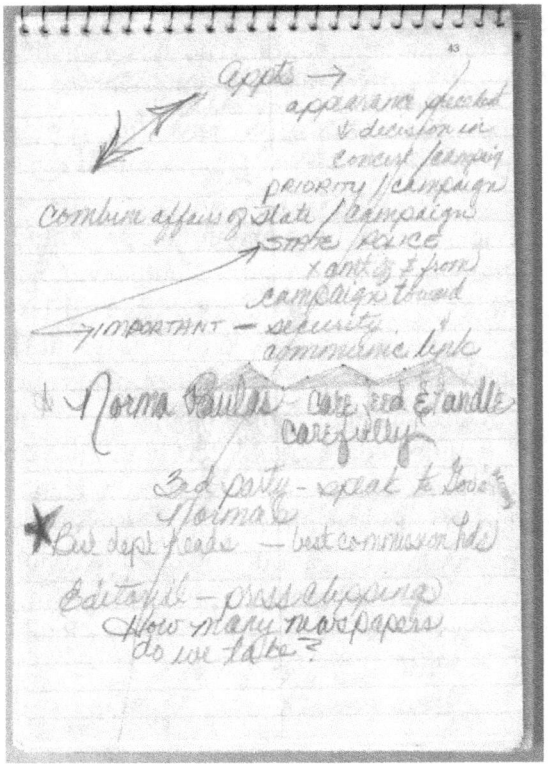

Gerry Thompson's observation about Secretary of State Norma Paulus. Atiyeh Collection, Pacific University Archives.

What really stuck with Atiyeh in the 1986 election, however, was presumptive Democratic nominee Neil Goldschmidt's referring to the people in state government as "dry rot" that needed to be removed from their jobs. Goldschmidt named names in his March 1986 talk with the Oregon Democratic Party Platform Convention.[2133] Reporter Peter Wong said, "I remember

---

[2133] Brad Cain, "Democratic Faithful Cheer Goldschmidt," *Salem (OR) Statesman-Journal*, 17 March 1986; Foster Church, "Goldschmidt Hits Top State Administrators," *Oregonian*, 17 March 1986.

that got Atiyeh's goat" and "contributed to the bad relations between the two of them."[2134] Atiyeh stated that he "now plans to play a more active role this year than originally planned in campaigning" for Paulus.[2135]

Emphasizing his three statewide campaigns, all of which were hard hitting, Atiyeh felt Goldschmidt went too far. "Trembl[ing] with anger and stammer[ing] as he read" to a Salem audience,[2136] Atiyeh argued, "If you bypass me to engage in bureaucrat-bashing of people who have dedicated their working lives to serving the citizens of this state, you are spoiling for a fight with Vic Atiyeh. As a matter of fact, Mr. Goldschmidt, you have just invited me into the ring where I now plan to stay until the bell rings on Nov. 4."[2137] It looked like Goldschmidt was attempting to tie Atiyeh to Paulus, in effect creating the 1982 race between Atiyeh and Goldschmidt that Atiyeh had wanted at the time.[2138] However, Paulus continued to be ambivalent at best about Atiyeh campaigning for her, and she began to openly attack some of his policies.

Paulus' campaign strategy was to blame Atiyeh for missing the boat on smaller Oregon towns and economic growth. The *New York Times* writer Tom Wicker picked up on the reasons for this. "Employment in the vital timber industry has fallen…, and Oregon's share of national plywood production has dropped…. That little has been done to reverse this trend is one reason why the Atiyeh years are seen…as stagnant."[2139] At a campaign talk in Newport, Paulus "criticized Atiyeh and the Legislature for 'going after the razzle-dazzle,' in other words, trying to attract big

---

2134 Peter Wong, interviewed by Jim Moore, "Atiyeh interview," Rock Creek, OR, 4 August 2015. Summary notes, 11.
2135 UPI, "Atiyeh Lashes out at 'Demagoguery': Goldschmidt's Comments," *Coos Bay (OR) World*, 19 March 1986.
2136 Church, "Atiyeh's Anger May Carry Him Into Paulus Campaign."
2137 Foster Church, "Governor Rebukes Candidate," *Oregonian*, 19 March 1986.
2138 Victor Atiyeh, interviewed by Clark Hansen, "Tape 35," Oral history, recorded by Oregon Historical Society, Portland, OR, 15 June 1993. Transcript, 128, Atiyeh Collection, Pac. Univ. Archives.
2139 Tom Wicker, "'The Two Oregons'," In the Nation column, *New York Times*, 20 January 1986.

business and industry to the state" instead of focusing on timber and agriculture and small businesses.[2140] In March and April 1986 letters, Paulus' fund raising committee asked Atiyeh to "make a few contacts for us on behalf of Norma."[2141] In a direct response, Atiyeh wrote to Thompson,

> I have had enough of this kind of crap——!
>
> Please tell the Paulus campaign I will not oppose her but also I will not support her——
>
> VA[2142]

2140 Vic Atiyeh, "Reaction to Letter from Paulus Campaign, Relevant Newspaper article," Office of the Governor, State of Oregon, (26 April 1986), Dean Brickey, "Paulus Seeks to Promote Fishing," Newport (OR) News-Times, March 29, 1986, Atiyeh collection, Pacific University Archive, Forest Grove, OR.

2141 Vic Atiyeh, "Reaction to Letter from Paulus Campaign, Relevant Newspaper article," Letter from William E. Love, Schwabe, Williamson, Wyatt, Moore & Roberts Attorneys at Law, to Honorable Victor Atiyeh, "Contact List," March 13, 1986; Vic Atiyeh, "Atiyeh Response to Norma Paulus Gubernatorial Campaign Request for Support," Office of the Governor, State of Oregon, (March, April 1986), Letter from William E. Love to Gerry Thompson, "Re: List of Potential People for the Governor to Consider Calling on Norma's Behalf," April 7, 1986, Atiyeh collection, Pacific University Archive, Forest Grove, OR.

2142 Vic Atiyeh, "Reaction to Letter from Paulus Campaign, Relevant Newspaper article," Routing Slip, VA to Gerry, April 26, 1986.

> **OFFICE OF THE GOVERNOR**
> **ROUTING SLIP**
>
> To: Goody
> From: VE   Date: 4/26
>
> ___ For your information.
> ___ Prepare response for Governor's signature.
> ___ For your comments and return.
> ___ Reply direct to origin. Return original and copy of reply to this office.
>
> COMMENTS:
>
> I HAVE HAD ENOUGH OF THIS KIND OF CRAP——!
> PLEASE TELL THE PAULUS CAMPAIGN I WILL NOT OPPOSE HER BUT ALSO I WILL NOT SUPPORT HER ——

An adamant Atiyeh, April 1986. Atiyeh Collection, Pacific University Archives.

Later in the campaign, Paulus said she would abolish the state Department of Energy, the center of Atiyeh's efforts in his first years as governor. Peter Wong recalled that Atiyeh had to go public to defend the agency from the Republican nominee.[2143] This contributed to a sense, as Wong put it, that Paulus was a loose cannon in the political world. Paulus recalled that "she needed to distance herself from Atiyeh's economic policies… without alienating Atiyeh's loyalists and other mainstream

---

2143 Wong, "Atiyeh interview," 11; AP, "Atiyeh Disagrees with Paulus' Proposal," *Salem (OR) Statesman-Journal*, 29 August 1986.

Republicans"[2144] Her eventual tactic was to focus on the fractious legislature.[2145]

In mid-September, a memo from the governor's office began to consider the last few months of the Atiyeh governorship. The beginnings of lists of accomplishments (for example, appointments to the Oregon Supreme Court) were included, as well as thinking about "pardons if any at Christmas: comb the system to see if any lingering injustices."[2146]

There was a draft letter to Atiyeh's successor, whoever that might be. The draft started out, "Dear Neil/Norma" and suggested ways to make the transition smooth, finishing with, "I pledge to you our fullest cooperation. Anything less from my own staff or department heads should be reported to me personally."[2147]

Goldschmidt beat Paulus 52% to 48%, the closest race since the 1956 election to fill out Paul Patterson's term (and the first victory by a Democrat since 1934).[2148] Atiyeh's analysis of the race a few years later was that the result was "more that Norma let it slip from her fingers rather than Neil won."[2149] Goldschmidt positioned himself as the active candidate who could move Oregon forward out of the economic ruins, whereas Paulus' campaign centered around the idea that Paulus really knew state government well; she was competent. Phil Keisling saw that she

---

2144 Norma Paulus, Gail Wells and Pat McCord Amacher, *The Only Woman in the Room: The Norma Paulus Story*, (Corvallis, OR: Oregon State University Press, 2017), 189.

2145 Paulus, Wells and Amacher, *Only Woman in the Room*, 189.

2146 "Office Conversation of 9/15/86, Transition File," Office of the Governor, State of Oregon, Memo to VA, (18 September 1986), Atiyeh Collection, Pac. Univ. Archives.

2147 Victor Atiyeh, "Draft Letter to Successor," Office of the Governor, State of Oregon, Tickler File, Transition letter draft to Neil/Norma, (Spring 1986), Atiyeh Collection, Pac. Univ. Archives.

2148 *Oregon Blue Book, 1987–1988*, (Salem, OR: Oregon Secretary of State, 1987), 402; Jim Moore, "Gubernatorial Results in Oregon," (Unpublished manuscript, 9 December 2016), Table.

2149 Victor Atiyeh, interviewed by Clark Hansen, "Tape 47," Oral history, recorded by Oregon Historical Society, Portland, OR, 15 July 1993. Transcript, 492, Atiyeh Collection, Pac. Univ. Archives.

just did not seem to be able to inherit the Republican leadership mantle from Tom McCall or Vic Atiyeh.[2150] *Oregonian* editorial board member David Sarasohn attributed the outcome to Paulus' lack of dynamism.[2151] More relevant, perhaps, was that she was a liberal Republican, like McCall and Packwood. Ted Kulongoski saw that the 1978 Republican primary victory of moderate Vic Atiyeh was the beginning of the end for the dominance of liberal Republicans.[2152] Reagan's 1980 presidential victory helped push the party even further to the right—further from the center and Atiyeh's political identity. Liberal Republican Dave Frohnmayer would likewise lose to Democrat Barbara Roberts in 1990, with a much more conservative third-party candidate, the social conservative Al Mobley, providing a place for some Reagan Republicans to put their votes. Republicans would get close to retaking the governor's office—Chris Dudley was within about 1.5% in 2010, Kevin Mannix within 3% in 2002—but the seat has remained stubbornly out of reach to the party since 1987.

Atiyeh had his staff create a "transition book" and "offered to help whoever [Goldschmidt] wanted" to learn about the office of the governor. But Goldschmidt had different ideas about the process. When the governor-elect came to see the governor on November 14, Goldschmidt had just one question for Atiyeh: "How many computers do you have?"[2153] "That's the *only* question he asked," Atiyeh emphasized.[2154]

Atiyeh knew that each governor changed the ways state government functioned to a certain extent. It was human nature and part of the political process. But he "objected to the

---

2150 Phil Keisling, interviewed by Jim Moore, "Atiyeh interview," Portland, OR, 23 February 2015. Summary notes. 6.

2151 David Sarasohn, interviewed by Jim Moore, "Atiyeh interview," Portland, OR, 17 February 2015. Summary notes. 5.

2152 Ted Kulongoski, interviewed by Jim Moore, "Atiyeh interview," Portland, OR, 30 March 2015. Summary notes, 8.

2153 "Atiyeh Daily Index-Card Schedule, November 14, 1986," Office of the Governor, State of Oregon, (14 November 1986), Governor-Elect Goldschmidt, Atiyeh Collection, Pac. Univ. Archives; Victor Atiyeh, interviewed by Jim Moore, "Atiyeh interview #1," Raleigh Hills, OR, 19 December 2013. Summary notes, 5.

2154 Victor Atiyeh, "Tape 55," 697. Emphasis underlined, twice, by Atiyeh in original.

Goldschmidt style. ...Anybody that had anything to do with Atiyeh got dumped" when Goldschmidt became governor. Atiyeh said, "That's the wrong thing to do. ...It's wrong in the sense of just institutional memory, if nothing else."[2155] Atiyeh did not recall wholesale replacements of agency heads with governors Hatfield, McCall, or Straub. In 1993, he compared Goldschmidt's actions "to the Scarlet Letter, ...you know, where Hester had this A on her sweater. Well, ...if an A stood, not for adultery, but stood for Atiyeh, if you had an A on your sweater, out you go [laughter]."[2156]

Atiyeh did not seem to remember that people were somewhat amazed when he did not remove many Straub appointees at the beginning of his first term in office, an amazement that was amplified because Atiyeh was a Republican and Straub was a Democrat. By 1987, the differences between the two parties were becoming more pronounced in Oregon's state government. What annoyed Atiyeh had become the norm in many places in the United States.

In the middle of the transition, as one-sided as it was, Goldschmidt asked Atiyeh to forgo appointments to boards and commissions so that Goldschmidt could appoint his own people after inauguration day. Atiyeh felt this was a step too far. "I was going to be governor until the minute his hand went up [to be sworn in]. No, until he said, 'So help me, God.' ...I was offended he even suggested it. ...[H]e wanted to become governor before he was governor." Atiyeh pointed out that when he had taken over from Straub, "I respected the fact that he was governor up to the last minute, and I was going to be governor up to the last minute."[2157] When Atiyeh had been governor-elect in 1978, he consulted, and the Straub administration cooperated and made the

---

2155 Victor Atiyeh, interviewed by Clark Hansen, "Tape 28," Oral history, recorded by Oregon Historical Society, Portland, OR, 21 May 1993. Transcript, 802, Atiyeh Collection, Pac. Univ. Archives.
2156 Victor Atiyeh, "Tape 28," 803. Brackets in original.
2157 Victor Atiyeh, "Tape 55," 701.

actual appointments, in making some personnel choices.[2158] Goldschmidt did not want to consult; he just wanted Atiyeh to forgo his constitutional powers.

One of Atiyeh's last unofficial acts as governor was to gather with fellow members of the Pompous Twits, a group named by Salem columnist Ron Blankenbaker, consisting of "politicians, lobbyists, bureaucrats and governmental hangers-on who've committed acts of pomposity too outrageous to ignore."[2159] The Twits delivered Christmas gifts to needy Salem-area families each year, distributing donations from local businesses. Atiyeh, Secretary of State Barbara Roberts, and a former Salem mayor led the group in 1986, joined by over eighty fellow Twits. The Twits had become something of an honorary society, even sponsoring a dinner for Blankenbaker.[2160]

Atiyeh delivered his final state of the state address a week before leaving the governorship. He was back in Washington County, where his political career began. "It is with pride and a real sense of nostalgia that I return to Washington County today to deliver my final remarks on the state of our great state," he said to open his speech.[2161] He focused on the economic challenges of his time in office, when "we saw the traditional foundations of our livelihoods—timber, agriculture, fisheries—rocked by an

---

2158 "Fred Klaboe Named Transportation Chief," *Salem Oregon Statesman*, 1 December 1978; "Saalfeld Successor Named," *Salem (OR) Statesman Journal*, 2 December 1978.

2159 Ron Blankenbaker, "Twits Play Santa Again: Merry Christmas," Column, *Salem (OR) Statesman-Journal*, 24 December 1986.

2160 "Governor's Schedule, 22–28 October 1984," Office of the Governor, State of Oregon, Confidential, (18 October 1984), October 26 Gov. Atiyeh will deliver remarks at roast honoring Ron Blankenbaker sponsored by Pompous Twits Anonymous; Black Angus restaurant, Salem, Atiyeh Collection, Pac. Univ. Archives; "Monthly Diary Schedule, May 1984," Office of the Governor, State of Oregon, (1984), Pompous Twits: Meet Sen. Day in the Capitol coffee shop, Atiyeh Collection, Pac. Univ. Archives "Monthly Diary Schedule, December 1986," Office of the Governor, State of Oregon, (1986), December 23 Breakfast Deliveries: Pompous Twits, Atiyeh Collection, Pac. Univ. Archives.

2161 Vic Atiyeh, "State of the State" (speech, Washington County Public Affairs Forum, Beaverton, OR, 5 January 1987), 1, Atiyeh Collection, Pac. Univ. Archives.

economic earthquake."[2162] But with all the policy challenges, both successes and failures, Atiyeh had stayed in love with Oregon and Oregonians. "What I will miss most of all will be the people of my state: honest, hard-working people from all walks of life, who have confirmed for me that Oregonians are truly a breed apart."[2163] The same person who had been described as a reluctant campaigner at the beginning of his 1974 run for governor was now an unabashed people person—open with friends and strangers alike.

After years of recession and hard times, in 1986–87 Oregonians were hopeful that the state was moving to a more positive and less stressful economic future.[2164] As the new legislature met in January 1987, an editorial called for continuation of Atiyeh's goals of making taxation, economic development, and paying for vital services the center of policymaking "Economic development is a major issue facing this Legislature. ...Gov. Atiyeh has laid the basis for diversification of our timber-based economy. That push must be intensified."[2165]

On Atiyeh's last day in office, January 12, 1987, he recalled he "was well mentally prepared for that. ...I'd seen it happen before. ...I know how it works. I know that one minute you're governor and the next minute you're not."[2166] He did get emotional as he gave his short farewell address, "but it was not an emotion of leaving office," it was that he knew he would "miss the people [that he worked with], very much...."[2167] After Goldschmidt was inaugurated, Atiyeh and Dolores had lunch with his staff.[2168] Then

---

2162 Vic Atiyeh, "State of the State, 1987," 2.
2163 Vic Atiyeh, "State of the State, 1987," 5.
2164 Mike Thorne, interviewed by Jim Moore, "Atiyeh interview," Pendleton, OR, 23 June 2015. Summary notes, 6.
2165 *Statesman-Journal*, "Roll Up Your Sleeves: Welcome, 64th Legislature," Editorial, 12 January 1987.
2166 Victor Atiyeh, "Tape 55," 703.
2167 Victor Atiyeh, "Tape 55," 703.
2168 "Atiyeh Daily Index Card, Jan 12, 1987," Staff Luncheon; "Monthly Diary Schedule, January 1987," Office of the Governor, State of Oregon, (January 1987), January 12, Atiyeh Collection, Pac. Univ. Archives.

both his driving aides, Lon Holbrook and Darrell Berning "drove Dolores and me home in the [Oregon] number one car [the Oregon '1' license plate], turned around, and went back to Salem, and that was it."[2169]

Life after Government

For Atiyeh, January 13, 1987, started out as all his days for the past eight years had—he consulted the three-by-five index card typed out by his assistant Robin Shepherd to guide him through the day. On this morning there was just one event, a KXL radio interview. But at the top of the card Shepherd wrote, "You thought you were rid of me—but here I am again!"[2170] On January 24, 1987, Atiyeh wrote to the director of the Executive Department that his transition from governor to ex-governor would be complete "on June 30, 1987. That date will end 28 years and 6 months of an official, formal public relationship."[2171]

Home life back in the Atiyeh house in Raleigh Hills, however, was a blessing after the Winter Street house. Dolores, especially, was very happy to be done with life in Salem. Atiyeh recalled, "A couple of months after we'd been home, she said, 'Gee, it's nice to be home.'"[2172]

2169 Victor Atiyeh, "Tape 55," 704.
2170 "Atiyeh Daily Index-Card Schedule, January 13, 1987," Office of the Ex-Governor, (13 January 1987), Atiyeh Collection, Pac. Univ. Archives.
2171 "Transition Documents," Letter from Victor Atiyeh to Fred Miller, June 24, 1987.
2172 Victor Atiyeh, "Tape 55," 705.

Portrait by Don Gray. Is Vic more twinkly? Photo by Jim Moore.

On February 13, 1987, as part of an early state of Oregon birthday party (it was a Friday), Atiyeh's official portrait was unveiled in the capitol.[2173] "Dolores thought the portrait was far too grim and unsmiling."[2174] The artist, Don Gray, had lunch with the Atiyehs and "Vic smiled and twinkled a lot…so Don agreed to

---

2173 "Atiyeh Daily Index-Card Schedule, February 13, 1987," Office of the Ex-Governor, (13 February 1987), Unveiling: Governor's Portrait, 2nd floor, Senate side, State Capitol, Atiyeh Collection, Pac. Univ. Archives; "Atiyeh's Portrait Goes on View," *Salem (OR) Statesman-Journal*, 14 February 1987.

take the portrait back and lighten up." Salem columnist Gloria Bledsoe Goodman thought the new version showed "a far happier looking Vic."

Later in the winter of 1987, Atiyeh suddenly realized "this is the first time I haven't been down in Salem [...for a] legislative session in 28 years. ...It took me a couple of months to kind of finally dawn on me that I wasn't there."[2175] For Atiyeh, this showed he was not missing the process of governing, but he was missing the relationships he had with all those people. The first staff reunion took place on August 1, 1987.[2176] The ex-governor would greatly enjoy getting together for lunches and talks with his former staff until the end of his life.

Atiyeh had not been a governor who sought the limelight for much of what he did, and for certain major parts of his governorship, like the Rajneeshees, he actively sought to conceal his role. The Rajneeshee experience showed him at his best—balancing the rights of all with the desire for people to live in lawful and safe communities. His work during that crisis remained unknown.

He likened the way some other governors and politicians sought out publicity to the way football players celebrate after scoring a touchdown or sacking a quarterback. "God," Atiyeh observed, "that's his job. What are you strutting around about?"[2177] The former governor pointed out in 2014, "Atiyeh

---

2174 Gloria Bledsoe Goodman, "New Zealand Visitor Comes Up a Winner," Column, *Salem (OR) Statesman-Journal*, 24 February 1987.

2175 Victor Atiyeh, "Tape 55," 706.

2176 "Atiyeh Daily Index-Card Schedule, August 1, 1987," Victor Atiyeh and Company, (1 August 1987). Staff Reunion, Atiyeh Mountain Home, Atiyeh Collection, Pac. Univ. Archives; "Atiyeh Daily Index-Card Schedule, July 16, 1987," Victor Atiyeh and Company, (16 July 1987), Dinner: Lon and Karen Holbrook & Al and Gerry Thompson; Governor's House, Atiyeh Collection, Pac. Univ. Archives; "Atiyeh Daily Index-Card Schedule, July 29–30, 1989," Victor Atiyeh and Company, (29–30 July 1989), July 29, 1989 Staff Reunion: Champoeg Park, Atiyeh Collection, Pac. Univ. Archives.

2177 Victor Atiyeh, interviewed by Jim Moore, "Atiyeh interview #2," Raleigh Hills, OR, 2 January 2014. Summary notes, 7.

didn't want more press" when he was governor.[2178] He was well aware of the criticism directed toward Denny Miles by those who thought Atiyeh should have received more press coverage emphasizing his leadership during his time in office, but Atiyeh was quite clear that Miles was doing what the governor had wanted.

Atiyeh had some idea in his mind that as an ex-governor, he would be able to step into duty on boards of directors and the like, just like high-ranking ex-government officials in Washington, D.C. As early as August 1983—just seven months after being sworn in for his second term—Atiyeh had a meeting "regarding your career after politics."[2179] He thought to himself, "I'm young enough [just turning 64 when he left office in 1987], I've run the biggest business in the state, I could be on a board."[2180] But, he found "it just doesn't happen" with Oregon ex-governors.[2181] He found that his post-gubernatorial life meant the he would "have to work at what I do, and it doesn't come easy. It doesn't come any easier for me than it does anybody else."[2182] Atiyeh would serve stints on the boards of Riedel Environmental Technology,[2183]

2178 Victor Atiyeh, interviewed by Jim Moore, "Atiyeh interview #3," Raleigh Hills, OR, 26 March 2014. Summary notes, 15.

2179 "Atiyeh Daily Index-Card Schedule, August 8, 1983," Office of the Governor, State of Oregon, (8 August 1983), Jim Philo, Logan Int'l. & Dr. Terry Lowry, regarding your career after politics; business opportunities, Atiyeh Collection, Pac. Univ. Archives.

2180 Victor Atiyeh, interviewed by Clark Hansen, "Tape 60," Oral history, recorded by Oregon Historical Society, Portland, OR, 10 September 1993. Transcript, 79, Atiyeh Collection, Pac. Univ. Archives.

2181 Victor Atiyeh, "Tape 60," 79.

2182 Victor Atiyeh, "Tape 60," 80.

2183 "Atiyeh Daily Index-Card Schedule, September 6, 1989," Victor Atiyeh and Company, (6 September 1989), Board Meeting: Riedel Environmental Technologies, Atiyeh Collection, Pac. Univ. Archives; Victor Atiyeh, interviewed by Clark Hansen, "Tape 27, side 2," Oral history, recorded by Oregon Historical Society, Portland, OR, 21 May 1993. Transcript, 783, Atiyeh Collection, Pac. Univ. Archives.

Greenbrier Manufacturing,[2184] and Bank Audi,[2185] but nothing like what he initially anticipated in his future.

Victor also made it clear to his brothers that he was not coming back to Atiyeh Brothers in any capacity and told his gubernatorial staff of the decision just as his second term started in 1983.[2186] He found that he liked making decisions as a single decider, unlike the fraternal troika that ran Atiyeh Brothers. Vic Atiyeh, post-governorship, would work for himself.[2187] Ed and Richard still consulted with their brother on big company decisions—Ed recalled that they always valued Victor's opinion—but it was clear that Victor's future lay elsewhere.[2188] Atiyeh Brothers passed to the next generation while Atiyeh was governor. He and his brothers had intense conversations about who should run the company and their own retirements from actively working at the family business. The upshot was that Ed's oldest son, David, took over the management of Atiyeh Brothers while Vic's son, Tom, started Atiyeh International, a company that sourced the Oriental rugs to sell to retailers. Tom's business would come to specialize in rugs from China, just as Aziz Atiyeh had worked to specialize

---

[2184] Victor Atiyeh, "Atiyeh interview #1," 2; Tom Atiyeh, interviewed by Jim Moore, "Atiyeh interview," Sherwood, OR, 28 July 2015. Summary, 7.

[2185] "Atiyeh Daily Index-Card Schedule, March 9, 1988," Victor Atiyeh and Company, (9 March 1988), Board Meeting: Bank Audi (California)...; contact: William Hanna, Atiyeh Collection, Pac. Univ. Archives; "Atiyeh Daily Index-Card Schedule, January 9, 1989," Victor Atiyeh and Company, (9 January 1989), Tour: Hanna Car Wash International, Atiyeh Collection, Pac. Univ. Archives; "Atiyeh Daily Index-Card Schedule, January 25, 1989," Victor Atiyeh and Company, (25 January 1989), Meeting: International Yogurt with William Hanna and Marc Audi, Atiyeh Collection, Pac. Univ. Archives; "Atiyeh Daily Index-Card Schedule, March 22, 1989," Victor Atiyeh and Company, (22 March 1989), Lunch: Riedel Environmental Technologies Board, Atiyeh Collection, Pac. Univ. Archives; "Atiyeh Daily Index-Card Schedule, May 18, 1989," Victor Atiyeh and Company, (18 May 1989), Board Meeting: Bank Audi [in D.C.], Atiyeh Collection, Pac. Univ. Archives.

[2186] Gerry Thompson, Email to Jim Moore, "Question About Post-Gubernatorial Life," 29 December 2017.

[2187] Victor Atiyeh, "Tape 60," 73.

[2188] Edward Atiyeh, interviewed by Jim Moore, "Atiyeh interview #1," Raleigh Hills, OR, 18 October 2014. Summary notes, 1.

in rugs made in Persia. In effect, David took on grandfather George's role, while Tom took on great-uncle Aziz's role.

Atiyeh was proud of his leadership on economic development, so he started his own consulting firm, with several Japanese companies hiring him to keep pushing for international investment in Oregon. Atiyeh's idea was that "because of my travels and the fact that I'd met people overseas and already knew…how to go there and come back from there, and I didn't have to relearn something, that's what I thought I would do. So, I started my own business," Victor Atiyeh and Company.[2189] His product was himself as an intermediary and advisor. He was once asked by some Japanese how big his business was. "Well," he told them, "it's just big enough to take care of the business that I have."[2190] What that meant was that his employees were himself and his administrator. His office was in his son's suite of office space, upstairs from the Atiyeh Brothers retail store in downtown Portland in the building he and his brothers owned.[2191] As he put it, "That's the other part of me, as a former retail merchant. …I'm pretty cheap about the whole thing. I pay low rent, and…I'm not fascinated by fancy quarters."[2192]

His work was divided into consulting and trade, where he acted as a broker between buyers and sellers. He was on retainer with Fujitsu and Seiko-Epson for several years. He got involved in products that he knew about—like electronics—and products that he knew nothing about, like "some pantyhose from Czechoslovakia" one time, 81,000 cases of vodka another time.[2193] As a consultant he mainly worked the phones from his Portland office. He did go to D.C. for Fujitsu to testify before a congressional committee on proposals for tariffs, but that was an

---

2189 Victor Atiyeh, "Tape 60," 73.
2190 Victor Atiyeh, "Tape 60," 74.
2191 Victor Atiyeh, "Tape 60," 73, 77.
2192 Victor Atiyeh, "Tape 60," 74.
2193 Victor Atiyeh, "Tape 60," 75; Victor Atiyeh, interviewed by Clark Hansen, "Tape 63," Oral history, recorded by Oregon Historical Society, Portland, OR, 11 June 1998. Transcript, 32, Atiyeh Collection, Pac. Univ. Archives.

exception to his normal practice.[2194] He found a role as somebody who could cut through much of the political and business clutter to connect people with each other.

Traveling on his own was different than traveling as governor. He had headed up delegations of several dozen, he had also traveled with Tom Kennedy and Charles Swindells as a trio focused on getting investment for Oregon. For Victor Atiyeh and Company, he traveled by himself, and sometimes with Dolores. When he traveled after his governorship, Atiyeh's hosts figured they could take him to places he had not been while on official business. He sang in a karaoke bar with a trio, one from Japan and one from China.[2195] He went out with a Japanese businessman, "just the two of us. And he loved to dance. And we went to this place and there was dancing involved. But he just happened to like to dance, so that's what we did."[2196]

In the first several years after Atiyeh left office, he "did quite a bit of travel to Japan, Korea, and Taiwan…and Hong Kong, and a couple of trips to the Middle East."[2197] He had lunch with U.S. ambassador to Japan Mike Mansfield, just like he had done when

---

2194 Victor Atiyeh, "Tape 60," 76.

2195 Victor Atiyeh, interviewed by Clark Hansen, "Tape 51," Oral history, recorded by Oregon Historical Society, Portland, OR, 28 July 1993. Transcript, 603–604, Atiyeh Collection, Pac. Univ. Archives.

2196 Victor Atiyeh, "Tape 51," 604.

2197 "Atiyeh Daily Index-Card Schedule, September 28, 1988," Victor Atiyeh and Company, (28 September 1988), Taiwan, Atiyeh Collection, Pac. Univ. Archives; Victor Atiyeh, "Tape 60," 78; "Atiyeh Daily Index-Card Schedule, October 11, 1988," Victor Atiyeh and Company, (11 October 1988), Saudi Arabia, Atiyeh Collection, Pac. Univ. Archives; "Atiyeh Daily Index-Card Schedule, October 16, 1988," Victor Atiyeh and Company, (16 October 1988), Saudi Arabia, Atiyeh Collection, Pac. Univ. Archives; "Atiyeh Daily Index-Card Schedule, October 23, 1988," Victor Atiyeh and Company, (23 October 1988), Qatar, Atiyeh Collection, Pac. Univ. Archives; "Atiyeh Daily Index-Card Schedule, October 24, 1988," Victor Atiyeh and Company, (24 October 1988), Kuwait, Atiyeh Collection, Pac. Univ. Archives; "Atiyeh Daily Index-Card Schedule, October 29, 1988," Victor Atiyeh and Company, (29 October 1988), Syria, Atiyeh Collection, Pac. Univ. Archives; "Atiyeh Daily Index-Card Schedule, October 30, 1988," Victor Atiyeh and Company, (30 October 1988), Syria, Atiyeh Collection, Pac. Univ. Archives; "Atiyeh Daily Index-Card Schedule, October 31, 1988," Victor Atiyeh and Company, (31 October 1988), Syria, Atiyeh Collection, Pac. Univ. Archives.

he was governor.[2198] He returned to Syria in November 1988 and visited with President Hafez Assad again.[2199] And this time he was able to walk around his father's village of Amar on foot, tour a nearby monastery, and host the governor of the area in the Atiyeh family home.[2200] As he had in 1984, Atiyeh proposed that he play a role as "an unofficial channel of communication between the U.S. and Syria," as well as passing along a message from the South Korean government—given to Atiyeh by South Korea's ambassador to Kuwait.[2201] But a telephone conversation between President Bush and President Assad in April 1990 indicated that neither had any real need for Atiyeh to play a role in connecting them; they would "continue our communications through the channels [Bush had] suggested."[2202] In September 1989, Atiyeh traveled to Iraq. He did not meet with Saddam Hussein but did meet with several Iraqi government officials. He also spoke with the U.S. Ambassador to Iraq, April Glaspie,[2203] who would come

---

2198 "Atiyeh Daily Index-Card Schedule, September 17, 1987," Victor Atiyeh and Company, (17 September 1987), Luncheon: Ambassador Michael Mansfield, Atiyeh Collection, Pac. Univ. Archives; "Atiyeh Daily Index-Card Schedule, September 16, 1987," Victor Atiyeh and Company, (16 September 1987), Atiyeh Collection, Pac. Univ. Archives; "Atiyeh Daily Index-Card Schedule, September 15, 1987," Victor Atiyeh and Company, (15 September 1987), Atiyeh Collection, Pac. Univ. Archives.

2199 Victor Atiyeh, "Tape 60," 79–80; "Atiyeh Daily Index-Card Schedule, November 2, 1988," Victor Atiyeh and Company, (2 November 1988), 10:15 AM Meeting: President Hafez Assad (lasting until 12:40 PM), Atiyeh Collection, Pac. Univ. Archives.

2200 "Atiyeh Daily Index Card, Oct 30, 1988," Leave for Amar; "Atiyeh Daily Index Card, Oct 31, 1988," 5:30 AM Tour: Amar Village on foot; 10:30 AM Tour: …St. George Monastery…; 2 PM Lunch: Gov. Abuasley, head of party & security & other, our home.

2201 Victor Atiyeh, Summary of meeting "Typewritten notes from meeting with President Assad," 2 November 1988, Atiyeh Collection, Pac. Univ. Archives.

2202 George Bush and Hafez Assad, "Telephone Conversation with President Hafiz al-Assad of Syria," White House, U.S. Government, Memorandum of Telephone Conversation, (23 April 1990). http://bush41library.tamu.edu, 4, George H.W. Bush Presidential Library and Museum, Textual Archives.

2203 "Atiyeh Daily Index-Card Schedule, September 24, 1989," Victor Atiyeh and Company, (24 September 1989), Meet Deputy Minis. Nazir Hamdoon, Atiyeh Collection, Pac. Univ. Archives; "Atiyeh Daily Index-Card Schedule, September 25, 1989," Victor Atiyeh and Company, (25 September 1989), [Bazaars and museums], Atiyeh Collection, Pac. Univ. Archives; "Atiyeh Daily Index-Card

to public attention a year later for a famous meeting with Saddam Hussein, after which he felt free to invade Kuwait.

In the early months of 1991, Atiyeh found himself in Washington, D.C., part of a nationwide group of Arab-American leaders, hearing from President Bush himself that that American troops were on the ground in Iraq to push Saddam Hussein's forces out of Kuwait.[2204] Atiyeh had pride of place among the Arab Americans, sitting directly across from the president at the briefing table. Back at home, Atiyeh sat in as the FBI interviewed his relative Sam Kahl (Atiyeh's interpreter on the 1984 Middle East trip) in January 1991. The FBI was seeking information on possible terrorist groups in the United States, especially in the runup to the first Persian Gulf War. The ex-governor characterized the interviews of Arab Americans as disturbing, saying, "I am still indignant about the whole thing."[2205] Atiyeh, consistent with his calls for more fairness in U.S. dealing with Middle Eastern countries—a consistency known at the national level since he took on Senator Jacob Javits (NY) at the 1968 Republican National Convention—expressed his concerns in interviews with the reasons for U.S. foreign policy and the backlash that policy created against Arab Americans.[2206] In the summer of 2000, Atiyeh wrote his condolences to the Syrian government on the death of Hafez Al-Assad. He noted that he had been on the initial State Department list to attend Assad's funeral as part of the U.S.

Schedule, September 26, 1989,' Victor Atiyeh and Company, (26 September 1989), Meet with Amb. April Glaspie, Atiyeh Collection, Pac. Univ. Archives; "Atiyeh Daily Index-Card Schedule, September 27, 1989," Victor Atiyeh and Company, (27 September 1989), Meet w/Feham Aboul Razzar & Hanan Amin re. Lumber, Atiyeh Collection, Pac. Univ. Archives; "Atiyeh Daily Index-Card Schedule, September 28, 1989," Victor Atiyeh and Company, (28 September 1989), Meet with Mohamed Saleh, Minister of Trade, Atiyeh Collection, Pac. Univ. Archives.

2204 "Gov. Atiyeh Meets in the White House with President Bush and Delegation of Arab Americans," Exhibit Draft Portland International Airport: Victor G. Atiyeh International Concourse, Mayer/Reed Design Consultant, Port of Portland, Picture caption of ca. February 1991 event, (2007), Atiyeh Collection, Pac. Univ. Archives.

2205 AP, "Atiyeh Decries FBI Interviews Based Only on Arab Ancestry," *Salem (OR) Statesman Journal*, 12 January 1991.

2206 Dave Berns, "Arab-Americans are Anxious, Anguished," *Salem (OR) Statesman Journal*, 18 January 1991.

delegation, but he did not make the final cut.[2207] In a letter to the new president, Bashar Al-Assad, Atiyeh expressed the hope that he might play some role in helping the governments of Syria and the United States communicate with each other, adding, "I am proud to say that just days before your Presidency became official, I 'voted' for you in an unofficial election to show support for you among those of us of Syrian heritage in America. I am proud to say that I was the first one to cast a vote."[2208] Atiyeh would continue publicly writing and speaking about his Arab American point of view through the ongoing Middle East conflicts during the presidency of George W. Bush in the 2000s.[2209]

By 1998, when he was 75, Atiyeh's business was slowing down as his contacts also retired.[2210] Atiyeh moved into the role of elder statesman of Oregon and for the Republican Party, continuing to meet important Republicans when they came to Oregon, and he worked to elect George Bush in 1988, though Bush did not carry the state.[2211] He was interviewed about Tom McCall by reporter Brent Walth for what would become Walth's authoritative biography of the flamboyant former governor.[2212] He served as a Republican national committee person in the early

---

2207 Victor Atiyeh, to Rostom al- Zoubi and Bashar al- Assad, "Series of Letters from Atiyeh to Dr. Rostom Al-Zoubi and President Bashar Al-Assad After the Death of President Hafez Al-Assad of Syria," June–July 2000, Letter to Rostom Al-Zoubi, June 14, 2000, Atiyeh Collection, Pac. Univ. Archives.

2208 Victor Atiyeh to Zoubi and Assad, June–July 2000, Letter to Bashar Al-Assad, July 18, 2000.

2209 Doug Bates, "An American, An Arab," Q&A, *Oregonian*, 18 November 2001, Atiyeh Collection, Pac. Univ. Archives; Vic Atiyeh, "Former Governor Vic Atiyeh Cries 'STOP!': Lebanon Carnage," Opinion piece, *Oregonian*, 30 July 2006, Atiyeh Collection, Pac. Univ. Archives.

2210 Victor Atiyeh, "Tape 63," 32.

2211 "Atiyeh Daily Index-Card Schedule, July 8, 1987," Victor Atiyeh and Company, (8 July 1987), Reception: Vice President George Bush, Atiyeh Collection, Pac. Univ. Archives; "Atiyeh Daily Index-Card Schedule, August 23, 1988," Victor Atiyeh and Company, (23 August 1988), Rally: George Bush for President …(sit on podium), Atiyeh Collection, Pac. Univ. Archives; "Atiyeh Daily Index-Card Schedule, October 16, 1989," Victor Atiyeh and Company, (16 October 1989), [Vice President Dan Quayle activities in Portland], Atiyeh Collection, Pac. Univ. Archives.

1990s, representing Oregon at the national party meetings. He did not "really yearn…to do that." But he saw that the candidate to be Oregon's national committee representative was social conservative Jim Bunn, and "I thought, well, we've got to really kind of balance this thing out a little. And the only one I think could have won in those circumstances would be me, so I ran."[2213] Bunn would later serve one term in Congress—swept in by the Republican wave in 1994; swept out by questions over his personal life and management of his office in 1996.

The ex-governor also occasionally reached out to his successors, speaking his mind as he saw fit. Atiyeh wrote to newly inaugurated Governor John Kitzhaber in January 1995.

> Dear John,
>
> Since your inauguration in jeans I have weighed in my mind whether or not to write to you. Certainly I am aware of the public and media reaction to this form of dress. Some hailed it as "macho," some think it was "neat" and some even said it was "Oregon."
>
> As politely as I can say it-------------it was in very bad taste.
>
> You do, and should, treasure your individuality. However, you must remember that you are no longer just John Kitzhaber, you are now governor John Kitzhaber. There is a dignity and respect for the office that, in my mind, was demeaned on that solemn day of inauguration.
>
> As time moves along you will find yourself representing us as our Governor on important occasions such as national and regional Governors conferences, invitations to the White House, swearing in of judges, etc. It is my hope that at those times you will pay the proper respect to the office of Governor that it deserves.

2212 "Atiyeh Daily Index-Card Schedule, January 22, 1988," Victor Atiyeh and Company, (22 January 1988), Interview: Brent Walth, Willamette Week, re: Tom McCall, Atiyeh Collection, Pac. Univ. Archives; Brent Walth, Email to Jim Moore, "Question About Interview," 12 January 2018.

2213 Victor Atiyeh, "Tape 60," 54; David Steves, "Atiyeh, Bunn Will Clash at Oregon GOP Convention," *Salem (OR, Statesman Journal*, 17 July 1992.

You will hear no more from me on this subject. I know you have been applauded in some quarters for your casual dress. However, if I am the only one who feels as I do (and I do not think so), I felt obliged to give my view.

Respectfully,

Victor Atiyeh

P.S. The cleaning lady in the building across the street feels the same as I—she mentioned it first.[2214]

Atiyeh also used his friendships to move political issues he thought were important. One of these was the nomination of his 1962 Oregon House slate-mate Robert Jones to the federal court from the Oregon Supreme Court (where he sat after being appointed by Governor Atiyeh). As Jones put it in 2015, "He still had one more favor up his sleeve."[2215] Atiyeh had access to the Bush White House when he was in D.C. Jones's nomination was stalled, so, without consulting Jones at all, Atiyeh talked with President Bush on a trip to D.C. Jones' nomination began to move forward shortly thereafter and he was confirmed in the last week of April 1990.[2216]

The former governor also was asked to sit on many boards of organizations he supported—the Boy Scouts, the Japan-America Society, the Oregon World Affairs Council, the board of the Oregon Historical Society, the Warm Springs Museum board,[2217]

2214 Victor Atiyeh, to John Kitzhaber, "Letter from Governor Atiyeh to Governor Kitzhaber Criticizing His Casual Dress at His Inauguration," 11 January 1995, Atiyeh Collection, Pac. Univ. Archives.

2215 Robert Jones, interviewed by Jim Moore, "Atiyeh interview," Portland, OR, 21 July 2015. Summary notes, 3.

2216 Jones, "Atiyeh interview," 4; "State Supreme Court Race Thins Out," *Salem (OR) Statesman Journal*, 8 March 1990; Janet Davies, "Salem Lawyer Fills Court of Appeals Vacancy," *Salem (OR) Statesman Journal*, 5 May 1990.

2217 "Atiyeh Daily Index-Card Schedule, December 16, 1988," Victor Atiyeh and Company, (16 December 1988), Board Meeting: Warm Springs Indian Museum, Atiyeh Collection, Pac. Univ. Archives; "Atiyeh Daily Index-Card Schedule, June 23, 1989," Victor Atiyeh and Company, (23 June 1989), Museum Meeting: Warm Spring, Atiyeh Collection, Pac. Univ. Archives; "Atiyeh Daily Index-Card

Pacific University's board of trustees, the Special Olympics board, the Lone Fir Cemetery board,[2218] and many others. Atiyeh made it to the Pendleton Round-Up and Umatilla Pow Wow as often as he could.[2219] He joined the board of the Oregon Wildlife Heritage Foundation, the group that had coordinated the purchase of the Deschutes River properties for state parks.

He loved being a part of each of the boards, but he found as he approached his 70s that he "really [didn't] want to go meetings anymore."[2220] He negotiated roles with each board or gracefully left them at the end of his term.

An exception, however, was the Warm Spring Museum board. He happily went to Warm Springs for celebrations, meetings, and to see his friends. In 1988 he worked to combine his interests with an idea about linking the Warm Springs tribes and their various enterprises to Japan.[2221] He not only attended, he cajoled people into donating their time and money to this cause he supported so strongly. Eventually, he did leave the board, where his place was taken by Ted Kulongoski. But, as Kulongoski remembered, Atiyeh kept showing up to meetings where "he would participate" as a non-voting member.[2222]

Schedule, October 9, 1989," Victor Atiyeh and Company, (9 October 1989), Brian Burke—Architect for Warm Springs, Atiyeh Collection, Pac. Univ. Archives; "Atiyeh Daily Index-Card Schedule, October 27, 1989," Victor Atiyeh and Company, (27 October 1989), Middle Oregon Indian Historical Society Board Meeting, Atiyeh Collection, Pac. Univ. Archives. This was the name for the tribes on the Treaty of 1855.

2218 Marcus Lee, interviewed by Jim Moore, "Atiyeh interview," Portland, OR, 27 March 2015. Summary notes, 4.

2219 "Atiyeh Daily Index-Card Schedule, September 10, 1988," Victor Atiyeh and Company, (10 September 1988), [Pow Wow activities all day], Atiyeh Collection, Pac. Univ. Archives.

2220 Victor Atiyeh, "Tape 60," 71.

2221 "Atiyeh Daily Index-Card Schedule, February 14, 1988," Victor Atiyeh and Company, (14 February 1988), Council Meeting: re: strategy of potential link with Japan, Atiyeh Collection, Pac. Univ. Archives.

2222 Dave Miller et al., "Oregon Remembers Former Governor Vic Atiyeh," Live interview, recorded by Think Out Loud, KOPB radio, Salem, OR, 3 September 2014. MP3, 7:30.

Atiyeh kept up his relationships with his onetime political foes in many ways. Many within a generation of Oregon leaders had respected each other across party lines from the 1960s to the 1980s. That respect led to friendships that lasted for years. Atiyeh sat on the board of the Bob Straub archives. He wrote the foreword to Charles K. Johnson's biography of Straub, emphasizing his respect for the years of service Straub gave to Oregon in the legislature, as state treasurer, and as governor.

At Dorchester in 2003, after five gubernatorial elections without a Republican winner, the annual show featured

> state GOP Chairman Kevin Mannix, who narrowly lost last November's governor's race to Democrat Ted Kulongoski, asking what it would take for him to win a statewide office. Several women on stage went about giving Mannix a makeover, and when the process was completed and a giant sheet was pulled away, there sat former Gov. Vic Atiyeh, smiling and waving to the crowd.[2223]

As Roger Martin, who Atiyeh beat in the 1978 gubernatorial primary, put it, "The longer he lived, the bigger a hero he became."[2224]

In May 2004, Nigel Jaquiss of *Willamette Week* broke the news that Neil Goldschmidt had repeatedly raped an underaged girl during the 1970s.[2225] Atiyeh, who had a long and fractious

---

2223 Brad Cain, "Republicans Reflect on Cost of 'Litmus Test' for Abortion," *Oregonian*, 3 March 2003, Atiyeh collection, Pacific University Archive, Forest Grove, OR.

2224 Roger Martin, interviewed by Jim Moore, "Atiyeh interview," Lake Oswego, OR, 23 April 2015. Summary notes, 1.

2225 Nigel Jaquiss, "The 30-Year Secret: A Crime, a Cover-Up and the Way It Shaped Oregon," *Portland (OR) Willamette Week*, 11 May 2004, http://www.wweek.com; Steve Law, "Goldschmidt Resigns, Admits Sex With Teen," *Salem (OR) Statesman Journal*, 7 May 2004; Brad Cain, "Goldschmidt Scandal Blow to Longtime Ally: Oregon Governor Kulongoski 'Shocked, Mad'," *Seattle Times*, 9 May 2004; Colin Fogarty, "Why Goldschmidt Abuse Went Unreported for 30 Years?," *Portland (OR) OPB News*, 12 May 2004, http://www.opb.org.

relationship with Goldschmidt, was stunned, as were all who learned of the story. Atiyeh stopped referring to Goldschmidt by name, calling him "my successor."

A real camaraderie and affection developed among former governors Atiyeh, Roberts, and Kulongoski, what Atiyeh called "good and strong feelings."[2226] He asked that Roberts speak at his memorial service, and he gave Kulongoski one of his highest accolades: "We get along real well. We could go camping together without any problem."[2227] Barbara Roberts found that the ex-governors were drawn together because "there are less than a handful of people who have had that experience in a state." Ex-governors "look at another governor and…know what they have been through. …There is a bond that comes from that understanding."[2228] She recalled that Bob Straub, even as his health deteriorated, was part of this. Later, it was "the boys and me," she said, referring to Atiyeh and Kulongoski.

By the early 2000s, the end of Kitzhaber's first two terms as governor, and while Kulongoski served in the governor's office—and especially after Goldschmidt's downfall in 2004—Atiyeh and Roberts were the two ex-governors at all the major events—Oregon's February 14 birthday parties, state awards ceremonies, parades, holiday celebrations at the state capitol.[2229] When Kulongoski left office in 2011, he joined the two of them to make an ex-gubernatorial trio at all the happenings.

Political Reputation

Even while Atiyeh was still in office, news stories assessing his tenure began to appear. A laudatory piece in the *Oregon Business* magazine focused on the ways the governor guided the state through the recessions, with the result that employment had not

---

[2226] Victor Atiyeh, "Atiyeh interview #3," 10.
[2227] Victor Atiyeh, "Atiyeh interview #3," 10–11.
[2228] Barbara Roberts, interviewed by Jim Moore, "Atiyeh interview," Portland, OR, 23 February 2015. Summary notes, 2.
[2229] Roberts, "Atiyeh interview," 9–10.

only recovered, but that by 1986 there were almost 136,000 more people employed than before the recessions started in 1980. Atiyeh said, "When I look at Oregon as it was when I became governor and look at it today, I can tell you I think Neil Goldschmidt is getting a real good deal."[2230] Polls, however, showed that the public was evenly split on Atiyeh's job performance, a sharp difference from the overwhelming support he received from voters in the 1982 election and from polling in December 1981 indicating that approval for the work Atiyeh was doing stood at about 60%.[2231]

An examination of Atiyeh's relationships with the Democratic-controlled legislature during his eight years in office noted that relations between the two constitutional parts of state government "were remarkably stormy, especially in his first term."[2232] After a relatively genial first session in 1979,[2233] the special sessions, from 1980 on, were times during which the governor and the legislature butted heads. Democratic leaders criticized the way the first, and longest, special session was handled in 1980. A business leader denounced Atiyeh's 1982–83 tax reform: "He made up his plan by himself, in consultation with himself. The net receipts tax was to increase; the tax on cigarettes was to be dropped, as he stood there with a cigarette in his hand."[2234] Others saw Atiyeh's willingness "to propose unpopular taxes that directly affected his own best supporters…as a mark of political courage." Former Assistant Attorney General Stan Long, a Democrat who supported Goldschmidt's election, was impressed when "this conservative [was] saying: 'I've cut enough. We're past the fat, and into the muscle and into the bone.

2230 Gary Eisler, "Farewell to Governor Vic," *Oregon Business*, December 1986, Atiyeh Collection, Pac. Univ. Archives.

2231 Alan R. Hayakawa, "Poll Shows Public Divided on Atiyeh," *Oregonian*, 28 December 1986, Atiyeh Collection, Pac. Univ. Archives.

2232 Alan Hayakawa, "Governor's Relationship with Legislature Stormy: Mixed Triumphs, Defeats Mark Tenure," *Oregonian*, 29 December 1986, B1.

2233 Gary Wilhelms, "Vic Atiyeh" (speech, Trumpeters, Portland, OR, 5 September 2014), 3, Atiyeh collection, Pac. Univ. Archives.

2234 Hayakawa, "Governor's Relationship with Legislature," B1.

I don't want to cut any more; we need some revenue sources.' That was not a change in philosophy, that was a change in fact."[2235]

The Medford paper editorialized about Atiyeh's two terms as governor, arguing that he did not "get the credit he deserves. His steady, underpublicized leadership prevented us from heading for the lifeboats in panic, although at times that seemed like the most reasonable thing to do."[2236] Atiyeh referred to his governorship by pointing out that "I wasn't trying to be a Tom McCall. I'm Vic Atiyeh. I was the right governor for the time."[2237] The laudatory *Medford Mail Tribune* editorial gave the governor "credit for holding state government together when financial disasters and political struggles had many talking major demolition" and for his "efforts both at home and abroad" to let people know that Oregon was open to all, "including new business."[2238]

When Atiyeh left office, even his supporters among editorialists wrote about the "forced retrenchment" years of reacting to economic crises and the "cultivation" and sowing of economic "seedlings" that he hoped "will grow and bear fruit."[2239] By the 1990s it became clear that Oregon's economic future was with the global economy, not with timber and natural resources, although those were still major sectors. Phil Keisling, who became secretary of state in 1991, came to understand that even Democrats who ran against Atiyeh and his policies in the 1980s did not understand that Oregon's economy was fundamentally changing, and the state was becoming more complex. Even Neil Goldschmidt, with his experience at global brand company Nike,

---

2235 Hayakawa, "Governor's Relationship with Legislature," B1.
2236 R. A. S., "Nice Job, Gov. Atiyeh," Editorial, *Medford (OR) Mail Tribune*, January 1987, Atiyeh Collection, Pac. Univ. Archives.
2237 Debbie Howlett, "Atiyeh Tallies His Score," *Salem (OR) Statesman-Journal*, 4 January 1987, 1A.
2238 R. A. S., "Nice Job, Gov. Atiyeh."
2239 *Oregonian*, "Vic Worked for State," Editorial, 9 January 1987; *Statesman-Journal*, "Governor Sets Pace: Steady Economic Progress," Editorial, 4 January 1987.

seemed to run on a platform of "a return to Eden," in Keisling's estimation.[2240]

Ted Kulongoski grew to understand Atiyeh in much the same way as Keisling. As Atiyeh left office in 1987, Kulongoski observed, "The man gets too much criticism. People are judging him now—and you have to wait for history to decide."[2241] Almost thirty years later, he said of his one-time rival, "…[H]e was a long-term thinker. I don't think…a lot of people… realized that Vic had a better sense…of trade and the global economy than" any subsequent governor.[2242] Kulongoski knew very well that there had been international trade going on before Atiyeh took office. But he saw that it was Atiyeh's work that really got Oregon out there in the international economic world. Since the late 1990s it has been Intel and Nike that have been Oregon's big international brands.[2243] Kulongoski "always thought [Atiyeh] never got the credit he deserved" for planning the diversification of Oregon's economy. He was the one, in Kulongoski's estimation, who saw into the future. It was reforming the tax code through the repeal of the unitary method of taxation, laying the groundwork for international trade, and opening Oregon to the world that was Atiyeh's true legacy.[2244]

Atiyeh was essentially the same political person when he died in 2014 as he had been in 1958. Those who were part of his professional political life saw this. He was pragmatic, he was at home in the Oregon Republican Party of that moderate to liberal era, and he felt that there were solutions for Oregonians, regardless of party affiliation. In 1993 Atiyeh observed the social conservatives in the Oregon Republican Party pressuring their opponents. He characterized it as, "Constant intimidation," the party was "not doing all the things they normally would do, not

---

2240 Keisling, "Atiyeh interview," 3.
2241 Howlett, "Atiyeh Tallies His Score," 1A.
2242 Kulongoski, "Atiyeh interview," 1.
2243 Kulongoski, "Atiyeh interview," 1.
2244 Kulongoski, "Atiyeh interview," 1.

being the umbrella that they should be."[2245] He had seen this split begin with the rise of Walter Huss in the 1970s. It saddened Atiyeh that the Oregon Republican Party was still so split twenty years later.[2246]

Atiyeh updated his argument in 1998. "My problem was that the right wing said, 'We want to be included.' And I have no problem with that. But they say they want to be included, which means they want me excluded, and that I have a problem with."[2247] Through all of this, however, Atiyeh was loyal to his party even as the Republican Party changed.[2248] Part of this, as former legislator Norm Smith observed, was that Atiyeh was the last person to win the governorship as a Republican, something that became more and more stark as the years and elections passed.[2249] Former House Republican leader Gary Wilhelms saw Atiyeh as a big-tent Republican, somebody who would actually work with the different parts of the party. Not only did the ex-governor say he did not want rifts in the party, but he would also actively work to heal those rifts.[2250]

The change in the nature of the Republican party led many of the Atiyeh family to switch parties or work against Republican nominees. Notably, in 2004, the spouse of Bob Atiyeh (Vic's nephew), Deb Atiyeh, formed a "Republicans for [John] Kerry" group when George W. Bush ran for his second term.[2251] Victor was blindsided by a reporter's question about the Atiyeh name being associated with the group. Bob recalled that there was a frosty family birthday party attended by his uncle and himself and

---

2245 Victor Atiyeh, "Tape 60," 55, 64.

2246 Victor Atiyeh, "Tape 60," 65.

2247 Victor Atiyeh, "Tape 63," 29.

2248 Charles E. Beggs, interviewed by Jim Moore, "Atiyeh interview," Salem, OR, 12 March 2015. Summary notes, 1.

2249 Norm Smith, interviewed by Jim Moore, "Atiyeh interview," Roseburg, OR, 28 April 2015. Summary notes, 8.

2250 Gary Wilhelms, interviewed by Jim Moore, "Atiyeh interview," Rock Creek, OR, 5 March 2015. Summary notes, 4.

2251 Bob Atiyeh, interviewed by Jim Moore, "Atiyeh interview," West Linn, OR, 4 February 2015. Summary notes, 4.

his wife. It was Bob's sense that his uncle was angrier about not being told in advance about the group rather than the political stance itself. But Victor got over it.

Atiyeh clearly saw that there were what he called "nuts" on the left and on the right so that both parties had their share of them. But he saw that Democratic nuts tended to leave the party while "our nuts are still here" in the Republican Party.[2252] The March 2014 Dorchester meeting was mirrored by an alternative meeting of Republican social conservatives in Portland that same weekend.[2253] Atiyeh was clear about his feelings: "In my view, they swept all the crap out" of Dorchester.[2254] There might have been something to that. Atiyeh has become known as Oregon's last Republican governor. Because of the sense of finality in that phrase, and with a twinkle in his eye, he would correct people and say he was Oregon's *latest* Republican governor.

Former legislator Norm Smith knew all the governors after Atiyeh. He saw that Atiyeh "still wanted to be visible and engaged" and that Atiyeh, "like his peers, hungered to be called" by those serving in government, especially those elected officials in areas where Atiyeh's expertise could really add something.[2255] Former legislator Tony Van Vliet added, "People did not appreciate what a great contribution Vic made as a manager." As far as Van Vliet knew, nobody ever asked Atiyeh for his input on managing various parts of state government. He thought part of that might have been Atiyeh's Boy Scout image, so people may not have thought that Atiyeh knew the details of making hard managerial decisions.[2256] But he did.

2252 Victor Atiyeh, "Atiyeh interview #3," 12.
2253 Harry Esteve, "Conservatives Blast GOP Dorchester Conference, Plan Their Own Oregon 'Freedom Rally'," *Portland OregonLive*, 25 February 2014, http://www.oregonlive.com; Peter Wong, "Dorchester Conference Tracks Changing Role of GOP," Column—Peter Wong's Oregon, *Salem (OR) Statesman Journal*, 1 March 2014, http://www.statesmanjournal.com.
2254 Victor Atiyeh, "Atiyeh interview #3," 12.
2255 Smith, "Atiyeh interview," 8.
2256 Tony Van Vliet, interviewed by Jim Moore, "Atiyeh interview," Corvallis, OR, 11 March 2015. Summary notes, 4.

In 1987, after Atiyeh left office, he was walking in the capitol and saw his friend Jill Thorne. She had been in the middle of Goldschmidt's 100-day agenda to shake up government, an effort that Speaker of the House Vera Katz later characterized as Goldschmidt not understanding "the process, and you don't do it in 100 days in Salem."[2257] Thorne looked Atiyeh and said, "This job is tougher than you made it look."[2258]

Of A Certain Time and Place

Jill Thorne was right: Atiyeh did bring a certain calmness to a tough job. He came into the governorship with a focus on implementing all the ideas that had been scattered across state government during Tom McCall's years in the office—ideas that originated in the legislature or the governor's office. Atiyeh did that by insisting that the land-use system be applied at every level, by continuing the fight to mesh Oregon's messy taxation system with the services voters wanted and demanded, and by seeking a balance between the natural resource economies of yesteryear and the new high-tech industries that were beginning to become vital drivers of Oregon's economy. He stayed true to these goals throughout his eight years in office. It was these types of continuing issues that Goldschmidt inherited from Atiyeh, just as Atiyeh has inherited them from Hatfield, McCall, and Straub.

But Atiyeh faced much bigger challenges than his immediate predecessors had. There was the challenge to Oregon's constitution and laws by the Rajneeshees. Atiyeh governed as Oregon was forced to change from a natural resource–dependent economy to a more diversified set of businesses and jobs. The change had already begun to happen when he took office in 1979 —high tech was a major employer in Washington County and large timber companies were already either planning to move their operations or had begun the process of leaving Oregon—but

---

[2257] Jill Thorne, interviewed by Jim Moore, "Atiyeh interview," Pendleton, OR, 23 June 2015. Summary notes, 2.

[2258] Jill Thorne, "Atiyeh interview," 2; Victor Atiyeh, "Atiyeh interview #1," 1; Victor Atiyeh, "Atiyeh interview #2," 7.

the recessions of 1980 and 1982 accelerated the process. Atiyeh was forced to manage the downturn *and* reach out for new economic players to come to the state. In 2007, his work to integrate Oregon into the world economy was honored with the naming of the Governor Victor G. Atiyeh International Concourse at Portland International Airport along with an almost life-sized statue of the governor heading for a flight.[2259]

Atiyeh's twenty years in the legislature taught him that in times of abundant tax revenue (through much of the 1960s and 1970s), reform does not happen because it is impossible to show the need for change when everything is working well.[2260] The cries for reform only come during downturns, and then the options are fewer and the stakes seem higher. Atiyeh attributed some of this to politicians who governed to win the next election instead of governing for the good of the entire state. In 2013, fifty-five years after running for that first House seat, he saw this as a major problem that had become worse.[2261] Those same good economic years in the 1960s and 1970s seemed to encourage an activist legislature, one that played its true constitutional role as the creator of policies. Land use planning, the Beach Bill, the Bottle Bill, but also ideas that did not make it through—major tax reform and rethinking how Oregon funds education—were all hallmarks of this strong legislature. Since the mid-1970s, however, Oregon's governor has been the primary source of big policy ideas—or the people have been the source through the initiative process (e.g. assisted suicide in the 1990s). During Atiyeh's eight years in office, the Democratic legislature was adept at either blocking him or working with him, but it did not generate the same big ideas as the Democratic and Republican

---

2259 Gerry Thompson, "Dedication of PDX International Concourse, Governor Vic Atiyeh" (speech, Honorees Vic and Dolores Atiyeh and Dedication Audience, Portland International Airport, 18 July 2007), Atiyeh Collection, Pac. Univ. Archives.

2260 Victor Atiyeh, "Atiyeh interview #1," 7.

2261 Victor Atiyeh, "Atiyeh interview #1," 7; Victor Atiyeh, "Atiyeh interview #3," 10; *Statesman Journal*, "Vic Atiyeh, Truth Teller," Editorial reprinted from *Oregonian*, 2 August 2014.

legislatures from fifteen years earlier. The last big idea to rise primarily from the Oregon legislature was health care reform, led by Senate President John Kitzhaber in the early 1990s, and then nurtured and pushed further by Governor John Kitzhaber in his first eight years in the office from 1995 to 2003.

Between Atiyeh's time in office and the present the culture of the capitol changed tremendously. Partisanship has intensified since the 1980s. During Atiyeh's time in the legislature and as governor, as Gerry Thompson put it, even bitter partisan enemies put all that aside at the end of the day and socialized with each other, played card games, and ate together. Jackie Winters, who served in 2018 in Atiyeh's old post as Senate Republican leader (and like Atiyeh, was a leader of the minority), agreed. She found the trust level to be different. Ted Kulongoski has pointed out that Atiyeh focused on what "he thought was the right thing to do, even if there was a political consequence."[2262] The post–1980 Republican mantra of "no new taxes"—a phrase that contributed to Atiyeh's friend George Bush losing his 1992 presidential re-election bid—was not who Atiyeh was. When budgets were cut to the bone, Atiyeh knew it was time to raise taxes. Voters seemed to trust Atiyeh. He promised that the income tax surcharge would be temporary, and there were no efforts to refer the vote to the people.[2263]

Vic Atiyeh was a product of his time. He forged his political outlook when Washington County was firm in electing Republicans and Multnomah County had large Republican and Democratic contingents going to the state legislature. Washington County Republicans had a lead in voter registration until the early 1970s when the Vietnam War and Watergate gave the lead to the Democrats while also contributing to significant expansion of the number of voters unaffiliated with either major party.

When Atiyeh first ran for statewide office, in the Watergate year of 1974, statewide voter registration clearly favored Democrats, with an 18% lead in party registration. Atiyeh also

---

2262 Miller et al., "Oregon Remembers Former Governor Vic Atiyeh," 29:20.
2263 Miller, et al., "Oregon Remembers Former Governor Vic Atiyeh," 30:00.

faced strong Democratic registration leads in 1978 (+21%), when he won, and in 1982 (+14%), when he set records with his re-election victory. There were significant declines in Democratic registration during those years, but the beneficiary appeared to be more non-affiliated voters. The growth in Republican voters did not recover from the Watergate hit until 1986, just as Atiyeh was leaving office. Atiyeh was clearly successful at winning enough Democrats and most of the non-affiliated voters in his two successful statewide victories.

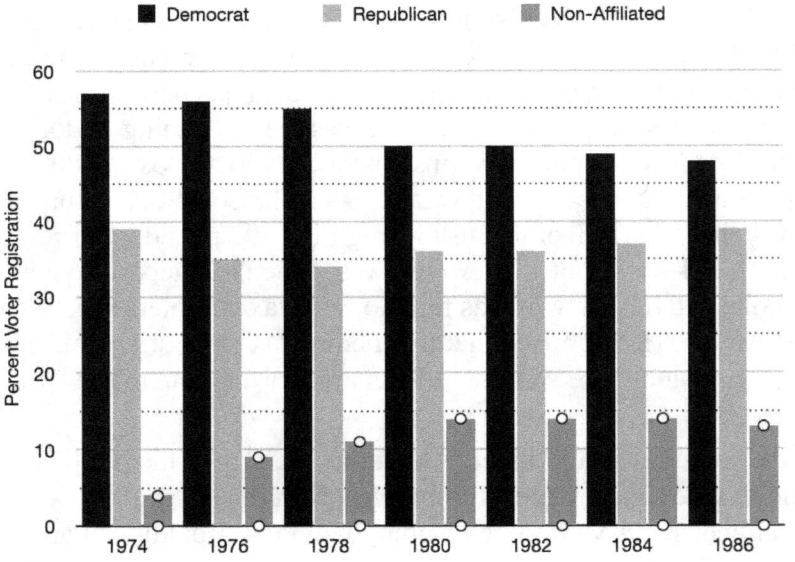

Oregon statewide voter registration, Atiyeh as gubernatorial candidate and serving in office.

One of the biggest drivers of change in Oregon's electorate since the 1980s has been population growth. The state grew 59% between 1987 and 2020—just enough to get a sixth congressional district, with one of the top growth rates in the country. However, measuring the difference between Democratic registrations and Republican registrations, the state electorate did not change in any major way (this omits the rise of the non-affiliated). In 1988 there was a 9.6% advantage for Democrats; in 2021 there was a 10.1% advantage for Democrats—a 0.5% shift their way. It was if the new arrivals split along the exact same party lines as those who already lived there.

But in Atiyeh's old political base, Multnomah and Washington counties, something very different occurred. Multnomah was overwhelmingly Democratic in 1988, but 31% of voters were Republicans. By 2021, the Republicans were down to 11%. The change over time was a 16.9% shift toward the Democrats. But then there was Washington County. In 1988 the Republicans had 4.1% registration advantage over the Democrats. In 2021, the Democrats had a 17.4% advantage over the Republicans, a shift of 21.5%.[2264] That shift to Democratic registrations, combined with Washington County's high growth rate, contributed mightily to the continued victories of Democrats for statewide office and to keeping the legislature in Democratic hands. Vic Atiyeh's home county had become crucial to statewide Democratic control.

Newcomers were arriving in Oregon because of the McCall era's reputation for change and quality of life, but they were working in an Oregon that diversified during the Atiyeh era. It was as if McCall still drew immigrants, but Atiyeh provided them jobs and careers. Atiyeh's call to diversify the economy appears to have spelled the end of Republican dominance where that newly diversified economy took off.

Vic Atiyeh's great political ambition was to diversify Oregon's economy. Part of this was by intention, part was by necessity as the recessions of 1980 and 1982 crashed down on the state. He succeeded in laying the groundwork for Oregon more fully participating in the global economy. The fruits of his work were in the new facilities constructed in the last years of his time in

---

2264 1988 Multnomah County, Ds 55.6%, Rs 31 %: +Ds=24.6%. 2021 Multnomah County, Ds 52.5%, Rs 11%: +Ds=41.5%. 1988 Washington County, Ds 40.6%, Rs 44.7%: +Rs=4.1%. 2021 Washington Country, Ds 38.2%, Rs 20.8%: +Ds=17.4%.

office, as well as the growing knowledge about Oregon and its opportunities in Japan, Taiwan, South Korea, and Fujian province in China. Oregon transformed from an exporter of natural resources and goods made from natural resources into an exporter of manufactured goods. The industry that got all the attention were the computer chips, computer printers, and circuit boards of high tech, but Oregon also continued to export barges and train cars, trucks, and steel. Oregon agriculture continued as it had before Atiyeh—its markets, especially for wheat, were across state and country borders. The timber industry was still a major player, but it was one among several, in effect sharing top billing with high technology.

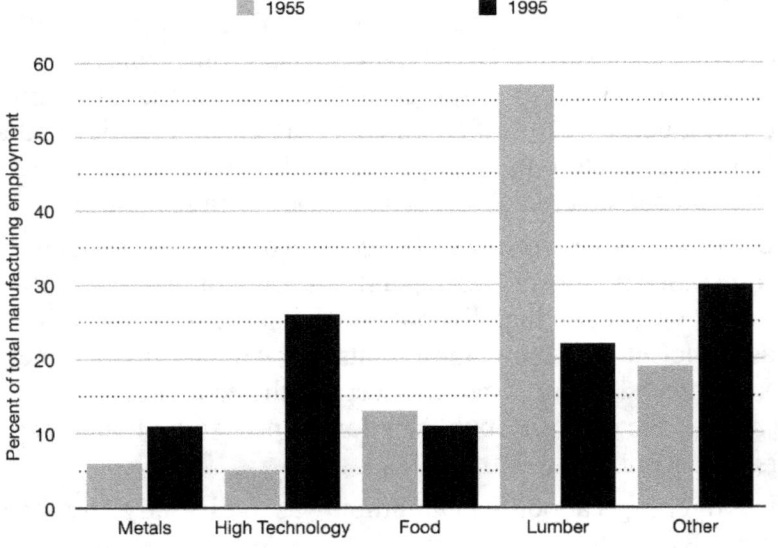

Oregon's diversified economy, 1955, 1995, based on employment numbers. "A key to Oregon's strong economy . . . is the increase in diversity of employers." Adapted from Oregon Blue Book, 1997–1998, 225.

Did this actually diversify Oregon's economy? The evidence is mixed. On the positive side, more high-tech manufacturing meant being part of new markets. But those new markets carried their own dangers. The international investment was so heavily focused on Asia that Oregon suffered when Japan's economy stopped growing in the early 1990s. Asia's economy was also ravaged during the Asian financial crisis of 1997–1998. South Korea's economy, in particular, plummeted by 7% in 1998.[2265].

By the turn of the millennium in 2001, several of the big Japanese firms had shut down their Oregon facilities.[2266] The manufacture-export model that had done so well for the country since the 1940s, and that Oregon and Atiyeh had pushed hard to be a part of, was changing. China was becoming the world's factory.[2267] Oregon's bet on high tech manufacturing was hit hard. Oregon found that it could not shelter itself from economic storms that originated in either the national or global economies. Atiyeh had emphasized this in his 1982 re-election bid, when one of his biggest opponents appeared to be the Reagan administration's policies on interest rates and the national debt. Oregon became a place with good reasons for investment—land-use laws, quality of life, lower housing costs—but it was simply not in control of any of those larger economic impacts.

Corporations can, and do, threaten to leave Oregon for other areas with more favorable conditions, whether that be tax policies, costs of employment, or better access to shipping. As Atiyeh discovered when he built personal relationships with business and government leaders in the United States and in other countries, there must be some strong reason for companies to come to Oregon rather than anywhere else. Atiyeh's big advantage in the 1980s was the repeal of the unitary tax. By being

---

2265 "Economy—Overview," South Korea, CIA World Factbook, http://www.cia.gov, last modified 3 January 2018.

2266 Christopher Foss, "'I Wanted Oregon to Have Something': Governor Victor G. Atiyeh and Oregon-Japan Relations," *Oregon Historical Quarterly* 118, no. 3 (2017): 360, https://doi.org.10.5403/oregonhistq.118.3.0338.

2267 Howard W. French, "Japan Learns the Sun May Not Come Out Tomorrow," Week in Review, *New York Times*, 8 April 2001, http://www.nytimes.com.

the first U.S. state to change this method of taxation, Oregon sent a powerful message that it was open for investment and business. It is difficult to maintain that kind of reputational momentum over decades. Since the early 2000s, China has had the economic power and freedom to seek what it wants anywhere in the world. Oregon's geographic advantage means very little in this new globalized world.

Legacy

Atiyeh began thinking about his place in history in a serious way in the late 1990s. He began to work with a writer on a potential biography.[2268] In 2011, Atiyeh approached Pacific University and began the process of donating his papers and memorabilia to the newly created Atiyeh Collection in the university's archives. His 90th birthday in 2013 was celebrated with gatherings in many venues, ranging from reunions with staff members to parties with those he had known for decades and lunches with well-wishers. He made the effort to seek out those who had been important to him, and to speak to groups for what he thought might be one last time.

The Atiyeh Collection at Pacific University opened in October 2013 with a gathering of people from Atiyeh's political life. Denny Miles and Paul Phillips spoke, former staffers flew in from their far away homes, and Atiyeh gave a heartfelt speech—off the cuff—as Dolores and his family looked on from the table of honor. Atiyeh declared that the event was as important to him as his wedding day and the election night in 1978 when he was first selected as Oregon's governor.[2269] Atiyeh also talked with Scott

---

2268 Margie Hunt, "Atiyeh Book Outline," (Unpublished manuscript, ca 2000), Book outline, interview list, draft of newspaper op-ed piece, Oregon Historical Society, Atiyeh collection, Pac. Univ. Archives.

2269 Peter Wong, "Gov. Atiyeh's Collection Gets Digital Revolution," *Salem (OR) Statesman Journal*, 5 October 2013, http://www.statesmanjournal.com; Laura Frazier, "Pacific University Opens Former Gov. Vic Atiyeh's Collection," *Oregonian*, 7 October 2013, E-edition; Eva Guggemos, ed. *Atiyeh! The Governor Victor Atiyeh Collection at Pacific University*, (Forest Grove, OR: Pacific University, 2013).

Jorgensen in 2014 for a series of conversations that became a book distilling some of the ex-governor's political wisdom as he looked back on his life.[2270]

Atiyeh closed his downtown office in the summer of 2013, emptied of much of its contents because of the donation to the Atiyeh archive, and began to run the rest of his life from his house.[2271]

On Victor and Dolores' seventieth wedding anniversary, in July 2014, Atiyeh fell and broke some ribs. Atiyeh was admitted to the hospital for internal bleeding after initially being sent home to heal. Dolores, whose health had been failing for a while, joined him in the hospital with a broken hip.[2272] On Sunday evening, July 20, 2014, he died after spending his last days with his wife, his children, his grandchildren, his brother Edward, and close friends, including those from the Warm Spring Reservation. Lon Holbrook was there as well, serving his governor to the end.[2273]

Governor Victor G. Atiyeh was laid to rest in a Portland cemetery with other members of his family after a private service. Several weeks later, on September 3, 2014, there was a gathering in the Oregon House chambers for the state he loved to remember, for people to smile and say goodbye to the former legislator and governor. Atiyeh had fine-tuned what he wanted in the memorial service for years. Atiyeh picked the music (sung by the chamber choir from Pacific University), he picked the speakers (Governor Barbara Roberts, U.S. Representative Greg Walden, State Senator Jackie Winters, Gerry Thompson, his children Tom and Suzanne Atiyeh), with Denny Miles serving as the master of ceremonies. One of the blessings at the end of the

---

[2270] W. Scott Jorgensen, *Conversations with Atiyeh*, (Carlton, OR.: Ridenbaugh Press, 2014).

[2271] Victor Atiyeh, interviewed by Pat Amedeo, "Arlington Club Oral History," Oral history, recorded by Arlington Club, Portland, OR, 10 September 2013. Transcript, 42, Atiyeh Collection, Pac. Univ. Archives.

[2272] Carol McAlice Currie, "Atiyeh's Expected to Leave Hospital: Former Governor, Wife Injured in Separate Falls," *Salem (OR) Statesman Journal*, 18 July 2014.

[2273] "State Memorial for the Honorable Vic Atiyeh," Memorial service, recorded by Oregon Legislative Media, Salem, OR, 3 September 2014. DVD, 6:45.

ceremony was from the Episcopal Bishop of Oregon. The other was from Chief Delvis Heath of the Warm Springs. Heath sang a 10,000-year-old song from the Creator of "the laws that we must live by."[2274]

Upon Victor George Atiyeh's death, "the Confederated Tribes of the Warm Springs requested that they wrap his body with Pendleton blankets and perform a ritual drum and chanting ceremony." Atiyeh's children "were honored to accept."[2275] This gesture of respect was a continuation of a great conversation between the governor and the tribes stretching back decades. Almost a year after Atiyeh's death, at the 2015 Pi-Ume-Sha, "the tribe presented the Atiyeh family with ceremonial Pendleton blankets honoring Governor Victor G. Atiyeh."[2276]

2274 "State Memorial," 1:43:50.
2275 Tom Atiyeh, Recollection to Jim Moore, "Textiles for VA Funeral," 14 January 2018; Donna Campbell, interviewed by Jim Moore, "Atiyeh interview," Raleigh Hills, OR, 26 June 2015. Summary notes, 10; Tom Atiyeh, Email to Jim Moore, "Your Father," 9 January 2018.
2276 Tom Atiyeh to Moore, 14 January 2018.

Warm Springs Pendleton blanket. Photo by Tom Atiyeh.

A rare antique silk rug. Photo by Denny Miles.

As Atiyeh's casket sat before the altar for the family service in July 2014, an oriental rug covered it, representing the continuity of family, of identity, and his impact on the larger world.[2277] The antique silk rug was to represent in spirit Victor's older brother Richard, who died in 2013, as well as Richard's son, George, who was severely injured in an airplane crash that July of 2014. The rug was "interlaced with gold and silk threads" and "purchased by Aziz Atiyeh after being alerted by George [Aziz' brother, Victor's father] upon finding a small stash of these rare rugs in Istanbul."[2278] In a larger sense, the family heirloom linked Victor

---

2277 Denny Miles, Photograph to Jim Moore, "Atiyeh's Casket," July 2014, Sent January 2018.
2278 Tom Atiyeh to Moore, 14 January 2018.

to his Arab roots, his retail life, and his role as a trailblazer for Arab American politicians in the United States.

On September 3, 2014, the people of Oregon wrapped their former governor in respect and fondness. The stories and smiles of people from the political world, the business world, the tribal world, the world of gun collectors, the world of organizations that had been involved with Atiyeh for decades, told of a person who made Oregon a better place.

His imprint on the state was all around. Yes, there were still big issues of economic development outside of the Portland area, yes, there were still ongoing issues of bigotry, unfairness, and the underside of human nature. But there was also a more diverse economy, a model of openness in government, and an aspiration of respect for all the people of the state.

Acknowledgments

A project of this size depends on the willingness of people to be interviewed, access to documents, and the help of those who read the many, many drafts of chapters.

Vic Atiyeh's decision to donate his archive to Pacific University, the only university in his old Oregon legislative district, was the beginning. Boxes began to appear, each with a set of stories and memories that Atiyeh shared with the university's library team.

Juliette Brosing, my Pacific colleague, was adamant that I apply for a sabbatical to get this project jump started. She was right.

Special thanks to the over eighty interview subjects. Their insights into work and life with Vic Atiyeh were invaluable. Atiyeh aides Gerry Thompson and Denny Miles were always available for questions and memories during this entire process.

There was a group of readers who looked over every chapter as it was completed. Thank you to the Pacific library staff who played this role: Former Director Marita Kunkle, Archivist Eva Guggemos, and Librarian (and later Dean) Isaac Gilman.

John Bloss worked many months to check and double check every citation.

Katie van Heest of Tweed Editing turned a huge manuscript into something that could be published in a single volume. She and I know where the 500,000+ words she cut are still on file....

Heartfelt appreciation to the over 100 donors who contributed to the Pacific University Atiyeh Archive initiative. This book project was funded by those donations as well, paying for the expert help of John and Katie.

This project was supported, endured, and critiqued by Dawna Warren. She not only read every draft, but she also pushed when pushing was needed and helped to celebrate when it was all over.

I was humbled to be asked to write this biography by Governor Atiyeh. His words to me: "You are the writer. If I tell you what to do, feel free not to do it. I have to have you as objective as you can." It was a delight to interview him four times before his death. I only wish I could have consulted with him on more issues I uncovered while researching.

All this help was amazing. I alone am responsible for any errors that still exist in the book.

Index

Amar, Syria, 7, 16, 432-33, 437, 498
Amedeo, Pat, 119, 123, 130, 132, 169, 184, 196, 197, 198-99, 204, 353, 401
Appling, Howell, 39n, 46, 100
Arab American, 145, 344-45, 499, 500, 523
Assad, Hafez, 50, 430, 432, 433, 435-37, 440, 498
Atiyeh (Hewitt), Dolores, 17-18, 20-21, 24, 41, 48, 63, 66, 77, 97, 114, 192, 193, 339, 345, 346, 348n, 430, 433-34, 437, 439, 490-91, 492, 497, 512n, 518, 519
Atiyeh Bros. Fine Carpets, 7-12, 20, 22-23, 25-26, 28, 30, 35-37, 40, 66, 69, 74, 90-91, 118, 121n, 313, 346, 428, 472, 495, 532n
Atiyeh House 1958 election, 31-37
Atiyeh, Aziz, 7-8, 9, 11, 25, 496, 522
Atiyeh, Bob, 25n, 99n, 101, 196, 221, 376, 436, 437, 509
Atiyeh, David, 25n, 28n, 32
Atiyeh, Edward, 10, 13n, 26n, 121n
Atiyeh, George (father), 10-12, 21, 22, 28, 29
Atiyeh, George (nephew), 194, 195, 197, 199
Atiyeh, Linda, 9-10, 25, 29n, 31
Atiyeh, Richard, 10, 13, 16, 18, 20, 22-23, 25, 26-28, 98, 194, 455, 522
Atiyeh, Suzanne, 27, 28, 41
Atiyeh, Tom, 27n, 41, 94, 193-195, 432
Atiyeh, Vic, principles, 7, 31-33, 38, 53, 56, 76, 111, 243, 320, 333
Barton, Clarence, 43
Bhagwan Shree Rajneesh, 350-415
Boe, Jason, 59, 92, 136, 143, 304, 423
Bonneville Power Administration (BPA), 130, 154, 156, 159
Bush, George H.W., 186, 274, 339-40, 343, 345, 440, 498, 499, 500
Campbell, Jim, 17, 18, 24, 30, 69n, 75, 132, 252-53
Carter, Jimmy, 167, 170, 175, 185, 190, 226, 263, 274, 339, 425
China (PRC), 24, 307, 421, 425, 442-59, 464-65, 495, 497, 516, 517-18, 520
Columbia Gorge, 217-21
Cross, Travis, 117, 119
Davis, Bob, 324, 354, 361
Deschutes River, 200-07, 208, 503
Domestic and Rural Power Authority (DRPA), 156-57,161, 163-64, 165
Duncan, Verne, 373-74
Economic development, 47, 81-82, 154-55, 175, 178, 189, 222-25, 230, 243, 247, 250, 265, 268, 273, 290, 293-94, 297-308, 330, 419-76, 478-79, 489
Egypt, 9, 197, 427-31, 435, 439-40, 441
Energy, 153-77, 444, 485
Faust, Jack, 100, 135, 292, 440
Ford, Gerald, 87-89, 223, 274, 340
Forestry, 177-200, 299
Frohnmayer, Dave, 235, 251, 261, 348, 371-72, 373, 377, 381, 384, 404, 409, 414, 415, 416, 487

Galt, Tom, 17, 18, 24, 132
Gary, Bill, 362, 372, 377, 381, 384, 396, 401, 403, 414
Goldschmidt, Neil, 472, 474, 476, 482-83, 485-89, 490, 504-05, 506, 507, 511
Green Bay Packers, 19-20, 97, 119, 121
Gubernatorial 1974 election, 64-85
Gubernatorial 1978 election, 92-115
Gubernatorial 1982 election, 263-69, 273-87
Hatfield, Mark, 37, 38, 41, 43-44, 49, 51, 74, 104, 130, 163, 169, 174, 183, 185-86, 192, 196-97, 198, 200, 202, 219, 289, 312, 314, 323, 338, 348, 365, 421, 442, 471, 478, 511
Hemmingway, Roy, 156, 162, 164, 165-66
Hong Kong, 307, 458, 497
Hydropower, 153-77, 444, 485
Israel, 49, 426-27, 430-32, 435, 437-40
Jackson, Henry "Scoop", 160, 162
Japan, 296, 307-08, 311, 421, 423-25
Javits, Jacob, 50, 499
Johnson, Lee, 118, 121, 123, 124, 129, 131, 201, 231, 233, 262, 303, 347
Katz, Vera, 2, 80, 304, 325, 332, 511
KD, mayor of Rajneeshpuram, 353, 363, 377, 378, 381, 390, 392-94, 396, 401, 408
Kicker, the, 143-44, 331n
Kitzhaber, John, 2, 3, 286, 325, 331, 332, 476, 501, 505, 513
Kulongoski, Ted, 242, 256, 258, 264-87, 316, 476, 487, 503, 504, 505, 508
Land Conservation and Development Commission (LCDC), 57-58, 292-95
Land Use Board of Appeals (LUBA), 292-95
Land use system, 57-58, 292-95
Lang, Phil, 90n, 215
Listening posts, 122, 146-47
Livermore, Roy, 258-59
Ma Anand Sheela, 351, 354
Mansfield, Mike, 460-61, 469, 497
Martin, Roger, 92, 94, 100, 102, 104, 105, 273, 275, 504
McCall 1973 Tax Plan, 58-64, 72, 73
McCall, Tom, 58-65, 68, 93-98, 100-02, 104-06, 128, 155, 163, 177, 269-70, 272-73, 284, 288-89, 304, 323, 354, 421, 449, 473, 487, 500, 507, 511
Measure 11, 110-11, 139, 143
Measure 6, 110-11, 134-35, 138, 141-42, 294, 295
Miles, Denny, 96, 116, 119, 120, 123, 124, 150, 197, 237, 248, 270, 276, 280, 283, 333, 369, 401, 403, 407, 430, 458, 471, 481, 494, 518, 519
Montgomery, F. F. "Monte", 37, 253, 258, 259, 260-61, 263, 352
Mubarak, Hosni, 429-30, 435, 440
Munn, Richard, 44, 61, 137, 228, 331, 451
Myers, Clay, 64, 65, 66-69, 71, 98, 303
Newbry, Lynn, 51, 77, 117, 118, 258
Northwest Power and Planning and Conservation Act, 158-61, 167-68, 171, 263
Nuclear power, 140, 154-55, 156, 160-62, 166, 167, 170-77, 410
Oliver, Bob, 119, 271, 354, 379, 380, 388, 389, 399, 401
Ombudsman, 146-48, 150
Opal Creek, 192-200
Open office, 132-34
Oregon Food Share, 148, 209
Oregon Welcome sign, 16, 270, 272, 273
Packwood, Bob, 46, 114, 264, 276, 280, 487
Paulus, Norma, 2, 80, 94, 114, 155, 180, 259, 260, 360, 364, 383, 389-90, 397-98, 405, 409, 474-75, 480-87
Press corps 1-2, 125-26, 369, 430, 494

Prison overcrowding, 230-39
Property tax reform, 245-47, 263, 279
Racial harassment legislation, 240
Rajneeshees, 350-415
Rajneeshpuram, 350-415
Ray, Dixy, 162, 218, 421
Reagan, Ronald, 167, 171, 181-82, 184, 185, 199, 219, 220, 254, 265, 266-67, 274, 289, 337-41, 342, 440
Republican National Convention of 1968, 48-50, 499
Roberts, Barbara, 86-87, 91, 128, 134, 348, 349, 408, 487, 489, 505, 519
SAIF Raid, 249-60
SAIF scandal, 258-63
Samples, Duane, 236-38
Saudi Arabia, 289, 427-28, 430, 437, 441
Senate 1964 election, 39, 46
Senate Minority leader, Atiyeh as, 50-52
Shamir, Yitzhak, 438, 440
Smith, Bob (legislator, congressman), 37, 39, 48
South Korea, 311, 423-25, 442, 443-44, 458, 498
Stockman, David, 182, 266-67, 337, 341
Straub, Bob, 66, 73, 74, 75-84, 93-94, 99, 102, 106-115, 117, 121, 124, 126, 149, 156, 159, 163, 165, 177, 226, 285, 335, 348, 421-22, 476, 488, 504-05
Sullivan, Mike, 360, 361, 363, 368-69, 375, 399, 409, 411, 412, 417
Taiwan (ROC), 307, 413, 414, 421, 423, 424-26, 442-43, 458, 465
Thompson, Gerry, 67, 74, 113, 123, 130, 131
Thorne, Jill, 211, 511
Thorne, Mike, 56, 236, 300
Trader Vic, 469-76
Transition team (1978), 115-23, 487, 488
Unitary tax, 442-57, 459, 462, 467-68
Warm Springs Tribe, 210, 212-17, 464, 502, 503, 520
Watergate, 65, 70, 76, 77-78, 84, 513
Weaver, Jim, 163, 164-66, 195, 263-64
Whitney, Carol, 95-96, 97, 107, 113, 114
Wilderness areas, 189-92
Woodrow, Shirley, 75, 84, 114, 119, 133, 335
Yunker, Jon, 127, 128, 324, 348, 357

Jim Moore has been an independent political analyst in the Portland area since 1990. He worked with several Portland-area television and radio stations and his analysis appeared in regional, national, and international media outlets. Moore teaches politics at Pacific University in Forest Grove where he is the political outreach director of the Tom McCall Center for Civic Engagement.

www.ingramcontent.com/pod-product-compliance
Lightning Source LLC
Chambersburg PA
CBHW051932290426
44110CB00015B/1948